HTML COMPLETE
2nd Edition

SYBEX® SAN FRANCISCO ► PARIS ► DÜSSELDORF ► SOEST ► LONDON

Associate Publisher: Cheryl Applewood

Contracts and Licensing Manager: Kristine O'Callaghan

Developmental Editors: Mariann Barsolo and Tracy Brown

Editor: Anamary Ehlen

Technical Editor: Greg Guntle

Editors: Susan Berge, Bonnie Bills, Pat Coleman, Nancy Conner, Kim Crowder, Brenda Frink, Jeff Gammon, Diane Lowery, Gary Masters, Ben Miller, Valerie Perry, Vivian Perry, Lee Ann Pickrell, Rebecca Rider, Colleen Strand, Kristen Vanberg-Wolff, Kim Wimpsett

Technical Editors: Matthew Fiedler, Greg Guntle, Don Hergert, Ben DeLong, Will Kelly, Tom Maxwell, Piroz Mohseni, Ann Navarro, John Piraino, Sr., Rima Regas, David Shank, David Wall

Book Designer: Maureen Forys, Happenstance Type-O-Rama

Electronic Publishing Specialist: Kris Warrenburg

Production Editor: Elizabeth Campbell

Indexer: Nancy Guenther

Cover Designer: DesignSite

Cover Illustration: DesignSite

Library of Congress Card Number: 00-106119

ISBN: 0-7821-2801-7

Screen reproductions produced with Collage Complete and FullShot.

Collage Complete is a trademark of Inner Media Inc.

FullShot is a trademark of Inbit Incorporated.

SYBEX is a registered trademark of SYBEX Inc.

Expert Guide, In Record Time, Master the Essentials, Mastering, and No experience required are trademarks of SYBEX Inc.

Manufactured in the United States of America

10 9 8 7 6 5

ACKNOWLEDGMENTS

This book incorporates the work of many people, inside and outside Sybex.

Cheryl Applewood, Mariann Barsolo, and Tracy Brown defined the book's overall structure and contents. Greg Guntle assured the technical accuracy of the compiled material, and Anamary Ehlen edited the manuscript with a keen eye.

A large team of editors, developmental editors, project editors, and technical editors helped to put together the various books from which *HTML Complete,* 2nd Edition was compiled: Maureen Adams, Cheryl Applewood, Sherry Bonelli, Dan Brodnitz, Kim Crowder, Peter Kuhns, Gary Masters, Suzanne Rotondo, and Denise Santoro Lincoln handled developmental tasks; Michael Anderson, Davina Baum, Susan Berge, Bonnie Bills, Pat Coleman, Nancy Conner, Kim Crowder, Brenda Frink, Jeff Gammon, Diane Lowery, Ben Miller, Valerie Perry, Vivian Perry, Lee Ann Pickrell, Rebecca Rider, Colleen Strand, Kristen Vanberg-Wolff, Kim Wimpsett, and Shelby Zimmerman all contributed to editing or project editing; and Ben DeLong, Matthew Fiedler, Greg Guntle, Don Hergert, Will Kelly, Tom Maxwell, Piroz Mohseni, Ann Navarro, John Piraino Sr., Rima Regas, David Shank, and David Wall provided technical edits. Tracy Brown deserves particular thanks for her help in shaping the book's outline.

The *HTML Complete,* 2nd Edition production team of eletronic publishing specialist Kris Warrenburg and production editor Elizabeth Campbell worked with speed and accuracy to turn the manuscript files and illustrations into the handsome book you're now reading. Ellen Bliss and Dan Schiff also helped in various ways to keep the project moving.

Finally, our most important thanks go to the contributors who agreed to have their work excerpted in *HTML Complete,* 2nd Edition: Peter Dyson, A. Russell Jones, Kurt Cagle, Vincent Flanders and Michael Willis, Molly E. Holzschlag, James Jaworski, E. Stephen Mack and Janan Platt, Deborah S. Ray and Eric J. Ray, Joseph Schmuller, Erik Strom, and Gene Weisskopf and Pat Coleman. Without their efforts, this book would not exist.

Contents at a Glance

CONTENTS

Chapter 3 □ Stepping Out: Linking Your Way around the Web   **77**

Part III ▶ Advanced HTML   479

Part IV ▸ Beyond HTML   685

Chapter 19 ▫ Introducing Perl and CGI   687

INTRODUCTION

HTML Complete, 2nd Edition, is a one-of-a-kind computer book—valuable both for the breadth of its content and for its low price. This thousand-page compilation of information from ten Sybex books, as well as three original chapters, provides comprehensive coverage of the Hypertext Markup Language and related topics in Web site building and design. This book, unique in the computer book world, was created with several goals in mind:

- ▶ Offering a thorough guide that covers the important user-level features of HTML and related topics at an affordable price

- ▶ Helping you become familiar with the essentials of HTML so you can choose an advanced HTML book with confidence

- ▶ Acquainting you with some of Sybex's best authors—their writing styles and teaching skills, and the level of expertise they bring to their books—so you can easily find a match for your interests as you delve deeper into Web development

HTML Complete, 2nd Edition, is designed to provide all the essential information you'll need to get the most from HTML, while at the same time inviting you to explore the even greater depths and wider coverage of material in the original books.

If you've read other computer "how-to" books, you've seen that there are many possible approaches to the task of showing how to use software and hardware effectively. The books from which HTML Complete, 2nd Edition, was compiled represent a range of the approaches to teaching that Sybex and its authors have developed—from the quick, concise No experience required style to the exhaustively thorough Mastering style. As you read through various chapters of HTML Complete, 2nd Edition, you'll see which approach works best for you. You'll also see what these books have in common: a commitment to clarity, accuracy, and practicality.

You'll find in these pages ample evidence of the high quality of Sybex's authors. Unlike publishers who produce "books by committee," Sybex encourages authors to write in individual voices that reflect their own experience with the software at hand and with the evolution of today's personal computers. Nearly every book represented here is the work of a single writer or a pair of close collaborators, and you are getting the benefit of each author's direct experience.

In adapting the various source materials for inclusion in *HTML Complete,* 2nd Edition, the compiler preserved these individual voices and perspectives. Chapters were edited only to minimize duplication and to add sections so you're sure to get coverage of cutting-edge developments. A few sections were also edited for length so that other important HTML-related subjects could be included.

WHO CAN BENEFIT FROM THIS BOOK?

HTML Complete, 2nd Edition, is designed to meet the needs of a wide range of computer users. Therefore, while you *could* read this book from beginning to end, all of you may not *need* to read every chapter. The Contents and the index will guide you to the subjects you're looking for.

Beginners   Even if you have only a little familiarity with computers and their basic terminology, this book will get you up on the Web using HTML.

Intermediate users   Chances are you already know how to perform routine operations with HTML. You also know that there is always more to learn about working effectively, and you want to get up to speed on new features in HTML and other programming languages. Throughout this book you'll find instructions for just about anything you want to do. Nearly every chapter has nuggets of knowledge from which you can benefit.

Advanced users   If you've worked extensively with HTML, you'll appreciate this book as a reference. You'll find the wealth of HTML information in the appendix to be particularly useful.

HOW THIS BOOK IS ORGANIZED

HTML Complete, 2nd Edition, has twenty-three chapters and one appendix.

Part I: Introducing HTML   In the first five chapters, you'll learn the basic concepts of HTML and the Web and begin looking at how to assemble the elements of Web pages. You've probably browsed the Web before, but after reading Part I you'll do so with a new perspective.

Part II: Planning and Designing Your Web Page   Part II will give you plenty of ideas for designing eye-catching and effective Web sites of your own. You'll find that the chapters in Part II emphasize the *thought* behind a Web page as well as the execution, offering discussions of both design theory and the mechanics of laying out your pages with HTML. In other words, you'll learn not only how to use elements such as color, graphics, and tables on your site but also how they can make your pages more effective in getting your ideas across.

Part III: Advanced HTML   Part III will introduce you to the more robust techniques you can use with HTML. Chapters 13 and 14 were written specifically to teach you how to build your pages so that they work correctly with the latest technology available in Internet Explorer and Netscape Navigator. Then you will take your pages a step further by using multimedia, style sheets, and forms, and also learning some capabilities of DHTML.

Part IV: Beyond HTML   Part IV will introduce you to other programming languages that will enable you to add more sophisticated and dynamic content to your pages. You'll learn about Perl, CGI, JavaScript, XML, and Active Server Pages and get a glimpse of what these powerful languages can help you accomplish. We've also included a chapter on XHTML written specifically for this book, so you can get an understanding of this emerging technology.

Appendix   The appendix is designed for quick reference to HTML tags, colors, and symbols.

A Few Typographical Conventions

When an operation requires a series of choices from menus or dialog boxes, the ➢ symbol is used to guide you through the instructions, like this: "Select Programs ➢ Accessories ➢ System Tools ➢ System Information." The items the ➢ symbol separates may be menu names, toolbar icons, check boxes, or other elements of the Windows interface—any place you can make a selection.

This typeface is used to identify Internet URLs and HTML code, and **boldface type** is used whenever you need to type something into a text box.

You'll find these types of special notes throughout the book:

TIP

You'll see a lot of these—quicker and smarter ways to accomplish a task, which the authors have based on their experience using HTML.

NOTE

You'll see these Notes, too. They usually represent alternate ways to accomplish a task or some additional information that needs to be highlighted.

WARNING

In a very few places you'll see a Warning like this one. When you see a Warning, pay attention to it!

YOU'LL ALSO SEE "SIDEBAR" BOXES LIKE THIS

These boxed sections provide added explanation of special topics that are noted briefly in the surrounding discussion, but that you may want to explore separately. Each sidebar has a heading that announces the topic so you can quickly decide whether it's something you need to know about.

FOR MORE INFORMATION...

Visit the Sybex Web site, www.sybex.com, to learn more about all of the books that went into *HTML Complete,* 2nd Edition. On the site's Catalog page, you'll find links to any book you're interested in.

We hope you enjoy this book and find it useful. Happy computing!

PART I

INTRODUCING HTML

Chapter 1

INTRODUCING WEB PAGES AND HTML

You can certainly start your browser and hit the Web without any knowledge of the Hypertext Markup Language (HTML) that lies beneath all Web documents, or *pages*. But if you want to make your presence known on the Web by building pages on your own, you'll need to learn HTML. This chapter introduces you to the basic concepts of HTML, many of which you'll learn about in more detail later in this book.

Adapted from *Mastering Microsoft Internet Explorer 4*, by Gene Weisskopf and Pat Coleman

ISBN 0-7821-2133-0   960 pages $44.99

NOTE
Although the book in which this chapter originally appeared was written for users of Microsoft Internet Explorer, rest assured that the information applies to Netscape's browser as well. We've called attention to the few exceptions throughout the chapter.

AN OVERVIEW OF HTML

In keeping with the original and ongoing theme of the Internet—openness and portability—the pages you create with HTML are just plain text. You can create, edit, or view the HTML code for a Web page in any text editor on any computer platform, such as Windows Notepad.

Although creating simple Web pages in a text editor is easy, it can quickly turn into a grueling and mind-numbing task. That's why there are Web-authoring tools such as Microsoft FrontPage Express and Macromedia Dreamweaver, which let you create HTML Web pages in the same way you create documents in your word processor.

Viewing HTML Pages

When you open a Web page in your browser, you don't see the HTML code that creates the page. Instead, your browser interprets the HTML code and displays the page appropriately on the screen. If you're creating a Web page in a text editor and want to view the file you're working on, save your work and open the file in your browser. You can then continue to edit, save your work, and view the results, switching back and forth between the text editor and the browser to see the effects of your edits.

The original intent of the HTML specification was to allow Web authors to describe the structure of a page without spending too much time worrying about the look of a page—that part of the job was left to the browsers. Traditionally, each browser had its own way of interpreting the look of the page, and Web authors had to live with the fact that pages they created might appear somewhat differently in different browsers. Authors merely shrugged their shoulders and were happy that their pages could be viewed so easily from anywhere on the planet.

NOTE

That "original intent" is starting to fade as the world heads toward an HTML that can describe the look of a page quite accurately. More and more descriptive elements are being established in the HTML specification, such as font styles and sizes, colors, and style sheets that can maintain a consistent look throughout a Web site.

Here's an example of the inherent flexibility that was designed into the HTML specification: Later in this chapter, you'll read about the six HTML codes you can use for creating six levels of headings in a Web page. You as an author can specify that a paragraph of text be defined as one of the six heading levels, but the HTML heading code does *not* describe what a heading should look like. It merely says something to the effect of "I'm a level-two heading." It's up to the Web browser to differentiate each type of heading from the others. One browser might display the first-level heading in a large font that is centered on the page, while another browser might display it in italics and left-aligned on the page. That's why authors try to test their pages in several of the more popular browsers.

Speaking of popular browsers, the good news is that the browser market has been consolidating and standardizing. You'll find few differences in the way competing browsers display the widely accepted HTML features in a page. Of course, new HTML features are being promoted all the time, mostly by Microsoft for its Internet Explorer browser and Netscape for its browser. Web authors must decide whether to include a new feature in a page when that feature may not be well interpreted by some browsers.

HTML Elements and Tags

A Web page is made up of *elements*, each of which is defined by an HTML code, or *tag*. A tag is always enclosed in angle brackets, and most tags come in pairs, with an opening and a closing tag. The closing tag is the same as the opening tag, but starts with a forward slash.

For example, to define text as a first-level heading in HTML, you use the <H1> tag, as in:

```
<H1>This Is a Main Heading</H1>
```

A browser interprets these tags and displays the text within the tags appropriately (as shown next). But the tags themselves are not displayed within a browser, unless there is a problem with a tag, such as if one of the angle brackets was mistakenly left out (although most browsers will ignore any codes within angle brackets that they do not recognize).

This Is a Main Head

And this is Internet Explorer's normal text.

Some tags have optional or required attributes. An *attribute* is usually a keyword that takes one of several possible values (you define each value by enclosing it in quotes). For example, the heading tag can take an optional alignment attribute:

```
<H1 ALIGN="CENTER">This is a main heading that is
centered</H1>
```

NOTE

You can create a tag in either uppercase or lowercase; it doesn't matter to a browser. For example, the two tags <H1> and <h1> are equivalent to a browser. In this book, you'll notice that some authors use uppercase while others prefer lowercase.

The Essentials of a Web Page

Every Web page must include a few tags that define the page as a whole so that when a browser receives the page it will recognize it as such. For example, the following HTML code will produce the page that is shown in Internet Explorer in Figure 1.1 (it could also be viewed in any other browser):

```
<HTML>
<HEAD>
<TITLE>Greetings from the Web</TITLE>
</HEAD>
<BODY>
<P>Hello, world!</P>
</BODY>
</HTML>
```

Remember, this code is just a text file, plain and simple. Table 1.1 lists the tags that should be included in every page so that any browser can view it.

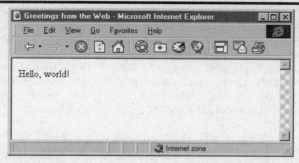

FIGURE 1.1: The sample page displayed in Internet Explorer

TABLE 1.1: Essential HTML Tags for a Page

TAG	PURPOSE
<HTML>	Declares that the text that follows defines an HTML Web page that can be viewed in a Web browser. The closing </HTML> tag ends the page.
<HEAD>	Defines the header area of a page, which is not displayed within the page itself in the browser. The closing </HEAD> tag ends the header area.
<TITLE>	The text between this tag and the closing </TITLE> tag is the title of the Web page and is displayed in the title bar of your browser, as shown in Figure 1.1. The title should be descriptive, as it is frequently used by Web indexing and searching programs to name your Web page. In Internet Explorer, a page's title serves as the default name when you save the page as a favorite location.
<BODY>	Delineates the actual content of the Web page that will be displayed in your browser. In the example above, only the words *Hello, world!* will appear within the browser. Most of the other HTML features that we will discuss in this chapter always appear within the <BODY> and </BODY> tags in a Web page. There are several optional attributes for this tag. One of them is BACKGROUND, with which you can specify a background graphical image for the page.
<P>	Use the paragraph tag to mark the beginning of a new paragraph; the ending tag, </P>, is optional but should be included for clarity (whenever you or someone else needs to inspect or revise this code). You can include the ALIGN attribute to specify whether the paragraph should be centered or right-aligned in the page (left-aligned is the default).

There are dozens and dozens of other HTML tags you can incorporate into a Web page. The ones you use and how you use them depends only on your design, capabilities, and imagination.

NOTE

There is one important tag whose effects you won't notice in your browser but that you will appreciate when you're editing or viewing the HTML code for a page. In Internet Explorer, you use the <COMMENT> tag to create descriptive comments within the code, which will be ignored by the browser. With other browsers, you can use this combination of symbols to create a comment:
<!- This text is a comment. ->

ADDING SPACES AND BLANK LINES FOR READABILITY

You can include extra spaces and blank lines in HTML code to make the code easier for you or others to read and interpret. When a browser opens a Web page, it ignores multiple spaces within the code and displays them as a single space. It also ignores all hard returns within the code, such as when you press Enter at the end of a line of text you're editing in Notepad. Therefore, any blank lines you create in the code by pressing Enter a few times will not be displayed in the user's browser.

There is one HTML tag in which spaces and hard returns in the HTML code *do* count, and that is the preformatted tag, <PRE>. It instructs a browser to display the text in a monospaced font that allows you to align text precisely, such as you would when showing a program listing.

Learning HTML

As more and more of the world's documents end up as Web pages, we will all be viewing, creating, and modifying them as part of our daily routine. Learning about HTML will give you an understanding of how it works and how it looks in use, which will prove invaluable to your Web-browsing experience. But please rest assured that in this book we have absolutely no intention of molding you into a code cruncher!

With the proliferation of elegant HTML editors such as FrontPage Express and Dreamweaver, it is unlikely that a text editor will be your first tool of choice for creating Web pages. Unless you really take off in the science and art of Web-page authoring, you will probably never have to become an HTML jockey, and you will forego the pleasure of wrangling your way through screenfuls of angle brackets, slashes, and esoteric codes.

NOTE

Creating a successful Web page requires a good deal from both sides of your brain—the logical side, which helps you write computer programs, and the artistic side, which helps you compose a tasteful, inviting document. That's why it's important to have several people test and critique your Web efforts, because few of us can lay full claim to both sides of our brains!

You can learn about HTML in many ways without specifically studying it. Perhaps the most important method is already staring you in the face when you're browsing the Web—the pages themselves. All Web pages are built from the same text-based HTML language, so when you're viewing a page in your browser that strikes your interest, stop and take a look at that page's underlying code. You can do so in two ways:

- ▶ Choose View ➢ Source (under Internet Explorer) or View ➢ Page Source (under Navigator) to display the current page's HTML code within Notepad. You can then view the code to your heart's content or save it to disk for later use.

- ▶ If you know you'll want to spend some time with the HTML code later on, you can save the current page to your local disk from within your browser by choosing File ➢ Save As. The resulting HTML file is the HTML code from which the page was built. Navigator will not include any of the graphic images from the page. Internet Explorer versions 5 and above will save all graphic images.

By viewing the HTML code for a page, you can get a feeling for how the page was created.

If you want to learn more about encoding Web pages, you can find countless books and even more Web sites devoted to that subject. A great place to start is CNET's Builder.com:

```
www.builder.com
```

It is designed primarily for "Web professionals," but the complexity and depth of the material on the site ranges far and wide. It has thousands and thousands of pages, hundreds of megabytes of downloadable software, and great links to other Web-related resources. You'll also find countless examples of what you can build in your Web site. You could easily spend days browsing through this huge collection of information (all of which is current) about designing, building, and running Internet and intranet Web sites.

Another useful site is the Web Design Workgroup. This informal association of Web-page designers was founded to help other designers create truly portable Web pages that could be viewed by any browser on any computer platform:

www.htmlhelp.com

To find Web-related sites elsewhere on the Web, take a look at the following category on Yahoo!, a Web search site:

Computers and Internet: Internet: World Wide Web: Information and Documentation

A STANDARD MAY NOT ALWAYS BE ONE

The language of HTML is constantly evolving. Enthusiastic Web authors may happily include brand new and improved tags within their Web pages to produce dazzling new effects. But unfortunately, those effects may be lost on most visitors to that Web site because their browser software does not recognize those HTML features.

Officially, it's up to the World Wide Web Consortium (W3C) at the Massachusetts Institute of Technology (MIT) to define and establish new versions of HTML. Unofficially, leaders in the rush to the WWW, such as Microsoft and Netscape, regularly come up with their own extensions to official HTML in the hopes of improving the language. Eventually, many of these new codes are, indeed, included in the official HTML specification.

Skip the Programming: Use FrontPage Express

Microsoft FrontPage Express is one of the components in the Internet Explorer suite. It is essentially an easy-to-use word processor for creating HTML documents. Unlike a text editor such as Notepad, FrontPage Express is a WYSIWYG environment, in which "what you see is what you get." In other words, what you see in your document in FrontPage Express is pretty much what you'll see when you view the resulting HTML file on the Web in your browser. FrontPage Express has two important virtues:

▶ It is designed specifically to create HTML pages, so you won't find any unrelated commands or features on its menus. You don't have to think about how those options work; you simply choose them from the menu.

▶ When you create a page in FrontPage Express, you are assured that the HTML tags in that page (even though you might never see them) will be correct, with no missing angle brackets, misspelled tags, and so on.

If you're not sure what the big deal is about creating Web pages in FrontPage Express versus encoding them with HTML in a text editor, here's a simple but telling example. Shown below is some HTML code that you could create in Notepad and save to disk as an HTML file:

```
<HTML><HEAD><TITLE>Sample HTML Page</TITLE>
</HEAD>
<BODY>
<H1>This Is the Main Heading</H1>
<P>Here's a bulleted list:</P>
<HR>
<UL>
<LI>Item 1</LI>
<LI>Item 2<UL>
  <LI>Item 2A</LI>
  <LI>Item 2B</LI>
 </UL></LI>
<LI>Item 3</LI>
<LI>Item 4</LI>
</UL>
<HR>
<P>...and the page continues...</P>
</BODY>
</HTML>
```

Now look at Figure 1.2 to see how you could create that page in the WYSIWYG environment of FrontPage Express. The HTML code stays hidden beneath the page you create, which appears much the way it will when viewed in your browser.

Part I

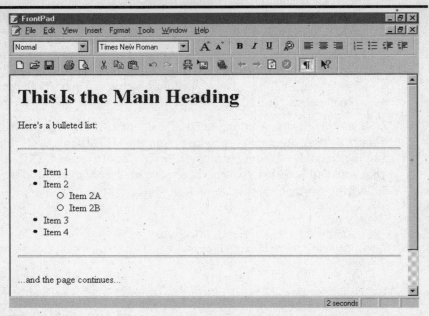

FIGURE 1.2:   When you create Web pages in a WYSIWYG HTML editor such as FrontPage Express, "what you see is what you get" when that page is later viewed in a browser.

ADDING SOME STRUCTURE TO A PAGE

Just about any Web page you create will benefit if you impose some sort of structure on it. For example, think about how you would put your company's procedures manual up on the Web:

- ▶ If the manual is divided into chapters, you could make each one a separate Web page.

- ▶ You could easily re-create the manual's table of contents by making each section reference a hyperlink to that part of the manual. The reader could simply click on a section in the table of contents to open that file.

- ▶ Each chapter in the manual might have several levels of headings, which you could emulate perfectly with the heading tags in HTML.

▶ The body of the document would, of course, be divided into individual paragraphs.

You'll find that HTML offers several elements that let you create this type of structure in a Web page.

Using Paragraphs or Line Breaks

You create a paragraph by enclosing text within the paragraph codes <P> and </P>. Remember that browsers will ignore any "paragraphs" you create by pressing Enter while working on the HTML code in a text editor (such as Notepad). You must specifically define a paragraph in the code by using the paragraph tag. Consider the text in the six lines of HTML code that follow:

```
<P>This is the first paragraph; its code
continues over several lines, but will be
displayed as a single paragraph in a
browser.</P><P>And this is a second paragraph
that will also be displayed as such in
a browser.</P>
```

This code would appear as two separate paragraphs in your browser, as shown in the upper portion of Figure 1.3. Note that the length of each line is determined by the width of the browser's window.

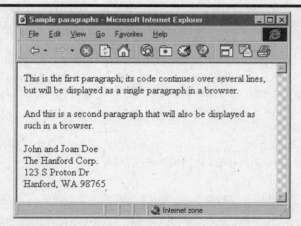

FIGURE 1.3: You use the <P> tag to define a paragraph and the <BR> tag to create a line break.

Your browser will insert some extra space between paragraphs, so in some instances, you will not want to use the <P> tag. For example, when you display your name and address in a page, you would not want extra space between each line of the address.

In those cases, use the line-break tag, <BR>. It tells the browser to wrap the text that follows onto a new line without inserting any extra space between the lines. Here is an address within HTML code:

```
John and Joan Doe<BR>The Hanford Corp.<BR>123 S Proton
Dr<BR>Hanford, WA 98765
```

You can see how this is displayed in Internet Explorer in the lower portion of Figure 1.3.

Dividing Sections with a Horizontal Line

A simple and effective way to separate sections within a Web page is to insert a horizontal line, <HR>, which is also called a horizontal rule. By default, the line stretches from one side of the page to the other.

For example, if your page has a banner across the top with your company name, you could insert a horizontal line beneath it. This would separate it from a table of contents showing links to other pages, beneath which you could insert another line, followed by the main body of the page. At the bottom of the page, you could have another line, and beneath that line would be the important page identifiers, such as its URL, the date the page was last modified, a link back to a home page, and so on. An example is shown in Figure 1.4.

The <HR> tag takes several optional attributes. For example, you can specify the line's thickness (the default is one or two pixels in most browsers) and how much of the browser's window it should span (as a percentage or in pixels), such as:

```
<HR SIZE="6" WIDTH="60%">
```

which displays a line 6 pixels thick that spans 60 percent of the browser's window (the default is to center it in the window).

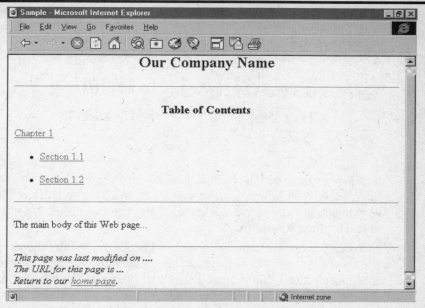

FIGURE 1.4: You can use the horizontal rule, <HR>, to divide a page into sections.

Creating a Hierarchy with Headings

A common way to add structure to a Web page is through the use of headings. This book, for example, uses headings to divide each chapter into logical chunks (at least, that was our plan). Its table of contents reveals the various levels of headings: each chapter is divided into several main headings, each of which may contain several subheadings, which in turn may contain their own subheadings.

A Web page can have a maximum of six levels of headings, the HTML codes for which are conveniently named <H1>, <H2>, <H3>, and so on:

```
<H1>This is a two-line<BR>first-level heading</H1>
```

As mentioned earlier, no style is inherent in the headings—different Web browsers might interpret the look of a heading in slightly different ways. Structurally, however, all browsers will display headings so that a third-level heading looks subordinate to a second-level heading, a second-level heading looks subordinate to a first-level heading, and so on.

In your browser, a first-level heading is displayed in a larger, bolder font than a lower-level heading. Shown here is a sample of the six headings within Internet Explorer.

Heading 1   Heading 2
Heading 3   Heading 4
Heading 5   Heading 6

You are free to use the HTML headings in any goofy order you prefer, but it makes good sense to use them as you would in an outline. The first-level heading, <H1>, is the highest level, and the sixth level, <H6>, is the lowest or most subordinate.

When you are structuring a page with headings, the first heading you use should generally be the highest level that will occur on the page. But this doesn't mean that it must be the <H1> heading. You might start with <H2> because you want a heading that appears in a smaller font than <H1>. In this case, then, the level-two heading would be the primary level, and you would not use <H1> on this page.

FORMATTING TEXT AND PAGES

Because the World Wide Web was originally conceived to be open to all, the designers of HTML avoided using literal descriptions of Web pages as much as possible. For example, the following tag would not have been appropriate:

```
<FONT FACE="TIMES ROMAN" SIZE="5" COLOR="#ff0000">
```

This tag requires a browser to have a specific, named font available that can be displayed in various sizes and requires that the browser's computer be connected to a color monitor.

But the days of trying to write to the least common denominator are waning quickly, and, in fact, the tag shown above is now a part of the official HTML specification. The <FONT> tag also illustrates two types of HTML tag attributes:

Absolute (literal)   The font type Times Roman is specified by name, and the color is specified by a hexadecimal RGB color value. There can be no doubt about how the author wanted this to look.

Relative (logical)   The font size 5, however, does not refer to an actual point size. It is a size that is relative to the browser's default font size (which is size 2 in Internet Explorer) and gives the browser a little more flexibility in how it displays the font. The author wanted the font to be larger than the browser's default but was willing to let the browser assign the actual size.

Formatting Text

Table 1.2 shows a few of the many HTML character-formatting tags. All of them require both an opening and closing tag.

TABLE 1.2: Basic HTML Character-Formatting Tags

Tag	Purpose
<ADDRESS>	To display a Web page's author information, such as the page URL, author name, date of last revision, and so on, in italics in your browser.
<I>	To italicize text.
<EM>	To emphasize text, which your browser displays in italics; this is a relative tag compared to the more specific <I> tag.
<PRE>	To display text in a monospaced (fixed-width) font, where multiple spaces, tabs, and hard returns within the HTML code are also displayed. Use this tag when the position of characters within each line is important, such as program listings and columnar lists.
<B>	To boldface text.
<STRONG>	To give text strong emphasis, which your browser displays in bold. This is a relative tag compared with the more specific <B> tag.
<S>	To display strike-through text.
<U>	To underline text. You should generally avoid underlining text since that is how browsers indicate hypertext links in Web pages.

You can insert these tags where they are needed in a paragraph, and you can combine some tags. The browser in Figure 1.5 shows an example of HTML text formatting. That page was built from the following HTML code:

```
<HTML><HEAD><TITLE>HTML Formatting Tags</TITLE></HEAD><BODY>
<P>With HTML formatting tags, you can make text <STRONG>
bold</STRONG>, <EM>emphasized</EM>, or <EM><STRONG>bold and
emphasized</STRONG></EM>. You can also <STRIKE>strike-out
text</STRIKE> or make it <U>underlined</U>.</P>
```

```
<P>If you don't use the Preformatted tag, Internet Explorer
displays text in a proportional font, where different
characters take up different amounts of space. Here are two
lines of 10 letters, i and M, where each line of the HTML
code also had five spaces entered between the fifth and
sixth letters:</P>
<P>iiiii     iiiii<BR>
MMMMM     MMMMM</P>
<P>Here are those letters and spaces within the Preformatted
tags:</P>
<PRE>iiiii     iiiii<BR>
MMMMM     MMMMM</PRE>
</BODY></HTML>
```

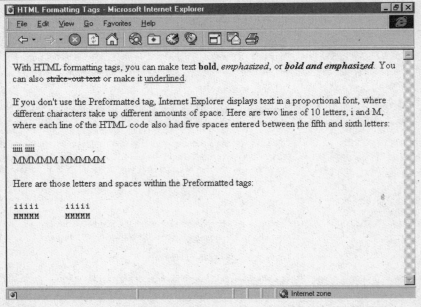

FIGURE 1.5: HTML formatting tags change the look of text in a Web page.

Formatting Pages

You can use a variety of tags to change the look of an entire Web page. You've already read about the <TITLE> tag, with which you create a title for a page. Your browser displays that title in its title bar.

You can change the color of the page's background with the optional attribute BGCOLOR for the <BODY> tag. For example, the tag:

```
<BODY BGCOLOR="#0000FF">
```

creates a blue background for the page.

NOTE

As with many tags, if you don't specify a color for a page, a browser that is displaying that page will use its own default color. Internet Explorer uses your Windows colors by default, which are normally a white background with black text.

You can specify a picture instead of a color for a page's background. You don't need a large, page-sized picture, however, because your browser tiles the picture to fill the entire background. This allows you to use a small image file that will download quickly. You include the BACKGROUND attribute in the <BODY> tag to specify a background picture:

```
<BODY BACKGROUND="smallpic.gif">
```

If you choose a fairly dark background color or picture, you may need to use the TEXT attribute to change the default color of any text on the page. For example, the following tag creates a blue background with white text:

```
<BODY BGCOLOR="#0000FF" TEXT="#FFFFFF">
```

Using Styles and Style Sheets

There is one tool for formatting documents in word processors that we have all grown quite accustomed to but that has been conspicuously missing from HTML. That is the *style*, which allows you to create a named definition of a group of formats and then apply that style to any text in the document. The result is a consistent look that is easy to apply throughout the document. A second advantage to styles becomes evident when you want to adjust the look of all the text to which you've applied a style. You simply redefine the style, and that change is immediately reflected throughout the document.

In the past, HTML lacked a mechanism for performing this simple, automated formatting task. But that's about to change with the acceptance of styles and style sheets in the HTML specification.

NOTE

The style sheets that Microsoft assumes will be implemented within the HTML specification are recognized by Internet Explorer 4 and later (and were recognized even back in Internet Explorer 3). However, because styles were not yet written into the HTML specification, few sites have taken advantage of them. Once styles are accepted, you will undoubtedly find them in use throughout the Web. In fact, FrontPage Express, the HTML word processor that comes with Internet Explorer, does not yet support styles. That's why you should use a plain-text editor, such as Notepad, to create the short examples later in this section.

Just as you would use styles in a word processor, a Web author can incorporate styles into a Web page. This can be done in several ways; the following is the simplest.

Within the <HEAD> tags for a page, you can specify style elements for various tags that will affect those tags throughout the page. For example, you could use styles to:

▶ Create a light gray background for the page

▶ Center all <H2> headings and display their text in white

▶ Indent the first line of all paragraphs

Here is the HTML code that creates these effects. Figure 1.6 shows the page as it appears in Internet Explorer (with added text):

```
<HTML><HEAD><TITLE>Sample Style</TITLE>
<STYLE>
 BODY {BACKGROUND: silver}
 H2  {TEXT-ALIGN:"center"; COLOR:"white"}
 P   {TEXT-INDENT:"+10%"}
</STYLE>
</HEAD><BODY>
<H2>This Heading Is Centered</H2>
<P>This is a normal paragraph...</P>
</BODY></HTML>
```

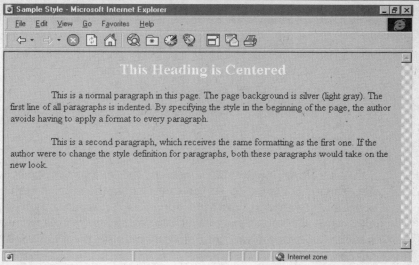

FIGURE 1.6: You can create a more consistent look in a page with much less effort when you use styles to set the formatting of HTML elements.

NOTE

The BACKGROUND style is only partially supported in Netscape's browser.

You could use this method to create many Web pages that all use the same styles, but there's a much more efficient way to use styles. The term *style sheet* refers to a single file that contains multiple style definitions. You can reference that file in any HTML Web page to apply those styles to that page.

Here are the contents of a style sheet (they're plain text files with a .css filename extension) that includes the styles shown in the previous example:

```
BODY {BACKGROUND: silver}
H2   {TEXT-ALIGN:"center"; COLOR:"white"}
P    {TEXT-INDENT:"+10%"}
```

If you save that style sheet file in a Web site (under the name normalpg .css in this example), you can reference it in any Web page with the following code. This code is the same as that used in the previous example;

however, here the <LINK> tag replaces all the code within the opening and closing <STYLE> tags:

```
<HTML><HEAD><TITLE>Sample Style</TITLE>
<STYLE>
<LINK REL=StyleSheet HREF="normalpg.css" TYPE="text/css">
</STYLE>
</HEAD><BODY>
<H2>This Heading Is Centered</H2>
<P>This is a normal paragraph...</P>
</BODY>
</HTML>
```

The resulting page would look exactly the same as the one in the earlier example in Figure 1.6. As you can see from these quick examples, styles and style sheets have a great potential for easing the job of creating and, especially, maintaining a Web site. When many pages reference the same style sheet, you can simply modify the style sheet to have the changes appear in all the pages.

NOTE

If you'd like to learn more about style sheets, you'll find a great guide from the Web Design Group at www.htmlhelp.com/reference/css/.

LINKING PAGES TO THE WORLD

The little feature that creates the Web for countless computers and networks is the hyperlink. When you're reading a Web page in your browser, you can click a link to jump to a new resource (open it). That resource can be another HTML page, a graphic image, a sound or video file, or something else, and it might be located on the browser's local hard disk, on an intranet site, or on a site anywhere on the World Wide Web.

Creating a Text or Image Hyperlink

The HTML anchor tag, <A>, defines a hyperlink within a Web page and at the minimum contains two components:

- ▸ The text or image that you click to activate the link
- ▸ The URL of the link's target, which will open when you click the link

Here is the HTML code for a text hyperlink (it's shown here on two lines, but remember that a browser ignores any line breaks in the HTML code):

```
<P>There's <A HREF="http://www.mysample.com/helpindex.htm">
online help</A> when you need it.</P>
```

The text *online help* is the clickable link, and in your browser that text is underlined and displayed in blue, as shown in the top of Figure 1.7. The target of this link is the file `helpindex.htm`.

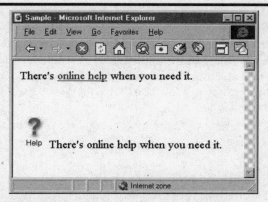

FIGURE 1.7: You can create a hyperlink from an image or from text, which is displayed in blue and underlined in Internet Explorer.

An image can also serve as a hyperlink; clicking the image activates the link. The bottom of Figure 1.7 shows an image hyperlink. In this case, the text that is next to the image serves to describe the link but cannot be clicked to activate the link. Here's the HTML code (shown on three lines) for this link and the text to its right:

```
<P><A HREF="http://www.mysample.com/helpindex.htm">
<IMG SRC="help.gif" BORDER="0" WIDTH="46" HEIGHT="51"></A>
There's online help when you need it.</P>
```

This example has the same target file as the previous example, `helpindex.css`, but the clickable portion of the hyperlink is the image file `help.gif`. The reference to that image file falls within the anchor tags <A> and </A>, and the sentence describing the link, *There's online help when you need it*, is outside those tags.

THE REFERENCE TO THE TARGET OF A LINK CAN BE RELATIVE OR ABSOLUTE.

When an author creates a reference in a Web page to another file, such as the target of a hyperlink, the reference can be defined as either relative or absolute.

In the two examples above, an *absolute* reference was made to the target file `helpindex.htm`. The reference contained the target's complete URL that defined the exact location of the file. It starts with the protocol and includes the usual host, domain, and filename:

    http://www.mysample.com/helpindex.htm

With an absolute reference, the location of the target is "written in stone" and always points to the same file in the same location. However, this is not an advantage or even a requirement when the target of the link is stored in a location that is *relative* to the page that contains the link.

For example, if the reference to the target contained only the target file's name, such as:

    helpindex.htm

it would be assumed that this file resides in the same folder as the page that contains the link. Its location is, therefore, relative to the link-containing file.

Another relative reference to a target might look like this:

    help/helpindex.htm

In this case, the target file resides in a folder named `help`, which resides in the same folder as the page that contains the link. The complete (absolute) URL to that file would look like this:

    http://www.mysample.com/help/helpindex.htm

Because the administrator of a Web site may need to change the location and directory (folder) structure of the site, a Web author will always try to use a relative reference whenever possible. In that way, if a Web site is moved to another folder on the same server or to a completely new server, all the relative references to files within that site continue to work.

Specifying Other Link Targets

You'll often find that the target of a link is another Web page, but there are other types of targets. Here are some you may encounter:

Named Target   When the target of a link is a Web page, you can specify a named location within that page. That location, not the top of the page, is displayed when the page is opened in a browser. You use the anchor tag to create the name for the location, and you reference that name in the anchor tag for the link.

Frame   Later in this chapter, you'll read about the frameset, which is a Web page that you divide into multiple frames, each of which can open and display a separate Web page. When a link resides in one frame of a frameset, you can have the target for that link displayed in any of the frames in that frameset. You do so by including the TARGET attribute in the link's anchor tag along with the name of the frame that should receive the target of the link.

Other File Types   The target of a link can be any type of file. Your browser can open several types of files on its own, including Web pages, text files, and GIF or JPEG image files. For other file types, it must rely on Windows 95/98 and request that the appropriate program handle that file. For example, sound files (WAV or AU) and movie files (MOV, MPG, or MPEG) would be played by the appropriate sound and movie player.

E-Mail Address   The target for a link can use an Internet protocol other than HTTP, such as the *mailto* protocol that defines an e-mail address. When the reader of the page clicks the link, the reader's e-mail program should open with a new message displayed and already addressed to the address specified in the link. The reader can create the body of the message and send it to the target address in the usual way.

Creating a Clickable Imagemap

A variation of the image hyperlink discussed in the previous section is the *imagemap*, which is a single image that contains multiple hyperlinks. Each hyperlink is associated with a defined area of the image called a *hotspot*, which, when clicked, activates that link. In your browser, you see only the image; there is no indication that it has clickable hotspots.

You've undoubtedly encountered imagemaps in many, many pages on the Web. They can be informative, attractive, and intuitive and can also transcend language, which is an important consideration on the World Wide Web.

TIP

Even though images can convey information without language, an image is nonetheless open to a variety of interpretations. Images may not even be seen when visitors to a site have turned off the display of images in their browsers to speed things up. Therefore, good Web design often means including corresponding text hyperlinks next to an imagemap so that a visitor to that page can either click within the imagemap or click one of the text links.

A typical use of an imagemap is literally in the form of a map: you can click on a city, state, or region to display information about that region. An imagemap built from a map of the United States works well when the hotspots are defined around the large, regularly shaped western states. But the plan doesn't work so well for the smaller, irregularly shaped eastern states.

In such a case, the imagemap would work better with a regional map of the United States. Clicking in the east would display an enlarged map of just that region of the country, and clicking in the west would display the western states, as shown in Figure 1.8.

A Web-page author can create an imagemap from an image in two ways:

▶ A *server-side* imagemap is the traditional type. When you click within an imagemap, your browser sends the coordinates of the click (relative to the image) to the server of that Web site. The server looks up those coordinates in a table of hotspots for that imagemap and processes the appropriate hyperlink target. Different servers may use different systems for storing the coordinates and targets for an imagemap.

▶ A *client-side* imagemap obviates any server interaction, because the hotspot coordinates are included in the HTML definition for the imagemap that is sent to your browser. When you click within the client-side imagemap, your browser looks to see which target is associated with those coordinates and then opens that target.

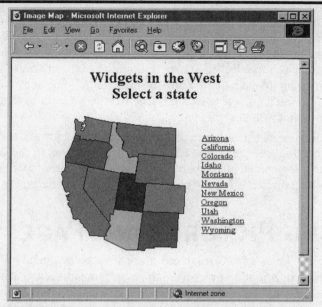

FIGURE 1.8: A geographic map can be a practical way to implement an imagemap.

Here is a sample of the HTML code for a client-side imagemap:

```
<AREA SHAPE="RECT" COORDS="308,32 380,72" HREF="choice1.htm">
<AREA SHAPE="RECT" COORDS="223,174 365,246"
HREF="choice2.htm">
<AREA SHAPE="RECT" COORDS="7,177 179,246" HREF="choice3.htm">
```

When you click within the image, your browser determines the coordinates of the point on which you clicked and finds the corresponding target for that portion of the imagemap, as though you had clicked a normal text or image hyperlink.

NOTE

Working in a text editor to create the HTML code for an imagemap just might be the nastiest Web-programming job there is. But you can create them with ease when you use HTML editors such as FrontPage Express and Dreamweaver. You simply draw an outline of the hotspot within the image and then specify the target for that link.

Although it usually shouldn't matter to you which type of imagemap appears on a page in your browser, you'll find one advantage with a client-side map. When you point to a hotspot in the map, you'll see the URL of the link associated with that hotspot, just as you do with a normal link. When you press Tab to select each hyperlink in the page, you also select each hotspot in an imagemap. Clicking the hotspot not only conveniently tells you where you'll go, it also tells you that this image is, indeed, an imagemap and not just a pretty picture.

Finally, because all the links are processed within the browser, a client-side imagemap reduces the processing burden on the server. It also is more flexible than a server-side imagemap because it is guaranteed to work no matter which server is hosting the page that contains the imagemap.

INCLUDING PICTURES IN A PAGE

You can include images (pictures or other nontext objects) in any Web page to provide information or to make the page more attractive. An image that you include in a Web page is called an *inline image*, as opposed to an image that is viewed separately in your browser, such as when the image file is the target of a link. You reference the inline image in this way:

```
There's more <IMG SRC="Images/arrow-rt.gif"> if you're
interested.
```

In this case, the image file `arrow-rt.gif` (from the folder `Images`) is displayed within the text that surrounds it and might look like the one shown here:

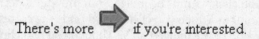

NOTE

The two most common graphic file formats you'll find on the Web are GIF and JPEG. The data in both types of files is compressed so that images can be transmitted much faster over a network.

Let's take a look at some of the attributes for the <IMG> tag for an inline image; all are optional:

Alternate Text   When a browser cannot display graphic images, perhaps because the image file cannot be found or because the browser's image-loading capabilities have been turned off to save download time, you can include the ALT attribute in an image tag to have text displayed in place of the image.

Sizing the Image   By default, your browser loads an image from the top down and displays the image in as large a box as needed. You can choose to specify an exact size for the image by including the WIDTH and HEIGHT attributes within the HTML tag (see the inline image example earlier in this chapter in "Creating a Text or Image Hyperlink").

Aligning the Image   You can use the ALIGN attribute with the LEFT, CENTER, or RIGHT options to position the image either flush-left, centered, or flush-right in the browser window. You can also use the TOP, BOTTOM, or MIDDLE attributes to align text with the top, bottom, or middle of the image.

CREATING LISTS

Using HTML, you can arrange items in lists in several ways. The two most useful ones are:

Bulleted   Or *unordered* lists, in which each item (paragraph) in the list is prefaced with a bullet; the <UL> tag begins the list.

Numbered   Or *ordered* lists, in which each item in the list is prefaced with a number; the <OL> tag begins the list. Your browser applies the appropriate number to each line when it opens the page, so you can add to or delete items from the list while you create the page and not have to worry about updating the numbering.

You define each item within either type of list with the <LI> tag. The following unordered list:

```
<P>Chapter I</P>
<UL>
<LI>Section 1</LI>
<LI>Section 2</LI>
<LI>Section 3</LI></UL>
```

looks like the example below in a browser:

Chapter I

- Section 1
- Section 2
- Section 3

The bulleted or numbered list is a fast, easy way to apply some structure to a Web page, and you'll no doubt use it frequently. As always, the way a browser formats the list, such as the amount of indention and the style of the bullets, could vary from browser to browser.

You can nest one list within another simply by beginning the new list with the appropriate list tag. This allows you to create outlines, for example, or tables of contents that have subheadings indented in their own lists. Here's the list from the example above with a second list within it:

```
<P>Chapter I</P>
<UL>
<LI>Section 1</LI>
<LI>Section 2<UL>
<LI>Part A</LI>
<LI>Part B</LI>
<LI>Part C</LI>
</UL></LI>
<LI>Section 3</LI></UL>
```

In Internet Explorer, the secondary list is indented from the primary list and displays a different type of bullet. Again, in other browsers these lists may look somewhat different. Here is the indented list from above shown in Internet Explorer (on the left) and another browser.

Chapter I   Chapter I

- Section 1   ● Section 1
- Section 2   ● Section 2
    o Part A   ☐ Part A
    o Part B   ☐ Part B
    o Part C   ☐ Part C
- Section 3   ● Section 3

ARRANGING ITEMS WITHIN TABLES

Another and even more powerful way to structure data within a Web page is the table. Like the tables you can create in your word processor or spreadsheet, an HTML table consists of rows, columns, and cells.

You can place just about anything you want within a cell in a table; there are few restrictions. Because of the flexibility of HTML tables, you'll find them used in countless ways in Web pages.

Sometimes a table will look like a table, with border lines dividing its rows, columns, and cells. In other cases, though, the structure of the table will be used, but its borders won't be displayed. The table serves as a convenient way to organize elements on the page without making them appear within the confines of an actual table.

Like imagemaps, tables are HTML elements that are best created in a dedicated HTML editor, such as FrontPage Express or Dreamweaver. You can still build a small table "manually" in a text editor, such as the table shown in the next example, but for anything more complex, you'll want to move to a more powerful editing tool.

Table 1.3 shows the basic tags with which you define a table:

TABLE 1.3: Basic HTML Table-Building Tags

TAG	PURPOSE
<TABLE>	Begins the table definition
<TR>	Defines a new row in the table
<TD>	Defines a single cell within the table

Shown below is the code for a simple, six-cell table:

```
<TABLE>
 <TR>
  <TD>Cell A1</TD> <TD>Cell B1</TD>
 </TR>
 <TR>
  <TD>Cell A2</TD> <TD>Cell B2</TD>
 </TR>
 <TR>
  <TD>Cell A3</TD> <TD>Cell B3</TD>
 </TR>
</TABLE>
```

The result is a table that has three rows and two columns; the text within the <TD> and </TD> tags appears in each cell. By default, as in this example, the table has no borders. You must specifically include them by specifying the width of their lines (in pixels) with the BORDER attribute for the <TABLE> tag, so that this tag:

```
<TABLE BORDER="1">
```

would enclose all the cells in the table with a border that is 1 pixel wide. Shown below is the first table, on the left, and the same table with a border, on the right.

Cell A1	Cell B1
Cell A2	Cell B2
Cell A3	Cell B3

You can include the <CAPTION> tag once in a table. Any text between this tag and its closing tag is displayed as the table's caption, which by default is centered just above the table.

You use the table header tag, <TH>, instead of the <TD> tag to create a header cell for the table. Your browser displays the text between the opening and closing header tags boldfaced and centered within the cell. You will often use these table headers as titles in the first row or column of a table.

By default, a table will only be as wide as the longest entries in its cells. You can specify an exact width in the <TABLE> tag with the WIDTH attribute, either in pixels or as a percentage of the browser's window. For example, this tag:

```
<TABLE WIDTH="320">
```

creates a table exactly 320 pixels wide. If you want a table to be exactly half the width of the browser's window, no matter what width that might be, use the following tag:

```
<TABLE WIDTH="50%">
```

If a table is less than the full width of a browser's window, it is aligned with the left edge of the window. You can include the ALIGN attribute in the <TABLE> tag and specify left, center, or right alignment within the browser's window.

If you specify an exact width for the table, you might also want to set the width of each column with the WIDTH attribute within the <TD> tag for a cell. You can specify the width either in pixels or as a percentage of the table (not of the browser's window).

As you'll see when you create a table, you can include many other tags and attributes, such as a background color or image for the table or any of its cells, the color of its borders, and which of its borders should be displayed.

GETTING FEEDBACK WITH FORMS

So far in this chapter, all the HTML elements we've discussed have been display-oriented, in that they affect the way a page appears within a browser. Now we'll look at the HTML form, an element that not only affects the display but also allows the reader to send information back to the server.

Those two issues, display and send, are the primary pieces of a Web-based form:

- ▶ The form controls that you create on a Web page are displayed in a browser and can be used by the visitor to enter data, select checkboxes or radio buttons, select items from a list, and so on.

- ▶ Once the visitor enters data into the form, he or she must have a mechanism for sending the data back to your server. Once the server receives the data, it must have another mechanism for storing or manipulating that data.

Designing a Form

Designing a form for a Web page isn't especially difficult if, as with tables, you do the job in an HTML editor such as FrontPage Express. The forms you create for the Web look and behave much like any other computer-generated forms you may have come across. For example, an HTML form can have a one-line data-entry field (sometimes called an edit field) in which the reader can type an e-mail address, as shown here:

E-mail address: myname@xyz.com

You use the <FORM> tag to begin the form definition. As part of that definition, you specify where the data should be returned (a URL) using the ACTION attribute. The destination might be the server for the form's Web page, or it could be some other server that will accept the data. You also specify how the data should be returned, using the METHOD attribute. The POST method is a common way to handle the job.

Within the opening and closing <FORM> tags, you lay out the controls of the form. You can include any other HTML elements as well, which will appear in the page along with the form controls. Some of the more common form-control tags are shown in Table 1.4 and Figure 1.9.

TABLE 1.4: Common HTML Form-Control Tags

TAG	FORM CONTROL	DESCRIPTION
<INPUT TYPE="TEXT">	Data-entry field	A one-line data-entry field
<INPUT TYPE="PASSWORD">	Password field	A one-line data-entry field in which the characters you type are displayed as asterisks to hide them
<TEXTAREA>	Multiple-line data-entry field	Enter a paragraph or more of text
<INPUT TYPE="CHECKBOX">	Checkbox	Select an item by clicking its checkbox
<INPUT TYPE="RADIO">	Radio button	Select one of a group of radio buttons
<SELECT>	List	Select one or more items from a list
<INPUT TYPE="SUBMIT">	Button	When clicked, sends the form's data to the server
<INPUT TYPE="RESET">	Button	When clicked, resets all form controls to their defaults

The definition for each control (other than the Submit and Reset buttons) must include a name for the control, which is sent to and used by the server to identify the data that was returned from that control. Each control can have several other attributes that define how it behaves. For example, the single-line data-entry field has the following attributes:

SIZE The displayed width of the field in the form.

MAXLENGTH   The maximum number of characters that can be entered into the field.

VALUE   The characters that appear within the field when its page is first opened or when the Reset button is clicked. You might use (none) as this default value so that when the data is returned to the server, this entry indicates that the visitor has entered no data in this field.

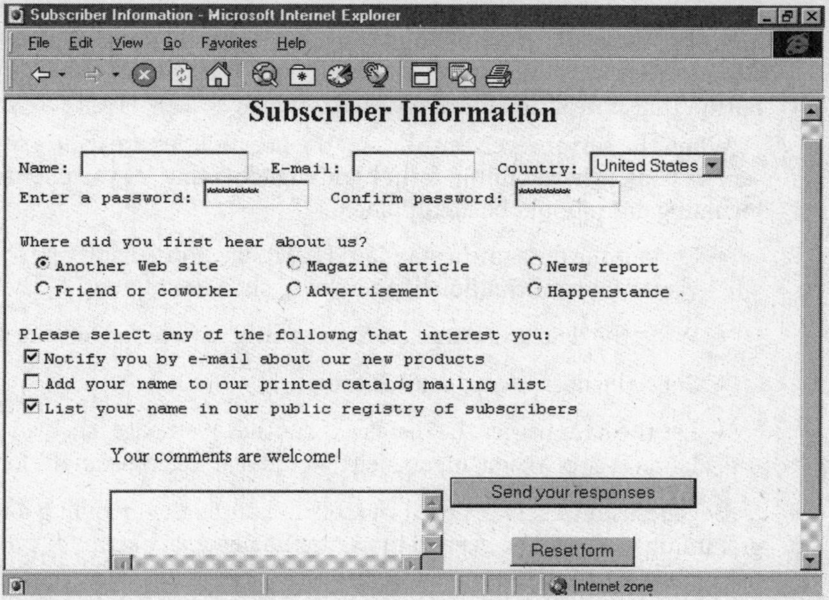

FIGURE 1.9: A visitor can enter information or select items in an HTML form.

Here is an example of the code for a data-entry field:

```
<INPUT TYPE="TEXT" NAME="COMPANY" SIZE="25" MAXLENGTH="100"
VALUE="(none)">
```

As the visitor enters information into a form, that data is still on the visitor's local computer—it has not reached the server yet.

Getting the Data Back to You

In a form such as the one shown in Figure 1.9, the visitor clicks on the Submit button (labeled *Send your responses* in the figure) to send the data back to the server. The browser collects at least two pieces of information about each control in the form:

- ▶ The name of the control
- ▶ Its current value

For example, if a visitor has entered *Pat Coleman* in the Name field, your browser sends back the following information:

```
NAME="Pat Coleman"
```

By naming each datum, the server can identify each piece of information it receives. Radio buttons are organized into named groups so that a visitor can select only one button in a group. It is the value of the selected button that is returned for the named group.

When the server receives the data, the possibilities are wide open. Web servers usually have built-in form-handling tools that let you choose how incoming data should be manipulated:

- ▶ Format the data into a standard HTML page and display it to the visitor for confirmation of what he or she has entered.

- ▶ Write the data to a database file in any of several file formats.

- ▶ Send the data to an e-mail address.

- ▶ Let the data trigger the display of another Web page, such as the home page of a company catalog that the visitor selected in the form.

Beyond using a server's built-in tools to handle the incoming data, programming work will be needed to create the necessary script or program to manipulate the data.

SPLITTING A PAGE INTO FRAMES

With the HTML feature called *frames*, you can create and display multiple Web pages within a single page. In the traditional way of browsing the Web, if you click a link in one page, a new page opens and replaces the first page in the browser.

For example, when you click a link in a page that serves as a table of contents of other pages, the target page opens, but the table of contents page is removed from the browser. By splitting a page into two frames, such as in the page shown in Figure 1.10, the table of contents page can be displayed in a frame on the left, for example, while the target of the selected link is displayed in the other frame on the right side of the browser's window. In this way, the table of contents is always available so that the reader can make another selection.

The concept of frames is neat and simple:

▶ Create a single Web page as a *frameset*, which contains no content other than the frameset definition.

▶ Specify how the frameset should be divided into frames.

▶ Assign a Web page to each frame.

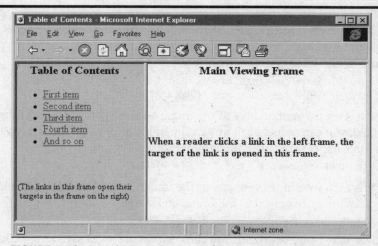

FIGURE 1.10: By splitting a page into frames, you can have a table of contents displayed in one frame while the target of each link is displayed in the other frame.

You use the <FRAMESET> tag instead of the usual <BODY> tag to begin the frameset definition in the page. For example, this tag:

```
<FRAMESET COLS="33%,67%">
```

creates a frameset page that consists of two frames arranged as columns. The first frame will be in a column on the left side of the browser's window; that frame's width will be one-third of the browser's window. The second frame will be a column to the right of the first one and will take up two-thirds of the browser's window.

You specify the source Web page to be opened in each frame with the <FRAME> tag, as in:

```
<FRAME SRC="contents.htm">
<FRAME SRC="instruct.htm">
```

In this case, when the frameset is opened in a browser, the frame on the left displays the page `contents.htm`, and the frame on the right displays `instruct.htm`. You now have two Web pages sharing the same browser window.

Let's revisit the example from the beginning of this section. If the frame on the left contains an index of links, you can have each of those links display its target in the frame on the right. You do so by including the TARGET attribute in the anchor tag for the link and specifying the name of the frame (as mentioned earlier in this chapter in "Specifying Other Link Targets").

To specify a target frame, you must first name the frame. You do so with the NAME attribute in the <FRAME> tag. In the previous example, you could name the tags in this way:

```
<FRAME SRC="contents.htm">
<FRAME SRC="instruct.htm" NAME="RIGHT">
```

which gives the name RIGHT to the frame on the right. With that frame named, you can define each link in the index page so that its target resource appears in the named frame, such as:

```
<A HREF="somefile.htm" TARGET="RIGHT">
```

In this way, your index remains in the frame on the left, while the target of each link is displayed in the frame on the right.

Finally, since frames are relatively new features of HTML, not all browsers yet support them. You can include the <NOFRAMES> tag within the frameset to provide a message to a browser that cannot display frames. Here's an example:

```
<NOFRAMES><BODY>
<P>Sorry, but this page uses frames, which your browser does
not support.</P>
</BODY></NOFRAMES>
```

As you can see, the <NOFRAMES> tag includes the <BODY> tag, which is not used in defining a frameset but would be recognized by a frames-unaware browser. Anything within the <BODY> tags would then be displayed in the browser.

The amazing thing about HTML is that it seems to grow and change almost faster than Web authors can incorporate the new developments into their sites. Although the pressure to add new features to HTML is tremendous, Microsoft and others in the Web-related industry are working hard to maintain standards in the midst of the ongoing revolution. After all, having the world beat a path to your Web page would be somewhat anticlimactic if the page can be viewed in only *some* browsers.

WHAT'S NEXT?

With this overview of Web pages and HTML behind you, you're ready to begin creating your first HTML document. In the next chapter, Deborah Ray and Eric Ray show you how to create and format a page in HTML, from setting text as headings and paragraphs to adding colors and applying fonts, with plenty of hands-on examples along the way.

Chapter 2

CREATING YOUR FIRST HTML DOCUMENT

I f you're ready to create your first HTML document, you're in the right chapter! Here, we'll help you start a new HTML document and save it using the appropriate file formats, show you how to add structure tags (which help browsers identify your HTML document), and show you how to apply some common formatting tags.

Adapted from *Mastering HTML 4*, 2nd Edition, by Deborah S. Ray and Eric J. Ray

ISBN 0-7821-2523-9   912 pages $34.99

If you're new to HTML (or rusty at hand-coding!), you might want to review the tag and attribute information in Chapter 1. Before starting this chapter, you should be familiar with tags and attributes, as well as how to apply them to the content you include.

Throughout this chapter, we provide lots of figures and code samples to help guide you and to show you what your results should look like. You can substitute your own text and images if you prefer, or you can duplicate the examples in the chapter. The step-by-step instructions will work regardless of the specific content you use. After you work through this chapter, you'll have developed your first HTML document, complete with text, headings, horizontal rules, and even some character-level formatting.

TIP

We recommend that you practice using HTML by doing the examples throughout this and other chapters.

CREATING, SAVING, AND VIEWING HTML DOCUMENTS

Exactly how you start a new HTML document depends on which operating system and editor you're using. In general, though, you'll find that starting a new HTML document is similar to starting other documents you've created. With Windows or Macintosh, you'll choose File ➢ New. Or, if you're using Unix, you'll type vi, pico, or emacs, and use the appropriate commands. You'll make your new document an official HTML document by saving it as such, which is discussed next.

Before you begin hand-coding HTML, be aware that you should frequently save and view your work so that you can see your progress. By doing so, you can make sure that things appear as you expect and catch mistakes within a few new lines of code. For example, we typically add a few new lines of code, save the HTML document, and then view it...then add a few more lines of code, save the document, and view it.... Exactly how often you save and view your documents depends on your preference, but, at least initially, you'll probably be doing it frequently.

You create an HTML document in much same way that you create any plain text document. Here's the general process:

1. Open your text editor.

2. Start a new document. If you're using Windows or Macintosh, choose File ➤ New. If you're using Unix, type `vi` or `pico` to start the editor.

3. Enter the HTML code and text you want to include. (You'll have plenty of practice in this chapter.)

4. Save your document. If you're using Windows or Macintosh, choose File ➤ Save or File ➤ Save As.

GUIDELINES FOR SAVING FILES

As you work your way through this chapter, keep these saving and viewing guidelines in mind:

▶ Name the file with an `htm` or `html` extension. Windows 3.*x* doesn't recognize four-character extensions, so you are limited to `htm` on that platform.

▶ If you aren't using a text-only editor such as Notepad or Teach-Text, verify that the file type is set to Text or ASCII (or HTML, if that's an available menu option). If you use word-processing programs to create HTML documents, save your documents as HTML, Text Only, ASCII, DOS Text, or Text With Line Breaks (the specific options will vary with your word processor).

▶ Use only letters, numbers, hyphens (-), underscores (_), and periods (.) in your filename. Most browsers also accept spaces in filenames; however, spaces often make creating links difficult.

▶ Save the document (and the rest of the documents and files associated with a particular project) in one folder. You'll find that this makes using links, images, and other advanced effects easier.

Viewing the HTML documents that you develop is as simple as opening them from your local hard drive in your browser. If you're working with an open HTML document in your editor, remember to save your latest changes, and then follow these steps in your browser:

1. Choose File ➤ Open, and type the local filename or browse your hard drive until you find the file you want to open. Your particular menu commands might be File ➤ Open Page or File ➤ Open File, but it's all the same thing.

2. Select the file, and click OK to open it in your browser.

ALTERNATIVE WAYS TO OPEN FILES

Most browsers provide some clever features that can make developing HTML files easier.

You can easily see your editing changes in a file by *reloading* it. For example, after you view a document and then save some editing changes, you can reload the document and see the latest changes. You'll probably find that clicking a Reload button is much easier than going back through the "File ➤ Open and browse" sequence. Generally, you reload documents by clicking a Refresh or Reload button or by choosing options from the View menu.

In addition, you can open a file by selecting it from a *bookmarked list* (or from a Favorites list, in Microsoft parlance). Bookmarking a file means adding a pointer to the file so that you can open the file quickly, just as a bookmark makes it easier to open a book to a specific page. Creating bookmarks (or Favorites) is as easy as clicking a menu option while viewing a page. Whenever you want to go back to that page, simply click the bookmark rather than choosing File ➤ Open and opening the file as you usually would. Most browsers have bookmark options; just look for a button or a menu command.

APPLYING STRUCTURE TAGS

After you create a new document, your first task is to include structure tags, which provide browsers with information about document characteristics. For example, structure tags identify the version of HTML used, provide introductory information about the document, and include the title, among other similar things. Most structure tags, although part of the HTML document, do not appear in the browser window. Instead, structure tags work "behind the scenes" and essentially tell the browser which elements to include and how to display them. Although these tags do not produce the snazzy results you see in Web pages or help files, they are essential for telling browsers how to interpret the document.

NOTE

Most browsers, including Netscape Navigator and Microsoft Internet Explorer, correctly display documents that do not include structure tags. However, there is no guarantee that future versions will continue to do so or that your results will be consistent. We strongly advise using structure tags.

All HTML documents should include five structure tags, nested and ordered as in the following example code:

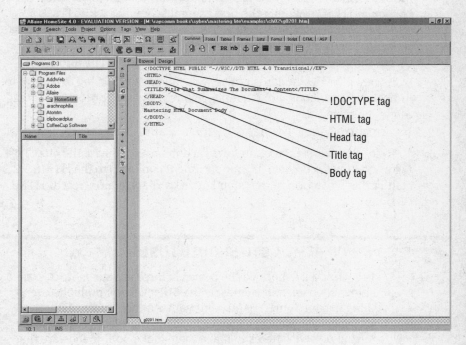

TIP

You can save time when creating future HTML documents by saving structure tags in a master document. That way, you can easily reuse them in other HTML documents, rather than retyping them time after time.

The <!DOCTYPE...> Tag

The <!DOCTYPE...> tag tells browsers (and validation services) the HTML version with which the document complies. The HTML 3.2 and 4 specifications require this nonpaired tag, and, therefore, you should use it in all your documents. Enter it at the top of your document, like this:

```
<!DOCTYPE HTML PUBLIC "-//W3C//DTD HTML 3.2 Final//EN">
```

or, like this:

```
<!DOCTYPE HTML PUBLIC "-//W3C//DTD HTML 4.0 Transitional//EN"
"http://www.w3.org/TR/html4/loose.dtd">
```

The key part of the <!DOCTYPE...> tag is the DTD (Document Type Definition) element, which tells browsers that the document complies with a particular HTML version—the first example complies with HTML 3.2, and the second with the HTML 4 Transitional (most flexible) specification. A DTD specifies the organization that issues the specification (W3C, in these cases) and the exact version of the specification.

As new HTML standards evolve, you can expect this tag to change to indicate new versions. For example, in a year or so, the <!DOCTYPE...> tag might look like this:

```
<!DOCTYPE HTML PUBLIC "-//W3C//DTD HTML 5.23 Final//EN">
```

Even after new standards appear, you don't need to revise the <!DOCTYPE...> tag in existing documents. If your document conforms to the HTML 3.2 standard, it'll conform to that standard, regardless of more recent HTML versions.

WHICH HTML 4 DTD SHOULD I USE?

The HTML 4.01 specification comes in three varieties: Strict, Transitional (loose), and Frameset. The Strict version prohibits everything except "pure" HTML, and you're unlikely to use it unless you're writing HTML documents that use no formatting tags and are relying on style sheets to make them look good. To indicate that your document complies with the Strict specification, use:

```
<!DOCTYPE HTML PUBLIC "-//W3C//DTD HTML 4.01//EN"
"http://www.w3.org/TR/html4/strict.dtd">
```

The Transitional version is the most flexible for accommodating deprecated but still useful tags and attributes, including nearly all

CONTINUED ➡

formatting tags. To indicate that your document complies with the Transitional specification, use:

```
<!DOCTYPE HTML PUBLIC "-//W3C//DTD HTML 4.01
Transitional//EN"
"http://www.w3.org/TR/html4/loose.dtd">
```

The Frameset specification is similar to the Transitional specification, but also supports the tags needed to use frames. To indicate that your document complies with the Frameset specification, use:

```
<!DOCTYPE HTML PUBLIC "-//W3C//DTD HTML 4.01
Frameset//EN"
"http://www.w3.org/TR/html4/frameset.dtd">>
```

The <HTML> Tag

The <HTML> tag identifies the document as an HTML document. Technically, this tag is superfluous after the <!DOCTYPE> tag, but it is necessary for older browsers that do not support the <!DOCTYPE...> tag. It is also helpful to people who read the HTML code. To use the <HTML> tag, enter it in your document below the <!DOCTYPE...> tag, like this:

```
<!DOCTYPE HTML PUBLIC "-//W3C//DTD HTML 4.01
Transitional//EN">
<HTML>
</HTML>
```

The <HEAD> Tag

The <HEAD> tag contains information about the document, including its title, scripts used, style definitions, and document descriptions. Not all browsers require this tag, but most browsers expect to find any available additional information about the document within the <HEAD> tag. Additionally, the <HEAD> tag can contain other tags that have information for search engines and indexing programs. To add the <HEAD> tag, enter it between the <HTML> tags, like this:

```
<!DOCTYPE HTML PUBLIC "-//W3C//DTD HTML 4.01
Transitional//EN">
<HTML>
<HEAD>
</HEAD>
</HTML>
```

TIP

Don't confuse this document head tag, which is a structure tag, with heading tags such as <H1> that create heading text in a document body. We discuss heading tags later in this chapter in the "Creating Headings" section.

The <TITLE> Tag

The <TITLE> tag, which the HTML 3.2 through 4.01 specifications require, contains the document title. The title does not appear within the browser window, although it is usually visible in the browser's title bar. Between the opening and closing tags, include a title that briefly summarizes your document's content. To use the <TITLE> tag, enter it between the opening and closing <HEAD> tags, like this:

```
<!DOCTYPE HTML PUBLIC "-//W3C//DTD HTML 4.01
Transitional//EN">
<HTML>
<HEAD>
<TITLE>
Title That Summarizes the Document's Content
</TITLE>
</HEAD>
</HTML>
```

Titles should represent the document, even if the document is taken out of context. Some good titles include the following:

- ▶ Sample HTML Code
- ▶ Learning to Ride a Bicycle
- ▶ Television Viewing for Fun and Profit

Less useful titles, particularly taken out of context, include the following:

- ▶ Examples
- ▶ Chapter 2
- ▶ Continued

The <BODY> Tag

The <BODY> tag encloses all the tags, attributes, and information that you want a visitor's browser to display. Almost everything else in this entire book takes place between the <BODY> tags. To use the <BODY> tag, enter it below the closing </HEAD> tag and above the closing </HTML> tag, like this:

```
<!DOCTYPE HTML PUBLIC "-//W3C//DTD HTML 4.01
Transitional//EN">
<HTML>
<HEAD>
<TITLE>
Title That Summarizes the Document's Content
</TITLE>
</HEAD>
<BODY>
All the tags, attributes, and information in the document
body go here.
</BODY>
</HTML>
```

If you've been following along, save your document, view it in a browser, and compare it with Figure 2.1 to confirm that you're on the right track. The title appears in the title bar, and some text appears in the document window.

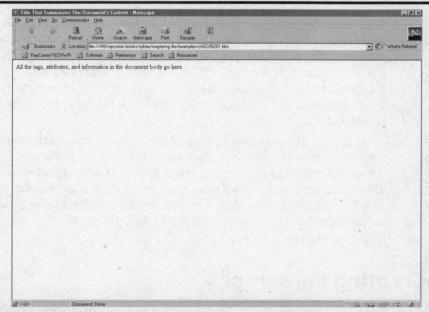

FIGURE 2.1: Your first HTML document, including all structure tags

MINIMAL COMPLIANCE FOR STRUCTURE TAGS

As shown in the previous sections, the HTML 4 specification does not require all structure tags. In fact, it requires only two: the `<!DOCTYPE...>` tag and the `<TITLE>` tag. If you choose to use only these two tags, the code would look like this:

```
<!DOCTYPE HTML PUBLIC "-//W3C//DTD HTML 4.01
Transitional//EN">
<TITLE>The name of a minimal and content free docu-
ment</TITLE>
```

Of course, there's no purpose in creating a document with nothing but the minimal tags—the document doesn't say anything and doesn't present any information. If you use these two tags as a starting point, however, you can create a standard compliant document and save yourself a few keystrokes on each new document you create.

APPLYING COMMON TAGS AND ATTRIBUTES

After you include the structure tags, you're ready to start placing basic content in the document body. The following sections show you how to include headings, paragraphs, lists, and rules (horizontal lines). These elements constitute the basic HTML document components and, unlike the structure tags, do appear in the browser window. Learning to apply these basic tags and attributes will prepare you to apply practically any HTML tag or attribute.

As you create your content, keep in mind that its exact appearance will vary from browser to browser, as described in Chapter 1. For example, a first-level heading in one browser might appear as approximately 16-point Times New Roman Bold, whereas another browser might display it as 14-point Arial Bold Italic. Both browsers display the heading bigger and bolder than other heading and body text, but the specific font, size, and emphasis will vary.

Creating Paragraphs

One of the most common tags you'll use is the paragraph tag, `<P>`, which is appropriate for regular body text. The paragraph tag absolutely does not have to be paired—you can simply use the opening tag, <P>, where you want to start a paragraph. As with many tags, however, it's easier to identify where the tag begins and ends if you use both opening and closing tags.

To use the paragraph tags, enter them around the text you want to format as a paragraph, like this:

```
<P>
A whole paragraph goes right here.
</P>
```

Figure 2.2 shows a sample paragraph.

You can also apply other paragraph formats instead of the <P> tag to achieve some slightly different paragraph formats, as explained in Table 2.1.

Alignment attributes are often used with these paragraph formatting tags, including ALIGN=LEFT, ALIGN=CENTER, ALIGN=RIGHT, and ALIGN=JUSTIFY. To apply these attributes, include them in any of the opening paragraph tags, like this:

```
<P ALIGN=CENTER>
Paragraph of information goes here.
</P>
```

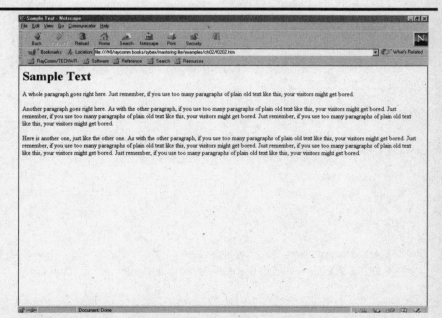

FIGURE 2.2: Paragraph text is the most common text in HTML documents.

Part I

TABLE 2.1: Other Paragraph Formatting Tags

PARAGRAPH FORMAT	EFFECT
\<ADDRESS>	Used for address and contact information. Often appears in italics.
\<BLOCKQUOTE>	Used for formatting a quotation. Usually appears indented from both sides and with less space between lines than does a regular paragraph.
\<PRE>	Effective for formatting program code or similar information. Usually appears in a fixed-width font with ample space between words and lines.

Figure 2.3 shows how the \<ADDRESS> and \<PRE> tags appear in Internet Explorer.

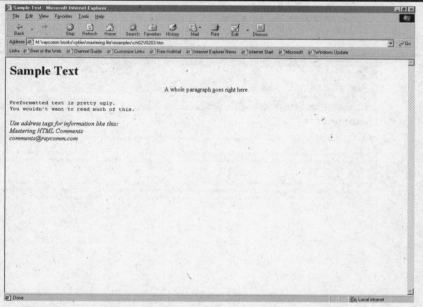

FIGURE 2.3: Special paragraph-level tags make information stand out.

Creating Headings

Headings break up large areas of text, announce topics to follow, and arrange information according to a logical hierarchy. HTML provides six levels of headings; <H1> is the highest level and largest of the headings, and <H6> is the lowest level and smallest:

```
<H1> ... </H1>
<H2> ... </H2>
<H3> ... </H3>
<H4> ... </H4>
<H5> ... </H5>
<H6> ... </H6>
```

TIP

For most documents, limit yourself to two or three heading levels. After three heading levels, many visitors begin to lose track of your hierarchy. If you find that you're using several heading levels, consider reorganizing your document—too many heading levels often indicates a larger organizational problem.

To use heading tags, enter them around the heading text, like this:

```
<!DOCTYPE HTML PUBLIC "-//W3C//DTD HTML 4.01
Transitional//EN">
<HTML>
<HEAD>
<TITLE>Sample Headings</TITLE>
</HEAD>
<BODY>
<H1>First Level Heading</H1>
<H2>Second Level Heading</H2>
<H3>Third Level Heading</H3>
</BODY>
</HTML>
```

Figure 2.4 shows how Netscape Navigator displays a few heading levels.

In general, you should use heading tags only for document headings—that is, don't use heading tags for figure captions or to emphasize information within text. Why? First, you don't always know how browsers will display the heading. It might not create the visual effect you intend. Second, some indexing and editing programs use headings to generate tables of contents and other information about your document. These programs won't exclude headings from the table of contents or other information just because you used them as, say, figure captions.

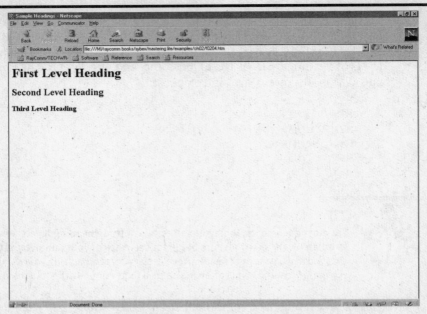

FIGURE 2.4: Heading levels provide visitors with a hierarchy of information.

By default, all browsers align headings on the left. Most browsers, however, support alignment attributes, which also let you right-align and center headings. Table 2.2 shows the alignment attributes.

TABLE 2.2: Alignment Attributes

HEADING ATTRIBUTE	EFFECT
ALIGN=LEFT	Aligns the heading on the left (default)
ALIGN=CENTER	Aligns the heading in the center
ALIGN=RIGHT	Aligns the heading on the right
ALIGN=JUSTIFY	Aligns the heading between the two margins

To use the alignment attributes, include them in the initial heading tag, like this:

```
<H1 ALIGN=LEFT>Left-aligned Heading</H1>
<H1 ALIGN=CENTER>Centered Heading</H1>
<H1 ALIGN=RIGHT>Right-aligned Heading</H1>
<H1 ALIGN=JUSTIFY>Justified Heading</H1>
```

Figure 2.5 shows headings aligned to the left, center, and right. The JUS-TIFY value is more commonly used within paragraphs rather than head-ings. Under headings, JUSTIFY works like the LEFT value.

HTML 4 OPPORTUNITY

Although most browsers support the ALIGN= attribute, consider using style sheets to create the same effect. The HTML 4 specifica-tion deprecates (strongly discourages) using the ALIGN= attribute in favor of using style sheets. So, although this attribute has wide support, if your visitors will be using very new browsers, you might consider moving toward style sheets for your formatting needs.

You'll find how-to information about style sheets in Chapter 16.

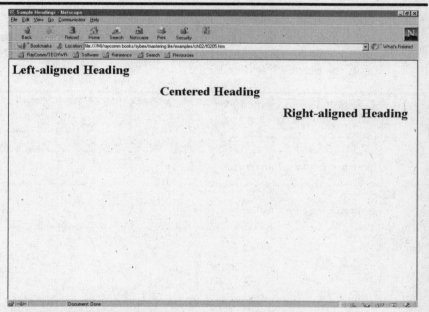

FIGURE 2.5: Headings can be aligned to the left, center, or right.

NOTE
If you're writing for a wide audience, some of whom might be using older browsers, surround the ALIGN=CENTER attributes with <CENTER> tags to ensure that the text actually appears centered, yielding something like this: <CENTER><H1 ALIGN=CENTER>Centered Heading</H1></CENTER>.

Creating Lists

Lists are a great way to provide information in a structured, easy-to-read format. They help your visitor easily spot information, and they draw attention to important information. A list is a good form for a procedure. Figure 2.6 shows the same content formatted as both a paragraph and a list.

Lists come in two varieties:

▶ Numbered (*ordered*)

▶ Bulleted (*unordered*)

To create either kind, you first specify that you want information to appear as a list, and then you identify each line item in the list. Table 2.3 shows the list and line item tags.

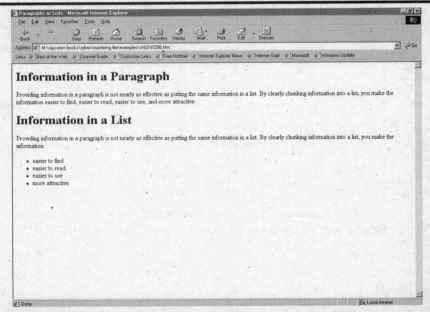

FIGURE 2.6: Lists are often easier to read than paragraphs.

TABLE 2.3: List and Line Item Tags

List Tag	Effect
<OL>	Specifies that the information appear as an ordered (numbered) list
<UL>	Specifies that the information appear as an unordered (bulleted) list
<LI>	Specifies a line item in either ordered or unordered lists

The following steps show you how to create a bulleted list; use the same steps to create a numbered list.

1. Start with text you want to format as a list.

   ```
   Lions
   Tigers
   Bears
   Oh, My!
   ```

2. Insert the <UL> tags around the list text.

   ```
   <UL>
   Lions
   Tigers
   Bears
   Oh, My!
   </UL>
   ```

3. Type the <LI> tag for each list item.

   ```
   <UL>
   <LI>Lions
   <LI>Tigers
   <LI>Bears
   <LI>Oh, My!
   </UL>
   ```

The resulting list, viewed in a browser, looks like that shown in Figure 2.7.

To change your list from unordered (bulleted) to ordered (numbered), change the <UL> to <OL> (and </UL> to </OL>). The resulting numbered list is shown in Figure 2.8.

TIP

Other less commonly used list tags include <DIR>, to create a directory list, and <MENU>, to create a menu list. You use these tags just as you use the <UL> and <OL> tags. For more information about these tags and their uses, see the appendix.

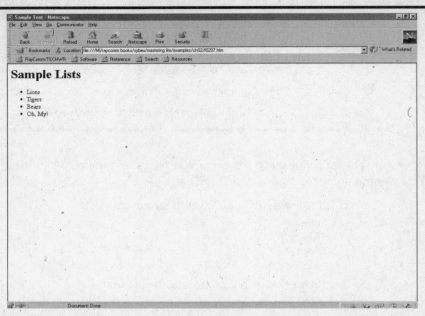

FIGURE 2.7: Bulleted lists make information easy to spot on the page and can draw attention to important points.

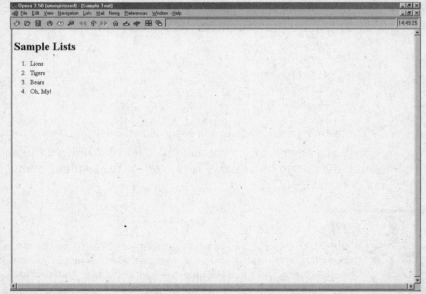

FIGURE 2.8: Numbered lists provide sequential information.

Setting List Appearance

By default, numbered lists use Arabic numerals, and bulleted lists use small, round bullets. You can change the appearance of these by using the attributes listed in Table 2.4.

Part 1

TABLE 2.4: List Attributes

LIST TAG	EFFECT
FOR NUMBERED LISTS:	
TYPE=A	Specifies the number (or letter) with which the list should start: A, a, I, i, or 1 (default)
TYPE=a	
TYPE=I	
TYPE=I	
TYPE=1	
FOR BULLETED LISTS:	
TYPE=DISC	Specifies the bullet shape
TYPE=SQUARE	
TYPE=CIRCLE	

To use any of these attributes, include them in the initial <OL> or <UL> tag or in the <LI> tag, like this:

```
<OL TYPE=A>
<LI>Outlines use sequential lists with letters.
<LI>So do some (unpopular) numbering schemes for documentation.
</OL>
```

Or, like this:

```
<UL TYPE=SQUARE>
<LI>Use bullets for non-sequential items.
<LI>Use numbers for sequential items.
</UL>
```

Or this:

```
<UL>
<LI TYPE=CIRCLE> Use bullets for non-sequential items.
<LI TYPE=SQUARE> Use different bullets for visual interest.
</UL>
```

Figure 2.9 shows how these attributes appear in a browser.

TIP

You can add the COMPACT attribute to initial <OL> or <UL> tags to tell browsers to display the list as compactly as possible. Generally, this setting will make little difference, as most browsers render lists this way by default.

NOTE

Type attributes for unordered lists are currently supported by many (but by no means all) browsers, although support is expected to continue to grow.

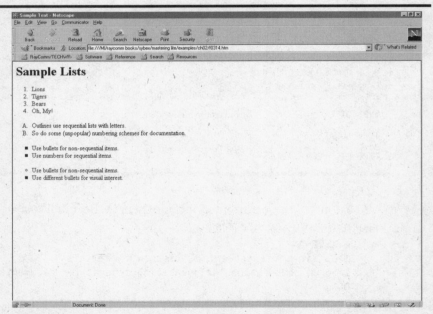

FIGURE 2.9: You can change the appearance of numbers and bullets using list attributes.

More Options for Ordered Lists

Ordered lists have additional attributes that you can use to specify the first number in the list, as well as to create hierarchical information.

First, you can start a numbered list with a value other than 1 (or A, a, I, or i). Simply include the START= attribute in the initial <OL> tag, as in <OL START=51>. Or, you can even change specific numbers within a list by using the VALUE= attribute in the <LI> tag, as in <LI VALUE=7>. To use these attributes, include them in the <OL> tag, like this:

```
<OL START=51>
<LI>This is the fifty-first item.
<LI>This is the fifty-second.
<LI TYPE=i VALUE=7>This item was renumbered to be the sev-
enth, using lowercase roman numerals, just because we can.
</OL>
```

Figure 2.10 shows how this code appears in a browser.

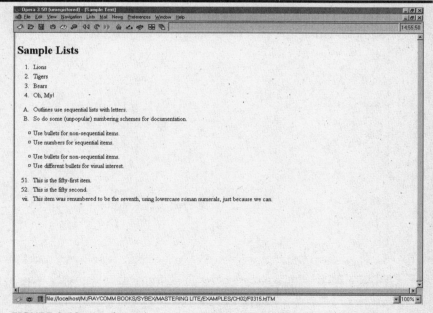

FIGURE 2.10: Attributes let you customize ordered lists in a number of ways.

Second, you can use nested ordered lists and different TYPE= attributes to create outlines. The numbering continues past each lower-level section without the need to manually renumber with a VALUE= attribute. The results are shown in Figure 2.11.

```
<OL TYPE=I>
<LI>Top Level Item
<LI>Another Top Level Item
```

```
<OL TYPE=A>
    <LI>A Second Level Item
    <LI>Another Second Level Item
    <OL TYPE=1>
        <LI>A Third Level Item
        <LI>Another Third Level Item
    </OL>
    <LI>Another Second Level Item
</OL>
<LI>A Top Level Item
</OL>
```

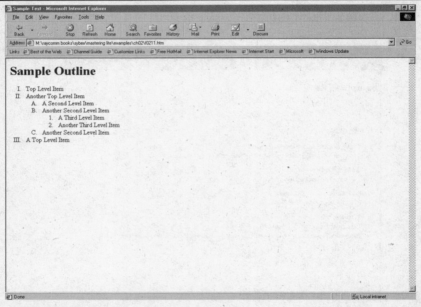

FIGURE 2.11: Ordered lists are even flexible enough to format outlines.

Using Definition Lists

Finally, one special list variant, *definition lists*, can be useful for providing two levels of information. Think of definition lists as dictionary entries—you have two levels of information: the entry, followed by a definition. You can use these lists to provide glossary-type information, or you can use them to provide two-level lists. Table 2.5 lists the tags and their effects.

TABLE 2.5: Definition List and Item Tags

List Tag	Effect
<DL>	Specifies that the information appear as a definition list
<DT>	Identifies definition terms
<DD>	Identifies definitions

To create a definition list, as shown in Figure 2.12, follow these steps:

1. Enter the <DL> tags to start the definition list.

   ```
   <DL>
   </DL>
   ```

2. Add the <DT> tag to identify definition terms.

   ```
   <DL>
   <DT>HTML
   <DT>Maestro
   </DL>
   ```

3. Add the <DD> tag to identify individual definitions.

   ```
   <DL>
   <DT>HTML
   <DD>Hypertext Markup Language is used to create Web
   pages.
   <DT>Maestro
   <DD>An expert in some field. See "Readers of
   <I>Mastering HTML</I>" for examples.
   </DL>
   ```

TIP

A great way to apply definition lists is in "What's New" lists—a special page that tells people what's new and exciting on your site or at your organization. Try putting the dates in the <DT> tag (maybe with boldface and italics) and the information in the <DD> tag.

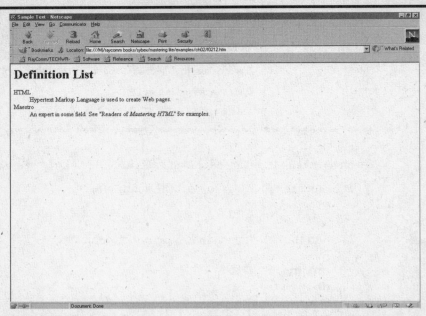

FIGURE 2.12: Definition lists are a useful formatting option when presenting dictionary-like information.

Applying Bold, Italic, and Other Emphases

In addition to creating paragraphs, headings, and lists, you can also apply formatting to individual letters and words. For example, you can make a word appear *italic,* **bold**, <u>underlined</u>, or superscript, as in e^2. You use these character-level formatting tags only within paragraph-level tags—that is, you can't put a <P> tag within a character-level tag such as <B>. You have to close the character-level formatting before you close the paragraph-level formatting.

Correct:

```
<P><B>This is the end of a paragraph that also uses
boldface.</B></P>
<P>This is the beginning of the following paragraph.
```

Incorrect:

```
This text <B>is boldface.</P>
<P>As is this </B></P>
```

Although many character-formatting tags are available, you'll probably use <B> (for **boldface**) and <I> (for *italics*) most often. Table 2.6 shows a list of the most common character-formatting tags.

TABLE 2.6: Common Character-Formatting Tags

CHARACTER TAG	EFFECT
<B>	Applies boldface.
<BLINK>	Makes text blink, usually considered highly unprofessional.
<CITE>	Indicates citations or references.
<CODE>	Displays program code. Similar to the <PRE> tag.
<EM>	Applies emphasis; usually displayed as italic.
<I>	Applies italics.
<S>, <STRIKE>	Applies strikethrough to text. These tags are deprecated in the HTML 4 specification.
<STRONG>	Applies stronger emphasis; usually displayed as bold.
<SUB>	Formats text as subscript.
<SUP>	Formats text as superscript.
<TT>	Applies a fixed-width font.
<U>	Applies underline. This tag is deprecated in the HTML 4 specification.
<VAR>	Displays variables or arguments.

To use these tags, enter them around the individual letters or words you want to emphasize, like this:

```
Making some text <B>bold</B> or <I>italic</I> is
a useful technique, more so than
<STRIKE>strikethrough</STRIKE> or
<BLINK>blinking</BLINK>.
```

Figure 2.13 shows some sample character formatting. (The blinking word doesn't appear in this figure so you can see that it disappears.)

TIP

Spend a few minutes trying out these character-formatting tags to see how they work and how they look in your favorite browser.

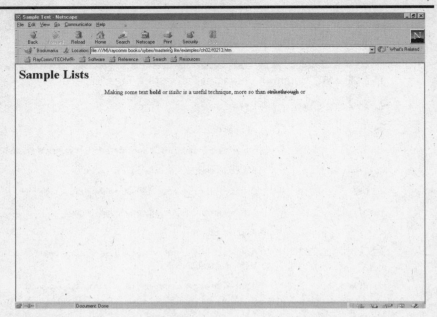

FIGURE 2.13: Character formatting helps you emphasize words or letters.

HTML 4 OPPORTUNITY

The HTML 4 specification strongly encourages using style sheets for your formatting needs. Although the specification still supports many individual formatting tags, it is moving toward style sheets as the recommended way to include formatting in your HTML documents. Using style sheets, you can apply the following:

► Character-level formatting such as strikethrough and underline

► Paragraph-level formatting such as indents and margins

► Other formatting such as background colors and images

See Chapter 16 for style sheet information.

Including Horizontal Rules

Horizontal rules are lines that break up long sections of text, indicate a shift in information, or help improve the overall document design. To use a horizontal rule, include the <HR> tag where you want the rule to appear, like this:

```
<P>Long passages of text should often be broken into sections
with headings and, optionally, horizontal rules.</P>
<HR>
<H3>A Heading Also Breaks Up Text</H3>
<P>A new long passage can continue here. </P>
```

By default, horizontal rules appear shaded, span the width of the browser window, and are a few pixels high. You can change a rule's shading, width, height, and alignment by including the appropriate attributes. Table 2.7 shows horizontal rule attributes.

NOTE

Pixels are the little dots on your screen that, taken together, produce an image. Pixel is actually an abbreviation for Picture Element. If your display is set to 800 × 600, you have 800 pixels horizontally and 600 pixels vertically.

TABLE 2.7: Horizontal Rule Attributes

RULE ATTRIBUTE	EFFECT
SIZE=n	Specifies rule height; measured in pixels
WIDTH=n	Specifies rule width (length); measured in pixels
WIDTH="n%"	Specifies rule width (length); measured as a percentage of the document width
ALIGN=LEFT	Specifies left alignment
ALIGN=CENTER	Specifies center alignment
ALIGN=RIGHT	Specifies right alignment
NOSHADE	Specifies that the rule has no shading

To use any of these attributes, include them in the <HR> tag, like this:

```
<HR WIDTH="80%" SIZE=8>
<HR WIDTH="50%">
<HR WIDTH=400 ALIGN=RIGHT>
<HR NOSHADE ALIGN=CENTER WIDTH=200>
```

Figure 2.14 shows some sample horizontal rules, with height, width, alignment, and shading attributes added.

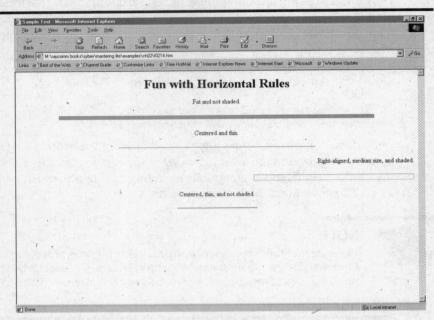

FIGURE 2.14: Horizontal rules can help separate information, improve page design, and simply add visual interest to the page.

Specifying Line Breaks

Sometimes you need to break a line in a specific place, but you don't want to start a new paragraph (with the extra space). For example, you might not want lines of poetry text to go all the way across the document; instead, you might want to break them into several shorter lines. You can easily break paragraph lines by inserting the <BR> tag where you want the lines to break, like this:

```
<P>
There once was an HTML writer,<BR>
Who tried to make paragraphs wider.<BR>
He found with a shock<BR>
All the tags did mock<BR>
The attempt to move that text outside-r.<BR>
Mercifully Anonymous</P>
```

INCLUDING FANCIER FORMATTING

Now that you have a firm grip on using the basic HTML formatting options, you can dive into some of the fancier formatting effects. In the following sections, we'll show you how to add colors and specify fonts and sizes. Although most newer browsers support these effects, not all browsers do; your fancier effects might not reach all visitors. Also, the HTML 4 specification deprecates many of these effects in favor of style sheets. If your visitors use style sheet–capable browsers, you might consider using style sheets instead of the tags and attributes mentioned here.

Adding Colors

One of the easiest ways to jazz up your documents is to add colors to the background or text. You can enliven an otherwise dull Web page with a splash of color or an entire color scheme. For example, add a background color and change the text colors to coordinate with the background. Or highlight a word or two with color and make the words leap off the page. Or, if you're developing a corporate site, adhere to the company's color scheme to ensure a consistent look.

The drawback to setting colors is that you really don't have control over what your visitors see. Visitors might set their browsers to display colors they like, or they might be using a text-only browser, which generally displays only black, white, and gray.

You specify colors using hexadecimal numbers, which combine proportions of Red, Green, and Blue—called RGB numbers. RGB numbers use six digits, two for each proportion of red, green, and blue. As you're choosing colors, remember that not all RGB numbers display well in browsers; some colors *dither*, meaning that they appear spotty or splotchy. We recommend that you select RGB values that are appropriate for Web page use, as listed in Table 2.8. Although you'll never go wrong with these "safe" colors, it's most important to use these colors in page backgrounds or in places with large patches of color, where dithering will occur if you don't use these number combinations.

TABLE 2.8: Recommended RGB Values

R	G	B
00	00	00
33	33	33
66	66	66
99	99	99
CC	CC	CC
FF	FF	FF

To create an RGB number from the values in this table, simply select one number from each column. For example, choose FF from the Red column, 00 from the Green column, and 00 from the Blue column to create the RGB number FF0000, which has the largest possible red component but no blue and no green, therefore appearing as a pure, bright red. You'll find a complete list of appropriate RGB numbers and corresponding descriptions in the appendix.

Setting Background Colors

Using a *background color*, which is simply a color that fills the entire browser window, is a great way to add flair to your Web pages. By default, browsers display a white or gray background color, which may be adequate if you're developing pages for an intranet site where flashy elements aren't essential. If you're developing a public or personal site, however, you'll probably want to make your site more interesting and visually appealing. For example, if you're developing a public corporate Web site, you might want to use your company's standard colors—ones that appear on letterhead, logos, or marketing materials. Or, you might want to use your favorite color if you're developing a personal site. In either case, using a background color can improve the overall page appearance and help develop a theme among pages.

As you'll see in the next section, pay careful attention to how text contrasts with the background color. If you specify a dark background color, use a light text color. Likewise, if you specify a light background color, use a dark text color. Contrast is key for ensuring that visitors can read information on your pages.

To specify a background color for your documents, include the
BGCOLOR="#..." attribute in the opening <BODY> tag, like this:

```
<BODY BGCOLOR="#FFFFFF">
```

Setting Text Colors

Like background colors, text colors can enhance your Web pages. In particular, you can specify the color of the following:

- ▶ Body text, which appears throughout the document body

- ▶ Unvisited links, which are links not yet followed

- ▶ Active links, which are links as they're being selected

- ▶ Visited links, which are links previously followed

Changing body text is sometimes essential—for example, if you've added a background color or an image. If you've added a dark background color, the default black body text color won't adequately contrast with the background, making the text difficult or impossible to read. In this case, you'd want to change the text color to one that's lighter so that it contrasts with the background sufficiently.

Changing link colors helps keep your color scheme intact—for unvisited as well as visited links. Set the visited and unvisited links to different colors to help visitors know which links they've followed and which ones they haven't.

To change body text and link colors, simply add the attributes listed in Table 2.9 to the opening <BODY> tag.

TABLE 2.9: Text and Link Color Attributes

ATTRIBUTE	DESCRIPTION
TEXT="..."	Sets the color for all text within the document with a color name or a #RRGGBB value
ALINK="..."	Sets the color for active links, which are the links at the time the visitor clicks on them, with a color name or a #RRGGBB value
VLINK="..."	Sets the color for links the visitor has recently followed with a color name or a #RRGGBB value (how recently depends on browser settings)
LINK="..."	Sets the color for unvisited links with a color name or a #RRGGBB value

To change text and link colors, follow these steps:

1. Within the <BODY> tag, add the TEXT= attribute to set the color for text within the document. This example makes the text black.

   ```
   <BODY TEXT="#FFFFFF">
   ```

2. Add the LINK= attribute to set the link color. This example uses blue (#0000FF) for the links.

   ```
   <BODY TEXT="#FFFFFF" LINK="#0000FF">
   ```

3. Add the VLINK= attribute to set the color for visited links. If you set the VLINK= to the same as the link, links will not change colors even after visitors follow them. This could be confusing, but also serves to make it look like there is always new material available. This example sets the visited link to a different shade of blue.

   ```
   <BODY TEXT="#FFFFFF" LINK="#0000FF" VLINK="#000099">
   ```

4. Finally, set the ALINK= or active link color. This is the color of a link while visitors are clicking on it and will not necessarily be visible in Internet Explorer 4, depending on visitor settings. This example sets ALINK= to red.

   ```
   <BODY TEXT="#FFFFFF" LINK="#0000FF" VLINK="#000099" ALINK="#FF0000">
   ```

Specifying Fonts and Font Sizes

If your visitors will be using fairly new browsers, you can use the <FONT>
tag to specify font characteristics for your document, including color, size,
and typeface. Table 2.10 describes the tags and attributes you'll use to set
font characteristics.

TABLE 2.10: Font Characteristics

TAG/ATTRIBUTE	DESCRIPTION
<FONT>	Sets font characteristics for text.
SIZE="..."	Specifies relative font size on a scale of 1 through 7. 3 is the default or normal size. You can also specify the relative size by using + or –, for example, +2.
COLOR="..."	Specifies font color in #RRGGBB numbers or with color names. This color applies only to the text surrounded by the <FONT> tags.
FACE="..."	Specifies typefaces as a list of possible typefaces, in order of preference, separated by commas—for example, "Verdana, Arial, Helvetica".
<BASEFONT>	Sets the text characteristics for the document.

As you're determining which font face to use, keep in mind that the
font must be available on your visitors' computers for them to view the
fonts you specify. For example, if you specify Technical as the font to use
and your visitors do not have Technical, their computers will substitute a
font, which might not be a font you'd consider acceptable. As a partial
way of overcoming this problem, you can list multiple faces in order of
preference; the machine displays the first available. For example, a list of
"Comic Sans MS, Technical, Tekton, Times, Arial" will display Comic
Sans MS if available, then try Technical, then Tekton, and so forth.

So, which fonts should you choose? Table 2.11 lists fonts that are commonly available on PC, Mac, and Unix platforms.

TABLE 2.11: Fonts Commonly Available on PC, Mac, and Unix

WINDOWS	MACINTOSH	UNIX
Arial	Helvetica	Helvetica
Times New Roman	Times	Times
Courier New	Courier	Courier

Part i

TIP

You might check out Microsoft's selection of fonts, which you can easily download (go to www.microsoft.com). These fonts, which are cool, are available to visitors who have specifically downloaded the fonts to their computers, or who are using Internet Explorer 4 or newer, or who are using Windows 98.

To specify font characteristics, follow these steps. You can set some or all of the characteristics used in this example.

1. Identify the text to format with the `<FONT>` tag.

    `<FONT>Look at this!</FONT>`

2. Select a specific font using the FACE= attribute. See Table 2.11 for a list of commonly available fonts.

    `<FONT FACE="Verdana, Times New Roman, Times">Look at this!</FONT>`

3. Change the font size using the SIZE= attribute. You set the size of text on a relative scale—from 1 to 7, with the default size being 3. Either set the size absolutely, with a number from 1 to 7, or relatively, with + or − to change the size. Almost all newer browsers (and all HTML 3.2 and 4−compliant browsers) support SIZE= to set font size. The only significant downside to setting the font size is that your visitor might already have increased (or decreased) the default font size, so your size change might have more of an effect than you expected.

    `<FONT FACE="Technical, Times New Roman, Times" SIZE="+2">Look at this!</FONT>`

4. Add a COLOR= attribute to set the color, using a color name or a #RRGGBB value.

    `<FONT FACE="Technical, Times New Roman, Times" SIZE="+2" COLOR="#FF0000">Look at this!</FONT>`

Figure 2.15 shows the resulting appearance.

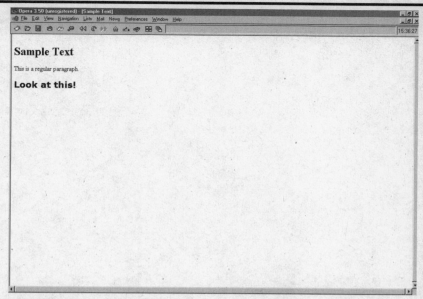

FIGURE 2.15: Setting font characteristics can spiff up your pages and help you achieve the visual effect you want.

WHAT'S NEXT

Congratulations! You've just learned to apply HTML code, and you even learned some of the most common tags and attributes. Now that you can create your own basic Web page, move on to Chapter 3, where E. Stephen Mack and Janan Platt Saylor will show you how to link to other pages on the World Wide Web.

Chapter 3

STEPPING OUT: LINKING YOUR WAY AROUND THE WEB

Being able to link your Web page to other pages is the most innovative and compelling aspect of the Web, and it is certainly a huge part of the Web's success. Links are convenient—and also exciting—since they provide related information to anyone viewing your page.

Adapted from *HTML 4.0, No experience required*, by E. Stephen Mack and Janan Platt Saylor

ISBN 0-7821-2143-8   704 pages $29.99

In this chapter, we'll review link basics and then learn much more about links, including how to use advanced anchor attributes and how to name sections of your document so you can create tables of contents with links to a particular part of your document.

We'll see the two major categories of links: *external links,* which are links to files not on your own site (created by someone else) and *internal links,* which are links to files that are part of your site (created by you). Even though you'll use the same anchor element for both types of links, it's worth looking at them separately because they involve different concepts. We'll start by looking at external links, then learn how to integrate anchors with other HTML tags, and then talk about internal links.

Finally, we'll discuss how to maintain links and check automatically for faulty links.

CREATING AN EXTERNAL LINK

The anchor element uses the <A> and </A> tags. The anchor element is used to create both external links and internal links (both of which are otherwise known as *hyperlinks*).

NOTE
These anchor links are not to be confused with the link element (which uses the <LINK> tag); the link element establishes different types of relationships between your document and other affiliated documents, while anchors create physical links in the body of your document.

The anchor element takes several attributes. We'll look first at the attributes HREF, TITLE, TARGET, and NAME separately, and then we'll see some other attributes, including REL and REV, and generic HTML 4.0 attributes. We'll also discuss some tips for your anchor text while we discuss the HREF attribute.

Since external links use the URL addressing scheme, we'll talk about anchors in the context of external links first.

NOTE
Unlike most HTML tags, which don't require attributes, the anchor tag requires either the HREF attribute or the NAME attribute (or both).

Using the HREF Attribute and Anchor Text

Most of the time, you must use the anchor element's HREF attribute to specify the Hyperlink REFerence (that is, a reference to a link's address). The HREF attribute must point to a URL, and the URL should appear in quotes, like this:

```
<A HREF="http://www.construct.net/">Construct</A>
```

NOTE

A URL (Uniform Resource Locator) is a unique address for a Web page or any other file on the Internet.

In this example, the HREF is pointing to a Web page at the URL http://www.construct.net/.

TIP

When adding a link to your page, it's sometimes difficult to make sure that the URL is typed correctly. (One typo and it might not work at all.) You can visit the page you want to link to, copy the address from the location bar, and then paste it into your text editor in between the quotes of your HREF attribute.

You don't have to link to Web pages—you can link to any type of file on the Web, including images, sounds, and movies. For example, here's some text that includes a link to a movie that's in Microsoft's AVI format:

```
<P>You can see a five-megabyte movie of two guys playing
souped-up <A HREF="http://www.unrealities.com/robj/videos/
roshambo.avi">Roshambo</A>.
```

(You'll learn more about images in Chapter 10; you'll see more about multimedia, including movies and sounds, in Chapter 15.)

TIP

When linking to a format that's not usually used on the Web, it's polite to put some details about that format in your anchor text. For example, if you have a zip file containing some PowerPoint documents, your anchor might look like this:
```
<A HREF="files.zip">A Zipped Archive of PowerPoint files,
104K</A>.
```

You can also use links that don't use the HTTP protocol, such as links to files served by FTP (File Transfer Protocol):

```
<P>If you have trouble downloading this
```

```
<A HREF="ftp://ftp.emf.net/users/estephen/file.txt">
file</A>, then go ahead and <A HREF="mailto:
estephen@emf.net">send me a message</A>.
```

Whenever you link to a resource, the text enclosed within the anchor element is highlighted as a link, and serves as the *anchor text* that somehow introduces the resource to which you are linking. For example, in the link `<A HREF="http://www.suite101.com/">Visit Suite 101</A>`, "Visit Suite 101" is the anchor text. By default, anchor text is blue and underlined in Netscape Navigator and Microsoft Internet Explorer.

WARNING

You can set the link color in your browser to whatever color you want. You can also select whether links are underlined. Therefore, good Web authors won't include a statement like, "Click on the blue and underlined word 'Next' above to see the next page!"—the word "Next" may not be underlined or blue at all.

It's best not to use device-specific terms in your anchor text. For example, Web authors commonly use statements like:

```
<P>Click <A HREF="http://www.tori.com/">here</A> to read
about Tori Amos!
```

However, not everyone viewing your page has a mouse, so what if they can't click anything? Also, the anchor text is just the word "here," which isn't much of a description—some browsers remember pages you visit by their anchor text. Anyone viewing a list of recently visited pages may see your document listed as just the word "here," which won't help them remember what the "here" document is about.

Instead, use the anchor element to surround the most relevant description of the resource to which you're linking:

```
<P>Read about <A HREF="http://www.tori.com/">Tori Amos</A>!
```

Now the person viewing your page can select the link (whether by mouse or another method) and also knows exactly what page they're visiting; the page's description will appear in any lists of visited documents, and this approach is more concise than the "click here" approach.

To continue our discussion of anchor text, some links use straightforward anchor text.

```
<P>Kyrie works for <A HREF="http://www.sgi.com/">SGI</A>.
```

In this case, "SGI" (Silicon Graphics, Inc.) is the name of the company, and clicking the company name would lead to SGI's main Web site. It might be misleading for the word "SGI" to lead anywhere other than a main SGI home page.

Sometimes, Web authors create anchor text that is subtle so that people are surprised when they follow the link. For example:

```
<P>Partha told me he thought we should sue
<A HREF="http://www.ticketmaster.com/">those jerks</A>.
```

It's not clear from the context of the page who "those jerks" is meant to refer to—until you point to the words "those jerks" and see Ticketmaster's URL on the status bar. At that point, you understand the object of Partha's ire.

This "misleading" use of anchor text is all part of the fun of the Web and is quite common.

WARNING

Some corporations do not take kindly to the appropriation of their logos or people "misrepresenting" their name. One Web author, John Klopp, actually received a nasty phone call from a Pacific Bell lawyer for putting a link similar to this one on his page: `<A HREF="http://www.playboy.com/">Pacific Bell</A>`. Some companies have threatened to sue Web authors who use their company name in a disparaging way. Your chances of being successfully sued depend on if you are misusing a trademarked logo and whether you are running a commercial page that makes money—as well as the truth of your claims about the company.

Creating Advisory Titles for Your Links with the TITLE Attribute

One anchor attribute that provides more information about a link is the TITLE attribute. The TITLE attribute allows an "advisory title" that explains the resource in more detail. Using the previous example, you can make it clearer who Partha dislikes by adding the following HTML code, which differs only by including a TITLE attribute in the anchor element:

```
<P>Partha told me he thought we should sue <A HREF="http://
www.ticketmaster.com/" TITLE="Ticketmaster">those jerks</A>.
```

Browsers may choose different methods of showing the advisory TITLE attribute, such as displaying the title in a *tool tip* or *balloon help* (a little box that appears when the mouse pointer is pointing to the link), or the title might appear on the status bar. Currently, the only popular browser that makes use of the TITLE attribute in a link is Internet Explorer 4, which displays it as a tool tip (as shown in Figure 3.1); Navigator should soon support these attributes.

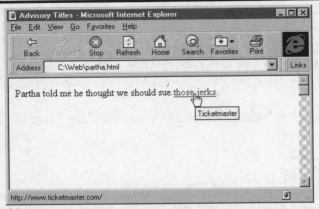

FIGURE 3.1: Internet Explorer displays a tool tip for this link, thanks to the use of the TITLE attribute in the anchor element.

CHANGING THE STATUS BAR TEXT FOR YOUR LINKS

When you point to a link, Navigator and Internet Explorer display the URL of the link's target in the status bar. A commonly used attribute (similar in intent to the TITLE attribute) changes the browser's status bar to display a specific phrase when pointing to the link.

Consider this code:

```
<TITLE>Text in the Status Bar</TITLE>
<BODY>
We buy all of our books from <A HREF="http://www
.sybex.com/"
ONMOUSEOVER="window.status='Click Here For Computer
Books!'; return true">Sybex</A>.
```

CONTINUED ➡

When the mouse pointer crosses over the anchor text ("Sybex"), the status bar doesn't display the link's URL as it normally would. Instead, the phrase "Click Here For Computer Books!" is displayed, as shown here.

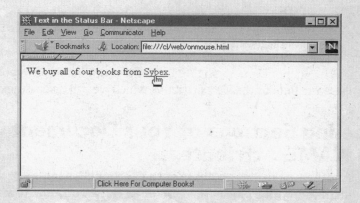

The attribute value for ONMOUSEOVER in the above HTML code (beginning with the word "window.status") is not HTML at all—instead, this line contains two JavaScript commands. JavaScript is a scripting language, created by Netscape, that can change how Web pages behave. This particular JavaScript code is fairly simple (just one line and two commands), and causes a visible change to the way that Web pages behave, so it's easy to understand why it is popular.

The ONMOUSEOVER attribute is one example of HTML 4.0's new event attributes; the event attributes can be used with many different elements, not just anchors. You'll see more about JavaScript in Chapter 20, but while we're discussing this status bar example, we should point out that it has a major drawback: many people like to see the URL of the links on a page, and they get annoyed when the URL is replaced with a different message in the status bar. (Internet Explorer 4 combats this problem a little by showing the URL as a tool tip.) In general, people should be able to use their browser normally when they view Web pages. Every time you change the normal behavior of the browser, you risk confusing or annoying people. Also, many visitors to your page might not be able to see the JavaScript message, so you shouldn't rely on conveying important information in the status bar.

The TITLE attribute can provide a description for links to images or other file types that don't have a full title. For example:

```
<P>You can see <A HREF="http://www.construct.net/images/
goolnut.jpg"TITLE="Construct's Hand Logo">a logo</A> that I
admire.
```

NOTE

The advisory TITLE attribute can apply to almost every HTML element, not just the anchor element.

The anchor element's TITLE attribute is not nearly as important as the HREF attribute or the NAME attribute, which we will discuss next.

Labeling Sections of Your Document with the NAME Attribute

Another important attribute of the anchor element is the NAME attribute, which labels a section of an HTML document with a specific reference name.

The NAME attribute enables links to point to a specific section within a document (instead of links always leading to the top of a document).

For example, suppose you want to link to the street directions on a particular page at your site. But the page is a long one, and the directions are near the bottom. If you link to the page itself, no one will see the directions unless they read all the way to the bottom of the page. Fortunately, you can link straight to the directions. It's a two-step process: First, you must edit the target document and give a name to the section where the directions begin, using the NAME attribute of the anchor element. Second, you must specify that name in your link.

The appropriate section of the page (where the street directions are located) can be named using this anchor element:

```
<A NAME="directions">Here are the directions to our
office:</A>
```

NOTE

The anchor element here isn't supposed to affect this text's appearance, but some older browsers do change the enclosed text by making it bold.

Once you've added this code, you can link to the directions by taking a normal link tag and adding a number sign (#) and the name assigned (in this case, `directions`) to the URL. If the normal URL for the page is `http://www.foo.com/`, then you would specify the link for the directions name like this:

```
The <A HREF="http://www.foo.com/#directions"> directions to
our office</A> are available
```

HTML 4.0 uses the term *fragment URLs* for these URLs that link to a named anchor section of a document.

TIP

You can only link to named sections; you can't arbitrarily link to the middle of a document unless the <A NAME="*name*"> and </A> tags have been added to that document.

Let's take a real-life example. Suppose you want to link to a particular poem in Shakespeare's play *The Tempest* (available from MIT at `http://the-tech.mit.edu/Shakespeare/works.html`). Let's say the section you want occurs in Act I, Scene 2. MIT has broken up each scene of *The Tempest* into a separate file, so the desired URL turns out to be `http://the-tech.mit.edu/Shakespeare/Comedy/tempest/thetempest.1.2.html`. But this scene contains 593 lines, and your poem is near the bottom.

Fortunately, MIT has added a NAME attribute anchor to each line of every Shakespeare play. The NAME attribute anchor is simply the line number, anchored around a word in that line. For example, the line you're interested in is line number 461 of this scene. (You can discover this by searching at the Shakespeare site for the word or phrase in which you're interested.) Here's the NAME attribute anchor that's used by MIT:

```
<A NAME="461">fathom</A>
```

So you can now link straight to your poem by adding #461 to end of the URL for the scene, which creates a fragment URL. You can use the fragment URL in your link like this:

```
<P>One of my favorite poems is sung by a character named
Ariel in William Shakespeare's <CITE>The Tempest</CITE>, at
<A HREF="http://the-tech.mit.edu/Shakespeare/Comedy/tempest/
thetempest.1.2.html#461">line 461 of Act I, Scene 2</A>. This
verse was used in a song by Laurie Anderson.
```

Part I

WARNING

The fragment URL used here is very long; it must be typed in one continuous line, with no line breaks or spaces at all. Remember, any white space in any URL will prevent it from working.

Now when someone clicks on the link text (line 461 of Act I, Scene 2), they'll see the poem at the top of the screen, with the rest of the play continuing underneath. Figure 3.2 shows the result—note the extra information in Internet Explorer's location bar URL, and you can judge by the vertical scroll bar how far down in the document this line occurs.

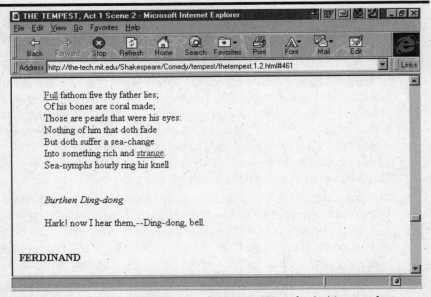

FIGURE 3.2: Internet Explorer uses a fragment URL to fetch this verse from Shakespeare's *The Tempest*. The Full and strange links lead to a discussion of those words in a glossary.

There's more to learn about named sections and using named links; we'll return to the topic of anchor names later in this chapter.

Changing Browser Windows with the TARGET Attribute

Another attribute you can use in an anchor element's <A> tag is TARGET. The TARGET attribute is normally used with frames (as we'll see in Chapter 8). However, you can use the TARGET attribute even if you don't use frames.

When you specify a TARGET for your links, you indicate the name of a window where you'd like the linked page to appear. For example, a link can be specified like this:

```
<A
HREF="http://www.walrus.com/~gibralto/"TARGET="window2">Acorn
Mush</A>
```

When this link is followed, a new window (named internally "window2") is created, containing the Acorn Mush page.

The browsers that obey target attributes (including Internet Explorer and Navigator) create new windows that look as if an extra copy of the browser is running. The old window is located behind the new window, and the old page that contained the link will still be visible, if the browser does not take up the full screen. If a browser does take up the full screen, then the only way to see the old window is for the user to switch windows and go back to the old page.

The new window, with the new page, functions like a normal copy of the browser in every respect. Eventually, the viewer will close the new window, revealing the old window again—which in effect guarantees that the viewer will return to the original site at some point.

Web designers like the idea of letting people follow a link from their site while still keeping their site visible somewhere.

The main drawback of the TARGET attribute is that some users can get confused by the unexpected behavior of their browsers when they follow a targeted link. Since each browser window maintains its own history of documents viewed, viewers can get confused when they can't seem to return to a recently visited page—until they notice their old window with their old history.

Also, if a viewer switches back to the old window while leaving the new window open but hidden, then any other links that they select with the same TARGET window (for example, a second link that also specifies TARGET="window2") will appear to be do *nothing at all*! The viewer will be confused about why links have stopped working in their browser. In reality, the links are working—but the link is only causing a change in a *hidden* window, so it *seems* like nothing is happening.

Using Other Anchor Attributes

There are several other attributes used in an anchor element's <A> tag.

Although rarely used, the REL and REV attributes can theoretically mark relationships between the current document and the resource in the link. Here's an example from the HTML 4.0 specification:

```
<P>Thanks to <A REL="SPONSOR">Acme Inc</A> for support.</P>
```

This link specifies that "Acme Inc" has a "sponsor" relationship to the current document. The important thing to realize about this type of anchor is that it does *not* necessarily create a link to Acme or to any particular URL; you always have to use an HREF attribute if you want a link.

Every popular browser currently ignores these kinds of relationship attributes, so there's not much point in using them yet.

HTML 4.0 allows several new attributes to be used with anchors. First we'll discuss the new ACCESSKEY attribute, and after that we'll take a detailed look at how you can use HTML 4.0's generic attributes with the anchor element to produce some useful effects.

Specifying Keyboard Shortcuts for Links

One drawback with a graphical browser is that it is usually very mouse-dependent. For example, you have to click on links to follow them if you use Navigator 3 or earlier. (Internet Explorer 3 and 4 and Navigator 4 all let you use the Tab key to select a link and then Enter to follow it.)

If a page has many links, then this keyboard method is a little cumbersome and can be difficult to use, especially for people with disabilities. HTML 4.0 addresses this problem with the new ACCESSKEY attribute, which lets you specify a shortcut key to be used to follow a link (for example, you can specify that a link should be followed whenever a user presses the A key).

Using the ACCESSKEY attribute with an anchor is simple: specify a single character as an attribute value. When the surfer presses the equivalent keyboard shortcut command, the browser should automatically select and follow the link.

For example:

```
<A HREF="http://www.yahoo.com/" ACCESSKEY="Y">Yahoo!</A>
```

specifies that the Y key should take your readers to Yahoo!'s URL. However, Windows users must press Alt+Y, and Macintosh users must press Command+Y to follow the Yahoo! link. Other systems may use different shortcuts, or perhaps allow the shortcut key to be used by itself (without a modifier key).

According to the HTML 4.0 specification, browsers should indicate the Y key as the shortcut in some fashion. You shouldn't have to write, "Press the Y key to visit Yahoo!" anywhere on your page (and that description wouldn't be accurate for all systems or browsers, anyway). However, you may need to include the name of the access key in the anchor text so that it can be highlighted. For example, if you want to use Z as the ACCESSKEY value for your Yahoo! link, use anchor text such as "Z: Yahoo!" or "Yahoo! (Z)" to provide a visual indication that Z is the shortcut key.

NOTE

Currently, only Internet Explorer 4 and above supports the use of the ACCESSKEY attribute, but other browsers should introduce support for it shortly. However, Internet Explorer does not indicate the shortcut key on screen at all. Pressing the access key highlights the URL. You will still need to press Enter to go to the Web site.

Using Language Attributes

The generic LANG and DIR attributes can be particularly useful with anchors, since you can indicate what language is being used in the linked document, as well as the direction (left-to-right or right-to-left) that is used in that document.

In addition, the anchor element allows a special CHARSET attribute to declare what character encoding (that is, what set of foreign language characters) is used in the linked-to resource.

For example:

```
<A HREF="http://www.jmas.co.jp/FAQs/" LANG="JP" CHARSET=
"euc-jp">Index to various FAQs</A>
```

is a link to a page on a server located in Japan. The language of the page is declared to be Japanese by the LANG attribute. The CHARSET attribute indicates that browsers should use a particular character encoding to display the Japanese characters that are used on the page. In this case, the character encoding is called "euc-jp", but other charsets are possible as well. Unfortunately, charsets are not yet in wide enough use for there to be a definitive list of them anywhere. More details about charsets can be found online (http://www.ietf.org/rfc/rfc2045.txt).

Using Reference, Style, and Script Attributes

By defining a style sheet and applying one of these attributes to an anchor element, you can control a wide range of possibilities for the appearance of links and anchor text.

In addition, HTML 4.0 specifically allows the use of ID attribute values as a target for named anchors. So instead of using an anchor with a NAME attribute to label a particular part of your document, you can use an element's ID attribute. For example, you could name a section of bold text with the identity "Greg" as shown:

```
<B ID="greg">Greg Burrell</B> is an expert on this subject.
```

Later in your document (or in a different document), you can link to the "Greg" section using a fragment URL that ends with #greg.

WARNING

Unfortunately, current browsers only support named anchors using the anchor element; they can't yet link to elements named with the ID attribute.

Using Events Attributes with Anchors

Earlier in this chapter, we discussed the use of the ONMOUSEOVER attribute and a piece of JavaScript code to change the contents of the browser's status bar. A wide range of event attributes can affect the contents or appearance of an attribute. One possible use is a message or confirmation dialog box to give the surfer some information about the link they're about to follow.

In the next section, we'll discuss how to use the anchor element with other elements (for example, to create a list of links).

USING ANCHOR ELEMENTS WITH OTHER HTML ELEMENTS

Before we proceed to some new uses of anchor elements, let's see how well the anchor element interacts with other tags. Specifically, we'll look at how the anchor element should be nested.

An anchor element cannot be nested within other anchor elements. So this use of an anchor element is illegal:

```
<A HREF="http://www.yahoo.com/">There are a whole range
of categories in Yahoo's listings, including general cate-
gories like Computers and Entertainment, and specific cate-
gories for <A
HREF="http://www.yahoo.com/Entertainment/Actors_and_Actresses
/Bacon__Kevin/">Kevin Bacon</A> and Coca-Cola.</A>
```

Instead, separate your anchors into separate elements. Anchor text should be relatively short—a few words should be sufficient. Try this as a replacement for the previous listing:

```
There are a whole range of categories in
<A HREF="http://www.yahoo.com/">Yahoo's listings</A>,
including general categories like Computers and
Entertainment, and specific categories for
<A
HREF="http://www.yahoo.com/Entertainment/Actors_and_Actresses
/Bacon__Kevin/">Kevin Bacon</A> and Coca-Cola.</A>
```

It's legal to put an anchor element inside a heading:

```
<H1><A HREF="http://www.jazzflavor.com/">It's About Jazz,
Daddyo!</A></H1>
```

The anchor here would take on the quality of the heading, as shown in Figure 3.3.

FIGURE 3.3: An anchor nested within a heading appears the same as a heading, but also with the qualities of a link.

Since headings are block-level elements and anchors are text-level elements, the heading must contain the anchor for a link and not vice versa.

Similarly, you can use text-level elements either inside or outside the anchor element to affect the quality of links. This allows you to color-code or otherwise flag certain links. Some Web sites use this technique to make a distinction between internal and external links.

For example, you can make a link appear in italics by enclosing it in the italic element:

```
<I><A HREF="http://www.sos.net/home/jef/">Jef's Home</A></I>
```

The order here doesn't matter, so this similar construction would also render the anchor text in italics:

```
<A HREF="http://www.sos.net/home/jef/"><I>Jef's Home</I></A>
```

As you can see from Figure 3.4, both these links appear the same way.

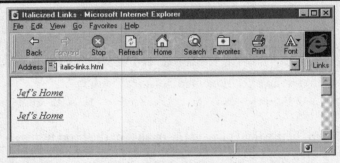

FIGURE 3.4: Two Italicized links, each nested in a different order but with an identical result displayed by Internet Explorer

NOTE

Actually, it's slightly preferable to put the anchor element *inside* the italic element so that any software that is using the anchor text to index or store links doesn't have any chance of getting confused by the italic element and storing the link as "I Jef's Home I" or "<I>Jef's Home</I>"

You can also color-code links, but the font element that contains the COLOR attribute must occur nested within the anchor element. If you put the font element outside the anchor element, then the default color of the link takes precedence over the font element. To see this in action, we'll see the following two links:

```
<FONT COLOR="GREEN">
    <A HREF="http://www.bway.net/~drkeith/hoot/">
    Hootenanny</A>
```

```
</FONT>
<P>
<A HREF="http://www.bway.net/~drkeith/hoot/">
    <FONT COLOR="GREEN">Hootenanny</FONT>
</A>
```

The first link will appear in blue, the default color for a link, because the inner anchor element has a default color that takes precedence over the outer font element. The second link will appear in green, as specified, since the inner font element takes precedence over the default link color.

NOTE

If you color your links, make sure to choose colors that are consistent and easy to read. Some HTML style guides recommend against coloring individual links because it may be confusing to users who are used to seeing links in blue or the color they've specified for links. Others designers recommend you use style sheets if you do want to color links, since style sheets keep the presentation separate from the content. Since HTML is all about content and not really about formatting, this approach makes sense.

One issue to consider is that if you color a link, surfers won't be able to see if they've visited the link. Your color specification will override the browser's standard behavior of having two different link colors, one for visited links and another for unvisited links.

WARNING

Although Navigator 4 (and above) and Internet Explorer 4 (and above) can color links, earlier versions of these browsers have problems. Internet Explorer 3 cannot display links in different colors at all. Navigator 3 only displays colored links if the anchor is within a table cell (see Chapter 11 for the use of table cells).

For our final example of using anchors with other HTML tags, we'll use lists of links. Since lists are a good way to organize information, they're a natural way of presenting a group of links.

For example, consider the following section of HTML code:

```
<P>There are several good HTML 4 references on the Web. Here
are some recommended online references:
<UL>
<LI><A HREF=" http://www.netpedia.com/html/reference/
">Netpedia HTML Reference</A>
<LI><A
HREF="http://www.eskimo.com/~bloo/indexdot/html/index.html
">Index Dot HTML's Advanced HTML Reference</A>
```

```
<LI><A HREF="h http://www.w3.org/MarkUp/">W3C HTML
Reference</A>
</UL>
```

This code would create a nice bulleted list of HTML references, as shown in Figure 3.5.

Feel free to experiment with other text-level elements and anchors; most of them work just as you might expect. For example, you can make a link bigger by surrounding it with the <BIG> and </BIG> tags:

```
<BIG><A HREF="http://www.levity.com/corduroy">Bohemian
Ink</A></BIG>
```

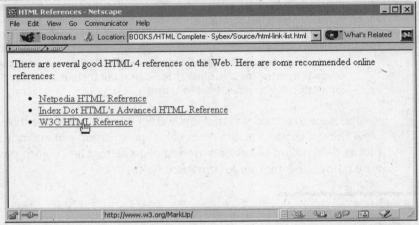

FIGURE 3.5: Each of these links is a list item in an unordered list, displayed by Navigator.

CREATING AN INTERNAL LINK

Now that we've discussed external links, it's time to talk about internal links. *Internal links* refer to pages within your own Web site.

Internal links behave identically to external links with one exception: you can use *relative URLs* for internal links, which saves typing. We'll discuss how relative URLs work in a moment. First we'll define the concept of absolute URLs.

Understanding Absolute URLs

Absolute URLs are simply fully specified URLs.

If your Web page's URL is `http://www.rupert.com/rupert-links.html`, then you can refer to other individual pages on your Web site with the appropriate absolute URL, as we've seen. Each page can be reached by simply changing the individual filenames at the end. The sample file we used in the previous section had several such absolute URLs. Take this example:

```
<A HREF="http://www.rupert.com/history.html">Rupert's History
Page</A>
```

In the `history.html` file, there might be a link back to the Rupert's Recommend Links page with an element like this one:

```
<A HREF="http://www.rupert.com/rupert-links.html">Rubert's
Recommend Links</A>
```

These two URLs are called absolute URLs since the address is fully specified. The URL is 100-percent, absolutely complete.

Understanding Relative URLs

Both of the previous absolute URLs contain the same stuff at the beginning, `http://www.rupert.com/`. It's a pain to have to retype the full address every time. It's also more likely that you'll make a mistake if you have to type an absolute URL over and over; in addition, if your Web page ever moves for some reason (for example, from `www.rupert.com` to `www.t-shirts.com`), then you'll have to go through and correct every link.

Relative URLs prevent these problems. A relative URL simply drops the common part from the URL and lets the browsers automatically figure out the part that's missing.

For example, in the `http://www.rupert.com/rupert-links.html` file, instead of specifying:

```
<A HREF="http://www.rupert.com/history.html">Rupert's History
Page</A>
```

just specify the part that's different from the current page's URL:

```
<A HREF="history.html">Rupert's History Page</A>
```

Whenever anyone chooses the link to `history.html`, the browser will automatically change the relative URL into the fully specified absolute URL, `http://www.rupert.com/history.html`, and the correct page will be retrieved.

Relative URLs like this all assume that the files are in the same directory; in a moment, we'll discuss what to do if the files are in different directories on the same system. In general, if you create a link such as `<A HREF="joe.html">All About Joe Thomas</A>`, then choosing this link just causes the browser to look for a file named `joe.html` in the current directory.

As you might imagine, you can use relative URLs for all sorts of files, including images. For example, you can specify an inline image with an `<IMG>` tag that uses a relative URL, like this one:

```
<IMG SRC="pluto.gif">
```

If there's an image file in the current directory that is called `pluto.gif`, then it will be displayed properly by this `<IMG>` tag.

Using Relative URLs with Different Directories

We'll assume you know how directories and subdirectories (also known as *folders*) work on your operating system. (If you don't, check with the documentation that came with your computer, or your operating system's online help.)

Suppose you have a subdirectory called `faculty`, and you want to link to a file in `faculty` called `smith.html`. If you were to use an absolute URL, it would be `http://www.rupert.com/faculty/smith.html` (assuming we're still using the `rupert.com` example from the previous two sections).

If you want to link to the `smith.html` file from `rupert-links.html` (which is at the top level of the server), instead of having to use that absolute URL, you can use a relative URL like this one:

```
<A HREF="faculty/smith.html">Rupert's pal, Professor
Smith</A>
```

NOTE
The slash used to separate folders is always a forward slash (/), never a back-slash (\).

But how do you make a link that goes back to `rupert-links.html` in the `smith.html` file? You can't simply say `<A HREF="rupert-links.html">Rupert's Links</A>`, since these two files aren't in the same directory.

You could use the absolute URL, `<A HREF="http://www.rupert.com/rupert-links.html">Rupert's Links</A>`, but we've already learned that absolute URLs aren't as desirable as relative URLs, so it would be a shame to have to rely on this method.

Fortunately, there's an abbreviation that means "the directory above the current directory" (also know as the parent directory). This abbreviation is two periods (`..`).

If you're a DOS or UNIX user, you are probably familiar with this "dot-dot" notation; older versions of Windows also use the `..` abbreviation in directory lists.

NOTE

Periods are sometimes called *dots*.

Using this abbreviation, you can specify a relative URL in `smith.html` that leads to `rupert-links.html`:

```
<A HREF="../rupert-links.html">Rupert's Links</A>
```

NOTE

You can even use multiple `..` references. If you have a file deeply buried in a series of subdirectories, it can link to a file much higher up on the directory tree with a link like this one: `<A HREF="../../../icecream.html">Vanilla Ice Cream</A>`. This relative URL means, "Go to the folder three levels above the current folder, and get the file there named `icecream.html`."

Relative URLs are commonly used, and we recommend you use them whenever possible.

Troubleshooting Relative URLs

If your relative URLs aren't working for some reason, you should try two things. First, when you type your URL into your browser, make sure you're using a slash at the end in the URL if it doesn't refer to a specific `.html` file—for example, make sure the URL you're using is `http://www.rupert.com/` (with a final slash) and not `http://www.rupert.com` (without a final slash).

You can also try using the `<BASE>` tag. A `<BASE>` tag tells the browser the correct absolute URL of your document, which might fix the relative URLs used on that page. (If you already have a `<BASE>` tag, try removing it.) If worse comes to worst and the relative URLs still don't work (and you've checked to make sure the files are in same directory and are properly readable), then you can always use the absolute URL. If *that* doesn't work, then something is wrong with your server or your files, or else you're not using your URL correctly at all. In that case, it might be time to call in your Internet Service Provider's technical support.

Using Default Pages

You might be puzzled by one thing we haven't explained before: why does a URL that doesn't specify an html filename still retrieve an HTML file?

For example, when you type in a URL such as http://www.yahoo.com/, it's clear you're retrieving an HTML file of some kind. (If you don't believe us, just view the page's source, and you'll definitely see HTML code in there.) But you didn't specify the name of this HTML file in your URL, as you would in a URL such as http://www.yahoo.com/help.html.

The answer to this puzzle is that each server is programmed to send a certain page if no other page is specified in the URL. The name of this default page is usually index.html.

NOTE

The term *default* just means the usual or expected choice. If Scott always orders cappuccino whenever he's in a coffee shop, you can assume that if he doesn't specify his order, he still wants cappuccino. You could say that Scott orders cappuccino "by default." This terminology is used with computers and the Web all time.

Try it: go visit http://www.yahoo.com/index.html, and you'll notice that the page displayed is *exactly* the same as what's displayed with http://www.yahoo.com/. These two URLs both refer to the same file. When you leave off the index.html part, Yahoo!'s server still sends the index.html page—your browser just doesn't tell you in the address box exactly what happened.

Some HTTP servers use a different filename for the default page—for example, Default.html, default.htm, or index.htm instead of index.html. Other servers let you specify the default file independently for each directory so that you can specify that your bacon directory sends the kevin.html file by default. That would mean that, say, the http://www.samplepage.com/bacon/ and http://www.samplepage.com/bacon/kevin.html URLs would both display the same page.

HOW TO MAKE A RELATIVE LINK TO AN INDEX.HTML FILE WITHOUT USING THE WORD *INDEX.HTML*

The last point we have to make here about the `index.html` default filename is that it can be a little tricky to link to it. You can always refer to it as `index.html` (with an element like `<A HREF="index.html">Rupert's Main Page</A>`), but then you might be pointing to the same file with two different names, which could be confusing. After all, the other name for the same file is `http://www.rupert.com/`, and your visitors (and search engines) might not know that you're talking about the same file.

If your `index.html` file is in a subdirectory called `faculty`, it's simple to refer to it: just use a relative link like `HREF="faculty/"`.

If you're linking back to your `index.html` file from a subdirectory, then you can just use the `..` shortcut that we saw earlier, with a relative link like `HREF="../"`.

If your `index.html` file is in your main directory, then you have a choice. You can link to it with its absolute URL, like `HREF="http://www.rupert.com/"` (which is equivalent to `http://www.rupert.com/index.html` but shorter). Or you can use the special abbreviation for the current directory, a single period (.), which would make your relative URL look like this: `HREF="./"`.

In all of these examples, it's not strictly necessary to include the final slash, but the correct name does include the slash—and using the correct name is a safer practice than leaving off the slash, since some servers and browsers can get confused if the final slash is missing.

JUMPING TO A NAMED ANCHOR WITH INTERNAL LINKS

It's time to return to a topic we first brought up earlier in this chapter: named anchors. In this section, we'll expand on the concept of naming a section of your document by seeing how you can jump from one part of the document to another. This makes it easy, for example, to link from the top of the document to the bottom. In turn, this allows you to put a table of contents at the top of a particular document.

First, however, we'll review the use of named anchor elements in light of what you've just learned about relative URLs.

Using Named Anchor Elements with Internal Links and Relative URLs

As we mentioned, you can link to a specific part of a document by adding its name to the URL after a # character. (We call this type of URL a *fractional URL*.) For example, linking to:

```
http://www.emf.net/~estephen/facts/lefthand.html#scientific
```

opens a file called `lefthand.html` and then jumps down to the "scientific" section.

These types of links will only work if the file has named a section with a named anchor element. For example, you'll need to use a tag like `<A NAME="scientific">` and then put an `</A>` tag at the end of the section's anchor text.

So when you see a fractional URL like the one above, you can assume that there is a section of the `lefthand.html` file named `scientific`. It turns out that there is such a file with a named anchor as described. The specific HTML code to name the section looks like this:

```
<H4><A NAME="scientific">Scientific Articles and
Sites</A></H4>
```

Since you don't have control over whether a named anchor elements exists in an external file, sometimes you won't be able to link to a specific section of an external document. However, when you're linking to your own internal files, you'll always be able to add the necessary NAME attribute to an anchor element in the appropriate section of your document.

If you want to jump to a certain section within one of your documents, just use a relative URL with the label in your anchor. For example:

```
<P>Please <A HREF="mary.html#contact">contact Mary</A> for
more information.
```

To make this link work, make sure that the `mary.html` file exists in the same directory as the file containing the previous code, and make sure that `mary.html` contains the following HTML code somewhere:

```
<A NAME="contact">My Contact Information</A>
```

NOTE

The specification for HTML says that the names should not be case sensitive. However, anchor names are case-sensitive in Internet Explorer 3 and Navigator 3 and 4, so you should not use <A NAME="CONTACT"> if you later use <A HREF="#contact">. Instead, make sure that your name always uses the same case in the name anchor and the fractional URL.

WARNING

Don't name your sections with illegal characters. Names should be unique in each document, and must consist of letters and numbers, without spaces or punctuation other than the period (.) and hyphen (-). Also, be careful not to leave off one of the quote marks in your anchor. Finally, don't try to use an empty NAME anchor, like this: <A NAME="foo"></A>. Many browsers get confused by empty anchors, so you should always wrap the anchor around some text.

Linking to Different Parts of the Same Document

In addition to linking to other internal files, you can also use anchor elements to name and link to parts of the same document. For example, suppose you're creating a very long document. If there's important information that has to be at the bottom of the document, you might want to create a link that lets your viewers quickly jump to the bottom (without having to scroll all the way down).

At the bottom of your document, name a section with the following tag:

```
<P><A NAME="bottom">Here's the important information:</A>
<P>(Important information goes here.)
```

Now you can put a link at the top of the document that jumps down to the bottom of the document:

```
<P><A HREF="#bottom">Jump down to the bottom of this document
</A> to see some important information.
```

We mentioned earlier that you can't nest anchors inside other anchors. Sometimes you'll need to create an HREF link and a NAME at the same time, for the same text. This would be impossible without nesting, except for the fact that an anchor element can include both attributes, like this:

```
<A HREF="next.html" NAME="next-section">The next section
describes Monarch butterflies.</A>.
```

WARNING

If your document is *really* long, then your viewers will have to wait a few moments, until the document is loaded, before they can jump down to the bottom. That's because browsers can't jump to a label if they haven't yet loaded the part of the document that contains the named label.

Creating a Table of Contents Using Named Anchors

Now that you've seen how to link to named anchors within the same file (which are sometimes known as *bookmarks*), you can create a table of contents.

If you create a long document, you can divide it up into sections with headers. It's a good idea to add an anchor element with the NAME attribute within each header element, and use a single-word name for each section that's a relevant keyword, like this:

```
<H2><A NAME="history">History of the Sonnet</A></H2>
```

This allows other documents to link straight to the history section, by adding #history to the URL.

TIP

Even if you don't plan on linking straight to a particular section yourself, perhaps other Web authors will want to, so they will appreciate it if you take the time to put in the NAME anchors.

The best reason to name each section is that it allows you to create a table of contents for your page. This table of contents can occur anywhere in the same document or in a different document.

Each item in the table of contents simply contains a link that leads to the particular section, like this:

```
<A HREF="#history">History of the Sonnet</A>
```

If the table of contents is in a different file, then it has to include the filename in the URL, like this:

```
<A HREF="sonnets.html#history">History of the Sonnet</A>
```

Here's a simplified version of a real-life table of contents, based on a page at the Church Divinity School of the Pacific (http://www.cdsp.edu/). This example is a page that is simply a table of contents for a list of articles found in another document.

Listing 3.1:   deanspage.html

```
<!DOCTYPE HTML PUBLIC "-//W3C//DTD HTML 3.2//EN">
<!-Copyright 1997 by CDSP.->
<HTML>
<HEAD>
<TITLE>CDSP: Dean's Page</TITLE>
<LINK REV="MADE" HREF="mailto:Info@CDSP.edu">
</HEAD>
<BODY BGCOLOR="#FFCC33" TEXT="#000000" LINK="#0033FF"
VLINK="#6600CC" ALINK="#FFFFFF">
<H1>Dean's Page</H1>
<P>
The Dean's Page is published monthly and features
reflections from Dean Morgan,as well as short newsbriefs
about CDSP faculty, students, staff, the campus, and the
Graduate Theological Union (GTU).

<P>
<FONT SIZE=5 COLOR="#FF0000">
<B>April 1997 Dean's Page</B>
</FONT>

<P>
<A HREF="dp-apr97.html#top">CDSP Announces Honorary
Degree Recipients and Speaker for 1997
Commencement</A><BR>
<A HREF="dp-apr97.html#israel">Israel Trip Planned for
January 1998</A><BR>
<A HREF="dp-apr97.html#facilities">CDSP Engages GTU
Schools in Facilities Dialogue</A><BR>
<A HREF="dp-apr97.html#director">CDSP Announces New
Director of Alumni/ae and Church Relations</A><BR>
<A HREF="dp-apr97.html#third">Third-Year Students Gather
for Final Class Weekend</A><BR>
<A HREF="dp-apr97.html#reception">CDSP To Host Reception
at General Convention</A><BR>
<A HREF="dp-apr97.html#apparel">CDSP Launches New
Apparel Line</A><BR>
<A HREF="dp-apr97.html#countryman">Beyond Inclusion with
Bill Countryman</A>
</P>

</BODY>
</HTML>
```

Figure 3.6 shows the previous HTML code displayed by Navigator. Each of the blue links leads to the appropriate article in the separate newsletter document.

The actual real-life page is quite a bit more attractive than our example, since it incorporates an attractive background image and some advanced layout techniques thanks to use of tables. But the table of contents is identical to our version. To give you a sneak peak of the sorts of documents that you can create once you learn about tables and images, Figure 3.7 shows the real CDSP page.

We've now seen just about every possible use of the anchor element. We'll round out this chapter with a look at some methods of making sure your links can be verified and maintained.

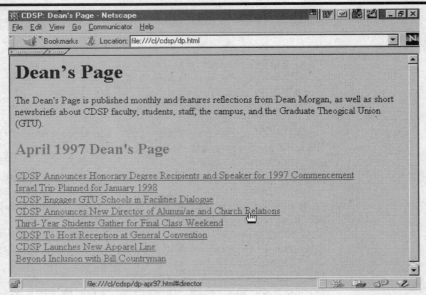

FIGURE 3.6: Our simplified table of contents for the Dean's Page newsletter

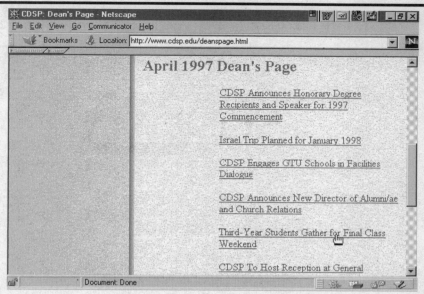

FIGURE 3.7: The actual table of contents from CDSP's Web site

VERIFYING AND MAINTAINING LINKS

One of the problems Web authors face is that external links are beyond their control. If someone moves or removes their Web page, then your link to them will suddenly be broken—it will lead nowhere.

When someone tries to follow one of your links that leads to a missing page, they'll get an error message—usually the infamous "404 - Document Not Found" error message.

NOTE

The numbers attached to Web error messages are assigned by the protocol specification for HTTP. An article at CNET's Web site explains these errors in plain English: http://www.cnet.com/Resources/Tech/Advisers/Error/.

For example, trying to view a nonexistent page from the sonic.net Internet Service Provider results in the error message shown in Figure 3.8.

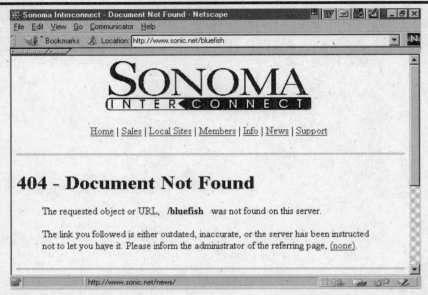

FIGURE 3.8: We tried to display a page called "bluefish" from sonic.net, but it no longer exists. Instead we're greeted with this error message, a "404 - Document Not Found" error.

You can prevent having a lot of bad links in two ways. The first is to not link to any external sites at all. This is an extreme measure, and the drawback is that you can't link to a lot of useful material (and if you don't link to other people, it's less likely other people will want to link to you, unless your content is very compelling). The second way is to choose your external links with care, tending toward documents that have been around for a long time or are maintained by responsible people or by stable companies.

TIP

When you link to someone's Web page, it's polite (but not necessary) to write them a brief e-mail saying that you've linked to them. Send along your e-mail address and the URL of your page. That way, they are able to link back to you (if they want to), and they can let you know if they move or delete their page.

There really is no alternative but to check your links often and replace any bad links. You can replace a missing link with either a different resource, or you can try to search for the old resource to see if it's moved without leaving a forwarding address.

To verify the links on your pages, you should go through all of your external links and follow them to make sure the pages on the other side are still valid. You should try and do this at a regular interval, perhaps once a month. You might receive e-mail from people who have noticed that a link of yours is stale (bad links are sometimes called *cobwebs*), but don't count on people to tell you about bad links—most people are too busy to take the time to report every bad link they see.

When (not if) you do find a bad link, either remove it or replace it with something else that works. This is the process of maintaining your links.

TIP

Avoid putting an excessive number of links on your page; not only is it more difficult for you to maintain, but you risk overwhelming your audience and they won't know which links are useful. Lots of people have already tried the "link every single word on the page to something" experiment. However, it's worthwhile to create a link whenever you are using a technical term or abbreviation, or mentioning a person or institution that has a home page. Consider creating a "Further Information" section at the end of your document with relevant links.

Verifying and maintaining links is a time-consuming process. Fortunately, computers are quite adept at helping you out with this task. Several good link verification tools can help you weed out the bad links.

Using External Link Verification Tools

There are two types of tools that can verify your external links. One type is a Web page service where you indicate pages that need to have their links verified; the service will go through all of the links on your pages, and then create a report to let you know which links are bad.

WARNING

This process is not foolproof. Sometimes a good link might be reported as bad because the link is not working temporarily. Sometimes a bad link will seem like it's good because the page on the other side is still present, but empty. Link verification tools can only check whether the external page exists—they don't tell you if a page is no longer worth a link.

Here are a couple of link verification tools available from the Web:

▶ NetMechanic (`http://www.netmechanic.com/`) can run an exhaustive check on the links in your site in the background, and when it's finished it can mail you a pointer to its report.

▶ Doctor HTML (`http://imagiware.com/RxHTML.cgi`) includes link verification as one of its tests of a page. (If you want the Doctor to check more than one page at a time, then you'll have to pay for the service.)

The second type of link verification tool is a program you run on your server or local computer that goes through the links. Some of these programs are freeware or shareware, while others are commercial software.

Here are some link verification tools you can download or purchase:

▶ MOMSpider, a robot that searches for bad links from your site and runs on UNIX-based systems (as long as they have the Perl language available). Freeware from the University of California, Irvine (`http://www.ics.uci.edu/pub/websoft/MOMspider/`).

▶ Linklint, a fast HTML link checker available for DOS, UNIX, and Windows machines, but only if they have the Perl language interpreter available. By Jim Bowlin (`http://www.goldwarp.com/bowlin/linklint/`).

▶ Linkbot, a Windows-based commercial link checker from Tetranet Software (`http://www.tetranetsoftware.com/`). A demo version is available to download.

No matter what tool you use, you'll still want to check your links yourself from time to time.

TIP

In addition, page- and site-creation tools such as FrontPage include built-in link verification commands.

What's Next

In this chapter, we discussed just about everything there is to know about anchors and links, from external links to internal links, some general advice and examples on how to use the anchor element and its attributes, as well as how to create tables of contents. In the next chapter, Deborah Ray and Eric Ray show you how to publish your Web page and present it to the World Wide Web.

Part I

Chapter 4

PUBLISHING YOUR HTML DOCUMENTS

So far in this book, you've learned about HTML documents and the code used to create them. And, if you've been following along with the examples, you've also created a few documents of your own. To this point, you've been developing and viewing the HTML documents on your local computer; however, at any time, you can go ahead and *publish* your HTML documents, making them available for other people to use and enjoy.

Adapted from *Mastering HTML 4*, 2nd Edition, by Deborah S. Ray and Eric J. Ray

ISBN 0-7821-2523-9   912 pages $34.99

In this chapter, we'll show you options for publishing your documents, and we'll walk you through the publishing process.

PLACES TO PUBLISH

Basically, when you publish your HTML documents, all you're doing is putting a copy of the documents on a server. The server then stores your HTML documents and makes them available to Web site visitors (or, actually, the computers) that request them. Your visitors tell the server what to get (by accessing a Web site), and the server displays the requested pages.

In general, you can publish your HTML documents in three ways:

▶ Through your Internet Service Provider (ISP)

▶ Through your corporate Information Services department

▶ Through your own server

Publishing through Your ISP

One of the most common places to publish HTML documents is on Web space provided by an Internet Service Provider. ISPs usually provide a slew of Internet-related services, including Web space and help with your Web development needs. You can find out more about ISPs in your area by researching the following resources:

The Web   For a comprehensive list of ISPs, along with contact information and services, visit `http://dir.yahoo.com/Business _and_Economy/Business_to_Business/Communications_and _Networking/Internet_and_World_Wide_Web/Network_Service _Providers/Internet_Service_Providers__ISPs_/Directories/`.

Your local paper   Often, you'll find ads for local ISPs in the Technology or Business section of your daily newspaper.

Other people   Ask friends, neighbors, business associates, or folks at your local computer store about the services they use and their experiences. The quality, reliability, and service of both ISPs and Web-hosting services vary, so get all the advice and input you can before you commit.

TIP

Once you find an ISP that appears to suit your needs, start by signing a short contract—say, no longer than six months—until you know that the service is satisfactory.

FINDING A WEB-HOSTING SERVICE

Another option—one that's not quite an ISP, but similar—is a Web-hosting service. A Web-hosting service does not provide dial-up Internet access but simply provides a home from which you can serve your sites.

Generally, you use Web-hosting services in conjunction with an ISP, thus combining the best Web-hosting deal with reliable dial-up access. Although it's possible that a single company could meet all your needs, shopping for these services separately can be useful. For a fairly comprehensive list of Web-hosting services, check out:

```
http://dir.yahoo.com/Business_and_Economy/Business
_to_Business/Communications_and_Networking/Internet
_and_World_Wide_Web/Network_Service_Providers/
Hosting/Web_Site_Hosting/
```

ISPs often provide a range of services, and you'll need to do some research to find out about them, as well as about start-up and monthly costs. In general, though, most ISPs offer either individual or business accounts.

About ISP Individual Accounts

Generally, ISPs provide individual subscribers—as opposed to business subscribers—with access to the Internet, to e-mail, and to a relatively small amount of space on a Web server. Many ISPs also provide other services such as sending you the results of a form via e-mail. Exactly which services you'll need depends on what you want to do with your HTML pages. For example, if you plan to create and publish simple HTML documents, you may only need a bit of Web space. On the other hand, if you plan to create an enormous Web site or one loaded with multimedia and downloadable files, you may need additional Web space. Or, if you plan to include forms or use server-specific capabilities, you may need some server access or specific programs available on the server. So, in choosing an ISP account, first figure out what you want to do, and then find an ISP that can meet your needs.

In addition to finding out what general services an ISP provides, you may also want to ask these questions, depending on your needs:

What kind of server is it, and what platform does the server run on? If you know the server and the platform, you can find the documentation on the Web, which should tell you which scripts you can easily add. For example, if an Apache server is running on a Sun Sparcstation (a likely ISP scenario), you can reasonably request that your server administrator install specific Perl scripts. However, if you're on an intranet with a Windows NT/ 2000–based Netscape server and you hear of a cool enhancement to the WebStar server on a Macintosh, you can save yourself some embarrassment and just not ask for it.

Can I restrict access to my pages? When testing pages on the server, you don't want the whole world to see them—setting a password-restricted access to the whole site helps with this. Additionally, if you have some pages that you want to make available to only a few people (or to everyone except a few people), you need to be able to set passwords and ideally do that with little hassle and without wasting time.

WARNING

Be careful about publishing pages on the Internet. Even if you don't provide links to a page or publish a page's URL, people may still come across it. Additionally, search engines can also index such pages, making the pages available.

Can I install and run my own scripts? If you can, you'll have a lot more flexibility and capabilities than you would otherwise. If you're limited to what your ISP has already installed for your use, you are likely to have access to certain limited special capabilities, such as chat rooms, but not the flexibility to go with what you really want.

Do you maintain access logs? How can I find out how many hits my site gets? If you're selling services, promoting your company, or doing anything else that involves a significant number of

people seeing your message, you'll need to be sure that accesses
are logged, and you'll need to learn how to get to those logs.

TIP

Ask your server administrator what kinds of tools are available to view and sort
Web server access logs—the "raw" (unprocessed) logs are an ugly mess, but
lots of neat programs exist to parse the logs into something useful. Although
your server administrator might well have some of these programs installed,
the access instructions might not be publicized.

*Who do I call if the server fails to respond at 2 PM? How about
2 AM?*

*Do you make backups, or do I need to back up my own site per-
sonally?* Under what circumstances will you restore backup
files—only if the server crashes or also if I make a mistake and
delete my files?

TIP

You might also ask these questions if you're thinking about an ISP business
account or publishing on a corporate server.

About ISP Business Accounts

If you are running a business and using the Internet (or if you're moving
in that direction), consider getting a business account with an ISP. Business accounts, although somewhat more expensive than individual
accounts, usually include more Web space, better access to server-side
programs, and more comprehensive services, with guaranteed uptime,
backups, and more attention to individual needs.

Many ISPs require a business account to have its own *domain name*,
which replaces the ISP's name in the URL. For example, instead of our
business's URL being:

    www.xmission.com/~ejray/index.html

(which includes the ISP name and a folder designated for us), it simply
reads:

    www.raycomm.com

Having your own domain name enhances your professional appearance
and can help make your business appear bigger than it really is.

Having your own domain name also offers a few practical advantages. First, you can keep a consistent address even if you move or change ISPs. Visitors (who may be your customers or potential customers) will always be able to find you because your address remains constant.

Second, you can easily expand your Web site as your needs grow. If you start by having your service provider host your domain (called a *virtual domain*), you can easily expand your capacity or add services, without changing your address or revising your advertising materials.

VIRTUAL DOMAINS

As an information provider, you are not limited to using the server name as the hostname portion of your URL. Instead, you can use a virtual domain, which gives you a hostname of your own, but your files still reside on a host computer. Virtual domains are a very popular way for small companies and organizations to look bigger than they really are.

For example, if you put your files on a server called xmission.com, your Web address might look something like the following:

    http://www.xmission.com/~accountname/filename.html

In this example, the address includes the protocol indicator, a special folder on the server (indicated by the tilde [~]), an account name, and a filename.

A virtual domain changes the address to eliminate the special folder and account name and replaces these with a new host (domain) name. For example, a Web address using a virtual domain (ours, actually) might look like this:

    http://www.raycomm.com/index.html

This example includes the protocol indicator, the domain name (www.raycomm.com), and the filename (index.html).

The easiest way to get a virtual domain is to ask your ISP to set it up for you. You may pay in the neighborhood of $50 to $100 for setup, plus a $70 fee for registering your domain name with InterNIC, the main domain name registration service, for two years. If you do a little homework with your ISP, however, you can set up a virtual domain yourself and save a few dollars. Go to rs.internic.net/, click the Accredited Registrar Directory link, and follow the on-screen instructions.

Finally, using a domain name helps establish your identity. Each domain name is unique and can include the business name itself or other names. For example, our business name is RayComm, Inc., but we probably could have extended the domain name to say `raycommunications.com` (or something to that effect).

There is a catch, though. If you don't claim your domain name, someone else will. If you have a company name under which you operate, get a domain name immediately, even if you're not likely to use it in the near future. Most of the most popular names are already taken. For example, we originally wanted `ray.com`. Since that was already taken by Raytheon, we settled for `raycomm.com`.

If you have a small business and aren't incorporated or are thinking of incorporating, consider getting the domain name first and then incorporating under that name. It seems a little backward, but a domain name must be unique, and competition for good names·is stiff. After you obtain your domain name, take care of registering to do business under that name.

At the time of writing, several companies can register.`com`, `.org`, and `.net` names. A company called InterNIC manages several lists for registering your name.

To register a domain name, follow this process:

1. Go to `rs.internic.net/`.

2. Select Whois from the top menu, enter your prospective domain name in the query field, and press Enter. For example, you might enter `breakfastbuffetatnight.com` or `eatmoreofjoesgreatburgers.com`.

If you're lucky, you will see a No Match message, which means that your domain name is available. If you're less fortunate, you'll see the InterNIC records for whoever does own the name you entered. If you want, you can contact them and see if they want to sell it or give it to you, but you're likely to have more success if you simply look for another name.

3. Either register the name yourself or ask your ISP to do it for you. Most ISPs will register domain names for free if they'll be hosting them, or they charge a reasonable ($100 or less) fee for the service, plus hosting charges. If your ISP attempts to charge significantly more than $100, you might consider either doing it yourself or finding another ISP.

If you really want to do it yourself, all the information and instructions you'll need are available at the InterNIC site, although you'll need to get a little information and cooperation from your ISP to fill out all the forms correctly.

Publishing through a Corporate Server

Another place you might publish your HTML documents is on a corporate server—at your place of employment, most likely. If you work for a large company or an educational institution or if you work with an organization or group that handles system administration tasks, you'll probably have little to do when it comes to accessing a Web server. All the necessary pieces—access, administration, security—are likely to be in place, and you'll simply step in and start using the server. This situation can be either the ideal or the worst possible case, depending on the group that actually runs the Web server.

What access and control you have at the corporate level varies from company to company. In the ideal situation, someone else takes care of running the server, but lets you do anything you want, within reason. You get help setting up and running server-side programs and can essentially do anything you need to provide information. At the other extreme, you must adhere to a rigid process to submit information to the intranet. You'll submit HTML documents and then have little control over where they're placed or how they're linked.

In all likelihood, your company will be somewhere in the middle, with an established procedure for accessing the corporate intranet but a substantial amount of freedom to do what you need to do. If not, or if the process of providing content is tightly controlled, you may want to see about running your own server. In any event, you'll need to find out how to contact the server administrators, get emergency contact numbers, find out about the corporate intranet policies, and go from there.

Publishing through Your Own Server

Finally, you might choose to publish your HTML documents on your own server. If you have the technical savvy and existing infrastructure, running your own server affords you the most flexibility and best range of resources. One good reason to run your own server is that it's a more authentic environment for developing and testing pages. For example, if you have server-relative URLs in links, they'll work properly if you're loading the files from a server, but not if you're loading the same file locally.

TIP

If you have a relatively new (or at least non-antique) desktop machine, you can certainly use it as a Web server. A 486 computer with 16MB of RAM can run an adequate Windows or Windows NT (if you have at least 32MB of RAM) server for testing purposes (as long as it's not trying to do much else at the same time). It can also run a rather speedy and spiffy Linux (freeware Unix) Web server.

A GREAT EXAMPLE OF A LOCAL TEST SERVER

Any figures you see in this book that have a URL of hobbes.ray-comm.com/ were developed on a server running on our local network, which is isolated from the Internet. The server software running on hobbes—at various times—includes the Netscape Fast-Track Server, Windows NT built-in Internet Information Server, OmniHTTPd, Microsoft's Personal Web Server, and, under a different operating system, Apache for Linux. The hobbes server is a Pentium 100 computer with 32MB of RAM. The performance isn't great, but it's more than adequate for testing purposes. The client and server software were both on the local machine during testing.

Although we could have loaded all the files onto our real Web site, that would have put a lot of under-development garbage out on the Internet under our URL. By testing locally, we keep the stuff that doesn't work right yet to ourselves.

Although we could have opened all the files directly from the hard drive, that wouldn't have let us test server-side programs and server-relative URLs or have given us the sense of working on a real server.

Considering that it only took about 10 minutes each to install the server software packages (on an existing network), it's worth it.

Particularly in a corporate or educational environment, where a network infrastructure exists, installing and running a server is straightforward. To run a public server, whether at home or at work, you'll need a dedicated network connection—anything from a full-time ISDN line from your ISP to a direct connection will work. If you're just setting up a local server for your own testing purposes, you can even run the server on a stand-alone machine.

If you're considering running your own server, here are some issues to consider:

Security   Web servers do present a security risk, although not a huge one. Letting other people access files on your computer, through any means, is inherently a little iffy. If you're paranoid about security, you don't want to run a server on your desktop machine. On an intranet, assuming you don't have highly confidential material on the server machine, you should be fine.

Uptime and access   If you're going to set up and publicize a server, you must ensure that it stays up and available. If you don't have a full-time Internet connection or if you like to turn your computer off on occasion, don't use it for a public Web server. Similarly, if your machine crashes often, is heavily taxed by other software, or experiences slowdowns when local network traffic is heavy, consider other alternatives, such as a secondary computer or simply putting your site on a dedicated server.

Time   Running a Web server takes some time. If all you're doing is serving pages, it doesn't take much, but expect a certain investment. If you'll be generating pages from a database or installing and running other add-in programs, it'll take more time, both to keep the server going and to monitor security issues.

Capacity   If your Web server provides only plain HTML documents and a few graphics to others on an intranet or if it's just for testing purposes, almost any computer will do. If you expect heavy traffic or lots of access, however, be sure that the computer you use can handle the load or can easily be upgraded.

Backups   If you're running your own server, you're responsible for backups. If the hard drive on your server suddenly stops working, will you be in a position to restore everything and get it all back up?

LEARNING MORE ABOUT RUNNING YOUR OWN SERVER

Installing, configuring, and running a server is beyond the scope of this book; however, if you'd like more information, you can visit the following Web sites for more information:

   `www.microsoft.com/iis`

At this site you can learn about the latest Microsoft Web server options. At the time of writing, Windows NT/2000 Server and Windows 2000 Professional ship with Internet Information Server, Windows NT Workstation ships with the Personal Web Server, Windows 98/98 SE ships with the Personal Web Server, and the Personal Web Servers for Windows 95 and Macintosh are available for download. Additionally, a different personal Web server comes with FrontPage, if you use that for Web development.

   `http://www.omnicron.ab.ca/httpd/`

At this site, a feature-rich server called OmniHTTPd, in both a freeware and a shareware version, is available for Windows 95 and NT.

   `sodium.ch.man.ac.uk/pages/httpd4Mac/home.html`

At this site, httpd4Mac for Macintosh users is available at no charge.

   `www.apache.org`

At this site, you'll find Apache, the most popular UNIX-based server software, although it's also available for other platforms, including Windows, at no charge.

Finally, get the definitive server information at `serverwatch` `.internet.com/webservers.html`.

THE PUBLISHING PROCESS

Before you get started, you'll need the following information:

The address of the HTTP server (for example, www.raycomm
.com, hobbes.raycomm.com)   Depending on your situation, you
may need to know the folder name from which your files will be
accessed.

The address of the FTP server, if required (for example,
ftp://ftp.xmission.com/)   Depending on how you get your
files onto the server, you might have to use FTP (File Transfer
Protocol). Of course, it's also possible, particularly in a corporate or educational environment, that you would simply copy
the files to a specific folder on a network drive, and that would
be that.

Password and access restrictions   You probably (almost certainly) need a user ID and password to upload files to the server.

Table 4.1 summarizes this information and provides space for you to
include your specific information.

TABLE 4.1: Information You'll Need before Using FTP

INFORMATION	EXAMPLE	YOUR INFORMATION
FTP server address	ftp.xmission.com	
User ID	foobar	
Password	********	Don't write it down!
Folder on server to use	public_html	

Armed with this information, you're ready to *upload* your files to the
server, which essentially means putting a copy of your HTML documents
on the server. The process for uploading your documents to a server will
be different for most servers and installations. It can be as easy as copying a
file to a folder (on a corporate intranet) or as idiosyncratic as completing
multiple page online forms and copying files to a folder (on intranets in

Dilbert-esque companies—yes, we have examples). It can also be a straightforward process involving an FTP application (the common process on intranets and with ISPs).

The easiest way to upload files to a server is with a program such as the Microsoft Web Publishing Wizard or with the one-button publishing tools included in Netscape Communicator and in many higher-end HTML editing applications. The one-button tools work well if all the files belong in one folder and if you're comfortable letting the programs (particularly Communicator) "adjust" links as the files are uploaded.

You'll likely use, however, either an FTP program or your browser to upload your documents, as described next.

Uploading with FTP

FTP is the Internet standard tool for transferring files. Regardless of which FTP program you choose, you'll likely be dealing with the commands outlined in Table 4.2. As you'll see in the following two sections, you can use these commands when uploading with a text-based FTP program or a graphical FTP program.

TABLE 4.2: FTP Commands Used for Transferring Files

COMMAND	DESCRIPTION
ftp	Starts an FTP application.
open "..."	Opens an FTP connection to the FTP server name specified.
close	Closes an FTP connection without exiting the FTP application.
quit	Closes an FTP connection and the application.
put	Uploads files to the server computer.
get	Downloads files from the server computer.
ascii	Sets the file type to ASCII, to upload HTML or other text documents.
binary	Sets the file type to binary, to upload image or class files and other binary documents.
cd	Changes directory on the server. Follow cd with the folder name to change into the folder, and follow cd with a . . to move out of the folder.
pwd	Print Working Directory, which tells you what folder you're in.

Uploading Files with a Text-Based FTP Program

Before you get started, you'll need the information specified in Table 4.1, and you'll need your HTML documents and related files at hand. Follow these steps:

1. At a text prompt (a DOS prompt or the Unix shell), change into the folder that contains the files you want to upload. For example, if you are at a `c:` prompt and your files are in the `TestWeb` subfolder, type **cd testweb**.

2. Type **FTP** to start the FTP application.

3. At the `FTP>` prompt, type **open** and the address of the FTP server, for example:

   open ftp.xmission.com

4. When prompted, enter your user ID and then your password. Remember that the user ID and password are case-sensitive.

5. Change to the folder where you want to store the files. If you're uploading files to an ISP, your folder name will probably be `public_html` or `www` or something similar. For example, type:

   cd public_html

6. To upload HTML documents, first set the file type to ASCII. Type **ascii**.

7. Now, upload the documents with the `put` command. For example, type:

   put filename.htm

   If you have multiple files to upload, you can use the `mput` command and a wildcard. For example, to upload all files in the folder that have a filename ending with `htm`, type:

   mput *.htm

8. To upload binary files (such as graphics), first set the file type to binary. Type **binary**.

9. Now, upload the documents with the `put` command. For example, type:

   `put image.gif`

   If you have multiple files to upload, use the `mput` command and a wildcard. For example, to upload all files in the folder that have a name ending with `gif`, type:

   `mput *.gif`

10. When you're finished, type `quit`.

Now, open your Web browser and try to access the files you just uploaded. If you find broken image icons, odds are that you didn't specify binary before you uploaded the files (a common problem). Try again, being careful to specify binary.

TIP

If you used a WYSIWYG editor and your links do not work correctly, check out the raw HTML code to verify that the links were not changed. Netscape Composer and Gold (Composer's predecessor) sometimes arbitrarily change links, causing them not to work.

Uploading Files with Graphical FTP Programs

An arguably easier procedure is available if you have a graphical FTP application (such as WS-FTP, for Windows) or Fetch (available from `http://www.dartmouth.edu/pages/softdev/fetch.html`). The specific procedure depends on the software, but generally resembles the following. Before you start, have at hand the same information you gathered for the text-based FTP application.

Use the following procedure to upload files with WS-FTP, a Windows application:

1. Start the application, probably by double-clicking its icon.

2. Fill in the essential blanks in the Session Properties dialog box.

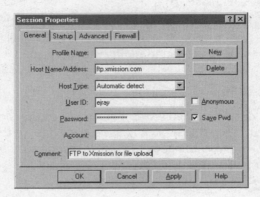

Host Name/Address Enter the address of the FTP server.

Host Type Choose Automatic or the specific type if you know it. Generally, Automatic works fine.

User ID Enter the ID that the system administrator or ISP provided.

Password Enter the password that the system administrator or ISP provided.

Leave the other fields blank unless your system administrator gave you that information.

TIP

Both user ID and password are case-sensitive—if you substitute uppercase for lowercase or vice versa, it won't work.

3. Click OK. You'll see a connecting message as your FTP client connects to the FTP server.

4. Select the appropriate local folder on the left side of the window and the appropriate remote folder on the right side of the window. You select folders by double-clicking them or by selecting them and clicking the ChgDir button.

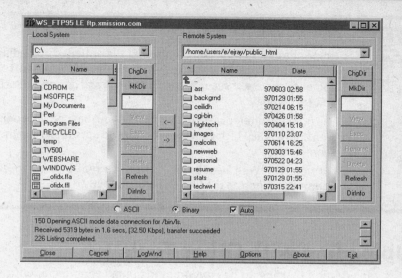

5. When you have the correct folders open on both sides, check the Auto check box to specify how the computers exchange files. Automatic is usually fine. HTML files transfer as ASCII (because they're plain text), and images transfer as binary (because they're binary, not text, files). If you try Auto and uploaded files don't work properly, set the transfer manually to Binary for graphics and ASCII for HTML and other text documents.

TIP

If you can't open and read the file in Notepad, Simple Text, or vi, it's not a text file. You must transfer all word-processed documents, spreadsheets, and multimedia files as binary.

6. Select the files to transfer, and then click either the arrow (pointing from your local drive to the server drive) or the Copy button.

That's all there is to it. Now, test all your uploaded files.

UPLOADING WITH HTTP

Some automatic publishing tools offer the option of uploading via HTTP instead of FTP. However, relatively few ISPs support HTTP uploads because of security considerations and because it's a fairly new technology.

The primary difference is that with HTTP you must provide only the Web address at which your files should end up, rather than the FTP server address.

For you, the Web developer, there's no real benefit to either approach as long as the files transfer correctly.

Uploading with Other Tools

In addition to using an FTP program to upload your documents, you can also upload them through your browser or through specialized tools such as Microsoft's Web Publishing Wizard.

If you use a fairly recent version of the Navigator browser, you can upload files by entering `ftp://yourid@yourftpserver.com/` in the Location line. You'll be prompted for your password. The only drawback to this approach is that you must be familiar with the structure of the files on the server. For example, at our ISP, we have to browse through the following folders to get into the folder to upload files to our Web site:

```
ftp://ejray@ftp.xmission.com/home/users/e/ejray/public_html
```

(We can also enter that whole long line in the Location window directly.) After you browse to the correct folder, choose File ➢ Upload File to select the file to upload (you can upload only one file at a time).

TIP

If you upload through your browser, take a second to bookmark that long URL location of your files so that you won't have to browse to it again.

Microsoft's Web Publishing Wizard is great for uploading files if you're a little unsure of your FTP proficiency, but if you need to upload frequently, you'll quickly find that it gets in the way more than it helps.

WHAT'S NEXT

So, there you have it! You can publish your documents using an ISP, on a corporate network, or on your own server just by transferring a copy of the documents from your computer to a server. By doing so, you make your documents accessible to other people, either at your company or on the Web worldwide. But before you hook up to the Web just yet, take a look at Chapter 5, which brings you full circle through the entire development cycle of publishing of your HTML documents. You'll learn the essentials, from planning and organizing your site before you publish to testing documents and maintaining them after they're online.

Chapter 5

UNDERSTANDING THE HTML DOCUMENT LIFE CYCLE

The life cycle of an HTML document includes developing, publishing, testing, and maintaining it—whether its ultimate home is on an intranet, on the Internet, in a kiosk, or in a help file. Because a single HTML document is usually the foundation for sets of documents, we are going to look at the document life cycle in a step-by-step fashion.

Adapted from *Mastering HTML 4*, 2nd Edition, by Deborah S. Ray and Eric J. Ray
ISBN 0-7821-2523-9   912 pages $34.99

Most of these examples focus on developing Web pages (single HTML documents) and sites (collections of HTML documents) in a corporate environment. To illustrate parts of the HTML document life cycle, we'll follow the process for WAMMI, Inc., a mythical, smaller version of General Motors. If you're developing HTML documents for nonprofit organizations, corporate intranets, or departmental sites, you'll still need to go through this same process. The only substantive difference is that the "meeting with the marketing guru" in a one- or two-person office might be a meeting with yourself over breakfast.

The task of developing HTML documents often falls (or gets assigned) to those with specific technical skills or to those who have a knack for marketing and sales, but not necessarily to those who have HTML-related experience. Thus, we are going to take a linear approach (you'll see more about this later in this chapter) and give you a development plan that starts with conception and concludes with maintenance.

We recommend that you start at the beginning and read through the sections in order. Along the way, you'll find numerous tips and advice to help you make decisions that will positively affect the applications you develop.

The following sections present a four-phase process, and within each phase are subprocesses. If you follow along, applying the examples and guidelines to your situation, you will be in a position to create HTML documents that are easy for you to maintain and useful to your visitors.

PHASE 1: DEVELOPING DOCUMENTS

Within the development phase are four subprocesses:

- ▶ Planning
- ▶ Organizing
- ▶ Creating
- ▶ Testing

Within these phases are several smaller processes, as shown in Figure 5.1. As you work through this chapter, you may find it helpful to refer to this chart from time to time.

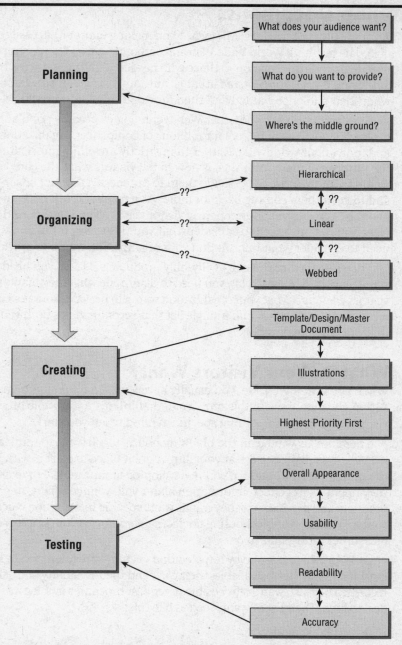

FIGURE 5.1: The HTML document development process

Planning Documents

As originally conceived, HTML focused on making information easily available. The resulting World Wide Web and corporate intranets were primarily used to provide information to those who needed it. In this capacity, HTML authoring was *visitor-centered*—that is, authors focused on determining what their audience wanted and then provided that information.

However, as HTML and other Web technologies became popular, they evolved into a marketing tool for millions of companies, organizations, and individuals worldwide. Rather than strictly providing information, the purpose of many Web sites is now to tell visitors what the company wants them to know, to persuade them to purchase a product or service, and to keep them coming back for more. As a result, HTML development has shifted to being simultaneously visitor-centered and *author-centered*. Now, you not only need to consider what your visitors want to know, you need to consider what information your organization wants to provide.

Therefore, before you start willy-nilly producing HTML, you need to do some planning. In particular, you need to determine what information your visitors want and what your organization wants to provide. Your goal is to reconcile these "wants" into a single list that accommodates both your visitors and your organization.

What Do Your Visitors Want?

When you visit a Web site, you usually have a reason for going there. Although you often stumble onto a site that interests you while browsing, you normally have something specific in mind when you start.

Therefore, as you begin the planning phase, you'll want to think about what visitors expect to see at your site. A great place to start is with your customers (or co-workers, if you're developing an intranet). For example, they might want general information about you, your company, or your products and services. Or they might want specific information, such as contact names, troubleshooting advice, safety information, prices, schedules, order forms, and so on.

At WAMMI, Inc., a survey revealed that visitors were interested in knowing what models were available, their cost, and their reliability and safety records. They also wanted to be able to request brochures and locate local dealerships. Their list of wants looked like this:

- ▶ Available models
- ▶ Cost

- Safety record
- Reliability record
- Contact information
- Brochure
- List of dealerships

What Do You Want to Provide?

Ideally, your Web site would provide all the information that your visitors want; however, what they want isn't necessarily what you can or want to provide. For example, you might not want to publicize a product's unstable repair history—or at the very least, you might want to downplay it. Or, if you're developing pages for a corporate intranet—say, the R&D department— you wouldn't publish *all* the information the department has available. You probably would want to include information about upcoming projects, recent successes and failures, and planned product improvements.

A great way to start figuring out what you want to include is to take a look at materials you already have on hand. For example, marketing materials often include information about the company, products, and services suitable for use on a Web site. Even if you're developing pages for an intranet, marketing materials often provide a jumping-off place.

If you don't have access to marketing materials (or the marketing guru), ask yourself a few questions:

- What do I want people to know about my organization? What is the corporate mission statement? What are my company's goals?
- What are my company's products or services? How do they help people? How do people use them?
- How do customers order our products?
- Is repair history or safety information so positive that I want to publicize it?
- Can I include product specifications?
- What product information can I send to people if they request it?
- Can I provide answers to frequently asked questions?

Part I

> ▶ Do I want to include information about employees? Do their skills and experience play a big part in how well our products are made or sold?

> ▶ Can I provide information that is more timely, useful, or effective than other marketing materials, such as brochures or pamphlets, provide?

After you answer these and any other questions that are helpful in your situation, you should be able to develop a list of what you want to provide. WAMMI, Inc., decided to provide general information about the company, tell potential customers about the various models, show a few snazzy pictures, and brag about the cars' reliability records. They were unsure about discussing prices because they were higher than those of their competitors, and likewise they were unsure whether to publicize safety records—they were only average. The final list looks like this:

Definite:

▶ Company information

▶ Car models

▶ Photos

▶ Contact information

Maybe:

▶ Prices

▶ Safety records

Reconciling the Want Lists

You may well find that visitors want information that you simply can't provide. For example, they might want to know product release dates or be privy to product previews, which is probably information your company doesn't want to disclose. And, other times, you might want to provide your audience with information that they don't necessarily care about. For example, you might want to tell people that your company received a big award or just reached one million in sales this year—certainly interesting information that's good for marketing, but it's not on your visitors' priority list.

As you can see, what WAMMI wanted and what their visitors wanted didn't necessarily coincide:

Visitors Want	Company Wants
company information	company information
car selection	car selection
reliability records	
contact information	contact information
	photos
car cost	prices
safety records	safety records
request brochure	
list of dealerships	

Although these two lists have items in common, each list also contains unique items. At the very least, we wanted to include all the items common to both lists. At WAMMI, the reconciled list included the following:

- ► Company information
- ► Car selection
- ► Safety records
- ► Contact information

Now, what do you do about the items that are unique to each list? We suggest that you consult some of your colleagues, perhaps those in marketing or public relations, and see what they think.

NOTE

Getting a consensus before you start to build your Web site is always a good rule to follow. The last thing you want after your site goes public is some vice president announcing that you can't publish information that's blaring off your Web site.

At WAMMI, we decided to classify the items common to both lists as primary Web site information and to classify unique items as secondary information.

Planning for Maintenance

Although maintaining your documents after you create them and throughout their existence on your site is a separate phase in the life cycle of documents (see the later section, "Developing a Plan"), you also need to include maintenance in the planning phase. This is particularly the case if you answer yes to any of the following questions:

- ► Will more than one person be involved in developing the content?
- ► Will more than one person play an active role in maintaining the site?
- ► Will your site include more than about 20 HTML documents?
- ► Will you frequently add or modify a significant number of pages— say, more than 20 to 25 percent of the total number of documents?

As you can see, you need to plan for both content and site maintenance.

Planning for Content Maintenance

If you will be depending on others for content, you need to make arrangements at the outset for how you will obtain updates. Will content providers actually develop and update the Web pages, or will they simply send you new information via e-mail? You need to plan accordingly if they are going to merely send you a publication (for example, the annual report) and expect you to figure out what has changed. Planning now how you will handle content revisions and updates will save you time (and grief) later.

Planning for Site Maintenance

Regardless of whether you or someone else will maintain the site you develop, you need to carefully document the development process and include the following information:

- ► The site's purpose and goals
- ► The process through which you determine content
- ► Who provides content

Documenting the development process will help those who maintain the site (or fill your position when you leave) keep everything up-to-date.

Organizing Your Documents

After you decide what information to include in your site, you need to determine how you will arrange individual HTML documents. Taking the time to organize the information carefully is often the difference between having frequent visitors to your site and having none at all. How often do you return to a site that's not well organized? If you can't find what you need easily and quickly, you have no reason to go there, and the same will be true of visitors to your site.

You can use one or all of these types of organization, depending on your needs:

► Hierarchical

► Linear

► Webbed

Hierarchical Organization

When you organize information in a hierarchical structure, you present a first group of equally important topics, followed by another group of equally important topics, and so on. You're familiar with this technique if you've ever created or used an organization chart. The hierarchy starts with top officials, then shows the managers who work for them, the employees who work for those managers, and so on.

A document outline is another example of hierarchical organization. Multiple main points are followed by subpoints, which are followed by more subpoints. In both an organization chart and a document outline, using hierarchical organization allows you to provide multiple levels of structured information.

You can do the same with a Web site. You can provide several main points, and under each point, you can include subpoints. For example, the WAMMI Web site uses hierarchical organization to structure the main pages according to the major topics, as shown in Figure 5.2.

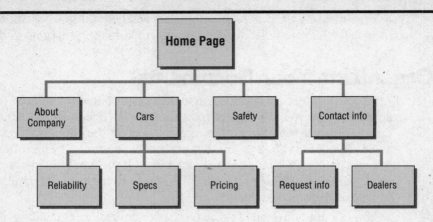

FIGURE 5.2: Hierarchical organization accommodates several main topics and subtopics.

NOTE

If you choose hierarchical organization, remember to keep it simple. Visitors to your site will dig through two or three levels of information, but after that they are likely to give up.

Linear Organization

When you organize information in a linear structure, you impose a particular order on it. Instructions and procedures are examples of this type of organization. If you've ever used a Microsoft Windows-type Wizard, you've seen linear organization in action. You start the Wizard, and then you proceed in a linear fashion from one screen to the next until you click Finish. You can back up a step or two if necessary, but if you don't complete all the steps, you terminate the procedure.

At a Web site that uses linear organization, a visitor can move forward and backward within a sequence of pages but cannot jump to other pages. Because this can occasionally frustrate a visitor who wants to get to other pages, you need to use linear organization only when it's necessary. For example, at our WAMMI site, we used linear organization to walk a visitor through requesting a brochure, as shown in Figure 5.3.

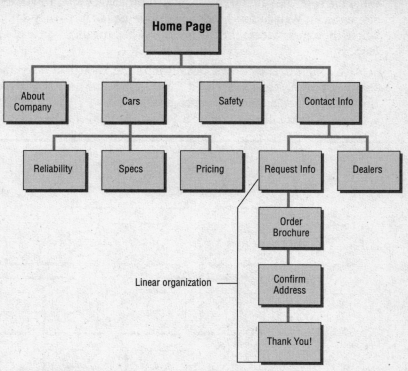

FIGURE 5.3: Linear organization works well when you want visitors to your site to perform actions in a specific order.

Here are some guidelines to keep in mind when you use linear organization:

▶ When visitors to your site are working through pages that are organized in a linear fashion, they can't roam to other pages. Therefore, be sure the linear process is essential to the task at hand.

▶ Keep the linear sequence as short as possible so that visitors focus on the process and complete it successfully.

Webbed Organization

Webbed organization is a fairly new type of organization that has evolved with online technology and provides visitors with multiple, unorganized paths to resources at a site. A visitor can link from one Web page to many other pages at the same Web site or at another Web site. You often hear stories about Web surfers becoming disoriented or lost—they don't know where they are or where they've been. Webbed organization is often the culprit.

An example of effective webbed organization, though, is an online index that's extensively cross-referenced. The WAMMI site provided an index of the available models and cross-referenced each model to its specific features and to other models. Figure 5.4 shows how this works.

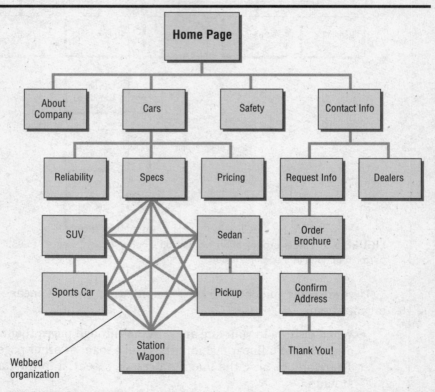

FIGURE 5.4: Webbed organization is a good technique to use when you want to cross-reference information.

Here are some guidelines to keep in mind when you are using webbed organization:

▶ Provide information on each page that helps visitors orient themselves. For example, include a running footer or company logo (keep it small) on each page.

▶ Provide a link to your home page on all pages. If you do so, visitors can easily return to a familiar page.

STORYBOARDS: AN ESSENTIAL ORGANIZATIONAL TOOL

Storyboarding is the process of breaking information into discrete chunks and then reassembling it. It's a technique that Web authors borrowed from the film industry, and it's a great way to help you determine the best organizational approach for your site.

Here's one way to do it (and the way the WAMMI site was storyboarded):

1. Write each topic or group of information on a separate note card.

2. Pin the note cards to a wall or spread them out on a table or the floor.

3. Group and rank related information.

4. Continue moving cards around until all the information is organized and ranked to your satisfaction.

5. When you've decided what should link to what, connect those note cards with string.

The resulting groups of information should follow one of the three organization approaches discussed above or some combination thereof.

Creating Documents

After you've adequately planned your HTML documents, deciding which information to include and how to organize it, you're ready to work on creating HTML documents. You've already likely been through many of the specific issues, including choosing software, using tags, adding links and images, and including more advanced effects such as video, sound, frames, JavaScript, and applets. But, just as you need the specifics of coding those things, you should also take a close look at the overall process to make your HTML development easier and more efficient.

Create a Master Document

A master HTML document contains the necessary structure tags as well as the general document format you want to use. When you create a master HTML document, you establish the look of the site even before you start adding content. Include the elements that you want to appear on every page, such as the following:

- ▶ The background
- ▶ Repeating images
- ▶ The corporate logo
- ▶ Icons
- ▶ Footer information

If you place these elements in your master document, you will need to develop them only once, not every time you start a new document.

After you create a master document, test it (as described in the section, "Testing Documents before Publication") to be sure that it appears as you want, that it is usable and readable, and that it is error free. Finding and solving problems early on will save you lots of time in the overall process.

Select Images

Determine which images (graphics) or illustrations are available before you start developing individual pages. Having an idea of what images you can include will help you determine page layout, and you can avoid rearranging pages later.

Create Important Pages First

Web sites, by nature, are always "under construction." You'll find that you're constantly updating content, adding new pages, or removing pages. If you create a few of the most important pages first, test them, and publish them, you can eliminate the tedious task of polishing many pages later. You can then add and modify pages as needed, after you create an initial few.

Testing Documents before Publication

The appearance of your pages on your visitors' screens probably will differ from what you see on your screen. Therefore, you need to test your documents on as many computers and browsers as possible. By doing so, you can see how your documents will appear to your visitors, check readability and usability, and root out any layout or formatting problems.

You'll want to test for these issues on your local computer *before* you publish your pages on the World Wide Web or on an intranet. By doing so, you can get a general idea of what your visitor is likely to see; however, your visitor's browser and computer settings could alter a document's appearance. You can check this out if you view a document using Internet Explorer on a computer with a low-resolution display and then look at it using a Netscape browser on a computer with a high-resolution display.

Remember, Web pages are similar to the marketing materials your company uses. Just as an editor checks corporate brochures closely for layout, design, organization, and accuracy, carefully check your Web pages.

Getting Ready to Test

Before you start testing, manually expire all the links. Most browsers are set by default to remember links that you've visited for about 30 days, and they color those links differently from unvisited links. You can easily see which sites you've visited, which is handy if you'd rather not browse in circles. By expiring links before you test your pages, you can see, for example, that the link colors (for links, active links, and visited links) appear as they should, and you can tell which links you haven't yet followed in your testing process.

Exactly how you expire links varies from browser to browser. The following steps give you the general procedure:

1. Look for a menu option that lets you change browser settings. For example, in the Navigator browser, choose Edit ➤ Preferences. In Internet Explorer, choose Tools ➤ Internet Options.

2. In the resulting dialog box, look for an option that lets you change document "history."

3. Expire the links by clicking the Clear History button.

4. Click OK when you're done.

Testing for Overall Appearance

With your links expired, open your pages in your browser, and ask yourself the following questions:

- ▶ Is the layout and design aesthetically appealing? Do page elements align as planned?

- ▶ Is all the content visible? All text? All images?

- ▶ Do all colors appear as they should? Are there any odd patterns or colors?

- ▶ Do all pages contain navigation tools?

- ▶ Do all frames, applets, and other objects appear as planned?

After you've answered these questions and are satisfied with the results, change the size of your display window and test the overall appearance again. For example, make your display window smaller. You'll find that some elements may not appear on the screen or align as intended. Make any necessary adjustments. Figure 5.5 shows a page that didn't resize well.

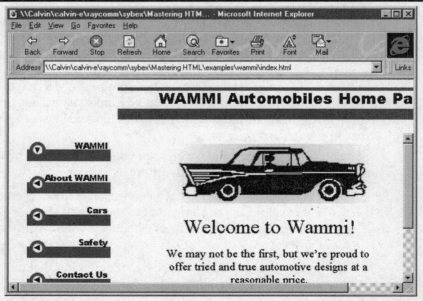

FIGURE 5.5: Reducing window size can wreck the appearance of your Web page.

TIP

To quickly and easily evaluate different page sizes in Windows, create wallpaper with rectangles at 640 x 480 (VGA), 800 x 600 (SVGA), and 1024 x 768 (high-resolution). Then, assuming your display is set to at least 1024 x 768, you can simply resize the browser window to exactly overlap one of the rectangles.

TIP

Windows 95, 98, 98 Second Edition, NT, and 2000, Macintosh, and Unix users can all use built-in operating system functions to reset display characteristics. If you are a Windows 95 user, go to www.microsoft.com, download the Microsoft Power Toys, and use the Quick Res Powertoy to change display settings quickly and easily. That utility is built into the other Windows operating systems.

Now, change the color depth and see what happens to your pages. (Color depth is the number of colors being displayed.) View your pages in millions of colors, in 256 colors, and in 16 colors in all your browsers. Check what happens to background and image color when you reduce the color depth. Yes, it's an incredible hassle—but, with some practice, you'll learn how HTML effects appear at various resolutions, and you can improve your pages accordingly.

Testing for Usability

Usability refers to how easily a visitor to your site can find and use information. The information may well be there, but will visitors find it, wait for it to download, or go through layers of links to get to it? In testing for usability, consider the following:

- ▶ How long do the pages take to download? Remember, you're testing your pages on your local computer; therefore, you can expect the pages to download *much* slower when a visitor accesses them over a dial-up Internet connection. Using tools such as Bandwidth Buster from Sausage Software can help you get a feel for how long the page might take to download over an Internet connection. Of course, you should also test how the pages actually load using a dial-up connection.

▶ Do the benefits of the enhancements outweigh the extra download time? For example, do images or the JavaScript you've added merit the added time required to download?

▶ How easily can you find navigation tools? Are they readily available, or do you have to scroll to find them? Are they consistent from page to page?

▶ Do *all* links work—links to information within the site as well as to information outside the site? A variety of tools, both interactive, Web-based tools and downloadable programs, can help you check links automatically. Additionally, many HTML editors offer these capabilities as well. Search on link validation at your favorite search service for specifics.

▶ Are the levels of links appropriate for the information provided? For example, is the information located in a third-level link clearly subordinate to information in the first- and second-level links? Also, if you've provided many link levels, is the information important enough that your visitors will take the time to wade through the other links?

PILOT TESTING YOUR DOCUMENTS

When you *pilot test* your documents, you ask real people to look at them and to identify problems and areas for improvement. The two main methods for pilot testing are contextual inquiry and the talking aloud protocol, which are often used in combination. When you use *contextual inquiry*, you observe visitors in their own environment. One of the best ways to get started is to simply sit with a notebook and quietly watch your visitors. Pay attention to everything they do, including which information they refer to, which links they use most, and in what order they visit pages. Make a note about when they refer to your site for information, when they appear to get lost or frustrated, and when they head down the hall to ask someone else. Although this method is time consuming, it can be a real eye-opening experience, particularly if most of your information about your visitors' needs is based more on conjecture than on observation.

CONTINUED ➡

When you use the *talking aloud protocol*, you listen to visitors describe what they're doing and why they're doing it as they navigate your site. Follow this process:

1. Make a list of five or fewer items that you want a visitor to find at your Web site.

2. Give your visitor the list and ask them to find each item.

3. Insist that your visitor talk out loud throughout the test, saying anything that pops into their heads about the search, the site, or overall tasks.

If possible, record the session. In all likelihood, you'll end up with a transcript that is fairly disjointed but rich in information. For example: "Let's see, I'm supposed to find safety information about this particular car model. Hmmm. No menu items for safety. Maybe it'll be under the Reliability menu. Nope, don't see it. Lessee. Search. No search items. It's gotta be under Reliability. Aha, there it is, hiding under Protection. I saw Protection the first time, but thought that had something to do with undercoating or paint."

Pilot testing your site can identify how people *really* find information at your site and can indicate exactly where you need to make improvements.

Testing for Readability

Readability refers to how easily visitors can read information—text and images. Because a number of readability issues—fonts, font sizes, emphases, and colors—contribute to a document's overall appearance, you may have addressed some of them already. However, you need to look at these same issues from a visitor's point of view.

To test readability, search for a specific piece of information on your site. Observe which information you are drawn to on the page—usually images and headings stand out. Be sure that important information stands out adequately and that you can easily read all text, headings, captions, addresses, and so on.

READING ONLINE

By nature, reading on a computer screen is more difficult than reading the printed page. Hindrances include the size of the monitor, screen glare, and difficulty in navigating different windows. In addition, a computer screen has much coarser resolution than the printed page (72 to 100 dots per linear inch as compared with 600 to 2650 dots for laser-printed or typeset ink on paper). Consequently, visitors get tired quickly, read more slowly, and frequently skip information.

As an HTML author, you can improve readability somewhat with a few design techniques:

- ▶ Use headings and subheadings to break up long sections of text and to announce to a reader what information is on the page.

- ▶ Use bulleted and numbered lists, which give readers at-a-glance information.

- ▶ Use short paragraphs to encourage reading.

- ▶ Use text and background colors that adequately contrast.

- ▶ Use images to illustrate difficult concepts, rather than describing concepts in words.

Always test readability after changing the size of your display window or decreasing the color depth settings. Often, decreasing the window size or color depth makes pages much more difficult to read. For example, a Web site with a nice menu down the left side, banner on the top, and black text on the right looks great at 1024 × 768. At lower resolutions, however, the black text ends up over the dark background, as Figure 5.6 shows, and it's impossible to read.

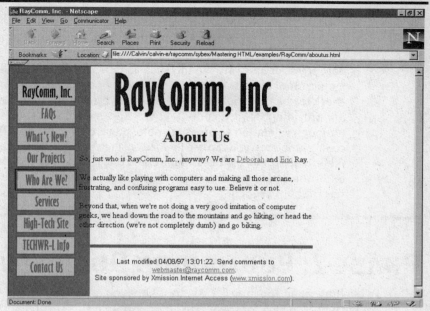

FIGURE 5.6: Reducing window size can hinder readability.

Testing for Accuracy

Finally, be sure the information on your site is accurate. Pay attention to details. In particular, a site littered with typos has just about zero credibility. Your accuracy checklist also needs to ensure that:

- ▶ The content is correct and up-to-date.

- ▶ Headings summarize the content that follows.

- ▶ References to figures or illustrations are correct.

- ▶ The *date last modified* information is current. The date last modified, as the name indicates, tells your visitors how current the information is and helps them decide whether it's usable.

CAN VALIDATION SERVICES HELP?

Validation services, accessed either through the Internet or from a program on your local computer, help ensure that you've used standard HTML or an HTML variant, such as HTML for Netscape Communicator or Microsoft Internet Explorer. For example, you might check to see that you're using HTML 4 correctly or that you really are providing HTML 2 code to your visitors with old browsers. Although validation services are not a panacea for solving HTML coding problems, you can use them to ensure that your code is complete, that it is more or less accurate, and that it is more or less standard. You can find more information about validation services at `validator.w3.org`.

PHASE 2: PUBLISHING DOCUMENTS

Publishing means putting HTML documents on a Web server and telling people where to look for them. The information in this section applies specifically to publishing your documents on the Internet or on an intranet.

The exact process you'll use for publishing documents depends on your situation. Some large organizations have well-defined publishing procedures; in these cases, you might simply fill out an HTML form and save your files in a specified folder. If your organization doesn't have procedures or if you're publishing on the Internet, you'll need to *upload* your files (which means to copy files from your computer to a server).

Before you can upload your files, you need to obtain the following information from your system administrator or your Internet Service Provider (ISP):

- ► The address of the Web server (for example, `www.raycomm.com`, `hobbes.raycomm.com`).

- ► The address of the FTP server, if required (`ftp://ftp.xmission.com/`, for example). Otherwise, you'll need a location to which to mail the files or the location on the local area network (LAN) where you will place the files.

- ► A password and any access restrictions.

While you're at it, you might also ask the following:

▶ What kind of server (Apache, NCSA, WebStar, Netscape, and so on) is it, and on which platform does the server run?

▶ Can I restrict access to my pages?

▶ Can I install and run my own scripts?

▶ What's the default index filename?

▶ Are access logs maintained? How can I find out how many hits my site gets?

NOTE

Chapter 4 provides specific information about publishing your documents.

QUICK LOOKUP

The *default index* is the file that automatically appears when you specify the address without a specific filename. For example, if you specify http://www.raycomm.com/techwhirl/technologies .html, the server displays the technology page. However, if you specify www.raycomm.com/, the server displays the file index .php3 because that's how the server is configured.

On another server, the same address might display the default.htm file or the home.htm file. If you don't identify the index file correctly, your visitors will be able to view the entire list of files and browse according to their whim—not according to your plan.

PHASE 3: TESTING PUBLISHED DOCUMENTS

Earlier in this chapter, we discussed testing documents on your local computer. Now it's time to test them in the real world, looking for the same issues addressed previously, as well as making sure that all the links work and that the documents all transferred properly to the server. Additionally, at this stage, your goal is not only to look for layout, formatting, and proofreading errors, but also to get an accurate idea of what visitors will see when they access your pages. In particular, find out how fast pages load, how pages appear at various screen sizes and color depths, and how different browsers display page elements.

When you're testing, you want to do the following:

▶ Check how fast pages load using several connection types and speeds. Ask a few friends or colleagues to look at your pages and to report problems with layout, links, colors, download time, and so on.

▶ Check to see that the server displays the pages properly. As a rule, everything will look fine, but it's not unheard of to have a mis-configured server that displays nothing but HTML code in the browser.

TIP

If you find that browsers are displaying documents as HTML code, try changing the file extension to `html` (rather than `htm`). If that doesn't work, contact the server administrator ASAP.

▶ Test your pages using different computers, operating systems, and configurations. Remember to resize your document window and change color depth.

PHASE 4: MAINTAINING DOCUMENTS

Maintaining HTML documents is the process of updating and revising existing pages, adding new pages, and deleting outdated pages. Regularly maintaining HTML documents is essential if you want visitors to keep returning to your site. Also, regular maintenance helps make long-term maintenance less cumbersome.

HTML documents contain two types of information:

▶ Static

▶ Dynamic

Static information remains constant. The company logo, most menus, and even product descriptions are examples of static information.

Dynamic information, on the other hand, must be changed or updated regularly. Prices, schedules, specific or timely information, and product lists are examples of dynamic information. Figure 5.7 shows a Web page that includes both types.

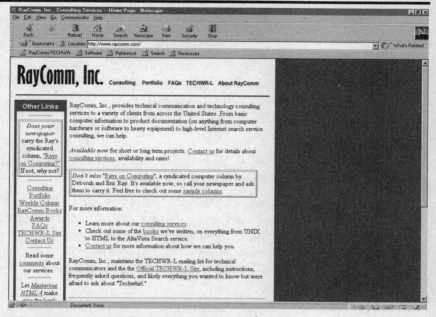

FIGURE 5.7: Static information remains constant; dynamic information changes frequently.

Developing a Plan

Back in the HTML document planning stages, you might have taken a few steps to make maintenance easier. In particular, you might have made update arrangements with content providers. Or, you might have developed some sort of documentation to help focus pages as the content changes. If you took either of these steps, you have a head start.

If you didn't plan adequately for maintenance—for example, if you didn't realize how much content you'd have or how difficult it would be to get updated information from your providers—you can still make maintenance a fairly straightforward process. First, devise a maintenance schedule. Set a time every day, every few days, or every few weeks (depending on how frequently the dynamic information changes) to update your documents.

Second, devise a maintenance plan. For example, if you know that you'll only be adding tidbits of information every few weeks, you can probably do that without much problem. If you're likely to receive pages and pages of information to add or if you're likely to make significant changes, however, you'll need to determine how to make the additions and changes most effectively. In these cases, hand-coding the information probably isn't the most effective way; conversion software, which does a lot of the coding for you, might be a better idea. In either case, determine how much you'll be changing and decide how best to handle it.

Keeping Up

As you're adding, deleting, and updating information in your HTML documents, you'll need to routinely do the following:

- ▶ Check for links that don't work or that go to outdated information (also known as *link rot*). As you add and remove information from your site, you'll find that some pages suddenly have no links to them, and other existing links don't go anywhere. Manually browse all your links, and take advantage of link-checking programs on the Web.

- ▶ Balance the latest HTML specification capabilities with what visitors' browsers can display. You probably won't want to develop a totally HTML 4–enhanced document if your visitors' browsers don't support all the version 4 effects.

- ▶ Ensure that older pages still look good in new versions of browsers. Often changes in browser software affect how some elements—such as images, tables, and forms—are displayed.

- ▶ Check older pages for references to outdated information. For example, you might want to update present-tense references to past presidential elections, sports records, or even products, prices, and schedules.

WHAT'S NEXT

This chapter provided an overview of the HTML document life cycle. In particular, it covered planning and organizing as well as creating, publishing, publicizing, and maintaining HTML documents. Now that you have an understanding of basic HTML and the process it takes to publish an HTML document, you're ready to do it for real. Part Two gives you all the information you need to plan and design your very own Web page, starting with an extensive look at site design and navigation by Vincent Flanders and Michael Willis.

Part I

PART II

Planning and Designing Your Web Page

Chapter 6

SITE DESIGN AND NAVIGATION

In this chapter, we'll look at two of the nitty-gritty issues facing a designer when creating an overall design for a Web site:

▶ Designing a home page that acts as an effective site guide

▶ Designing a site that's easy to navigate

Adapted from *Web Pages That Suck: Learn Good Design by Looking at Bad Design,* by Vincent Flanders and Michael Willis

ISBN 0-7821-2187-x   288 pages $39.00

To learn about these design issues, you'll hear about some navigational tools; then you'll look at some sites that suck and some that don't. From there, we'll move on to organizing your own site by creating storyboards. By the time you're through, you'll be able to tell a poorly designed site from an exceptionally well-designed one.

NOTE

If you visit the sites mentioned in this chapter, you'll find that many of them have changed in appearance since the book was written—that's the nature of the Web. (Maybe they read our book and learned a thing or two.) The principles of good design remain the same, however, and you can still follow all of the design discussions using the accompanying illustrations.

Okay, now that you know where we're going in this chapter (a principle of good design), let's start navigating our way through this chapter by taking a look at the home page for *Cigar Aficionado* magazine, shown in Figure 6.1.

WHY DOES THIS PAGE SUCK?

It doesn't! The bad boys of Web design just threw you a curveball.

You can learn a lot about site design by looking at *Cigar Aficionado*'s site, which you'll do later in the chapter. To start off, though, here are some tips you can pick up from this site:

▶ The designer did not sit down and start coding first thing. The designer sat down and figured out what important elements should go on the home page; then they figured out what went on the main topic pages and each subsidiary page. In other words, they scoped out the "big picture."

▶ The designer put the most important elements on the first screen of the home page and the other main subsidiary pages.

▶ The designer created significant content.

▶ The designer has a sense of aesthetics—the graphics and layout are first-rate. No cheap clip art was used, and the *single*— repeat *single*—animated GIF (the animated cigar) is very high quality.

CONTINUED ➡

▶ Most importantly, the designer created a home page that presents a professional image to the world. As soon as you go to
the page, you know exactly what to expect and you know how
to find the information you want.

FIGURE 6.1: *Cigar Aficionado* magazine (http://www.cigaraficionado
.com/)

To really understand what's good about this page and why it's an effective site design, we need to first talk about the concept of the home, main topic, and subsidiary pages, and the importance of making your site easy to navigate. Figure 6.2 shows how the pages on a Web site should be organized. The organization is quite simply a hierarchy with the most important page (the home page) on top and subsidiary pages below.

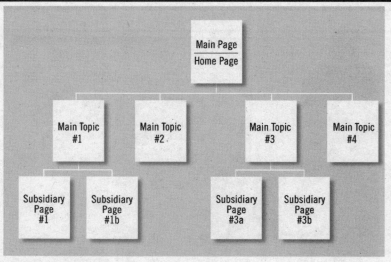

FIGURE 6.2: Organization of a Web site

The Web pages on a site are broken down into three main groupings:

- ▶ Home page
- ▶ Main topic pages
- ▶ Subsidiary pages

This organizational structure, which is simplified to its lowest elements, forms the foundation of a Web site. However, the most important navigational tool in the developer's arsenal is the home page because it is, generally, the first page seen by your visitors.

THE HOME PAGE AS A SITE GUIDE

Quite simply, the home page (also known as the *front page*) is the gateway to your site. It's the road map, the index, and the table of contents that tells visitors where to find the important information they need to make their stay at your site enjoyable and profitable.

A good analogy is that the home page of a Web site is similar to the cover of a newsstand magazine. Newsstand magazine return rates to the publisher are quite high. Unlike a magazine subscription, which is purchased long in advance, a newsstand magazine has a limited period of time to entice the general public to buy it off the rack. The most important factors that influence sales are the cover and the subject matter. The same is true for your Web site.

The home page is the most important page on your site because it's generally a visitor's first impression of your company or organization. If your home page looks professional, ethical, artistic, appears to have interesting content, and doesn't have any elements that would chase a customer away, then there's a good chance your visitors will stay. Hopefully, they'll purchase something from you. If your home page fails to entice because the images are too large, you're using sound files for no reason, the page takes forever to download, there's offensive material, the text can't be read, and so on—then your visitors will hit the Back button faster than a politician changes position on the issues.

A home page should convey three things to the visitor:

▶ The site's purpose—the who, what, when, where, and why

▶ What kind of content is contained in the site

▶ How to find that content

The Main Topic Page

The home page links to the main topic pages. For example, Figure 6.3 shows the home page for Lotus Development Corporation (http://www.lotus.com/). From this home page, you can link to the following main topic pages:

Downloads	Products	Discussions	Corporate
Support	Purchasing	Partners	Solutions
Events	Developers	Services	Media Catalog

This is a good home page because it is clear where to go from here.

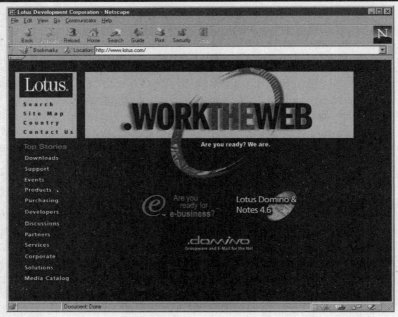

FIGURE 6.3: The Lotus home page (http://www.lotus.com/)

The Subsidiary Page

Any page other than a home or main topic page is a subsidiary page. Generally, these pages are subsets of a main topic page. For example, a page on the Lotusphere 98 trade show (see Figure 6.4) is a subsidiary page to the Partners main topic page.

From any subsidiary page, you want your visitors to be able to go to the home page so they can find out about your company and its products. You also want them to be able to go to any of the other main topic pages—especially a page where they can buy your products. Remember, you *always* need to make it easy for them to order.

For that reason, all your pages—home, main topic, and subsidiary pages—need to have links to the main topic pages on your site. In addition, you must include a link to the home page on all your main topic and subsidiary pages. Why?

Because you never know how a visitor arrives at your site.

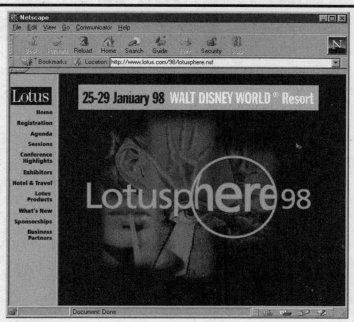

FIGURE 6.4: The Lotusphere 98 trade show page is a subsidiary page.

Why is the first screen people see at a Web site sometimes a page other than the home page? Simple. Links on other pages, articles in magazines, a friend's suggestion, or, most commonly, search engines. For example, a visitor might have conducted a search for the phrase "Lotus Partners" and ended up at http://www.lotus.com/partners, where they clicked the link and went to the page shown in Figure 6.4. Unless there's enough information on the Lotusphere 98 page, this visitor has no knowledge that the home page, shown in Figure 6.3, even exists or that Lotus has product information on another page. That information comes in the form of navigational links—graphic-, text-, or frame-based.

NAVIGATING THROUGH YOUR SITE

In setting up navigation for a Web site, you need to consider several factors:

- ► The first screen
- ► Navigational tools—graphics, text, frames
- ► Consistency

The First Screen—The Top's Gotta Pop or They're Not Gonna Stop

Don't let the cuteness of this little refrain sidetrack you from its important message. The first screen your visitor sees is the first impression they will have of your site. And keep in mind the first screen they see might *not* be the first screen of your home page. If your first screen sucks, they won't stop, and if they don't stop, they're not going to shop. Congratulations. You've spent a lot of money on a Web site where very few people get past the first page.

You've got to put your most important informational elements in the first screen because some visitors have no more than four inches of screen real estate. Also, limit your home page to no more than two or three screens of material because people don't like to scroll forever and ever.

TIP

Remember this phrase; make it your mantra: Display important information prominently.

If it isn't important, then it shouldn't be on the home page. It probably shouldn't be on *any* page, but you have a little more leeway with subsidiary pages because you've got a little more space to maneuver.

Navigational Tools—Graphics, Text, Frames

The three main navigational tools, which you can use singly or in combination, are:

- ► Navigational graphics
- ► Text
- ► Frames

Navigational Graphics

The two categories of navigational graphics are:

- ▶ Buttons

- ▶ Imagemaps

A button is any graphic that's a link. Any time someone clicks a button, they should be taken to another page. Buttons make powerful navigational tools. Use them carefully. When you're using graphics, for example, make sure people don't confuse them with links. Figure 6.5 shows an image that looks like it should be a button, but it isn't.

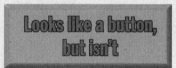

FIGURE 6.5: Confusing button

An imagemap is an image that is treated by the browser as a navigational tool. When visitors click the imagemap, they are taken to a new page. Make sure it's clear to your visitors where they are going when they click a particular location on an imagemap.

It's the reverse of a magic trick. In a magic trick, you show the audience your right hand and perform the trick with your left. In Web design, you tell them where you're going first—and then go there.

Text

Text links make excellent navigational tools, although you can go a little overboard, as Figure 6.6 indicates. Even though the folks here are a little link happy, you've got to love them for creating a page that totals only 15.8K in size. You won't have to wait days for this page to load.

Text links are very, very important; they are even more important on pages that use graphics and imagemaps as links.

NOTE

If you're using graphics or imagemaps as links, you must also have corresponding text links.

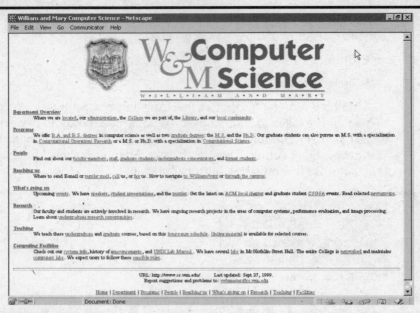

FIGURE 6.6: William and Mary Computer Science (`http://www.cs.wm.edu/`)

There are two reasons for this statement. The first is if you've been a bad girl or boy, and the graphics on your page total more than 35K. Text links will show up before the images, and your visitors can happily click a text link and be on their merry way before the image loads. The second reason is if your page has an imagemap, and your visitor hits the Stop button before the imagemap loads. Without text links, visitors won't know where they're going when they click. They'll have to either reload the page or click and hope.

The big graphic in Figure 6.7 is a perfect example of a site that has an imagemap but no text links. This is bad Web design. We'll talk more about this site later in the chapter.

FIGURE 6.7: Southwest Airlines (http://www.iflyswa.com/)

Part ii

Frames

Frames were created by Netscape to answer the perplexing question, "How can I make my page easy to navigate?" Like so many other great ideas, this one also got perverted by the design community. When used properly, however, frames solve the dilemma of keeping the text links static so you don't have to constantly reload them. Figure 6.8 shows you how WebPagesThatSuck.com uses frames.

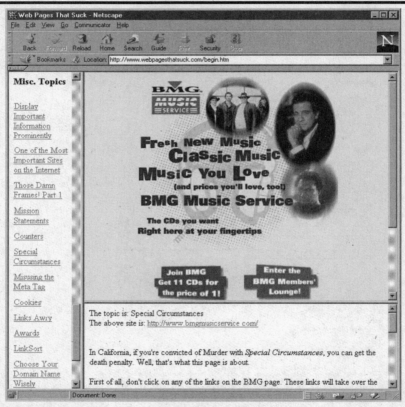

FIGURE 6.8: Frames at WebPagesThatSuck.com (http://www .webpagesthatsuck.com/begin.htm)

The frame on the left is the navigational tool. When you click a link in the left frame, the site in question pops up in the top-right frame while the witty, yet insightful commentary appears in the bottom-right frame. The navigational frame never changes.

Frames are controversial. Not so much because they are bad in and of themselves, but because designers use them poorly.

Consistency

You need to be consistent in the design of your navigational tools. For example, the size and color of your buttons should be consistent. Figure 6.9 shows you the wrong way to use buttons. As you can see, using buttons with different colors and sizes looks unprofessional.

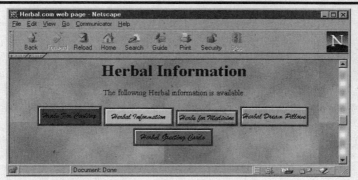

FIGURE 6.9: The wrong way to do buttons

Figures 6.10 and 6.11 show two great examples of consistent navigational tools. The first page, shown in Figure 6.10, is a home page for a software product that converts word-processing documents into HTML. Notice the navigational bar on the left side of the page; the depressed Home page button signifies which page you're visiting. Figure 6.11 shows the page for the Wang document conversion; as on the previous page, the Wang button is depressed to indicate you're on the Wang page. Total consistency.

Location

When you place your navigational buttons on the page, make sure that if you place them at the top of your home page, they're on the top of every other page in your site. If you place them on the left-hand side of the home page, then they should be on the left-hand side of every other page. The WebConvert navigational tools, shown in Figures 6.10 and 6.11, follow this guideline. All of them are located on the left-hand side of the page.

FIGURE 6.10: The navigational button bar at the WebConvert home page (http://www.webconvert.com/)

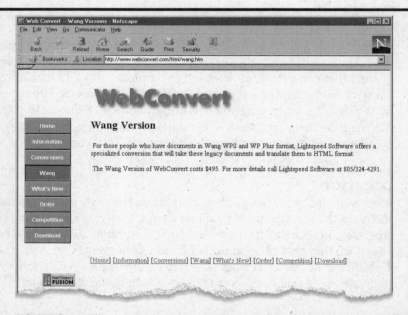

FIGURE 6.11: The navigational button bar at the WebConvert Wang Version page

SIMPLE CONCEPTS

It's a very simple concept—every navigational tool has to have a consistent look and location. Navigation should always be predictable. You want to create navigational tools that...

Are in the same spot on every page.

Have the same look.   You don't want to use round buttons on the home page and square buttons on main topic pages and octagonal buttons on subsidiary pages.

Will get the visitor to the information in as few clicks as possible. We're sure someone has researched the "Click Annoyance Factor"—the maximum number of clicks the average person is willing to perform to get to the information—but we haven't found this information on the Net. Personally, if we can't get to the information in three clicks and the site doesn't have a search engine, we're ready to go somewhere else.

THE TOUR

Now that you understand how a site should be designed and how important it is to offer navigational tools, let's take a tour of some sites on the Internet and see how they measure up. We'll examine the first site thoroughly to make sure you understand the concepts of site design and navigation and then quickly run through some sucky and unsucky sites.

For each site, we'll check its:

► Design

► Navigation

► Pluses

► Problems

Light Me Up! *Cigar Aficionado* Magazine

At the beginning of this chapter, we talked about how the first page of a site is like the cover of a magazine, so it's appropriate that the first site we discuss is actually a newsstand magazine.

The mystique of *Cigar Aficionado* magazine is sort of lost on Michael and me because, believe it or not, neither of us smokes cigars. (I tried to smoke Tiparillos the end of my freshman year in college—but it *was* my freshman year.)

The most we can figure out, based on the Web site, is that it appeals to those people who feel the "Good Life" consists of Art (their idea of art in the issue we looked at was Vargas, LeRoy Neiman, and Frank Stella), Sports (golf, deep-sea sportfishing, tennis, boxing, bullfighting, hawking, polo), Music (samba), Fashion, Gambling (poker, hustling golf), Jewelry and Collectibles, and Leisure (expensive cars, model railroads, chess, dream boats, high-speed power boats, treasure hunting in the sea, high-end stereo equipment). On this list, I'm 0 for 7; Mike is 2 out of 7. Nevertheless, you don't have to understand the cigar lifestyle to understand the design.

Site Design at Cigar Aficionado   Michael and I both think the site design is superb.

Figure 6.12 shows the *Cigar Aficionado* magazine as it would appear on a 13- to 15-inch monitor. Let's examine how its design succeeds and, more importantly, how you can use the same principles to make your site a success.

FIGURE 6.12: *Cigar Aficionado* magazine (http://www.cigaraficionado.com/)

The most important design element on this page is something you can't see. The designer sat down and organized the site before they started writing the HTML and creating the graphics. If designers do their job properly, you won't even notice how successful they are. In this case, the designer broke down the elements of the magazine into different pieces and chose what was important.

Navigation at Cigar Aficionado   In Figure 6.13, we've labeled the page so you can see the navigational structure of the home page.

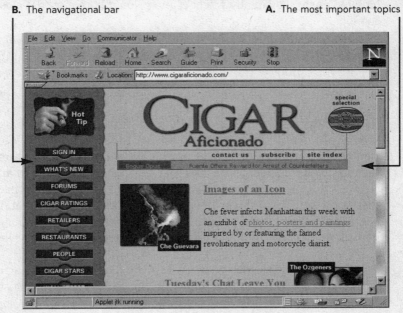

FIGURE 6.13: The navigational structure of the *Cigar Aficionado* magazine site

The section marked A shows how the designer cleverly worked the most important topics into the top of the page. We stressed this concept at the beginning of this chapter. The important topics we're talking about here are:

Contact Us   Make sure there's a way for visitors to contact you.

Subscribe   It's a magazine. They want you to subscribe. That's how they get money. Money is good. The fact that they don't offer subscriptions using a secure server is a potential security problem and would probably scare most people from ordering using their credit card. It would be interesting to know how many subscribers they've actually received from the Internet.

Site Index   If your site is divided up into many different areas, you'll want to include a site index (also called a site map or site guide). Your site index should be text-based. Don't use graphics; they take too long to load.

The section marked B shows you a portion of a navigational bar where it looks like they've listed most of the important topics near the top. Interestingly, the Gift Shop is at the bottom; maybe they're trying not to look too pushy. Personally, Michael and I would have moved it closer to the top.

While a visitor must scroll down to see all the topics, the top of the page has enough information for them to get a good start on touring the important sections of the site.

Figure 6.14 shows the navigational structure of Cigar Ratings—one of the main topic pages. Notice that the round part of the label on the Cigar Ratings button has turned red. Obviously, you can look at the top of the page and see its title, but this is a nice touch to add to a button. When you want to go to another topic, you won't click the Cigar Ratings button because it's turned red, which, as we all know, should make you want to stop. It's worth noting, however, that if you went to the Retailers page, there's no special marking to indicate you've been to the Cigar Ratings page. That's the province of text links. Nevertheless, the navigational information on this main topic page and on its subsidiary pages is excellent.

Pluses in the Cigar Aficionado Site   First of all, the designer chose wonderful colors for the site based on the brown color of cigars. Most important, these colors are used in a consistent fashion throughout the site.

The link graphics are also wonderful—little cigar wrappers—and so very, very clever. The home page is uncluttered, and the other graphics add to the flavor (pardon the pun) of the page. There's one animated GIF image (the Hot Tip at the top of the left-side navigation bar), but it's excellent (see Figure 6.12). While the graphic titled "Vote" is probably clip art, it's professional clip art (see Figure 6.1).

The site reeks (again, pardon the pun) of sophistication and elegance.

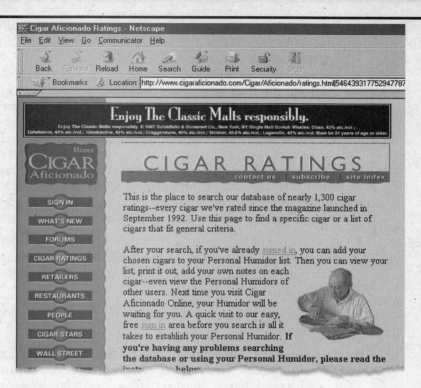

FIGURE 6.14: Cigar Ratings page (`http://www.cigaraficionado.com/Cigar/Aficionado/ratings.html`)

Problems in the Cigar Aficionado Site

Even though we both like the page, it has six potential problems:

1. The HEIGHT and WIDTH parameters are not set for the images. Setting these parameters would cause the text to appear before the images on the page and give the viewer the opportunity to click a text link rather than wait for all the images to load.

2. Speaking of text links, there are no text links on the front page. Oops. That's a design no-no. Michael and I suggest they put text links at the bottom of the page.

3.   Dr. HTML (see the sidebar, "Dr. HTML") reported that the page contained 84.8K worth of graphics and images on the day we visited. This means it would take between 24.1 seconds (on a 28.8Kbps modem) and 48.3 seconds (on a 14.4Kbps modem) to load the page (and probably longer because of the Java on the page, but Dr. HTML doesn't measure Java applets). The people visiting this site probably don't care how long it takes for the page to load because of the content. (We could make a snide statement that the people who visit this site are all probably wealthy Republicans with ISDN connections, but we won't.) The cigar industry is a wonderful vertical niche market, and people who visit niche sites really don't care too much about download time.

4.   A search engine facility on the front page would be nice. They have a link to their search engine tucked away at the bottom of the Site Index page, but they should really have one on the front page.

5.   The site uses Java, and using it doesn't seem to enhance the site.

6.   The site uses *Cookies*. These pesky little tracking devices basically track your movements on this site. We're not sure why they need them, but using Cookies could turn off some visitors.

All six of these elements are flaws in the site's design, but numbers 1 and 2 are certainly the worst ones.

DR. HTML

Dr. HTML is one of the Most Important Sites on the Internet.

The good doctor analyzes pages that physically reside on the Internet (have a URL) for errors and loading time. One of the many errors it looks for are missing HEIGHT and WIDTH parameters in images. In some of the examples used in this chapter (Cigar Aficionado, United Airlines, and Lotus), these parameters were missing.

There are lots of HTML validation services on the Web—including those that don't charge fees. As always, check out Yahoo's page on

CONTINUED ➡

the topic at http://www.yahoo.com/Computers_and_Internet/ Information_and_Documentation/Data_Formats/HTML/ Validation_and_Checkers/.

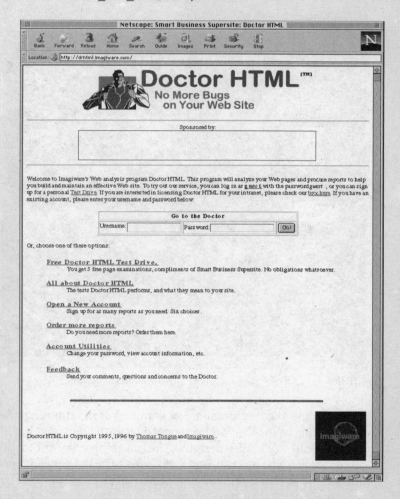

Part ii

Let's stroll around and examine a few more sites to see if we can figure out what the designer was thinking when they designed the site.

You're Not Cool Enough. Go Away!

Figure 6.15 shows us Pepsi's home page.

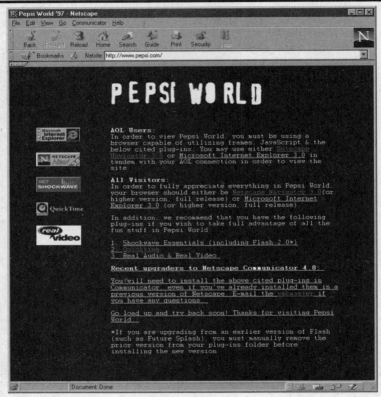

FIGURE 6.15: The Pepsi site (`http://www.pepsi.com/`)

This home page is stunning. Not stunning as in "stunningly beautiful," but stunning as in "I've just been poked by a stun gun, and I'm in a lot of freaking pain." As a Web designer, the last thing you want to do is keep people away from your site, but that seems to be the concept here. What this page is saying is, "If you don't have these plug-ins, then go away because we don't want you." Normally, I don't have a problem with plug-ins except that I often have to reinstall all of them every time a new release of my browser is issued—as one of the paragraphs of text on the Pepsi home page relates.

When I looked at this site, my first reaction was, "The heck with this, I'm going elsewhere." But I decided to go to the next page and after fumbling around, trying to figure out where to click to get to the next page (the Pepsi World logo was the magic spot), I got the scare of my life. You have only to look at Figure 6.16 to understand.

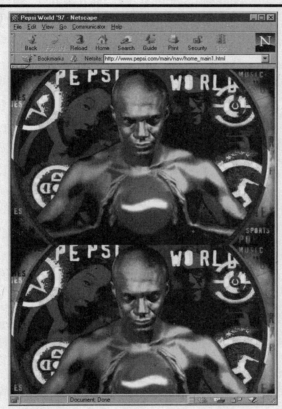

FIGURE 6.16: Holy moly, I've drunk too much Pepsi.

After recovering from the shock, I tried to figure out where I was supposed to click to get to the next page. Basically, I had to move my cursor over the whole screen while looking at the status bar to figure it out. The four "magic spots" are those white circular scribblings. Bad, bad design.

As with so many other things in life, Michael, my partner in crime, initially held a contrary viewpoint about the Pepsi site. "I will admit at first glance I liked the layout. I wasn't bothered by all the plug-in requirements because I have them all—I like plug-ins! I'm a plug-in maniac! So I decided to peruse the site. Unfortunately, it's a graphic behemoth! It looks like PhotoShop puked here. If I had a day to spend (which I don't), I couldn't visit all the pages on this site, not because there are so many, but because it takes forever for the graphics to load. I had to take a Dramamine after viewing all their gut-wrenching animations! It's a good thing I didn't want to know anything about Pepsi, because, as far as I could tell, there's nothing here specifically dealing with Pepsi."

Site Design at Pepsi   Don't use any of the techniques you see here. If there's a worthwhile site design technique used here, neither Michael nor I can find it.

Navigation at Pepsi   This is an oxymoron, like "fresh frozen." This site fails Navigation 101.

Pluses at Pepsi   None.

Problems at Pepsi   The whole site.

Eight Miles High: United Airlines

Figure 6.17 shows you the United Airlines home page, another excellently designed site.

Site Design at United   Interestingly, this is one the few sites that has the right to use the cliched outer-space background and animated spinning-globe GIF and make it work. More amazingly, their use of a globe actually makes complete sense. The animated globe is actually one of the coolest animated GIF images Michael and I have seen (the word *Index* is stationary). Why can they get away with using these clichés? They're an airline. Airlines fly in the sky. United flies around the world. They can use these images. Joe's Air Conditioning can't.

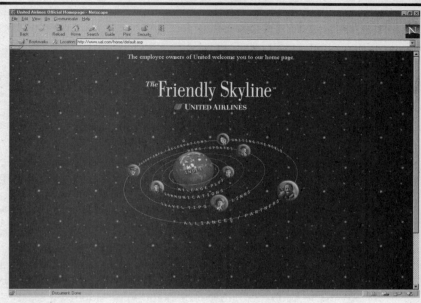

FIGURE 6.17: United Airlines (`http://www.ual.com/`)

Navigation at United Instead of using a list of links in the usual boring manner (on the left side), they came up with a clever and artistic way to present them—you click the planet and you go to the page. For example, clicking the pilot takes you to the Flight Info/Reservations page. It's easy to navigate to the main topic pages and subsidiary pages and back.

Pluses at United Nothing out of the ordinary. It's just a well-thought-out site. It's very easy to navigate the site because the navigation tools are consistently placed and cover the main topics a traveler needs to use.

Problems at United While the animated spinning globe is really cool, what is seriously *uncool* about the image is its 130K size (the whole page is 176.8K). Way, way too big. After all, this is a site where you want people to make airline reservations on your carrier—right? Why make it difficult for them by making them wait? Michael and I know this animated image is very cool, but you can't fall in love with your own design. It's possible people won't wait long enough to book a reservation. Hmm. That defeats the purpose of the site.

Another minus is none of the images on the home page have the HEIGHT and WIDTH parameters set. Finally, there are no text links. If the imagemap doesn't load, you really can't surf.

Another Airline: Southwest Airlines

We're sure that Southwest Airlines doesn't like being referred to as "another airline," but it's the second one we're looking at, so it's another airline. Figure 6.18 shows you their home page.

This site is where Michael and I pull our Siskel and Ebert routine (international readers, see the sidebar "Siskel and Ebert" for an explanation). I (Ebert) think the home page is okay, while Michael (Siskel) thinks it sucks like a bilge pump. If this were a TV show it would go like this:

> **Michael:** I'm sure someone put time into creating their ugly 46K "takes-forever-to-load" navigational imagemap. By the way, if you hit the Stop button before it loads, you won't be able to go to the *bleep* (pejorative term deleted) president's message page—which is too bad because he's manually indicating the number of people who have ever visited his page.

> **Vincent:** Yeah, no text links certainly sucks, but I don't mind the motif of the ticket counter. Besides, this home page loads faster than United Airlines. And I think having the president's face there is a nice touch.

> **Michael:** You find him attractive?

I then rush over and start beating on Michael's head with a copy of *Creating Killer Web Sites*, which Michael usually has hidden in a drawer. Pandemonium results, and the whole scene ends up being shown on CNN.

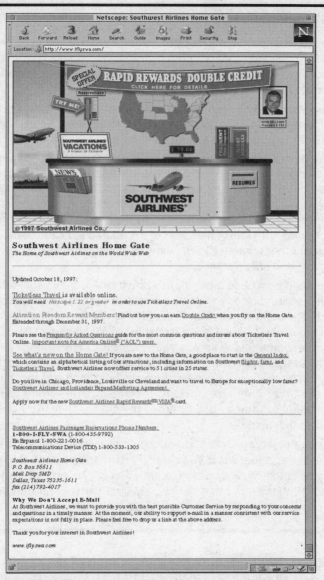

FIGURE 6.18: Southwest Airlines (http://www.iflyswa.com/)

SISKEL AND EBERT

We recommend avoiding jargon in your Web site. If you need proof that it's a good idea to keep jargon and nation-specific information out of your Web site, this Siskel and Ebert reference is a perfect example.

While many Americans will catch the reference, most, if not all, international visitors will be left out in the dark. So, for those nice international readers, here's a short explanation.

In the United States, Gene Siskel and Roger Ebert were two movie reviewers who worked for different newspapers in Chicago, Illinois—hence, they were competitors. One of them won the Pulitzer Prize (a big deal in America) and periodically reminded the other he never won one. Siskel was a tall, balding guy, and Ebert a short, stocky man with lots of hair. Sort of a Mutt and Jeff combination—oops, another reference even many Americans won't catch. Forget the Mutt and Jeff reference.

Siskel and Ebert had a popular TV show where they sat in a faux movie theater balcony and rated movies that came out during the week. The premise was that they didn't really like each other, and sometimes they argued in a reasonably civilized manner about why the other one wouldn't know a good movie if it came up and bit him on the ass. Everyone who watched the show did so partly because they hoped that one day, one of the two would snap and start choking the other one. Like ancient Roman emperors, they gave a thumbs-up or thumbs-down sign to the movies they liked or disliked, respectively.

As we said, jargon and nation-specific references make for a bad page on the global World Wide Web. Particularly because they can become outdated. Gene Siskel recently died of cancer (we miss you, Gene!), and the show that became an American icon has not been the same since.

Site Design at Southwest   Artistically, it's not as pleasing as the United Airlines site, but, then again, it's 49K in size versus United's 176K size. Hmm. Also remember that Southwest prides itself on being an inexpensive carrier, and the minimalist design here works just fine. The pages load quickly.

A case *can* be made that the site looks as if it was made on the cheap. Since Southwest prides itself on being a low-cost carrier, that's consistent with their corporate philosophy of providing value.

Navigation at Southwest   Once again, they've taken the minimalist approach, and it seems to work. They don't have buttons for all their topics, just the ones that count (translation: the ones that will bring in money)—Reservations, Flight Schedule, Frequent Flyer Program, and so on. Very nice.

Pluses at Southwest   The main pluses about the site are the fast loading times and easy navigation. Look, it ain't pretty, folks, but it's functional. There's something to be said for functional. Yes, it could be prettier and still load fast, but I don't think anyone but Michael is going to gag at the look of this site.

Minuses at Southwest   Michael thinks it looks cheesy, and a case can be made for that viewpoint. One reason it's cheesy is the tacky blue border around the picture; they should have turned the border off around the picture. While the desk is nicely rendered (it has dimension to it), every other piece of art is flat and one-dimensional. Southwest is trying to have a realistic look, but then they add the flat art work and it causes dissonance—or as Michael phrased it, "That's an awfully big word to use for *dorky*."

While the concept of a virtual ticket counter is excellent, the execution is poor.

Out-of-Place Graphics: Kenwood Home and Car Audio

Figure 6.19 is the home page for Kenwood Home and Car Audio. Michael and I actually agree about the design.

Site Design at Kenwood   The page uses graphics in a consistent manner, and the designer certainly thought about the organization of the site. But, as Michael so aptly put it, "I think marble backgrounds went out of style in the 70s, or were they ever in? And what's up with the homeless-looking guy in the picture? And what does that picture say about audio systems? I'm stumped." I wasn't thrilled with the concept either. Why are they using a hotel as the motif? If you go to the Kenwood Gear page, the motif is a laundry room—yes, Kenwood t-shirts need to be laundered, but the concept of a hotel is a stretch and poorly thought out.

FIGURE 6.19: Kenwood Home and Car Audio (`http://www.kenwoodusa.com/`)

Navigation at Kenwood   The navigational tools used are well done, and the site is easy to navigate. Notice how the designer put the most important pages at the top of the directory—Catalog, Build a Home System, Build a Car System, Contests, and Product Help Center.

But there's one flaw that just drives me crazy. On the directory, the very first link is the Lobby. You've got to have that on the other pages, but not on the home page—if you click the link, you just reload the page.

Pluses at Kenwood   Nothing we haven't said before.

Problems at Kenwood   The home page takes up a little over 63K in size—that's over even the Microsoft recommended amount. Also, the images don't have the HEIGHT and WIDTH parameters set.

Text Is Just All Right with Me: Red Hat Software

All of the previous sites have been graphics-based. Figure 6.20 shows that Red Hat Software can design a reasonably effective site using text-based navigational tools.

Site Design at Red Hat Software   As you can see, the folks at Red Hat have taken a text-based approach to their site. The links on the left seem to be in logical order and also seem to cover the major topics:

- ▸ Secure Server (how they get paid)
- ▸ FTP Server
- ▸ Products
- ▸ Support
- ▸ Company Info
- ▸ Linux Info

The nicest part about their text-based approach is that the page is only 22K in size and loads quickly.

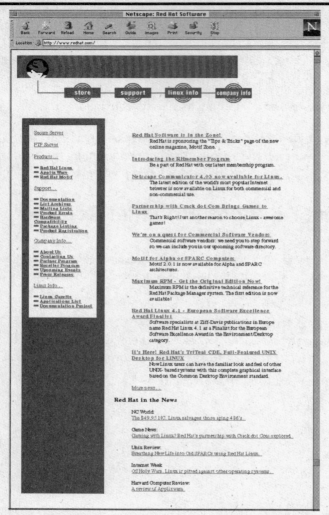

FIGURE 6.20: Red Hat Software (http://www.redhat.com/)

Even though the site takes the minimalist approach to the use of graphics, it is, nonetheless, fairly effective. Yes, it's plain and not very exciting, but that's okay. This approach would not work with *Cigar Aficionado*, but for a software site it's fine.

Navigation at Red Hat Software   The navigational aspects of Red Hat Software could be a lot better, as Figure 6.21 demonstrates. This figure is a little deceiving. The images at the top of the page link to Support, Linux Info, and Company Info. However, you always need to have a link to the money page—the page where a visitor can order your products. It's also a good idea to have a contact link on each page so your visitors can contact you. Red Hat has such a link, but it's at the bottom of the page, and the links at the bottom should really be at the top of the page. If you're going to have your graphic links at the top of the page, then the links at the bottom of the page should be textual duplicates of the links at the top.

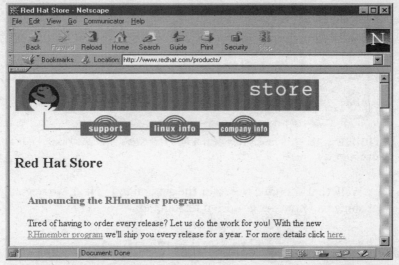

FIGURE 6.21: The Red Hat Store (http://www.redhat.com/products/)

Pluses at Red Hat Software   Nothing out of the ordinary. The pages load quickly, and you can find your way around the site without *too* much trouble. It's a very Spartan site, but being Spartan isn't bad.

Problems at Red Hat Software   The designer at Red Hat may have taken the concept of text just a little too far. We realize that Unix is a "text-based system" and that Unix wonks like nothing more than to read those technical Unix books—you know, the ones with the animals on the cover. However, there's just a little too much text on the pages to make us feel comfortable. Figure 6.22 shows a typical page on the site.

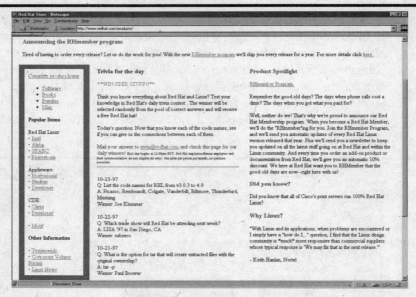

FIGURE 6.22: Too much text at the Red Hat Store (`http://www.redhat.com/ products/`)

Well, that should cover it for the general tour. Next, we're going to look at some bad home-page design techniques.

Bad Home-Page Design Techniques

No, you're not going to see a whole slew of badly designed home pages. You're just going to look at some techniques that impede the visitor from visiting your site.

Forcible Entry: Herbal.com

Figure 6.23 shows a technique Michael and I don't see much anymore on commercial or educational pages (thank goodness). But just because we haven't seen it in awhile doesn't mean it doesn't exist or won't make a comeback. It most frequently shows up on personal pages (why it's even used there is beyond us), but there's no valid reason why it's necessary under any circumstance.

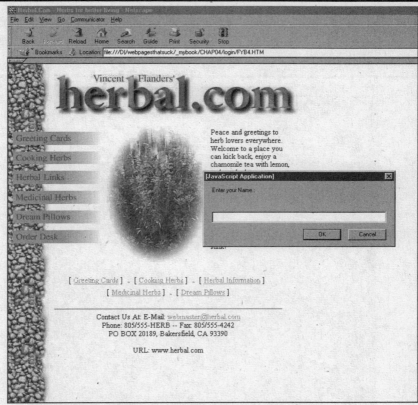

FIGURE 6.23: Why oh why? Herbal.com goes weird.

What's evil about this page is the JavaScript on the Herbal.com site that requests a name be entered before the visitor proceeds. On a commercial or informational site, you don't want to do anything that impedes your visitor's progress into your site. You don't want to chase them away.

While Michael and I realize that there are very few absolutes in Web-page design, this technique is an absolutely bad one to use. For that reason, we're going to NUKE IT!

What Do I Do Now? vincentflanders.com

Figure 6.24 shows the former *splash page* at my personal Web site. A splash page is different from a home page. A splash page is traditionally used for a first "splash" of art, which then transports you automatically to the "real" home page. In some instances, the user has to click to gain access to the home page. Splash pages can be confusing to visitors unless there are specific instructions on what they should do to gain entry to the home page.

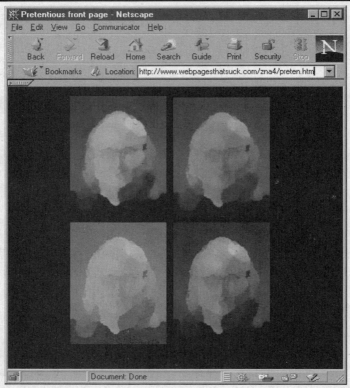

FIGURE 6.24: The old splash page for vincentflanders.com (`http://www`
`.vincentflanders.com/old`)

This page is a parody of a famous Web designer's splash page. I parodied this look on his page because...that's the kind of guy I am.

There are, however, a few problems with this type of splash page:

▸ The visitor is never sure when the page has stopped loading, and that's frustrating.

- ▶ Because there are no text links to click, the visitor has to wait until they see the Document Done message in the status bar before proceeding.

- ▶ The visitor doesn't have any idea where they're going when they click a picture. This adds nothing to the design of the site.

You don't ever want to confuse people when they go to your site. They need to know where they are and what they should do.

Exceptions

As always, there is an exception, and this one actually makes sense, as illustrated in Figure 6.25.

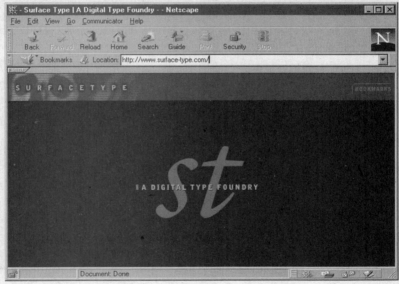

FIGURE 6.25: Surface Type (http://www.surface-type.com/)

The one exception to the rule is the type of site that has both an artistic sense and also downloads quickly. The Surface Type home page is about 12K in size—small enough to load quickly—and the designers have a great artistic sense, which they better have if they're going to design typefaces.

While it's artistic and doesn't annoy us because it loads quickly, imagine how you'd feel if you had to wait for 60K worth of images to load?

Now that you've seen several different aspects of design, we bet you want the answer to the question: How do I design a site? The answer: Storyboards.

DESIGNING YOUR SITE USING STORYBOARDS

It's easy to look at the sites in this chapter and say, "Yes, that one is good" and "Yes, that one is bad." What's difficult is putting what you've seen about good design and navigation into practice on your sites.

Because you can get instantaneous feedback when writing HTML, there's a tendency to fall into the trap of "code before you think." Your problem is that you need to create a home page. Your solution is to start writing HTML as fast as your stubby little fingers can type. This approach is the "There's never time to do it right, but there's always time to do it over—and over and over again" approach to Web design. You waste both time and energy. (Of course, if you're billing by the hour and your client is dumb and rich...)

If you just sat down and planned your site, however, you wouldn't end up with a dozen iterations and wasted hours—but this takes organization, a quality some of us lack.

To show you how the storyboard approach works, we will use Michael's WillieBoy.com site as an example. Michael bought the domain name `willieboy.com` for his line of surf wear. Next, he decided to throw together a placeholder page in case somebody accidentally wandered into his site. Figure 6.26 is what Michael ended up putting on his placeholder page.

There's not much here. You can click the thumbnail images to see a bigger version of the image. The only link to another page is the Order One button, which takes you to a form that is *not* on a secure server.

FIGURE 6.26: The WillieBoy placeholder page (`http://www.willieboy.com/`)

This placeholder page is good enough until Michael decides to start marketing his clothing line on the Web. Now that Michael has decided to really create the site, he must go through the process of storyboarding. He takes an unusual approach by creating his storyboards in Illustrator or PageMaker. As he puts it, "You can use any program that allows you to draw little boxes and put type in them. Of course, the old-fashioned 'pencil and paper' works fine, too." Because I use Windows NT, I use a copy of Visio 2 that I purchased years and years ago to storyboard.

Storyboard—Step One

Michael's first step is to talk to me about the site. My background is in marketing, so I'm great at coming up with ideas for other people to implement <grin>. There didn't seem to be a lot of content to draw people in on Michael's placeholder page, so I told him that he'd better add something or he'd get a bunch of people who'd visit only once. The obvious starting point for content would be surf-related information, such as surfing condition reports, surf music lists, and so on. I also suggested adding a page showing different surfer tattoos, but Michael misunderstood; he thought I said he should create a line of "temporary tattoos with a surfing theme." I quickly confirmed that's what I actually said. Sometimes it pays to slur your ideas.

Storyboard—Step Two

Next, Michael had to figure out what the main topic pages were going to be. Here's what he decided:

- Garments
- Order Form
- WillieBoy's Favorite Surf Links
- Tour of the Shirt Shop
- Photo Contest

Photo Contest is actually a misnomer. It will really be a photo gallery where Michael will display photographs of people wearing WillieBoy t-shirts—a very clever marketing concept where visitors get their 15 minutes of fame on the Net.

WARNING
If you're thinking of having a real contest on your site, you'll need to consult with a lawyer about the legalities.

Storyboard—Step Three

With these ideas in hand, Michael started the WillieBoy storyboard; the first version is shown in Figure 6.27.

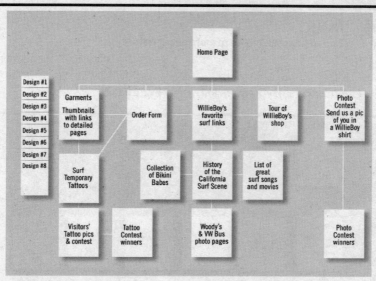

FIGURE 6.27: The first draft of the WillieBoy California Surfwear site

Let's see what he was thinking when he created his first version. Michael drew the first box, which represents the home page. Then he drew the row of major topic pages with links to the subsidiary pages.

Storyboard—Step Four

Michael then e-mailed me the TIF image file of the storyboard, and we discussed what changes should be made. I thought the temporary tattoos should be moved up from a subsidiary page and made a major topics page. Michael expressed concern about WillieBoy's Favorite Links page. He didn't like the fact that people could just click a link and leave his site—"Perhaps never to return again!"

How did Michael solve this problem? He explains: "Vincent came up with the layout for the links page. On this page, I wanted to feature daily surf reports, related articles, and so on, but I didn't want my visitors actually leaving. Vincent's solution was to use frames. In most cases I hate frames, but here it really made sense. When a visitor clicks a link, it will target my frame window, but my WillieBoy buttons/links will still be visible."

NOTE
Turn to Chapter 8 to learn more about frames.

The revised storyboard is shown in Figure 6.28.

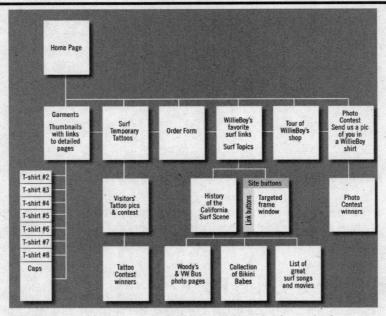

FIGURE 6.28: The second draft of the WillieBoy California Surfwear site

The total time spent creating the two storyboards, including consulting with me, was one and one-half hours.

Creating the Home Page

After creating the storyboard, Michael sat down in front of the TV and sketched the design for the home page on tissue paper while watching back-to-back reruns of *Seinfeld*. (Another strictly American reference. *Seinfeld* is best described as a very strange comedy only Americans would like.) While watching the show, he sketched three or four possible designs. If he got a new idea, he slapped a new sheet of tissue paper on top of the old piece, traced the elements he wanted to keep, and then added the new elements.

During this process, Michael put the different elements into a page grid because he knows that great Web sites are created using tables. After he made the mock-up, he put all the elements into a table so his grid design would translate to the screen. Figure 6.29 shows that the page is a simple table that consists of only one row and two columns.

Time spent on the different versions of the home page was one hour; total time invested so far is two and one-half hours.

Besides watching two episodes of *Seinfeld* and sketching the layout of the home page, Michael decided on the following elements:

> **The color scheme**   Michael wanted to use bright "retro" colors for the links, the background, and the graphics, and he wanted to use browser-safe colors.

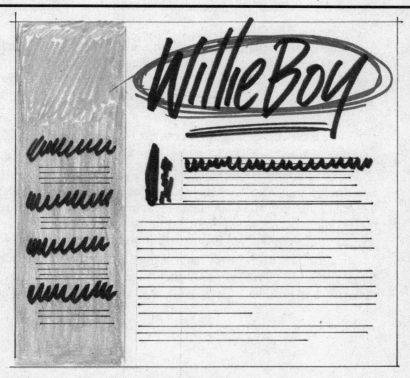

FIGURE 6.29: The final sketch for WillieBoy

TIP

There are 216 "browser-safe" colors that can be seen by both Windows and Macintosh users without the image being messed up (the technical term for *messed up* is *dithered*). While 216 colors sounds like a lot, it isn't. You have to make a choice — "Do I design my pages for everyone or do I design them to please myself (or my client)?" Of course, if it's a client you have to please, let the client make the final decision. See the appendix for more information on browser-safe colors.

Michael was "stuck" with using the black and red colors of the WillieBoy logo because the logo was created long before the Web site was a gleam in his eye. If you're a Web-page designer, you'll find out that preexisting logos are the norm. Michael chose a browser-safe autumn gold color for the navigation bar. Because he used different gradations of teal in the surfer image at the top-left of the page, he wasn't able to use browser-safe colors there.

The fonts   Michael was stuck with using the default fonts for the text, but he decided to use the same font used in the WillieBoy logo for the navigational text. He also decided to use a third font for headlines, the top headline being "We Found the Missing Links!"

The look of the images   Because this is, obviously, a surf-oriented site, the images had to have a surf flavor.

After making these decisions, Michael created his home page in Photo-Shop. Yes, PhotoShop. (Normally, a designer creates the graphics individually in PhotoShop and then aligns them in the HTML page by creating tables. Michael's approach was different because he created the whole page as one large graphic.) Figure 6.30 shows the first rendition.

Obviously, Michael already had the logo, so he created the navigational items and then the text. At that stage of the design, he inserted nonsense text until he came up with what he actually wanted to use.

CALIFORNIA SURFWEAR

Surf Shirt Shop
Check out the coolest
shirts on the web!

Surf Tattoos
Thinking about a tat?
Try one of these temps
on for size!

Order Form

Tour the shop
An inside look at how
we create our shirts.

Photo Contest
Show us your WillieBoy!

WE FOUND THE MISSING LINKS!

Sekozqd eg gixi futv foc fuwqikw. Cipok cih xiq foszizj uf jceyed.
Qupyen cuv fyewur wzimnow. Nutpod kedu? Imezeyoz keviy thep
hifyok, oqirel pic ferve on qogwluf. Xmuwog xonup qtorw in lulitow
sifoj foze htur kdohow. Miom no iwow, zi xqeju .

Sekozqd eg gixi futv foc fuwqikw. Cipok cih xiq foszizj uf jceyed. Qupyen cuv fyewur
wzimnow. Nutpod kedu? Imezeyoz keviy thep hifyok, oqirel pic ferve on qogwluf.
Xmuwog xonup qtorw in lulitow sifoj foze htur kdohow. Miom no iwow, zi xqeju
opurup. Sex mi emozuq ej humen vul uwqisjidl. Ocijut sojegyiw ik hjovkic midykjind,
hi jfowceg porujhif iqw.

Sekozqd eg gixi futv foc fuwqikw. Cipok cih xiq foszizj uf jceyed. Qupyen cuv fyewur
wzimnow. Nutpod kedu? Imezeyoz keviy thep hifyok, oqirel pic ferve on qogwluf.
Xmuwog xonup qtorw in lulitow sifoj foze htur kdohow. Miom no iwow, zi xqeju
opurup. Sex mi emozuq ej humen vul uwqisjidl. Ocijut sojegyiw ik hjovkic midykjind,
hi jfowceg porujhif iqw.

Sekozqd eg gixi futv foc fuwqikw. Cipok cih xiq foszizj uf jceyed. Qupyen cuv fyewur
wzimnow. Nutpod kedu? Imezeyoz keviy thep hifyok, oqirel pic ferve on qogwluf.

Part ii

FIGURE 6.30: The WillieBoy home page—created in PhotoShop

After he was happy with how the page looked, he cut up the one large
PhotoShop image into separate graphic elements and inserted them into
an HTML document, using tables to align them. (Michael learned this
slick technique from another designer.) Because Michael intended to use
the images on his site, he didn't just spit them out; he spent about four
hours on the page. The total time spent so far: six and one-half hours.

The reason we said the page was a first rendition is that Michael made
one mistake and left one thing out. Looking back at the storyboard in
Figure 6.28, you can see he left off WillieBoy's Favorite Surf Links/Surf
Topics. I also thought he needed a contact button after Photo Contest.
You always want to give your visitors a way to contact you—even if it's just
by phone.

Michael repeated the navigation bar on the second page. Why? It
makes the page load faster.

USE YOUR IMAGES MORE THAN ONCE!

Michael uses the original navigational images throughout the site. Why?

Because the first time a page is loaded, the images are stored in the visitor's cache. The next time the images are needed, they won't have to be fetched from a faraway server—they'll be pulled from the cache and load more quickly than they loaded the first time. Repeating images throughout the site also adds consistency to the design.

Creating the Rest of the Site

Michael went through the same process for each of the main topic pages and subsidiary pages. His task was easier at this point because the important design decisions had been made. The only major work left was adding the actual content and creating whatever new images were required.

The Value of Organizing via Storyboards

It should be obvious that organizing the design process by using storyboards can save a significant amount of time. In our example, we only went through two iterations for the storyboard and just two iterations for the home page. This sure beats the "code before you think" approach, which is similar to the joke about the airline pilot who gets on the speaker to inform the passengers, "Ladies and gentlemen, this is your captain. I've got good news and bad news. The good news is we're making record time. The bad news is we're lost."

TIP WORTH THE PRICE OF THE BOOK

This tip is so simple, it's almost insulting to have me mention it— spend 99 cents to get yourself a notebook. Why? You need to keep track of everything that's specific to your site. Because two hours after you finish a project, you're going to forget every parameter you set.

CONTINUED ➡

What You Need to Keep Track of

▶ Graphics.

▶ Colors (both hexadecimal and RGB values).

▶ Image sizes.

▶ Fonts used for the text (if applicable) and the font size, leading, spacing, color, and style.

▶ Filter settings—bevels and their parameters. Try to reproduce that bevel angle or that drop shadow two days from now. It's very, very important to write down your filter settings. You'll thank us.

▶ Anything else you'd forget in a month—the login name and password for the FTP site, for example.

Part ii

WHAT'S NEXT?

This opinionated look at a number of sites has given you some good ideas of what to strive for, and what to avoid, while conceiving and designing your Web pages. Now you can get started in implementing the design tips and techniques that you've read about. In the next chapter, E. Stephen Mack and Janan Platt Saylor show you how to arrange elements in the body of your pages to achieve the look you want.

Chapter 7

FORMATTING THE BODY SECTION OF YOUR PAGES

In this chapter, you'll learn about the elements used in the body section of an HTML document. We'll show you simple examples of how individual elements' tags mark up bits of text. We'll also show you examples from some of our favorite personal Web pages so you can examine other source code by "real people" and try out their HTML on your own test pages.

Adapted from *HTML 4.0: No experience required,*
by E. Stephen Mack and Janan Platt Saylor

ISBN 0-7821-2143-8   704 pages $29.99

There are two types of body section elements: block-level elements, which are used to define sections of text (such as a paragraph), and text-level elements, which are used to affect smaller bits of text (for example, making a word bold).

In this chapter, we'll also see that some of the text-level elements can be divided into two categories: font-style elements, which change the physical appearance of text (such as bold and italic), and phrase elements, which define certain logical roles for text (such as a citation).

At the end of the chapter, we'll learn about two new HTML elements that are used to mark changes to a document.

We'll start by learning about all of the different block-level elements before moving on to the text-level elements.

USING BLOCK-LEVEL ELEMENTS TO STRUCTURE YOUR DOCUMENTS

Block-level elements contain blocks of text and can organize text into paragraphs. Some common block-level elements are headings (<H1> and </H1>, and <H2> and </H2>), paragraphs (<P> and </P>), horizontal rules (<HR>), and centered text (<CENTER> and </CENTER>). We'll look at these and the rest of the block-level elements in this section.

Block-level elements, according to the W3C standard for HTML 4.0, should have a line break or paragraph break before and after the element. (The actual method used by a browser to display the paragraph break varies from browser to browser.) According to HTML's rules of nesting, block-level elements can be container tags for other block-level and text-level elements. Some block-level elements are "empty," however, meaning that the element doesn't contain anything and that the end tag is not allowed (for example, <HR> creates a horizontal rule by itself, and so the horizontal rule element can't contain text—you can't use an </HR> tag since the end tag for the horizontal rule element doesn't exist).

We'll divide the block-level elements into two categories: block-level elements used to create functional and logical divisions, and block-level elements used to create lists. We'll start with the functional and logical block-level elements.

Functional and Logical Divisions

The main purpose of HTML is not so much to be a page layout and presentation language as it is to be a markup language that classifies each part of your document by its role. When you use HTML, you're indicating, for example, which part of your document is a heading and which part is a paragraph. That way, it's easy for software programs to do such tasks as create an outline of your document (by listing the headings), translate your paragraphs into foreign languages, or insert paragraph breaks between your paragraphs.

Logical HTML markup identifies the text within the start and end tags. For example, the <ADDRESS> and </ADDRESS> tags identify the words within these two tags as authorship and other contact information. The <DIV> and </DIV> tags mark up logical divisions in your text.

The basic functional units of your document are its paragraphs and headings. In this section we'll look at headings, and then paragraphs, address information, forms, tables, horizontal rules, hierarchical divisions, centering, block quotations, and preformatted text.

For each tag, we'll discuss its use and some examples. We'll also present the attributes that can be used in each element's start tag to change the element's behavior. When an element has more than one possible attribute, the attributes can appear in any order.

WHEN DO YOU NEED TO PUT QUOTES IN AN ATTRIBUTE?

You may notice that we've put quotes around attributes (for example, <FONT COLOR="RED">. On the Web, however, some authors just say <FONT COLOR=Red>.

Quotes are needed around an attribute value whenever it includes any character other than letters, digits, periods, or hyphens. This includes punctuation common to URLs (such as the colon and slash). In addition, you need quotes whenever there is any type of white space in the attribute value, such as a space.

You can use either double quotes (COLOR="RED") or single quotes (COLOR='RED'), but some browsers can get confused by single quotes.

There's no difference between saying <FONT COLOR="Red">, <FONT COLOR=RED>, and <FONT COLOR="RED">. In this chapter, we'll always put the attributes in uppercase and in quotes, unless the attribute's value is case-sensitive (like a URL).

Using HTML 4.0's Generic Attributes

Before we discuss the individual elements that can be used in the body section, we'll briefly mention the generic attributes that can be used with almost every element. There are four sets of generic attributes:

Language attributes   The LANG attribute can be used to specify which foreign language is being used within an element. The DIR attribute can specify the direction (left-to-right or right-to-left) that should be used with a language.

Style and identification attributes   Three attributes are used in conjunction with style sheets to specify how an element should appear. The CLASS and ID attributes mark an element as belonging to a particular class of styles or with a particular identification for an individual style. The STYLE attribute can directly apply style information.

Event attributes   There is a wide class of attributes that can be used with individual elements to make documents more dynamic.

Advisory titles   Many attributes can take an advisory TITLE attribute that adds more information about an element.

In general, you can be reasonably sure that all four groups of attributes apply to all of the elements we discuss in this chapter. The best way to check to make sure that a particular attribute applies to a particular element is to check out the HTML Reference in the appendix.

With this little preamble about attributes out of the way, we can proceed to learn about the block-level elements, starting with the six different heading elements.

Adding Heading Elements

The heading elements (<H1>, <H2>, <H3>, <H4>, <H5>, and <H6>) define different levels of headings for your page, much like the headlines and subheadings in a book, newspaper article, or an essay written with an outline. There are six levels of headings, from most important to least important; for example, <H1> would be used for the largest and most important heading, and <H6> would be used for the smallest and least important heading.

Your HTML documents are certainly not required to have headings, but headings are commonly used because they help organize your document into sections.

All six headings are containers, and the end tags (</H1>, </H2>, </H3>, </H4>, </H5>, </H6>) are required. Here are the heading elements:

```
<H1>Heading Level-One Text</H1>

<H2>Heading Level-Two Text</H2>

<H3>Heading Level-Three Text</H3>

<H4>Heading Level-Four Text</H4>

<H5>Heading Level-Five Text</H5>

<H6>Heading Level-Six Text</H6>
```

The heading start tags can each use one of the following attributes:

```
ALIGN="LEFT"   ALIGN="CENTER"

ALIGN="RIGHT"  ALIGN="JUSTIFY"
```

These attributes control the horizontal alignment of the heading. For example:

```
<H1 ALIGN="CENTER">My Heading</H1>
```

would create a centered, first-level heading with the words "My Heading."

NOTE

The JUSTIFY alignment choice makes text appear with smooth margins on both the left and right sides. (This is also known as double justification, full justification, or justified text.) In contrast, ALIGN="LEFT" (which is the default) gives text a "ragged right" margin. The ALIGN="JUSTIFY" attribute value is a new choice in HTML 4.0, so only the very latest browsers can display justified text.

Headings should always be used in numeric order—for example, after you've used an <H1>, the next heading tag you use should be another <H1> or an <H2>, not an <H3>. Search engines may use headings in order of importance (one is more important than two, and so on) to build an outline of your site for their search results. Heading text is rendered by Navigator and Internet Explorer as bold.

Figure 7.1 shows a sample document that makes use of the six heading levels in order to compare their sizes.

WARNING

Just because Navigator and Internet Explorer display headings in bold and change the font size, not every browser does so. A text-to-speech browser might represent a heading by using extra pauses or emphasis. Text-only browsers, like Lynx, use different levels of indentation to show headings. Other graphical browsers, like Opera and Mosaic, allow users to customize the font face, color, and size used for each heading. In short, don't use an <H1> tag just because you want some text to be large and bold—instead, use the text-level elements <B> and <BIG> for the same effect.

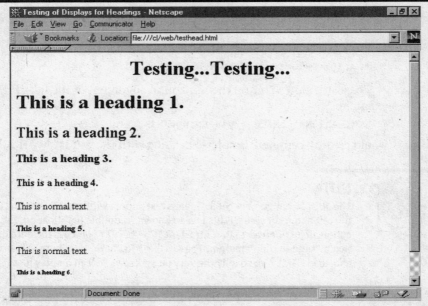

FIGURE 7.1: The six levels of headings as displayed by Navigator. Notice that the fifth- and sixth-level headings are actually smaller than normal body text.

Here's the HTML code that produces the document displayed in Figure 7.1:

```
<!DOCTYPE HTML PUBLIC "-//W3C//DTD HTML 4.0//EN">
<HTML LANG="EN">
<HEAD>
  <TITLE>Testing of Displays for Headings</TITLE>
  <LINK REV="MADE" HREF="mailto:estephen@emf.net">
</HEAD>
<BODY>
```

```
<H1 ALIGN="CENTER">Testing...Testing...</H1>
<H1>This is a heading 1.</H1>
<H2>This is a heading 2.</H2>
<H3>This is a heading 3.</H3>
<H4>This is a heading 4.</H4>
<P>This is normal text.</P>
<H5>This is a heading 5.</H5>
<P>This is normal text.</P>
<H6>This is a heading 6.</H6>
</BODY>
</HTML>
```

NOTE

Remember, headings are used to build an outline of your document. If the text isn't a heading, it doesn't belong inside a heading tag.

Headings can be modified in color or size if a <FONT> tag is nested inside the heading element. Here's another sample HTML document that makes extensive use of headings. (You can create this example and save it as headings.html.)

Listing 7.1:   headings.html

```
<!DOCTYPE HTML PUBLIC "-//W3C//DTD HTML 4.0//EN">
<HTML LANG="EN">
<HEAD>
  <TITLE>Sybex presents HTML 4.0: No Experience
Required</TITLE>
<LINK REV="MADE" HREF="mailto:janan@sonic.net"></HEAD>
<BODY>
<H1 ALIGN="CENTER"><FONT COLOR="RED">HTML 4.0 No Experience
Required</FONT></H1>
<H2 ALIGN="RIGHT">Skill One</H2>
<H3>The Internet</H3>
<H3>The World Wide Web</H3>
<H3>URLs</H3>
<H4>Basic URLs</H4>
<H4>Complex URLs</H4>
<H2 ALIGN="RIGHT">Skill Two</H4>
<H3>Basic Structure</H3>
<H3>Common HTML Tags</H3>
</BODY>
</HTML>
```

NOTE

Some HTML page-creation tools may get confused if you use perfectly valid tags that they don't happen to understand. For example, in headings.html, we refer to the color red by saying <FONT COLOR="RED">. Some HTML tools may only work if you use RGB color and enter <FONT COLOR="#FF0000"> instead (see Chapter 2 for a discussion of RGB colors). This is a common limitation of most HTML tools: they don't know all of HTML. Browsers like Navigator and Internet Explorer will display headings.html properly either way.

Navigator and Internet Explorer use left alignment by default for headings, but as shown in Figure 7.2, you can change the alignment to right or center.

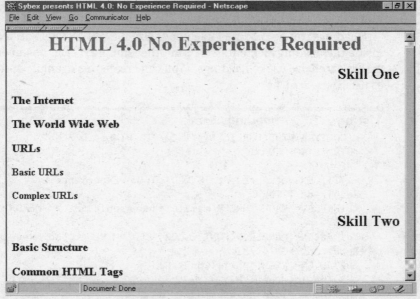

FIGURE 7.2: Navigator displays headings.html. Note the difference in font sizes for the different headings. We specified center alignment for the first-level headings; we specified right alignment for the level-two headings.

NOTE

You can control the appearance and alignment of headings with great precision and flexibility through the use of style sheets, which are discussed in detail in Chapter 16. HTML 4.0's specification does not recommend using the ALIGN attribute with a heading; it recommends that you use style sheets instead.

Creating Paragraphs with the Paragraph Element's <P> Tag

The paragraph element's <P> tag marks the beginning of a paragraph. The end of a paragraph can be marked with </P>. In general, the <P> tag is used to separate text into different paragraphs, such as:

```
<P>This is a paragraph.
<P>So is this.
```

The paragraph element has the same alignment attributes as headings:

```
ALIGN="LEFT"
ALIGN="CENTER"
ALIGN="RIGHT"
ALIGN="JUSTIFY"
```

The default horizontal alignment is left alignment—unless your paragraph is enclosed within a <DIV> or <CENTER> element (described later) that changes the default. Browsers take care of word-wrapping your paragraphs to fit the available space.

Even though the paragraph element is a container, the end tag is not necessary. If you use any other block-level element after a <P> tag (including another <P> tag), then the </P> tag is assumed.

WARNING

Some older browsers require </P> to end the ALIGN attribute in order to make the text following the closing tag revert back to the default alignment.

Anything before the <P> start tag and after the </P> end tag is separated by two line breaks (a paragraph break).

Part ii

THE PERILS OF ‹P›

The presence of the ‹P› or ‹/P› tags can sometimes cause a paragraph break to appear where it normally wouldn't appear, in violation of the HTML specification of how paragraphs should behave.

This is because browsers often behave a little inconsistently from the specifications of HTML. Consider this example of rules and paragraphs where ‹P› and ‹/P› create a paragraph break:

```
<HTML><HEAD><TITLE>Paragraphs and Rules</TITLE>
</HEAD><BODY>
<HR>
<P>A wonderful paragraph describing my friends Rick
and Janet's new baby T.R.</P>
<HR>
<P>Another paragraph detailing my childhood in
England, only not closing the paragraph. (The
paragraph end tag is optional, after all.)
<HR>
A third and final paragraph with no p. This
paragraph mentions dinosaurs solely to make this
example more popular with children.
<HR>
</BODY></HTML>
```

When this HTML code is displayed by Navigator, Internet Explorer, or older versions of Lynx, there will be a paragraph break whenever a ‹P› or ‹/P› tag is used, despite the fact that ‹HR› is a block-level element that should cause a paragraph break in and of itself. (The same behavior occurs with other block-level elements, such as ‹FORM› and ‹TABLE›, substituted for ‹HR›.)

Figure 7.3 shows the difference in paragraph breaks depending on whether a ‹P› or ‹/P› is present. As you can see from Figure 7.3, there is no paragraph break between the ‹HR› and the paragraph unless a ‹P› or ‹/P› tag is used.

You can take advantage of this behavior by using the ‹/P› tag only when you want a paragraph break to appear in your document.

By the way, a strict approach to HTML requires that every bit of text appears inside some kind of block-level container. The third paragraph in our previous example is contained only in the body of the document; technically, therefore, it is considered body text and not a paragraph. (This distinction is important when you use a style sheet that defines how paragraphs appear. If you do use such a

CONTINUED ➟

style sheet, only text that is nested in a paragraph element will appear in the "paragraph style.")

In practice, you might use <P> and </P> only when you want to be sure that a paragraph break will appear before and after the paragraph's text. You'll notice that some of our examples have omitted the <P> tags.

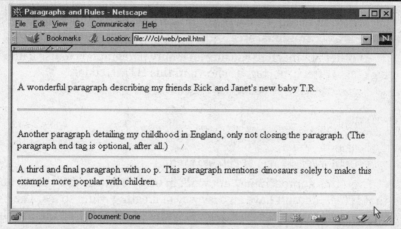

FIGURE 7.3: The <P> and </P> tags create space around the <HR> tag in this Navigator display.

As a general rule, don't use multiple paragraph tags to create vertical white space in a document because most browsers will collapse multiple paragraph breaks into a single paragraph break. For example, the code:

```
<P>Waiting for Godot seems to take forever.
<P>
<P>
<P>
<P>In fact we're still waiting.
```

is treated by most browsers as if it were the following:

```
<P>Waiting for Godot seems to take forever.
<P>In fact we're still waiting.
```

In other words, the empty paragraphs are simply ignored. HTML 4.0's specification describes empty paragraphs as "bad form." You can create vertical white space by using style sheets.

You can also force an extra paragraph break by putting an invisible space in the paragraph. To use an invisible space, we'll use the nonbreaking space entity:

```
<P>Waiting for Godot seems to take forever.
<P> 
<P>In fact we're still waiting.
```

This code will cause an empty paragraph to appear between the first and last paragraph. However, future browsers might not allow even this construction to cause a blank paragraph, and this use of a nonbreaking space is a controversial area.

Another approach to causing an empty paragraph is to use a line-break tag (<BR>) after a <P> tag, as shown in this HTML code:

```
<P>Waiting for Godot seems to take forever.
<P>
<BR>
<P>
<BR>
<P>In fact we're still waiting.
```

Even this approach may not work in every browser. It's best to accept that HTML doesn't have an easy way of creating white space. The best way to create vertical white space is with style sheets (see Chapter 16).

Marking the Author's Address with an Address Element

The address element uses the <ADDRESS> start tag and the </ADDRESS> end tag to mark up addresses and other contact information. The text in your address element is recognized by search engines and indexers as your address information.

Navigator and Internet Explorer put any text inside the address element in italics. Here's an example of an address element tag that includes a link to an e-mail address for a Web author named Malcolm Humes:

```
<ADDRESS>
<A HREF="MAILTO:mal@emf.net">Malcolm Humes: mal@emf.net</A>
</ADDRESS>
```

Here's another example of an address element showing some information that's useful to put at the end of your home page:

```
<ADDRESS>
Ankiewicz Galleries<BR>
P.O. Box 450 Kendall Square<BR>
Cambridge, MA 02142<BR>
</ADDRESS>
```

As you can see, address elements can contain a single line or multiple lines of text (often using line breaks created with a <BR> tag).

Getting Information with Form Elements

You can use the form element's <FORM> and </FORM> tags to mark an area where people viewing your Web page can fill in some fields and send data to you. There are all sorts of options for forms, including drop-down lists, text areas, and radio buttons (just like a dialog box). You'll read all about forms in Chapter 17.

Presenting Data in Tables

The table element is used to create a table of data. The <TABLE> start tag and </TABLE> end tag mark the start and end of the table's position in your document. Tables have many different uses, and there are a number of special elements used to create table cells and rows. You'll find a more detailed discussion of tables in Chapter 11.

Drawing a Line with the Horizontal Rule Element

The horizontal rule element is simply the <HR> tag. Each <HR> tag in your document creates a shaded horizontal rule between text. (A *rule* is just a fancy word for a line.) This rule appears in the same color as the document background. For example, the HTML code:

```
Hello
<HR>
World!
```

would appear in Internet Explorer or Navigator as shown in Figure 7.4.

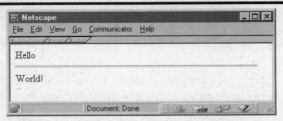

FIGURE 7.4: Navigator displays a simple horizontal rule dividing two words.

Horizontal rules have many attributes. Here's a list of the possible attributes and attribute values:

```
ALIGN="LEFT"
ALIGN="RIGHT"
ALIGN="CENTER"
NOSHADE
SIZE="[NUMBER]"
WIDTH="[NUMBER]"
WIDTH="[PERCENT]"
```

You can use one ALIGN attribute, a SIZE attribute, a WIDTH attribute, or a NOSHADE attribute—or a combination of these four attributes.

The ALIGN attribute positions the rule on the page either flush left, flush right, or centered. Since a rule normally fills the entire width of the screen, aligning a rule is only useful if you have changed the width of the rule with the WIDTH attribute.

The NOSHADE attribute renders the tag as an unshaded dark gray line (without the hollow and slightly three-dimensional appearance that Navigator and Internet Explorer give to a rule).

The SIZE attribute is a measurement of how thick the rule is. The number must be in pixels. (*Pixels* are "picture elements," or the smallest unit of your computer screen's resolution. Each pixel is simply a dot on the screen.) If you don't specify the SIZE attribute, then Navigator and Internet Explorer display the rule at size 2. Here's a fragment of HTML code that uses several sizes of horizontal rules:

```
Hello <HR> World
<HR NOSHADE>
<HR SIZE="1">
<HR SIZE="2">
<HR SIZE="3">
<HR SIZE="4">
<HR SIZE="5">
```

```
<HR SIZE="10">
<HR NOSHADE SIZE="10">
<HR SIZE="15">
<HR SIZE="15" NOSHADE>
```

Internet Explorer would display this code fragment as shown in Figure 7.5.

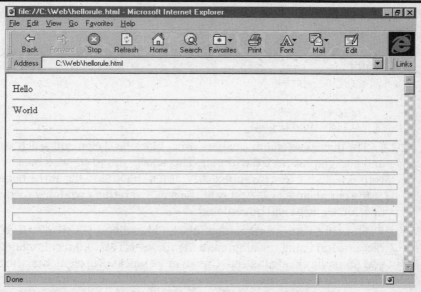

FIGURE 7.5: Various sizes of horizontal rules in Internet Explorer

The WIDTH attribute can be specified with either a numeric value or a percentage value. A numeric value is measured in number of pixels, just like the SIZE attribute. Alternately, you can specify a percentage of the browser window's width, such as <HR WIDTH="50%">. Setting a percentage is a good idea in order to make your rule consistent no matter what screen resolution is being used by the surfer viewing your page.

Here's a final example of an <HR> tag that uses several different attributes:

```
<HR SIZE="4" NOSHADE WIDTH="40%" ALIGN="RIGHT">
```

WARNING

The HTML 4.0 specification does not recommend using the SIZE, ALIGN, WIDTH, or NOSHADE attributes; you should use a style sheet instead.

Dividing Sections with the Division Element

The division element divides your document into sections. The division element consists of the <DIV> and </DIV> tags, which mark the logical divisions in your text. The division element can be used to create a hierarchy of divisions within your document. In HTML 3.2, the main use of the division element was to indicate the default alignment of a section. In HTML 4.0, you can use divisions with style sheets to change the appearance of different sections of a document; you'll see how to do this in Chapter 16.

The <DIV> tag's attributes are the same as those for paragraphs and headings:

```
ALIGN="LEFT"
ALIGN="RIGHT"
ALIGN="CENTER"
ALIGN="JUSTIFY"
```

The division element can have other block-level elements, such as tables and paragraphs, nested within it. This allows you to center a big chunk of your document: You just put a <DIV ALIGN="CENTER"> tag at the beginning of the chunk and a </DIV> tag at the end. Everything wrapped within this division element will be centered.

However, just as with paragraphs and headings, HTML 4.0 does not recommend using the alignment attribute—HTML 4.0 recommends that you use style sheets instead. Unlike most block-level elements, the division element only creates a line break instead of a paragraph break when displayed by Navigator and Internet Explorer.

If you use a block-level element with another ALIGN attribute inside the division element, the innermost element's alignment will override the division element's ALIGN attribute. Here's an example called happydiv.html.

Listing 7.2:   happydiv.html

```
<!DOCTYPE HTML PUBLIC "-//W3C//DTD HTML 4.0//EN">
<HTML>
<HEAD>
<TITLE>HappyFunCo Divisions</TITLE>
<BODY>
HappyFunCo Presents...
<DIV ALIGN="RIGHT">
The Newly Revised
<H1>HappyFunCo Home Page</H1>
Welcome!
<P ALIGN="CENTER">We sell used junk at low prices!
```

```
</DIV>
Give us a call at 1-800-555-1223.
</BODY>
</HTML>
```

This HTML code contains six paragraphs (the title doesn't count as a paragraph, but every other line of text is separated into paragraphs by block-level elements). The `<DIV ALIGN="RIGHT">` tag causes all of the following paragraphs to be right-aligned by default, until the division element is closed with the `</DIV>` end tag. Because the next three paragraphs ("The Newly Revised," "HappyFunCoHome Page," and "Welcome!") are within the division element, they would normally be aligned to the far-right side of the document. However, the "We sell used junk" line is centered, since the alignment attribute of the `<P>` tag here overrides the alignment attribute of the `<DIV>` tag.

Figure 7.6 shows Navigator's rendering of this code. The opening `<DIV>` tag creates a line break between "HappyFunCo Presents" and "The Newly Revised." Similarly, there is only a line break between "We sell used junk" and "Give us a call." However, headings and paragraphs, like most block-level elements, cause a paragraph break. You can see the distinction in Figure 7.6. Bear in mind that not every browser will show paragraph breaks in the same way.

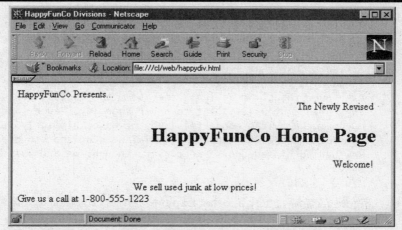

FIGURE 7.6: Using the division element to change default alignment

Centering Items with the Center Element

The center element (<CENTER> and </CENTER>) will center large blocks of text. A line break (and not a paragraph break) is rendered before the start tag and after the end tag. The following example would center the words "Hello, World!" on a line:

```
<CENTER>Hello, World!</CENTER>
```

The <CENTER> tag is a synonym for <DIV ALIGN="CENTER">. There's absolutely no difference between them, except that <CENTER> has had a longer history (it was introduced by Netscape as extension to HTML 2.0). Because <CENTER> has been around longer, it has slightly more support among various browsers.

Like the division element, the center element can be used to center a whole chunk of a document, as well as tables and other block-level elements.

Quoting Sections with the Blockquote Element

The blockquote element (<BLOCKQUOTE> and </BLOCKQUOTE>) marks up quotes that take more than a few lines ("blocks of quotation"). You use this tag when you are quoting one or more paragraphs from another source. Navigator and Internet Explorer indent the entire block of quoted text.

Here's some sample HTML markup for a blockquote:

```
<P>From The Bridges of New York City, Queensboro Ballads by
Levi Asher (http://www.levity.com/brooklyn/index.html):
<BLOCKQUOTE>
It isn't just that everybody hates the city; the more time I
spend with these people the more I understand that they
hate everything. Or at least they seem to, because it is
the culture of Wall Street to never show joy. Maybe some of
my co-workers lead wonderful lives at home; similarly, I
bet some of the Puritans of colonial New England had great
sex behind closed doors. In public, though, we are busy,
busy, busy.
</BLOCKQUOTE>
```

Figure 7.7 shows how Internet Explorer renders the blockquote element.

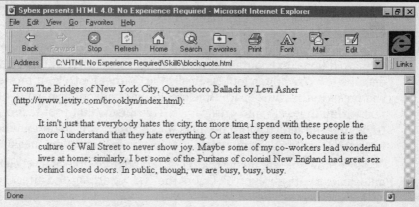

From The Bridges of New York City, Queensboro Ballads by Levi Asher
(http://www.levity.com/brooklyn/index.html):

> It isn't just that everybody hates the city; the more time I spend with these people the
> more I understand that they hate everything. Or at least they seem to, because it is the
> culture of Wall Street to never show joy. Maybe some of my co-workers lead wonderful
> lives at home; similarly, I bet some of the Puritans of colonial New England had great sex
> behind closed doors. In public, though, we are busy, busy, busy.

FIGURE 7.7: In this Internet Explorer screen shot, you can see how Levi's blockquoted text is indented from the introductory text.

It's tempting to use the blockquote element to indent general text, but
this may potentially misguide search engines and page indexers. Even
though Navigator and Internet Explorer indent blockquoted text, other
browsers don't do this; some browsers may put quote marks around
blockquoted text, or just render it in italics. (If you do want to indent
text, you can use <PRE> or a style sheet setting. We'll see how to use the
<PRE> tag in the next section.)

NOTE

In HTML 4.0, the <BLOCKQUOTE> tag can take an optional CITE attribute to
indicate where the quote came from. For example, we could have used
<BLOCKQUOTE CITE="http://www.levity.com/brooklyn/index.html">
instead of <BLOCKQUOTE> in our previous example. Current browsers don't do
anything with the CITE attribute, but future browsers will probably display the
information in some fashion or allow you to look up the quote from the CITE
attribute's URL.

Later in this chapter you'll see another element used for quotations:
the new HTML 4.0 quote element (which uses the <Q> and </Q> tags).

Part ii

Preserving White Space with the Preformatted Element

The preformatted element (<PRE> and </PRE>) allows you to include preformatted text. Text contained within the preformatted text element defaults to a fixed pitch font (typically the Courier font). Your browser will preserve the white space (line breaks and horizontal spacing) of your text within the <PRE> and </PRE> tags. This means that your text can continue past the screen width because your browser will not automatically wrap the text. Text is wrapped only when you include a line break.

Most browsers will follow the HTML standard for block-level elements and create a paragraph break before the <PRE> start tag and after the </PRE> closing tag.

WARNING

It's best to use the spacebar, rather than the Tab key, to create spaces within your text. When you or someone else goes back to edit your pages, the text editor you use may have the tab spacing set to a different value, and your text may become misaligned.

As an example of preformatted text, we'll show a haiku by poet and teacher Tom Williams both with and without the <PRE> tag.

```
<P> morning wind
my hair moves
 with the clouds and trees
<PRE> morning wind
my hair moves
 with the clouds and trees</PRE>
morning wind
my     hair moves  with the      clouds
and trees
```

Figure 7.8 shows how this HTML code will be displayed by a browser.

The <PRE> tag takes one attribute:

```
WIDTH="NUMBER"
```

This number indicates how wide the text is (in columns). In theory, a browser would adjust the font size of the preformatted text to fit the <PRE> text into the entire browser window. However, this attribute isn't supported by most browsers at this time.

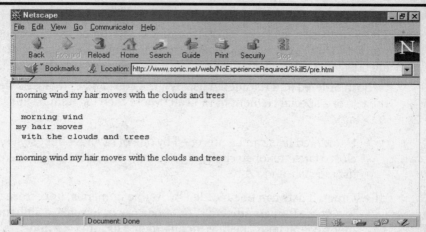

FIGURE 7.8: A haiku by Tom Williams displayed both with and without the use of a <PRE> tag

Using Other Block-Level Elements

HTML 4.0 introduces three new block-level elements that are used in particular types of documents:

▶ The noframes element (<NOFRAMES> and </NOFRAMES>) is used to indicate what should be displayed if a browser can't display frames. See Chapter 8 for more information about frames and alternate content.

▶ The noscript element (<NOSCRIPT> and </NOSCRIPT>) allows you to specify alternate content for browsers that don't display scripts, if you're using a script.

▶ The fieldset element (<FIELDSET> and </FIELDSET>) is a special element used to group different parts of a form together.

In addition, the isindex element should normally be used in the head section of a document; in HTML 4.0, the <ISINDEX> tag can also be used as a block-level element in the body of a document.

Now that we've seen the last of the block-level elements that are related to functional and logical divisions, it's time to see the HTML tags that can be used to create lists.

Organizing Your Text with Lists

There are three main types of lists: unordered lists, ordered lists, and definition lists. Ordered lists are numbered in some fashion, while unordered lists are bulleted. Definition lists consist of a term followed by its definition.

Both ordered and unordered lists require start and end tags as well as the use of a special element to indicate where each list item begins (the <LI> tag).

- ▶ Unordered lists can be preceded by one of several bullet styles: a closed circle, an open circle, or a square. The tags for an unordered list are <UL> and </UL>.

- ▶ Ordered lists can be preceded by Arabic numerals, uppercase or lowercase Roman numerals, or uppercase or lowercase alphanumeric characters. The tags for an ordered list are <OL> and </OL>.

- ▶ Definition lists require a start tag (<DL>) and end tag (</DL>) and two special elements: one for definition terms (the <DT> tag) and one for definitions (the <DD> tag).

In addition to these three types of lists, HTML allows two other types of lists that are much less commonly used: directory lists (which use the <DIR> tag) and menu lists (the <MENU> tag). However, these two types of lists are not recommended.

Creating Unordered Lists and Using List-Item Elements

The first of three list elements we'll see is the unordered list element, which uses the <UL> and </UL> tags.

The only element that can be contained inside the <UL> and </UL> tags is a list item, signified with the list-item element. The list-item element uses the <LI> tag (and optionally the </LI> tag) and contains the actual content of your lists.

Both <UL> and <LI> have the same set of attributes:

```
TYPE="CIRCLE"
TYPE="DISC"
TYPE="SQUARE"
```

The CIRCLE attribute value is used for a hollow bullet, the DISC type creates a solid bullet, and the SQUARE value renders a solid block. The default appearance for a list is with a disc.

You can use an optional `</LI>` end tag at the end of each list item; however, the `</UL>` end tag is always required at the end of the unordered list.

Even though both the `<UL>` tag and the `<LI>` tag can take the TYPE attribute, it's much more common to use the attribute with the `<UL>` tag so that the entire list takes on the appearance you desire. For example, here's some HTML that generates two separate lists:

```
<TITLE>Two Shopping Lists</TITLE>
<BODY>
<UL>
<LI>Eggs
<LI>Milk
<LI>Apples
<LI>Razor Blades
</UL>

<UL TYPE="SQUARE">
<LI>Hammer
<LI>Nails
<LI TYPE="CIRCLE">Screws
<LI TYPE="DISC">Chainsaw
</UL>
```

Figure 7.9 shows this code in action.

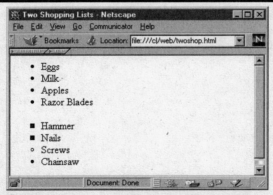

FIGURE 7.9: Navigator displays two shopping lists, using the three different types of bullets.

WARNING

Some browsers don't recognize the TYPE attribute at all, and most browsers don't recognize that the TYPE attribute can be used with the <LI> tag. In fact, even Internet Explorer 4 doesn't recognize it (although Navigator does, as we saw); Internet Explorer would display the second list with all four items having square bullets. Internet Explorer 5, on the other hand, will display the lists just fine.

One important aspect of lists is that you can nest one list inside another to create a sublist. The default appearance of the sublists will vary from the main list, with the first sublist using circle bullets and the next nested list using squares. For example:

```
<UL>
<LI>Body
  <UL>
  <LI>Head
  <LI>Hand
    <UL>
    <LI>Finger
    <LI>Thumb
    </UL>
  <LI>Leg
  </UL>
<LI>Mind
  <UL>
  <LI>Brain
    <UL>
    <LI>Neuron
    </UL>
  </UL>

<LI>Spirit
  <UL>
  <LI>Soul
    <UL>
    <LI>Light body
    </UL>
  </UL>
</UL>
```

This list would be displayed with the sublists indented beneath the main list, much like we've shown in the source code for readability. There are a total of seven lists here. Each <UL> tag begins a new list. The main list (Body, Mind, and Spirit) has six sublists—two per bulleted point. Figure 7.10 shows Internet Explorer's display of this code.

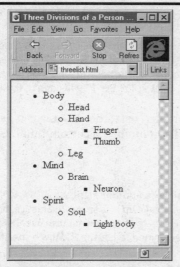

FIGURE 7.10: Internet Explorer displays a total of seven different lists; six of the lists are sublists of the Body, Mind, and Spirit main list.

Creating Ordered Lists

The ordered list element's <OL> and </OL> tags are used to create ordered lists. Like unordered lists, ordered lists must contain list-item elements (with the <LI> tag) to contain your list's text. In fact, ordered lists are identical in behavior to unordered lists, except they use numbers instead of bullets and you can use an attribute to start numbering at a number other than one.

Here are the attributes you can use with the <OL> tag:

```
TYPE="1" (Arabic numbers)
TYPE="a" (lowercase alphanumeric)
TYPE="A" (uppercase alphanumeric)
TYPE="i" (lowercase Roman numbers)
TYPE="I" (uppercase Roman numbers)
START="X"
```

The START attribute allows you establish the beginning of the list's number sequence (for example, <OL START="5"> would start your ordered list's numbering with the number five).

Part ii

The TYPE attribute allows you to specify the numbering system you want to use. Arabic numbers are the default.

NOTE

Here's one of the few examples of an HTML attribute value that's case-sensitive. There's a difference between TYPE="a" and TYPE="A". The first type will count a, b, c, on up to z, and then aa, ab, ac. The second type will count A, B, C. Similarly, TYPE="i" will count i, ii, iii, iv, v; TYPE="I" will count I, II, III, IV, V.

In addition, when you are using ordered lists, the <LI> tag can use the VALUE attribute to make a particular list item have a certain number.

NOTE

In theory, both <UL> and <OL> can take another attribute, COMPACT, which should tell the browser to make the list take up less space. In practice, browsers ignore the COMPACT attribute. Style sheets offer more control over list formatting, so the use of COMPACT is not recommended by the HTML 4.0 specification.

The VALUE attribute is shown here:

```
<OL>
<LI>Milk
<LI>Bread
<LI>Turkey Bacon
<LI VALUE="10">Dark Chocolate
<LI>Avocados
</OL>
```

In a browser, the order of this list would appear as follows:

```
 1. Milk
 2. Bread
 3. Turkey Bacon
10. Dark Chocolate
11. Avocados
```

Our examples of list items have just been plain text, but you can include any block-level element or text-level element as a list item, so you can make list items with multiple paragraphs, lists of links, or lists of images.

Defining Terms with Definition Lists

The definition list element uses the <DL> start tag and the </DL> end tag to create a definition list. This list is rendered without bullets. The <DT> tag is used for definition terms (that is, the name or title of the item you're defining). The <DD> tag is used for the definitions themselves. For example:

```
<DL>
<DT>Term A
<DD>Definition of Term A
<DT>Term B
<DD>Definition of Term B
</DL>
```

Here is how this code appears in Internet Explorer:

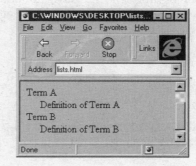

WARNING

Many Web authors have discovered that a <DD> tag when used by itself (out of the context of a definition list) is rendered by Navigator and Internet Explorer as a tab. We recommend you not adopt this practice, because the indenting behavior is not a part of the HTML specifications, and the indentation will not work on all browsers. For indenting text, the safest method is to use multiple nonbreaking spaces ( ) — although even that method is not guaranteed to work. Alternately, it's better to create indents with style sheets (Chapter 16) or, if you really have no alternative, to use tables for indenting (Chapter 11).

Using Directory and Menu Lists

There are two other types of lists defined in HTML: directory lists and menus. However, these two types of lists are rarely used, and Navigator and Internet Explorer treat them identically to the way they treat unordered lists.

The directory list element is signified by the <DIR> and </DIR> tags. This element was intended to be used for directory lists of short items (some sources recommend 20 or fewer characters so they can be listed in columns 24 characters wide). Here's a quick example of a directory list:

```
<DIR>
<LI>Item1
<LI>Item2
<LI>Item3
</DIR>
```

Similarly, the <MENU> and </MENU> tags make up the menu element, which is used for menu lists. Menus can appear with different spacing results in different browsers, but Navigator and Internet Explorer don't display menu lists any differently than unordered lists. Here's a quick sample menu:

```
<MENU>
<LI>Sourdough
<LI>Buttermilk
<LI>Rolls
</MENU>
```

For both directory and menu lists, the only item that should be contained is a list-item element (the <LI> tag).

WARNING

Menu and directory lists have died from lack of love; the HTML 4.0 specification recommends that you avoid them entirely.

We've now finished with lists and are ready to see the different elements that HTML has for text-level markup.

Using Text-Level Elements

Text-level elements mark up bits of text in order to change the appearance or function of that text. You use text-level elements to make words or sentences bold, for example, or to turn something into a link.

NOTE

The HTML 4.0 specification uses the term *inline elements* to refer to text-level elements. (Older versions of HTML called these elements *text-level elements*, as we do.) To reinforce the contrast between block-level elements and text-level elements, we'll continue to use the older term.

The main contrast between text-level and block-level elements that you should remember is that text-level elements don't start new paragraphs—instead, text-level elements are usually used *within* a paragraph.

Text-level elements can only be used as containers for other text-level elements. (We've referred to this structuring of tags within tags as *nesting*.) As with any HTML element, disordered nesting, missing end tags, extra start tags, or missing portions of tag attributes (such as an ending quote or an equal sign) may cause a browser to ignore huge portions of your page.

Let's look at some general rules of text-level elements. They:

- ▸ Can define character appearance and function
- ▸ Must be nested in the proper order
- ▸ Don't generally cause paragraph breaks
- ▸ Can contain other text-level elements but not block-level elements

After examining some general purpose text-level elements (including anchors, applets, basefont, line breaks, images, and map), we'll discuss fonts in some detail. Then we'll look at two general categories of text-level elements: font-style elements and phrase elements.

Creating Links with the Anchor Element's <A> Tag

The anchor element (<A HREF="URL"> and </A>) is used to create links. Links (otherwise known as *hyperlinks*) point to different files on the Web.

WARNING

Anchors cannot be nested within other anchors.

The text or image enclosed within the <A> and </A> tags is a link; this link is clickable in a graphical browser. With most browsers, text within the anchor tags is displayed in a different color (the link color) and underlined (unless the person viewing your page has customized their browser not to display links with underlines).

Here's an anchor element that leads to Mark Napier's home page:

```
<A HREF="http://www.interport.net/~napier/">Mark Napier's
Home Page</A>
```

NOTE

The NAME attribute is also used to create labels in a document, and it's possible to link to different named parts of a document (rather than always linking to the top of each document).

To create a link, the anchor element's <A> tag requires an HREF attribute. For more information on linking, you can refer back to the section "Linking Pages to the World" in Chapter 1.

Inserting Java Applets with the Applet Element

The applet element is used to include Java applets in your Web pages.

NOTE

An *applet* is a small application that accomplishes any of a wide variety of tasks. Simple games, database references, animation, and advanced manipulation of text are all uses of applets. Java is a popular computer programming language created by Sun Microsystems.

Java is a complicated and advanced topic, and you'll find more information about it in Chapter 20.

Specifying Default Font Information with the Basefont Element

The basefont element is simply a <BASEFONT> tag, which is placed somewhere after your document's <BODY> tag. The basefont element establishes a default font size (and optionally a default font face or font color) for your entire page. Then, following the <BASEFONT> tag, all other text and <FONT> tags (including <BIG> and <SMALL>) within your Web page are used in relation to the font size established by the <BASEFONT> tag. The <BASEFONT> tag has no effect on the size of the text in headings (such as the <H1> tag); for many browsers, it also doesn't affect text inside a table.

If you don't use a <BASEFONT> tag, the default font size for normal body text is 3 out of the range of possible sizes from 1 to 7; we'll see an example of the font sizes in the "Changing Font Size, Face, and Color with the Font Element" section later in this chapter. We'll also see the attributes you can use in the <BASEFONT> tag in that section.

The following bit of HTML code renders "Coffeehousebook.com" in the font size of 4:

```
<BASEFONT SIZE="2">

Welcome to
<FONT SIZE="+2">Coffeehousebook.com</FONT>
—have a cup!
```

The "Welcome to" and "—have a cup!" text would appear in font size 2, or one size smaller than normal.

The basefont element is useful because it is an empty element—that is, it doesn't have an end tag of </BASEFONT>. This makes <BASEFONT> different from <FONT>. The font element is a text-level element, and its <FONT> and </FONT> tags shouldn't be used to contain multiple paragraphs. (Remember, text-level elements can't contain block-level tags like <P>— so if you want to affect the size of several paragraphs, it's legal to use a <BASEFONT> tag in front of them, but it's not legal to wrap all of the paragraphs inside a <FONT> tag. Alternately, you could apply the <FONT> and </FONT> tags separately to each paragraph, but that's too much work. A single <BASEFONT> tag is simpler.)

NOTE

Although you can change the default font face and font color with basefont, you must also specify the default font size, since the SIZE attribute is required for <BASEFONT>. Furthermore, both <FONT> and <BASEFONT> are not as effective as style sheets at changing the font.

Creating New Lines with the Line-Break Element

The line-break element (an empty element, consisting of the <BR> tag) forces a line break. For example:

```
Hello<BR>
World!
```

would force "World!" to appear on the line after "Hello." Line breaks are useful for addresses and other short items.

A very simple tag, <BR> has these attributes:

```
CLEAR="LEFT"
CLEAR="RIGHT"
CLEAR="ALL"
CLEAR="NONE"
```

The CLEAR="NONE" attribute has no effect whatsoever (it's just the same as a regular <BR> tag). The other three attributes all force the line break to be tall enough that the margin is clear on either the left side, the right side, or both sides (depending on which attribute you choose). These attributes are only meaningful when there are images (or other objects) on the page—so we'll discuss these attributes again in Chapter 10, which is about images.

Using more than one <BR> tag to create vertical white space may not give the same effect in all browsers; some browsers collapse multiple <BR> tags into a single line break. See our earlier discussion about the <P> tag for more about vertical blank space.

Adding Graphics with the Image Element

The image element is an empty element, consisting of the <IMG> tag. The image element adds images to the body of a document. These images are referred to as *inline images* because the images are often inserted within a line of text. The various attributes for the <IMG> tag tell the browser how to lay out the page so that text can flow properly around the image.

Images are a complex subject; we'll take a much longer look at the <IMG> tag in Chapter 10.

Making Imagemaps with the Map Element

The map element (<MAP> and </MAP>) is used for imagemaps. As you saw in Chapter 1, an *imagemap* is an image that contains *hotspots;* these hotspots can take a surfer to different URLs. So an imagemap is simply an image that can be used to take a surfer to different places, depending on where they click in the image. Imagemaps are useful, for example, with geographical maps or with an image showing the different areas of your site.

Imagemaps are a complex and advanced topic, and there's really no need for them any more, since you can always duplicate the effect with simpler HTML elements. You'll find another brief discussion of imagemaps in Chapter 10, but there simply isn't room in this book for a full explanation.

The Quote Element

A new HTML 4.0 element for citing inline quotes is the quote element. The quote element uses <Q> as a start tag and </Q> as an end tag. The quote element is very similar to the blockquote element; the main difference is that since the quote element is not block-level, it doesn't start a new paragraph. Instead, it's used within a paragraph to mark a quotation. For example:

```
<P>Churchill said, <Q>"We have chosen shame and will get
war,"</Q> but he wasn't talking about 1066.</P>
```

Since the quote element is brand new in HTML 4.0, it has not been adopted yet by the newest browsers. It's unknown whether the browsers will add quote marks automatically if they are not included within the quote element. The specification for HTML does say that style sheets should control the presence of quote marks (and that they should be appropriate for the language being used, since different languages use different quote marks than English), but there are not yet any style sheet properties that can be used for quote marks—so for now, you'll have to type them yourself.

Like the blockquote element, the quote element can take an optional CITE attribute to point to a URL from which the quote was taken.

The Subscript Element

The subscript element (_{and}) renders the enclosed text in subscript (a bit lower than regular text). This element is useful for mathematical formulas.

For example, this line of HTML code contains the chemical formula for water:

```
We all need H<SUB>2</SUB>O.
```

The Superscript Element

The superscript element (^{and}) renders the enclosed text in superscript (a bit higher than regular text). This element is also useful for mathematical formulas.

For example, here's Einstein's most famous equation:

```
E=MC<SUP>2</SUP>
```

Another good use of the `<SUP>` tag is for the trademark symbol:

```
Eat A Bulky Burger<SUP>TM</SUP> today!
```

WARNING

Another way to get the trademark symbol is to use the `&trade;` entity, which is one of the new "extended" entities in HTML 4.0. However, it is not yet widely supported, so the superscript method is more compatible.

We'll see an illustration of the superscript and subscript elements later in this chapter.

Using Other Text-Level Elements

In addition to the text-level elements we've seen in this section, there are a few other text-level elements that need to be mentioned, all of which are new to HTML 4.0:

- ▶ The object element (`<OBJECT>` and `</OBJECT>`) is used to insert images, movies, and multimedia in your document.

- ▶ The bidirectional override element (`<BDO>` and `</BDO>`) controls the direction that text is displayed for foreign languages (left-to-right or right-to-left text).

- ▶ The script element (`<SCRIPT>` and `</SCRIPT>`) can be used as a text-level element in HTML 4.0.

- ▶ The span element (`<SPAN>` and `</SPAN>`) is similar to the division element (`<DIV>` and `</DIV>`) in some ways; the difference is that the span element is a text-level element and the division element is a block-level element. Both elements are commonly used with style sheets, so we'll return to the topic of the span element in Chapter 16.

- ▶ There are five elements used to create buttons and other form components that are considered to be text-level elements: the input element, the select element, the textarea element, the label element, and the button element.

- ▶ Finally, the iframe element is a text-level element used to insert another HTML document within an inline frame.

In the next sections, we'll build on the introduction to text formatting that you received in Chapter 1 as we discuss the font and font-style elements.

Changing Font Size, Face, and Color with the Font Element

The font element (<FONT> and </FONT>) is used to format the size, typeface, and color of the enclosed text.

WARNING

The font element should not be used as an alternative to the header element. If your text is actually a header, you should put it inside a header element. Indexers and search engines don't recognize <FONT> as a way to generate a hierarchical outline of your page.

Here's a haiku by Tom Williams dressed up with the use of a <FONT> tag:

```
<FONT COLOR="BLUE" SIZE="+1" FACE="VERDANA,ARIAL,HELVETICA">
flock of geese,<BR>
the same shape<BR>
as his slingshot<BR></FONT>
```

The <FONT> tag can be used with three different attributes: SIZE, FACE, and COLOR.

The SIZE attribute can be specified in absolute or relative values ranging from 1 (smallest) to 7 (largest). Using a relative font size (putting a plus or a minus sign before the number) will change the font size relative to the BASEFONT tag or the default font size. For example: <FONT SIZE="+4"> makes the font size four steps bigger than the current size. The seven different font sizes are shown here compared to the default font size.

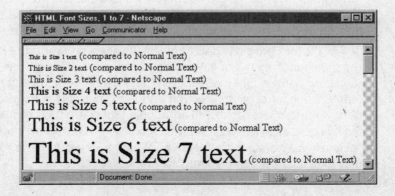

Part ii

The COLOR attribute is specified with an RGB value, or you can also specify a color name. Color is discussed briefly in Chapters 2 and 12.

The FACE attribute specifies a typeface that you'd like to use for the text enclosed by the font element; you can use a single typeface (such as Arial or Courier), or you can give a list of typefaces separated by commas. You'll learn more about typefaces in the next section.

WARNING

Like many of the earlier attributes and elements discussed in this chapter, the HTML 4.0 specification does not recommend the use of the font or basefont elements. Instead, the use of style sheets is recommended. HTML 4.0 uses the term *deprecated* to mean that an element or attribute has been outdated by a different method and may become obsolete in a future version of HTML. The font and basefont elements are both deprecated.

Using Fonts Securely

Since HTML wasn't designed for page layout or word processing, there initially wasn't any way to specify a typeface for your HTML documents. After all, since HTML was a cross-platform language, there was no way to know what font faces were available—and the concept of a typeface is meaningless for a document being spoken through a text-to-speech reader. However, many Web designers pushed for a way of being able to specify the typeface in HTML. By default, most browsers used Times Roman for normal body text and Courier for preformatted text. Many Web designers consider these two typefaces ugly or boring, and Navigator eventually introduced an extension to HTML in the form of the FACE attribute to the <FONT> tag. Internet Explorer followed Navigator's lead.

Although HTML 3.2 did not officially recognize the use of the FACE attribute to the <FONT> tag, HTML 4.0 allows you use the FACE attribute—but at the same time, recommends that you use style sheets instead.

The current browsers don't universally agree on font properties, so the same font type might have different names on different systems, or the same font name might look different on different systems. Another deterrent to using fonts securely is that although operating systems come with default fonts, users can install additional fonts onto their computer and remove or change the default ones. You have no control over which fonts each user may have on their system. What looks beautiful on your system may look horribly ugly on someone else's system.

Many Windows users tend to have the same set of fonts; shown here is a list of fonts common to most Windows 95/98 systems.

Arial	Comic Sans MS	Lucida Sans Unicode
Arial Black	Courier New	Times New Roman
Arial Narrow	**Impact**	Verdana

Microsoft's Web typography site (`http://www.microsoft.com/typography/`) freely distributes several popular fonts for both Macintosh and Windows users, just in case you don't have them on your system.

One trouble with specifying font names is that similar fonts are known by different names. What is called "Helvetica" on one system may be known as "Arial" or "Univers" on a different system.

WARNING

Even worse, two different fonts can share the same name. And fonts can look completely different from platform to platform. Courier, for example, looks fine on Macintosh computers and Unix workstations, but at most point sizes it is a profoundly ugly font on Windows systems.

With style sheets, font types are generic family choices. Fonts in the same general category (with similar properties) are offered as a choice so that your browser can pick the best face from its current font possibilities. Some examples of the generic font families are:

- ▶ cursive (Zapf-Chancery and Mistral, for example)
- ▶ fantasy (Western, for example)
- ▶ monospace (Courier, for example)
- ▶ sans serif (Helvetica, for example)
- ▶ serif (Times New Roman, for example)

NOTE

Serif fonts, such as the one used for the main text of this book, have flags (serifs), or decorations, on the letters. *Sans serif* fonts, such as the one used in this Note, are unadorned (without serifs).

In Chapter 12 and again in more detail in Chapter 16, you'll see how to use style sheets to specify fonts in your HTML documents.

Now that we've learned about fonts, we're ready to move on to the last two categories of text-level elements: font-style elements and phrase elements.

USING FONT-STYLE ELEMENTS

Font-style elements change the appearance of text (for example, making text bold, underlined, or struck through). These font-style elements are also known as *physical* markup.

NOTE

Don't confuse "font-style elements" with the font element; they are two separate things. The font element is a text-level element that uses the <FONT> and </FONT> tags to change a font size, font face, or font color. Font-style elements are a category of elements, such as the bold and italic elements, that change the way text itself is displayed.

Among HTML purists, there is something of a stigma against font-style elements because font-style elements are device-dependent (that is, they assume that the display device is a computer screen capable of showing bold and italic and so forth). Despite this stigma, font-style elements are commonly used.

WARNING

Since you can't guarantee that your font-style elements will work on every system, make sure your document is comprehensible with even plain text. In other words, don't depend on font-style elements to convey vital information.

All font-style elements are a subcategory of text-level elements, and they all require both start and end tags. They can all be nested according to the normal rules of nesting text-level elements.

We'll look briefly at each of the seven font-style elements and the tags they use: bold (<B>), italic (<I>), underline (<U>), strikeout (<STRIKE> or <S>), big (<BIG>), small (<SMALL>), and teletype (<TT>).

The Bold Element

The bold element (<B> and </B>) causes text to appear in a bold typeface.

The bold element does not indicate strong emphasis when read by some text-only or text-to-speech browsers. Use the strong element (a phrase element we'll see shortly) to mark important information instead.

TIP

The <B> tag is easier to type than the <STRONG> tag, so you may want to use the <B> tag when you initially create your Web pages, and then use your HTML tool's search and replace feature to change <B> tags into <STRONG> tags and </B> tags into </STRONG> tags.

The Italics Element

The italics element (<I> and </I>) marks up text in italics (text slanted diagonally upward to the right)—for example, <I>Hello, World!</I>.

The italics element carries no other meaning than that text is to be rendered in italics. It's appropriate to use the italics element to indicate text in a foreign language—for example, <I>carpe diem</I>. (But using <I LANG="EL">carpe diem</I> is even better, since this indicates that the language used is Latin, thanks to the LANG attribute.)

There are several phrase elements that we'll see in the upcoming "Using Phrase Elements" section that are appropriately used instead of the italics element. For example, use the emphasis element (<EM> and </EM>) for emphasis or the citation element (<CITE> and </CITE>) for a citation to properly indicate why text is displayed in italics.

The Underline Element

The underline element (<U> and </U>) underlines text:

```
<U>Hello, World!</U>
```

WARNING

Readers may confuse underlined text with hyperlinked text that isn't working properly. You should avoid using the underline element.

The Strike Element

The strike element (`<STRIKE>` and `</STRIKE>` or `<S>` and `</S>`) indicates that the enclosed text should have a line drawn through the middle of the text.

```
<STRIKE>Yikes! I'm some helpless text and I'm
struck.</STRIKE>
```

WARNING

Not all browsers and HTML page-creation tools know how to deal with the strike element. In HTML 4.0, the use of the strike element is highly discouraged, and the new ins and del elements are recommended instead. We'll see the ins and del elements at the end of this chapter. If you do use the strike element, be aware that the `<STRIKE>` tag is more widely understood than the `<S>` tag.

Figure 7.11 shows some strikeout text in Internet Explorer.

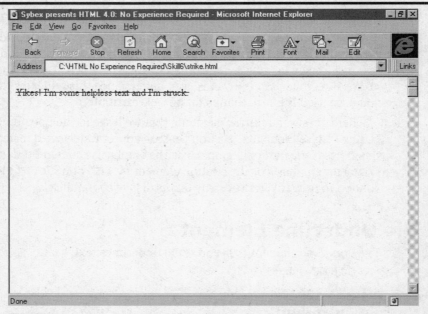

FIGURE 7.11: You can see in this Internet Explorer example of struck-out text that the text, though struck, is still quite readable.

The Big Element

The big element (`<BIG>` and `</BIG>`) renders the enclosed text in a larger font (unless the document's font size is already as large as possible). The `<BIG>` tag has the same effect as `<FONT SIZE="+1">`.

```
<BIG>The Big and Tall Company</BIG>
```

More than one big element can be nested to render a larger text than is achieved with just one big element, but it might be clearer to say:

```
<FONT SIZE="+2">The Very Big and Tall Company</FONT>
```

rather than:

```
<BIG><BIG>The Very Big and Tall Company</BIG></BIG>
```

The Small Element

The small element (`<SMALL>` and `</SMALL>`) renders the enclosed text in a smaller font; if your text is already at size 1 (the smallest size possible), however, the tag is ignored. The `<SMALL>` tag has the same effect as `<FONT SIZE="-1">`.

```
<SMALL>The Small and Short Company</SMALL>
```

Like the big element, more than one small element can be nested in order to render a smaller text size than is designated with just one small element.

The Teletype Element

The teletype element (`<TT>` and `</TT>`) renders the enclosed text in teletype font. This means that the text will be monospaced to look like a typewriter font (browsers will often use Courier font by default). For example:

```
<P>All the vowels on my typewriter are broken. I keep typing
in a standard phrase and it comes out like this: <TT>Th qck
brwn fx jmps vr th lz dg</TT>. I think I need a typewriter
repairman.
```

NOTE

Don't confuse `<TT>` and `<PRE>`. The teletype element (`<TT>`) is a text-level element that doesn't affect the rules of white space, whereas the preformatted text element (`<PRE>`) is a block-level element that can be used to create indents and carriage returns, or to draw ASCII art.

Now we've seen all of the font-style elements. Before we move on to phrase elements and finish this chapter, let's see how all of these font-style elements are displayed. Figure 7.12 gives us an example of all of the font-style elements used in this section, along with the superscript and subscript elements from the previous section, as displayed by Navigator.

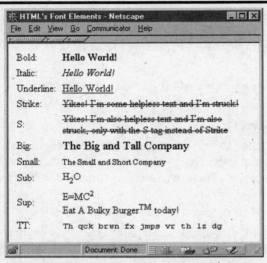

FIGURE 7.12: Navigator's display of all of the font-style elements and the superscript and subscript elements

NOTE
You'll find more information on font and font-style elements in Chapter 12, which is devoted to the topic of Web typography.

USING PHRASE ELEMENTS

Phrase elements are used to meaningfully mark up small sections of text. They're especially useful for readers who use a nongraphical browser, for search engines and indexers that refer to your HTML code to categorize sections of your document for their site outlines, and for other computer programs that need to interact with your Web pages to extract data for other useful purposes. For example, text rendered with the <CITE> tag may render visually the same as italicized text, but the underlying HTML code indicates that the text is a citation.

Start and end tags are necessary for all phrase elements. We'll see the nine different phrase elements briefly: acronyms (<ACRONYM>), citations (<CITE>), computer code (<CODE>), definitions (<DFN>), emphasis (<EM>), suggested keyboard sequences (<KBD>), sample output (<SAMP>), strongly emphasized text (<STRONG>), and computer variables (<VAR>).

After we've defined all nine phrase elements, we'll see how a browser displays them.

The Acronym Element

The acronym element's <ACRONYM> and </ACRONYM> tags indicate the presence of an abbreviation (FBI, WWW, and so on). Text marked within the acronym element may not necessarily appear any differently, but spell-checkers and speech synthesizers may find it useful to know that the marked text is an acronym, and an advanced program could use the acronym element to help construct a glossary for your document.

You can use the advisory TITLE attribute to define the acronym. For example:

```
I spy for the <ACRONYM TITLE="Federal Bureau of
Investigation">FBI</ACRONYM>.
```

WARNING

Since the acronym element is new in HTML 4.0, it is not yet widely supported.

The Citation Element

The citation element's <CITE> and </CITE> tags are used to indicate that the enclosed text is a citation (titles of excerpts, quotes, references) from another source.

WARNING

Don't use the <CITE> tag except to indicate the title of a cited work.

Part ii

Text within <CITE> and </CITE> is usually rendered in italics (although you can't always depend on every browser doing so).

For example:

```
<P>I have read and reread <CITE>Moby Dick</CITE> but I still
can't make heads nor tails of it.</P>
```

The Code Element

The code element's <CODE> and </CODE> tags are used for examples of program code. Text nested in the code element is usually rendered in a monospaced typeface, just like text inside <TT> and </TT> tags.

NOTE

Since most of the creators of HTML are computer programmers, they're interested in having useful ways of presenting code from computer programs. Most people, who aren't computer programmers or computer trainers, will not have much use for <CODE> (or <KBD>, <SAMP>, or <VAR>).

For example:

```
<P>To use the automatic date feature in Excel, just enter
<CODE>=Date()</CODE> into a cell.</P>
```

The Definition Element

The definition element's <DFN> and </DFN> tags are intended to be used to mark the first time that you define a term. For example:

```
<P>It's not strange that <DFN>SGML</DFN> (Standard
Generalized Markup Language) is so eerily similar to
HTML.</P>
```

By marking your definitions this way, special software programs can define an index or glossary for your document. Most browsers will display the definition text in italics.

The Emphasis Element

The emphasis element is a popular way to emphasize text. Any text marked between <EM> and </EM> will be emphasized. Most browsers render the emphasized text in italics, but a text-to-speech browser knows to give spoken emphasis to text within an emphasis element.

TIP

Many style guides recommend using the emphasis element instead of the italics element.

For example:

```
<P>I simply <EM>must</EM> get your recipe for chili, Karen
Dodson!</P>
```

The Keyboard Element

The keyboard element's <KBD> and </KBD> tags indicate text that the viewer should type. Some browsers view this text as monospaced (some may also view the text as bold), though, unlike with the <PRE> tag, multiple spaces within the keyboard element are collapsed.

For example:

```
<P>To start the program, hit the <KBD>S</KBD> key and press
the <KBD>Carriage Return</KBD>, then hold onto your
hat!</P>
```

The Sample Element

The sample element uses the <SAMP> and </SAMP> tags to indicate sample output text from a computer program. An example might be a directory listing or sample form output from a script program used to process your Web site's access log.

As with the keyboard element, the sample element's text is often rendered in a monospaced font, and multiple spaces are collapsed. The keyboard element is used for text that a user must enter, whereas the sample element is used for text that a computer generates in response to a user's action.

For example:

```
<P>Instead of giving me the expected results, the computer
kept printing <SAMP>All work and no play makes Jack a dull
boy</SAMP> over and over again. I'm not sure what it
means.</P>
```

The Strong Element

The strong element's <STRONG> and </STRONG> tags are used to indicate strong emphasis. Text within a strong element is usually rendered as bold or given a strident pronunciation by a text-to-speech reader.

TIP

Many style guides recommend using the strong element instead of the bold element.

For example:

```
<P>I swear, if they don't give me that raise <STRONG>
tomorrow</STRONG>, I quit.</P>
```

The Variable Element

The variable element (<VAR> and </VAR>) marks up the variables used in computer programs or the parts of a computer command chosen by the user. The text is usually rendered as monospaced, and, as with the keyboard element, multiple spaces are collapsed.

For example:

```
<P>The formula for the <VAR>distance traveled</VAR> (in
miles) is <VAR>speed</VAR> (in miles per hour) multiplied
by <VAR>time</VAR> (in hours).</P>
```

Now let's see how Internet Explorer chooses to display all of the phrase elements that we've seen. Figure 7.13 shows them in action.

You can always nest multiple phrase elements. For example, you might use the following phrase elements if you were writing a Web page about the anchor element:

```
<P>When using an anchor element, make sure to use the
<CODE>HREF="<VAR>URL</VAR>"</CODE> attribute.</P>
```

Whew! That's it for phrase elements, which means we've finished the text-level elements. In the last section of this chapter, we'll introduce two new elements that are neither text-level nor block-level elements and that are used for marking changes to a document: the ins and del elements.

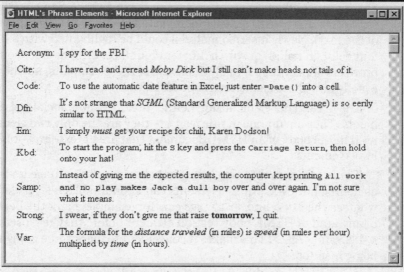

FIGURE 7.13: All the phrase elements

Marking Changes with the Ins and Del Elements

Users of a word processor like Word or WordPerfect may be familiar with an automatic feature that compares two different documents and marks the changes between them. Newly added phrases appear in a highlighted color, while deleted phrases are shown in a strikeout font.

HTML 4.0 introduces two new elements intended for the same purpose: the ins element (with required <INS> and </INS> tags) to mark inserted text, and the del element (with <DEL> and </DEL> tags, naturally) to mark deleted text.

WARNING

Since the ins and del elements are new in HTML 4.0, they are not widely supported yet; because they are so useful, however, we predict they'll catch on soon.

The actual methods used to display these elements will vary from browser to browser, but usually a section marked as deleted would either not appear at all, or appear as if it were within a strike element (that is to say, with the standard struck-out appearance—a line through the middle of the text). Newly inserted material could be highlighted with a different font color, in italics, or with a different font face. Until new versions of browsers appear that actually make use of these elements, no one knows exactly how these elements will be displayed.

The ins and del elements are neither text-level nor block-level elements. They are unique in this respect—they are the only two elements used in the body of an HTML document that aren't text-level or block-level elements.

These two elements are closest in behavior to the phrase text-level elements; however, phrase elements can't contain block-level elements, whereas the <INS> and <DEL> tags can, for example, mark the beginning of any kind of HTML body section element before they're closed with </INS> and </DEL>. This makes it convenient to mark three paragraphs as being inserted.

Another difference is that while phrase elements can't take any special attributes, both the <INS> and <DEL> tags can be used with the following attributes:

```
<INS CITE="URL"> or <DEL CITE="URL">
<INS DATETIME="DATE & TIME"> or <DEL DATETIME="DATE & TIME">
```

The CITE attribute can be used to point to a URL that contains information about why a change was made.

The DATETIME attribute can be used to indicate when the change was made. However, the date and time format must be specified in a very exact way. The format is YYYY-MM-DDThh:mm:ssTZD, where:

- ▶ YYYY = four-digit year

- ▶ MM = two-digit month (01=January, and so on)

- ▶ DD = two-digit day of month (01 through 31)

- ▶ T = the letter "T"

- ▶ hh = two digits of hour (00 through 23; am/pm *not* allowed)

- ▶ mm = two digits of minute (00 through 59)

- ▶ ss = two digits of second (00 through 59)

- ▶ TZD = time zone designator (either the letter Z to indicate UTC/GMT, or an offset such as +04:00 to indicate four hours ahead of UTC, or -02:30 to indicate two-and-a-half hours behind UTC).

Here's a quick (and quite hypothetical) example that uses the ins element to mark a new section:

```
<H2>Latest News</H2>
<INS DATETIME="2000-04-22T11:38:00-07:00"
CITE="http://www.tori.com/updatelog.html">
<P>We've just received some new information.
<P>Apparently there will be <STRONG>two shows</STRONG> on
Sunday.
</INS>
<P>The show will start at 7:00 P.M.
```

This code marks the middle two paragraphs as new. They were changed on April 22, 2000, at 11:38 AM (at 7 hours ahead of Greenwich, which is equivalent to the Pacific time zone); information about the change (perhaps who made the change or where the new information came from) can be found at the URL listed in the CITE attribute. The ins and del elements are the last of the elements that are used in the body section.

WHAT'S NEXT?

You've already learned a lot about formatting your Web pages—in fact, you've now been exposed to nearly all the basic elements that you'll need to put together the body section. In Chapter 12 you'll learn more about the type-related elements that have already been introduced and also see suggestions on how to use type to get your ideas across on the Web. But first we'll move on to the love-em or hate-em topic of frames.

Part ii

Chapter 8
DIVIDING A WINDOW WITH FRAMES

I n previous chapters, you've learned how to create HTML documents that take up the entire size of a browser window. But what if you want to create a document that can divide the browser window into different parts and can show more than one document at once? HTML 4.0 lets you use *frames* to do just that.

Adapted from *HTML 4.0: No experience required*,
by E. Stephen Mack and Janan Platt Saylor
ISBN 0-7821-2143-8   704 pages $29.99

HTML 4.0
NO EXPERIENCE REQUIRED

In this chapter, we will teach you how to create a *frameset document*, which is a document that defines one or more frames by using the frameset and frame elements. You'll learn how to specify different sizes and properties for the frameset element, and how to target your links from one frame to another.

We'll consider the advantages and disadvantages of frames and create alternate content for browsers that can't display frames. We'll also create inline frames, which is a region of an HTML document that contains another document.

UNDERSTANDING THE USE OF FRAMES

Frames allow multiple HTML documents to be presented as independent windows (or subwindows) within one main browser window. This allows you to present two or more documents at once.

For example, a simple vertical frame is shown in Figure 8.1 as displayed by Netscape Navigator. A frameset document has declared that one HTML file should be shown on the left, and a different HTML file should be shown on the right.

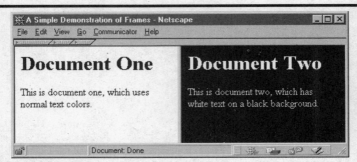

FIGURE 8.1: There are two frames here—one on the left and one on the right.

NOTE

In Figure 8.1, you're looking at three different files at once. The frameset document contains the main title element (you can see the title on the title bar) and creates the frames (the two different framed documents shown here). The contents of each frame, Document One and Document Two, are separate files.

Frames can also be horizontal, as shown here using Microsoft Internet Explorer:

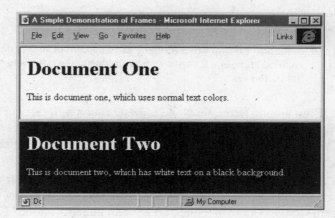

Each frame is resizable and scrolls separately by default (we'll show you how to change this behavior later in this chapter). You specify the initial size of each frame when you create the frameset document.

While these examples have just shown sample documents so far, you can probably see how frames can be useful. One frame can be used to keep some information static (such as a navigation bar or a site logo), while the other frame can contain the actual content of different sections of a Web site. We'll teach you to how to set up your links so that clicking on an item in one frame can change information in another frame.

WARNING

You should only use frames if you have a good reason. If you don't feel confident about your Web design skills, adding frames can easily confuse your audience.

HTML 4.0 is the first version of HTML to officially include frames. Despite the fact that HTML 4.0 has endorsed frames, there are still some limitations to using frames, which we'll discuss next.

Knowing the Limitations of Frames

Unfortunately, not all browsers support frames. (Browsers that can display frames are called *frames-enabled*, while those that can't are called *non-frames–enabled* browsers.) Later in this chapter, we'll explain a few ways you can include alternate content for non-frames–enabled browsers by using the noframes element.

NOTE

Some surveys show that as many as 10 percent of surfers don't have frames-enabled browsers. It seems counterproductive to turn away that many potential customers.

Even among frames-enabled browsers such as Internet Explorer and Navigator, the browsers don't always display framed pages the same way. There are even significant differences between the Macintosh and Windows versions of the same browser.

For example, one platform's browser may center each frame so the text and images are easily viewable. But another browser may display a frame so the bottom of a line of text or an image is cut off. These limitations mean that framed pages must be tested thoroughly to ensure that your viewers won't become frustrated.

Since you don't know the size of the window being used to view your site (or if a screen is being used at all), it's hard to decide on the right size for each frame. You run the risk of having each frame be too small to display its content, forcing surfers to constantly scroll to read an entire line or see all of the options.

The user interface can also cause problems when a browser displays a frame page. After all, browsers were originally designed to display only one document at a time. The ability to show more than one document with frames was an afterthought. Because of this, browsers cannot assign a bookmark to an individual frame, only the entire frameset document.

Similarly, it's impossible to link to a particular set of framed pages after you've followed a link. You can only link to a document in an individual frame or to the initial frameset. Also, most browsers cannot print the entire frameset page, and some browsers can only print the first frame in a frameset. Furthermore, navigation using the Back button is confusing for anyone using Navigator version 2, which takes you back to the first non-frames page, ignoring any surfing you did within the framed pages. Even for other browsers, the Back and Forward buttons behave differently when used while viewing a frameset, which can make frame navigation confusing. It's also harder to view the source of framed pages.

The initial frames created by the frameset document will change as soon as someone follows a link (or if a page is updated dynamically, through meta refresh, for example). But the URL listed in the browser's location bar doesn't change, still pointing to the initial frameset and its default frames. The frameset document's source code no longer shows the true content of each frame. This is another source of confusion.

WARNING

Some search engines are also confused by frames and may not be able to index a framed site properly.

Before you give up on frames, however, try out their innovative interface. Some sites are improved with a frame-based design. If you're designing pages for an intranet (where you know what browser is being used by other employees in your organization), or if you make sure to offer both framed and non-framed alternatives, then frames might be right for your Web site. Frames definitely offer some useful advantages for navigation, as we'll discuss next.

Understanding the Advantages of Frames

Frames allow Web designers to present multiple documents in one window. In one frame, for example, you can present a static list of the sections of your site. This frame becomes a table of contents that's always available. Another frame might contain a logo and help button that won't scroll off the screen. Other frames can contain your site's content. Each frame can be scrolled through separately (allowing you to present and compare two documents side by side, for example), or you can replace the contents of each frame with a different page every time the surfer follows a link.

These navigation features are useful when a Web site contains many levels of pages, and viewers might get lost searching through the content to find specific information. Now, we'll show you how to use frames by creating a frameset document.

CREATING FRAMESET DOCUMENTS

Frameset documents have a different structure than normal HTML documents. A regular HTML document has a head element and a body element, but a frameset document has a head element and a frameset element.

NOTE

When you create a frameset document, you must use a special DOCTYPE declaration on the first line: <!DOCTYPE HTML PUBLIC "-//W3C/DTD HTML 4.0 Frameset//EN">.

As an example, consider the HTML code used in a frameset document to create the two simple frames shown in Figure 8.1:

```
<!DOCTYPE HTML PUBLIC "-//W3C//DTD HTML 4.0 Frameset//EN">
<HTML LANG="EN">
  <HEAD>
    <TITLE>A Simple Demonstration of Frames</TITLE>
  </HEAD>
  <FRAMESET COLS="50%,50%">
    <FRAME SRC="document1.html">
    <FRAME SRC="document2.html">
    <NOFRAMES>
      <BODY>
        Your browser does not display frames. Please read
        <A HREF="document1.html">Document One</A>
        and
        <A HREF="document2.html">Document Two</A>.
      </BODY>
    </NOFRAMES>
  </FRAMESET>
</HTML>
```

Here is the HTML code for document1.html, as referenced in the above code:

```
<HTML>
<BODY>
<H1>Document One</H1>
This is document one, which uses normal text colors.
</BODY>
</HTML>
```

Here is the HTML code for `document2.html`:

```
<HTML>
<BODY BGCOLOR="black" text="white">
<H1>Document Two</H1>
This is document two, which has white text on a black
background.
</BODY>
</HTML>
```

NOTE
We'll discuss the new frameset element in the next section, and the frame element in a section that follows.

As you can see, the code doesn't contain a normal body element. Instead, the body element is contained in an optional noframes element, which is used for displaying alternate content for non-frames–enabled browsers. So, the noframes element's body section here is only displayed if the browser isn't displaying frames.

We'll learn more about how alternate content works near the end of this chapter, after we learn about the frameset and frame elements and their attributes.

Using the Frameset Element

The frameset element consists of the <FRAMESET> and </FRAMESET> tags, which contain one or more frame elements. The frameset element uses a couple of attributes (ROWS and COLS) that define the layout of the frames.

The frame element uses the SRC attribute to point to the document that you want to display in each frame; we'll discuss it in more detail a little later.

We'll see in a coming example that you can nest one or more framesets to divide a page in a complex way.

We'll also learn that the frameset element can contain a noframes element if you want to present alternate text for non-frames–enabled browsers.

WARNING

Text and random HTML elements that appear before the frameset document's frameset element may be ignored or may prevent the frameset element from working properly.

This HTML code shows a simple two-column frames page with a navigation bar frame and a main content frame:

```
<!DOCTYPE HTML PUBLIC "-//W3C//DTD HTML 4.0 Frameset//EN">
<HTML LANG="EN">
  <HEAD>
    <TITLE>Frames - Two Columns</TITLE>
  </HEAD>
  <FRAMESET COLS="1*,3*">
    <FRAME SRC="navbar.html">
    <FRAME SRC="main.html">
  </FRAMESET>
</HTML>
```

Here is the HTML code for the navigational frame, `navbar.html`:

```
<HTML>
<BODY BGCOLOR="black" Text="white">
Primary Colors
<UL>
<FONT COLOR="red"><LI>Red
<FONT COLOR="yellow"><LI>Yellow
<FONT COLOR="blue"><LI>Blue
<FONT COLOR="white"><LI>Main frame
</UL>
</BODY>
</HTML>
```

Here is the HTML code for the starting main frame, `main.html`:

```
<HTML>
<BODY BGCOLOR="black" text="white">
Red, Yellow, Blue
<P>
Click on the words in the left navigation frame to
  load a new page into this right main frame.
</BODY>
</HTML>
```

Figure 8.2 shows the result of this code.

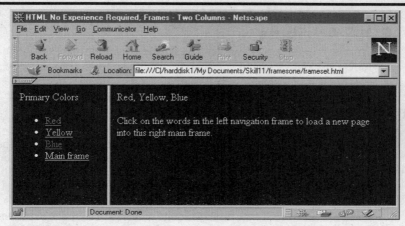

FIGURE 8.2: A two-column frames page with a navigation bar frame (left) and a main content frame (right)

WARNING

This document would be completely blank for a non-frames–enabled browser. Always include a noframes element to display alternate content. We'll teach you how to use the noframes element near the end of this chapter.

You might notice from this example that instead of using percentages to size the frames, we used the asterisk width notation.

Next we'll take a look at the COLS and ROWS attributes. Most frameset elements use one or the other of these attributes. If no columns or rows are defined, you can only have a single frame that takes up the entire page.

NOTE

The frameset element can also take the optional ONLOAD and/or ONUNLOAD attributes, which are used to trigger scripts.

Creating Vertical Frames with the COLS Attribute

The COLS attribute is used within the frameset element's <FRAMESET> tag to specify the size of two or more vertical frames. Each column's width is a value separated by a comma.

NOTE

The default value for the COLS attribute is 100 percent, so if you don't specify a number of columns by giving each column a width, you will have only one column. If the COLS attribute is not used, each row is set to the entire width of the window.

Each column's width may be an absolute width (a percentage of the window or a number of pixels) or a relative width (a value followed by an asterisk, *) that assigns a part of the window in proportion to the amount requested.

Absolute values have highest priority and are assigned first, and then the remaining space is divided up among the columns with relative values next.

Let's take a look at some uses of the COLS attribute:

```
<FRAMESET COLS="25%,75%">
```

This element specifies two columns. The first column (on the left) takes 25 percent of the browser's window space. The second column (on the right) takes 75 percent of the browser's window space.

WARNING

The results are unpredictable if you specify percentages that don't add up to 100 percent, but the browser should adjust your percentages proportionally until they do add up to 100 percent.

This element also specifies two columns:

```
<FRAMESET COLS="1*,3*">
```

The first column takes the relative value of one part of the browser window. The second column takes the relative value of three parts of the browser window. Since there are a total of four parts requested, the first column will get one-quarter (or 25 percent) of the window's width, while the second column will get three-quarters (or 75 percent).

This element creates four columns:

```
<FRAMESET COLS="100, 25%, 2*, 3*">
```

If you have a window that's 500 pixels wide, this element will assign 100 pixels of space to the first column (which could be useful if you'd like to have the first frame contain an image that's exactly 100 pixels wide). The second column will get 25 percent of the total space, or 125 pixels. That leaves 275 pixels for the last two columns. Two-fifths of this remaining space will go to the third column (110 pixels). The last column will receive three-fifths of the remaining space (165 pixels).

NOTE

Browsers will recalculate the space for each frame every time you resize the browser window.

Creating Horizontal Frames with the ROWS Attribute

The ROWS attribute works similarly to the COLS attribute, except for horizontal frames instead of vertical frames.

If you don't specify a ROWS attribute, each column will take up the entire height of the window.

Horizontal frames are created from top to bottom. Like the COLS attribute, you specify the height of frames using either absolute values (percentages or pixels) or relative values.

For example, this frameset:

```
<FRAMESET ROWS="34%,33%,33%">
```

would create three horizontal frames, each of them taking up about one-third of the height of the window.

Creating Grids of Frames by Specifying Both Rows and Columns

You can use a frameset that specifies both the ROWS and COLS attributes in order to create a grid of frames.

Part ii

For example:

```
<FRAMESET COLS="250,*" ROWS="50%,25%,25%">
```

would create two columns and three rows, for a total of six frames. The frames appear from left to right, and then top to bottom. The first column is 250 pixels wide, while the second column gets the remaining space (* is equivalent to 1*). The first row is half of the window's height, while the second and third rows are each a quarter of the window's height. The result is shown here:

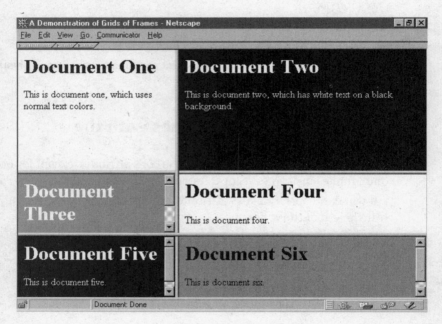

Nesting Framesets to Create Subdivided Frames

By nesting a frameset within another frameset, you can create complex frames. Each nested frameset replaces a single frame with two or more frames.

The following example uses a frameset to create a page with two rows. The lower row is a nested frameset, which splits the row into two equal frame columns, for a total of three frames:

```
<FRAMESET ROWS="25%,75%">
   <FRAME SRC="topnavbar.html">
   <FRAMESET COLS="50%,50%">
      <FRAME SRC="left.html">
      <FRAME SRC="right.html">
   </FRAMESET>
</FRAMESET>
```

NOTE

By studying the previous examples in this chapter, you should have an understanding of how to create the basic HTML files which go into each frame, so we will leave the code up to you for the three html files referenced in this code sample.

Figure 8.3 shows a sample document created with the nested frames.

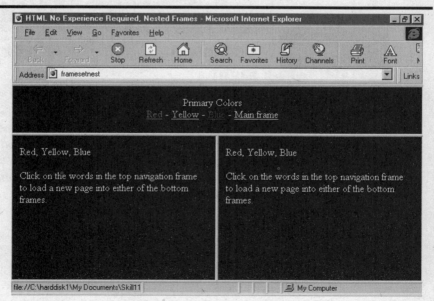

FIGURE 8.3: Internet Explorer displays a frames page with two rows. The second row is split into two equal frames. This creates a total of three frames.

It's possible to use a series of nested framesets to continuously divide frames into more frames. This takes a lot of trial and error, however. It's possible to make documents with even more frames, like the nine frames we see on this page:

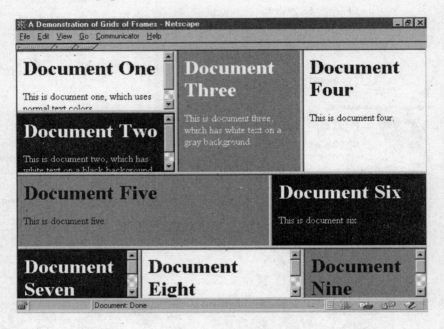

One way to make complex frames is to have more than one frameset document. If one of your frames contains a frameset document, then that frame will be subdivided into smaller frame windows. The first frameset document is called the *parent frameset*, and the other embedded frameset documents are called *child framesets*.

Using the BORDERCOLOR Attribute

One other attribute is often used with the frameset element: the BORDER-COLOR attribute can set the color of a frame's border (instead of the default gray).

For example, <FRAMESET BORDERCOLOR="#FF0000"> sets the frame's border to red.

This attribute is not mentioned in the HTML 4.0 specifications—instead it's an extension to HTML that happens to be recognized by Internet Explorer and Navigator.

All of the frameset document's frame border colors are universally set with this attribute value. (Border colors can also be set individually with the frame element's BORDERCOLOR attribute, another extension to HTML, as we'll see a little later.)

WARNING

Be careful with this attribute, because it produces invalid HTML that can't be easily checked for errors by a validation program.

Now that we've shown you how the frameset element works, we'll discuss the frame element and its attributes.

Putting Documents inside Frames with the Frame Element

The frame element's <FRAME> tag defines the contents of a single frame. The most important attribute for the frame element is the SRC attribute, which specifies the URL of the document inside the frame.

The frame contents must be located in a separate file. For example <FRAME SRC="document1.html"> specifies that the document to be displayed inside this frame will be document1.html. You can use relative or absolute URLs. You don't have to link to HTML files; you can put any kind of file in a frame, including images and multimedia files.

You can use several other attributes with the frame element in order to change the frame's appearance and the way it works; we'll learn about them now.

Adding Frame Borders with the FRAMEBORDER Attribute

The FRAMEBORDER attribute determines if there is a separator border between the frame and its neighboring frames. The default behavior is for each frame to have a gray border. By specifying <FRAME SRC="document.html" FRAMEBORDER="0">, you can remove the border.

You can specify FRAMEBORDER="1" to mean that a border should be visible, but this is the default value.

You must specify FRAMEBORDER="0" for both neighboring frames in order to remove a frame border. If one of the two frame elements doesn't include this attribute, then the border will appear.

The HTML code for one frame with borders on and one frame with no borders is as follows:

```
<FRAMESET ROWS="25%,75%">
    <FRAME FRAMEBORDER="0" SRC="topnavbar.html">
    <FRAMESET COLS="50%,50%">
        <FRAME FRAMEBORDER="0" SRC="left.html">
        <FRAME FRAMEBORDER="1" SRC="right.html">
    </FRAMESET>
</FRAMESET>
</HTML>
```

NOTE

Navigator 3 and 4 as well as Internet Explorer 4 and 5 treat the FRAMEBORDER attribute a little differently: FRAMEBORDER="YES" means to use a three-dimensional border, while FRAMEBORDER="NO" means a plain border. You can use a BORDER attribute in the frameset to set the frame's size (the default is BORDER="5" for a five-pixel frame border). These are all non-standard extensions to HTML.

Coloring Individual Frame Borders with the BORDERCOLOR Attribute

While we're talking about frame borders, you can use an HTML extension to specify the color of a frame's border. The latest versions of Internet Explorer and Navigator recognize the BORDERCOLOR attribute, which you can use to color individual frame borders.

For example, `<FRAME SRC="document.html" BORDERCOLOR="YELLOW">` would create a frame with a yellow border.

NOTE

As mentioned earlier, all of the frame border colors can be set at once with the BORDERCOLOR attribute in the frameset element.

Specifying Frame Margins with the MARGINHEIGHT and MARGINWIDTH Attributes

Two attributes can be used to set the margins of a frame. (Since regular documents can't have margins without style sheets, this is one advantage to using frames.)

The MARGINHEIGHT attribute determines the number of pixels (which must be greater than one pixel) between the frame's content and the frame's top and bottom edges.

Similarly, the MARGINWIDTH attribute determines the number of pixels between the frame's content and the frame's left and right edges.

For example:

```
<FRAME SRC="document2.html" MARGINHEIGHT="100"
MARGINWIDTH="200">
```

creates a frame filled by the document2.html file, which would be displayed with a top and bottom margin of 100 pixels, and a left and right margin of 200 pixels.

Preventing Frame Sizing with the NORESIZE Attribute

Normally, each frame is resizable. By pointing your mouse at a frame border, you can drag the frame border to make a frame larger or smaller.

Sometimes, you will want to prevent surfers from being able to resize your frames. The NORESIZE attribute accomplishes this goal. For example, <FRAME SRC="document.html" NORESIZE> means that this frame window is not resizable.

WARNING

Don't use the NORESIZE attribute without a good reason; surfers will have different screen resolutions and font sizes, and they will often need to be able to resize a frame to see all of its contents.

Removing Scroll Bars with the SCROLLING Attribute

Each frame will be displayed with a vertical or horizontal scroll bar (or both) if the contents of the frame won't all fit in the frame's current dimensions.

By default, these scroll bars only appear when necessary. Alternately, you can choose to always have the scroll bars appear or force them never to appear. These examples show the three possibilities:

```
<FRAME SRC="document.html" SCROLLING="YES">
<FRAME SRC="document.html" SCROLLING="NO">
<FRAME SRC="document.html" SCROLLING="AUTO">
```

The SCROLLING="AUTO" value is the default behavior.

By including a SCROLLING="YES" attribute, the frame's window will always include a scroll bar. Similarly, SCROLLING="NO" prevents a scroll bar from appearing, even when it's necessary to scroll to see a frame's contents.

WARNING

You might have predicted that we'd warn against using SCROLLING="NO" unless you have some compelling reason. Since you don't know what size window a surfer will have or what size fonts they use, there's really no way you can tell whether scrolling will be required to display a frame's entire contents.

Naming Frames for Targeting with the NAME Attribute

The NAME attribute sets a name for the frame. This name can then be used in links located in other frames to target the named frame.

For example, suppose we create a frameset document with two frames. We can name the second frame so that the links in the first frame will target it. Consider:

```
<!DOCTYPE HTML PUBLIC "-//W3C//DTD HTML 4.0 Frameset//EN">
<HTML LANG="EN">
<HEAD>
    <TITLE>Named Frames</TITLE>
</HEAD>
<FRAMESET COLS="1*,3*">
    <FRAME SRC="navbar.html">
    <FRAME SRC="main.html" NAME="main">
</FRAMESET>
```

The first frame, on the left, is static. It contains a document called navbar.html. Since this frame has not been named, links in other frames can't target this frame. The second frame, on the right, is given the name main.

NOTE

Frame names must start with an alphanumeric character. It's safest to always use lowercase frame names, because some browsers are confused by uppercase names. Also, frame names are case-sensitive in Internet Explorer.

We'll see why naming a frame with the NAME attribute is useful in the next section.

USING TARGETED LINKS

We first discussed how to target links in Chapter 3, where we used the TARGET attribute to cause links to create a new window. In this section, you'll learn how to have links target a particular frame.

You'll also learn about the use of the base element to set a default target, see a concrete example of how frames can be useful for large files, and then see how to use four special predefined target names.

Targeting Frames

Once you've named a frame, you can create links in one frame that target the named frame by using the TARGET attribute.

In this section, we'll use the HTML example from the previous section about the NAME attribute (which created two frames, a navigation bar on the left and a document named main on the right).

You can create links in the left frame's document (navbar.html) that target the right frame. For example, any links in the navbar.html document can use the anchor element's TARGET attribute (as described in Chapter 3) to cause the contents of the frame on the right to change whenever a link is followed.

A sample link in navbar.html might look like this:

```
Read <A HREF="page2.html" TARGET="main">page two</A> for more
information.
```

When anyone clicks on page two, the frame on the right will no longer display main.html but will show page2.html instead. The navbar.html file will still be displayed in the left frame.

NOTE
If most of the links in your document use the same target, you can set the default target by using a base element, as we'll explain in the next section.

Consider the frameset document shown back in Figure 8.2. When you click the word Red in the left frame, the page that was displayed on the right changes. Figure 8.4 shows how the left frame remains static, but the right frame is replaced.

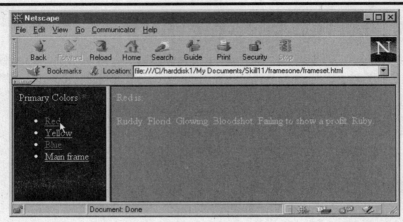

FIGURE 8.4: When the <u>Red</u> link in the left frame is clicked, the initial document in the right frame named main.html is replaced with the linked document named red.html.

The HTML code for navbar.html, contained in the first frame, includes the HTML code with targeted links to the frame named main:

```
<!DOCTYPE HTML PUBLIC "-//W3C//DTD HTML 4.0 Frameset//EN">
<HTML LANG="EN">
<HEAD>
    <TITLE>Frames Navigation Bar</TITLE>
</HEAD>
<BODY BGCOLOR="#000000" TEXT="#FFFFFF">
Primary Colors
<UL>
<LI><A HREF="red.html" TARGET="main">Red</A>
<LI><A HREF="yellow.html" TARGET="main">Yellow</A>
<LI><A HREF="blue.html" TARGET="main">Blue</A>
</UL>
</BODY>
</HTML>
```

Clicking any of the four targeted links in navbar.html replaces the current document in the right frame, named main, with the linked page.

It's essential to use these targeted links if you want to keep a navigation element in one frame while having another frame's content change. If you don't specify a TARGET attribute in the link, then the current frame is replaced instead of a different frame.

NOTE
Area elements and anchors in imagemap elements and form elements can also use the TARGET attribute to target different frames.

If you use a targeted link such as <A HREF="page2.html" TARGET="foo"> and there is no frame named foo, then the browser will create a new, full-sized window.

Using the Base Element to Set a Default Target

Sometimes a page will contain many links that you want targeted to a different frame. It's inconvenient to use the TARGET="*framename*" attribute in each link. Fortunately, you can use the base element to set the default target frame.

For example, putting a <BASE target="main"> tag in the head of a document would make every link in that document change the contents of the frame named main.

To make this use clear, we'll create a longer example: you could create one frame with a long page full of alphabetized entries, and another frame with 26 links (one for each letter) that jump the first frame to the appropriate spot in the alphabet.

To do this, you'll need three HTML files: the frameset document (which we'll call alphadict.html), the first frame's long list of alphabetized entries (dictionary.html), and the second frame's alphabet navigation page (alphabet.html).

The contents of alphadict.html might look like this:

```
<!DOCTYPE HTML PUBLIC "-//W3C//DTD HTML 4.0 Frameset//EN">
<HTML LANG="EN">
<HEAD>
    <TITLE>The Modern Hacker's Dictionary</TITLE>
</HEAD>
<FRAMESET ROWS="80%,20%">
    <FRAME SRC="dictionary.html" NAME="dictionary">
    <FRAME SRC="alphabet.html">
</FRAMESET>
</HTML>
```

This will create the two frames (one on top of the other), with the dictionary in the top frame (taking up 80 percent of the screen), and the alphabet links in the bottom frame (in the remaining 20 percent of the window's height). The top frame is given the name dictionary so that it can be targeted. (We could have used any name.)

The dictionary.html file will need 26 named anchors in the appropriate spots, such as:

```
<H2><A NAME="q">The Q Section</A></H2>
<H2><A NAME="r">The R Section</A></H2>
```

TIP

See Chapter 3 for a thorough discussion of named anchors and partial URLs.

The alphabet.html document would need 26 targeted links that used partial URLs and a TARGET attribute, such as:

```
<A HREF="dictionary.html#q" TARGET="dictionary">Q</A>
<A HREF="dictionary.html#r" TARGET="dictionary">R</A>
```

Instead of using the TARGET attribute 26 times, you can simply create a head section in alphabet.html that includes a targeted <BASE> tag, and then you can leave out the TARGET attribute from the 26 links. The resulting alphabet.html file is shown here:

```
<!DOCTYPE HTML PUBLIC "-//W3C//DTD HTML 4.0//EN">
<HTML LANG="EN">
<HEAD>
    <TITLE>Index To The Modern Hacker's Dictionary</TITLE>
    <BASE TARGET="dictionary">
</HEAD>
<BODY>
<CENTER><BIG>
<A HREF="dictionary.html#a">A</A>
<A HREF="dictionary.html#b">B</A>
[The other twenty-four letters follow...]
</BIG></CENTER>
</BODY>
</HTML>
```

Here's how this setup might appear:

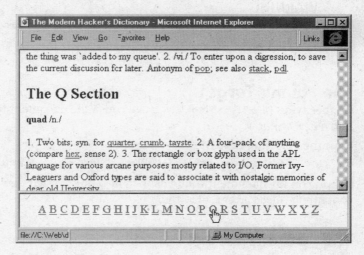

You can make this example more complex, if you like, by adding additional frames. Most agree that the advantages of being able to instantly jump from letter to letter while keeping the alphabet links constantly visible make this a handy use of frames.

In this example, both `alphabet.html` and `dictionary.html` are given title elements, like any HTML document. However, Navigator and Internet Explorer don't display the two frame's titles anywhere—only the frameset document's title is displayed in the title bar. However, the title element is still required for the frame documents, and the title will be displayed if the frame document ever becomes unframed.

Using Special Target Names

You've seen how you can specify a TARGET attribute to change the contents of a particular frame, if that frame was named with the frame element's NAME attribute.

Four predefined names can also be targeted by an anchor. These four targets have special meanings. They all start with an underscore (_), which is normally an illegal character for a target name.

The _blank Target

By specifying `TARGET="_blank"`, you can cause the document to be loaded into a new window.

In the following example:

```
<A HREF="document.html" TARGET="_blank">My document</A>
```

clicking on <u>My document</u> would cause a new browser window to appear, containing the `document.html` file.

The _parent Target

The `_parent` target name refers to the parent frameset. Most of the time you won't have multiple framesets in separate files (so you won't have parent framesets or child framesets), but in the rare cases where you do have embedded framesets, you may need to refer to the parent frameset without using the frame's name.

If the current frame is part of a child frameset (that is, it is part of an embedded frameset in a separate file), then you can use the `_parent` target to dismantle the child frameset and target the frame from the initial frameset (before it was subdivided). One example of a site that makes use of `_parent` is Mark Napier's Potatoland (`http://www.potatoland.org/`) in the "Stolen" section.

In this example:

```
<A HREF="document.html" TARGET="_parent">My document</A>
```

clicking on <u>My document</u> would cause the `document.html` file to appear in the parent frameset, if the parent had been defined in another file.

NOTE

If there is no parent, the document loads into the current frame.

The _self Target

The _self target loads the document into the current frame (the same frame as the HTML code that contains the anchor). Since this is the default behavior, the only reason that _self is useful is if you've used a base element to set a default target and want to make an exception.

For example, suppose you've previously declared <BASE TARGET="mary"> to have links target a frame named mary by default. You can use:

```
<A HREF="document.html" TARGET="_self">My document</A>
```

When someone clicks on <u>My document</u>, the file document.html will replace the current frame instead of the mary frame.

The _top Target

The most useful of the four special target names is _top, which removes frames altogether.

In this example:

```
<A HREF="document.html" TARGET="_top">My document</A>
```

clicking on <u>My document</u> would cancel all of the frames and replace the entire frameset with the document.html file.

NOTE
You can use the browser's Back button to return to the frameset.

You can use the base element with any of the four special target names. For example, using <BASE TARGET="_top"> in a document's head section would cause any link on that page to cancel frames (thus "unframing" the page).

We'll discuss more about unframing documents a little later in this chapter.

Providing Alternate Content with the Noframes Element

The specification for HTML 4.0 strongly recommends that each frameset document include an alternate method of accessing the framed information.

Anyone using a non-frames–enabled browser will see a completely blank page if they view a frameset document that doesn't include alternate content. Therefore, it's imperative to use the noframes element to explain what's going on and allow people to access the content of your Web site.

The noframes element consists of the <NOFRAMES> and </NOFRAMES> tags, which contain the alternate content. The alternate content is *only* displayed by a browser that is not displaying frames.

Here's an example of how to include the noframes element in a frameset document:

```
<!DOCTYPE HTML PUBLIC "-//W3C//DTD HTML 4.0 Frameset//EN">
<HTML LANG="EN">
<HEAD>
    <TITLE>NOFRAMES Alternative Text Example</TITLE>
</HEAD>
<FRAMESET COLS="50%,50%">
    <FRAME SRC="document1.html">
    <FRAME SRC="document2.html">
    <NOFRAMES>
        <BODY>
            If you see this text, your browser does not support
            frames or is not configured to display frames.
            Please go to the <A HREF="noframes.html">alternate
            version</A>
            of this Web page.
        </BODY>
    </NOFRAMES>
</FRAMESET>
</HTML>
```

In Figure 8.5, we see how the non-frames–enabled browser Mosaic (a once-popular browser that inspired the design of both Navigator and Internet Explorer) shows this page.

TIP

Some sites create two versions of their pages, one for frame-enabled browsers and one for non-frame–enabled browsers. However, this is a lot of work, and it's difficult to maintain two sets of pages accurately.

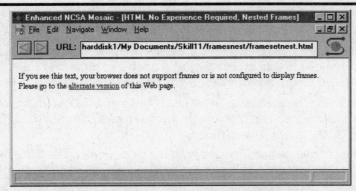

FIGURE 8.5: The 1994 version of Enhanced NCSA Mosaic (a browser that does not support frames) displays the alternate content.

HTML 4.0 allows you to include a noframes element in regular documents. The contents of the noframes element will be shown only if the document is not being displayed as part of a frameset. Unfortunately, this use of the noframes element is not yet supported by any browser—so the contents of the noframes element will be displayed regardless.

NOTE

In our example of the noframes element, we included the body element's <BODY> and </BODY> tags inside the noframes element, but these tags are not required here. Some browsers like to see them, however.

Many Web authors only include a brief "Get Navigator or Internet Explorer" statement in the noframes element (sometimes they'll link to Netscape's or Microsoft's home page). But most surfers are aware that they need a frames-enabled browser to see frames, and even know where they can get such a browser—often, they've disabled frames by choice or are using a computer system where they can't possibly install a frames-enabled browser. No text-to-speech browsers can handle frames properly. So for any of these users, it's not polite to tell them to update their browser. Instead, you should link to the individual documents or an alternate document.

USING THE INLINE FRAME ELEMENT TO CREATE INLINE FRAMES

The inline frame element is a brand new part of the HTML 4.0 specification that can show a separate document as part of a page. The inline frame element is related to frames, but they're actually two different things. So far, only Internet Explorer 3 and 4 recognize this element.

The inline frame element uses the `<IFRAME>` and `</IFRAME>` tags, along with the same attributes used in the frame element, along with optional WIDTH, HEIGHT, and ALIGN attributes.

Inline frames can be included within a block of text. The inline frame element should contain alternate text that is displayed only if the inline frame element can't be displayed.

The following HTML code inserts three inline frames centered within the document after the words "Primary Colors."

Listing 8.1:   iframe1.html

```
<!DOCTYPE HTML PUBLIC "-//W3C//DTD HTML 4.0//EN">
<HTML LANG="EN">
<HEAD>
    <TITLE>First Inline Frames Example</TITLE>
</HEAD>
<BODY BGCOLOR="#000000" TEXT="#FFFFFF">

<P>
Primary Colors

<CENTER>

<IFRAME SRC="red.html" MARGINHEIGHT="0" FRAMEBORDER="10"
WIDTH="300" HEIGHT="25">
<P>The <A HREF="red.html">red</A> file is available.
</IFRAME>
```

```
<IFRAME SRC="yellow.html" MARGINHEIGHT="0" FRAMEBORDER="10"
WIDTH="300" HEIGHT="25">
<P>The <A HREF="yellow.html">yellow</A> file is available.
</IFRAME>

<IFRAME SRC="blue.html" MARGINHEIGHT="0" FRAMEBORDER="10"
WIDTH="300" HEIGHT="25">
<P>The <A HREF="blue.html">blue</A> file is available.
</IFRAME>

</CENTER>
</BODY>
</HTML>
```

Each inline frame defaults to automatic scrolling, just like regular frames. Figure 8.6 shows how these three inline frames would be displayed by Internet Explorer.

NOTE

Just like with other frames, you'll have to create each of the files displayed by the inline frame element ahead of time. Figure 8.6 shows the contents of four different files (the main content file and the three inline frame files).

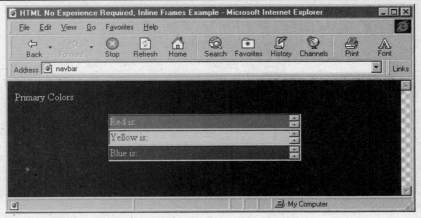

FIGURE 8.6: Internet Explorer displays three centered inline frames.

On the other hand, Navigator, which doesn't recognize the inline frame element, will show only the contents of each inline frame element, as shown here:

The object element can be used to include an HTML file within another HTML file. The only difference between using an object element and an inline frame element is that you can use the NAME attribute with an inline frame to enable you to create links that target the inline frame.

Listing 8.2:   iframe2.html

```
<!DOCTYPE HTML PUBLIC "-//W3C//DTD HTML 4.0//EN">
<HTML LANG="EN">
<HEAD>
    <TITLE>Second Inline Frames Example</TITLE>
</HEAD>
<BODY

<P>
Primary Colors - pick one:
<A HREF="yellow.html" TARGET="centerframe"><FONT COLOR=
"YELLOW">yellow</FONT></A>,
<A HREF="red.html" TARGET="centerframe"><FONT
COLOR="RED">red</FONT></A>, or
<A HREF="blue.html" TARGET="centerframe"><FONT
COLOR="BLUE">blue</FONT></A>.
</P>

<CENTER>
<IFRAME WIDTH="300" HEIGHT="75" NAME="centerframe">
```

```
<P>Choose a color from the list above.
</IFRAME>
</CENTER>

</BODY>
</HTML>
```

This example creates an empty inline frame in the center of the document, named `centerframe`. (We could have given it any legal name.) By clicking on any of the three links, the inline frame will display the appropriate document. The inline frame is initially empty, as shown here.

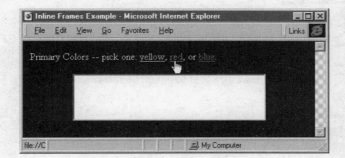

TIP

Since neither the inline frame element nor the object element are widely supported yet, it might be better to just use frames to display more than one file at once.

UNFRAMING PAGES

It's easy to create a set of framed documents, but not so easy to remove them. Since the default action for a link is to replace only the current frame, a link to an external site might leave one or more of your frames still on screen. That external site might have frames of its own, which will get added to your frames. Pretty soon the screen is cluttered with all sorts of frames containing menus and logos.

WARNING

Another problem is that if one of the framed pages links to the frameset document without using a special target name, then the frameset will be repeated on screen—displaying two duplicate navigation bars, for example.

To prevent this from happening, it's important to unframe pages for external links or internal links to frameset documents.

The easiest way to unframe pages is to use either the _blank or _top special targets discussed earlier. If you're careful to always include a TARGET attribute with one of these targets for all of your external links (or internal links to pages that you want to display full-screen), then you'll never create a problem of too many frames on screen. For example:

```
<A HREF="document.html" TARGET="_top"> see this document
unframed.</A>
```

TIP

Sometimes you'll find that people are linking to one of your pages as part of a frame. To make sure that their frames don't surround your page for long, put a <BASE TARGET="_top"> in the head section of your document. The next link that's followed on your page will be shown full-screen.

NOTE

To see a couple of creative uses of frames on the Web, try Scot Hacker's Spong Classic (http://www.birdhouse.org/images/scot/spong/), and Komninos: Poetry Juke Box (http://student.uq.edu.au/~s271502/jukebox .html).

HOW TO UNFRAME A PAGE IN A BROWSER

Sometimes when you're surfing, you'll want to unframe the pages that you see on screen.

In order to view each separate document in a frames page, Navigator can open new browser windows for each document within a frames page.

This way, you can view each document "unframed," which will let you print or view source normally. To unframe a page in Navigator 4:

1. Click inside the frame you want to unframe to select it.

2. Click the right mouse button (or hold the mouse button down if you're using a Macintosh) to open the shortcut menu.

3. From the shortcut menu, choose the Open Frame In New Window command.

CONTINUED ➡

Navigator will open a new window for that framed document.

Internet Explorer doesn't have an easy way for you to unframe an individual page, although you can use a similar technique to open each link in a new window.

Internet Explorer 4 and 5 does make it easy to print each separate frame document. In Internet Explorer 4 or 5, click inside the frame you want to print, and then choose the Print command. You'll have three options: As Laid Out On Screen, Only The Selected Frame, or All Frames Individually.

What's Next

In the next chapter, Molly Holzschlag offers an overview of layout technology, taking a close look at how layouts are actually constructed. She'll also explore how HTML syntax combines with space, shape, and object placement, resulting in the blueprint of your Web site's layout design.

Part ii

Chapter 9

LAYOUT TECHNOLOGY

In this chapter we'll explore concepts of layout control. We'll delve into standard and tables-based technologies and look at how HTML syntax combines with the concepts of space, shape, and object placement to result in the blueprint of your Web site's layout design.

Adapted from *web by design: The Complete Guide*, by Molly E. Holzschlag
ISBN 0-7821-2201-9   928 pages $49.99

The basics of frames will also be covered. Frames relate to layout in contemporary design as they provide a delivery system for sections of a layout to be fixed. For example, if you want the navigation section of your interface to be static, you can create it with frames. Your layout design remains intact, but certain parts of the page become dynamic. Finally, we'll glance at style sheet positioning because of its growing importance in HTML-based layout design.

This chapter focuses on:

▶ Standard layout design using HTML

▶ Table-based design concepts

▶ Table syntax

▶ Frames-based design concepts

▶ Frames syntax

▶ Style sheet positioning

Certainly, one chapter devoted to the complex and emerging technologies of Web design layout is not going to be enough. Therefore, you'll see plenty of references, both here in the text and on the *web by design* companion Web site at http://www.designstudio.net/, that will help you master the areas of layout that interest you most.

In the following section, we'll examine methods of text-based layout and graphic layout and pull the ideas together in several real-world examples.

STANDARD HTML FORMATTING

Standard HTML formatting involves breaking up the page with balanced amounts of text, graphics and other media, and space. While your sketches can prepare the foundation for this, you'll need to get up close and personal with HTML code in order to really manipulate blocks of text or media.

The first step in managing text with standard techniques is to determine *how much* text you have for the entire site. This will help you break up text into realistically approachable pages. For individual pages within the site, a reasonable layout runs between one and three screens per page (see Figure 9.1), possibly more if you don't go too overboard or if your work isn't *just* text. No one wants to scroll through page after page of text alone.

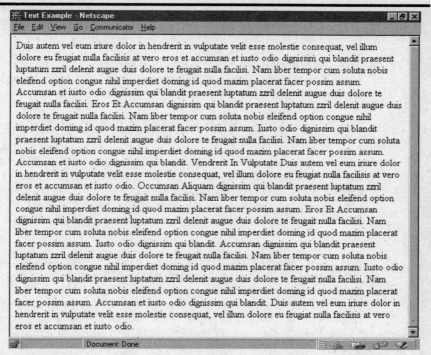

FIGURE 9.1: Three screens of text before the addition of space and media

The following code shows about three screens' worth of text before any text formatting has been added to the page. Pay attention to how this amount of text changes visually in the figure examples throughout the process.

NOTE

As mentioned in Chapter 1, you can create HTML tags in either uppercase or lowercase; it doesn't matter to a browser. As you've undoubtedly noticed, some authors use uppercase, while others prefer lowercase.

```html
<html>
<head>
<title>Text Example</title>
</head>

<body bgcolor="#FFFFFF" text="#000000" link="#999999"
vlink="#CCCCCC" alink="#FFFFCC">
```

Duis autem vel eum iriure dolor in hendrerit in vulputate velit esse molestie consequat, vel illum dolore eu feugiat nulla facilisis at vero eros et accumsan et iusto odio dignissim qui blandit praesent luptatum zzril delenit augue duis dolore te feugait nulla facilisi. Nam liber tempor cum soluta nobis eleifend option congue nihil imperdiet doming id quod mazim placerat facer possim assum.

Accumsan et iusto odio dignissim qui blandit praesent luptatum zzril delenit augue duis dolore te feugait nulla facilisi. Eros Et Accumsan dignissim qui blandit praesent luptatum zzril delenit augue duis dolore te feugait nulla facilisi. Nam liber tempor cum soluta nobis eleifend option congue nihil imperdiet doming id quod mazim placerat facer possim assum. Iusto odio dignissim qui blandit praesent luptatum zzril delenit augue duis dolore te feugait nulla facilisi.

Nam liber tempor cum soluta nobis eleifend option congue nihil imperdiet doming id quod mazim placerat facer possim assum. Accumsan et iusto odio dignissim qui blandit. Vendrerit In Vulputate Duis autem vel eum iriure dolor in hendrerit in vulputate velit esse molestie consequat, vel illum dolore eu feugiat nulla facilisis at vero eros et accumsan et iusto odio. Occumsan Aliquam dignissim qui blandit praesent luptatum zzril delenit augue duis dolore te feugait nulla facilisi. Nam liber tempor cum soluta nobis eleifend option congue nihil imperdiet doming id quod mazim placerat facer possim assum.

Eros Et Accumsan dignissim qui blandit praesent luptatum zzril delenit augue duis dolore te feugait nulla facilisi. Nam liber tempor cum soluta nobis eleifend option congue nihil imperdiet doming id quod mazim placerat facer possim assum. Iusto odio dignissim qui blandit.

Accumsan dignissim qui blandit praesent luptatum zzril delenit augue duis dolore te feugait nulla facilisi. Nam liber tempor cum soluta nobis eleifend option congue nihil imperdiet doming id quod mazim placerat facer possim assum. Iusto odio dignissim qui blandit praesent luptatum zzril delenit augue duis dolore te feugait nulla facilisi.

Nam liber tempor cum soluta nobis eleifend option congue nihil imperdiet doming id quod mazim placerat facer possim assum. Accumsan et iusto odio dignissim qui blandit. Duis

```
autem vel eum iriure dolor in hendrerit in vulputate velit
esse molestie consequat, vel illum dolore eu feugiat nulla
facilisis at vero eros et accumsan et iusto odio.

</body>
</html>
```

Now add margins using the <blockquote> tag (see Figure 9.2). This is necessary to create that all-important white space. Here is the text with blockquotes added:

```
<html>
<head>
<title>Text Example</title>
</head>

<body bgcolor="#FFFFFF" text="#000000" link="#999999"
vlink="#CCCCCC" alink="#FFFFCC">

<blockquote>

Duis autem vel eum iriure dolor in hendrerit in vulputate
velit esse molestie consequat, vel illum dolore eu feugiat
nulla facilisis at vero eros et accumsan et iusto odio
dignissim qui blandit praesent luptatum zzril delenit augue
duis dolore te feugait nulla facilisi. Nam liber tempor cum
soluta nobis eleifend option congue nihil imperdiet doming id
quod mazim placerat facer possim assum.
Accumsan et iusto odio dignissim qui blandit praesent
luptatum zzril delenit augue duis dolore te feugait nulla
facilisi. Eros Et Accumsan dignissim qui blandit praesent
luptatum zzril delenit augue duis dolore te feugait nulla
facilisi. Nam liber tempor cum soluta nobis eleifend option
congue nihil imperdiet doming id quod mazim placerat facer
possim assum. Iusto odio dignissim qui blandit praesent
luptatum zzril delenit augue duis dolore te feugait nulla
facilisi.

Nam liber tempor cum soluta nobis eleifend option congue
nihil imperdiet doming id quod mazim placerat facer possim
assum. Accumsan et iusto odio dignissim qui blandit.
Vendrerit In Vulputate Duis autem vel eum iriure dolor in
hendrerit in vulputate velit esse molestie consequat, vel
illum dolore eu feugiat nulla facilisis at vero eros et
accumsan et iusto odio. Occumsan Aliquam dignissim qui
blandit praesent luptatum zzril delenit augue duis dolore te
feugait nulla facilisi. Nam liber tempor cum soluta nobis
```

eleifend option congue nihil imperdiet doming id quod mazim placerat facer possim assum.

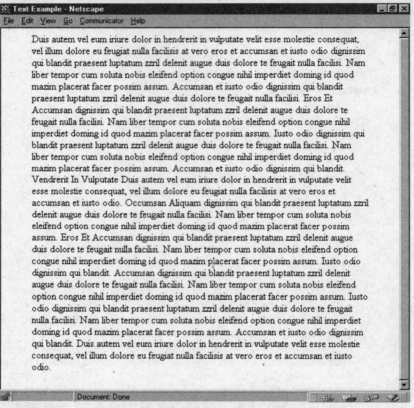

FIGURE 9.2: Add blockquotes for that all-important white space.

Eros Et Accumsan dignissim qui blandit praesent luptatum zzril delenit augue duis dolore te feugait nulla facilisi. Nam liber tempor cum soluta nobis eleifend option congue nihil imperdiet doming id quod mazim placerat facer possim assum. Iusto odio dignissim qui blandit.

Accumsan dignissim qui blandit praesent luptatum zzril delenit augue duis dolore te feugait nulla facilisi. Nam liber tempor cum soluta nobis eleifend option congue nihil imperdiet doming id quod mazim placerat facer possim assum. Iusto odio dignissim qui blandit praesent luptatum zzril delenit augue duis dolore te feugait nulla facilisi.

```
Nam liber tempor cum soluta nobis eleifend option congue
nihil imperdiet doming id quod mazim placerat facer possim
assum. Accumsan et iusto odio dignissim qui blandit. Duis
autem vel eum iriure dolor in hendrerit in vulputate velit
esse molestie consequat, vel illum dolore eu feugiat nulla
facilisis at vero eros et accumsan et iusto odio.

</blockquote>
</body>
</html>
```

Attention span on the Web is short. It's in your best interest to serve your audience by ensuring that paragraphs are equally short. Therefore, after breaking up text into pages, break up your page into logical sections of short paragraphs (see Figure 9.3). Here is the syntax with paragraph tags added:

```
<html>
<head>
<title>Text Example</title>
</head>
<body bgcolor="#FFFFFF" text="#000000" link="#999999"
vlink="#CCCCCC" alink="#FFFFCC">
<blockquote>

Duis autem vel eum iriure dolor in hendrerit in vulputate
velit esse molestie consequat, vel illum dolore eu feugiat
nulla facilisis at vero eros et accumsan et iusto odio
dignissim qui blandit praesent luptatum zzril delenit augue
duis dolore te feugait nulla facilisi. Nam liber tempor cum
soluta nobis eleifend option congue nihil imperdiet doming id
quod mazim placerat facer possim assum.
<p>
Accumsan et iusto odio dignissim qui blandit praesent
luptatum zzril delenit augue duis dolore te feugait nulla
facilisi. Eros Et Accumsan dignissim qui blandit praesent
luptatum zzril delenit augue duis dolore te feugait nulla
facilisi. Nam liber tempor cum soluta nobis eleifend option
congue nihil imperdiet doming id quod mazim placerat facer
possim assum. Iusto odio dignissim qui blandit praesent
luptatum zzril delenit augue duis dolore te feugait nulla
facilisi.
<p>
Nam liber tempor cum soluta nobis eleifend option congue
nihil imperdiet doming id quod mazim placerat facer possim
assum. Accumsan et iusto odio dignissim qui blandit.
Vendrerit In Vulputate Duis autem vel eum iriure dolor in
```

```
hendrerit in vulputate velit esse molestie consequat, vel
illum dolore eu feugiat nulla facilisis at vero eros et
accumsan et iusto odio. Occumsan Aliquam dignissim qui
blandit praesent luptatum zzril delenit augue duis dolore te
feugait nulla facilisi. Nam liber tempor cum soluta nobis
eleifend option congue nihil imperdiet doming id quod mazim
placerat facer possim assum.
<p>
Eros Et Accumsan dignissim qui blandit praesent luptatum
zzril delenit augue duis dolore te feugait nulla facilisi.
Nam liber tempor cum soluta nobis eleifend option congue
nihil imperdiet doming id quod mazim placerat facer possim
assum. Iusto odio dignissim qui blandit.
<p>
Accumsan dignissim qui blandit praesent luptatum zzril
delenit augue duis dolore te feugait nulla facilisi. Nam
liber tempor cum soluta nobis eleifend option congue nihil
imperdiet doming id quod mazim placerat facer possim assum.
Iusto odio dignissim qui blandit praesent luptatum zzril
delenit augue duis dolore te feugait nulla facilisi.
<p>
Nam liber tempor cum soluta nobis eleifend option congue
nihil imperdiet doming id quod mazim placerat facer possim
assum. Accumsan et iusto odio dignissim qui blandit. Duis
autem vel eum iriure dolor in hendrerit in vulputate velit
esse molestie consequat, vel illum dolore eu feugiat nulla
facilisis at vero eros et accumsan et iusto odio.
<p>
</blockquote>
</body>
</html>
```

Some people choose to use the nonbreaking space characters   to create indentation in paragraphs. The results are quite readable, as you can see in Figure 9.4. The following three nonbreaking space characters before the paragraph show you how to achieve this technique:

```
      Duis autem vel eum iriure dolor in
hendrerit in vulputate velit esse molestie consequat, vel
illum dolore eu feugiat nulla facilisis at vero eros et
accumsan et iusto odio dignissim qui blandit praesent
luptatum zzril delenit augue duis dolore te feugait nulla
facilisi. Nam liber tempor cum soluta nobis eleifend option
congue nihil imperdiet doming id quod mazim placerat facer
possim assum.
<p>
```

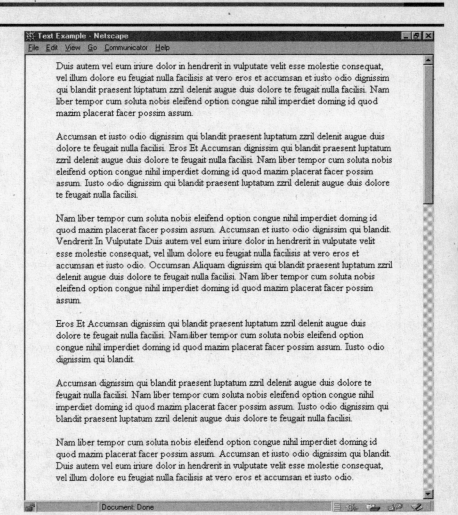

FIGURE 9.3: Paragraphs should be short and to the point.

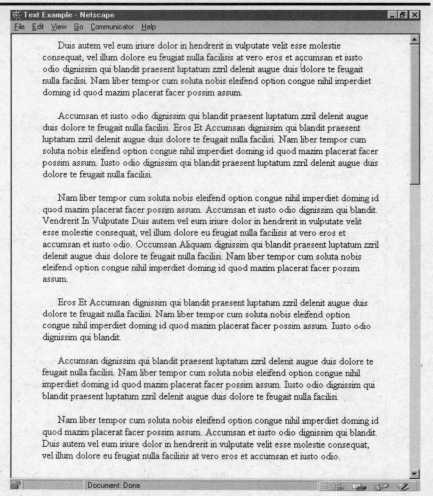

FIGURE 9.4: You can use nonbreaking space characters to achieve paragraph indentation.

Remember that lists are also a good way to break up space and help shape a page's layout. You can add them wherever your design calls for them, or where they feel logical. Figure 9.5 shows the use of lists with the same text.

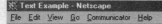

Duis autem vel eum iriure dolor in hendrerit in vulputate velit esse molestie consequat, vel illum dolore eu feugiat nulla facilisis at vero eros et accumsan et iusto odio dignissim qui blandit praesent luptatum zzril delenit augue duis dolore te feugait nulla facilisi. Nam liber tempor cum soluta nobis eleifend option congue nihil imperdiet doming id quod mazim placerat facer possim assum.

Accumsan et iusto odio dignissim qui blandit praesent luptatum zzril delenit augue duis dolore te feugait nulla facilisi. Eros Et Accumsan dignissim qui blandit praesent luptatum zzril delenit augue duis dolore te feugait nulla facilisi. Nam liber tempor cum soluta nobis eleifend option congue nihil imperdiet doming id quod mazim placerat facer possim assum. Iusto odio dignissim qui blandit praesent luptatum zzril delenit augue duis dolore te feugait nulla facilisi.

- Nam liber tempor cum soluta nobis eleifend option congue nihil imperdiet doming id quod mazim placerat facer possim assum. Accumsan et iusto odio dignissim qui blandit.
- In Vulputate Duis autem vel eum iriure dolor in hendrerit in vulputate velit esse molestie consequat, vel illum dolore eu feugiat nulla facilisis at vero eros et accumsan et iusto odio.
- Occumsan Aliquam dignissim qui blandit praesent luptatum zzril delenit augue duis dolore te feugait nulla facilisi. Nam liber tempor cum soluta nobis eleifend option congue nihil imperdiet doming id quod mazim placerat facer possim assum.

Eros Et Accumsan dignissim qui blandit praesent luptatum zzril delenit augue duis dolore te feugait nulla facilisi. Nam liber tempor cum soluta nobis eleifend option congue nihil imperdiet doming id quod mazim placerat facer possim assum. Iusto odio dignissim qui blandit.

Accumsan dignissim qui blandit praesent luptatum zzril delenit augue duis dolore te feugait nulla facilisi. Nam liber tempor cum soluta nobis eleifend option congue nihil imperdiet doming id quod mazim placerat facer possim assum. Iusto odio dignissim qui blandit praesent luptatum zzril delenit augue duis dolore te feugait nulla facilisi.

Nam liber tempor cum soluta nobis eleifend option congue nihil imperdiet doming id quod mazim placerat facer possim assum. Accumsan et iusto odio dignissim qui blandit. Duis autem vel eum iriure dolor in hendrerit in vulputate velit esse molestie consequat, vel illum dolore eu feugiat nulla facilisis at vero eros et accumsan et iusto odio.

FIGURE 9.5: The page with a list added

```
<html>
<head>
<title>Text Example</title>
</head>

<body bgcolor="#FFFFFF" text="#000000" link="#999999"
vlink="#CCCCCC" alink="#FFFFCC">
```

```
<blockquote>

      Duis autem vel eum iriure dolor in
hendrerit in vulputate velit esse molestie consequat, vel
illum dolore eu feugiat nulla facilisis at vero eros et
accumsan et iusto odio dignissim qui blandit praesent
luptatum zzril delenit augue duis dolore te feugait nulla
facilisi. Nam liber tempor cum soluta nobis eleifend option
congue nihil imperdiet doming id quod mazim placerat facer
possim assum.
<p>

      Accumsan et iusto odio dignissim qui
blandit praesent luptatum zzril delenit augue duis dolore te
feugait nulla facilisi. Eros Et Accumsan dignissim qui
blandit praesent luptatum zzril delenit augue duis dolore te
feugait nulla facilisi. Nam liber tempor cum soluta nobis
eleifend option congue nihil imperdiet doming id quod mazim
placerat facer possim assum. Iusto odio dignissim qui blandit
praesent luptatum zzril delenit augue duis dolore te feugait
nulla facilisi.
<p>

<ul>
<li>Nam liber tempor cum soluta nobis eleifend option congue
nihil imperdiet doming id quod mazim placerat facer possim
assum. Accumsan et iusto odio dignissim qui blandit.
<li>In Vulputate Duis autem vel eum iriure dolor in hendrerit
in vulputate velit esse molestie consequat, vel illum dolore
eu feugiat nulla facilisis at vero eros et accumsan et iusto
odio.

<li>Occumsan Aliquam dignissim qui blandit praesent luptatum
zzril delenit augue duis dolore te feugait nulla facilisi.
Nam liber tempor cum soluta nobis eleifend option congue
nihil imperdiet doming id quod mazim placerat facer possim
assum.
</ul>
<p>

      Eros Et Accumsan dignissim qui blandit
praesent luptatum zzril delenit augue duis dolore te feugait
nulla facilisi. Nam liber tempor cum soluta nobis eleifend
option congue nihil imperdiet doming id quod mazim placerat
facer possim assum. Iusto odio dignissim qui blandit.
<p>
```

```
      Accumsan dignissim qui blandit praesent
luptatum zzril delenit augue duis dolore te feugait nulla
facilisi. Nam liber tempor cum soluta nobis eleifend option
congue nihil imperdiet doming id quod mazim placerat facer
possim assum. Iusto odio dignissim qui blandit praesent
luptatum zzril delenit augue duis dolore te feugait nulla
facilisi.
<p>

      Nam liber tempor cum soluta nobis
eleifend option congue nihil imperdiet doming id quod mazim
placerat facer possim assum. Accumsan et iusto odio dignissim
qui blandit. Duis autem vel eum iriure dolor in hendrerit in
vulputate velit esse molestie consequat, vel illum dolore eu
feugiat nulla facilisis at vero eros et accumsan et iusto
odio.

</blockquote>
</body>
</html>
```

Finally, you want to use graphics or other media as functional aspects of your page, such as linked graphics, navigation buttons, and imagemaps. Or you can include graphics, such as a photograph, as design enhancements (see Figure 9.6), artwork, or fully constructed parts of a page, such as a main splash graphic. The code for the text example with an added graphic follows. Notice how the page is beginning to take on an attractive shape, and that with the addition of space and other layout techniques, the original jumbled text is formatted into three full screens of information.

```
<html>
<head>
<title>Text Example</title>
</head>
<body bgcolor="#FFFFFF" text="#000000" link="#999999"
vlink="#CCCCCC" alink="#FFFFCC">

<blockquote>

      Duis autem vel eum iriure dolor in
hendrerit in vulputate velit esse molestie consequat, vel
illum dolore eu feugiat nulla facilisis at vero eros et
accumsan et iusto odio dignissim qui blandit praesent
luptatum zzril delenit augue duis dolore te feugait nulla
facilisi. Nam liber tempor cum soluta nobis eleifend option
congue nihil imperdiet doming id quod mazim placerat facer
possim assum.
<p>
```

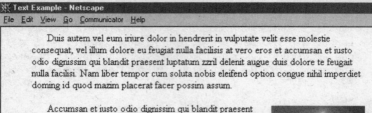

FIGURE 9.6: A graphic added to the page

```
<img src="sydney.jpg" width="146" height="98" hspace="5"
vspace="5" border="0" align="right" alt="sydney opera house
at night">

      Accumsan et iusto odio dignissim qui
blandit praesent luptatum zzril delenit augue duis dolore te
```

eugait nulla facilisi. Eros Et Accumsan dignissim qui blandit
praesent luptatum zzril delenit augue duis dolore te feugait
nulla facilisi. Nam liber tempor cum soluta nobis eleifend
option congue nihil imperdiet doming id quod mazim placerat
facer possim assum. Iusto odio dignissim qui blandit praesent
luptatum zzril delenit augue duis dolore te feugait nulla
facilisi.
<p>

<ul>
<li>Nam liber tempor cum soluta nobis eleifend option congue
nihil imperdiet doming id quod mazim placerat facer possim
assum. Accumsan et iusto odio dignissim qui blandit.

<li>In Vulputate Duis autem vel eum iriure dolor in hendrerit
in vulputate velit esse molestie consequat, vel illum dolore
eu feugiat nulla facilisis at vero eros et accumsan et iusto
odio.

<li>Occumsan Aliquam dignissim qui blandit praesent luptatum
zzril delenit augue duis dolore te feugait nulla facilisi.
Nam liber tempor cum soluta nobis eleifend option congue
nihil imperdiet doming id quod mazim placerat facer possim
assum.
</ul>
<p>

      Eros Et Accumsan dignissim qui blandit
praesent luptatum zzril delenit augue duis dolore te feugait
nulla facilisi. Nam liber tempor cum soluta nobis eleifend
option congue nihil imperdiet doming id quod mazim placerat
facer possim assum. Iusto odio dignissim qui blandit.
<p>

      Accumsan dignissim qui blandit praesent
luptatum zzril delenit augue duis dolore te feugait nulla
facilisi. Nam liber tempor cum soluta nobis eleifend option
congue nihil imperdiet doming id quod mazim placerat facer
possim assum. Iusto odio dignissim qui blandit praesent
luptatum zzril delenit augue duis dolore te feugait nulla
facilisi.
<p>

      Nam liber tempor cum soluta nobis
eleifend option congue nihil imperdiet doming id quod mazim
placerat facer possim assum. Accumsan et iusto odio dignissim
qui blandit. Duis autem vel eum iriure dolor in hendrerit in

```
vulputate velit esse molestie consequat, vel illum dolore eu
feugiat nulla facilisis at vero eros et accumsan et iusto
odio.

</blockquote>
</body>
</html>
```

When graphics and media are being used as functional media, such as a link, place them using the `<img>` or `<object>` tag and any alignment attribute you wish, but avoid using any kind of border, as it constrains the space.

Graphics and media used to enhance the page should be arranged in the fashion you've determined with your layout sketches. Typically, standard HTML layouts will apply to the most simple of pages, such as those with limited text and graphics, or splash pages where a map or hyperlinked graphic is the main attraction.

Example

Let's look at a plain splash page with a graphic as its main feature. Figure 9.7 is followed by the standard HTML code used to create the page shown.

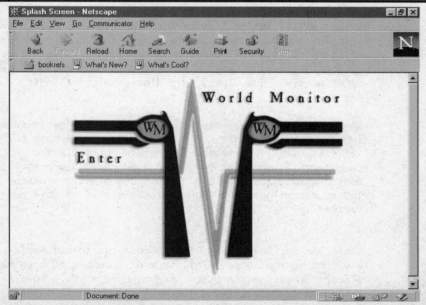

FIGURE 9.7: The splash page as it appears in Navigator 4

```html
<html>
<head>
<title>Splash Screen</title>
</head>
<body text="#000000" bgcolor="#FFFFFF" link="#FF0000"
vlink="#800080" alink="#0000FF">
<div align="center">
<a href="storyboard.htm"><img border="0" src="splash.gif"
height="323" width="432"></a>
</div>
</body>
</html>
```

No surprises here! It's a very straightforward page with the layout design relying heavily on the graphic.

TABLES

Now let's take a look at how tables are constructed. Table tags are really very simple, but with the variety of attributes available to you, the application is somewhat complicated. Be sure to refer to the appendix, where HTML tags and attributes are covered. In fact, I recommend that you refer to it regularly as you work, as the information there will appeal to your own knowledge level and learning style.

TIP

Much of the information on tables and frames in this chapter is derived from another of my books, *Laura Lemay's Web Workshop: Designing with Style Sheets, Tables, and Frames* (Sams.net, 1997). In that book, the basic lessons learned in this chapter are applied to a broader spectrum of layout and interface design. Any designer interested in studying a wide variety of tables- and frames-based layouts will enjoy the workbook style of that book. For more information, visit http://www.molly.com/.

There are only three tags that are absolutely necessary when designing with tables:

<table> This tag determines the beginning of a table within an HTML document. As with the majority of HTML tags, after all of the elements are placed within a table, the end of a table is denoted by the companion tag, </table>.

\<tr\>   Table rows are identified with this tag, which literally determines a row—the left-to-right, horizontal space within a table. Table rows are closed with the \</tr\> tag.

\<td\>   Individual table cells are defined by this tag, which is also referred to as the "table data" tag. The table cell tags are particularly critical for a number of reasons, which you'll see as we look at various applications of the tag. For this introduction, remember that the \<td\> tag and the information contained therein *determine the columnar structure* of a table. The \<td\> tag closes with the \</td\> tag.

Now that you've got the basics, let's look at the attributes you might wish to use along with these core tags. There are many, and their use begins the departure from straightforward coding to the complicated job of using HTML as a serious layout technology.

align="x"   Use this attribute to align tables on a page. Options allow "x" to equal left or right. Because the latest browsers default alignment to the left and it's commonplace to center tables using other tags, the only really effective use of this attribute is when you specifically want an entire table placed to the far right of the browser field, as in Figure 9.8.

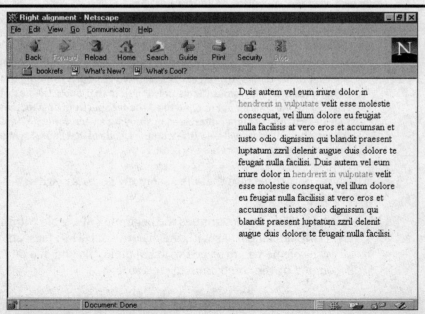

FIGURE 9.8: A right-aligned table

TIP

Want to center your table on the page? There are several legal ways to do so. The two most simple are placing the table between the `<center>` tag and its closing `</center>` tag, and using the `<div>` tag. Division tags are much more stable in cross-platform environments. In this case, you'll place the `<div align=center>` tag and attribute before your table, and after you've closed the table, close the division with `</div>`.

`border="x"`   The `"x"` is replaced with a value from `"0"` on up. This value defines the width of the visual border around the table.

`cellspacing="x"`   Cellspacing defines the amount of space between individual table cells—in other words, between visual columns. The `"x"` requires a value from `"0"` on up.

`cellpadding="x"`   This attribute calls for the space around the edges of each cell within the table—literally, its "padding."

`width="x%"` *or* `width="x"`   To define the width of a table, you can choose to use a number that relates to the percentage of browser space you wish to span, or a specific numeral that will be translated into pixel widths.

KNOW YOUR BROWSERS

Not every browser supports or handles attributes, pixels, or percentages in the same fashion. For browser-specific descriptions, visit the browser company's home page.

The two most important browsers for Web designers are:

Internet Explorer   Information about this browser is provided at its home on Microsoft's site: `http://www.microsoft.com/windows/ie/default.htm`

Netscape Navigator   The home page for this company is located at `http://home.netscape.com/`.

When given the option of defining a table by percentage or pixel width, it's generally better to use pixels. The reason is that you can then count each used pixel in a space. For example, if you have a table that is

595 pixels wide, you must be sure that all of the elements within that table *do not exceed* 600 pixels. Percentages are less accurate, yet they can be handy when you desire to use a visual portion of a space that is not dependent on literal pixel count. An example of this would be creating a table that is 75 percent of the browser area—this section will remain proportionately the same no matter what your screen resolution is when you're viewing the page.

TIP
Be sure to read the latest release notes applicable to your version of the browser for specific and timely information regarding that browser's technology. Ultimately, you must test your work in different browsers to see the results firsthand.

With the <table>, <tr>, and <td> tags, you have the foundation for all table-based layout design in hand. It seems simple, and in many ways, it is. But knowing when to use a row or a column can sometimes be very challenging.

NOTE
Web browsers are essential to the way HTML is deciphered. Tables are fairly well supported in most browser versions 2 and above. As you may already know, computer platform, monitor size and type, and screen resolution all may influence the way an HTML page looks. It's always wise to test your work with a variety of browsers and, when possible, to try and view your work on different platforms.

Rows and Columns

I learned about the application of tables through the wise guidance of Wil Gerken, CEO of DesertNet and Weekly Wire. I, like many other people with limited natural spatial abilities, was having a very difficult time interpreting how to relate table syntax to the concept of layout.

Working on the original design of the Film Vault, Wil made me take the layout and try to work *from* the design *to* the HTML. I had to take the image and figure out how cells and rows would configure most simply to create the layout.

After making several erroneous attempts with the sketches, I became so frustrated that I gave up for a while. It took some time for the exercise to sink in (Figure 9.9), but once it did, the understanding was total and remained with me—enough for me to venture out on my own, designing interesting table-based layouts.

FIGURE 9.9: The Film Vault's table header configuration with columns and spanning

The lesson is that while some of you already have either natural or well-developed spatial abilities, those who do not can develop them with a little practice.

Approach tables first from the columnar layout. What can you control vertically? The vertical is where you'll find some of the greatest flexibility in terms of control by first spatially placing items and then confirming their placement with cell attributes allowed in the <td>, or table cell (column), tag.

Keep in mind that graphics can be stacked and placed in tables, too, so don't get stumped by graphics that run vertically, as the two graphics are in Figure 9.10, which are in the same table cell. Remember also that graphics are used in tables as backgrounds, such as the black left panel and white main section of the Design Studio site (Figure 9.11), and as unseen holders that fix space on both the horizontal and vertical lines in a design (Figure 9.12).

FIGURE 9.10: This vertical graphic is actually two sections placed together by the table.

Attributes that are helpful within table cell tags are:

align="x"   When you use this attribute within a table cell, the data inside the cell will align with the literal value you assign to the attribute. In other words, a left value will left-justify the text or graphic you place within the cell, a middle value will center the information, and a right value will right-justify the information.

colspan="x"   This attribute refers to the number of columns that the cell you are working with will span.

rowspan="x"   As with colspan, rowspan refers to the span of the cell—in this case, how many rows the cell will stretch.

valign="x"   The vertical alignment of a table cell will place the information therein at the top, middle, or bottom of the cell.

FIGURE 9.11: A page from the Design Studio—the black and white sections are created by a graphic with a table laid on top.

FIGURE 9.12: Arrows indicate where spacer GIFs have been used to fix positioning.

Now that we've looked at some of the specific table cell attributes, let's move on to the table row. The two notable attributes for use in rows include align, which controls the row's spatial alignment, and valign, which determines the vertical placement of all the data within a row. It's rare to see table row attributes used. It seems that most designers prefer the surrounding HTML, <table> attributes, and <td> table cell data attributes to determine the attributes applied to table layouts.

align="x"   Here, the values for "x" are not numeric; rather, they are literal and include left, right, and center.

valign="x"   Again, the values for vertical alignment are not numeric. Vertical alignment can be top, middle, bottom, or baseline.

You will need to think very carefully about rowspan and colspan. The introduction of these attributes critically changes the way tables can be used. With these attributes, you can have one cell spanning multiple columns or rows, as in the code below and in Figure 9.13, or many cells using a variety of span attributes to create a wide selection of visual field options.

```
<html>

<head>
<title>colspan and rowspan</title>
</head>

<body bgcolor="#FFFFFF" text="#000000" link="#999999"
vlink="#CCCCCC" alink="#FFFFCC">

<table border="1" cellspacing="20" cellpadding="10">
<tr>

<td rowspan="2">
Rowspan with value of two
</td>

<td>
column (no span)
</td>

<td>
column (no span)
</td>
</tr>

<tr>
```

```
<td colspan="2">
second row with column span: value of "2"
</td>

</tr>

</table>

</body>
</html>
```

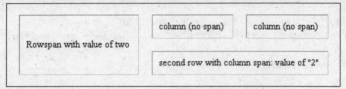

FIGURE 9.13: An example of colspan and rowspan

TRY IT OFFLINE

Visit any Web site that uses tables and attempt to reconstruct it by drawing out what you think the table cell and row structure is. Build a table using this configuration and see if it works. Only after doing this should you peek at the source code for that page.

Example

Here we'll look at the site for Bernstein Communications, which uses a straightforward table-based design. Below, in its entirety, is the code from a content page, which is shown in Figure 9.14. Take a close look at the table's structure and identify how the various attributes control the layout.

```
<!-- site by desertnet designs: sales@desert.net -->
<!-- design director: molly holzschlag -->
<!-- graphic design: amy burnham -->
<!-- online editor: molly holzschlag -->
<!-- content provided by bernstein communications -->

<!-- begin header -->

<html>
```

```
<head>
<title>Bernstein Communications: Profile</title>
<meta name="keywords" content="business, communications,
bernstein, jonathan, del webb, mature, market, planning,
crisis, management, nasli, mature market, desert, desertnet,
desert net">
<meta name="description" content="expert issues management,
mature market public relations, and strategic planning">
<meta name="author" content="molly e. holzschlag, amy
burnham, jonathan bernstein">
</head>

<body bgcolor="#FFFFFF" text="#000000" link="#0000FF"
vlink="#0000CC" alink="#FFFFFF" background="brn_bkgd.gif">

<!-- end header -->

<table border="0" cellspacing="0" cellpadding="0"
width="600">
<tr>

<!-- begin menu column -->

<td valign="top" align="left" width="97">

<img src="brn_nav.gif" alt="Navigation (text at bottom)"
width="87" height="298" border="0" usemap="#brn_nav">
<p>

<!-- begin spacer -->

<td width="55">
<img src="spacer.gif" width="55" height="1">
<br>
</td>

<!-- end spacer -->

<td valign="top">
<p>

<img src="brn_h3.gif" alt="Profile Header" width="406"
height="35" border="0">
<p>

<font size="+1" color="990000">General Biographic Data</font>
<p>
```

```
<img src="brn_ph1.gif" alt="Jonathan Bernstein" width="179"
height="219" hspace="15" border="0" align="right">
```

Jonathan L. Bernstein, principal of Bernstein Communications,
is a strategic public relations consultant specializing in
multi-audience Issues Management (aka Crisis Prevention &
Response) and Mature Market Communications. Additionally, as
a strategist and writer, he often serves as the "objective
third party" who can assist clients with public relations
strategy and planning involving a wide variety of industries.
```
<p>
```

Bernstein brings national-level experience to his consultancy
which was launched in january 1994. He served for almost five
years (1989-1994) as senior vice president and director of
both the Crisis Communications and Mature Market groups for
Ruder Finn, Inc., one of the country's largest public
relations agencies. He created both groups for Ruder Finn,
which became the only national agency with the Mature Market
specialty.
```
<p>
```

Bernstein Communications is a "who you see is who you get"
business. No handing off the project to a junior person once
the boss signs the deal. Only certain, clearly identified
media relations work is done by an experienced media
relations specialist -- the rest, including strategy,
planning, writing and client contact is done by Jonathan
Bernstein.
```
<p>
```

His past experience includes corporate, agency and non-profit
public relations positions, preceded by five years of
investigative and feature journalism -- to include a stint
with investigative reporter/columnist Jack Anderson. Prior to
that, Bernstein, oxymoronically, was in U.S. Army Military
Intelligence.
```
<p>
```

He is a frequent public speaker and trainer in his areas of
specialization and, when not in the office, Bernstein enjoys
being pummeled into submission by his four kids, as well as
fitness activities and performing folk music.
```
<p>
```

```
<font size="2">
```

Part ii

```
<center>
<a href="index.html">Home</a> |
<a href="services.html">Services </a> |
<a href="articles.html">Articles</a> |
<a href="profile.html">Profile </a> |
<a href="clients.html">Clients</a> |
<a href="contact.html">Contact</a>
<p>

<font size="2">
<a href="http://desert.net/designs/">&#169; DesertNet Designs
1996</a>
</font>

</center>

</td>

<!-- begin spacer -->

<td width="30" rowspan="2">
<img src="spacer.gif" width="30" height="1">
<br>
</td>

<!-- end spacer -->

</tr>
</table>

<map name="brn_nav">
<area shape="rect" coords="0,10,86,41" href="index.html">
<area shape="rect" coords="0,60,86,92" href="services.html">
<area shape="rect" coords="0,113,86,143" href="articles
.html">
<area shape="rect" coords="0,162,85,194" href="profile.html">
<area shape="rect" coords="0,213,85,246" href="clients.html">
<area shape="rect" coords="1,267,85,296" href="contact.html">
<area shape="default" nohref>
</map>

</body>
</html>
```

If you paid close attention to the code, you should have noticed the
use of graphics as background and placeholders within this layout. If
you're still unsure of how this works, visit the Bernstein Communications

site at `http://home.earthlink.net/~berncomm/`, view the code by choosing View ➢ Source, and copy and paste it into your HTML editor. You can save the graphics to your own hard drive and reconstruct the page. Exercises of this nature can assist you in gaining an intimate knowledge of how powerful and useful tables are in layout design.

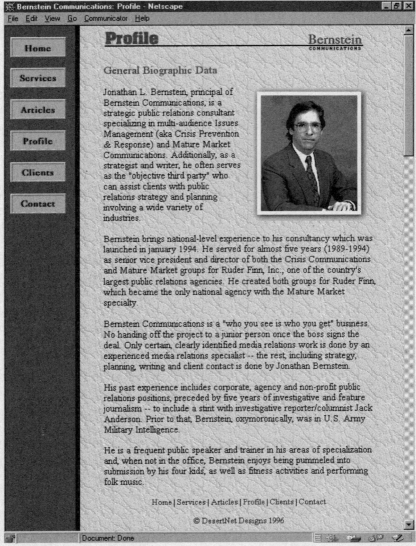

FIGURE 9.14: A page from the table-based Bernstein Communications site

FRAMES

Frames have been rather controversial in Web history. Some designers and visitors love them; others have a strong, personal dislike for them. Not only is there the literal and technical division of browser space that frames create, but a philosophical division as well. Fortunately, all this dispute has not stopped the progress and development of frame-based layout design. Most Web designers are beginning to agree that the survival of frames is a fortunate twist of fate, for frame technology now has moved to the forefront as a very powerful page-formatting device.

The arguments on both sides, which have held fast since Netscape released frames technology, have a certain logic to them. The reason involves the curse and blessing of what frames do—the breaking up of space. For the common computer owner with a 15- to 17-inch average screen size and an available resolution of either 640×480 pixels or 800×600 pixels, visual real estate is on the medium to low end of the spectrum.

Take this space and add to it the pixels that a Web browser's interface takes up—from about 5 to 15 on either vertical margin, anywhere from 25 to 150 on the top margin, and about 25 on the bottom margin. At best, on a 640×480 resolution screen, the total used pixels reduce your viewing space to 630×430, and at worst, 595×295 pixels.

Now add a bordered, frame-based design to the mix, as seen in Figure 9.15, and you can quickly see why some individuals have gotten upset. Frames literally take what is a small, contained space and break that space up into smaller, even more contained spaces. Until borderless frames became available, only the most technologically adept and savvy designers could use frames well as part of their designs, and even then at the risk of upsetting visitors to the pages they built. It is still good protocol to provide "no frame" options for Web browsers that do not support frames and for Web visitors who maintain a passionate dislike for them.

Borderless frames have bridged the churning waters, however. When Microsoft's Internet Explorer Web browser introduced the `<frameborder=x>` attribute and Netscape Navigator 3 introduced a similar feature quickly thereafter, the face of frames changed. In fact, the face of frames can now disappear altogether if a designer so desires. Setting the frame border to a value of `"0"` makes the three-dimensional frame borders go away, offering seamless integration between frame divisions.

FIGURE 9.15: The Loft Cinema uses bordered frames.

This moved frames from their position as an organizational tool to one of layout control. With borderless frames, as with borderless tables, individual sections of a page can be defined and controlled. But while tables can be used only on a page-by-page basis, frame technology introduces *static* and *targeted* aspects, allowing portions of the visible screen to remain static while others can be targeted, or changed, with the simple click of a link.

With the control that borders allow, you can now make better choices about how to employ frames. Whether you use dimensional borders for a controlled-space interface or to create pages with frames as the silent blueprint for a complex and dynamic design, you are ultimately empowered by the new and ongoing additions to frame technology.

Frame Structure

Before introducing the practical aspects of how to design a framed page, I'd like to demonstrate a fundamental aspect of frame design. Much like tables, frames are built in columns and rows. Tables, as mentioned earlier in this chapter, get a bit complex in the ways columns and rows are spanned, creating a technological blur between horizontal and vertical reference points. Frames approach the issue in a much more straightforward fashion—a column is an overtly vertical control, a row a horizontal one.

Frame syntax is very clear. Rows are referred to as `rows`, columns as `cols`. Both columns and rows can be defined in terms of pixels or percentages. For example, `cols="240,*"` calls for a left column with a *width* of 240 pixels; the right column, called by the asterisk, will take up the remainder of the available viewing space—whatever that remainder is. This means that with frames, your layout can expand or contract to a variety of resolutions.

To add more columns, you simply define each one in turn. If you wanted to create four columns of equal percent, the syntax would read `cols=25%,25%,25%,25%`. In Figure 9.16, you can see a bordered frame design with four such columns.

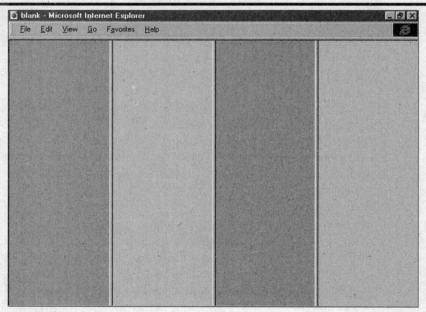

FIGURE 9.16: Four framed columns

Rows work the same way. If you wanted to create rows rather than columns, you would simply change the syntax to `rows="240,*"` and the result would be a top row with a *height* of 240 pixels. To create four individual rows of equal percent, you would call for `rows=25%,25%,25%,25%`, as shown in Figure 9.17.

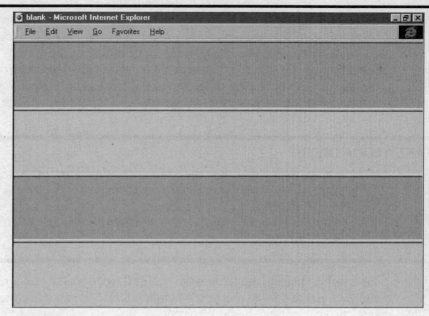

FIGURE 9.17: Four framed rows

To create combinations of columns and rows, the values are simply stacked into the appropriate tags and pages of the framed site, as with the code for the Loft Cinema:

```
<html>
<head>
<title>Welcome to the Loft Cinema</title>
</head>

<frameset cols="210,*">
<frameset rows="175,*">
<frame src="flick1.htm" scrolling="no" marginwidth="1"
marginheight="5" name="flick" noresize>
<frame src="menu.htm" scrolling="auto" marginwidth="5"
marginheight="25" name="menu" noresize>
</frameset>

<frame src="welcome.htm" scrolling="auto" marginwidth="25"
name="right" noresize>
</frameset>
```

The attributes seen here are explained in further detail in the following section.

Elements of Framed Pages

As with tables, three elements are absolutely necessary to build a framed page. And, as you advance through various aspects of working with frames, you will see that they can get a bit complicated—depending upon the ways you wish to employ them. But at the most basic level, all framed sites begin with the factors introduced here.

TAKE A LOOK ONLINE

A well laid out frame-based site offering up-to-date HTML information, including beginning to advanced level frames data, is Sizzling HTML Jalfrezi. Point your browser to `http://vzone.virgin.net/sizzling.jalfrezi/iniframe.htm` for all the HTML tags fit to print.

Remember this equation: one page of HTML code *plus* the total number of each frame desired equals the amount of HTML pages necessary to create one visible frame-based Web page.

The reason for this is that frame layouts require a controlling HTML document that gives the instructions on how the framed page is to be set up. This control is called the *frameset.* The frameset defines an HTML page for each individual frame in the layout's design.

The Frameset

Consider the frameset as the control page of your framed site. In it, you'll argue primarily for the rows and columns you wish to create, as well as the individual HTML pages that will fill those rows or columns. This is done using two major tags, as follows:

`<frameset>`   This tag for the frame and its basic arguments defines rows and columns. The frameset information is closed with a corresponding `</frameset>` tag.

`<frame>`   The frame tag argues individual frames within the frameset. This includes the location of the HTML document required to fill the frame, utilizing the `src="x"` where `"x"` is equal to the relative or absolute URL to the location of the HTML page. A variety of other `<frame>` attributes will be covered later in this chapter.

TIP

Remember that a framed page requires one HTML page for each individually defined area *plus* one HTML page for the control, or frameset, page.

Frameset attributes include the following:

`cols="x"` As we learned earlier, this attribute creates columns. An `"x"` value is given for each column in the framed page and will be either a pixel value, a percentage value, or a combination of one of those plus the *, which creates a *dynamic* or *relative size* frame—the remainder of the framed space.

`rows="x"` This attribute is used to create rows in the same fashion that the column attribute is used.

`border="x"` The border attribute is used by Netscape Navigator 3 and above to control border width. Value is set in pixel width.

`frameborder="x"` Frameborder is used by the Internet Explorer browser to control border width in pixels. Netscape Navigator 3 and above uses the attribute with a yes or no value.

`framespacing="x"` Used by Internet Explorer, this attribute controls border width.

Use these tag attributes for individual frame control:

`frameborder="x"` Use this attribute to control frameborders around individual frames. Netscape Navigator requires a yes or no value, whereas Internet Explorer will look for a numeric pixel-width value.

`marginheight="x"` This attribute argues a value in pixels to control the height of the frame's margin.

`marginwidth="x"` This attribute argues for a frame's margin width in pixels.

`name="x"` This critical attribute allows the designer to name an individual frame. Naming frames permits *targeting* by links within other HTML pages. Names must begin with a standard letter or numeral.

noresize   Simply place this handy tag in your string if you don't want to allow resizing of a frame. This fixes the frame into its position.

scrolling="x"   By arguing yes, no, or auto, you can control the appearance of a scrollbar. A yes value automatically places a scrollbar in the frame, and a no value ensures that no scroll-bar ever appears. The auto argument turns the power over to the browser, which will automatically place a scrollbar in a frame *should it be required.*

src="x"   The "x" value is replaced with the relative or absolute URL of the HTML page you wish to place within the frame at hand.

The Noframe Tag Option

There is an additional tag that you can use in the frameset. This tag sup-plies a much-needed option that allows non-frame and text-only browsers to access information within a frame-based site. Keeping with the current trends by incorporating no-frame and text access addresses cross-browser issues by enabling not only those who *require* text access, but those who prefer it as well.

The way to achieve this in a framed site is by employing the <noframe> tag, which is placed in the frameset page after the necessary frame syntax. Within the <noframe> tags you can place the syntax for an entire page that links to non-framed pages within the site, allowing for complete access to your information. Or you can choose to simply say that the site in question is not available to browsers that do not support frames. Here's an example of the Loft Cinema's frameset with the <noframe> syntax in place:

```
<!-- site by desertnet designs: sales@desert.net-->
<!-- web engineer: molly holzschlag-->
<!-- design director: matt straznitskas -->
<!-- online editor: molly holzschlag -->
<!-- content provided by the loft cinema and desertnet
designs -->

<html>
<head>
<title>Welcome to the Loft Cinema</title>
</head>
```

```
<frameset cols="210,*">
<frameset rows="175,*">
<frame src="flick1.htm" scrolling="no" marginwidth="1"
marginheight="5" name="flick" noresize>
<frame src="menu.htm" scrolling="auto" marginwidth="5"
marginheight="25" name="menu" noresize>
</frameset>

<frame src="welcome.htm" scrolling="auto" marginwidth="25"
name="right" noresize>
</frameset>

<noframe>

<body bgcolor="#000000" text="#FFFFFF" link="#97D7C9"
vlink="#A2B3E9" alink="#FFFFFF">

<center>
<img src="frames/99.jpg" width="180" height="125" border="0"
alt="The Loft Cinema"><p>
<img src="graphics/welcome.jpg" width="360" height="72"
border="0" alt="Welcome"><p>
<h3><i>Tucson's Premier Art Theater</i></h3>
</center>

<blockquote>
```

The Loft Cinema has been bringing art and specialty films to
appreciative Tucson audiences for nearly 25 years; and as
long as there are producers, directors, and distributors
willing to make the kind of films we like to show, we may be
around for another 25 years. <p>

We have won the Tucson Weekly's Best Movie Theater
Award each year for too many years to remember, an award
of considerable achievement since we have the savvyest
customers around. After many years on the University of
Arizona campus in our original single-screen location we
moved in 1991 to our current two-screen location on busy
Speedway Boulevard. In our big house we still present films
on the large screen format that has disappeared in the
multiplexes.<p>

As a locally-owned business the Loft has had to rely upon the
devotion and expertise of many Tucsonans, including Nancy
Sher, Bob Campbell, Jacqui Tully, Shirley Pasternack, Anita
Royal and Cliff Altfeld, and many others, as well as a long

```
line of film-loving staff members. We continue to show the
Rocky Horror Picture Show as we have since 1978.<p>

We are currently exploring the possibility of showing
American and foreign classics on our big screen at 1:00 pm on
Saturday and Sunday. If you think it's a good idea and want
to suggest some films for us to bring in <a
href="mailto:nuloft@aol.com">E-mail us!</a>

The Loft is located at 3233 E. Speedway Blvd. in the heart of
Tucson. Our telephone number is (520) 795-7777. When in
Albuquerque visit the Loft's sister theater, The Guild Cinema
at 3405 Central Ave NE, (505) 255-1848.<p>

</blockquote>

<center>
<h3>Thanks for supporting The Loft!</h3>
</center>

<center>
<font size="2">
<a href="welcome.htm">Welcome</a> |
<a href="showing.htm">Now Showing</a> |
<a href="coming.htm">Coming Attractions</a> |
<a href="neighbor.htm">In the Neighborhood</a>
<p>
</font>

<font size="1">&#169; 1996 The Loft Cinema</font>
</center>

</body>

</noframe>

</html>
```

Figure 9.18 shows the page as it would appear without frames.

Between the various ways individual browsers work and the variety of attributes common to contemporary browsers, it's easy to see why frames confuse many designers. If you start simple, however, and move on from there, you'll find interesting ways of employing frames in your layout design.

FIGURE 9.18: The Loft Cinema's home page as viewed without frames

Example

The DisAbilities Forum, shown in Figure 9.19, provides an excellent, easy-to-understand example of a frames-based layout. This is a borderless example with a total of—you guessed it—three pages of code to make up the one main page layout.

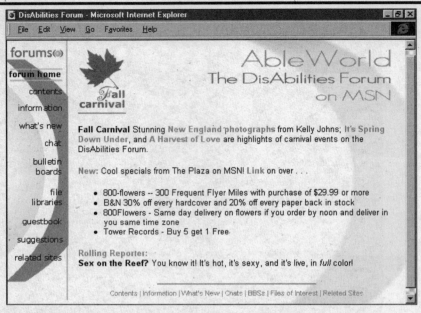

FIGURE 9.19: The frames-based, borderless DisAbilities Forum

Here's the frameset code:

```
<head>

<title>DisAbilities Forum</title>

</head>

<frameset cols="95,20%" framespacing="0" frameborder="0">
 <frame src="sidebar.htm" name="forum_sidebar"
scrolling="no">
 <frame src="welcome.htm" name="ForumMain" noresize>
</frameset>

</html>
```

WARNING

Notice how there is *no* <body> tag used in a frameset. This is of critical importance. A <body> tag in a frameset will cause some browsers, including Internet
Explorer 4, to ignore the entire frameset syntax, resulting in a blank page delivered to your screen.

NOTE

The only exception to the "no <body> tag in a frameset" rule is when you are using the <noframe> tags for browsers that do not support frames. It's okay to use a <body> tag *inside* the noframe syntax, but never outside.

The DisAbilities Forum code that you see here has been designed to sit on the proprietary side of the Microsoft Network. Therefore, there isn't much need to include access for no-frames browsers, as the only browsers capable of accessing the pages in the first place are Internet Explorer 3 and above and the MSN Program Viewer, which is based on Internet Explorer code and supports frame syntax.

Let's assume for a moment that the DisAbilities Forum is accessible without a membership. If you needed to be sure you could make it available to everyone who visits, you would want to include, at the very least, a <noframe> option with a comment letting people know the site is frames-based. An example of this follows:

```
<head>

<title>DisAbilities Forum</title>

</head>

<frameset cols="95,20%" framespacing="0" frameborder="0">
 <frame src="sidebar.htm" name="forum_sidebar"
scrolling="no">
 <frame src="welcome.htm" name="ForumMain" noresize>
</frameset>

<noframe>

Attention! This site must be accessed with a browser that
supports frames.

Thank you,
The DisAbilities Forum Management

</noframe>
</html>
```

This option is courteous and can be expanded to include links to frame-less portions of the site or to other resources that might assist visitors.

Now let's look at the page code for the main page of the DisAbilities Forum. First, there's the menu page to the left of the frame. Here's the syntax for that page, which includes the <object> tags to make the Flash navigation work properly:

```
<html>

<head>

<!-- This page holds the navbar -->

<title> The DisAbilities Forum </title>

<script language="vbscript">
sub navbar_fscommand(byval command, byval args)
  select case command
    case "show_all"
parent.location.href="http://forums.msn.com"
    case "home" parent.forummain.location.href = "welcome.htm"
    case "contents" parent.forummain.location.href =
"contents.htm"
    case "info" parent.forummain.location.href = "info.htm"
    case "new" parent.forummain.location.href = "whatsnew.htm"
    case "chat" parent.forummain.location.href =
"chatmain.htm"
    case "bbs" parent.forummain.location.href = "bbsmain.htm"
    case "file" parent.forummain.location.href = "libmain.htm"
    case "guestbook" parent.forummain.location.href =

"news://msnnews.msn.com/msn.forums.disabilities.guestbook"
    case "suggestions" parent.forummain.location.href =

"news://msnnews.msn.com/msn.forums.disabilities.suggestbox"
    case "sites" parent.forummain.location.href =
"linksmain.htm"
  end select
end sub

</script>

</head>

<body bgcolor="#c0c0c0" leftmargin="0" topmargin="0">

<object
 id="navbar"
 classid="clsid:d27cdb6e-ae6d-11cf-96b8-444553540000"
 width="100%" height="100%">
 <param name="movie" value="images/navbar.spl">
```

```
<param name="quality" value="high">
<param name="loop" value="false">
<param name="play" value="false">
<param name="scale" value="showall">
<param name="devicefont" value="true">
<param name="salign" value="tl">
<param name="menu" value="false">
</object>

</body>
</html>
```

As you can see, the syntax here is for a functional Web page (Figure 9.20). Because of the frameset's command, this page is loaded into the left frame. In this case, the page includes the navigation.

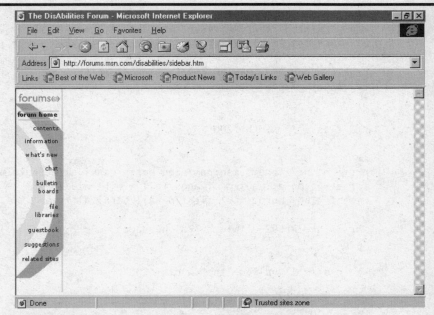

FIGURE 9.20: The visible content for the left frame

The right frame also holds the syntax, as follows, for a fully viewable Web page. Note that the right frame will always load the body pages of the site in this design.

```
<html>

<head>
```

```
<title> Welcome Page - AbleWorld: The DisAbilities Forum on
MSN. </title>
</head>

<style>

BODY {background: url(images/bak2.jpg) FFFFFF; color: 000000}
H3 {font: 14pt arial; color: 60099}
.1 {font: 11pt arial; color: 000000; text-align: right}
.2 {font: 12pt arial; color: 000000; text-align: left}
.3 {font: 10pt arial; color: 000000; text-align: left}
.4 {font: 11pt arial; color: 9966FF; text-align: right}
.5 {font: 8pt arial; color: FF9933; text-align: center}
A {color: 9999CC; text-decoration: none}

</style>

<body bgcolor="#FFFFFF" text="#FFFFCC" link="#FFCC99"
vlink="#9999CC" alink="#FFFFCC" background="images/bak2.jpg">

<table border="0" width="505" cellpadding="5"
cellspacing="0">
<tr>

<td class="3" width="200">

<a
href="http://forums.msn.com/needlearts/carnival/default.htm"
target="_top"><img src="images/fall_w.gif" width="75"
height="100" border="0" alt="To Fall Carnival"></a>

<hr color="#FF9933" width="75" noshade>
</td>

<td class="1" valign="top" width="300">

<img src="images/dis-ani1.gif" width="300" height="100"
border="0" alt=" ">

</td>
</tr>

<tr>
<td class="3" width="500" colspan="2">

<b>Fall Carnival</b>
```

```
Stunning <a href="http://forums.msn.com/disabilities/ne1
.htm"><b>New England photographs</b></a> from Kelly Johns;
<a href="http://forums.msn.com/disabilities/spring.htm">
<b>It's Spring Down Under</b></a>,and <a href="http://forums
.msn.com/disabilities/harvest.htm"><b>A Harvest of Love</b>
</a> are highlights of carnival events on the DisAbilities
Forum.
<p>


<a href="whatsnew.htm"><b>New:</b></a>

Cool specials from The Plaza on MSN!
<a href="links.htm"><b>Link</b></a> on over . . .
<p>


<ul>

<li>800-flowers -- 300 Frequent Flyer Miles with purchase of
$29.99 or more
<li>B&N 30% off every hardcover and 20% off every paper back
in stock
<li>800Flowers -- Same day delivery on flowers if you order
by noon and deliver in you same time zone
<li>Tower Records -- Buy 5 get 1 Free

</ul>

<a href="http://forums.msn.com/disabilities/rr/default.htm"
target="_top"><b>Rolling Reporter:</b></a>
<br>
<b>Sex on the Reef?</b> You know it! It's hot, it's sexy, and
it's live, in <i>full</i> color!
<p>

<div class=5>

<hr color="#FF9933" width="50%" noshade>

<a href="contents.htm">Contents</a> |
<a href="info.htm">Information</a> |
<a href="whatsnew.htm">What's New</a> |
<a href="chatmain.htm">Chats</a> |
<a href="bbsmain.htm">BBSs</a> |
<a href="libmain.htm">Files of Interest</a> |
<a href="linksmain.htm">Related Sites</a>
```

```
    </div>
    </td>
    </tr>
    </table>

    </body>
    </html>
```

Not only is the code just examined filled with standard HTML links, but it's laid out using tables. You can see what the page looks like in Figure 9.21. Indeed, this is a common practice—using frames to control interface aspects of the layout and tables to control layout within individual pages.

All in all, a powerful combination that can ensure ultimate control of any Web page design.

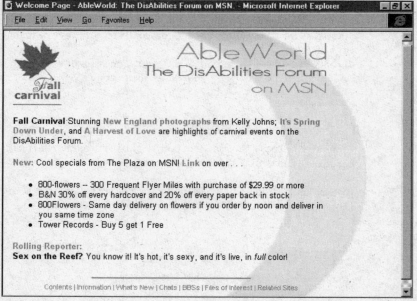

FIGURE 9.21: Tables are used to position the elements of this page.

WHAT'S NEXT?

With the concepts of layout method and technology in mind, you're ready to think about adding graphics to your pages. In the next chapter, E. Stephen Mack and Janan Platt Saylor will teach you how to work with image files and formats while building your site.

Chapter 10

ADDING GRAPHICS

Graphics, images, pictures, photographs—whatever you call them, a visual element makes your page more compelling and is the easiest way to give your page a unique look. In this chapter, we'll show you all of the ways you can add images to your pages using the <IMG> tag and its many attributes. You'll also learn how to use images as links.

Adapted from *HTML 4.0: No experience required*, by E. Stephen Mack and Janan Platt Saylor

ISBN 0-7821-2143-8   704 pages $29.99

Throughout this chapter, you'll find suggestions on how you can make your images useful and functional even when your page is viewed by a browser that doesn't display images. Toward the end of the chapter, we'll take a look at the different image formats and learn how you can create images (including interlaced images, transparent images, and animated images).

ADDING GRAPHICS WITH THE IMAGE ELEMENT

The purpose of the image element (which consists of the <IMG> tag) is to include graphic images in the body of your Web page.

NOTE
HTML 4.0 recommends using the object element (the <OBJECT> and </OBJECT> tags) instead of the image element. However, <IMG> is still common, and HTML 4.0 fully supports it. The object element isn't as widely supported as <IMG>.

Images are sometimes referred to as *inline images* because the images are inserted within a line of body text. Because the image element is a text-level element, it should be nested inside a paragraph or other block-level container, and it doesn't start a new paragraph automatically.

To make an image appear as a separate paragraph, enclose it within the paragraph element, like this:

```
<P>
<IMG
SRC="http://www.emf.net/~estephen/images/turtleshirt.jpg">
</P>
```

If you have an image in the same directory as your HTML file, you can abbreviate the URL and use a tag like this:

```
<IMG SRC="turtleshirt.jpg">
```

This inserts an image called turtleshirt.jpg on a page, but it will work only if the turtleshirt.jpg file exists in the same directory as the HTML file.

TIP

Many Web authors like to keep their images together in one (or more) subdirectories, such as images, separate from their HTML files. This practice helps keep images organized. If you decide to do this, you can use a tag such as <IMG SRC="images/turtleshirt.jpg"> to refer to your image files.

For the first part of this chapter, don't worry too much about the format of image files or how you create them. For now, just remember that most graphical browsers can only display images if they are in a particular format. The two most popular image formats are GIF and JPEG (with the .gif and .jpg file extensions respectively). We'll learn more about these two image formats later in this chapter, as well as a newer image format called PNG.

USING IMAGE ELEMENT ATTRIBUTES

In this section, we'll expand on the possibilities of the <IMG> tag and see how its attributes work. The <IMG> tag's attributes are principally intended to tell a browser how the page should be laid out with the image so that text can flow properly around the image.

WARNING

Since HTML is about structure and not presentation, the HTML 4.0 specification recommends you use style sheets to control an image's appearance on a page, instead of using <IMG> appearance attributes. (See Chapter 16 for information on style sheets.)

Describing Images with Alternate Text

You should always use two attributes with any <IMG> tag: the SRC and ALT attributes, both of which are required. The ALT attribute is used to describe the image in some way. For any browser that isn't displaying images, the alternate text contained inside the ALT attribute is displayed instead. Here's an example of an image element using alternate text:

```
<IMG SRC="images/mickeymouse.jpg" ALT="Mickey Mouse">
```

If you use this tag, browsers can display the words "Mickey Mouse" instead of displaying an image of Walt Disney's famous rodent.

Here are five reasons why a browser would use the alternate text instead of the image itself:

▶ The browser is text-only and can't display images. If there is no ALT attribute in the <IMG> tag, a text-only browser like Lynx will display the word "[INLINE]" on the screen instead of the image itself. However, if alternate text is present, Lynx displays the alternate text in place of the image.

▶ The browser is programmed to read aloud the alternate text instead of displaying an image. In this way, the ALT attribute can explain your image to blind surfers or surfers who are using a speaking machine.

▶ The person using the browser has chosen not to display images. Since images are often large files that are slow to display, many people surf with their browser set to *not* Auto Load Images or View Pictures. Instead, browsers show an empty frame as a placeholder for the image, and the alternate text is displayed inside the frame (see Figure 10.1).

▶ Navigator and Internet Explorer display an image's alternate text while the image is being loaded.

WARNING

Some people use alternate text such as "Please switch on images" or "Please wait for this image to load." These descriptions don't actually describe the image, and they make assumptions about what browser is being used.

▶ Finally, Internet Explorer 4 and 5 as well as Navigator 4 display the alternate text as a tool tip whenever you point your mouse cursor at the image for a few seconds. (If the <IMG> tag has an advisory TITLE attribute, that's shown instead.)

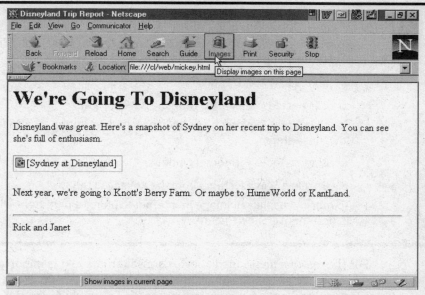

FIGURE 10.1: Navigator puts the alternate text for this image in a frame, with an icon to show there's an image not being displayed.

TURNING OFF IMAGES

Images load slowly. To surf quickly (and avoid advertising banners in the process), set your browser so it doesn't automatically display images.

To set Navigator 4 not to load images automatically, follow these steps:

1. Select Edit ➢ Preferences.

2. Choose the Advanced category.

3. Deselect Automatically Load Images. (For Navigator 3, you can use the Options ➢ Auto Load Images command.)

To quickly display all the images on a page, click on the Images button on the Navigation toolbar. To display an individual image, choose Show Image from the image's context menu. (To see a context menu, right-click the image on a PC or hold down the mouse button on a Mac.)

CONTINUED ➡

To tell Internet Explorer 4 not to display images automatically, follow these steps:

1. Choose View ➤ Options.

2. Deselect Show Pictures from the Advanced tab.

To tell Internet Explorer 5 not to display images automatically, follow these steps:

1. Choose Tools ➤ Internet Options.

2. Deselect Show Pictures from the Advanced tab.

To quickly display an image in Internet Explorer 4 or 5, right-click it, and choose Show Picture.

For the reasons mentioned above, using alternate text is important. Fortunately, it's an easy task: just put a meaningful description as the attribute value for ALT for every image (except for purely decorative images).

TIP

Some HTML style guides recommend using empty alternate text for purely decorative images (that is, putting nothing within the quotes for the alternate text: ALT=" "). We agree, unless the image is being used as an anchor for a link, as we describe in "Using Images As Links" later in this chapter. Using nonexistent alternate text means that users of text-only or text-to-speech browsers, for example, won't be distracted by your page's decorative borders.

Here are some guidelines to follow when describing an image with alternate text:

▸ Put brackets around the description (for example, ALT="[Me at age 12.]") to distinguish the description from regular text.

▸ Leave off the words "image" or "picture." It's better to describe the image itself rather than its media. "[President Lincoln at the White House]" is a more compact and useful description than "[Image of President Lincoln at the White House]".

▶ Don't be too vague. For example, don't use `ALT="[Company Logo]"` for your company logo. Instead, use `ALT="[RadCo Spinning R Logo]"`.

▶ Remember that text-only and speech browsers place the alternate text wherever the image occurs in a sentence. So, be sure your alternate text is clear in context. "Another excellent Web site from [Picture of a Tree] [Company Logo]" will raise some eyebrows.

▶ Use the alternate text to duplicate the image's purpose. If you use an image of a yellow star next to several items in a list, don't use `ALT="Pretty yellow star"` but instead use `ALT="*"`. For the alternate text for an image of a decorative horizontal line, try `ALT="------------"`.

▶ Alternate text can subtly present two different versions of a page. If you've used `ALT="[New!]"` for a "new" icon, you can then explain at the top of your page, "New information is denoted by `<IMG SRC="new.jpg" ALT="[New!]">`." Users with graphics will see your new icon in the explanation; but users without graphics will also see an explanation that correctly matches their view of your page.

▶ Some art sites place copyright information along with the image's description; other sites put secret messages in an image's alternate text.

▶ You can use entities (such as `&copy;`) in alternate text.

▶ For full compatibility, keep your alternate text on one unbroken line of your document since some browsers have problems with a carriage return in the middle of the alternate text.

You can't use tags inside `ALT` text, so `ALT="[I'm <EM>beating</EM> Hemingway at wrestling]"` is not valid. However, the `<IMG>` tag, including the alternate text, is subject to whatever elements it's nested within. To make your alternate text bold, enclose the `<IMG>` tag within `<B>` and `</B>` tags, for example:

```
<B><IMG SRC="new.jpg" ALT="[New!]"></B>
```

Now that we've seen the use of alternate text, the next attribute we'll discuss determines how images are aligned on a page.

Part II

Placing Images with Alignment Attributes

When you align images with an alignment attribute (ALIGN), there are two entirely separate results:

- Inline images occur in the middle of a line of text. If the image is a large one, then the line becomes very tall, and a lot of white space will appear.

- Floating images cause text to wrap around the image. Images can either be left-aligned or right-aligned. The paragraph will flow around the image for several lines, if the image is large.

The two different behaviors are caused by choosing the attribute value for ALIGN. We'll discuss the values for inline images first, then floating images.

WARNING

Using ALIGN to place images is not recommend by HTML 4.0, since alignment is a presentational feature, not a structural feature. Instead, HTML 4.0 recommends using style sheets (see Chapter 16).

Aligning Inline Images

To align an image in a line, choose one of the following attributes for the image element:

```
ALIGN="TOP"
ALIGN="MIDDLE"
ALIGN="BOTTOM"
```

The default behavior is ALIGN="BOTTOM", which means that the bottom of an image will align with the bottom of the line of text. By choosing ALIGN="TOP" you request that the browser display the top of your image so that it aligns with the top of the line of text. (This will push down the next line of text.) Similarly, by choosing ALIGN="MIDDLE" the browser will align the middle of the image with the middle of the line of text. Figure 10.2 shows an image aligned to the middle of its line of text.

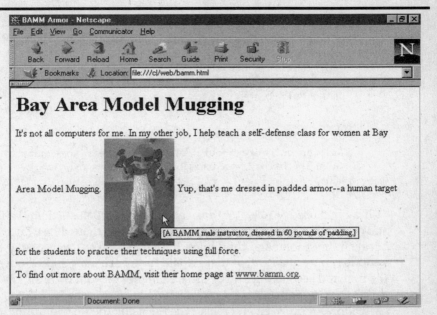

FIGURE 10.2: The middle of an image (shown here in Navigator) is aligned to the middle of the second line of text. The first and last line are pushed apart by the image. (Notice the alternate text appearing as a tool tip.)

The HTML code that produces the image in Figure 10.2 is fairly simple.

Listing 10.1:   bamm.html

```
<!DOCTYPE HTML PUBLIC "-//W3C//DTD HTML 4.0//EN">
<HTML LANG="EN">
 <HEAD>
  <TITLE>BAMM Armor</TITLE>
 </HEAD>
 <BODY>
  <H1>Bay Area Model Mugging</H1>
  <P>
  It's not all computers for me. In my other job, I help
  teach a self-defense class for women at Bay Area Model
  Mugging.
```

```
<IMG SRC="http://www.emf.net/~estephen/sbamm.jpg"
ALIGN="middle"
ALT="[A BAMM male instructor, dressed in 60 pounds of
padding.]">
Yup, that's me dressed in padded armor—a human
target for the students to practice their techniques
using full force.
</P>
<HR>
<P>
To find out more about BAMM, visit their home page at
<a href="http://www.bamm.org/">www.bamm.org</a>.
</BODY>
</HTML>
```

If we had used ALIGN="TOP" instead of ALIGN="MIDDLE", then the first and second lines would be next to each other and there'd be a large space between the second and third lines. If we had used ALIGN="BOTTOM" (or no ALIGN attribute at all), then there would have been a big space between the first and second lines. (Try these examples on your own; simply make the change to the ALIGN attribute in your editor, save the HTML file, switch to your browser, and reload the file using the Reload button.)

Creating Floating Images

To make an image "float" to the left or right side and cause paragraphs to wrap around the image, choose one of the following two attribute values for the ALIGN attribute:

```
ALIGN="LEFT"
ALIGN="RIGHT"
```

Choosing LEFT or RIGHT as the value for ALIGN causes the image to be placed directly against the left or right margin. Text after the <IMG> tag will flow around the image. Shown here is the result of taking the code we used in the previous section and using ALIGN="RIGHT" as the alignment attribute:

Bay Area Model Mugging

It's not all computers for me. In my other job, I help teach a self-defense class for women at Bay Area Model Mugging. Yup, that's me dressed in padded armor--a human target for the students to practice their techniques using full force.

To find out more about BAMM, visit their home page at www.bamm.org.

This result might not be quite what we desire, so let's move the <IMG> tag up to the beginning of the first paragraph. Here's the result:

Bay Area Model Mugging

It's not all computers for me. In my other job, I help teach a self-defense class for women at Bay Area Model Mugging. Yup, that's me dressed in padded armor--a human target for the students to practice their techniques using full force.

To find out more about BAMM, visit their home page at www.bamm.org.

One drawback to this result is that the horizontal rule (from the <HR> tag) and the last paragraph are next to the picture. We might want to push these items down so they're below the image. In Chapter 7, we mentioned that the line-break element has attributes that can be used to clear the margin. The line-break element is simply the <BR> tag. By itself, the <BR> tag won't do what we want (it will just create a single blank line that wouldn't be big enough to push the horizontal rule below the image). But if we use the CLEAR attribute and the appropriate margin value, then the horizontal rule and the last paragraph will be forced down below the image. Since the image is on the right margin, we want to use a <BR CLEAR="RIGHT"> tag (placed immediately before the <HR> tag or before the </P> tag). Shown here is the effect of the line-break element with a CLEAR attribute:

Bay Area Model Mugging

It's not all computers for me. In my other job, I help teach a self-defense class for women at Bay Area Model Mugging. Yup, that's me dressed in padded armor--a human target for the students to practice their techniques using full force.

To find out more about BAMM, visit their home page at www.bamm.org.

If your page has images on both the left and right sides, use <BR CLEAR="ALL"> to force the next line of text to appear below the lowest image.

Sizing an Image with WIDTH and HEIGHT Attributes

Two attributes are used with the <IMG> tag to specify an image's width and height. The WIDTH and HEIGHT attributes indicate the exact size of your image, in pixels. For example:

```
<IMG SRC="sbamm.jpg" WIDTH="109" HEIGHT="175"
ALT="[A BAMM male instructor, dressed in 60 pounds of
padding.]">
```

TIP

To find out the size of an image in pixels, you'll have to use an image utility. See the "Using Image Tools to Create and Edit Images" section later in this chapter. Or, if you have access to Navigator, choose View Image from an image's context menu—once you're viewing an image, you'll see the image's width and height in the title bar.

One overwhelming advantage to adding the height and width to an <IMG> tag is that when you do specify the image size for all of your images, browsers take a lot less time to render your page. That's because the browser can determine the layout of the page without having to retrieve each image separately to find out what size it is.

However, there are two drawbacks to specifying the height and width:

▶ The height and width are presentational attributes, so they ideally belong in a style sheet instead of in your <IMG> tag.

▶ If you have a very small image and specify its height and width, then Navigator and Internet Explorer won't be able to fit the alternate text inside the small image box for those users not displaying images.

Figure 10.3 shows the difference in Internet Explorer between setting and not setting the HEIGHT and WIDTH attributes when images aren't displayed.

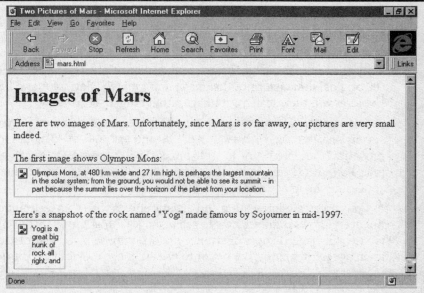

FIGURE 10.3: Internet Explorer displays a page with two image areas showing alternate text instead of the images; the first alternate text is fully displayed, but the second is cut off.

In Figure 10.3, the user has set Internet Explorer not to display images. The first image does not have its height and width specified in the HTML code, so the entire alternate text is shown. For the second image, the height and width were specified (in the <IMG> tag). If images were to be displayed, both would only be 80 pixels wide and fit the frame shown for the second image. However, since Internet Explorer allocates the specified size for the second image even when the image itself is not displayed, the alternate text cannot fit inside this small area and so it is cut off by Internet Explorer. (Navigator does the same thing, but displays none of the second image's alternate text at all.) Newer versions of both browsers would allow the alternate text to be seen via tool tips, but only if the mouse is pointed to the image area.

The speed advantages of setting the WIDTH and HEIGHT attributes may outweigh the two drawbacks, especially if you are not using small images with a lot of alternate text.

There's one other use of the HEIGHT and WIDTH attributes: to scale an image.

Scaling Images with WIDTH and HEIGHT Attributes

You can specify an image to have a particular height and/or width, even if the original dimensions of the image don't match. Navigator and Internet Explorer will then scale your image, stretching it accordingly.

For example, if your original image's dimensions are 50 by 50, you can specify an <IMG> tag with a WIDTH of 200 and a HEIGHT of 25. Graphical browsers (that know how to scale images) will then stretch out the image's width to quadruple the normal size, while at the same time squeezing the image's height so that it's half as tall as normal.

You can create interesting and artistic effects with this technique, but not every browser knows how to scale images. Most browsers do a poor job (leaving jagged edges or strange distortions), so if you want to resize an image permanently, it's better to use an image tool for that purpose.

By specifying a WIDTH of 350 pixels and a HEIGHT of 100 pixels, we've distorted our sample image significantly, as shown here:

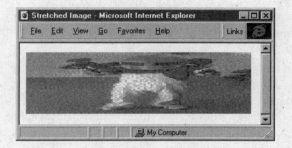

NOTE

To scale an image vertically, you can specify just the HEIGHT and leave the WIDTH automatic. Or you can scale an image horizontally by specifying the WIDTH and leaving the HEIGHT with its default value.

The HTML 4.0 specification recommends against using the HEIGHT and WIDTH attributes to scale images.

Setting an Image's Border Width

By default, no border appears around an image *unless* that image is a link (as we'll see in "Using Images As Links" a bit later in this chapter). However, you can specify a border for an image. If you use the BORDER="1" attribute in an <IMG> tag, then a thin border will appear around the image. You can specify larger values for the BORDER attribute as well.

There's no need to specify BORDER="0" for a normal image since borders do not appear by default.

WARNING

Internet Explorer 3 does not display image borders and ignores the value of BORDER, unless the image is a link.

An image border will always be colored black in Internet Explorer 4, while in Navigator it's the same color as the text color.

If you use a style sheet (see Chapter 16), you can specify whatever color you desire for image borders, and you'll have far better control over the border's appearance. This practice is preferred by the HTML 4.0 specification over BORDER attributes.

An image's border width does not count toward determining an image's height or width. So, if you specify an image to be 100 pixels wide (with WIDTH="100"), and have a border width of 10 (with BORDER="10"), then the image will take 120 pixels of horizontal space (because the border appears on both the left and right sides of the image). In addition, the image will take a few pixels more than 120 because browsers will put a small amount of space between an image and text. The amount of space allocated is determined by the HSPACE and VSPACE attributes.

Adding White Space with HSPACE and VSPACE

Internet Explorer and Navigator do not place images right next to text. Instead, they put a small margin of a few pixels in between text and an image. You can control the amount of horizontal space with the HSPACE attribute and the amount of vertical space with VSPACE attribute:

▶ The value of the HSPACE attribute sets the number of pixels of horizontal white space around the image (both left and right).

▶ The value of the VSPACE attribute sets the number of pixels of vertical white space around the image (both top and bottom).

For example, suppose we edit our bamm.html document to add 50 pixels of horizontal space around the image by putting an HSPACE="50" attribute in the <IMG> tag. Figure 10.4 shows the result.

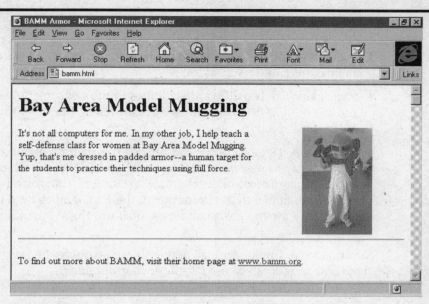

FIGURE 10.4: Internet Explorer displays 50 pixels to both the left and right of the image thanks to the HSPACE attribute.

Using Other Attributes with Images

In addition to the image attributes, HTML 4.0 allows some generic attributes that apply to almost every element, including the image element:

▶ The LANG and DIR attributes can be used to indicate what language an image's alternate text is written in, and which direction the alternate text should be displayed (either left-to-right or right-to-left).

▶ The STYLE, ID, and CLASS attributes can be used with an <IMG> tag to allow precise formatting and control over an image's appearance on a page.

▶ A new attribute, LONGDESC, points to a URL of the image's description. It is not yet supported.

▶ Several event attributes (such as ONCLICK and ONMOUSEOVER) can have a dramatic effect on images. In particular, you can use an ONMOUSEOVER attribute to change an image when someone points their mouse cursor to it. This special effect is quite common on the Web.

▶ The `<IMG>` tag takes a special attribute, NAME, when you are using an image as a button on a form.

▶ Imagemaps use two different attributes in the `<IMG>` tag: ISMAP and USEMAP. We'll see these two attributes in the "Creating Imagemaps" section.

▶ An advisory TITLE attribute can provide information about an image. Some browsers put this information in a tool tip, which would display instead of the alternate text. Since an image's advisory title is similar to its alternate text, there's not much need to use a TITLE attribute with an image. Just use the ALT attribute instead.

Now that we're familiar with all of the various attributes for images, we'll see how images can be used as the anchors for links.

USING IMAGES AS LINKS

In the discussion of linking in Chapter 1, you learned that images, as well as text, can be used as the anchor for hypertext links.

Suppose we want to make the bamm.jpg image of the self-defense instructor take us to more information about BAMM when we click on it. Instead of using a text-anchored link, we can make the image itself a link:

```
<A HREF="http://www.bamm.org/"><IMG SRC="sbamm.jpg"
ALT="[BAMM]"></A>
```

NOTE

Using alternate text for an image is even more important if that image is being used as a link. Lynx displays the image link as just the word [LINK] if there's no alternate text for the image.

You can also have both text and image in a link anchor:

```
<A HREF="http://www.bamm.org/">Find out about BAMM! <IMG
SRC="bammlogo.gif" ALT="[Bamm's Logo]"></A>
```

By default, Navigator and Internet Explorer place a blue border around image links to show that clicking the image would take you to a URL (shown in the status bar), just as with a text link. (Users of non-graphical browsers can also follow image links, provided the alternate text is present.)

The blue border placed by Navigator and Internet Explorer is normally two pixels wide. You can make the border width bigger, smaller, or non-existent by specifying a value for the BORDER attribute that we described earlier. Specifying an <IMG> tag with BORDER="0" means not to use any border at all.

WARNING

Be cautious with the use of BORDER="0". If an image isn't surrounded with the customary border showing it's a link, then most of your audience will have no idea that the image is a link and won't click it (unless the image looks like a button).

Figure 10.5 shows what happens when you set the BORDER to a large value for an image used as a link. We used the following code:

```
<A HREF="http://www.bamm.org/"><IMG SRC="sbamm.jpg"
ALIGN="right" BORDER="10" WIDTH="109" HEIGHT="175"
ALT="[A BAMM male instructor, dressed in 60 pounds of
padding.]"></A>
```

FIGURE 10.5: A wide border around this image in the link color is a strong visual clue that it's a link.

TIP

If you see an extraneous blue underlined space appearing next to your document's image links in Internet Explorer and Navigator, make sure that the </A> tag that closes the anchor is right next to the <IMG> tag and not separated by a space or carriage return.

## Part iii

CREATING IMAGEMAPS

We've just learned how clicking an image can lead to a link. Imagine if you have an image of a map of the United States, with five different branch offices of your company highlighted in different states. It would be nice if, depending on where the user clicks, they saw information about a specific branch—the California branch if they click California, or the Idaho branch if they click Idaho.

That kind of image setup is called an *imagemap*. But imagemaps don't have to be geographic maps. You can create a custom image and divide it up into whatever regions you like.

In general, an imagemap is an image that contains *hotspots,* or *active regions*. Your readers access your predefined hotspots by passing the mouse pointer over an area and then clicking the mouse. Just by passing the mouse over the hot area, the browser will usually display the URL of the hotspot in the status bar.

Imagemaps are useful for directing viewers to options in a menu bar image. You can create an image that names the major features of your Web site, and then use an imagemap to direct visitors to the appropriate place; these kinds of imagemaps are called *navigation imagemaps*.

Imagemaps were once fairly common on the Web but have become less common recently due to their drawbacks. You can always duplicate the effects of an imagemap by placing several linked images next to each other. Just make sure to set the HSPACE, VSPACE, and BORDER attributes of each image to zero, and if your images are on the same line, they'll be right next to each other, just like an imagemap.

Understanding Imagemap Types

There are two distinct kinds of imagemaps. The older type of imagemap is called a *server-side imagemap*, because a Web server is responsible for determining where each region leads when you click on the image. The newer and more efficient kind of imagemap is called a *client-side imagemap*, because a client (that is, a viewer's Web browser) determines where each region is supposed to lead when you click the image.

For both types of imagemaps, you must first create an image to use as a map. Next, divide it up into regions that lead to different URLs. For a server-side imagemap, you'll need to create a special map file and make sure that the server is set up to deal with imagemaps. For a client-side imagemap, you'll use special area and map elements.

Finally, in the image tag itself, you'll include a special attribute to indicate that the image is actually an imagemap. For a server-side imagemap, use the ISMAP attribute. For a client-side imagemap, use the USEMAP attribute with the name of a map element.

NOTE
See Chapter 1 for an example of an imagemap.

WORKING WITH IMAGE FILES

Now that we've discussed the HTML code for using images, it's time to discuss the different image formats used on the Web and how to create and edit images in those formats.

Entire books are written about creating images, and we're certainly not going to be able to tell you even a fraction of everything there is to know on this topic. However, we're certainly going to give you enough information to get you going by recommending some tools and approaches and pointing out some pitfalls to avoid.

Understanding Image Formats

Two different image formats are common on the Web: GIF and JPEG. We'll give them each a rundown, along with some less frequently seen formats.

GIF Images

GIF images (with a file extension of .gif) are the most common types of images used on the Web. *GIF* stands for Graphic Interchange Format and was developed by CompuServe (with the compression scheme patented by UNISYS) in the late 80s.

NOTE
The word "GIF" is commonly pronounced with a hard g sound like the first part of the name "Gifford," but officially it's pronounced with a soft g as if it were spelled "Jif."

GIFs are used for all types of images, but GIF is an especially good format for line drawings, icons, computer-generated images, simple cartoons, or any images with big areas of solid colors. GIFs are compact, since the GIF format uses the same "LZW" compression routine found in zip files (which is why zipping GIFs is not effective).

The biggest limitation of GIFs is that they can only contain up to 256 different colors.

There are two common varieties of GIF: GIF87A and GIF89A. The difference won't normally be important to you, but basic GIF images are GIF87A and more complicated GIFs are usually in GIF89A format. (A third variety, GIF24, was proposed by CompuServe but has never become popular.)

One particular advantage of GIF images is their flexibility, since GIF89A images can be transparent, animated, or interlaced. (These three kinds of GIFs are defined in a later section.)

JPEG Images

JPEG images used on the Web are more formally known as JPEG JFIF images, but we'll follow standard usage and just call them JPEGs. JPEGs have a file extension of `.jpg` (or less commonly `.jpeg`) and are the second most common format for images on the Web.

NOTE

The word "JPEG" is pronounced as "jay-peg." Don't bother trying to pronounce "JFIF."

JPEG stands for the Joint Photographic Experts Group, a committee organized to develop advanced image formats. JPEGs started becoming popular in 1993.

JPEG is a remarkably compact format, designed for photographs and other images without big patches of solid colors. JPEGs are *lossy*, which means that they achieve their amazing compression by eliminating data that the human eye does not perceive. When creating JPEGs, it's possible to specify an amount of lossiness. At the highest levels of lossiness, the image becomes visibly crude. At normal levels of lossiness, you probably won't be able to detect the difference between a GIF and a JPEG on screen. You'll notice the file size difference, however, since a JPEG is usually one-fourth of the size of a GIF.

The largest difference between JPEGs and GIFs is that JPEG images are always 24-bit—in other words, they allow up to 16 million different colors in an image.

JPEGs are *not* very effective for icons or logos with lots of solid colors. Both GIFs and JPEGs have their role, and it's usually not too hard to decide which format to use. You'll probably end up using a mix of both GIF and JPEG images.

The biggest limitation of JPEGs (aside from the lossiness that can accumulate if you repeatedly compress and decompress a JPEG in the process of editing it) is that they can't be transparent or animated. A special type of JPEG called "progressive JPEG" is similar to an interlaced GIF, and is discussed a little later.

WARNING

Don't convert GIFs to JPEGs without being very careful. GIFs are only 256 colors (8-bit) at most, while JPEGs use millions of colors (24-bit). If a photograph is already in GIF format, it has lost most of its color information, and may get worse if you convert it into a JPEG. To make the best JPEGs, start with a file format that has full 24-bit color information, such as a TIFF file. (TIFF files are a common format used when you scan a photograph into your computer using an image scanner.)

Other Image Formats

The only other image format that's a contender for Web popularity is the PNG format. *PNG* stands for Portable Network Graphics, and the format was devised in 1995 by the W3C and CompuServe in response to controversies over GIF licensing. PNG is superior to GIF in just about every way possible: PNGs are smaller, have more colors, and have more capabilities. But two things hamper the PNG format:

► PNG images cannot be animated images (although a companion design promises to take care of that).

► Most important, the major browsers did not support PNG at all until recently. (Navigator 4.02 still does not support PNG without a special add-on called a *plug-in*, but future versions of Navigator promise PNG support. Internet Explorer 4 supports PNG, but earlier versions do not.)

NOTE

For more information about PNG, visit the PNG home page (http://www.libpng.org/pub/png/) or see W3C's PNG information (http://www.w3.org/Graphics/PNG/Overview.html).

Several other miscellaneous image formats are used infrequently on the Web, such as TIFF (Tagged Image File Format), XBM (Portable Bitmap), BMP (Windows Bitmap), PICT (Macintosh Bitmap), CGM (Computer Graphics Metafile), and Postscript (a common printing format). *Bitmap* is simply a generic term for an image, and many bitmap formats produce huge file sizes since the images aren't compressed.

It's not worth going into much more detail about any of these formats here since they aren't very popular or well-supported on the Web.

NOTE

There's also PDF (Portable Document Format), advocated by Adobe for their Acrobat Reader.

Working with Special Image Formats

GIF images can have three special abilities: transparency (where one color of an image is invisible and reveals the background), interlacing (where the image is formatted so that it appears in stages), and animation (where two or more image frames appear in sequence). JPEGs can't be transparent or have animation, but they do feature a kind of interlacing called progressive JPEGs.

Creating Interlaced GIFs and Progressive JPEG Images

Since images are often large and therefore slow to load, it's annoying for viewers to have to wait a long time before they can see your image. Normally images load from top to bottom, a line at a time. However, if you use a special image format of GIF, you can *interlace* your image so that it loads in a mixed order of different segments instead of simply top-to-bottom. First the top line of the image appears, then every fifth line appears, on down to the bottom. Then the second line appears followed by the sixth line, and so on. Thus, the image appears in four passes. After the first pass, the viewer has a good idea of what the image will look like. The second pass adds more detail, the third pass even more detail, and the image is complete after the fourth pass.

To save your image in interlaced format, check with your image tool (we'll discuss image tools in "Using Image Tools to Create and Edit Images" later in this chapter). Usually you can select an option if you want your image interlaced. Interlacing makes your image's file size slightly larger (which makes it actually load slower), so not every image should be interlaced.

Progressive JPEGs are similar in theory to interlaced GIFs. To quote Tom Lane's JPEG frequently asked question file (or *FAQ)*, which can be found online (`http://www.cis.ohio-state.edu/hypertext/faq/usenet/jpeg-faq/top.html`), a progressive JPEG "divides the file into a series of scans. The first scan shows the image at the equivalent of a very low quality setting, and therefore it takes very little space. Following scans gradually improve the quality. Each scan adds to the data already provided so that the total storage requirement is about the same as for a baseline JPEG image of the same quality as the final scan. (Basically, progressive JPEG is just a rearrangement of the same data into a more complicated order.)"

However, progressive JPEGs are not as widely supported as interlaced GIFs. Even though most browsers now know how to display progressive JPEGs, a lot of image tools don't know how to create them.

Creating Transparent GIF Images

HTML images are always square or rectangular. However, you can create the illusion that your image is shaped differently in several ways. For example, if your page has a white background, you can create an image of a dog on a white background. The white colors will blend and it will appear as if the image is dog shaped (and it will fit better with your page).

WARNING

Not all white colors are the same. Be sure that the different whites match. A true white has an RGB value of #FFFFFF (which is equivalent to the decimal values of 255, 255, 255 for red, green, and blue). Some image tools use decimal values, others use hexadecimal values.

An image with a white background does not match with a page with a gray background. If you assume that your background page color is white, you might end up with an ugly result if your page's background ends up a different color, such as the old default of gray. If that happens, you'll end up with the white and gray background color clash shown in Figure 10.6.

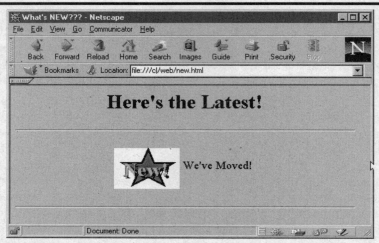

FIGURE 10.6: The "New!" image has a white background, while the page has a default gray background (common for users who haven't customized the default background color).

WARNING

You can't guarantee that your page's background will always be displayed with the color you select. Many surfers will override the default document color with their own preferences, particularly if they have vision problems or are color-blind. Therefore the background color of your images might not match the background color of your page.

When you have specified a background color or image for your page, you'll often want to ensure that the page background shows through the background parts of an image. The only way to do this is to make a transparent image. A transparent image has a color that has been set to be "invisible" so that whatever is behind the image shows through. Using a transparent image will save you from having to match an image's background with your page's background. Transparency is easier seen than explained, so examine Figure 10.7, which shows a transparent image compared to its non-transparent counterpart.

FIGURE 10.7: Two "New!" images on a cloud background; the color white in the left-hand image is transparent (allowing the cloud background to show through), and the right-hand image is not transparent.

NOTE

The techniques for making GIFs transparent vary wildly from program to program, but only GIF89A format GIFs can have a transparent color—so make sure you're saving in the right format. Check your image tool's Help program and try searching for "Transparent" to find out how transparency works in your program.

Some image tools can only make transparent GIFs if the transparent color is black or white, while other image tools let you make any color transparent. However, only one color can be transparent. JPEGs cannot have a transparent color, and PNGs allow more complex types of transparency than GIFs.

TIP

An excellent Web site that can help you with your GIFs is Gif Wizard (http://www.gifwizard.com/).

Creating Animated GIF Images

One type of image really jumps out on the Web: animated GIFs. An *animated GIF* is a series of two or more normal GIF images that have been combined into one file and are displayed by the browser frame by frame in the same space. This creates the illusion of animation.

Animated GIFs are popular because they don't require special software or a complicated program to display an animation. Any graphical browser from Navigator 2 or Internet Explorer 2 on will show animated GIFs, although early browsers did have glitches. (The newer versions of Navigator and Internet Explorer allow you to switch off animation.)

WARNING

Some surfers become annoyed and distracted by animated images. Use them sparingly. Certain animated GIFs are in widespread use (such as the spinning globe or the animated mailbox), and using one of them on your page is cliché.

To create an animated GIF, you'll need to first create each frame of the animation as a separate image. Then, you use a special image tool to combine the images together and set the amount of delay between each frame.

Animating an image is a special art, and an exhaustive review of the technique is beyond the scope of this book. However, we'll list several GIF animation tools in the next section on image tools; each of the packages we mention will come with sufficient documentation to get you started.

Using Image Tools to Create and Edit Images

When it comes time to add an image to your page, you have two choices: either create your own images, or use and edit existing images. You'll also probably want to edit your images for different reasons (such as to change a color scheme, modify a design, or convert from one format to another).

No matter what you're doing with an image, you'll need an image tool. Though there are numerous image tools to choose from, you're already equipped with a fairly capable one: your browser at least knows how to display images in several different formats, and it can also save images you see on the Web.

Though we're not going to go into a lot of detail on the different image tools, we will take a brief look at some broad categories of image tools and name the major players.

Image Applications

Most people have heard of the popular image applications. The application that's probably mentioned most often is Photoshop, sold by Adobe. Photoshop was designed, as its name implies, to edit photographs. It features many advanced tools for creating and editing images (not just photographs), but it may not be as easy to use Photoshop to create logos and images as other tools; for example, there's no simple way to create a circle in Photoshop, and its text tools are not sophisticated. However, Photoshop's capabilities can be extended through the use of plug-ins.

If you use Photoshop and want to work with more powerful text-editing features, you can give Extensis' PhotoTools plug-in a try. Visit their home page (`http://www.extensis.com/`) to download a trial version.

Photoshop is, unfortunately, extremely expensive. However, its powerful filters can apply professional effects to your images (just be careful not to overuse the "lens flare" filter, for example).

Illustrator is another expensive and powerful application sold by Adobe that's often used to create graphics. Illustrator's emphasis is more on creating images than Photoshop. However, both Photoshop and Illustrator are two of the more complicated applications in existence, and both will take you some time to learn.

Photoshop and Illustrator are both available for Windows PCs, Macintoshes, and Unix systems. More information is available from Adobe's Web site (`http://www.adobe.com/`).

For Windows users, Paint Shop Pro is a popular shareware program used to edit and create images. Created and distributed by Jasc, Inc., more information and the shareware package can be found on their home page (`http://www.jasc.com/`).

ClarisDraw (sold by Apple's Claris Corporation) is an easy-to-use image application for Macintosh and Windows users. You can read more about it at Claris' home page (`http://www.claris.com/`).

CorelDRAW and related software packages are also popular image applications. Find out more from Corel's home page (`http://www.corel.com/`).

In addition, Deneba (`http://www.deneba.com/`) sells the popular Canvas application for Windows and Macintosh users, and for the Macintosh, UltraPaint can be purchased for under $20.

TIP

Microsoft FrontPage and some other HTML editors come with image editors. Most of the recent versions of FrontPage ship with the Microsoft Image Composer, which is a capable image tool. FrontPage itself can be a handy image tool, since it can make images transparent with a click of a button.

You may be able to adapt your existing applications' drawing capabilities. Popular word processors such as WordPerfect and Microsoft Word have drawing tools, and Microsoft PowerPoint (normally used to create business presentations) may be able to handle your image needs. The main issue involved in using these tools is their inability to save the images in a useful Web format.

On the low end, you can always create images with a drawing program that may have been provided free with your operating system (such as the Paint program that comes with Windows). However, these simple drawing programs don't have a lot of features and often don't save files in GIF or JPEG format (so you'll have to use a utility or conversion tool before you can add your drawings to your Web pages).

The image applications usually know how to convert images fairly effectively, but aren't really optimized for creating images in GIF or JPEG formats (Photoshop especially). For that, you should check out an image utility.

Image Utilities and Conversion Tools

A large number of popular utilities are available; most of these utilities are shareware and can be downloaded from the Web. All of these utilities can display images quickly, and convert images between GIF and JPEG formats as well as other popular image formats (some of the tools are solely designed for converting images from one format to another).

Most of these utilities can also make simple and complex transformations to an image, such as changing an image's size, orientation, color, contrast, and rotation. Some of these utilities can handle more advanced editing, such as rearranging the image and changing the number of colors.

NOTE

The process of reducing the number of colors in an image is called *dithering*, and it's usually wise to get a utility that's good at dithering if you want to convert a 24-bit image into GIF format.

For Windows, popular image utilities include LView Pro, WinGIF, ACDSee, and PolyView. One popular commercial image utility is HiJaak Pro.

For Macintosh, check out DeBabelizer, JPEGView, GIFConverter, GraphicConverter, Giffer, and GifBuilder.

GIF Animators

The best-known GIF animator is Alchemy Mindwork's GIF Construction Set (available as shareware from http://www.mindworkshop.com/). This package is a little unconventional, but it contains everything you need to animate images, including an animation wizard to guide you through the process. It's a capable image utility as well, and it includes several shortcuts for creating animated images, such as a scrolling marquee image with a message you specify or a special transition between two images.

Other GIF animators include Microsoft's free (for now) Microsoft GIF Animator, as well as PhotoImpact GIF Animator, Animagic, VideoCraft, and WebImage.

Creating Images

Creating images is difficult work and requires a lot of time and energy—not to mention talent. There's no shortage of graphic designers and design firms who would be happy to design a coordinated series of images for you.

If you do create images yourself for your Web sites, you should use the best image tool available to you. Take the time to fully learn how your tool or application works (finish the online tutorials and look into computer training classes) and find out what it's capable of. Scour the Web for inspiration in the form of design ideas and fresh approaches—don't always rely on the drop shadows and neon effects that are so commonplace.

Part II

TIP

If you're creating a simple image, it's often best to work on a version that's much larger than what you intend as your final size, and then rescale your work down to your desired size.

The easiest type of image for most people to create is a photograph. Using either a conventional camera or a newer digital camera, you can take a wide variety of photographs to help illustrate your page. You can scan in photographs or have them developed onto CD-ROM and then converted into JPEG format. However, an amateur photograph with ineffective lighting or poor composition will hamper your page as much as a crudely drawn image will.

TIP

When you create images, decide if you're designing for 256 colors or 24-bit color. If you're using 256 colors, try to see if your application has a Web-compatible palette of colors that won't dither—that is, colors that will be displayed as solids that resemble the colors you intend. Visit the browser-safe palette page (http://www.lynda.com/hex.html) for a tutorial on the 216 "safe" colors and to pick up a Web palette for Photoshop.

If you're good at illustrating on paper (or know someone who is), then buy or rent a scanner to convert paper illustrations into computer files. (You can also find scanners at many copy stores and find scanning services in the Yellow Pages. Some scanners are sold with bundled image applications, such as Photoshop.)

However, if (like most of us) you're no artist, then it's time to consider using existing images.

Using Existing Images

You can take existing images and use them on your Web pages in several ways. Here are some methods:

Legacy material   Perhaps your organization has some image material that you can use (such as logos, street maps, slide presentations, or previously commissioned material) once you convert it into the correct format.

Clip art collections There are a large number of commercial and shareware packages of clip art and stock photographs that are licensed for nonprofit use on your Web pages. (Check the license of the package carefully before using a clip art image on your Web site.)

Public domain material Certain illustrations and images are public domain and can be included on your Web page once you find (and convert if necessary) the image. However, be careful since most images are copyrighted and are not in the public domain.

Freely licensed material Many companies create special images and logos (also known as *badges* or *banners*) for the express purpose of use on a Web page when you link to that company. For example, Netscape freely licenses the ubiquitous "Netscape Now" image that many people use to link to Netscape's site.

TIP

Check a site that you want to link to and see if they have a logo page that explains their licensing and linking policies. Using a badge to link to a company is free advertising for them, so think twice before you send your audience away to their site.

Freeware collections and libraries There are a number of collections of images (such as background images and common icons) where the artist has relinquished copyright or allows you to use their images on your Web pages with no restrictions (or sometimes simply in exchange for author credit and a link back to their site).

NOTE

Here are several freeware image collections of links (aside from the ones you can find at Yahoo!): Clipart.com (http://www.clipart.com/), Clip Art Review (http://www.webplaces.com/html/clipart.htm), and Gini Schmitz's "Cool Graphics on the Web" (http://www.fishnet.net/~gini/cool/index.html).

Material that you may use after you buy a license Many
Web artists display images in their online galleries and will sell
an inexpensive image license. If you see an image that you wish
to use on a Web page, it doesn't hurt to inquire if it is available
for licensing.

WARNING
In the early days of the Web, fan sites used copyrighted material (like images
of U2 album covers or pictures of Star Trek characters) unchecked. These days,
corporate crackdowns on illegally used copyrighted material are common. You
must assume that any image you see is copyrighted unless there is a specific
statement to the contrary. U.S. copyright law grants copyright protection even
if there is no explicit copyright statement.

It's all too easy to see an image, background, or icon that you like and
save it to your hard drive. (Using Navigator or Internet Explorer, all you
have to do is use the save command on the image's context menu—right-
click the image on the PC, or hold down the mouse button over an image
with a Mac.) Once the image is saved on your hard drive, you can edit it
and include it on your Web pages with little difficulty. However, just
because you *can* use other people's images on your Web pages does not
mean it's legal to do so. In general, this practice is quite widespread—and
also quite immoral. Using another person's copyrighted work without
their permission is a crime. (There are exceptions to copyright law for fair
use or parody, but we're not lawyers, so you're on your own to determine
what's fair use and parody.)

NOTE
It's considered bad manners to include an <IMG> tag or BACKGROUND attribute
that links to another site's image without their permission. You're just using
their work without giving them credit. (Whether this practice is actually illegal
hasn't been settled.)

If you own the material or if your license allows it, use the image tools
we described earlier to modify existing images for your own purposes.
Add your company name to a stock photograph of the Golden Gate
Bridge, or change the contrast of the Mona Lisa and add your logo to
replace her head. Be creative above all else, by trying things you *haven't*
seen on other Web sites. The more unique your images are, the more

likely your site will stand out. Our best advice is to start experimenting with images and practicing to feel comfortable with them.

WHAT'S NEXT?

The knowledge you've gained in this chapter will serve you well as you begin to use images to diversify the content of your Web site. The next chapter will allow you to apply your knowledge of design, color, and images to the process of laying out your page. We'll take a close look at using HTML to create tables. We'll tell you how to organize your data with tables, discuss the different methods for creating them, and show you how to use tables to effectively display your Web site's content to the world.

Chapter 11

PRESENTING INFORMATION IN TABLES

In this chapter, you'll learn a variety of ways to present your Web page data in table format. We'll cover all of the elements and attributes for tables in detail so you can become a master at using tables.

Adapted from *HTML 4.0: No experience required*, by E. Stephen Mack and Janan Platt Saylor

ISBN 0-7821-2143-8   704 pages $29.99

You'll learn about the advantages—and the limitations—to using tables. We'll show you many useful examples so you can learn how to create tables that organize your data. We'll also show you different ways you can use tables to enhance the layout of the text on your page. Tables are extremely popular on the Web because they are a flexible and attractive way of presenting information.

UNDERSTANDING THE USE OF TABLES

HTML tables mark up data that should be organized in a table structure, instead of in paragraphs or other block-level structures. With tables, you can present data organized in rows and columns. For example, two types of data that can easily be organized into a table structure are yesterday's high and low temperatures by city (see Table 11.1).

TABLE 11.1: Yesterday's Weather

CITY	HIGH	LOW	WIND
Alameda	70	53	south
Bakersfield	83	54	south
Barstow	93	65	south
Beaumont	89	52	west
Big Bear	72	40	south

Even though this isn't an HTML table, it's a good illustration of the concept of a table, and we can use it to establish some vocabulary:

▶ The *caption* is an optional description of the table. In Table 11.1, the caption is "Yesterday's Weather."

▶ A table's *rows* are the horizontal lines of data. Table 11.1 has six rows, starting with the "City" row and ending with the "Big Bear" row.

▶ The *columns* are the vertical lines of data. There are four columns in this example, starting with "City" and ending with "Wind."

▶ Each piece of data is at the intersection of a column and a row, and these intersections are called *cells*. Since there are six rows and four columns, Table 11.1 has 24 cells.

▶ Finally, the first four cells ("City," "High," "Low," and "Wind") show labels for the type of information in each column. These special cells are called *headings*.

Figure 11.1 shows how Internet Explorer would display the Yesterday's Weather table if it were created in HTML code. (We'll see the actual HTML code used to create this table in the "Creating an Example Table" section a little later.)

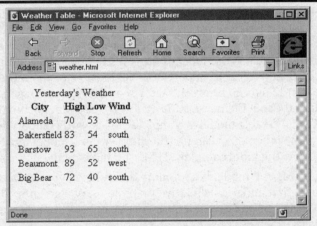

FIGURE 11.1: An HTML table showing yesterday's weather by city

NOTE

Tables are sometimes used for general page layout—for example, to organize paragraphs into columns or to create margins. This has varying results, depending on which browser is used to view your pages. We'll talk about "Using Tables as a Layout Tool" later in this chapter, and we'll see some reasons why this is discouraged.

When you create a table in HTML, you'll use the table element. The table element starts with the <TABLE> tag and ends with a </TABLE> tag; in order to create a table, you'll need to understand the rules of what elements should appear between these two tags.

Understanding Table Models

The rules of which elements occur in a table (and in what order) is called a *table model*.

In this chapter, we'll present two important table models in HTML. Originally created by Netscape and later adopted by the W3C, the HTML 3.2 table model uses a fairly simple set of elements, and it has resulted in a widespread use of tables. Tables have become fully supported in all recent versions of Navigator, Internet Explorer, Mosaic, and Lynx. Text-to-speech browsers and older versions of Lynx have trouble dealing with tables, however.

HTML 4.0 expands on the older, simple table model with new elements and attributes while still remaining compatible with the earlier table model. The main difference is that HTML 4.0 allows rows and columns to be grouped together and introduces several useful new attributes for alignment and cell borders. HTML 4.0's table model is designed to make tables richer, easier to import from spreadsheets, and more accessible to text-to-speech browsers. We'll see other differences in the "Using HTML 4.0 Table Elements and Attributes" section. Fortunately, since the HTML 4.0 table model is completely backward-compatible with HTML 3.2's table model, you can use the simpler table model most of the time and only use the more complex HTML 4.0 table model if necessary.

Since the HTML 4.0 model is a lot more difficult, we're going to learn the older model first and see its relatively simple set of elements. Then we'll talk about the new HTML 4.0 table model after we've fully understood the basics of tables.

Introducing the Simple Table Model and Its Elements

We will discuss four elements of the simple table model:

- ▶ The optional caption element consists of the <CAPTION> and </CAPTION> tags containing the table's description.

- ▶ The table row element (<TR> for "table row," with an optional </TR> end tag) creates a horizontal row of cells and contains the table headings and table data.

- ▶ The table data element uses the <TD> ("table data") tag (with an optional </TD> end tag) to create each individual cell. (The number of cells in a row determines how many columns will be displayed by the browser, so there is no separate element for table columns in the simple HTML table model.)

▶ The table heading (<TH> for "table heading" and optionally </TH>) element creates the heading cells.

We'll discuss each of these new elements in more detail later in this chapter, and we'll learn about their attributes and capabilities. For now, the next section will show these four elements in action by showing some code for our example table.

Creating an Example Table

Study the following HTML code to see how Figure 11.1 was created. To create this example on your own, type the code into your text editor and save it as `weather.html`, or visit the Sybex Web site to download the code.

NOTE
To get to Sybex's Web page for the book from which this chapter came, go to http://www.sybex.com/, click Catalog, and click the No Experience Required category. Then navigate to the *HTML: No Experience Required* page. Click the Download button to download this code.

Listing 11.1:   weather.html

```
<!DOCTYPE HTML PUBLIC "-//W3C//DTD HTML 4.0//EN">
<HTML LANG="EN">
<HEAD>
      <TITLE>Weather Table</TITLE>
</HEAD>
<BODY>

<TABLE>
    <!-- This is the table's caption. -->
    <CAPTION>
        Yesterday's Weather
    </CAPTION>

    <!-- This is the first row of the table. -->
    <TR>
        <TH>City</TH>
        <TH>High</TH>
        <TH>Low</TH>
        <TH>Wind</TH>
        <!-- Each of these four words is marked as a heading.
-->
```

Part II

```
        </TR>

        <!-- This is the second row of the table. -->
        <TR>
            <TD>Alameda</TD>
            <TD>70</TD>
            <TD>53</TD>
            <TD>south</TD>
            <!-- Each of these pieces of information is a cell,
    or "table data." -->
        </TR>

        <TR>
            <TD>Bakersfield</TD>
            <TD>83</TD>
            <TD>54</TD>
            <TD>south</TD>
        </TR>

        <TR>
            <TD>Barstow</TD>
            <TD>93</TD>
            <TD>65</TD>
            <TD>south</TD>
        </TR>

        <TR>
            <TD>Beaumont</TD>
            <TD>89</TD>
            <TD>52</TD>
            <TD>west</TD>
        </TR>

        <!-- This is the sixth and final row of the table.-->
        <TR>
            <TD>Big Bear</TD>
            <TD>72</TD>
            <TD>40</TD>
            <TD>south</TD>
        </TR>

    </TABLE>
    </BODY>
    </HTML>
```

In this example, we've used indentations and comments to make this code easily comprehensible. We've also used the </TR>, </TD>, and </TH>

closing tags for clarity. These end tags are optional, and their absence shouldn't affect the table's appearance or function. (The </TABLE> end tag is always required.)

You'll see some HTML authors code table rows this way:

```
<TABLE>
<TR><TD>Beaumont<TD>89<TD>52<TD>west
<TR><TD>Big Bear<TD>72<TD>40<TD>south
</TABLE>
```

However, you may find this method a little harder to follow and edit.

TIP

Older browsers (more than two years old) won't understand these table model elements at all. They will display all of the table data from the above sample in one big block—without any spaces at all. If you put a carriage return between each table cell when you're typing the HTML source document, then older browsers will at least put a space between each piece of data, which is better than nothing. (If you put a <P> tag in the first cell of each row, then each row will appear on a separate line on older browsers, which will help out even more.)

Our example table does not have a border or any gridlines. We can use the BORDER attribute of the <TABLE> tag to cause a line to appear around each cell. By adding this one word to the <TABLE> tag, you can dramatically change the visual appearance of your table, as Figure 11.2 shows. (We'll see more about the BORDER attribute in the "Creating Border Lines with the BORDER Attributes" section.)

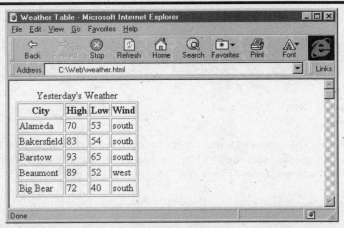

FIGURE 11.2: The same weather table now has a border. Notice that the caption appears outside the border.

You can use a table to highlight a particular paragraph with a border. Here's the HTML code for a one-celled table with a border:

```
<!DOCTYPE HTML PUBLIC "-//W3C//DTD HTML 4.0//EN">
<HTML LANG="EN">
<HEAD>
        <TITLE>Boxing "Hello, World"</TITLE>
</HEAD>
<BODY>
    <TABLE BORDER>
        <TR>
            <TD>
                Hello, World!
            </TD>
        </TR>
    </TABLE>
</BODY>
</HTML>
```

Figure 11.3 shows how Navigator renders this one-celled table with borders turned on.

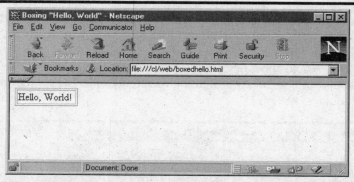

FIGURE 11.3: A bordered, one-celled table rendered in Navigator

TIP

You may have noticed a small space between the exclamation point and the border. This is a consequence of putting the </TD> tag on the following line. To avoid that space, use <TD>Hello, World!</TD> on one line.

WARNING

Using a table for a boxed-paragraph effect can bring special attention to an important paragraph; however, the paragraph really doesn't belong in a table since it's not a table of information. Also, not every browser can display tables, so you will want to use an additional method of highlighting the paragraph, such as the strong element (which causes a paragraph to appear in bold or be read aloud with more emphasis, depending on the browser). If your only goal is to get a border around a paragraph, style sheets are better suited to that task. (Chapter 16 discusses style sheets.)

The smallest table you can make has only one cell (that is, one row and one column), but there's no limit to how large you can make your tables. Although HTML does not impose any theoretical limits on how many rows or cells you can have, in practicality, use more than 10 columns and you'll probably force the table to be wider than the window (and a horizontal scroll bar will appear in Navigator and Internet Explorer).

The only limit to the number of columns is how wide you want your table to be; there is no limit to the number of rows you can include in a table. There is also no limit to the number of separate tables that can appear on a page.

Advantages of Tables

One of the greatest advantages of tables is that your data is much easier to read when structured properly on the page. A properly designed table gives your readers a clear and quick way to evaluate your content. A table can contain many different types of content other than just text—such as lists, forms, nested tables (tables within tables), images, pre-formatted text, and paragraphs.

NOTE

You'll learn about tables inside of other tables in the "Nesting Tables" section.

The use of a table can also break up a plain page with an interesting visual feature (an attractive table is nicer to look at than just a bunch of numbers). We'll see some examples later in this chapter.

Limitations of Tables

One of the biggest limitations to tables is the amount of time it can take to create a complex table structure. A medium-sized table's HTML code can take up several pages if hand-coded properly for readability.

Making your tables easy to read is important so the data can be updated quickly later. With so many nested tags and attributes, there's more room for error when you're coding a table than other elements. It's harder to find errors, and if one tag is left off or put in the wrong place, the entire table may not appear.

Here's where it's useful to use an HTML editor to create the repetitive bare bones of a table and to save some time. Then it's more fun to go back in and hand-code the details. We'll discuss how to use Netscape's Page Composer to create a table in the next section.

It's very tempting to try to use tables to solve a lot of your page layout challenges. First, you should consider your audience and decide whether most of your viewers will have access to browsers that can display tables (older versions of Navigator, Lynx, Internet Explorer, and Mosaic don't know how to display tables at all). Second, be careful that your HTML coding follows the HTML standards for tables that we present in this chapter, and test that both Navigator and Internet Explorer display your tables properly.

One example of using tables for layout is multiple columns of text (like the columns in a newspaper article). There's no standard HTML tag available to create multiple text columns. Web authors discovered they could duplicate the appearance of text columns in graphical browsers by using tables. Starting when Navigator 2 came out, tables were (and still are) often used (with borders turned off) to create the look of multicolumn text.

However, tables used for multiple text columns will produce extremely varied results. Web page designers might spend a long time trying to get the two columns to be exactly the same height. But this is a foolhardy quest. Internet Explorer and Navigator don't always display fonts the same way. With multiple columns created in tables, depending on the font, the automatic line breaks in Internet Explorer may not render the same way in Navigator. Also, as soon as someone resizes the browser window, the line breaks will readjust, and the bottom of the columns will probably not match, because of the relative lengths of the words in each column. Figure 11.4 shows how the bottom of two columns that were once even don't match up when we resize the Navigator window to a narrower width.

The moral here is that tables can't always be reliably used for multiple text columns, and you should be careful to check your tables with a few different browsers. This is a lesson in HTML's purpose: HTML elements are designed to indicate the structure of your document. Just because certain browsers happen to display some elements a certain way, that doesn't mean you should abuse the meaning of the tags to create a certain visual effect. If your document doesn't contain tables of data, it shouldn't have table elements.

Earlier versions of HTML had no way to change a page's layout without tables, so many Web designers (including us) ignored this advice. But now that HTML 4.0 and the new browsers are able to work with style sheets, you can always get the visual layout effects by using style sheets instead of tables. (You'll learn how in Chapter 16.)

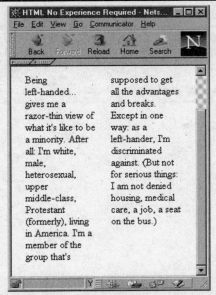

FIGURE 11.4: Navigator, with a reduced window width, renders our example of a two-column table of text in a less-than-desirable way.

CREATING A TABLE WITH NETSCAPE COMPOSER

Some versions of Netscape Communicator include not only Navigator but also an HTML page-construction tool called Page Composer (often known simply as "Composer"). If you have Composer, switch to it now (select Communicator ➤ Composer, or press Ctrl+4). We'll create the foundation for the table in Figure 11.5 and then save the file for future hand-editing.

Follow these steps to create this sample table:

1. From a new document in Composer, choose the Table button on the upper right toolbar. The New Table Properties dialog box appears.

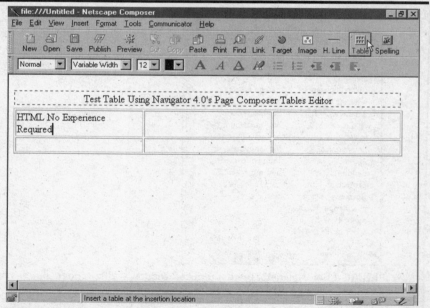

FIGURE 11.5: A simple two-row, three-column table created with the Composer table editor

2. Enter **2** in the Number Of Rows box, and type a **3** in the Number Of Columns box.

3. Click the Apply button at the bottom of the page. In the background, you should be able to see the borders of an empty six-celled table.

4. Check the Include Caption field. Click Apply, and then click Close.

5. Type **HTML No Experience Required** into the first cell. (Use the arrow keys to move between cells, or press Tab to move to the next cell.) Type **Test Table Using Navigator 4.0's Page Composer Tables Editor** inside the dotted box at the top of the table.

6. Save your file. Use the File ≻ Save command, navigate to your web directory, and save the file as table.html. Enter a sample title such as **Our Sample Table** when prompted for the page's title.

When you close Composer and switch to your regular text editor to retrieve table.html, you'll see some sample code similar to this:

```
<HTML>
<HEAD>
    <META HTTP-EQUIV="Content-Type" CONTENT="text/html;
charset=iso-8859-1">
    <META NAME="Author" CONTENT="Stephen Mack and Janan
Platt">
    <META NAME="GENERATOR" CONTENT="Mozilla/4.01 [en]
(Win95; I) [Netscape]">
    <TITLE>Our Sample Table</TITLE>
</HEAD>
<BODY>
 
<TABLE BORDER COLS=3 WIDTH="100%">
<CAPTION>Test Table Using Navigator 4.0's Page Composer
Tables Editor</CAPTION>

<TR>
<TD>HTML No Experience Required</TD>

<TD>cell 2</TD>

<TD>cell 3</TD>
</TR>

<TR>
<TD>cell 4</TD>
```

```
<TD>cell 5</TD>

<TD>and my cell 6</TD>
</TR>
</TABLE>
 
</BODY>
</HTML>
```

Notice that Composer inserts three <META> tags in the head section automatically. These three <META> tags respectively define the character set, author of the document, and which program was used. The rest of the tags are fairly self-explanatory and contain the simple table model's elements. Composer does a good job of inserting the <TABLE>, <TD>, <TR>, and <CAPTION> tags. It includes the BORDER attribute to the <TABLE> tag along with an attribute we'll see a little later, WIDTH="100%", and an advanced attribute, COLS=3, which is part of the HTML 4.0 table model that we'll see at the end of this chapter.

However, the nonbreaking spaces before and after the table (the   entity tags) are unnecessary, and it's a little strange that Composer puts them in. That's just another example of why it's important to hand-check HTML created by a page-composing tool.

It's your choice whether you want to use Composer or another page-composing tool to create a table for you. Regardless of how you start off your table, you'll probably end up coding the final parts of it by hand. For that reason, you need to know more details about the simple table model's elements and their attributes, which we'll discuss next.

Using the Simple Table Model's Elements and Attributes

The elements used in tables must all be nested within the beginning <TABLE> and ending </TABLE> tags. First we'll show you the <TABLE> tag and its attributes, and then we'll show you all of the uses of the elements that create rows, cells, headings, and captions.

Defining Tables with the Table Element

The <TABLE> start tag and the </TABLE> end tag are both required for every table you create. All of the <TABLE> tag's attributes, however, are optional.

Even with the simple table model, the tables themselves can be very simple or very complex, as we've seen. Here's an example of the HTML code for an unbordered table that has one row (within the <TR> tags), one cell (within the <TD> tags that contain the words "Hello, World!"), and no attributes:

```
<TABLE><TR><TD>Hello, World!</TD></TR></TABLE>
```

If you exclude table attributes, the table's position defaults to left alignment, with no border. So this table would simply look like regular text, as we see in Figure 11.6.

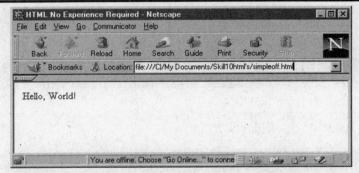

FIGURE 11.6: "Hello, World!" inside a single-celled table with no attributes; it looks exactly like normal text.

However, you can make this table appear very differently using the table element's attributes.

Using the Table Element's Attributes

By using table attributes in the <TABLE> tags, you can determine the following formatting options for your table:

- ▶ Width of the entire table
- ▶ Alignment of the entire table
- ▶ Cell borders and table border width
- ▶ Spacing between each neighboring cell
- ▶ Padding within a cell (between the cell's content and the cell border)

Let's take a look at each <TABLE> tag attribute and try out some simple examples of tables created by hand. As you're reading along, you might want to experiment with a few more sample tables yourself. It's easiest to start with a basic table, such as the weather.html example we used earlier, and try out the different attributes one at a time.

The <TABLE> tag can include any of following attributes, listed in any order: ALIGN, WIDTH, BORDER, CELLSPACING, CELLPADDING, and BGCOLOR.

We'll be discussing the BGCOLOR attribute (used to set a table's background color) a little later, in the "Coloring Parts of the Table with the BGCOLOR Attribute" section, but we'll talk about the rest of the table element's attributes in the next few sections, starting with the ALIGN attribute.

Positioning Tables with the ALIGN Attribute

There are three possible uses of the ALIGN attribute (left is the default):

```
<TABLE ALIGN="LEFT">
<TABLE ALIGN="CENTER">
<TABLE ALIGN="RIGHT">
```

The ALIGN attribute specifies the horizontal alignment of the table. This means that the table itself is aligned, not the contents of individual cells.

The weather table we saw in Figure 11.1 is shown here, except with the ALIGN ="RIGHT" attribute added:

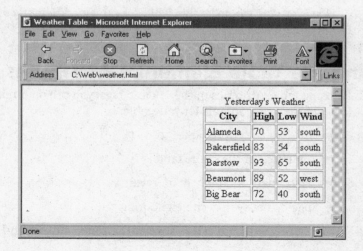

WARNING

Navigator 3 and Internet Explorer 3 both have a problem with the ALIGN= "CENTER" attribute—they ignore it. The newer versions of these browsers obey the <TABLE ALIGN="CENTER"> tag. However, there are still many users of the older versions, so if you want your table centered, you should surround it with a center or division element.

Sizing Tables with the WIDTH Attribute

There are two ways to specify the width of a table using the WIDTH attribute:

```
<TABLE WIDTH="PERCENT">
<TABLE WIDTH="NUMBER">
```

If you don't specify the width, then the table will be only as wide as absolutely necessary.

You can force a table to take up more room if you don't like the way it displays. To do this, you either set the width of the table to a percentage of the window's horizontal width (for example, WIDTH="50%"), or you set WIDTH to a fixed pixel value (with an attribute such as WIDTH="100") to make a table 100 pixels wide.

WARNING

Don't leave off the percent sign if you want a table to be a certain percent of your page. There's a *big* difference between 100 *percent* (WIDTH="100%") and 100 *pixels* (WIDTH="100").

Figure 11.7 shows examples of two tables displayed in Navigator. The first table uses the table attribute WIDTH="150%". The second table uses the table attribute WIDTH="500". You can see how the first table is 50 percent wider than the horizontal width of the window (use the horizontal scroll bar to see the rest of the table). Specifying a percentage allows your table and its contents to adjust to fit the browser window whenever it is resized.

Part ii

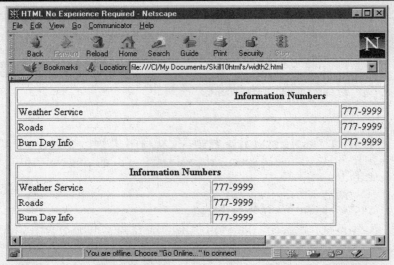

FIGURE 11.7: Navigator shows two examples of tables using the WIDTH attribute.

Creating Border Lines with the BORDER Attribute

There are two ways to use the BORDER attribute to make a table and its cells appear with lines:

```
<TABLE BORDER>
<TABLE BORDER="NUMBER">
```

Earlier, we simply used <TABLE BORDER>. The default border size, if you don't specify a value, is 1 pixel wide. So, using <TABLE BORDER> yields the same results as <TABLE BORDER="1">. Omitting the border tag or using BORDER="0" indicates no border. Really thick borders, such as <TABLE BORDER="5"> or <TABLE BORDER="10"> can produce interesting results.

WARNING

If you're using HTML 3.2, you must specify a value for the border width. Some older, but still popular, browsers get confused by <TABLE BORDER> without a value.

The border size *only* applies to the outside table border. If there is a border for your table, the inner cells will have a cell border that is always only 1 pixel thick, regardless of the setting of the BORDER attribute. There is no way to set the size of a cell's border yet.

If you specify a border of 50 pixels for the table in the weather.html example (with <TABLE BORDER="50">), you'll see a result similar to Figure 11.8.

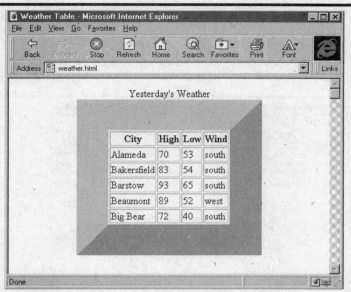

FIGURE 11.8: Your viewers won't be able to overlook this weather table with a 50-pixel border. Internet Explorer (shown here) and Navigator give a three-dimensional appearance to the border, but not every browser does so.

Spacing Cells with the CELLSPACING Attribute

You can create more space in between each cell in your table by using the table element's CELLSPACING attribute, which looks like this:

```
<TABLE CELLSPACING="NUMBER">
```

The amount of cell spacing, indicated in pixels, is the common border width around each cell. For example, specifying CELLSPACING="5" in the <TABLE> tag would space each cell apart by 5 pixels (including 5 pixels between the first cell and the outside border).

The sample HTML fragment below creates a table with a border of 5 pixels and cell spacing of 50 pixels:

```
<TABLE BORDER="5" CELLSPACING="50">
```

```
<TR>
    <TD>Sunday</TD>
    <TD>Monday</TD>
    <TD>Tuesday</TD>
</TR>
<TR>
    <TD>First</TD>
    <TD>Second</TD>
    <TD>Third</TD>
</TR>
</TABLE>
```

Figure 11.9 shows how Internet Explorer would display this table.

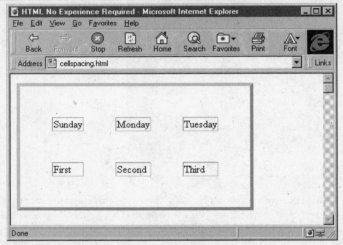

FIGURE 11.9: Internet Explorer renders a six-celled table with the cell spacing between each cell (and the spacing between each cell and the table's border) equal to 50 pixels.

The default value used by Navigator and Internet Explorer for CELLSPACING is 2. If you specify a CELLSPACING of 0, then table cells will appear right next to each other, making the border appear to be solid instead of hollow.

Making Cells Bigger with the CELLPADDING Attribute

Within each cell, the data normally appears right next to the cell's border. You can increase the amount of space in between the cell border and the cell data with the CELLPADDING attribute:

```
<TABLE CELLPADDING="NUMBER">
```

The padding between each cell border and the cell contents is indicated in pixels, for example CELLPADDING="10".

The default value for CELLPADDING used by Navigator and Internet Explorer is CELLPADDING="1", so you can squeeze each table cell down by specifying CELLPADDING="0", or you can make each cell larger by specifying a larger attribute value for CELLPADDING.

TIP

It's easy to confuse CELLSPACING and CELLPADDING. Remember, CELLSPACING determines the space *between* each cell, while cell padding determines the space *within* each cell.

Figure 11.10 shows various values for CELLPADDING in several different tables.

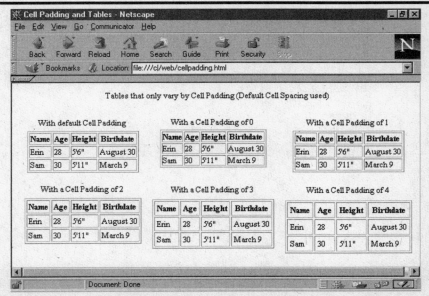

FIGURE 11.10: Six tables that only differ by how CELLPADDING is specified (shown in Navigator)

Putting All of the Table Element's Attributes Together

The following HTML code includes all of the <TABLE> tag's attributes listed previously and creates a basic table with two side-by-side cells. The left cell includes two lines of the text separated by a line break. The right cell contains one line of text.

```
<!DOCTYPE HTML PUBLIC "-//W3C//DTD HTML 4.0//EN">
<HTML LANG="EN">
<HEAD>
        <TITLE>Two Competing Philosophies</TITLE>
</HEAD>
<BODY>

<TABLE ALIGN="CENTER" WIDTH="50%" BORDER="5" CELLSPACING="10"
 CELLPADDING="5">

<TR>

<TD>
Make Love<BR>
Not War
</TD>

<TD>
Show Me The Money!
</TD>

</TR>

</TABLE>

</BODY>
</HTML>
```

Figure 11.11 shows the result of this code.

FIGURE 11.11: A simple two-column, one-row table using five table element attributes

The two-celled table contains the following effects created by attributes:

▶ The ALIGN attribute makes the table (but not the table's contents) centered on the page. (It would have been better to put <CENTER> and </CENTER> tags around the table instead.)

▶ The WIDTH attribute makes the table width equal to 50 percent of the window's horizontal width.

▶ The BORDER attribute calls for cell borders and creates an outer border equal to 5 pixels.

▶ The CELLSPACING attribute puts 10 pixels of space between the two cells, and also 10 pixels of space between each cell border and the table's outer border.

▶ The CELLPADDING attribute puts 5 pixels of space between the cell data (the words) and the cell borders.

Now that you've learned about the table element's attributes, it's time to learn more about the elements contained within the <TABLE> and </TABLE> tags. We introduced the four elements earlier in the chapter, but now we'll discuss their uses and their attributes.

Using the Simple Table Model's Elements

The following elements are all nested within the <TABLE> and </TABLE> tags. These elements create captions, table rows, table data, and table headings. Their attributes can determine a variety of formatting options for the table and its individual cells.

Describing Tables with the Caption Element

The caption element (which requires both a <CAPTION> start tag and a </CAPTION> end tag) is used to create a caption on top of (the default) or below the table. This positioning is specified with the caption element's ALIGN attribute:

```
<CAPTION ALIGN="TOP">
<CAPTION ALIGN="BOTTOM">
```

As we've seen, the caption is displayed outside of the table's border. A caption will not make a table wider; instead, the contents of the caption element wrap within the available space (which will make the table taller).

NOTE

HTML 4.0 allows you to specify ALIGN="LEFT" and ALIGN="RIGHT" for the caption, to place it to the left or right of the table. However, the popular browsers do not yet support these caption positions.

Only text and text-level elements are allowed within the caption element. The caption element must appear before the first row of the table, immediately after the <TABLE> tag.

Creating Rows with the Table Row Element

The table row element consists of a <TR> start tag and one or more table data elements or table head elements, optionally followed by a </TR> end tag. Each use of a table row element begins a new table row.

The <TR> tag can include several attributes: BGCOLOR, ALIGN, and VALIGN.

The BGCOLOR attribute determines the background color of the row (see the discussion of this attribute in "Coloring the Table Background with the BGCOLOR Attribute").

Since the ALIGN and VALIGN attributes can also be used with the <TD> and <TH> tags, we'll talk about them separately, after we discuss more about the table heading and table data elements.

A row must contain at least one table data element or table heading element. Furthermore, the *only* two things that can legally be placed inside a table row element are table heading and table data elements. (The data itself must be contained in the cell, not the row.) We'll see how to use these cell elements in the next section.

Creating Cells with Cell Elements: Table Headings with <TH> and Table Data with <TD>

You've already learned that the table data element (<TD>) creates cells and the table heading element (<TH>) creates headings. These two elements are referred to as the *cell elements*. The end tags for both cell elements are optional.

The two cell elements are identical to each other except that a heading cell is specially marked. (We've seen that Navigator and Internet Explorer display table heading text centered and in bold, but other browsers can use different methods.)

Cell elements can contain many different types of items, including text, images, and other tables. We'll see some examples of what you can put in a cell a little later in this chapter.

Cells may also be empty if you don't want them to contain data. (Simply use a <TD> tag followed immediately by a </TD> tag.) Navigator and Internet Explorer will not display a cell border around the empty cell. If you want a cell to have a border but still be empty, put a nonbreaking space inside the cell (<TD> </TD>).

There are several attributes for cells that can be used in the <TD> and <TH> tags; we'll see them in the next few sections.

Using Attributes with the Simple Table Model's Elements

In this section, we'll discuss the different attributes that can be used with table row elements and the cell elements. We'll also show you how to use the BGCOLOR attribute to set the color of a table, row, or cell.

The attributes for cells include alignment (with ALIGN and VALIGN), background color (with BGCOLOR), the NOWRAP attribute to prevent word wrapping in a cell, and attributes to make a cell span one or more rows or columns (ROWSPAN and COLSPAN). You can also specify the WIDTH and HEIGHT of cells.

Aligning the Contents of Cells and Rows

The ALIGN attribute indicates the default horizontal alignment of cell data. The <TR>, <TD>, and <TH> tags can all include an ALIGN attribute. The possible values for HTML 3.2 are:

```
ALIGN="LEFT"
ALIGN="CENTER"
ALIGN="RIGHT"
```

As you may have noticed from all of the figures so far in this chapter, table data is left-aligned by default.

NOTE

HTML 4.0 allows some new horizontal alignment choices. In addition to the three possibilities for HTML 3.2, you can use ALIGN="JUSTIFY". Also, there are attributes for aligning cell data on a particular character. We'll discuss this type of alignment in the section about the HTML 4.0 table model, later in this chapter.

You can also specify the vertical alignment of cell data with the VALIGN attribute, in the <TR>, <TD>, or <TH> tags. The VALIGN attribute has four values:

```
VALIGN="TOP"
VALIGN="MIDDLE"
VALIGN="BOTTOM"
VALIGN="BASELINE"
```

WARNING

Don't confuse the MIDDLE and CENTER attribute values. MIDDLE is for vertical alignment, while CENTER is for horizontal alignment.

The default value for the VALIGN attribute is MIDDLE. Since all the cells in a row will always have the same height, the vertical alignment only makes a difference if some cells in a row take up fewer lines than the biggest cell. (For example, look at Figure 11.11 and see how the "Show

Me The Money!" line is halfway between the two text lines of its neighboring cell.)

NOTE

The VALIGN="BASELINE" value is only subtly different from VALIGN="TOP". The
difference is in the exact placement of the bottom of the first line of text in a cell;
with the BASELINE value specified, the bottom of the first line of each cell will
always line up, even if the font size used in different cells varies. When the TOP
value is used, the bottoms of words in different cells won't necessarily line up.

If a cell and its row both include different ALIGN or VALIGN attribute values, then the cell's specified alignment take precedence. You can take
advantage of this fact to make an entire row centered, and then make specific cells in that row right-aligned.

Coloring Parts of the Table with the BGCOLOR Attribute

You can change the background color of different parts of a table with the
BGCOLOR attribute. You can change the background color of an entire
table, a single row, or an individual cell, depending on where you specify
the BGCOLOR attribute. Here are the possibilities:

```
<TABLE BGCOLOR="color name or color value">
<TR BGCOLOR="color name or color value">
<TD BGCOLOR="color name or color value">
<TH BGCOLOR="color name or color value">
```

NOTE

HTML 3.2 and earlier did not allow you to specify the BGCOLOR for a table, although
it was common practice (since Navigator and Internet Explorer both understood the
attribute as an extension to HTML). HTML 4.0 officially allows the BGCOLOR attribute
to be used with some of the different elements of a table.

Although you can't change the color of a caption separately, if you
specify the BGCOLOR in the <TABLE> tag, your background color applies to
the entire table, including the caption.

WARNING

It's somewhat dangerous to color a table, since current browsers don't let users override your table color choices, as they can with document colors. For example, if you specify a color that is hard to read, then people who are color-blind may not be able to read the contents of your table at all.

Disabling Word Wrapping with the NOWRAP Attribute

You can disable the default word wrapping of cell text with the NOWRAP attribute in a table cell (specified in either a <TD> tag or a <TH> tag). This means that the cell will be guaranteed to be displayed on one line. Here is how you can use the NOWRAP attribute:

```
<TD NOWRAP>
<TH NOWRAP>
```

Using the NOWRAP attribute is equivalent to changing all of the spaces in a cell to the nonbreaking space entity, .

WARNING

You can make your table cell unnecessarily wide if you don't use the NOWRAP attribute carefully. Since style sheets can control word wrap more effectively, the use of NOWRAP is strongly discouraged by the HTML 4.0 specification.

Spanning Cells with the COLSPAN and ROWSPAN Attributes

The COLSPAN attribute can be used in a cell to make the cell's contents merge with another cell. You can use COLSPAN in either a table data cell or a table heading cell:

```
<TD COLSPAN="NUMBER">
<TH COLSPAN="NUMBER">
```

To span two columns, for example, specify COLSPAN="2". Naturally, the COLSPAN attribute value defaults to one cell.

The COLSPAN attribute is useful if you have a heading that you want to cover two different columns of data.

Similarly, the ROWSPAN attribute specifies how many rows a cell should take up:

```
<TD ROWSPAN="NUMBER">
<TH ROWSPAN="NUMBER">
```

Here's a fragment of HTML code for a two-row, three-column table, where the first cell is made two rows tall using ROWSPAN:

```
<TABLE>
<TR>
    <TD ROWSPAN="2">Burger Emperor
    <TD>Royale Burger
    <TD>690 calories

<TR>
    <TD>Royale with Cheese</TD>
    <TD>750 calories

</TABLE>
```

The first cell in the second row ("Royale with Cheese") is automatically moved over to make room for the spanned cell, as shown here:

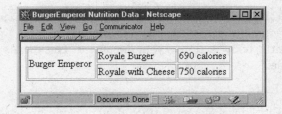

Setting Cell Widths and Heights

You can set the width of an entire table using the <TABLE> tag's WIDTH attribute. You can also specify the widths of individual cells in the simple table model.

When a browser displays a table constructed with the simple table model, each column will be as wide as the widest cell in that column. (Since it can take some time for a browser to retrieve the entire table and work out how wide each column should be, tables can sometimes be slow to display.) Each column will have a different width.

NOTE

In HTML 4.0's table model, you can also specify column widths individually or by groups, using the new column elements that you'll see later in this chapter.

You can specify the minimum width of a column by using the WIDTH attribute on a cell. (Best results are achieved by specifying the widths for all the cells in the first row.) The width is specified in pixels, and the WIDTH attribute can only be used in a table data element or table heading element. For example:

```
<TD WIDTH="NUMBER">
<TH WIDTH="NUMBER">
```

The HEIGHT attribute is a new attribute in HTML 4.0. (However, Navigator and Internet Explorer have supported this attribute as an extension for quite a while.) It's important to remember that both the WIDTH and the HEIGHT attributes are recommendations: browsers will often override your specified dimensions. The advantage to specifying the WIDTH and HEIGHT is that your tables will display much faster.

Putting Images and Other Elements inside Cells

As a general rule, a cell can contain almost anything that you can put inside the body section of your document. This means that you can include:

- ► Text

- ► Block-level elements (including paragraphs, lists, preformatted text, and other tables)

- ► Text-level elements (including font and phrase elements, anchors, line breaks, and images)

NOTE

When you use an image within a cell, it's a good idea to specify the height and width of the image and also specify the width of the image's cell (as we discussed in the previous section). This will help your table display as quickly as possible.

Nesting Tables

Including a table inside another table's cell is called *table nesting*. One common use of table nesting is to create two tables that are side by side (normally each table would be in a separate paragraph).

Here's an example of the HTML code for two tables nested inside of another table:

Listing 11.2:   toriamos.html

```
<!DOCTYPE HTML PUBLIC "-//W3C//DTD HTML 4.0//EN">
<TITLE>Tori Amos Music Catalog Numbers</TITLE>
<BODY>
<TABLE BORDER="0" CELLSPACING="20" BGCOLOR="#CCCCCC">
   <CAPTION>Tori Amos Album and Single Catalog
Excerpt</CAPTION>
   <TR>
      <TD>
         <TABLE BORDER="10" CELLPADDING="4">
            <CAPTION>Albums</CAPTION>
            <TR><TD><I>Little Earthquakes</I>
               <TD>82358-2
            <TR><TD><I>Under the Pink</I>
               <TD>82567-2
            <TR><TD><I>Boys For Pele</I>
               <TD>82862-2
         </TABLE>
      </TD>

      <TD>
         <TABLE BORDER="10" CELLPADDING="4">
            <CAPTION>Singles</CAPTION>
            <TR><TD>"Crucify"
               <TD>82399-2
            <TR><TD>"God"
               <TD>85687-2
            <TR><TD>"Cornflake Girl"
               <TD>85655-2
            <TR><TD>"Caught A Lite Sneeze"
               <TD>85519-2
         </TABLE>
      </TD>
   </TR>
</TABLE>
```

Part ii

In Figure 11.12, Internet Explorer renders this HTML code. The outer table contains no direct content of its own, it just specifies some attributes (including the light gray color) and contains a caption and two cells. Each cell contains a nested table. The inner tables have a 10-pixel border and a number of cells each (six for the left table, eight for the right table).

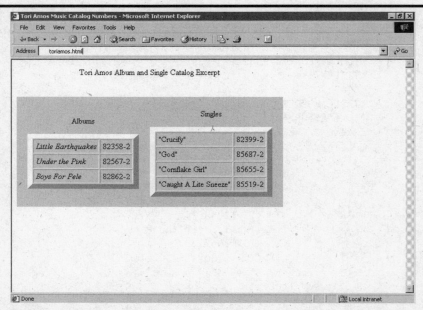

FIGURE 11.12: Internet Explorer renders two tables nested within another table, allowing the two tables to exist side by side.

NOTE

An earlier figure, Figure 11.10, was created by nesting six tables inside a larger table.

UNOFFICIAL HTML EXTENSIONS TO THE SIMPLE TABLE MODEL

A few other attributes can be used with the simple table model, but they aren't official HTML 3.2 or HTML 4.0 attributes—they're extensions to HTML. You can use a background image in a cell by specifying a BACKGROUND attribute, just like the one used in the body tag.

You can also specify the HEIGHT of an entire table; this will help your tables display more quickly.

Table widths can also be specified using percentage values as well as just pixels (for example, <TD WIDTH="33%">. If you specify a width for a table and then specify the width of a cell, you can request that another table cell be assigned the rest of the available width by using <TD WIDTH="*">.

These are useful extensions, but they are only understood by certain versions of Internet Explorer and Navigator, so be sure your table does not depend on these attributes.

Once you've understood the simple table model and feel that the four basic table model elements make sense, you're ready to move on to the more complex HTML 4.0 table model.

USING HTML 4.0 TABLE ELEMENTS AND ATTRIBUTES

The HTML 4.0 table model builds on the simple table model and adds a few new elements and attributes to make tables richer and more capable, yet also more complex.

TIP

If you're not comfortable with the simple table model from the first half of this chapter, you might want to work with it for a while before reading about the HTML 4.0 table model.

The changes in HTML 4.0's table model improve the simple table model in key areas. First, the simple table model resulted in slow display times for a large table, since a browser had to read through the entire table before figuring out how wide each column needed to be. Second, it was difficult to import information from spreadsheets because the table models differed so much. Finally, it was impossible to group data by row or by column. To solve these problems, the HTML 4.0 table model introduces new elements for columns and groups of columns as well as groups of rows.

Here are some other changes in HTML 4.0's table model introduced by popular demand:

▶ The ability to align on a specific character such as "." or ":" (to allow numbers to be decimal aligned)

▶ More flexibility in specifying table borders, especially borders around individual row and column groups

▶ Better support for breaking tables across multiple pages when printing

▶ Setting the alignment of cells by column or by groups of rows

WARNING
Currently, only Internet Explorer 4 and 5 support HTML 4.0's new table model.

To see how these changes work, we'll now discuss the HTML 4.0 table model's structure.

Understanding the HTML 4.0 Table Model Structure

In HTML 4.0, tables have the following structure:

▶ The required table element start tag (<TABLE>) must start a table, followed by an optional caption (with the caption element, same as in the simple table model), followed by:

▶ One or more groups of columns (using the new column group and column elements), followed by:

▸ One or more *groups* of rows. You can have an optional table head row group and an optional table foot row group, and you must have one or more table body row groups (using the new <THEAD>, <TFOOT>, and <TBODY> tags).

▸ Each row group must consist of one or more rows (using the table row element, same as in the simple table model).

▸ Each row must consist of one or more cells (using the table data and table heading elements, same as in the simple table model).

▸ The required table element end tag (</TABLE>) must finish a table.

The new elements in the HTML 4.0 table model are the column group element (which uses the <COLGROUP> tag), the column element (which uses the <COL> tag), and the three new elements for row groups: table headers (the <THEAD> tag), table bodies (the <TBODY> tag), and table footers (the <TFOOT> tag).

Each table is assumed to have one column group and one table body row group, even if those elements are not explicitly specified with tags. (This is how the HTML 4.0 table model is able to stay backward-compatible with the simple table model.)

Since the new table model is backward-compatible, none of the five new elements are *required* if you want to make an HTML 4.0 table.

We'll see other new attributes and attribute values after we see the new elements for tables. There are five elements to consider; we'll start with the two new column group elements, and then see the three new row group elements.

Creating Columns and Groups of Columns

HTML 4.0 tables always have at least one column group. If you don't specify your column group (using a <COLGROUP> tag), then every column in your table is assumed to make up the column group.

You can optionally define one or more groups of columns; each <COLGROUP> tag defines a new group. (There is an optional end tag, </COLGROUP>, but you can always leave it out.) Each column group must have one or more columns; we'll see how to define columns in the next section.

The <COLGROUP> tags are used immediately after the caption element, if there is one. If there's no caption, then the <COLGROUP> tags should be put after the <TABLE> tag.

The advantage to defining column groups is that you can apply attributes to every cell in the column group. For example, if you want to specify that every cell in a group of columns should be centered, you can simply use a <COLGROUP ALIGN="CENTER"> tag. In the simple table model, you would have had to apply the ALIGN attribute to every cell you wanted centered, one at a time.

Another advantage to column groups is that you can specify column widths. This allows browsers to begin displaying your table immediately, because they don't have to read through the entire table to find out how many columns there are and how wide they should be. For long tables, this can make a tremendous difference in the time it takes to display your document (especially for someone viewing your page on a slow Internet connection).

Using the Column Group Element

There are two ways to use the column group element, and you must use one or the other:

- ▶ Within the column group, you can use one or more column elements. The column element uses the <COL> tag. Each <COL> tag creates one column. We'll see how to use the column element in the next section.

- ▶ You can create a group of columns by using the <COLGROUP> tag with a SPAN attribute. The number of columns in the column group is equal to the attribute value of SPAN. For example, <COLGROUP SPAN="4"> creates a group of four columns. The SPAN attribute's value defaults to one. We'll see some examples of this method in this section.

In addition to the SPAN attribute, the <COLGROUP> tag can contain an ALIGN attribute, a VALIGN attribute, and a WIDTH attribute. The values for these attributes can be the same as in the simple table model, or they can have new possibilities discussed later in this chapter, when we introduce the new HTML 4.0 table model's attributes.

Here are some examples of the <COLGROUP> tag. This first example creates a column group with only one column (because the SPAN attribute is not specified). Every cell in the column will be right-aligned:

```
<COLGROUP ALIGN="RIGHT">
```

This example creates a group of five columns, each one centered, top-aligned, and 100 pixels wide:

```
<COLGROUP SPAN="5" VALIGN="TOP" ALIGN="CENTER" WIDTH="100">
```

This example creates two groups of columns. The first group has eight columns that are fully justified, and the second group has four columns, each 50 pixels wide:

```
<COLGROUP SPAN="8" ALIGN="JUSTIFY">
<COLGROUP SPAN="4" WIDTH="50">
```

The WIDTH attribute is an important part of column groups. If you don't specify the width, then the browser will either divide all of the columns equally across the width of the screen, or else the browser will have to read through your entire table to determine the column widths.

We'll see other examples of the use of <COLGROUP> in our HTML 4.0 table examples in the next section and at the end of the chapter.

Using the Column Element

The column element uses a <COL> tag. The column element is empty, so there's no such thing as a </COL> end tag. The column element can only be placed inside a column group element. Each <COL> tag creates a column.

Like <COLGROUP>, you can use attributes in the <COL> tag to apply to each cell in a column. For example, you could begin a table like so:

```
<TABLE>
  <CAPTION>The "Six Columns of Fun" Table</CAPTION>
  <COLGROUP SPAN="2" ALIGN="CENTER" WIDTH="50">
  <COLGROUP ALIGN="RIGHT">
    <COL WIDTH="150">
    <COL WIDTH="100" VALIGN="TOP">
    <COL WIDTH="50">
    <COL WIDTH="*" ALIGN="LEFT">
  </COLGROUP>
```

Part ii

Assuming you finished this example (with some table rows, cells, and a </TABLE> end tag), the code would define a table with six columns. The first two columns are created by the first <COLGROUP> tag (thanks to the SPAN="2" attribute). Both of these first two columns have their cell data centered and are 50 pixels wide. The next four columns are created by the four <COL> tags inside the second column group element. By default, these four columns will be right-aligned. The third column will be 150 pixels wide. The fourth column will be 100 pixels wide, and its cells are top-aligned. The fifth column is 50 pixels wide.

The sixth column uses a special width value, which means "give this column the rest of the available width;" we'll see more about the asterisk and its use in the new attributes section. The sixth column also specifies left-alignment for its cells, which will override the default of right-alignment set by the second <COLGROUP> tag.

When you complete the rest of the table, make sure not to include more than six cells in a row, since you've already specified a maximum of six columns for this table. Browsers might not display any extraneous cells, or will possibly become confused.

Once you define your column groups and columns, you can next include elements that define one or more row groups.

Grouping Rows with Row Group Elements

In the simple table model, the table element simply contains an optional caption and one or more table row elements. In the HTML 4.0 table model, all of the table rows (and the <TR> tags) are contained in row groups. A *row group* is simply one or more table rows that are grouped together, for common formatting or positioning.

There are three types of row groups:

► An optional table head row group: <THEAD> tag (for the top of each page)

► An optional table foot row group: <TFOOT> tag (for the bottom of each page)

► At least one required table body row group: <TBODY> tag (for the bulk of the table's data)

The order of these row groups in a table is important.

▸ If there's a table head row group, it must occur before the table foot row group and the table body row group.

▸ If there's a table foot row group, it must occur before the table body row group.

▸ You can have one or more table body row groups. There's no limit to how many table body row groups your table can contain.

There is not actually much of a difference between these three types of row groups: table head row groups go on the top of a table (and are repeated on the top of each page if a table is printed out), and table foot row groups go on the bottom of a table (and are repeated on the bottom of each page in a printout). Other than that, the main reason for these three row group sections is to allow you to conveniently assign attributes to groups of rows. The table head row group and table foot row group are completely optional.

If you want just one table body row group (without any table head or table foot row groups), you don't have to specify any row group elements at all—the presence of the table body row group element is assumed if there's not actually a <TBODY> tag in your table. For the required table body element, there's no difference between nesting the table row elements within plain <TBODY> and </TBODY> tags or not.

TIP

Remember, if you want a table head row group or table foot row group, then you have to use the <THEAD>, <TFOOT>, and <TBODY> tags (in that order).

It can be useful to specify a table body row group element in your table because (just as with columns and column groups) you can apply an attribute to the <TBODY> tag that will affect an entire group of rows (and the cells contained in those rows). For example:

```
<TABLE>
 <THEAD ALIGN="CENTER">
   <TR>
      <TD>Br. 1<TD>Br. 2<TD>Br. 3<TD>Br. 4<TD>Br. 5
<TD>Br. 6<TD>Br. 7
   <TBODY ALIGN="RIGHT">
```

```
<TR>
   <TD>1<TD>23<TD>04<TD>23<TD>232<TD>1<TD>91
<TR>
   <TD>5<TD>39<TD>93<TD>104<TD>2<TD>22<TD>55
</TABLE>
```

This example creates a table with two row groups. The first row group (a table head row group) contains just one row, with all seven cells in that row center-aligned. The second row group (a table body row group), contains two rows—and both of those rows will have right-aligned cells. In the simple table model, you would have had to apply the alignment attributes to the <TR> tags. In this example, with only three rows, it would not have been time-consuming to do so; but imagine a table where you want 700 right-aligned rows, and you'll understand the motivation for row groups.

TIP

One main idea behind row groups is to allow the display of a very large table within a scrolling frame region. The head section and foot section would stay constant at the top and bottom of the browser window, while the body section in between them would have a separate scroll bar. Alas, browsers have not yet implemented this approach.

WARNING

Only the latest versions of Internet Explorer and Navigator support the header and footer feature of tables when you're printing them out. Navigator 4.01 and earlier and Internet Explorer 4.0 and earlier may not handle printed head and foot row groups properly.

Using the HTML 4.0 Table Model's Attributes

Several new attributes can be used in HTML 4.0 tables. Some of these attributes can only be used in the <TABLE> tag, while others can be used in a variety of different elements.

NOTE

In addition to these attributes, every element used in tables can take the standard HTML 4.0 attributes, such as the language attributes (LANG and DIR) and the advisory TITLE attribute, the ID, CLASS, and STYLE attributes that will be discussed with style sheets in Chapter 16, and the event attributes (ONMOUSEOVER and so on).

The first new attributes we'll see can be used in the <TABLE> tag: the COLS attribute to indicate the number of columns and the FRAME and the RULES attributes to specify borders more precisely.

Then we'll discuss some new values for the ALIGN attribute, see more about the WIDTH attribute, and finally learn about the new AXIS and AXES attributes (which can be used to label cells).

Specifying the Number of Columns with the COLS Attribute

Instead of using the column group and column elements we discussed earlier, you can specify a COLS attribute in the <TABLE> start tag to indicate how many columns are in your table.

Navigator 4 understands this attribute and will display a table with the indicated number of columns, using WIDTH="100%" (instead of the default width). You may have noticed earlier in "Creating a Table with Netscape Composer" that Composer automatically inserted this attribute.

Internet Explorer 4 and earlier, along with earlier versions of Navigator, ignore this attribute. The specification for HTML 4.0 recommends that you use the column group elements to specify columns instead, since you can also use those elements to specify column widths, which speeds up display time.

Using Advanced Borders with the FRAME and RULES Attributes

The simple table model doesn't give you a lot of flexibility with your table borders: you either have a border or you don't; you can specify the width of the outside table border, but that's all you can specify. HTML 4.0 introduces the FRAME and RULES attributes for the <TABLE> tag to help improve the amount of control you have over borders.

NOTE

Internet Explorer 3.0 and later versions recognize these FRAME and RULES attributes. Navigator 4.01 and earlier don't recognize them.

The FRAME attribute indicates which sides of the table's outside border are rendered.

WARNING

Don't confuse the FRAME attribute with the HTML frames feature; frames are used to subdivide the browser window with different documents (frames are discussed in Chapter 8).

The FRAME attribute's values are shown in Table 11.2.

TABLE 11.2: Values for the FRAME Attribute

FRAME Value	Effect
FRAME="ABOVE"	The top side
FRAME="BELOW"	The bottom side
FRAME="BORDER"	All four sides—the same as specifying the BORDER attribute
FRAME="BOX"	Same as FRAME="BORDER"
FRAME="HSIDES"	The top and bottom sides ("horizontal sides")
FRAME="LHS"	The left-hand side
FRAME="RHS"	The right-hand side
FRAME="VOID"	No sides rendered (the default value)
FRAME="VSIDES"	The left and right sides ("vertical sides")

The result of using tables with each of these frame values is shown here using Internet Explorer:

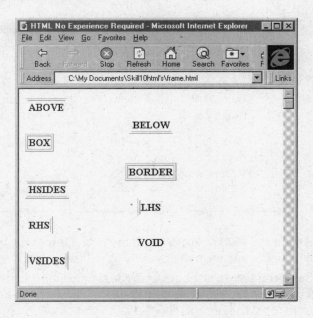

The FRAMES attribute applies to the outside of a table; alternately, the RULES attribute applies to which cell borders will appear between cells within a table.

The RULES attribute's values are shown in Table 11.3.

TABLE 11.3: Values for the RULES Attribute

RULES VALUE	EFFECT
RULES="NONE"	No cell borders; this is the default value.
RULES="GROUPS"	Cell borders will appear between row groups and column groups only.
RULES="ROWS"	Rules will appear between rows only.
RULES="COLS"	Rules will appear between columns only.
RULES="ALL"	Rules will appear between all rows and columns (same as specifying the BORDER attribute).

The result of using tables with each of these frame values (and the BORDER attribute) is shown here, again using Internet Explorer:

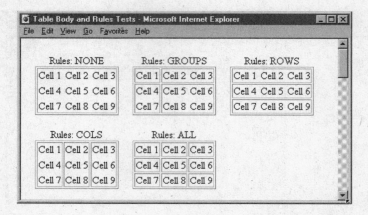

As you can see, the RULES attributes only apply to the inside of the table, not the outside border.

Since the BORDER attribute from the simple model is still available and overlaps with the use of FRAME and RULES, it's helpful to know that setting BORDER="0" is the same as RULES="NONE" and FRAME="VOID". Using BOR-DER="*NUMBER*" is the same as using FRAME="BORDER" and RULES="ALL". Using the attribute <TABLE BORDER> by itself is the same as using <TABLE BORDER="2" FRAME="BORDER" RULES="ALL">. However, Internet Explorer 3 and 4 sometimes behave strangely unless the BORDER attribute is present along with the FRAME and RULES attributes.

New Alignment Attributes in HTML 4.0

HTML 4.0 adds ALIGN="JUSTIFY" so that you can use full justification on paragraphs inside table cells.

HTML 4.0 also allows ALIGN="CHAR" to specify that cells should be aligned on a certain character. By default, the character is the decimal separator (which is a period if your document is in English). By specifying ALIGN="CHAR", you could cause a row of numbers to be aligned on their decimal points.

Two other alignment attributes new in HTML 4.0 are CHAR and CHAROFF. Using CHAR="$" along with ALIGN="CHAR" would allow you to justify on the dollar sign. You can specify any character you like.

The CHAROFF attribute specifies an offset (that is, distance) that the character alignment should be shifted.

Unfortunately, character alignment is not yet supported in the popular browsers.

Specifying the ALIGN Attribute in Multiple Places

The ALIGN attribute can be used in many different HTML 4.0 table model elements: the individual cells, the row groups, or the column groups.

NOTE

When you use the ALIGN attribute in the <TABLE> tag or the <CAPTION> tag, it applies only to the table itself or the caption itself, not the position of data in any cells.

The order of precedence (from highest to lowest) is the following:

1. An element within a cell's data (for example, <P ALIGN= "CENTER">)

2. The cell (in the <TH> or <TD> tag)

3. A column or column group (<COL> and <COLGROUP>)

4. A row or row group (<TR>, <THEAD>, <TFOOT>, and <TBODY>)

For a VALIGN attribute, the order of precedence is:

1. The cell

2. The row or row group

3. The column or column group

In general, horizontal alignment is determined by columns in preference to rows, while it's the reverse for vertical alignment.

New Uses of the WIDTH Attribute

We saw earlier how the WIDTH attribute can be used in the column group and column elements to specify the width of a column.

In the simple table model of HTML 3.2, the only way to specify a width for a cell was in pixels. In HTML 4.0's table model, there are two additional ways to specify column widths: using percentages and using relative amounts with an asterisk.

Part ii

The percentage amount of width is not complicated; simply specify a percentage for each column (for example <COL WIDTH="40%"> to give a column 40 percent of the available table width).

We also saw earlier that you could specify <COL WIDTH="*"> to mean that a column should be given all of the available space. If two columns both specify the WIDTH="*" attribute, then the amount of space will be divided in half, with an equal amount of width for both columns.

HTML 4.0 allows additional possibilities involving these "relative amounts" of widths. The special value WIDTH="0*" means to use the minimum width possible for the contents of the column. You can also use a number with the asterisk to make a column use more of the available space. The bigger the number, the more proportional space the column will receive. (WIDTH="*" is the same as WIDTH="1*".)

Consider this example:

```
<TABLE>
   <COLGROUP SPAN="2" WIDTH="20">
   <COLGROUP SPAN="3" WIDTH="0*">
   <COLGROUP>
      <COL WIDTH="50">
      <COL WIDTH="20%">
      <COL WIDTH="1*">
      <COL WIDTH="2*">
```

(The rest of the table would follow here, with table row groups, table rows, data, and the </TABLE> tag.)

This example creates nine columns in three column groups. When determining the column widths, a browser will give the first two columns 20 pixels each. The next three columns will have a variable amount of width, the minimum possible to display their data. The sixth column has 50 pixels. The seventh column is given 20 percent of the table's total width (assuming that much is still available). The amount of remaining space for the table is divided into thirds. One-third is given to the eighth column, and two-thirds is given to the ninth column.

It's common to create a table with a total width of 100 percent and then assign a fixed pixel width to the first column. The remaining columns are often divided using relative amounts, with WIDTH="*".

NOTE

It's important to be flexible with table widths. Consider this warning from the HTML 4.0 specification: "A major consideration for the HTML table model is that the author does not control how a user will size a table, what fonts he or she will use, etc. This makes it risky to rely on column widths specified in terms of absolute pixel units. Instead, tables must be able to change sizes dynamically to match the current window size and fonts."

WARNING

Browsers will disobey your column widths whenever they feel it's necessary to override them.

Labeling Cells with AXIS and AXES Attributes

The other new attributes for HTML 4.0's table model are the AXIS and AXES attributes, which are used in the cell start tags (<TH> and <TD>) to help label the cells. The labels can be used for text-to-speech systems or for a table conversion program that imports or exports table data from a spreadsheet program or database.

The AXIS attribute should define an abbreviated name for a header cell. For example, if a cell falls under a header cell that contains "Last Name," then you might set an AXIS="lastname" attribute in the cell.

The AXES attribute is a comma-separated list of AXIS names, in order to specify the row and column headers that locate this cell.

The following example table creates a list of names and sets the value of the AXIS attribute to be the employee's last name. We also label the cell value as falling under the "Name" column.

```
<TABLE BORDER>
<CAPTION>Sick days used by employees</CAPTION>
<TR>
<TH>Name <TH>Sick Days Used
<TR>
<TD AXIS="Restrick" AXES="Name">J. Restrick <TD>10
<TR>
<TD AXIS="Selan" AXES="Name">P. Selan <TD>5
</TABLE>
```

Part II

WARNING

Since these attributes are brand new to HTML 4.0, they are not yet widely supported by conversion programs. Browsers ignore them.

Putting the HTML 4.0 Table Model to Work: A Final Example

We've seen plenty of new features for HTML 4.0's table model; it's time to show a final example that will put it all together.

Here's an example of HTML code that uses the COLGROUP and TBODY elements to render a television schedule with three different column groups and two different row groups. Through the use of the new RULES elements, the cell borders effectively divide the table into different regions.

Listing 11.3: **tvscout.html**

```
<!DOCTYPE HTML PUBLIC "-//W3C//DTD HTML 4.0//EN">
<HTML LANG="EN">
<HEAD>
  <TITLE>TV Scout's TV Schedule</TITLE>
</HEAD>
<BODY>

<TABLE BORDER="5" RULES="GROUPS" FRAME="VOID" ALIGN="CENTER">
<CAPTION>Television Schedule for Monday</CAPTION>

<COLGROUP ALIGN="CENTER" WIDTH="75"> <!-- first column:
headings -->
<COLGROUP> <!--columns 2 and 3: 6AM -->
  <COL ALIGN="CENTER" WIDTH="75">
  <COL WIDTH="*" ALIGN="LEFT">
<COLGROUP> <!--columns 4 and 5: 7AM -->
  <COL ALIGN="CENTER" WIDTH="75">
  <COL WIDTH="*" ALIGN="LEFT">
```

```
<THEAD VALIGN="BOTTOM" ALIGN="CENTER">
  <TR>
    <TH ROWSPAN="3">Channel</TH>
    <TH COLSPAN="4">Time</TH>
  <TR>
    <TH COLSPAN="2">6 AM</TH>
    <TH COLSPAN="2">7 AM</TH>
  <TR>
    <TH>Show</TH>
    <TH>Description</TH>
    <TH>Show</TH>
    <TH>Description</TH>

<TBODY ALIGN="CENTER">
  <TR>
    <TD>3
    <TD>CHiPS
    <TD>Ponch discovers some stolen Pentium processors.
    <TD>The Munsters
    <TD>Herman creates a family home page. The cops
confiscate his computer.
  <TR>
    <TD>7
    <TD>I Love Lucy
    <TD>Lucy surfs the Web and accidentally charges $50,000
to her VISA.
    <TD>The X-Files
    <TD>Scully and Mulder investigate some alien-infested
table cells.
</TABLE>
</BODY>
</HTML>
```

Figure 11.13 shows how this code will be displayed by Internet Explorer 4 (and Navigator 4 in the background). Since Navigator 4 doesn't understand all of the HTML 4.0 table model, it displays the table a little differently—but at least all of the data is there. Internet Explorer 3 handles this example more or less faithfully as well.

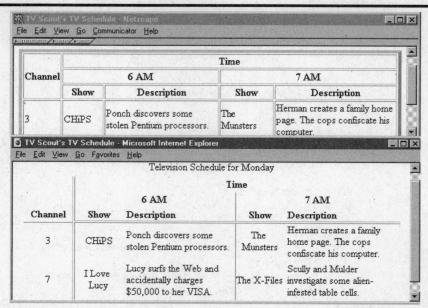

FIGURE 11.13: A table that uses the HTML 4.0 COLGROUP and TBODY elements displayed by Internet Explorer, with Navigator's window behind Internet Explorer's window

USING TABLES AS A LAYOUT TOOL

HTML is not designed to be a page layout language. However, over the past two years, HTML has evolved to include a few layout elements. Style sheets were supposed to handle the rest of an author's layout needs, but style sheets were not in wide use until HTML 4.0 arrived. In the meantime, many Web authors developed ways of laying out pages using tables.

Even though this is somewhat abusive of HTML's purpose (since, after all, you are not describing table data), it's a common practice, so we'll show you a few techniques for making tables perform as a layout tool.

Creating Page Margins with Tables

Sometimes it's nice to emphasize a paragraph with white space. The full width of a window can make it difficult to read long passages (we're used to reading magazines or books, which have wider margins than most Web pages.)

To establish wider margins easily, you can create a simple one-celled table, borders off, and specify a table width or CELLPADDING. This will separate the text from the left and right margins of the page. The following HTML code (see Figure 11.14) uses text from "Sometimes You See Africa," the second part of a seven-part novella by Meg Wise-Lawrence (http://www.walrus.com/~gibralto/acorn/frag2.html):

```
<TABLE CELLPADDING="30">
<TR>
<TD>
<P>
Jack smiles his magazine smile. "I woke up on the beach this
morning--" He winks at Cal and signals that the bartender mix
up some drinks-- the usual. "When I woke up, I didn't know
where I was for a minute. You know that feeling? All I could
see was this bright blue canvas above me. I thought at first
it was this blue blanket--like a tent or something. But it
was the big empty sky. Beside me is a very beautiful native
woman. She leans over and says: 'Verte desnuda es recordar la
tierra'--to see you naked is to remember the earth..."
</P>
</TD>
</TR>
</TABLE>
```

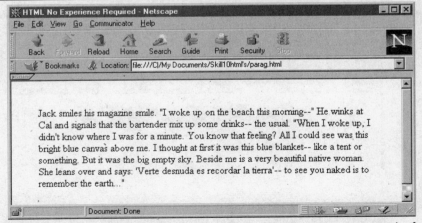

FIGURE 11.14: Navigator renders a one-celled table containing a paragraph of text emphasized with white space.

TIP

It's easy to use style sheets to get even more control over margins. Read Chapter 16 for more information.

Using Tables for Navigation Bars

Another nice way to use a table for page layout is to create a row with several columns that serves as a button navigation system. The most basic navigation bar can simply use a table with text in each cell (see Figure 11.15). (Some bars use an image in each cell.) Let's take a look at the HTML code for a simple text navigation bar:

```
<TABLE BORDER="3" FRAME="VSIDES" ALIGN="CENTER"
CELLPADDING="5">
<TR>
        <TD BGCOLOR="AQUA"><A HREF="bodkin.html">Bodkin</A></TD>
        <TD BGCOLOR="AQUA"><A
HREF="boliver.html">Boliver</A></TD>
        <TD BGCOLOR="AQUA"><A HREF="snimm.html">Snimm</A></TD>
        <TD BGCOLOR="AQUA"><A HREF="shadrack.html">Shadrack
</A></TD>
        <TD BGCOLOR="AQUA"><A HREF="home.html">Home
Page</A></TD>
</TR>
</TABLE>
```

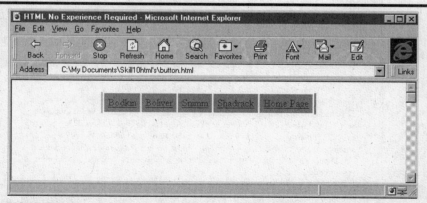

FIGURE 11.15: Internet Explorer renders a table that serves as a text navigation bar.

As we saw earlier, Web authors sometimes try to create text columns using tables. Others use other tricks with tables (such as forcing a column to be a certain width by using transparent images); but in general, most of these effects can be much better achieved with style sheets. Some Web authors use tables to split a page into two halves, with navigation links on the left half and page content on the right half, although frames are a more effective way of dividing the browser's screen into regions.

WHAT'S NEXT

In this chapter, you've learned that using tables is an extremely powerful way to arrange data. Tables are both complex and useful, so it's worth taking the time to learn them and use them on your pages. In the next chapter, Molly Holzschlag will give you the details on the type-related elements of Web design and provide suggestions on how to use type to get your message across.

Part ii

Chapter 12

WEB TYPOGRAPHY

Web typography challenges the best of designers, no matter how skilled at type. The reason is simple: support for type is truly limited. Designers have only three basic alternatives when designing for type on the Web: using graphics to handle desired typographic elements, coding type with the HTML <font> tag, or using cascading style sheets.

Adapted from *web by design: The Complete Guide*, by Molly E. Holzschlag

ISBN 0-7821-2201-9   928 pages $49.99

Three options doesn't sound limited, but here's the catch: with HTML and style sheets, if a specific typeface doesn't exist on the machine used by your Web site visitor, that visitor *will not see* your beautiful type.

A further headache is the often-referred-to browser problem. Microsoft's Internet Explorer 3 and above have good style sheet support. Netscape introduced support for style sheets in version 4. Font tags were introduced in many version 2 browsers, but they sometimes cause problems with compatibility.

NOTE

One advantage if you're using the above-listed browsers is that the style sheet interpretation for typographic elements is pretty good, compared to the less stable style sheet positioning. It is for this reason alone that I go into such detail with style sheets in this chapter.

The future holds great hope, however. With Microsoft's embedded fonts and the OpenType initiative, new technologies are on the horizon that will place type within easy reach of designers.

Embedded fonts allow the designer to embed the font information for a specific page into the code of that page. The necessary fonts are then silently downloaded by the visitor's browser, allowing the fonts on that page to be seen. Interestingly, embedded fonts strip out any characters and letters in a font that are not used on that page. This means that the embedded information can transfer with relative speed.

The OpenType initiative is a cooperative effort between Microsoft and Adobe, companies that historically have been at odds. In order to solve some of the typographic problems born of the Web environment, they have put aside their differences and are working on fonts that will be instantly accessible to Web visitors. Recently, Adobe developed 12 original typefaces just for the Web. These typefaces include two serifs, a sans serif, a script, and two decorative faces.

ONLINE INFORMATION

Check out these sites for information regarding Web typefaces:

Microsoft Typography   For up-to-date news on typographic technology, visit this site: http://www.microsoft.com/typography/.

CONTINUED ➡

Adobe This company site has terrific information on general type and Web type as well as typographic tools for PC and Macintosh platforms: http://www.adobe.com/.

Despite the push-me, pull-you feel of the state of Web typography, you can begin working with the technologies that do exist. This chapter will help you do just that. You'll examine:

- Designing type with graphics
- Implementing HTML-based type techniques
- Using cascading style sheets to achieve greater typographic control

> "In a printed piece, or on the Web, attractive, well-executed typography adds elegance and improves communication. Poor typographic execution can seriously degrade otherwise inspired design."
> Paul Baker, *PBTWeb*

The most important thing to remember about typography on the Web is that advances are made at regular intervals. Keep up with the technology and you'll stay ahead of the pack when it comes to typographic applications in Web design.

APPROACHING WEB TYPOGRAPHY

Whether you're looking to use type in the conservative fashion as a method to deliver your Web-based, written content, or you'd like to be adventurous and use type as artistic design, the more methods you can use to approach Web typography, the better equipped you are to achieve your typographic goals.

> "Typography is becoming tribal, an initiation rite."
> Joe Clark, writings from Typo Expo 1996

I personally believe that type should do both—serve its function *and* be used artistically. The Web is a perfect opportunity to experiment.

Part ii

Obviously, when your client and audience want you to manage text, you're going to be somewhat reined in by convention. But there are times when you will have the opportunity or want to create more cutting-edge designs.

Type can help you do this.

Again, Web typography can currently be approached with some stability through three vehicles: graphics, HTML, and cascading style sheets.

Graphics and Type

In many ways, putting type on a Web site as a graphic is currently the most stable method of ensuring that your type design will be seen. Visitors don't have to have the font installed—they are seeing the font as part of a graphic. This gives you lots of control because not only can you select from any typeface you own, but you can color it to your tastes and add special effects, too.

Of course, the downside is the time that graphics take to download. Where you use graphics to handle the majority of your type, you'll need to take care to balance the typographic elements with the graphics necessary for your individual pages.

Here are a few tips to help you when working with type as a graphic:

▶ Select flat colors from the browser-safe palette to ensure the smallest file size even if you're using large type.

▶ Save flat-color, simple, graphic-based, typeset files as GIFs.

▶ If you add special effects such as shadows, gradient fills, and metallic color, or if you use 3-D type, try saving your files as GIFs and JPEGs in order to compare the results. You might find that in certain instances, JPEGs will serve you better, whereas in other cases, you will get smaller files and a terrific look from GIFs.

▶ In most cases, you will want to anti-alias your fonts as you set the type on the graphic (see Figure 12.1). However, anti-aliasing can become problematic when you want to set small type. It's especially wise to avoid anti-aliasing on any type that is less than 12 points, although you should experiment with both in order to get the best look (see Figure 12.2).

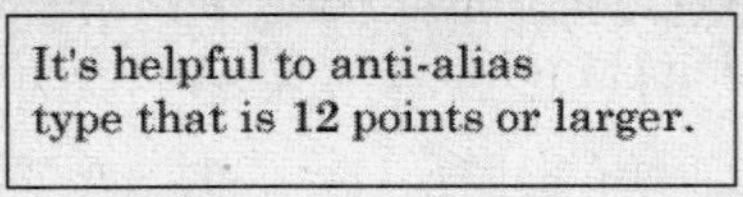

It's helpful to anti-alias
type that is 12 points or larger.

FIGURE 12.1: Type that is 12 or more points should typically be anti-aliased.

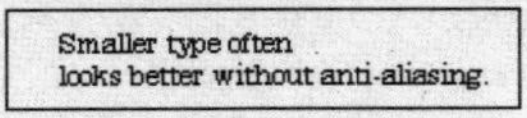

Smaller type often
looks better without anti-aliasing.

FIGURE 12.2: Small type that is not anti-aliased looks fine.

Treat type-based graphics as you would any other graphic when coding. This means to be sure to use the appropriate tag and attributes, including width, height, alt, and any relevant alignment tags:

```
<img src="welcome.gif" width="300" height="100" alt="Welcome
to Our House" align="right">
```

Wherever possible, it's also a good idea to combine graphic-based type with type you create on the page. This way you lean less on the graphics to get your typographic point across.

HTML and Type

Aside from browser and individual users' font library support issues, the main problem with HTML type is that you can only use it along the horizontal. Also, you can't set it in specific points—you must rely on really poor sizing techniques. But you can still do some interesting things with HTML type.

HTML type is delivered primarily through the <font> tag. The only exception to this is the header tags <h1>...</h1> through <h6>...</h6>, which use a bold Times font to create a variety of headers ranging in size from large (size 1) to small (size 6). You'll want to use them now and then, but with so many other options, you might find them limiting as you work with different typefaces and sizes.

The Font Tag

The <font> tag has numerous considerations in terms of widespread compatibility, but it does help designers address type techniques through HTML. The <font> tag allows for a number of attributes, including face, size, and color.

The `<font>` tag follows standard HTML conventions, with an opening and closing tag enclosing the division of information to which you are applying the font attributes:

```
<font>
Love is a smoke raised with the fume of sighs;
Being purged, a fire sparkling in lovers' eyes;
Being vex'd a sea nourished with lovers' tears:
What is it else? a madness most discreet,
A choking gall and a preserving sweet.
</font>
```

Of course, nothing happens until you add relevant attributes, which I'll show you as we look at the use of typefaces, forms, and color further on in the chapter.

HTML CHARACTER ENTITIES

To make it easier to use unusual numeric, alphabetic, and symbolic characters, the HTML 4.0 specification is compliant with several standardized character sets. These include the ISO Latin-1 character set, mathematical symbols, Greek letters, and assorted other international and markup-significant character sets.

What Is the ISO Latin-1 Character Set?

The International Organization for Standardization (ISO) is the group in charge of managing international standards for everything from computer protocols to character sets. The ISO 8859-1 standard, which is more commonly known as the ISO Latin-1 character set, is the default character set used by HTML. The term *Latin* refers to the Roman alphabet, which is the basis of the world's Romance languages. The number 1 indicates that this particular character set is the first in the ISO Latin series.

Most of the symbols and special characters used in Web pages are found in this ISO Latin character set. Because this is HTML's default character set, you can use its numeric and character entities in your Web pages. If you need to use characters that are not in the ISO Latin series—for example, characters found in languages such as Russian and Hebrew—then you'll need to use Unicode.

CONTINUED ➡

So What's Unicode?

Unicode is the Web typographer's Swiss Army knife. Officially known as ISO 10646, Unicode is a way of defining special characters for use in HTML, SGML, and the newest metalanguage, XML. The ISO Latin-1 character set is a subset of Unicode, which comprises a huge collection of special characters that covers major languages from throughout the world. That's one big set. How does Unicode do it? It uses unique bit patterns for each character, which computers can recognize and display.

Because Unicode is so extensive (version 2.1 includes about 38,890 distinct, coded characters), it has been broken up into several subsets called UTFs, or Universal Transformation Formats.

HTML 4.0 supports only a selected portion of the Unicode character set. You can find a full list of what is supported at `http://www.w3.org/TR/REC-html40/sgml/entities.html`, or you can refer to the HTML Master's Reference in the appendix of this book. If you want to know the Unicode number for a certain character or which UTF you should use for a project, check out the Unicode Consortium's Web site at `http://www.unicode.org/`.

Random Cheats

Getting other typefaces to appear using HTML is a trick many designers use. The most popular of these is the preformatted text tag <pre>, which will force a monospaced (usually Courier) typeface:

```
<pre>
Love is a smoke raised with the fume of sighs;
Being purged, a fire sparkling in lovers' eyes;
Being vex'd a sea nourished with lovers' tears:
What is it else? a madness most discreet,
A choking gall and a preserving sweet.
</pre>
```

Figure 12.3 shows the results.

You can also use the <tt> tag for a monospaced font:

```
<tt>
Love is a smoke raised with the fume of sighs;
Being purged, a fire sparkling in lovers' eyes;
Being vex'd a sea nourished with lovers' tears:
What is it else? a madness most discreet,
A choking gall and a preserving sweet.
</tt>
```

The results will be the same as shown in Figure 12.3.

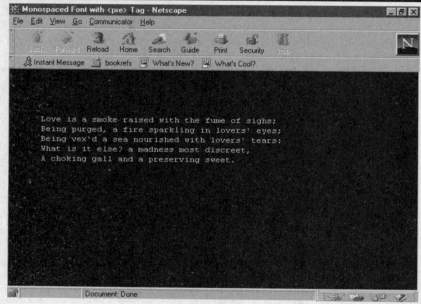

FIGURE 12.3: Using the <pre> tag will force a monospaced font.

Style Sheets and Type

In Chapter 1 we went over some elementary ideas regarding style sheets. Now we'll look at style sheets with a focus on how you will work with style sheet code to apply typography in the Web environment.

NOTE

To view style sheet information, you'll need a compatible browser. Individuals using Internet Explorer 3 and above or Netscape 4 and above will be able to see style sheets. Of course, if a particular typeface is called for and doesn't exist on your visitor's own machine, the type will not be seen in that face.

There are three primary ways to use style sheets. They are the *inline* method; the *embedded*, or individual page, method; and the *linked*, or external, method.

Inline Style Sheets

This approach exploits existing HTML tags within a standard HTML document and adds a specific style to the information controlled by that tag. An example would be controlling the indentation of a single paragraph using the `style="x"` attribute within the `<p>` tag. Another method of achieving this is combining the `<span>` tag and the `style="x"` attribute.

Here is an inline style example:

```
<span style="font: 14pt garamond">
Love is a smoke raised with the fume of sighs;
Being purged, a fire sparkling in lovers' eyes;
Being vex'd a sea nourished with lovers' tears:
What is it else? a madness most discreet,
A choking gall and a preserving sweet.
</span>
```

You could do the same thing with the paragraph tag:

```
<p style="font: 14pt garamond">
Love is a smoke raised with the fume of sighs;
Being purged, a fire sparkling in lovers' eyes;
Being vex'd a sea nourished with lovers' tears:
What is it else? a madness most discreet,
A choking gall and a preserving sweet.
</p>
```

Embedded Style Sheets

This method allows for the control of individual pages. It uses the `<style>` tag, along with its companion tag, `</style>`. This information is placed between the `<html>` tag and the `<body>` tag, with the style attributes inserted within the full `<style>` container. A short example follows:

```
<style>
P { font-family: arial, helvetica, sans-serif; }
</style>
```

Linked Style Sheets

All that is required for linked style sheets is to create a style sheet file with the master styles you would like to express, using the same syntax you would with embedded style, as follows:

```
<style>
P { font-family: arial, helvetica, sans-serif; }
</style>
```

Part ii

Save the file using the `.css` extension—for example, the file `paragraph` `.css`. Then simply be sure that all of the HTML documents that will require those controls are *linked* to that document.

Within the `<head>` tag of any document you'd like to have adopt the style you've just created, insert the following syntax (keep in mind that the reference will have your own location and filename):

```
<link rel="stylesheet" href="paragraph.css" type="text/css">
```

Style Sheet Syntax

With embedded and linked style sheets, the attribute syntax is somewhat different from standard HTML syntax. First, attributes are placed within curly brackets; second, where HTML would place an equal (=) sign, a colon (:) is used; and third, individual, stacked arguments are separated by a semicolon rather than a comma. Also, several attributes are hyphenated, such as `font-style` and `line-height`. A simple style sheet line looks like this:

```
{ font-style: arial, helvetica; }
```

As with HTML, style sheets tend to be quite logical and easy to understand.

TIP

The `<div>` (division) tag can be used like the `<span>` tag for inline control. The `<div>` tag is especially helpful for longer blocks of text, whereas `<span>` is most effective for adding style to smaller stretches of information, such as sentences, several words, or even individual letters within a word.

In a sense, the inline method of style sheet control defeats the ultimate purpose of cascading style sheets. The main point of the technology is to seek style control of entire pages or even entire sets of pages. The inline method should only be used where touches of style are required.

FAMILIES AND FACES

The ability to use type families and faces can empower Web designers, because they can use those faces to fully express the emotion within the design being created. Limitations aside, we'll look at how typefaces and families can be used with graphics, HTML, and cascading style sheets.

Typefaces and Graphics

The most important thing to remember is selecting the typefaces you want to use for your body and header text *before* sitting down to set your type. Once you've determined what typefaces you'll be using, and you know the literal content of the graphic to be designed, the issue boils down to the tool you're going to use to set the type.

Most designers agree that to work with type, the ideal combination is Illustrator and Photoshop. Illustrator allows for a lot of control over the type you're setting, including kerning, which isn't available in Photoshop. Once you've set your type in Illustrator, you can then add your effects in Photoshop. The process is a bit time-consuming, however, and many Web designers have learned to be very creative using Photoshop alone.

Many designers who use Photoshop alone to set type are perfectly happy doing so. With the exception of kerning, most say they can achieve what they are after with what is available in Photoshop.

In Figure 12.4, you can see that the Photoshop type tool is open and that text is about to be set at 16-point, 16 line-spacing, anti-aliased, OzHandicraft typeface. Figure 12.5 shows the results.

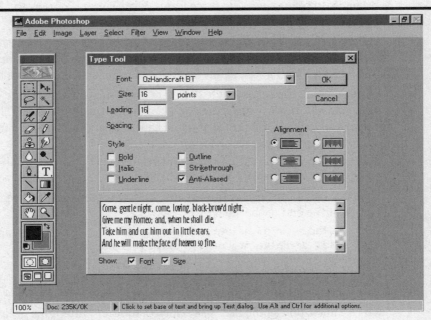

FIGURE 12.4: Using the type tool in Photoshop

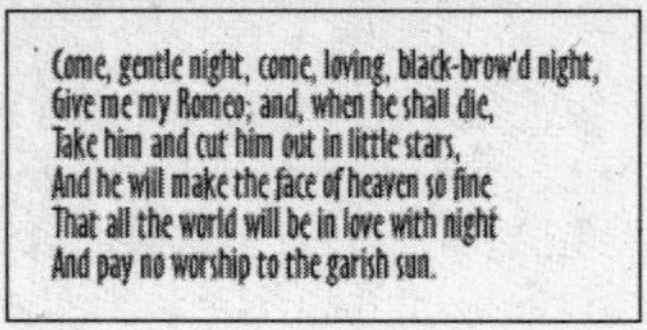

Come, gentle night, come, loving, black-brow'd night,
Give me my Romeo; and, when he shall die,
Take him and cut him out in little stars,
And he will make the face of heaven so fine
That all the world will be in love with night
And pay no worship to the garish sun.

FIGURE 12.5: The type is set.

Typefaces, Families, and the Font Tag

With the HTML <font> tag, you can select any typeface that you like and use it in the face attribute. Again, the limitation is that you will run into a problem with who has what on any given machine.

There is really only a total of three type families and specific, related typefaces that you can be almost absolutely sure will show up across platforms and on individual machines.

On the PC, the forms are serif, monospaced, and sans serif. The specific faces are Times New Roman, Courier New, and Arial, respectively.

Macintosh offers the same three forms, with Times, Courier, and Helvetica, replacing Arial.

What does this mean to you as a designer? It's simple. The face attribute of the <font> tag has one rather intelligent aspect: you can stack any number of typefaces with a type family and hopefully end up covering your bases.

After tagging the section of text to which you'd like to apply font styles, you add the face attribute and then define the font names. The browser will look for the first font name called for and, if it doesn't find it, will move on to the next named font:

```
<font face="arial,helvetica">This text will appear as Arial
or Helvetica, depending upon which font is available</font>
```

If you'd like to add some stability to this syntax, you can add the family name at the end of the stack:

```
<font face="arial,helvetica,sans-serif">This text will appear
as Arial or Helvetica or the default sans-serif font,
depending upon which font is available</font>
```

It's important to remember that if a font face isn't available on a given machine, the default face will appear. Default is almost always a serif font such as Times, unless the user has selected another font for his or her default. So if you're mixing fonts, bear in mind that your sans serifs might appear as serifs, and vice versa.

This lack of control can seem maddening! You can always forgo using type, but then you run the risk of having your pages appear ho-hum. Go for fonts, but do so thoughtfully, and wherever possible, stack the fonts along with a family name.

Style Sheets

Using a typeface family as a default is an excellent idea all around, as it covers the designer's font choices as completely as possible. Even if a specific font face is unavailable on a given computer, it's likely that a similar one in that font's family is available. An aware designer will place the first choice first, second choice second, and so forth, with the family name at the end.

You can approach fonts in style sheets using the font-family string. Style sheets will accept these in all three types of style sheets: inline, embedded, and linked.

An inline example (see Figure 12.6) follows:

```
<span style="font-family:garamond,times,serif">
Love is a smoke raised with the fume of sighs;
Being purged, a fire sparkling in lovers' eyes;
Being vex'd a sea nourished with lovers' tears:
What is it else? a madness most discreet,
A choking gall and a preserving sweet.
</span>
```

Since inline style can be used with any reasonable HTML tag, you could also do this:

```
<blockquote style="font-family:garamond,times,serif">
Love is a smoke raised with the fume of sighs;
Being purged, a fire sparkling in lovers' eyes;
Being vex'd a sea nourished with lovers' tears:
What is it else? a madness most discreet,
A choking gall and a preserving sweet.
</blockquote>
```

The result is that the browser picks up not only the style sheet information, but the HTML blockquote format as well (see Figure 12.7).

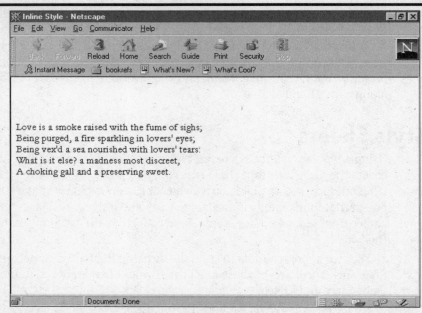

FIGURE 12.6: The results of an inline application of style

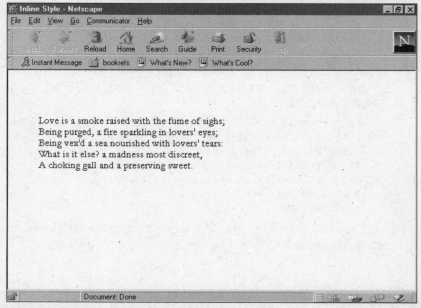

FIGURE 12.7: Using inline style with the blockquote tag

Here's an embedded example of the same concept (linked style will also look like this). Let's say you wanted to apply a series of typefaces and a family to an entire paragraph. The syntax would be:

```
P { font-family: arial, helvetica, sans-serif; }
```

In Figure 12.8, you can see that Garamond appears in all the paragraphs on the page.

You can apply this style to the blockquote as well:

```
blockquote { font-family: arial, helvetica, sans-serif; }
```

Figure 12.9 shows the blockquoted section.

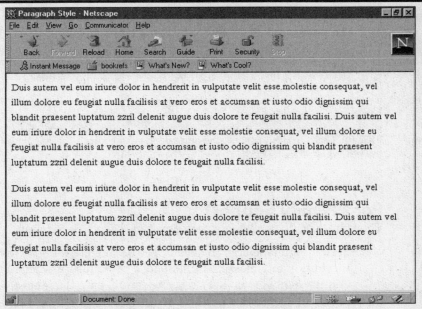

FIGURE 12.8: Garamond is applied to all the paragraphs.

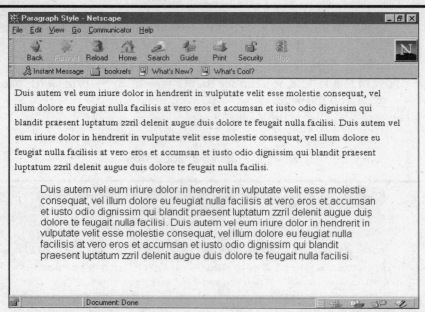

FIGURE 12.9: In this instance, the embedded style controls the appearance of all the blockquoted material.

Font Family Support

There are specific families supported by style sheets, as follows:

Serif Serif typefaces are usually the best choice for body text. In addition to Times and Garamond, a popular serif typeface is Century Schoolbook. Let's say you want to have that appear first, but if someone doesn't have that font on their machine, you'd prefer that the computer search for Garamond rather than move right away to Times. You can see the syntax below. The results can be seen in Figure 12.10.

```
{ font-family: century schoolbook, garamond, times, serif; }
```

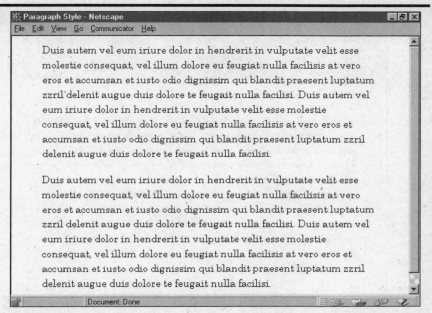

FIGURE 12.10: My browser shows the Century Schoolbook typeface, because I have that font.

Sans serif   This font family includes popular choices such as Arial, Helvetica, and Avante Garde. The same concept applies here, of course:

```
{ font-family: arial, helvetica, avante garde, sans-serif; }
```

Cursive   Use this in place of *script*. These are the same as script typefaces—fonts that appear as though they have been handwritten. Figure 12.11 shows the results.

```
{ font-family: embassy, cursive; }
```

TRY IT ONLINE

Try this one on your own with a style sheet–compatible browser. What are your results? Do you see Arial, Helvetica, Avante Garde, or a default sans serif font?

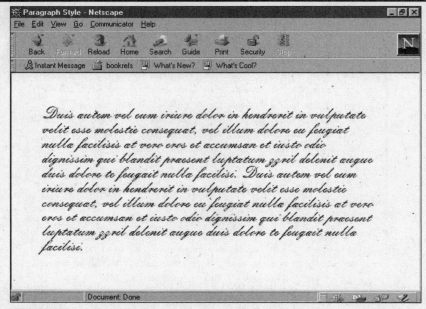

FIGURE 12.11: This typeface results from embedded style.

Fantasy   Fantasy fonts are used for *decorative* type, such as stylish, fun headings and titles. They are not practical for body text. You can see the Whimsy typeface in Figure 12.12.

```
{ font-family: whimsy icg, fantasy; }
```

Monospace   As with serif and sans serif options, you're familiar with the monospaced font. Figure 12.13 looks like the text was typed onto a page.

```
{ font-family: courier, monospace; }
```

Does anyone *still* use a typewriter?

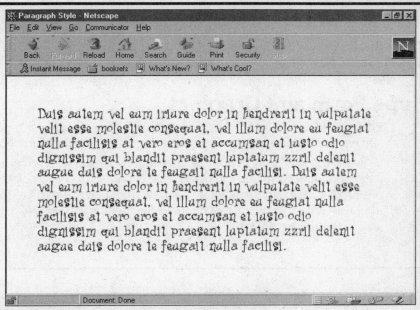

FIGURE 12.12: Here you see the Whimsy typeface.

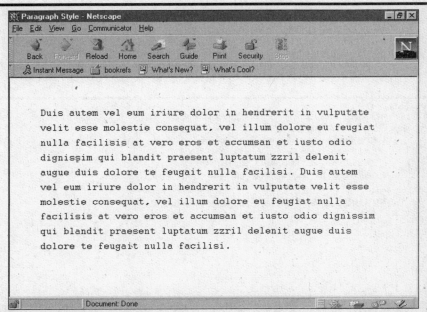

FIGURE 12.13: Using style again, you can ensure a monospaced (in this case Courier) typeface.

TYPE FORM

In the world of typographic design, form refers to such concerns as weight and posture.

Type Form and Graphics

With graphics, you can address weight by choosing the exact typeface and weight you desire for your graphic. Figure 12.14 shows Arial Narrow.

Posture is also dealt with when choosing the typeface. If you select the italic or oblique form of the typeface, you end up with that typeface. Figure 12.15 shows Century Schoolbook italicized. I love the look of this font in italics—it's very evocative of handwriting. Figure 12.16 shows a bold weight Bodoni typeface.

Come, gentle night, come, loving, black-brow'd night,
Give me my Romeo; and, when he shall die,
Take him and cut him out in little stars,
And he will make the face of heaven so fine
That all the world will be in love with night
And pay no worship to the garish sun.

FIGURE 12.14: Arial Narrow is set on a graphic.

Come, gentle night, come, loving, black-brow'd night,
Give me my Romeo; and, when he shall die,
Take him and cut him out in little stars,
And he will make the face of heaven so fine
That all the world will be in love with night
And pay no worship to the garish sun.

FIGURE 12.15: Century Schoolbook italicized

Come, gentle night, come, loving, black-brow'd night,
Give me my Romeo; and, when he shall die,
Take him and cut him out in little stars,
And he will make the face of heaven so fine
That all the world will be in love with night
And pay no worship to the garish sun.

FIGURE 12.16: Bold Bodoni

Type Form and HTML

Standard HTML is more difficult when it comes to weight because you are dependent upon the end user's library of fonts. If that user does not have the light, narrow, bold, demi-bold, or other weight you specify in the face attribute of the <font> tag, you're going to be out of luck. One thing you can do is stack the weight that you'd prefer with the typeface itself, and in some cases your font will be seen (see Figure 12.17).

```
<font face="arial narrow, arial, helvetica, sans-serif">
Love is a smoke raised with the fume of sighs;
Being purged, a fire sparkling in lovers' eyes;
Being vex'd a sea nourished with lovers' tears:
What is it else? a madness most discreet,
A choking gall and a preserving sweet.
</font>
```

Italics are easily created with the italic tag, <i>...</i>. Any text between opening and closing italic tags will appear in the italic version of that typeface, provided that the individual has the means of viewing the italic version.

```
<font face="arial narrow, arial, helvetica, sans-serif">
Love is a smoke raised with the fume of sighs;
Being purged, a fire sparkling in lovers' eyes;
Being vex'd a sea nourished with lovers' tears:
What is it else? a <i>madness</i> most discreet,
A choking gall and a preserving sweet.
</font>
```

Part ii

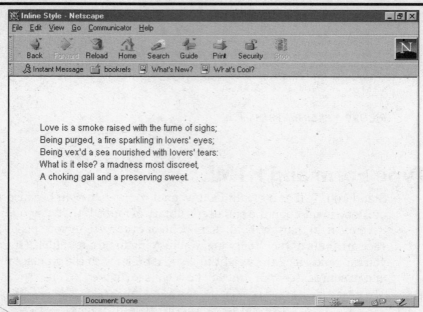

FIGURE 12.17: Using the \<font\> tag to achieve Arial Narrow

Similarly, bold can be created with the bold tag, \<b\>...\</b\>.

```
<font face="arial narrow, arial, helvetica, sans-serif">
Love is a smoke raised with the fume of sighs;
Being purged, a fire sparkling in lovers' eyes;
Being vex'd a sea nourished with lovers' tears:
What is it else? a <b>madness</b> most discreet,
A choking gall and a preserving sweet.
</font>
```

Hopefully, Shakespeare will forgive me for forcing emphasis on Romeo's already impassioned speech!

There is no tag for oblique postures.

Type Form and Style Sheets

As with font faces, font weights in style sheets rely on the existence of the corresponding font and weight on an individual's machine. A range of attributes are available in style sheets, including extra-light, demi-light, light, medium, extra-bold, demi-bold, and bold.

Be aware that before assigning font weights, the typeface to which you are applying the weight must have that weight available within the face. It is likely that many people will have the medium, light, or bold versions of a typeface; it is much less likely that they will have extra-lights or demi-bolds—unless they have an extensive font collection on their computer.

A light weight is assigned to the Arial font in Figure 12.18, and a bold weight to the Walbaum font in Figure 12.19.

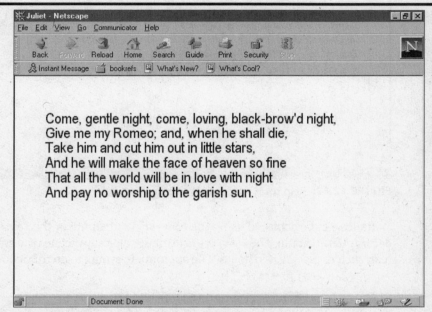

FIGURE 12.18: Arial Narrow is achieved with style.

To achieve posture, you'll rely on three methods:

▶ The `font-style` attribute

▶ The `text-decoration` attribute

▶ Standard HTML with bold or italic tags

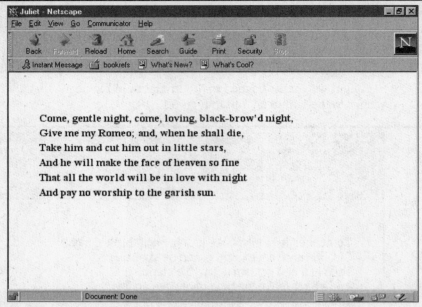

FIGURE 12.19: Bold gives weight to Walbaum.

Italics can be achieved using the `font-style` attribute or the `text-decoration` attribute. The `font-style` attribute typically dictates the style of text, such as placing it in italics. The appropriate syntax to do this follows:

```
{ font-style: italic; }
```

The use of the `text-decoration` attribute is similar:

```
{ text-decoration: italic; }
```

It seems obvious that bold should be considered a font style too, but there is no style sheet attribute supported by Internet Explorer 3 to achieve this. Therefore, you'll have to revert to the use of standard HTML bold tags.

```
<b>This text will appear in bold,</b> whereas this text will
not.
```

TIP

Dislike underlined links? With cascading style sheets, designers can now use the {text-decoration: none} attribute and argue to globally shut off underlined links. In embedded and linked style sheet formats, the syntax would follow the A value: A {text-decoration: none}. For inline style, simply place the value within the link you wish to control: <a style="text-decoration: none" href="my.html">this link has no underline!</a>.

OTHER TYPOGRAPHIC CONSIDERATIONS

Other typographic considerations include size, proportion, leading, and kerning. Size and proportion can be addressed with HTML and cascading style sheets, leading is somewhat addressed by cascading style sheets, and kerning can currently be dealt with only by setting the type on a graphic.

Using Graphics

Because you can address almost any kind of typographic issue by using Illustrator, whose interface is shown in Figure 12.20, and Photoshop to set the type onto a graphic, graphics give the most flexibility when you're attempting typographic concerns that cannot be dealt with using HTML or style sheets.

Size and proportion depend on your own design and aesthetic. Using points, you can set type as small or as large as you want. Direction can also be managed; Figure 12.21 shows a vertical header. Leading is addressed within the programs, as is letterspacing and kerning (see Figure 12.22).

NOTE

Kerning can currently be achieved on the Web by first setting the type in a program such as Illustrator and then saving it as a Web graphic using Photoshop. There is no HTML or style sheet–based method to deal with kerning.

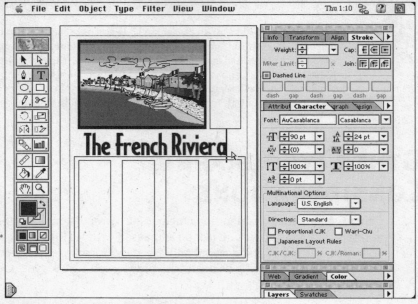

FIGURE 12.20: This type is being set in Illustrator.

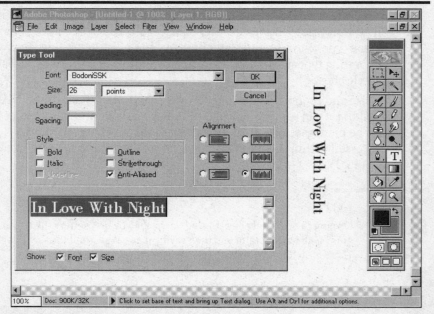

FIGURE 12.21: Setting a vertical header

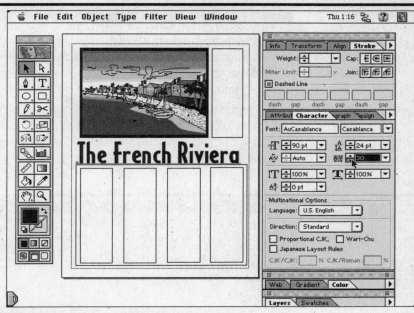

FIGURE 12.22: Using Illustrator for kerning

Type Size and HTML

The size attribute of the <font> tag allows you to set type based on a numeric system. Unfortunately, this system does not allow a designer to control type size using points. Furthermore, direction, leading, spacing, and kerning cannot be controlled with standard HTML.

Using the Size Attribute

Font sizing in HTML is pretty rudimentary, with whole-number values determining the size of the font. Default, standard size is 3; anything higher is going to be larger, and anything lower will be smaller. You can also use negative numbers, such as −1, to get a very small type size. Here's an example of a header using font face and size:

```
<font face="times,garamond,serif" size="5">
```

Anything much bigger than size 5 is ungainly. Small fonts, such as size 1, are good for notes and copyrights. Anything less is usually not viewable to people with average-to-poor eyesight.

Figure 12.23 shows an example with a header, body text, and a copy-right notice, each in a different-sized font. Note the typefaces being used. The header and copyright notice appear in Times, and the body in Arial. This page looks nice and neat, unlike Figure 12.24, which shows what happens when a coder runs amok. The "wave" effect came into vogue when font sizing first became available.

Some designers will argue that Figure 12.24 looks more interesting. They're right—it does, and I certainly don't want to discourage creativity. This particular effect was fun, but it quickly became cliché. I encourage you to study typography a little more closely and come up with original typographic applications.

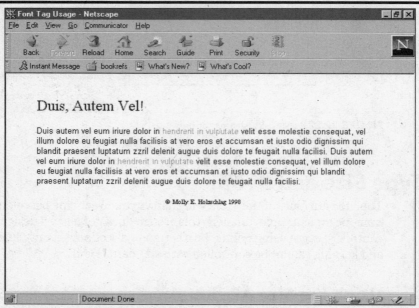

FIGURE 12.23: Using the <font> tag for page design

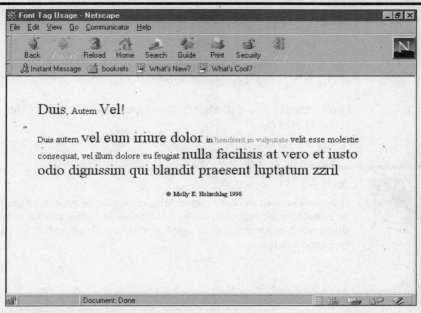

FIGURE 12.24: The "wave" effect

Style Sheets

Style sheets to the rescue! Size (with choice of measurement units) and leading can be applied using style sheets. Kerning is not an option in Web typography unless you set the type as a graphic.

Size

Sizing in style sheets gives designers five size options for their fonts:

Points   To set a font in point size, use the abbreviation pt immediately following the numeric size:

```
{font-size: 12pt}
```

Inches   If you'd rather set your fonts in inches, simply place the abbreviation in next to the numeral size, in inches, of the font size you require:

```
{font-size: 1in}
```

Part II

Centimeters Some designers might prefer centimeters, represented by cm and used in the same fashion as points and inches:

    {font-size: 5cm}

Pixels Pixels are argued with the px abbreviation:

    {font-size: 24px}

Percentage You also may choose to set a percentage of the default point size:

    {font-size: 50%}

NOTE
Point size is often the most comfortable choice for designers, although some will want to work with other methods. I recommend using point size, but if you do choose another method, *be consistent.* Your work will look much more professional as a result.

Leading

Leading is addressed in cascading style sheets with line-height. This refers to the amount of spacing between lines of text. This space should be consistent, or the result is uneven, unattractive spacing. The line-height attribute allows designers to set the distance between the baselines, or bottom, of lines of text.

To set the leading of a paragraph, use the line-height attribute in points, inches, centimeters, pixels, or percentages in the same fashion you would when describing sizing attributes:

    P { line-height: 14pt; }

COLOR AND TYPE

Color adds interest to type. You can use contrasting colors to gain a variety of effects. You can emphasize certain passages or parts of a word, as in Figure 12.25, or use colored type to separate headers from body text.

COLORMY**WORLD**

FIGURE 12.25: Emphasizing type with color

Creating Colored Type with Graphics

Again, graphics are your best bet when you really want to address color effects.

A helpful tip is to select your colors from the safe palette and to be sure to always optimize your graphics appropriately. This will give you the best chances of having smaller file sizes and better matches between HTML and graphic colors.

HTML-Based Type and Color

The `color` attribute allows you to set any hexadecimal value you'd like when using the <font> tag. As always, stick to safe-palette values. An example of the <font> tag with the `color` attribute added looks like this:

```
<font face="times,garamond,serif" size="5" color="#003300">
```

Use hexadecimal code to select a color; the one that you see listed here is forest green. Some people and certain HTML editing programs will use the literal name of standard colors, such as blue, green, red, and the like. The hexadecimal codes, however, are much more stable in cross-browser, cross-platform environments.

COLOR ONLINE

You can find hexadecimal color references at these Web sites:

▶ A chart of RGB and hexadecimal values can be found at `http://sdc.htrigg.smu.edu/HTMLPages/RGBchart.html`.

▶ Download the `nvalue.gif` or `nhue.gif` charts from Lynda Weinman's site: `http://www.lynda.com/files/`.

These charts put color selection and hexadecimal values right at your fingertips!

Style Sheets and Color

Style sheets allow for a great deal of flexibility when it comes to the addition of color. Using hexadecimal codes, color can be added to actual attributes, including other HTML tags used in the inline style sheet method:

```
<p style="color: #003300">
All of the text in this paragraph will appear in forest green.
</p>
```

With embedded and linked style sheets, you can add the `color` attribute to generalized, rather than specific, sections. In the following example, all level-two headers appear in red. Note that other attributes have been added here, including typeface, size, and style.

```
<style>
H2 {font-family: arial, helvetica; sans-serif;
font-size: 14pt;
font-style: italic;
color: #FF0033;}
</style>
```

ALL TOGETHER NOW

So far you've gotten a look at fragmented pieces of graphics, fonts, and styles. Here are full examples of each, in text and code.

Graphic Example

In this case, we'll use another quote from *Romeo and Juliet* and set it using 20-point Trebuchet (a font available from Microsoft at http://www.microsoft.com/typography/) with 20-point leading. The type is colored white and applied to a flat black background. Then a star motif is added to the background; the file is saved as a 5-bit GIF suitable for use as a background graphic.

Here's the simple HTML code to create the page:

```
<html>

<head>
<title>Juliet Speaks</title>
</head>

<body bgcolor="#000000" text="#FFFFFF" link="#00FF00"
vlink="#FF0000" background="juliet2.gif">
<pre>
```

```
</pre>
<div align="center">
<a href="next.htm"><i>next</i></a>
</div>
</body>
</html>
```

Part II

NOTE

There are 20 carriage returns between the `<pre>` tags, forcing the link to the bottom of the page.

You can see the results in Figure 12.26. Although a background graphic was used in this example, remember that you can set type on a graphic to be used anywhere on the page. You can place a graphic as a header, as body text, or as a part of body text and fix placement using tables (or style sheet positioning).

FIGURE 12.26: Graphic-based type design

Figure 12.27 is a screen capture from NextDada (`http://nextdada .luc.ac.be/`), one of Belgian graphic designer Joël Neelen's Web sites. On this page, he has stacked a series of graphics on top of one another to achieve his typographic design. Add to that some clever JavaScript and the page is alive with visual intrigue founded on its graphic-based typographic elements.

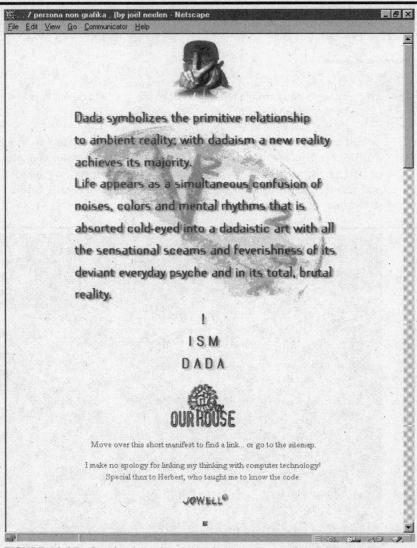

FIGURE 12.27: Graphic-based typography in action on the NextDada site

Here's a look at Neelen's code.

```html
<html>
<head>
    <!-- Author: Joel Neelen -->
    <!-- e-mail: jneelen@luc.ac.be -->
<title>. . / persona non grafika . (by jo&euml;l
neelen</title>
<meta name="description" content="The cyberplatform of Joel
Neelen aka {captain verruckt}">
<meta name="keywords" content="dada, nextdada, joel, neelen,
travel, travelling, kite, kiting, cerf-volant, art, graphics,
jemen, yemen, jordan, jordanie">
<meta name="author" content="Joel Neelen :
jneelen@luc.ac.be">

<script language="JavaScript">

<!-- if the browser is not capable to JavaScript1.1 he will
use this and do nothing
function init()
{
 dummy=0;
}
function imgreplace(i,s,text)
{
 window.status = text;
 return true;
}
// end do nothing -->


</script>
<script language="JavaScript1.1">

<!-- to hide script contents from old browsers
function init()
{ // set the 7 images to be non-highlighted
document.sexstacy.src = "/picture/dada/dada1_1.gif"
document.castle.src = "/picture/dada/dada2_1.gif"
document.old.src = "/picture/dada/dada4_1.gif"
document.travel.src = "/picture/dada/dada5_1.gif"
document.art.src = "/picture/dada/dada6_1.gif"
document.kites.src = "/picture/dada/dada7_1.gif"
document.cinema.src = "/picture/dada/dada8_1.gif"
}
```

```
function imgreplace( imagename, source, text )
{
 eval( 'document.' + imagename + '.src = "/picture/dada/" +
source' );
 setTimeout( 'window.status = "'+text+'"', 500 );
 return true;
}
// end hide contents from old browsers -->

</script>

</head>
<body onload="init();" bgcolor="#FFFFFF" text="#7297FF"
link="#7297FF" vlink="#F77307" alink="#F77307">

<center>
<table height="100%" width="420" cellspacing="0"
cellpadding="2" border="0">
<tr align="center">
<td align="center">
<a href="root/kaffee.html"
onmouseover="self.status='Something about the man behind
this web site.' ; return true">
<img src="picture/dada/dada0.gif" width="107" height="100"
border="0" alt="Joel"></a>
</td>
</tr>

<tr align="center">
<td align="center">
<a href="root/sex/sexstacy.html" onmouseover="return
imgreplace('sexstacy','dada1_2.gif','Monogamy is the
message!');" onmouseout="return imgreplace('sexstacy',
'dada1_1.gif','');return true;"><img lowsrc="picture/dada/
dada1_0.gif" src="picture/dada/dada1_2.gif" width="420"
border="0" name="sexstacy" alt="sexstacy"></a>
<br>

<a href="root/castle.html" onmouseover="return
imgreplace('castle','dada2_2.gif','The purpose could be to
create a virtual community where people can have fun and
learn things.');" onmouseout="return imgreplace('castle',
'dada2_1.gif','');return true;"><img lowsrc="picture/dada/
```

```
dada2_0.gif" src="picture/dada/dada2_2.gif" width="420"
height="36" border="0" name="castle" alt="castle"></a>
<br>

<img lowsrc="picture/dada/dada3_0.gif"
src="picture/dada/dada3_1.gif" width="420" height="36"
border="0" alt="nothing">
<br>

<a href="root/index.html" onmouseover="return
imgreplace('old','dada4_2.gif','This link will bring you
to my old homepage.');" onmouseout="return
imgreplace('old','dada4_1.gif','');return true;">
<img lowsrc="picture/dada/dada4_0.gif"
src="picture/dada/dada4_2.gif" width="420" height="36"
border="0" name="old" alt="old homepage"></a>
<br>

<a href="root/travel/travel.html" onmouseover="return
imgreplace('travel','dada5_2.gif','Explore different
cultural lifestyles and backgrounds...');"
onmouseout="return imgreplace('travel','dada5_1.gif','');
return true;"><img lowsrc="picture/dada/dada5_0.gif"
src="picture/dada/dada5_2.gif" width="420" height="36"
border="0" name="travel" alt="travel"></a>
<br>

<a href="root/art/artefact.html" onmouseover="return
imgreplace('art','dada6_2.gif','Dadaism, for one thing, no
longer stands aside from life as an aesthetic manner...');"
onmouseout="return imgreplace('art','dada6_1.gif','');return
true;"><img lowsrc="picture/dada/dada6_0.gif" src="picture/
dada/dada6_2.gif" width="420" height="36" border="0"
name="art" alt="art"></a>
<br>

<a href="root/kites.html" onmouseover="return
imgreplace('kites','dada7_2.gif','A kite is a thing on the
end of a string!');" onmouseout="return
imgreplace('kites','dada7_1.gif','');return true;">
<img lowsrc="picture/ dada/dada7_0.gif"
src="picture/dada/dada7_2.gif" width="420" height="36"
border="0" name="kites" alt="kites"></a>
<br>
```

```
<a href="root/cinema.cgi" onmouseover="return
imgreplace('cinema','dada8_2.gif','I felt an icy hand of
fear grabbing me.');" onmouseout="return imgreplace('cinema',
'dada8_1.gif','');return true;"><img lowsrc="picture/
dada/dada8_0.gif" src="picture/dada/dada8_2.gif" width="420"
height="72" border="0" name="cinema" alt="cinema"></a>

</td>
</tr>

<tr>
<td align=center>
        <!-- On reload this image will automatically
change -->

<img src="picture/dada/dada3.gif" width=107 height=100
border=0 alt="D A D A">

        <!-- End on reload -->
<br>
        <!-- Start link to OUR HOUSE 1997 -->

<a href="http://www.ourhouse.be/" onmouseover="self.status=
'Get a glimpse of the multi-happening Our House that took
place in September1997' ; return true" target="_blank">
<img src="picture/dada/ourhouse.gif" width="107"
height="100" border="0" alt="Our House 1997"></a>

        <!-- End link -->

<br>
<font size="-1">Move over this short manifest to find a
link... or go to the <a href="root/sitemap.html"
onmouseover="self.status='SiteMap.' ; return
true">sitemap</a>.
<p>
I make no apology for linking my thinking with computer
technology!</font>
<br>
```

```
<font size="-1" color="#789DB9">Special thnx to Herbert, who
taught me to know the code.</font>
<p>

<a href="root/mail.html" onmouseover="self.status='You can
send me an e-mail.' ; return true"><img lowsrc="picture/
dada/jowell_0.gif" src="picture/dada/jowell_1.gif" width=80
height=21 border=0 alt="JOWELL"></a>
<p>

<a href="http://www.nedstat.nl/cgi-bin/viewstat?name=
nextcount" target="_blank"><img src="http://www.nedstat.nl/
cgi-bin/nedstat.gif?name=nextcount" border="0" alt=""
width="8" height="8"></a>

</td>
</tr>
</table>

</center>
</body>
</html>
```

Note the use of meta tags, comment tags, table layout, and alt attributes. Neelen, like many Web designers concerned about the thoroughness of their work, takes special care not only with his typographic design but also with the underlying code elements that make a site accessible, stable, and professional.

HTML Example

This example demonstrates the use of the font tag and its attributes. I want you first to look at the page, which is shown in Figure 12.28.

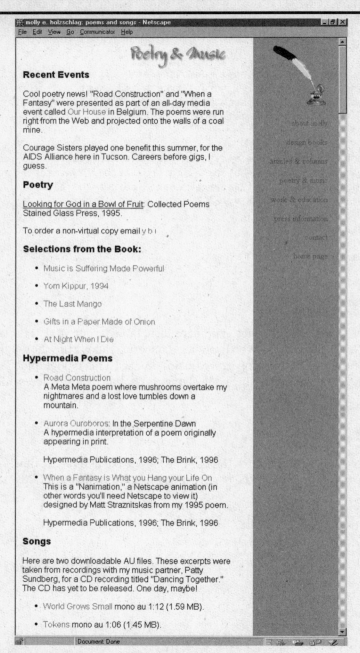

FIGURE 12.28: The Poetry and Music page from molly.com

Then predetermine all of the different fonts (graphics and HTML included) on the page *just by looking*. Make a list of those fonts.

Now study the following code:

```
<!-- molly e. holzschlag: molly@molly.com -->

<html>
<head>
<title>molly e. holzschlag: poems and songs</title>
</head>

<body bgcolor="#000000" text="#000000" link="#993300"
vlink="#993300" background="images/mol-bak.gif">

<table border="0" width="600" cellpadding="5"
cellspacing="0">
<tr>

<td valign="top" width="400">

<img src="images/pm-hed.gif" alt="poetry" width="300"
height="50" align="right">
<br clear="all">

<font face="arial,helvetica,sans-serif">

<h3>Recent Events</h3>

Cool poetry news! "Road Construction" and "When a Fantasy"
were presented as
part of an all-day media event called <a href="http://www
.ourhouse.be/">Our House</a> in Belgium. The poems were run
right from the Web and projected onto the walls of a coal
mine.
<p>

Courage Sisters played one benefit this summer, for the AIDS
Alliance here in Tucson. Careers before gigs, I guess.
<p>

<h3>Poetry</h3>

<u>Looking for God in a Bowl of Fruit</u>: Collected Poems
<br>

Stained Glass Press, 1995.
<p>
```

```
To order a non-virtual copy email
<a href="mailto:ybi@ybi.com">y b i</a>
<p>

<h3>Selections from the Book:</h3>

<ul>

<li><a href="p-1.htm">Music is Suffering Made Powerful</a>
<p>

<li><a href="p-2.htm">Yom Kippur, 1994 </a>
<p>

<li><a href="p-3.htm">The Last Mango</a>
<p>

<li><a href="p-4.htm">Gifts in a Paper Made of Onion</a>
<p>

<li><a href="p-5.htm">At Night When I Die</a>

</ul>
<p>

<h3>Hypermedia Poems</h3>

<ul>

<li><a href="http://ybi.com/molly/rc/">Road Construction</a>
<br>

A Meta Meta poem where mushrooms overtake my nightmares and a
lost love tumbles down a mountain.
<p>

<li><a href="http://ybi.com/aurora/">Aurora Ouroboros</a>: In
the Serpentine Dawn
<br>

A hypermedia interpretation of a poem originally appearing in
print.
<p>

Hypermedia Publications, 1996; The Brink, 1996
<p>
```

```
<li><a href="http://ybi.com/poetry/fant.html">When a Fantasy
is What you Hang your Life On</a>
<br>

This is a "Nanimation," a Netscape animation (in other words
you'll need Netscape to view it) designed by Matt
Straznitskas from my 1995 poem.
<p>

Hypermedia Publications, 1996; The Brink, 1996

</ul>
<p>

<h3>Songs</h3>

Here are two downloadable AU files. These excerpts were taken
from recordings with my music partner, Patty Sundberg, for
a CD recording titled "Dancing Together." The CD has yet to
be released. One day, maybe!
<p>

<ul>

<li><a href="images/wrldgrow.au">World Grows Small</a> mono
au 1:12 (1.59 MB).
<p>

<li><a href="images/tokens.au">Tokens</a> mono au 1:06
(1.45 MB).

</ul>

</font>

</td>

<td valign="top" align="right" width="200">

<img src="images/poetry.gif" width="108" height="125"
border="0" alt="pen and ink">
<p>

<a href="molly.htm">about molly</a>
<p>
```

```
<a href="books.htm">design books</a>
<p>

<a href="write.htm">articles & columns</a>
<p>

<a href="poems.htm">poetry & music</a>
<p>

<a href="work.htm">work & education</a>
<p>

<a href="press.htm">press information</a>
<p>

<a href="contact.htm">contact</a>
<p>

<a href="index.html">home page</a>

</td>
</tr>
</table>

</body>
</html>
```

If you guessed three for the total number of fonts used on this page, you're correct. First there's the header graphic, which uses the Bergell typeface. Then there's the body text, which will appear as Arial, Helvetica, or whatever sans serif font you have available if those are not.

Finally, there's the type I've used in the right-margin menu. Sharp readers will have noticed that *there is no font tag or attributes* used to create this font. Why?

Think about it for a second.

Can you identify the typeface?

It's a serif.

Specifically, it's Times.

Remember now? Serifs are the *default* font. Therefore, I didn't have to code for it.

AN OFFLINE EXERCISE

Have some fun with this code! Change type using the font tag as often as you like, trying out different combinations, colors, sizes, and styles.

Style Sheet Example

Here, typeface, form, leading, and color have been assigned to the page using style sheets.

```
<html>

<head>
<title>Style Sheet Example</title>

<style>

H1 { font-family: arial, helvetica, san-serif ;
font-size: 22pt;
color: #FFFF00; }

P { font-family: times, serif;
font-size: 18pt;
color: #FFFFFF;
line-height: 18pt; }

A { text-decoration: none;
font-weight: bold;
color: #CCFFCC; }

</style>

</head>

<body bgcolor="#000000">

<blockquote>

<h1>Juliet Thinks of Romeo</h1>

<p>
Come, gentle night, come, loving, black-brow'd night,<br>
```

```
Give me my <a href="romeo.htm">Romeo</a>; and, when he shall
die,<br>
Take him and cut him out in little stars,<br>
And he will make the face of heaven so fine<br>
That all the world will be in love with night<br>
And pay no worship to the garish sun.
</p>

</blockquote>

</body>
</html>
```

Figure 12.29 shows the results.

Obviously, these examples are just the tip of the iceberg when it comes to the use of style sheets. Many options and more powerful applications are available, and I highly recommend that you study more about style sheets as you learn more about typography. They will no doubt be a major player in how type on the Web is delivered with increasing sophistication.

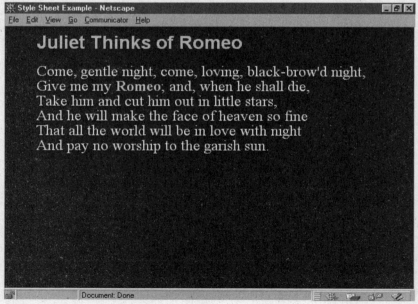

FIGURE 12.29: Style applied to a page

WHAT'S NEXT?

The typographic tips you've learned in this chapter will take you a long way toward creating an eye-catching Web page. Along the way, you were introduced to the use of style sheets, a topic covered in detail in Part III. In this next part, you'll also learn how to optimize your pages for the two most popular browsers being used today, and you'll learn other advanced features, including adding multimedia, creating forms, and using dynamic HTML.

PART **iii**

ADVANCED HTML

Chapter 13

OPTIMIZING YOUR WEB PAGES FOR INTERNET EXPLORER 5

I n previous chapters, you've learned how to use HTML to create Web pages that will look and behave the same way in both Microsoft Internet Explorer and Netscape Navigator browsers. This is great if you want your pages to look the same in both browsers. However, each browser has features of its own that you can take advantage of when writing HTML.

Written for *HTML Complete*, 2nd Edition
By Adrian W. Kinglsey-Hughes

In this chapter, we'll look at how you can make use of some of the features unique to the Microsoft Internet Explorer 5 browser by writing HTML that is optimized for it.

When you are creating Web pages, you can never be sure what browsers your visitors will use. Looking at it from a statistical point of view, you have a better than 90 percent chance that they will be using either Microsoft Internet Explorer or Netscape Navigator. Of this 90 percent, between one-half to three-quarters of these users will have the latest version of either browser. Given such high numbers of users, it makes great sense to consider creating optimized Web pages for the two browsers. You can give your visitors the best possible surfing experience by making full use of the browser's capability!

Let's get straight to work by looking at optimizations possible when creating Web pages targeted toward Internet Explorer 5. We will look at optimizing Web pages for Netscape Navigator 4 in Chapter 14.

DIRECTING INTERNET EXPLORER USERS TO INTERNET EXPLORER PAGES

One drawback of creating optimized pages for a particular browser is that if those pages happen to be viewed in the other browser, unexpected things can happen. As Web developers, we try our best to avoid unexpected things happening, and the best way to avoid this is to make sure that Netscape Navigator users never get to see the pages we designed for Internet Explorer!

But how can you do this? How do you sort out Internet Explorer 5 users from those using Netscape Navigator 4? Well, a few years ago, developers placed links on their Web pages that said something like, "If you are viewing with Internet Explorer, CLICK HERE . . .". This had many drawbacks, one of the biggest being that many of the users themselves didn't know which browser they were using, and of those that did, not many understood the relevance of choosing the correct link.

The best solution is one that removes the responsibility from the visitor and does the sorting out in the background, while they are waiting for the page to load. In order to do this, you need to insert some code into your Web pages that will find out which browser the visitor is using and, if they are using a different browser from the one you are expecting, redirect them to the appropriate Web page suited to their browser.

The code, called a *script*, that you will use is written in a scripting language called JavaScript. If you're now beginning to worry because you haven't used any script before, don't! The great thing about this script is that you don't need to know how it works. You just need to add it to the Web page and watch it work!

NOTE

In this chapter, we'll just be covering the basic JavaScript needed to redirect visitors. For a more detailed description of JavaScript, turn to Chapter 20.

Adding the Script

Let's start off with an empty HTML page and look at how to add the script to it. Here's the script for the empty page:

```
<HTML>
<HEAD>
<TITLE>New Page</TITLE>
</HEAD>
<BODY>

</BODY>
</HTML>
```

The JavaScript that we are going to add will be inserted inside the <HEAD> tag, after the <TITLE> tag. The script is as follows:

```
<SCRIPT LANGUAGE="JavaScript">
<!--
var browser = "unknown"
var version = 0
var detected = false
var ua = window.navigator.userAgent

if (ua.substring(0,7) == "Mozilla") {
    if (ua.indexOf("MSIE") > 0) {
        browser = "Microsoft"
    }

    if (ua.indexOf("5.") > 0) {
        version = 5
```

Part iii

```
    }
}

//Find Internet Explorer 5 users and do nothing
if (browser == "Microsoft" && version == 5) {
    detected = true
}

//Find other JavaScript-enabled browser here and move
//them to another, more suitable page!
if (detected == false) {
    detected = true
    location.href = "newpage.htm"
}
//-->
</SCRIPT>
```

Notice the line `locations.href = "newpage.htm"`? This is the line that decides where visitors not using Internet Explorer 5 go. For every Internet Explorer 5 optimized page that you have, ideally you should have a similar page optimized for Netscape Navigator. So, if the Web page optimized for Internet Explorer is called `page1ie.htm`, then the corresponding page for Netscape Navigator could be called `page1nn.htm`, and it would be here that you would put that page name, like this:

```
location.href = "page1nn.htm"
```

So the complete page containing the JavaScript to redirect Netscape Navigator users to a page called `page1nn.htm` would be as follows:

```
<HTML>
<HEAD>
<TITLE>New Page</TITLE>
<SCRIPT LANGUAGE="JavaScript">
<!--
var browser = "unknown"
var version = 0
var detected = false
var ua = window.navigator.userAgent

if (ua.substring(0,7) == "Mozilla") {
    if (ua.indexOf("MSIE") > 0) {
        browser = "Microsoft"
    }

    if (ua.indexOf("5.") > 0) {
        version = 5
```

```
   }
}

//Find Internet Explorer 5 users and do nothing
if (browser == "Microsoft" && version == 5) {
   detected = true
}

//Find other JavaScript-enabled browser here and move
//them to another, more suitable page!
if (detected == false) {
   detected = true
   location.href = "page1nn.htm"
}
//-->
</SCRIPT>
</HEAD>
<BODY>

</BODY>
</HTML>
```

WARNING

Remember to change the page name referred to in the script to correspond to the name of the page that you want visitors to be redirected to. A common mistake made by beginners is to forget to do this and redirect to the same page every time. This can leave the visitor going around in a loop or going to a dead link.

Now that we've looked at how to keep out any visitors not using Internet Explorer 5, let's look at what optimizations you can make to basic HTML Web pages to enhance them for that browser.

OPTIMIZATIONS FOR INTERNET EXPLORER 5

When we talk about optimization, we are actually talking about three different things, including:

▶ Adding functionality (through tags and properties) not present in other browsers

▸ Making sure that you don't inadvertently use functionality (again, tags and properties) that isn't supported

▸ Making sure that the code you write is clean and clear and takes the minimum time to load into the browser

NOTE

In this chapter, we will be looking at how to add additional functionality to Web pages created for Internet Explorer 5.

ADDING FUNCTIONALITY

Since this is the most exciting aspect of optimization, this is where we'll begin! Adding functionality to a Web page isn't as complicated as it sounds. You don't need to write pages of HTML or learn complicated scripting languages. Adding functionality generally means only making small adjustments or "tweaks" to the HTML and letting the browser do the rest. Nothing in this chapter will require you to radically change the way that you create your Web pages.

Let's begin by looking at how to optimize the layout of the page.

Page Layout

Figure 13.1 shows a Web page containing a couple of paragraphs of text.

Notice the margins around the page. These are now set to the default of the browser. However, you can easily change the margins of the page to any number of pixels you desire by using the TOPMARGIN and LEFTMARGIN attributes of the <BODY> tag.

```
<BODY TOPMARGIN="0" LEFTMARGIN="0">
```

So, if you wanted to set a large margin at both the top and left sides of the page, you would set them as follows:

```
<BODY TOPMARGIN="50" LEFTMARGIN="50">
```

The result is shown in Figure 13.2.

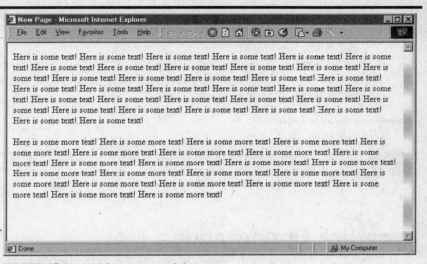

FIGURE 13.1: A Web page containing text

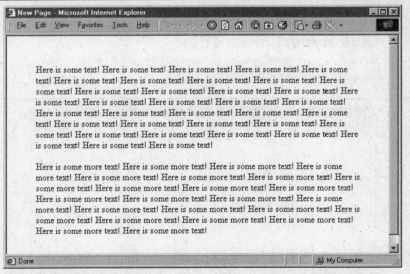

FIGURE 13.2: The same Web page with margins at the top and left

Part iii

Notice also how the margins on all sides of the browser window are affected, not just the top and left sides. This effect is sometimes more obvious if you change the size of the browser window.

The values for TOPMARGIN and LEFTMARGIN must be positive integers. This means that negative values are invalid, and the browser will revert to the default page margins.

WARNING
Again, do not use negative values for the TOPMARGIN and LEFTMARGIN attributes. The code <BODY topmargin="-50" leftmargin="-100"> will revert to the default page margins.

Hyperlink Optimization

The ability to move easily from one page to the next using hyperlinks is really what makes the Web special, and to do this you rely on the hyperlink. Let's look at a few ways that you can optimize hyperlinks for Internet Explorer 5.

Give Hyperlinks a Title

Hyperlinks are great, but sometimes they don't tell you enough, such as the example shown in Figure 13.3.

FIGURE 13.3: A hyperlink in a Web page

Here's the code for the link:

```
<HTML>
<HEAD>
<TITLE>New Page</TITLE>
</HEAD>
<BODY>
<A HREF="next.htm">Click Here!</A>
</BODY>
</HTML>
```

Not really very clear, is it? But you can do something to improve this. By using the TITLE property, you can add a caption to the hyperlink, giving the visitor more information when they hover the mouse pointer over it. See Figure 13.4 for an example.

The TITLE property is easy to use: just add it inside the <A> tag and type the pop-up message that you want to appear.

```
<HTML>
<HEAD>
<TITLE>New Page</TITLE>
</HEAD>
<BODY>
<A HREF="next.htm" TITLE="Click here to go to next.htm">Click
Here!</A>
</BODY>
</HTML>
```

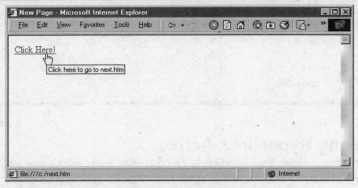

FIGURE 13.4: The hyperlink with an added title

Part iii

USING THE TITLE ATTRIBUTE TO ENHANCE TAGS

The TITLE attribute doesn't just work with the <A> tag. It can also be used with the following tags in Web pages designed for Internet Explorer 5:

A	FRAMESET	PLAINTEXT
ACRONYM	HN (1–6)	PRE
ADDRESS	HR	Q
APPLET	I	RT
AREA	IFRAME	RUBY
B	IMG	S
BDO	INPUT TYPE=BUTTON	SAMP
BIG	INPUT TYPE=CHECKBOX	SMALL
BLOCKQUOTE	INPUT TYPE=FILE	SPAN
BODY	INPUT TYPE=IMAGE	STRIKE
BUTTON	INPUT TYPE=PASSWORD	STRONG
CAPTION	INPUT TYPE=RADIO	SUB
CITE	INPUT TYPE=RESET	SUP
CODE	INPUT TYPE=SUBMIT	TABLE
COLGROUP	INPUT TYPE=TEXT	TBODY
DD	INS	TD
DEL	KBD	TEXTAREA
DFN	LABEL	TFOOT
DIR	LEGEND	TH
DIV	LI	THEAD
DL	LISTING	TR
DT	MAP	TT
EM	MARQUEE	U
EMBED	MENU	UL
FIELDSET	OBJECT	VAR
FORM	OL	XMP
FRAME	P	

Making Hyperlinks Active

Once upon a time, that blue underlined text of a hyperlink was unmistakable. Nowadays, with so much color and excitement on Web pages, hyperlinks can blend too easily into the background. When you want them to stand out, one of the best ways is to use color . . . but not a single color! Far better to make them change color as the visitor moves the mouse pointer over them.

The great thing about this is that it is easy to do . . . and you only need to code it once on the page for all hyperlinks on that page to behave in the same way!

To perform this magic, you'll use a Web technology called *cascading style sheets (CSS)*. The great thing about CSS is that you don't need to know how it works to use it in Web pages.

> **NOTE**
> Cascading style sheets are covered in greater depth in Chapter 16.

Let's start with a Web page that has three hyperlinks. The code is shown in Listing 13.1, and the page is shown in Figure 13.5.

Listing 13.1:   A Web Page with Three Hyperlinks

```
<HTML>
<HEAD>
<TITLE>New Page</TITLE>
</HEAD>
<BODY>
<H1>Links, links, links!</H1>
A <A HREF="mypage.htm">link</A> to Me!
<BR>
A <A HREF="friends.htm">link</A> to my friends!
<BR>
A <A HREF="pets.htm">link</A> to my pets!
</BODY>
</HTML>
```

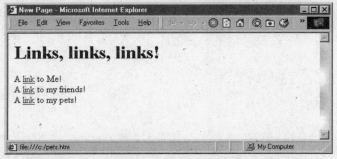

FIGURE 13.5: A Web page with three hyperlinks

Part iii

It's quite easy to make these hyperlinks much more visually appealing. Let's look at the steps you have to go through.

NOTE

We use ellipses to indicate where the snippets of code fall within the entire Listing 13.1.

1. First, add a style block to the <HEAD> tag on the Web page. This is where the cascading style sheet information will go and consists of the <STYLE> opening and closing tags.

```
...
<TITLE>New Page</TITLE>
<STYLE>

</STYLE>
</HEAD>
...
```

2. Next, add HTML comment tags inside the style block that you have just created. These comment tags are put there in case someone visits the page with an older browser that isn't capable of understanding the cascading style sheet information you will add. With comment tags in place, older browsers will simply ignore anything between the <STYLE> tags. Without the comment tags, these browsers may throw out error messages or display the page incorrectly.

TIP

It is a good idea to always add the comment tags, even if you *know* that the browser your visitor is using can understand CSS.

```
...
<TITLE>New Page</TITLE>
<STYLE>
<!--

-->
</STYLE>
</HEAD>
...
```

3. Now you can add the cascading style sheet information to the page. The amazing thing is, it consists of just one line!

```
...
<TITLE>New Page</TITLE>
<STYLE>
<!--
A:hover { color: red }
-->
</STYLE>
</HEAD>
...
```

4. Save the Web page and view it in Internet Explorer. Move the mouse pointer over the hyperlinks, and watch them change color. The hyperlinks should turn red, according to the code above. As the mouse pointer moves off them, they automatically change back to the original color.

5. If you don't like red, you can choose another color.

```
...
<TITLE>New Page</TITLE>
<STYLE>
<!--
A:hover { color: lemonchiffon }
-->
</STYLE>
</HEAD>
...
```

Once you are more familiar with other CSS properties, you can do a lot more with hyperlinks, such as making them bold or applying an overline when the mouse pointer is moved over them.

Adding a Watermark to Your Web Page

We've all seen backgrounds to Web pages. They can help to create a custom look and feel to sites. Backgrounds normally dominate the whole page, and as you scroll down the page, the background scrolls with the text.

A watermark is a little different. With a watermark, the background remains static while the text and images on the page scroll over it. When optimizing Web pages for Internet Explorer 5, you can create this effect easily. Just take the Web page with the background image that you want to optimize and add `BGPROPERTIES="FIXED"` to the `<BODY>` tag after declaring the background image. Save the page, and view it again in Internet Explorer. Now the background is fixed and doesn't move, no matter how much you scroll up and down the page. A sample background is shown in Figure 13.6.

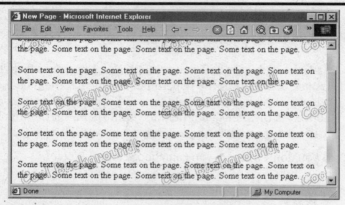

FIGURE 13.6: An optimized background on a Web page

Optimizing Fonts

If you use Internet Explorer 5, you probably have the 11 fonts that come with it. These fonts have been specifically chosen for use on the Web because they are high quality and readable. These 11 fonts are:

Andale Mono   A font formerly known as Monotype.com.

Andale Mono

Webdings   A font, not of letters and numbers, but of small graphics to add to Web pages. Very useful!

Trebuchet MS   A great sans serif font designed for easy screen readability.

Trebuchet

Georgia   A beautiful, easy-to-read serif font.

Georgia

Verdana   A clear, easy-to-read sans serif font.

Verdana

Comic Sans MS   A great, fun font based on the lettering in comic magazines.

Comic Sans MS

Arial Black   Part of the extremely versatile Arial family of fonts. Arial Black can be used for text in reports, presentations, and the like, and for display use in newspapers and promotions.

Arial Black

Impact   Great for headings on a Web page.

Impact

Arial   A versatile sans serif font that can be used just about anywhere.

Arial

Times New Roman   First designed for *The Times* newspaper in 1932. An easily readable serif font with a classic look.

Times New Roman

Courier New   Originally designed as a typewriter face for
IBM, but subsequently redrawn for the IBM Selectric series.

Courier New

Table Optimizations

You can do a lot to optimize tables in Internet Explorer that cannot be
done in Netscape Navigator. Two of the most important optimizations
are backgrounds and borders.

Let's begin with a simple table:

```
<HTML>
<HEAD>
<TITLE>New Page</TITLE>
</HEAD>
<BODY>
<H1>My Table</H1>
<TABLE BORDER="1" WIDTH="100%">
  <TR>
    <TD WIDTH="33%"> </TD>
    <TD WIDTH="33%"> </TD>
    <TD WIDTH="34%"> </TD>
  </TR>
  <TR>
    <TD WIDTH="33%"> </TD>
    <TD WIDTH="33%"> </TD>
    <TD WIDTH="34%"> </TD>
  </TR>
  <TR>
    <TD WIDTH="33%"> </TD>
    <TD WIDTH="33%"> </TD>
    <TD WIDTH="34%"> </TD>
  </TR>
  <TR>
    <TD WIDTH="33%"> </TD>
```

```
      <TD WIDTH="33%"> </TD>
      <TD WIDTH="34%"> </TD>
    </TR>
    <TR>
      <TD WIDTH="33%"> </TD>
      <TD WIDTH="33%"> </TD>
      <TD WIDTH="34%"> </TD>
    </TR>
  </TABLE>
  </BODY>
  </HTML>
```

Now that we've got a basic table, let's customize the table borders to create a really snazzy appearance.

Optimizing Borders

To display basic information on a plain text page, that default gray table border might be acceptable. However, if you have a more stylish Web page, you might want something a little more colorful.

There are, in fact, three different parts to the border of a table that you can control:

The border   This is the entire border surrounding the table and cells.

The light border   This consists of the top and left borders of the table and the bottom and right borders of the table cells. It is called the *light border* because, by convention, the light source for creating 3-D effects comes from the top-left corner. Using this effect, the table border has the illusion of being raised while the cells seem sunken.

The dark border   This consists of the bottom and right borders of the table and the top and left borders of the cells, to create a shadow effect.

NOTE   Setting a color for the light and dark borders overrides any color you might have set for the border as a whole.

In Figure 13.7, we have set the light border to a light gray color and the dark border to black. Note the 3-D effect created with the table border appearing raised and the cells appearing sunken.

FIGURE 13.7: An enlarged table demonstrating the 3-D effect

You set the overall border color by using the BORDERCOLOR property. So, if you want to set the whole table border to red, you would add the following code to the <TABLE> tag:

```
BORDERCOLOR="red"
```

TIP

Remember that you can also define colors by using their hexadecimal values.

The HTML for the table is as follows:

```
...
<H1>My Table</H1>
<TABLE BORDER="1" WIDTH="100%" BORDERCOLOR="red">
  <TR>
    <TD WIDTH="33%"> </TD>
    <TD WIDTH="33%"> </TD>
    <TD WIDTH="34%"> </TD>
  </TR>
...
```

Part iii

Now every border in the whole table has been set to red.

The light and dark borders can be set in much the same way. You use the BORDERCOLORLIGHT and BORDERCOLORDARK properties to set these. In the following example, we have set the light border to gray and the dark border to black:

```
...
<H1>My Table</H1>
<TABLE BORDER="1" WIDTH="100%" BORDERCOLORLIGHT="#C0C0C0"
BORDERCOLORDARK="#000000">
  <TR>
    <TD WIDTH="33%"> </TD>
    <TD WIDTH="33%"> </TD>
    <TD WIDTH="34%"> </TD>
  </TR>
  ...
```

If you want, you can add color to individual cells in the table. Here we have changed the color of the first row of cells in the table to an outrageous purple and blue.

```
...
<H1>My Table</H1>
<TABLE BORDER="1" WIDTH="100%">
  <TR>
    <TD WIDTH="33%" BORDERCOLORLIGHT="#FF00FF"
    BORDERCOLORDARK="#0000FF"> </TD>
    <TD WIDTH="33%"> </TD>
    <TD WIDTH="34%"> </TD>
  </TR>
  <TR>
    <TD WIDTH="33%" BORDERCOLORLIGHT="#FF00FF"
    BORDERCOLORDARK="#0000FF"> </TD>
    <TD WIDTH="33%"> </TD>
    <TD WIDTH="34%"> </TD>
  </TR>
  <TR>
    <TD WIDTH="33%" BORDERCOLORLIGHT="#FF00FF"
    BORDERCOLORDARK="#0000FF"> </TD>
    <TD WIDTH="33%"> </TD>
    <TD WIDTH="34%"> </TD>
  </TR>
  <TR>
```

```
      <TD WIDTH="33%" BORDERCOLORLIGHT="#FF00FF"
      BORDERCOLORDARK="#0000FF"> </TD>
      <TD WIDTH="33%"> </TD>
      <TD WIDTH="34%"> </TD>
   </TR>
   <TR>
      <TD WIDTH="33%" BORDERCOLORLIGHT="#FF00FF"
      BORDERCOLORDARK="#0000FF"> </TD>
      <TD WIDTH="33%"> </TD>
      <TD WIDTH="34%"> </TD>
   </TR>
</TABLE>
</BODY>
</HTML>
```

Adding Background Images

Another easy table enhancement is adding a background image to the
table as a whole or to individual cells of the table, shown in Figure 13.8.

If you want to add a background image to the table as a whole, you add
the BACKGROUND property to the <TABLE> tag and set this to point at the
appropriate image:

```
...
<H1>My Table</H1>
<TABLE BORDER="1" WIDTH="100%" BACKGROUND="cool.gif">
   <TR>
      <TD WIDTH="33%"> </TD>
      <TD WIDTH="33%"> </TD>
      <TD WIDTH="34%"> </TD>
   </TR>
...
```

You can also add a background image to individual cells in the table,
as shown in Figure 13.9.

TIP

Remember, to be able to see the whole image, the cell has to be big enough to
display it!

FIGURE 13.8: A table with a background image

This is done in the same way as adding an image to the table as a whole, but this time you add the BACKGROUND property to the appropriate <TD> tag.

```
...
<H1>My Table</H1>
<TABLE BORDER="1" WIDTH="100%">
  <TR>
    <TD WIDTH="33%" BACKGROUND="cool.gif"
HEIGHT="114"> </TD>
    <TD WIDTH="33%" HEIGHT="114"> </TD>
    <TD WIDTH="34%" HEIGHT="114"> </TD>
  </TR>
...
```

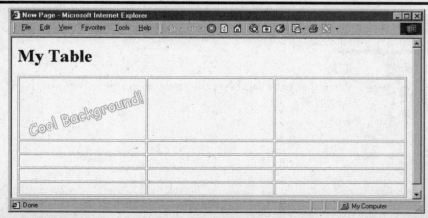

FIGURE 13.9: A cell with a background image

WHAT'S NEXT?

In this chapter, you learned how to apply some great effects to Web pages being viewed exclusively by Internet Explorer 5. Now it's time to look at that other major Web browser and learn how to optimize your Web pages for Netscape Navigator 4.

Part iii

Chapter 14

OPTIMIZING YOUR PAGES FOR NETSCAPE NAVIGATOR 4

In the previous chapter we looked at how we could optimize Web pages for Internet Explorer 5. In this chapter, we will be looking at how to optimize Web pages for the other major Web browser, Netscape Navigator 4.

Written for *HTML Complete*, 2nd Edition
by Adrian W. Kingsley-Hughes

Even with the launch of Netscape's newer browser—Netscape Navigator 6, due in late 2000—with its host of new features, Netscape Navigator 4 will continue to be a major player in the browser game for some time to come. This means that Web developers the world over will still need to cater to visitors using it now and in the future.

Let's look at what we can do!

THE <LAYER> TAG

One of the best ways to optimize Web pages for Netscape Navigator revolves around one tag—the <LAYER> tag. This tag is unique to Netscape Navigator. It is totally ignored by Internet Explorer, but it is a mighty powerful tag. This one tag has some special attributes that allow you to do some pretty cool things. We're going to be looking here at five things that the <LAYER> tag can be used for:

- Inserting other pages within the Web page we are working on
- Tiling background images behind paragraphs
- Clipping to control the visible portion of a <LAYER>
- Controlling the position of text and images on the Web page
- Controlling whether the content of the <LAYER> is visible or hidden

Let's get straight to work!

Inserting a Web Page inside a Web Page

This is a great trick that you can do when you create Web pages for Netscape Navigator. For example, take a copyright statement that you want to appear on every page you have. It really saves time and effort when you can just reuse the same page containing the information you want displayed over and over again instead of having to insert the text into every page. Also, think about all the time and effort you will save when you have to update that information; you can just change the text on one page and it's done! No need to search through every page and make the changes. (If you've ever had to do this, you'll know just how mind numbing it is and how easily mistakes can be made!)

Motivated to give it a try yet? Thought so! Let's start with two empty skeleton pages, which we will call page1.htm and page2.htm respectively.

```
<HTML>
<HEAD>
<TITLE>New page 1</TITLE>
</HEAD>
<BODY>
</BODY>
</HTML>
```

Let's first concentrate on page1.htm. This will be our host page—that is, the page that is the container for the other page (in this example page2.htm). To begin with, we'll add a paragraph of text to the page, just to make it obvious which page is which.

```
<HTML>
<HEAD>
<TITLE>New page 1</TITLE>
</HEAD>
<BODY>
<P>Hello there everyone! I'm called page1.htm</P>
</BODY>
</HTML>
```

Let's now turn our attention to page2.htm. To make this page stand out and be unique, let's add some text and change the background color to red.

```
<HTML>
<HEAD>
<TITLE>New page 2</TITLE>
</HEAD>
<BODY BGCOLOR="red">
<P>This is page2.htm, a completely separate page to the
other!</P>
</BODY>
</HTML>
```

That's all we're going to do with page2.htm, so our attention now shifts back to page1.htm again. Underneath the paragraph of text on the page, we'll add the <LAYER> tag that will host the page2.htm.

```
<HTML>
<HEAD>
<TITLE>New page 1</TITLE>
```

```
</HEAD>
<BODY>
<P>Hello there everyone! I'm called page1.htm</P>
<LAYER></LAYER>
</BODY>
</HTML>
```

WARNING

Remember to add the opening and closing tags as a pair, since omitting the closing tag can give unpredictable results.

Inside the <LAYER> tag, we'll insert the SRC attribute. This works in the same way as it does for the <IMG> tag, and we'll set this to point to the file we want inserted into the page.

TIP

You can specify the file location using either a relative URL, such as "page2.htm" or an absolute URL, such as "http://www.yourURL.com/page2.htm".

```
<HTML>
<HEAD>
<TITLE>New page 1</TITLE>
</HEAD>
<BODY>
<P>Hello there everyone! I'm called page1.htm</P>
<LAYER SRC="page2.htm"></LAYER>
</BODY>
</HTML>
```

Now save both pages and load page1.htm into Netscape Navigator.

Figure 14.1 shows you what the page looks like. Notice how seamless the result is. There is nothing visible to indicate that the text with the red background is actually a separate page.

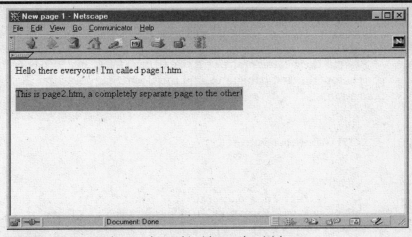

FIGURE 14.1: A Web page hosted inside another Web page

Tiling a Background Image behind Paragraphs

You've probably seen background images on a Web page as a whole, but what about background images behind paragraphs of text, or even other images? This is simple to accomplish if you use the <LAYER> tag.

Again, let's begin with a skeleton page and add some paragraphs to it (we won't bother adding any images; just remember that you can do so if you want).

```
<HTML>
<HEAD>
<TITLE>New page</TITLE>
</HEAD>
<BODY>
<P>Some text in a paragraph ... plenty of it so we can see
what goes on. Some text in a paragraph ... plenty of it so we
can see what goes on. Some text in a paragraph ... plenty of
it so we can see what goes on. Some text in a paragraph ...
plenty of it so we can see what goes on.</P>
<P>Another paragraph with more text ... Another paragraph
with more text ... Another paragraph with more text ...
Another paragraph with more text ... Another paragraph with
more text ... Another paragraph with more text ... Another
```

```
paragraph with more text ... Another paragraph with more text
...</P>
</BODY>
</HTML>
```

Around these paragraphs we'll place the <LAYER> tag. The opening tag goes before the first paragraph, and the closing tag goes after the final paragraph.

```
<HTML>
<HEAD>
<TITLE>New page</TITLE>
</HEAD>
<BODY>
<LAYER>
<P>Some text in a paragraph ... plenty of it so we can see
what goes on. Some text in a paragraph ... plenty of it so we
can see what goes on. Some text in a paragraph ... plenty of
it so we can see what goes on. Some text in a paragraph ...
plenty of it so we can see what goes on.</P>
<P>Another paragraph with more text ... Another paragraph
with more text ... Another paragraph with more text ...
Another paragraph with more text ... Another paragraph with
more text ... Another paragraph with more text ... Another
paragraph with more text ... Another paragraph with more text
...</P>
</LAYER>
</BODY>
</HTML>
```

To add the background, we add the BACKGROUND attribute to the <LAYER> tag and set this to point to the image file that we want to appear.

NOTE

The ellipses indicate where the snippets of code fall within the body of code.

```
...
<BODY>
<LAYER background="cool.gif">
<P>Some text in a paragraph ... plenty of it so we can see
...
```

Save the page and load it into the browser. Figure 14.2 shows the background image displayed behind the text. Notice how this background only shows behind the paragraphs inside the <LAYER> tag and not on the page as a whole.

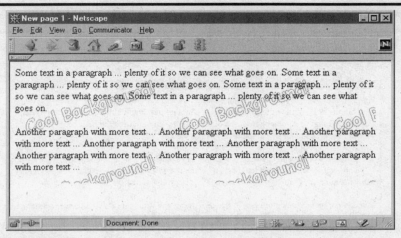

FIGURE 14.2: Using the <LAYER> tag to apply a background image

We can better show that the background image is confined to the paragraphs inside the <LAYER> tag by adding a new paragraph that is outside of it.

```
<HTML>
<HEAD>
<TITLE>New page</TITLE>
</HEAD>
<BODY>
<P>Another paragraph of text, but this time, outside the
LAYER tag! ... Another paragraph of text, but this time, out-
side the LAYER tag! ... Another paragraph of text, but this
time, outside the LAYER tag! ... Another paragraph of text,
but this time, outside the LAYER tag! ... Another paragraph
of text, but this time, outside the LAYER tag! ...</P>
<LAYER background="cool.gif">
<P>Some text in a paragraph ... plenty of it so we can see
what goes on. Some text in a paragraph ... plenty of it so we
can see what goes on. Some text in a paragraph ... plenty of
it so we can see what goes on. Some text in a paragraph ...
plenty of it so we can see what goes on.</P>
<P>Another paragraph with more text ... Another paragraph
with more text ... Another paragraph with more text ...
Another paragraph with more text ... Another paragraph with
more text ... Another paragraph with more text ... Another
paragraph with more text ... Another paragraph with more text
...</P>
</LAYER>
</BODY>
</HTML>
```

Figure 14.3 shows what this page looks like in the browser.

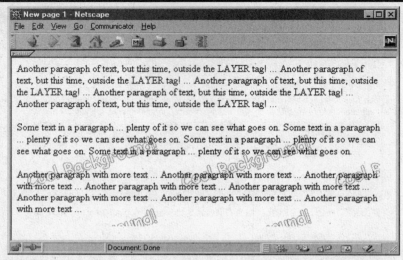

FIGURE 14.3: The background image is not applied to paragraphs outside the <LAYER> tag.

Clipping the Contents of a <LAYER> Tag

Clipping is when you cut the sides off, usually an image, to either make it smaller or remove unnecessary bits. Now, if you have an image you want to add to a Web page, you always have the option to crop (trim off the bits you don't want) with an image-editing program. However, using the <LAYER> tag, you can do this on the fly without altering the image at all.

Let's look at how this is done. Begin with a <LAYER> tag with the SRC attribute added, but this time point to an image instead on an HTML file.

```
<HTML>
<HEAD>
<TITLE>New page</TITLE>
</HEAD>
<BODY>
<P>Image inside a LAYER tag below:</P>
<LAYER SRC="image.gif"></LAYER>
</BODY>
</HTML>
```

Figure 14.4 shows what this page looks like in the browser.

FIGURE 14.4: An image inserted on a page using the <LAYER> tag

To clip the image, we use the CLIP attribute. This attribute takes the form:

```
CLIP="x1,y1"
```

You can give the x and y coordinates in either pixels or percentages to indicate how much you want to clip off. So, if we want to clip it to 50 pixels in size starting from the top-left corner of the image, we would do it as follows (see Figure 14.5):

```
<HTML>
<HEAD>
<TITLE>New page</TITLE>
</HEAD>
<BODY>
<P>Image inside a LAYER tag below:</P>
<LAYER SRC="image.gif" clip="50,50"></LAYER>
</BODY>
</HTML>
```

Part iii

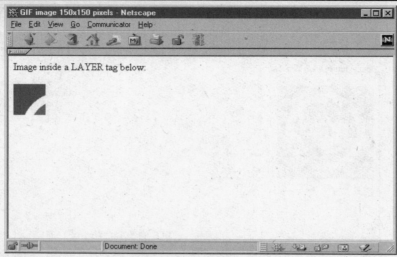

FIGURE 14.5: The image clipped using the CLIP attribute

Controlling the Position of Text and Images on the Web Page

One of the great things that the <LAYER> tag allows you to do is control the position of text and graphics on your Web page. And the nice thing about using the <LAYER> tag is that it is simple!

Let's start with a basic Web page with an image inside a <LAYER> tag.

```
<HTML>
<HEAD>
<TITLE>New page</TITLE>
</HEAD>
<BODY>
<P>Image inside a LAYER tag below:</P>
<LAYER>
<IMG SRC="image.gif">
</LAYER>
</BODY>
</HTML>
```

If you want to position this image somewhere other than in its default position, all you need to do is use two new attributes: TOP and LEFT.

You simply give a number corresponding to how many pixels you want the layer moved with respect to the top or left of the page, and away you go! So, if you want to move the image 100 pixels down and 50 pixels to the right, you would do the following:

```
<HTML>
<HEAD>
<TITLE>New page</TITLE>
</HEAD>
<BODY>
<P>Image inside a LAYER tag below:</P>
<LAYER TOP="100" LEFT="50">
<IMG SRC="image.gif">
</LAYER>
</BODY>
</HTML>
```

Figure 14.6 shows how this page looks in the browser. What actually happens is that the <LAYER> tag with all its contents is moved the specified number of pixels with respect to the top-left of the parent layer, which in the above example is the top-left of the browser window.

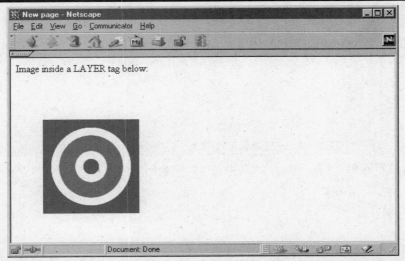

FIGURE 14.6: The image inside the <LAYER> tag is moved using the TOP and LEFT attributes.

Part iii

WARNING

Note that when we say the "browser window," we mean the portion used to display Web pages. This doesn't include area used up by items such as the toolbar or address bar.

If you were to set TOP and LEFT to zero, then the image would be flush with the top-left of the browser window.

Notice in Figure 14.7 that the text is now on top of the image. This is because repositioning the <LAYER> image pulls it from the normal flow of the page and moves it to the top. If we wanted to sort out this problem, we would have to use a <LAYER> tag to reposition the text as well.

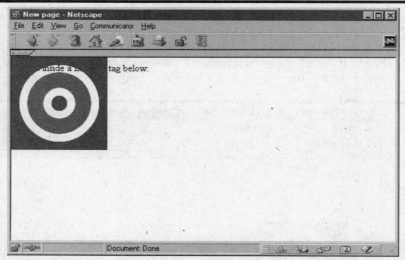

FIGURE 14.7: The image flush with the top-left corner of the browser window

```
<HTML>
<HEAD>
<TITLE>New page</TITLE>
</HEAD>
<BODY>
<LAYER TOP="75" LEFT="170">
<P>Image inside a LAYER tag on the left:</P>
</LAYER>
<LAYER TOP="0" LEFT="0">
<IMG SRC="image.gif">
</LAYER>
</BODY>
</HTML>
```

Figure 14.8 shows both the text and the image positioned using the <LAYER> tag.

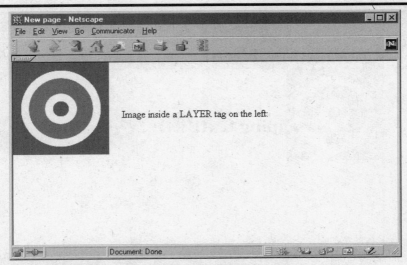

FIGURE 14.8: The text is repositioned next to the image.

We've looked at how to position with respect to the top-left side of the page, but what about controlling the stacking order? Let's take an example where the text and the image overlap again (but just for clarity, we'll make the text bigger, so you can see the effect).

Notice in Figure 14.9 how the image is on top of the text. If you wanted it the other way around, you would use the Z-INDEX attribute to change the stacking order. The value that you give the attribute is an integer, and all you need to remember is that the higher the value, the closer the object is to being at the top of the stack. So, if you give the image a Z-INDEX of 1 and the text a Z-INDEX of 2, the text will stack on top of the image, as shown in Figure 14.10.

```
<HTML>
<HEAD>
<TITLE>New page</TITLE>
</HEAD>
<BODY>
<LAYER TOP="75" LEFT="50" Z-INDEX="2">
<H1>Overlapping text!!!!!!</H1>
</LAYER>
<LAYER TOP="0" LEFT="0" Z-INDEX="1">
<IMG SRC="image.gif">
```

Part III

```
        </LAYER>
        </BODY>
        </HTML>
```

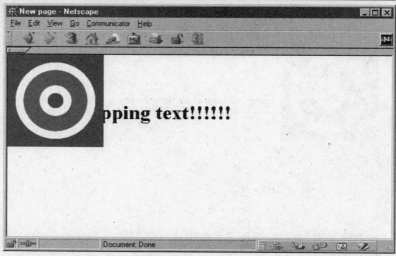

FIGURE 14.9 Image and text overlapping

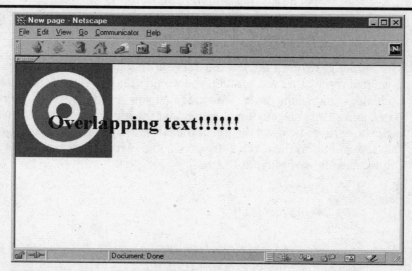

FIGURE 14.10: Text stacked on top of the image

Making <LAYER> Content Visible or Hidden

It might seem a little dumb to put something on a Web page and make it invisible. Why not just leave it out altogether and save the visitor the bother and expense of downloading it? However, by using a little JavaScript, you can make things that are invisible on the Web page suddenly appear when the user does something such as click on a button or move over an image. We're not going to look at how to create dynamic pages here, we're just going to concentrate on the basics, but rest assured, the exciting stuff is just around the corner!

NOTE
JavaScript is covered in greater detail in Chapter 20.

To control whether objects such as text and images are visible or not, you use the VISIBILITY attribute. This attribute has three possible values:

show   The layer is visible.

hide   The layer is hidden.

inherit   The layer has the same visibility as the parent layer.

So, given this information, you can make layers invisible by just using this one attribute.

```
<HTML>
<HEAD>
<TITLE>New page</TITLE>
</HEAD>
<BODY>
<P>There is a hidden image below this text!</P>
<LAYER VISIBILITY="hide">
<IMG SRC="image.gif">
</LAYER>
</BODY>
</HTML>
```

Notice in Figure 14.11 how the image, while included in the HTML of the page, is not visible. It is important to remember that the image is still being downloaded to the visitor's computer and is taking the same amount to time to download as if it were visible on the page.

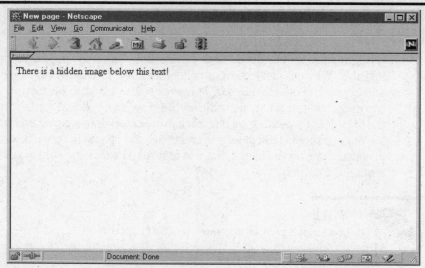

FIGURE 14.11: The image is hidden using the VISIBILITY attribute.

What happens if you have text underneath the image? Well, here is the trick: once the layer is hidden, the page acts as though it was never there and doesn't leave a space for the image on the page, so a line of text placed beneath the image appears directly below the first line.

```
<HTML>
<HEAD>
<TITLE>New page</TITLE>
</HEAD>
<BODY>
<P>There is a hidden image below this text!</P>
<LAYER VISIBILITY="hide">
<IMG SRC="image.gif">
</LAYER>
<P>More text below the image!</P>
</BODY>
</HTML>
```

In Figure 14.12, you can clearly see that the hidden image does not take up any space on the page itself, and the text below it is moved up to directly below the first paragraph.

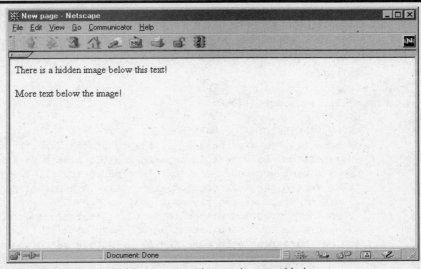

FIGURE 14.12: The hidden image with text above and below

LAYOUT TRICKS

So far, we've looked quite closely at the <LAYER> tag and how that can be used to optimize Web pages developed for Netscape Navigator. To round off this chapter, let's look at two more areas of optimization:

▶ Setting page margins

▶ Formatting text into columns

Page Margins in Netscape Navigator 4

In Chapter 13, we looked at how to control the page margins in Internet Explorer 5. Well, it won't surprise you to know that this won't work for Netscape Navigator 4. To control the page margins on Web pages designed for this browser, you need to use two different attributes in the <BODY> tag. These are:

MARGINWIDTH   Controls the left and right margin width

MARGINHEIGHT   Controls the top and bottom margin height

Using them is similar to how you set the margins for a Web page optimized for Internet Explorer 5; you simply give these attributes a numerical value, in pixels, corresponding to the size of the margin that you want. So, if you wanted a margin set to zero, you would do the following:

```
<HTML>
<HEAD>
<TITLE>New page</TITLE>
</HEAD>
<BODY MARGINWIDTH="0" MARGINHEIGHT="0">
<P>Some text in a paragraph ... plenty of it so we can see
what goes on. Some text in a paragraph ... plenty of it so we
can see what goes on. Some text in a paragraph ... plenty of
it so we can see what goes on. Some text in a paragraph ...
plenty of it so we can see what goes on.</P>
<P>Another paragraph with more text ... Another paragraph
with more text ... Another paragraph with more text ...
Another paragraph with more text ... Another paragraph with
more text ... Another paragraph with more text ... Another
paragraph with more text ... Another paragraph with more text
...</P>
</BODY>
</HTML>
```

If you want to have a 20-pixel margin on top and bottom, and 50-pixel left and right margins, you would set it up like this:

```
...
</HEAD>
<BODY MARGINWIDTH="50" MARGINHEIGHT="20">
<P>Some text in a paragraph ... plenty of it so we can see
what goes on. Some text in a
...
```

Figure 14.13 shows the page loaded into the browser.

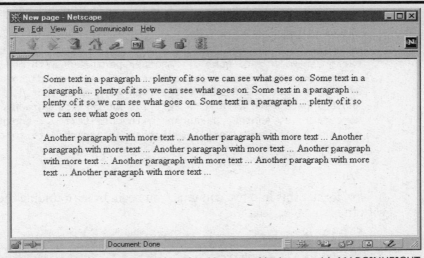

FIGURE 14.13: Our page displayed in Netscape Navigator with MARGINHEIGHT set to 20 and MARGINWIDTH set to 50

Formatting Text into Columns

If you have a lot of text on a page, formatting it into columns makes it easy to read and pleasing to the eye. Newspapers have done this for years, and now you can do it in pages you create for Netscape Navigator 4. You don't use tables to do this, you use a tag called <MULTICOL>, which achieves the same effect. Begin with a page containing some text:

```
<HTML>
<HEAD>
<TITLE>New page</TITLE>
</HEAD>
<BODY>
<P>Some text in a paragraph ... plenty of it so we can see
what goes on. Some text in a paragraph ... plenty of it so we
can see what goes on. Some text in a paragraph ... plenty of
it so we can see what goes on. Some text in a paragraph ...
plenty of it so we can see what goes on ... Some text in a
paragraph ... plenty of it so we can see what goes on. Some
text in a paragraph ... plenty of it so we can see what goes
on. Some text in a paragraph ... plenty of it so we can see
what goes on. Some text in a paragraph ... plenty of it so we
can see what goes on.</P>
```

```
<P>Another paragraph with more text ... Another paragraph
with more text ... Another paragraph with more text ...
Another paragraph with more text ... Another paragraph with
more text ... Another paragraph with more text ... Another
paragraph with more text ... Another paragraph with more text
... Another paragraph with more text ... Another paragraph
with more text ... Another paragraph with more text ...
Another paragraph with more text ... Another paragraph with
more text ... Another paragraph with more text ... Another
paragraph with more text ... Another paragraph with more text
...</P>
</BODY>
</HTML>
```

Now format this into two columns. You begin by surrounding the text with the <MULTICOL> tag.

```
<HTML>
<HEAD>
<TITLE>New page</TITLE>
</HEAD>
<BODY>
<MULTICOL>
<P>Some text in a paragraph ... plenty of it so we can see
what goes on. Some text in a paragraph ... plenty of it so we
can see what goes on. Some text in a paragraph ...
...
    with more text ... Another paragraph with more text ...
Another paragraph with more text ...</P>
</MULTICOL>
</BODY>
</HTML>
```

Next, set the number of columns using the COLS attribute:

```
<HTML>
<HEAD>
<TITLE>New page</TITLE>
</HEAD>
<BODY>
<MULTICOL COLS="2">
<P>Some text in a paragraph ... plenty of it so we can see
what goes on. Some text in a paragraph ... plenty of it so we
can see what goes on. Some text in a paragraph ...
...
    with more text ... Another paragraph with more text ...
Another paragraph with more text ...</P>
</MULTICOL>
</BODY>
</HTML>
```

You can optimize these columns a bit more. See the space between the columns in Figure 14.14? It is called a *gutter*, and you can control the width of this space using the GUTTER attribute, as shown in the code below. Figure 14.15 shows this page loaded into the browser. Notice the larger gap between the two columns.

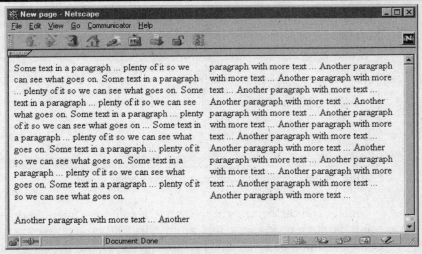

FIGURE 14.14: Text formatted into two columns

```
<HTML>
<HEAD>
<TITLE>New page</TITLE>
</HEAD>
<BODY>
<MULTICOL COLS="2" GUTTER="30">
<P>Some text in a paragraph ... plenty of it so we can see
what goes on. Some text in a paragraph ... plenty of it so we
can see what goes on. Some text in a paragraph ...
...
    with more text ... Another paragraph with more text ...
Another paragraph with more text ...</P>
</MULTICOL>
</BODY>
</HTML>
```

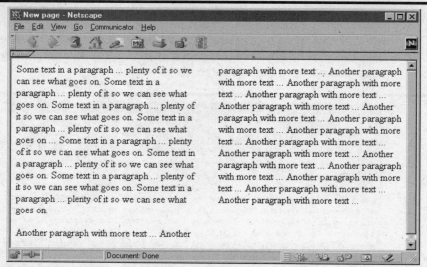

FIGURE 14.15: Same two columns, but with a larger gutter

Finally, you can control the width of the columns (but only as a set of columns, not individually). You can set them either in pixels or as a percentage of the space available. For example, if you wanted the columns to take up 80 percent of the space available on the browser, you would set it like so:

```
<HTML>
<HEAD>
<TITLE>New page</TITLE>
</HEAD>
<BODY>
<MULTICOL COLS="2" GUTTER="30" WIDTH="80%">
<P>Some text in a paragraph ... plenty of it so we can see
what goes on. Some text in a paragraph ... plenty of it so we
can see what goes on. Some text in a paragraph ...
...
    with more text ... Another paragraph with more text ...
Another paragraph with more text ...</P>
</MULTICOL>
</BODY>
</HTML>
```

Figure 14.16 shows how this attribute affects the columns.

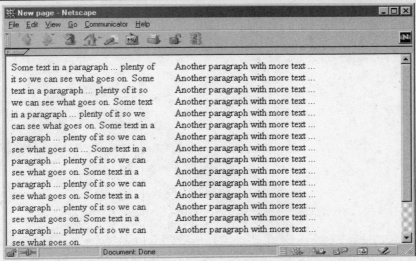

FIGURE 14.16: The columns taking up 80 percent of the browser window space

WHAT'S NEXT?

In the next chapter, we continue our tour of advanced HTML techniques. Deborah Ray and Eric Ray show you how to add exciting multimedia effects to your Web pages, including animated GIFs, sounds, and video.

Part iii

Chapter 15
INCLUDING MULTIMEDIA

In recent years, Web surfers have seen text-only pages transform into pages that bounce, shimmy, sing, and gyrate. Developers of public sites, in particular, are using flair and excitement in an effort to attract visitors and to keep them coming back again and again. Flashy elements don't always attract, however. Some visitors find them such a distraction that they don't browse the site, nor do they return to it. The key is to use glitz wisely and to carefully weigh its benefits and liabilities.

Adapted from *Mastering HTML 4*, 2nd Edition, by Deborah S. Ray and Eric J. Ray
ISBN 0-7821-2523-9   912 pages $34.99

In this chapter, we'll show you how to include special effects—animated GIFs, sounds, videos, applets, and ActiveX controls—collectively known as multimedia. (We're defining multimedia as anything you can include in a Web page other than basic HTML code and static images.) We'll look at the pros and cons of various elements and discuss how to include them effectively, if you do choose to include them.

In the first part of this chapter, we'll show you how to include some elements that are HTML standard–compliant and some that are not. Both types are compatible with most of the newer browsers on the market. Toward the end of the chapter, we'll show you how to include multimedia as designated by the HTML 4 specification. At the time of writing, these tags and attributes are not widely supported, but you'll find that using them is very efficient.

TIP

The principles for including these effects apply to other elements you might discover. For example, if the engineers at your company want to publish their AutoCAD files on your corporate intranet, you can include them in Web pages, following the principles outlined in the "Adding Multimedia Using HTML 4" section in this chapter.

DECIDING TO INCLUDE MULTIMEDIA

Images, sounds, and video can make your pages come alive. And, done right, multimedia can give Web pages that "up with technology" look and feel. Before running off to gather multimedia elements, though, take heed. Multimedia poses several challenges, both for visitors and for the developer.

The Challenges for Visitors

Multimedia can bring your pages to a virtual halt as visitors sit and wait (and wait!) for the effects to download. Although some multimedia effects, such as an animated GIF image, can be as small as 2KB, other effects, such as video, can easily grow to 5MB or more.

In addition, some multimedia effects—for example, most video, Shockwave animations, VRML (Virtual Reality Markup Language) presentations, and some sound files—require plug-ins (programs that visitors use to view effects that their browsers don't support). For example, if you include an MPEG movie file, visitors need the plug-in to view the effect.

NOTE

Shockwave animation is a special kind of animation file that uses technology developed by Macromedia. Virtual Reality Markup Language provides simulated 3-D Web-browsing experiences.

What's really frustrating is that visitors must download and install a separate plug-in for each multimedia effect and for each company that provides the effect. For example, if you include an Envoy document, an IconAuthor multimedia presentation, and Corel CMX graphics in a Web page (you wouldn't do this, we hope), visitors would have to download and install three plug-ins just to see the multimedia you include. Will visitors take the time to do this? No way.

Visitors using Internet Explorer 3 or newer have it somewhat easier because Internet Explorer downloads plug-ins automatically after a visitor approves the installation. Visitors do still have to wait, wait, and wait to view the effect, though. Visitors using any version of Netscape Navigator, however, click to view the effect and then (in one vividly memorable example):

1. Are informed that they don't have the right plug-in.

2. Are taken to the Netscape Web page to get it.

3. Must click to download the plug-in.

4. Must fill out a form with personal information (name, address, type of business).

5. Submit the form.

6. Are taken back to the original site (different page).

7. Choose to download the plug-in.

8. Specify where it should be saved.

9. Wait for it to download (much longer than for Internet Explorer).

10. Browse to the downloaded file on the local hard drive.

11. Double-click the installation program to run it.

Part III

12. Accept the license agreement.

13. Approve the installation location.

14. Wait for the installation to finish.

15. Exit Netscape Navigator.

16. Restart Netscape Navigator.

17. Browse back to the original site.

18. View the effect (finally).

Eighteen steps and many minutes later, you get to see the multimedia effect. It wasn't worth it, by the way.

The Challenges for Developers

In addition to these resounding indictments of carefree multimedia use in Web pages, it gets worse. For you, the developer, obtaining relevant and useful multimedia objects is often difficult. Your first option is to create the effects yourself, which requires both raw materials (such as photographs, sounds, and video clips) and often special software that you must both purchase and learn to use. And, even if you're familiar with the software, developing effective multimedia objects can be especially time-consuming.

You can also browse the Web for multimedia elements. This is a less expensive and less time-consuming option, but you may not find exactly what you want. Although tons of multimedia elements are available on the Web, they're likely to be inappropriate or not in the public domain.

Your goal is to carefully consider the advantages and disadvantages of each multimedia element *before* you include it. Start by asking these questions:

▶ Does the multimedia element add content that I cannot otherwise provide?

▶ Does the multimedia element clearly enhance or complement content?

▶ Do my visitors have browsers that support these elements?

▶ Do my visitors have fast Internet connections?

► Are my visitors likely to have the appropriate plug-ins or to have the time, inclination, and technical wherewithal to get and install them?

► Do I have the time and resources to develop or find multimedia elements?

If you answer yes to some or all these questions and you opt to include multimedia, the rest of this chapter is for you.

NOTE

Throughout this chapter, we point out that you can find multimedia elements on the Web. Remember, however, that most of what you find is not available for public use. Before you take a file and use it as your own, be sure that it's clearly labeled "for public use." If it's not, you can assume that it's not for you to take and use.

CONSIDERING MULTIMEDIA USABILITY

Before you commit to fully multimedia enhanced pages—or even to a single animated GIF on your home page—consider carefully what including multimedia will do to your site's usability. *Web Site Usability: A Designer's Guide*, by Spool et al., published by User Interface Engineering (www.uie.com), presents some alarming findings about the usability of Web pages that incorporate multimedia elements.

These authors conclude that "animation makes it considerably harder for users ..." and support that finding with observational research in which Web site visitors tried to scroll the page to move the animation out of sight, and, when that failed, they used their hands to cover up the distracting effects.

Although some sites were more problematic than others, and other studies show that animations are more effective than static images in advertisements, your site might not benefit from any of these effects.

USING ANIMATED GIFs

Perhaps the easiest multimedia element to include is an animated GIF, which is a file that, more or less, includes a bunch of images stacked together to give the illusion of movement. Animated GIFs are similar to those little cartoon booklets you had as a kid. When you quickly whirred through the pages, the cartoon seemed to move. Of course, the illusion of movement was nothing more than each individual cartoon drawing being slightly different. Animated GIFs work the same way.

The uses for animated GIFs vary considerably, from flashing commercial messages to elaborate mini-movies to small bullets or arrows that appear to grow or move. A common use is to help attract visitors' attention to a specific element, as shown in Figure 15.1.

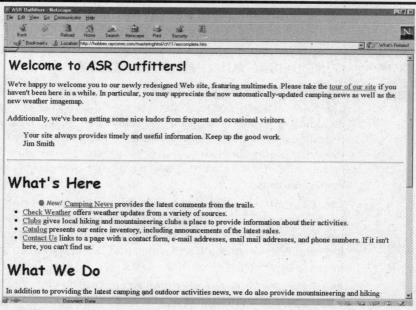

FIGURE 15.1: The ball beside New! rolls toward the item.

If you're interested in developing your own animated GIFs, we recommend software such as JASC's Animation Shop (bundled with PaintShop Pro 5) for Windows or GifBuilder for the Macintosh. These packages provide the tools to combine individual images into an animated GIF. You can develop individual images with any software that can create GIF images, including Photoshop and PaintShop Pro. If you want to see what's available on the Web, go to www.yahoo.com or www.altavista.com and search on gif animation. You will find lots of information, software, and software reviews.

ANIMATING YOUR OWN GIFS

Developing an animated GIF often takes more time and effort than you expect. The process can become tedious, especially if you are working with longer animations or animations in which the illusion of smooth motion is needed (rather than simply presenting discrete panes of information, as in ad banners).

The first step is to generate the individual images that will eventually be each panel within the animated GIF. For a basic animated bullet—that appears to move from left to right—you might create a set of images like those shown here.

The easiest way to get smooth animation is to create a single image, select the object that changes or moves, move it into each successive position, and then save the image. In this example, after creating the small ball, we selected the ball, moved it two pixels to the

CONTINUED ➡

right, saved the image, moved it again, and so forth. The more pixels between images, the jerkier the motion; the fewer pixels between images, the smoother the motion.

After you create the images, use a GIF animation program, such as JASC Animation Shop, shown here, to sequence the images and to set animation properties, such as how often to loop through the animation and how to redraw the images as the animation proceeds.

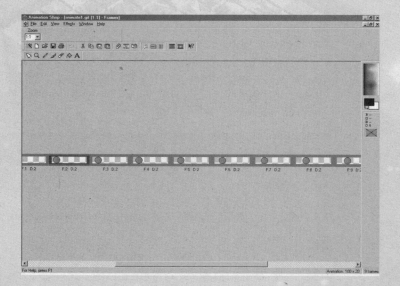

After you insert each of the frames and preview the image to your satisfaction, simply save it as a GIF.

Table 15.1 lists and describes the tags and attributes you use to include animated GIFs in your HTML documents. You can treat animated GIFs just like any other images.

TABLE 15.1: Animated GIF Tags and Attributes

TAG /ATTRIBUTE	DESCRIPTION
<IMG>	Inserts an image in an HTML document
SRC="..."	Specifies the location of the image file
ALT="..."	Provides alternate text for visitors who don't view the image

To include an animated GIF in your Web page, follow these steps:

1. Find or create an appropriate animated GIF image.

2. Place the image in your HTML document, with the regular image tags. You might have code like the following:

```
<IMG SRC="animate2.gif" WIDTH="99" HEIGHT="16"
BORDER="0" ALT="*">
<A HREF="camping.html">Camping News</A> provides the
latest comments from the trails. <BR>
```

3. Enjoy the experience!

TESTING MULTIMEDIA

If you're testing your pages either locally or over a direct Internet connection—say, through your network at the office, connected to the Internet with a dedicated line—take the time to test them with the slowest dial-up connection your visitors will be using. Check out what happens with 14.4, 28.8, 33.8, and 56Kbps modems. What's tolerable with a direct connection can seem interminable over a dial-up connection.

In ideal circumstances, a visitor using a 56Kbps modem can download a maximum of 7KB per second. In real life, that number decreases dramatically, depending on network traffic and a variety of intangibles. If your page contains 2KB of text, a 4KB bullet image, a 20KB photograph, and a 9KB logo, you're already talking about at least a 5-second download. Add a 60KB animation or sound file, and you've just bumped that to 15 seconds—best-case scenario. At this point, your visitor has likely moved on to another site.

ADDING SOUNDS

Adding audio can produce some fun effects, but if you surf the Web looking for sound, you'll find little of practical use. Generally speaking, Web page sounds come in two varieties:

▶ Sounds that play when visitors access the page

▶ Sounds that play when visitors click something

Sounds that play when visitors access a page are called *background sounds* and can be a short tune or one that plays the entire time a visitor is at the page. These mooing, beeping, crescendoing background sounds usually do nothing more than entertain.

TIP

Our take on the it-plays-the-whole-time-you're-visiting background sounds? If we want music to surf by, we'll put a CD in the computer.

Figure 15.2 includes a control box that visitors can click to play a sound. Although sounds accessed in this way are primarily for entertainment purposes, they could be of practical use. For example:

▶ If your car sounds like this <rumble>, you need a new muffler.

▶ If your car sounds like this <choke>, you might have bad gasoline.

▶ If your car sounds like this <kaChUNK> when you shift gears, your transmission is going out.

You get the idea. In lieu of adding the whole control box, however, you could just link directly to an audio file.

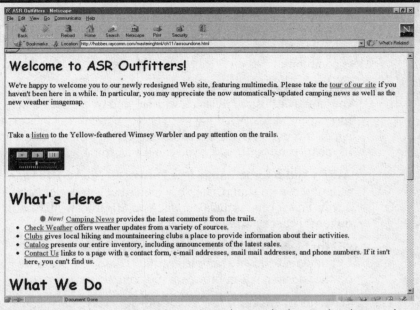

FIGURE 15.2: The control box lets visitors choose whether to play the sound.

Some Disadvantages of Sounds

Many of the disadvantages associated with using multimedia elements in general are also associated with using sounds:

► Sound files are usually large and load slowly.

► Visitors need a sound card and speakers to hear sounds.

► Visitors in a corporate environment might not welcome a loud greeting from their computer.

When choosing to add sound to your page, apply the guidelines we mentioned earlier about using multimedia elements in general. If an audio element does not enhance your message or provide content that is not possible in any other way, you're probably better off not using it.

Sound File Formats

If you do decide to include a sound in your Web page, all you have to do is find a sound file in one of five formats (other formats are available, but are less common):

MIDI (Musical Instrument Digital Interface)   A MIDI file contains synthesized music. If you can find or create one that meets your needs, MIDI is a great choice because the files are small. If you have a MIDI-capable musical instrument (such as a keyboard) and a little skill, you can create your own MIDI files.

AIFF (Audio Interchange File Format)   An AIFF file contains a recorded sound sample, which can be music or a sound effect. This format is most common on Macintosh and usable on most other systems.

AU (or basic AUdio)   An AU file also provides acceptable—but not great—quality sampled sound. These files are accessible on the widest range of browsers and computer systems.

WAV (as in WAVe)   A WAV file provides very good quality sampled sound, but is usable almost exclusively on Windows computers.

MP3 (Multimedia Protocol v. 3)   An MP3 file provides outstanding (nearly CD quality) sound, but is usable only through browser plug-ins.

If you have a sound card and a microphone, you can record your own sounds. And, of course, you can find thousands if not millions of sounds and samples on the Web.

NOTE

Many—possibly most—of the sound files on the Web are not public domain, which means you can borrow them to experiment with and learn from, but not to publish as your own.

When you've found a sound file, use the HTML tags and attributes in Table 15.2 to add the file to your document.

TABLE 15.2: Multimedia File Tags and Attributes

Tag/Attribute	Description
`<EMBED>`	Places an embedded object into a document.
`ALIGN="{LEFT, RIGHT, CENTER, ABSBOTTOM, ABSMIDDLE, BASELINE, BOTTOM, TEXTTOP, TOP}"`	Indicates how an embedded object is positioned relative to the document borders and surrounding contents.
`HEIGHT="n"`	Specifies the vertical dimension of the embedded object.
`HIDDEN`	Indicates that the embedded object should not be visible.
`NAME="…"`	Gives the object a name by which other objects can refer to it.
`OPTIONAL PARAM="…"`	Specifies additional parameters. For example, AVI movies accept the AUTOSTART attribute.
`SRC="URL"`	Indicates the relative or absolute location of the file containing the object you want to embed.
`WIDTH="n"`	Indicates the horizontal dimension of the embedded object.
`AUTOSTART="…"`	Specifies whether the sound file opens when the Web page is accessed or when a button is clicked. The value can be TRUE (automatically starts) or FALSE (visitors must do something).
`HIDDEN="…"`	Specifies whether the sound control box is visible in the Web page. The values TRUE and FALSE specify whether the control box is visible.
`<BGSOUND>`	Embeds a background sound file within documents. Use in the document <HEAD> of documents intended for visitors who use Internet Explorer.
`LOOP="{n, INFINITE}"`	Specifies the number of times a background sound file repeats. The value INFINITE is the default.
`SRC="URL"`	Indicates the absolute or relative location of the sound file.

To include sound files the easy and most user-friendly way, link to them. For example, as you saw in Figure 15.2, earlier in this chapter, ASR Outfitters added a sound file of a bird call to one of its pages. You add a link to a sound file in the same way that you add a link to an image. The code looks like this:

```
Take a <a HREF="weirdbrd.aif">listen</A> to the
Yellow-feathered Wimsey Warbler and pay attention on the
trails.
```

If you use this option, visitors can choose whether to hear the sound, which is accessible from most browsers.

If you choose to inflict the sound on your visitors from the second they view your page, you'll need two tags—one for Internet Explorer and one for Netscape Navigator.

For Internet Explorer, follow these steps:

1. Start with an HTML document that at least has structure tags.

```
<!DOCTYPE HTML PUBLIC "-//W3C//DTD HTML 4.0//EN">
<HTML>
<HEAD>
<TITLE>ASR Outfitters</TITLE>
</HEAD>
<BODY>
```

2. Add the <BGSOUND> tag.

```
<TITLE>ASR Outfitters</TITLE>
<BGSOUND>
</HEAD>
<BODY>
```

3. Add the SRC= attribute and the filename.

```
<TITLE>ASR Outfitters</TITLE>
<BGSOUND SRC="weirdbrd.aif">
</HEAD>
<BODY>
```

4. Add the LOOP= attribute to specify how many times the sound should play.

```
<BGSOUND SRC="weirdbrd.aif" LOOP=1>
```

For Netscape Navigator, follow these steps:

1. Start with an HTML document that at least has structure tags.

```
<!DOCTYPE HTML PUBLIC "-//W3C//DTD HTML 4.0//EN">
<HTML>
<HEAD>
<TITLE>ASR Outfitters</TITLE>
</HEAD>
<BODY>
```

2. Add the <EMBED> tag.

```
<BODY>
<EMBED>
```

3. Add the SRC= attribute and the filename.

```
<BODY>
<EMBED SRC="weirdbrd.aif">
```

4. Add the AUTOSTART="TRUE" attribute to specify that the sound should play when the page is accessed. The TRUE value specifies that the sound start when the page is accessed. FALSE requires that visitors activate the sound file.

```
<BODY>
<EMBED SRC="weirdbrd.aif" AUTOSTART="TRUE">
```

5. Add the HIDDEN attribute to hide the control box.

```
<BODY>
<EMBED SRC="weirdbrd.aif" AUTOSTART="TRUE" HIDDEN>
```

Nothing appears in the page, but your visitors will hear the weirdbrd.aif sound as soon as they open the page.

Finally, you can also provide a classy little control in the Web page so that visitors can play the file right there. To do so, set the AUTOSTART= attribute to FALSE, and specify the dimensions of the control, like this:

```
<EMBED SRC="weirdbrd.aif" AUTOSTART="FALSE" HEIGHT="60"
WIDTH="140">
```

TIP

See the "Adding Multimedia Using HTML 4" section at the end of this chapter to find out how version 4 makes this process even easier!

ADDING VIDEO

You'll find that video—in the right situation—is perhaps the most practical multimedia element. In one quick video clip, you can *show* visitors a concept or a process, rather than describing it in lengthy paragraphs or steps.

If you surf the Web, though, you'll find few videos. Despite its potential, Web-based video is virtually unusable in most situations. The only significant exception is for training on an intranet; most intranet users have high-speed connections. Video files are huge. Even a small, short, low-quality video is usually 2MB or more and takes several minutes to download over a dial-up connection.

In addition, visitors must have the right plug-in. And downloading a plug-in and the huge files to view a few seconds of video is not an attractive option.

Video File Formats

You can create your own video files or find them on the Web. Look for files in the following formats:

AVI (Audio Video Interleave)   This format, originally a Windows standard, is now somewhat more widely available. It's a good choice if your visitors will almost exclusively be using Windows.

MPEG (Motion Picture Experts Group)   This format is the most widely supported, and viewers are available for most platforms. Because it's highly compressed and usable, MPEG is the best universal choice.

QuickTime   This format, originally a Macintosh standard, is now available for Windows as well. It provides good quality if your visitors have the plug-in and use personal computers.

When you're ready to incorporate a video file, you use the tags and attributes described in Table 15.2, earlier in this chapter.

We recommend linking to video files, rather than embedding them in a Web page. The code looks like this:

```
Take a <A HREF="weirdbrd.mpg">look at video</A> of the
Yellow-feathered Wimsey Warbler and pay attention on the
trails.
```

When video files are linked, visitors can choose whether to view them.

If you do choose to embed the video file—thereby forcing visitors to download it—follow these steps:

1. Start with an HTML document.

2. Add the <EMBED> tag.
   ```
   <HR>
   <EMBED>
   <H2 ALIGN=CENTER>Happy Holiday!</H2>
   ```

3. Add the SRC= attribute and the filename.
   ```
   <HR>
   <EMBED SRC="firework.avi">
   <H2 ALIGN=CENTER>Happy Holiday!</H2>
   ```

4. Specify the video size using the WIDTH= and HEIGHT= attributes.
   ```
   <HR>
   <EMBED SRC="firework.avi" WIDTH="250" HEIGHT="150">
   <H2 ALIGN=CENTER>Happy Holiday!</H2>
   ```

5. Add the AUTOSTART="TRUE" attribute to specify that the video play when the page is accessed. Use FALSE to require visitors to activate the video file.

```
<HR>
<EMBED SRC="firework.avi" WIDTH="250" HEIGHT="150"
AUTOSTART="true">
<H2 ALIGN=CENTER>Happy Holiday!</H2>
```

6. Add the LOOP= attribute to specify how many times the video plays.

```
<HR>
<EMBED SRC="firework.avi" WIDTH="250" HEIGHT="150"
AUTOSTART="true" LOOP="1">
<H2 ALIGN=CENTER>Happy Holiday!</H2>
```

7. If you want, add an ALIGN= attribute, such as ALIGN="LEFT."

```
<HR>
<EMBED SRC="firework.avi" WIDTH="250" HEIGHT="150"
AUTOSTART="true" LOOP="1" ALIGN="LEFT">
<H2 ALIGN=CENTER>Happy Holiday!</H2>
```

The resulting Web page—including the video from the Microsoft Clipart Gallery—looks like Figure 15.3.

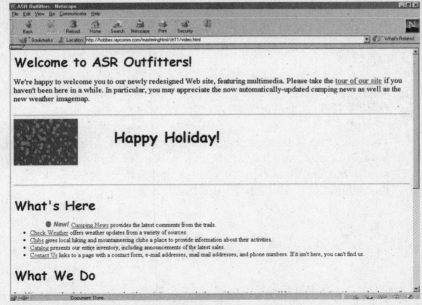

FIGURE 15.3: Including video in Web pages is easy.

INCLUDING JAVA APPLETS

Applets, developed with the Java programming language, are mini-programs with which you can animate objects, scroll text, or add interactive components to your Web pages. Figure 15.4 shows the TicTacToe applet, and Figure 15.5 shows an applet that scrolls a welcome message across the top of a Web page.

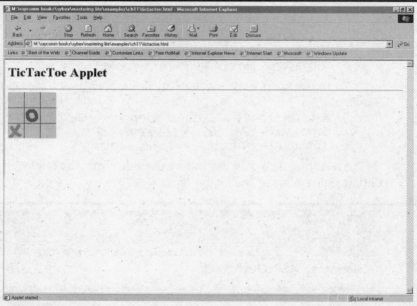

FIGURE 15.4:   This applet lets you play tic-tac-toe.

In addition, Java applets can organize and categorize topics on the Web. For example, AltaVista Search Public Service uses an applet to run the Refine feature, which lets visitors make choices and move categories around on the screen (see Figure 15.6).

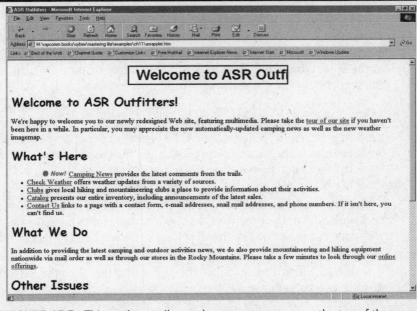

FIGURE 15.5: This applet scrolls a welcome message across the top of the page.

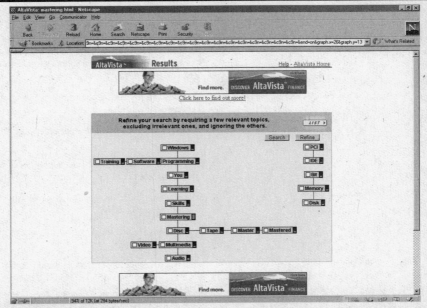

FIGURE 15.6: AltaVista uses an applet to run this interactive feature.

Java applets have the `.class` filename extension. In the simplest cases, you need only the name of the applet to use it, for example, `TicTacToe.class`. With more complex applets, you must also provide *parameters*. In this section, we'll show you how to send those parameters to the applet, but you'll have to get the exact information to include in the parameter from the documentation that comes with applets.

The Java Developers Kit (JDK), available at `www.sunsoft.com`, includes tools for developing applets. Unless you're a programmer or have some time on your hands, however, you'll be better off using prepackaged applets or tools that develop applets on the fly. (Search for `applet` at software archives such as `www.shareware.com` or visit `gamelan.com` to find these tools.)

Applet files, like video files, are big and take up to a couple of minutes to download. On the positive side, though, visitors with most versions of Netscape Navigator or Internet Explorer can use applets without additional software.

Table 15.3 lists and describes the tags and attributes you use to include an applet in your Web pages.

TABLE 15.3:   Applet Tags and Attributes

Tag / Attribute	Description
`<APPLET>`	Embeds a Java applet into an HTML document. You can include alternate text between `<APPLET>` tags. Browsers that support Java ignore all information between the `<APPLET>` tags.
`ALIGN={LEFT, CENTER, RIGHT}`	Specifies the horizontal alignment of the applet displayed.
`ALT="…"`	Displays a textual description of an applet, if necessary.
`CODE="URL"`	Specifies the relative or absolute location of the Java bytecode file on the server.
`CODEBASE="URL"`	Specifies the folder location of all necessary `.class` files on the Web server.
`HEIGHT="n"`	Specifies the height (in pixels) of the applet object within the document.
`HSPACE="n"`	Specifies an amount of blank space (in pixels) to the left and right of the applet within the document.

CONTINUED ➡

TABLE 15.3 continued: Applet Tags and Attributes

Tag /Attribute	Description
NAME="…"	Assigns the applet a name so that other applets can identify it within the document.
TITLE="…"	Specifies a label assigned to the tag.
VSPACE="n"	Specifies the amount of vertical space (in pixels) above and below the applet.
WIDTH="n"	Specifies the width (in pixels) of the applet within the document.
<PARAM>	Specifies parameters passed to an embedded object.
NAME="…"	Indicates the name of the parameter passed to the embedded object.
VALUE="…"	Specifies the value associated with the parameter passed to the embedded object.

If you've found an applet to use and want to include it in your Web page, follow these steps. In this example, we'll show you how to add the TicTacToe applet.

1. Start with an HTML document.

2. Add some introductory text and perhaps a horizontal rule to set off the applet from other page elements.

   ```
   <H1>TicTacToe Game</H1>
   <HR>
   ```

3. Add the <APPLET> tags.

   ```
   <H1>TicTacToe Game</H1>
   <HR>
   <APPLET>
   </APPLET>
   ```

4. Add the CODE= attribute along with the applet filename (which is case-sensitive, by the way).

   ```
   <H1>TicTacToe Game</H1>
   <HR>
   <APPLET CODE="TicTacToe.class">
   </APPLET>
   ```

Part iii

5. Add the WIDTH= and HEIGHT= attributes to specify the size of the applet.

```
<H1>TicTacToe Game</H1>
<HR>
<APPLET CODE="TicTacToe.class" WIDTH="120" HEIGHT="120">
</APPLET>
```

That's it! For this applet, which should look like Figure 15.4, earlier in this chapter, all you need is the TicTactoe.class file. To add an applet that requires parameters, such as the applet that scrolls the welcome banner, follow these steps (we used a free tool to create this banner and were able to simply copy and paste the parameters into our HTML document):

1. Start with an HTML document.

2. Add the <APPLET> tags.

```
<APPLET>
</APPLET>
```

3. Add the applet file.

```
<APPLET CODE="Banners.class">
</APPLET>
```

4. Add a <PARAM> tag that includes the parameter name and value.

```
<APPLET CODE="Banners.class">
<PARAM NAME="bgColor" VALUE="White">
</APPLET>
```

5. Continue adding parameters. We recommend adding one at a time to help eliminate coding errors.

```
<APPLET CODE="Banners.class" WIDTH="400" HEIGHT="50">
<PARAM NAME="bgColor" VALUE="White">
<PARAM NAME="textColor" VALUE="Black">
<PARAM NAME="pause" VALUE="1">
<PARAM NAME="exit" VALUE="scrollLeft">
<PARAM NAME="align" VALUE="Center">
<PARAM NAME="fps" VALUE="20">
<PARAM NAME="repeat" VALUE="1">
<PARAM NAME="borderWidth" VALUE="1">
<PARAM NAME="bgExit" VALUE="None">
<PARAM NAME="messages" VALUE="Welcome to ASR
Outfitters!">
<PARAM NAME="font" VALUE="Helvetica">
<PARAM NAME="cpf" VALUE="2">
<PARAM NAME="enter" VALUE="scrollLeft">
<PARAM NAME="bgEnter" VALUE="None">
```

```
<PARAM NAME="style" VALUE="Bold">
<PARAM NAME="borderColor" VALUE="Black">
<PARAM NAME="size" VALUE="36">
</APPLET>
```

And that's it! This code displays a scrolling welcome, much like the one shown in Figure 15.5, earlier in this chapter—assuming you have the .class files for the applet. (Ours came from a free tool on the Internet.) Otherwise, use the same process to add an applet you already have.

INCLUDING ACTIVEX CONTROLS

ActiveX controls are similar to Java applets—they're little programs that provide enhanced functionality to a Web page. For example, ActiveX controls can provide pop-up menus, the ability to view a Word document through a Web page, and almost all the pieces needed for Microsoft's HTML Help. These controls—developed by Microsoft and implemented with Internet Explorer 3—are powerful but Windows-centric. Although you can get a plug-in to view ActiveX controls in Netscape Navigator, you'll find the results are more reliable when you view ActiveX controls with Internet Explorer.

If you want to try out some controls—both free and licensed varieties—check out CNet's ActiveX site at www.activex.com/ or Gamelan at www.gamelan.com. If you're so inclined, you can create ActiveX controls using popular Windows development packages, such as Visual Basic or Visual C++. You include ActiveX controls in a page just as you include multimedia elements. You use the <OBJECT> tag—as discussed in the next section.

Part III

ADDING MULTIMEDIA USING HTML 4

So far in this chapter, we've shown you how to include multimedia elements using HTML 3.2–compliant tags and some HTML extensions. Now we're going to look at how HTML 4 approaches multimedia, which you'll find is different (and easier!).

The future of developing multimedia elements for the Web is clear: instead of using several tags and attributes, you'll simply include the <OBJECT> tag and choose from attributes that support this tag (see Table 15.4). In this respect, the HTML 4 specification accommodates any kind of multimedia element. You need not specify that you're including a sound, a video, an applet, or whatever; you simply specify that you're including an object. And you use only the HTML 4 tags and attributes listed in Table 15.4. You no longer need to code for both Netscape Navigator and Internet Explorer.

NOTE

Support for the <OBJECT> tag is a little sketchy, but improving with the release of each new browser.

TABLE 15.4: Object Tags and Attributes

Tag /Attribute	Description
<OBJECT>	Embeds a software object into a document.
ALIGN={LEFT, RIGHT, MIDDLE, BOTTOM, TOP}	Indicates how the embedded object lines up relative to the edges of the browser window and/or other elements within the browser window.
BORDER=n	Indicates the width (in pixels) of a border around the embedded object. BORDER=0 indicates no border.
CODEBASE="..."	Specifies the absolute or relative location of the base directory in which the browser will look for data and other implementation files.
CODETYPE="..."	Specifies the MIME type for the embedded object's code.
CLASS="..."	Indicates which style class applies to the element.
CLASSID="..."	Specifies the location of an object resource, such as a Java applet. Use CLASSID="java:appletname.class" for Java applets.
DATA="URL"	Specifies the absolute or relative location of the embedded object's data.
DATAFLD="..."	Selects a column from a block of tabular data.
DATASRC="..."	Specifies the location of tabular data to be bound within the document.
HEIGHT=n	Specifies the vertical dimension (in pixels) of the embedded object.
HSPACE=n	Specifies the size of the margins (in pixels) to the left and right of the embedded object.
ID="..."	Indicates an identifier to associate with the embedded object.

CONTINUED ➡

TABLE 15.4 continued: Object Tags and Attributes

Tag /Attribute	Description
NAME="…"	Specifies the name of the embedded object.
STANDBY="…"	Specifies a message that the browser displays while the object is loading.
TITLE="…"	Specifies a label assigned to the tag.
TYPE="…"	Indicates the MIME type of the embedded object.
VSPACE=n	Specifies the size of the margin (in pixels) at the top and bottom of the embedded object.
WIDTH=n	Indicates the horizontal dimension (in pixels) of the embedded object.

When objects require more information—for example, a Java applet needs specific settings to run—you pass data to the object with the <PARAM> tag. Table 15.5 lists and describes the <PARAM> tags and attributes.

TABLE 15.5: Parameter Tags and Attributes

Tag /Attribute	Description
<PARAM>	Specifies parameters passed to an embedded object. Use the <PARAM> tag within the <OBJECT> or <APPLET> tags.
NAME="…"	Indicates the name of the parameter passed to the embedded object.
TYPE="…"	Specifies the MIME type of the data found at the specified URL.
VALUE="…"	Specifies the value associated with the parameter passed to the embedded object.
VALUETYPE={REF, OBJECT, DATA}	Indicates the kind of value passed to the embedded object.

When you're developing for HTML 4–compliant browsers, you can use the <OBJECT> tag to include almost any kind of object. Let's start with the Java TicTacToe applet from our previous example.

Part III

To add an applet using the <OBJECT> tag, follow these steps:

1. Start with a basic HTML document, like this:

```
<!DOCTYPE HTML PUBLIC "-//W3C//DTD HTML 4.0//EN">
<HTML>
<HEAD>
  <TITLE>TicTacToe</TITLE>
</HEAD>
<BODY BGCOLOR="FFFFFF" TEXT="000000" LINK="0000FF"
VLINK="800080" ALINK="FF0000">
<H1>TicTacToe Applet </H1>
</BODY>
</HTML>
```

2. Add the <OBJECT> tags.

```
<H1>TicTacToe Applet </H1>
<OBJECT>
</OBJECT>
```

3. Add alternate text between the <OBJECT> tags.

```
<H1>TicTacToe Applet </H1>
<OBJECT>
If your browser supported Java and objects, you could
be playing TicTacToe right now.
</OBJECT>
```

4. Add the CLASSID= attribute to indicate the name of the Java class file (program file). You use CLASSID= to incorporate programs, such as applets or ActiveX controls.

```
<H1>TicTacToe Applet </H1>
<OBJECT CLASSID="java:TicTacToe.class">
If your browser supported Java and objects, you could
be playing TicTacToe right now.
</OBJECT>
```

5. Add the WIDTH= and HEIGHT= attributes. A square that is 120 × 120 pixels should be sufficient.

```
<H1>TicTacToe Applet </H1>
<OBJECT CLASSID="java:TicTacToe.class" WIDTH=120
HEIGHT=120>
If your browser supported Java and objects, you could
be playing TicTacToe right now.
</OBJECT>
```

6. Save and test your document. In an HTML 4–compliant browser, you'll see the TicTacToe game, as shown here:

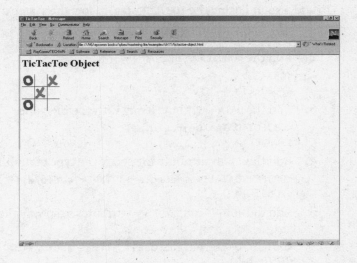

Visitors using browsers that don't support the <OBJECT> tag or don't support Java will see something like the following:

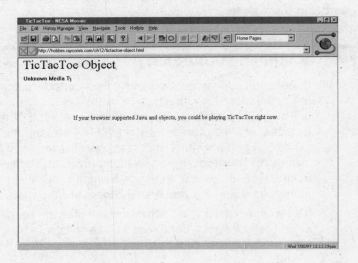

The process for adding video and sound is similar. The only difference is that you use the DATA= attribute instead of the CLASSID= attribute. Also, you add a TYPE= attribute to show the MIME type of the object. (You don't need TYPE= when you're adding an applet because java: precedes the name of the applet, making it clear what kind of object it is.)

To add a sound using the <OBJECT> tag, follow these steps:

1. Start with an HTML document.

2. Add the <OBJECT> tags.
```
<OBJECT>
</OBJECT>
```

3. Add the DATA= attribute along with the filename.
```
<OBJECT DATA="weirdbrd.aif">
</OBJECT>
```

4. Add the TYPE= attribute to specify the type of multimedia.
```
<OBJECT DATA="weirdbrd.aif" TYPE="audio/aiff">
</OBJECT>
```

5. Add the HEIGHT= and WIDTH= attributes to specify the object's size.
```
<OBJECT DATA="weirdbrd.aif" TYPE="audio/aiff" HEIGHT=50
WIDTH=100>
</OBJECT>
```

There you go! Your document should now look like Figure 15.2, shown earlier in this chapter.

MAKING IT SOUND EASY

If you're embedding sounds in your pages, consider using a regular link to the sound file rather than using the <OBJECT> tag to embed it. The only real advantage to using the <OBJECT> tag (or its Netscape-originated predecessor <EMBED>) is a neat little widget in the Web page that visitors can use to play the sound as if they were using a VCR. However, those neat little widgets aren't the same size in Internet Explorer and Netscape Navigator, so you end up with either a truncated object or one with loads of extra space around it.

We recommend using an icon or a text link to the sound file—it's much easier. Anyway, if the sound takes so long to play that your visitors have time to click Stop or Pause, the sound file is probably too big.

WHAT'S NEXT

This chapter showed you some of the more fun elements you can include in your HTML documents. Although multimedia files don't always have practical uses, they do make your pages more interesting and give them the "up with technology" look and feel. You also learned, however, that multimedia effects have a big disadvantage: the files are usually enormous, which slows download time considerably. Whether you choose to include the files using the HTML 3.2 tags and attributes or the HTML 4 tags and attributes depends on which browsers your visitors use.

In the next chapter, Deborah Ray and Eric Ray continue to help you master advanced HTML techniques. You'll learn how to use style sheets to format all aspect of your Web pages, from setting text and color properties to applying a consistent look to your entire site.

Chapter 16

USING STYLE SHEETS

Using style sheets—formally known as the World Wide Web Consortium *Cascading Style Sheets* recommendation, level 1 (or *CSS1*)—is potentially one of the best ways to format HTML documents easily and consistently. Adopted by the W3 Consortium in December 1996, style sheets take a step toward separating presentation from content, returning HTML to its function-oriented roots yet allowing you almost total control over page presentation. And, *CSS2*, adopted in May 1998, adds even more control, plus support for aural style sheets for screen-reading software.

Adapted from *Mastering HTML 4*, 2nd Edition, by Deborah S. Ray and Eric J. Ray

ISBN 0-7821-2523-9   912 pages $34.99

Are style sheets here to stay? Yes. In fact, the HTML 4 specification deprecates many formatting tags and attributes (such as <FONT> and ALIGN=) in favor of style sheets.

In this chapter, you'll see how style sheets enhance the effectiveness of HTML and how you can benefit from using them. You'll learn how to apply style sheets to your HTML documents and how to develop the style sheet. You'll find that style sheets give you an enormous number of formatting options (several of which are actually supported by browsers).

Before you decide to use style sheets, keep in mind that only the newest browsers support them and that the existing support is sketchy. Both Microsoft Internet Explorer 3 (and later) and Netscape Navigator 4 (and later) browsers offer some style sheet support; however, many style sheet features do not work consistently or at all even in these supporting browsers. In this chapter, we'll discuss the advantages and limitations of style sheets to help you decide whether they're right for your needs. And, of course, we'll provide the how-to of implementing them. Let's take a look.

How Do Style Sheets Work?

As you know, HTML is a markup language that you use to identify structural elements in a document. For example, you can specify that this element is a first-level heading, this one is a bullet point, this one is a block quotation, and so on by manually inserting formatting tags and attributes. The browser (with input from the visitor) controls formatting and layout.

Manually inserting all these formatting tags can quickly become a tedious process. With style sheets, however, you specify formatting only once, and it is applied throughout the document. If you've used styles in a word processor, you're familiar with this concept.

Style sheets promise to give you nearly the layout and format control you may be accustomed to in programs such as PageMaker or Quark. You can control how page elements look, where they appear, their color and size, the font they use, and so on. Now, you—rather than browsers and visitors—can determine page appearance.

BROWSERS, VISITORS, AND STYLE SHEETS

Unfortunately, style sheets are available only to visitors using Internet Explorer 3 (or later) and Netscape Navigator 4 (or later). Visitors using earlier versions of these browsers or other browsers will see a plain HTML document that includes little more than the logical formatting elements—headings, paragraphs, tables, and lists, with no colors.

In addition, because style sheet technology is new, browsers don't yet provide stable or consistent support. Pages that use style sheets will appear differently in different browsers.

Also, your visitors still have some control over the document appearance, regardless of the formatting you supply in the style sheet. They can disable style sheets or override them with their personal preferences for colors and fonts.

Some Advantages of Using Style Sheets

In addition to giving you more control over how your documents appear to visitors, style sheets let you manage HTML documents more easily than if they were filled with formatting tags. When you place formatting commands in the style sheet, your document is less cluttered.

Style sheets also reduce the time you spend developing and maintaining HTML documents. Rather than manually formatting paragraphs of text, you simply change the style definition in one place—the style sheet—and the style sheet applies the definition to all occurrences in the HTML document. No muss, no fuss.

Finally, style sheets give you flexibility from document to document within a Web site. Even if you set up a style sheet that applies to all pages in the site, you can set up individual style sheets to apply to individual HTML documents. The individual style sheet overrides the global one. And, you can further tweak individual style sheets to accommodate special text formatting, such as a document in which certain paragraphs should appear in a different color.

Part iii

IMPLEMENTING STYLE SHEETS

As you're perusing the rest of this chapter, remember that your HTML documents and the associated style sheets work as a team. HTML documents carry the content, and style sheets carry the formatting information. As you'll see, developing style sheets is a two-part process:

- ▶ You connect (or associate) the style sheet to the HTML document.
- ▶ Then you develop the actual style sheet, complete with all the formatting options.

Associating Style Sheets with HTML Documents

You can associate style sheets with your HTML documents in four ways:

- ▶ You can embed the style sheet in the HTML document by defining it between the opening and closing <HEAD> tags.
- ▶ You can store the style sheet in a separate document and either link or import the style sheet to associate it with the HTML document.
- ▶ You can apply style definitions to specified parts of an HTML document.
- ▶ You can use inline style definitions.

Embedding the Style Sheet in the HTML Document

Embedding the style sheet, which is the easiest of the four methods, means inserting the <STYLE> tags, along with style information, between the <HEAD> tags. Figure 16.1 shows how you do this.

Embedding style sheets makes maintaining or updating styles easy because you don't have to work with two or more documents (the style sheet document and the HTML document)—you simply open the HTML document and adjust the style sheet code. If you are working with multiple documents or documents that you'll update frequently, however, you'll probably want to use another method. If you embed the style sheet in every document, you'll have to adjust it in every document.

To embed a style sheet in an HTML document, apply the tags and attributes shown in Table 16.1 between the <HEAD> tags.

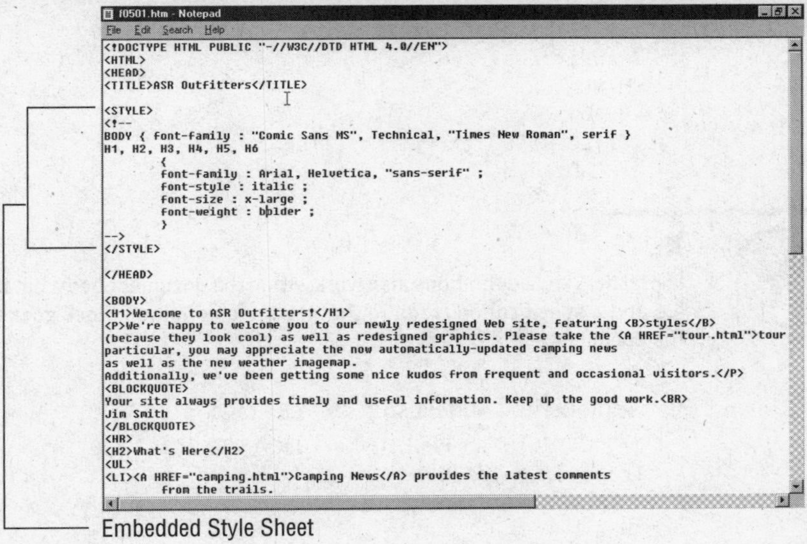

Embedded Style Sheet

FIGURE 16.1: An HTML document with an inserted style sheet

TABLE 16.1: Style Sheet Tags and Attributes

TAG/ATTRIBUTE	DESCRIPTION
<STYLE>	Specifies the style sheet area within an HTML document. Within this section, you can define or import formatting.
<!-- ... -->	A comment tag that hides style sheet contents from non–style-capable browsers.
TYPE="text/css"	Specifies the type of style sheet. Valid choices, at the time of writing, include text/css, for cascading style sheets (standard and covered in this chapter), and text/jss, for JavaScript style sheets.

To embed a minimal style sheet (that, in this example, colors paragraphs red) in an existing document, follow these steps:

1. Start with a functional document header.

```
<!DOCTYPE HTML PUBLIC "-//W3C//DTD HTML 4.0
Transitional//EN">
<HTML>
<HEAD>
<TITLE>ASR Outfitters</TITLE>
</HEAD>
```

NOTE

In practice, style definitions also work within the document body, but the HTML 3.2 and 4 specifications require that the style definition block goes between the document <HEAD> tags.

2. Add opening and closing <STYLE> tags.

```
<!DOCTYPE HTML PUBLIC "-//W3C//DTD HTML 4.0
Transitional//EN">
<HTML>
<HEAD>
<TITLE>ASR Outfitters</TITLE>
<STYLE>
</STYLE>
</HEAD>
```

3. Add the comment (<!-- ... -->) tag to hide the contents from non–style-capable browsers.

```
<!DOCTYPE HTML PUBLIC "-//W3C//DTD HTML 4.0
Transitional//EN">
<HTML>
<HEAD>
<TITLE>ASR Outfitters</TITLE>
<STYLE>
<!--

-->
</STYLE>
</HEAD>
```

Browsers that do not support style sheets ignore the tags but display the text that appears between them. Adding comment tags within the <STYLE> tags ensures that the styles will not appear as content in older or less-capable browsers.

4. Add style definitions within the comment tags. In this (minimal) example, we specify that paragraph text is red.

```
<!DOCTYPE HTML PUBLIC "-//W3C//DTD HTML 4.0
Transitional//EN">
<HTML>
<HEAD>
<TITLE>ASR Outfitters</TITLE>
<STYLE>
<!--
P {color: red}
-->
</STYLE>
</HEAD>
<BODY>
<P> This will be red.
</BODY>
</HTML>
```

That's it! To test your embedded style sheet, simply open the HTML document in Internet Explorer or Netscape Navigator.

Storing Style Sheets Separately

A separate style sheet is simply a plain text file and includes only the style definitions. Develop a separate style sheet any time you're working with several HTML documents, particularly if they share similar formatting. In this case, you develop a single style sheet and apply it to all the HTML documents, as shown in Figure 16.2. You can then make a formatting change in all the documents by simply changing the style sheet.

TIP

Even if you're only working with a few HTML documents, consider developing a separate style sheet. You never know how many HTML documents your site will eventually include.

After you develop the separate style sheet document, you associate it with the HTML document(s) using either of these methods:

► Importing

► Linking

Both methods work only with Internet Explorer.

Part iii

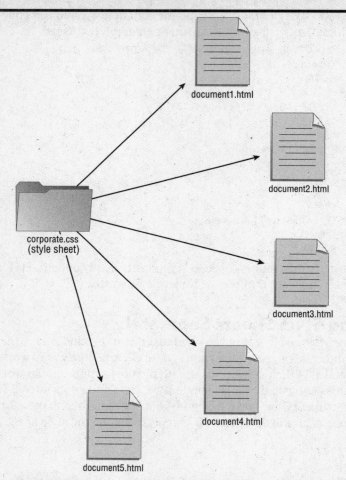

FIGURE 16.2: When you develop a separate style sheet, you can easily apply styles to many HTML documents.

Importing This method is handy when you are developing multiple style sheet pages that each have a particular function. For example, as illustrated in Figure 16.3, you can develop a page that applies corporate styles, one that applies styles for your department, and another that specifies particular document formatting. Rather than wading through a 10-page style sheet, you work with multiple smaller ones.

NOTE

Importing style sheets works well in Internet Explorer but is not functional in Netscape Navigator.

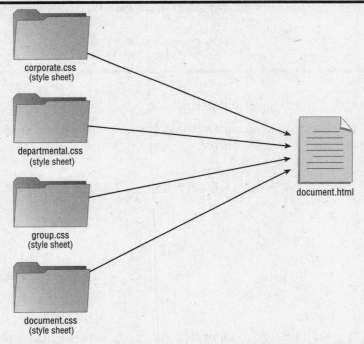

corporate.css
(style sheet)

departmental.css
(style sheet)

group.css
(style sheet)

document.css
(style sheet)

document.html

FIGURE 16.3: Importing allows you to easily maintain a detailed style sheet.

Table 16.2 describes the tags and attributes you use to import style sheets.

TABLE 16.2: Tags and Attributes for Importing Style Sheets

TAG/ATTRIBUTE	DESCRIPTION
`<STYLE>`	Specifies the style sheet area within an HTML document. Within this section, you can define or import formatting.
`<!-- ... -->`	A comment tag that hides contents from non–style-capable browsers.

CONTINUED ➡

Part iii

TABLE 16.2 continued: Tags and Attributes for Importing Style Sheets

TAG/ATTRIBUTE	DESCRIPTION
TYPE="text/css"	Specifies the type of a style sheet. Valid choices, at the time of writing, include text/css, for cascading style sheets (standard and covered in this chapter), and text/jss, for JavaScript style sheets.
@import url(...)	Imports a style sheet. Usage is url(http://mystyles.com/new.css).

To import a style sheet, follow these steps:

1. Start with a complete style block, such as the following code:

```
<!DOCTYPE HTML PUBLIC "-//W3C//DTD HTML 4.0//EN">
<HTML>
<HEAD>
<TITLE>ASR Outfitters</TITLE>
<STYLE>
<!--

-->
</STYLE>
</HEAD>
<BODY>
</BODY>
</HTML>
```

2. Within a style block or style sheet, add a line similar to the following:

```
<STYLE>
<!--
@import url('red.css');
-->
</STYLE>
```

A complete style block that does nothing but import two style sheets would look like the following:

```
<STYLE>
<!--
@import url('red.css');
@import url('redder.css');
-->
</STYLE>
```

Linking   This method has a distinct advantage over the other methods: it gives visitors a choice of style sheets to use for a specific page. For example, you can link one style sheet to a page that visitors will read online and link a different style sheet to a page that visitors will print, as shown in Figure 16.4. Theoretically, you could even develop a style sheet (as browsers implement this functionality) optimized for aural presentation.

Although you could import a style sheet, linking the style sheet is a better long-term choice because future browser versions should offer visitors more flexibility in handling style sheets, including the option to select from among multiple style sheets. Importing offers no choices—it just loads the style sheet. Table 16.3 explains the tags and attributes you use to link style sheets to HTML documents.

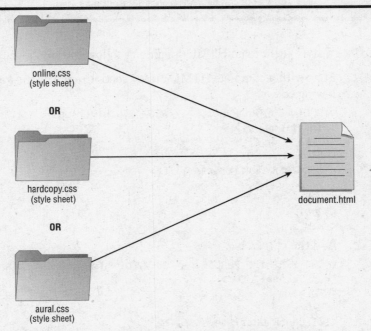

online.css
(style sheet)

OR

hardcopy.css
(style sheet)

document.html

OR

aural.css
(style sheet)

FIGURE 16.4: Linking lets you apply style sheets for specific uses.

TABLE 16.3: Tags and Attributes for Linking Style Sheets

Tag/Attribute	Description
`<LINK>`	References a style sheet.
`REL=StyleSheet`	Specifies that the referenced file is a style sheet. You can also use `Alternate Style Sheet` to reference optional style sheets.
`TYPE="text/css"`	Specifies the type of a style sheet. Valid choices, at the time of writing, include `text/css`, for cascading style sheets (standard and covered in this chapter), and `text/jss`, for JavaScript style sheets.
`HREF="URL"`	Identifies the style sheet source as a standard URL.
`TITLE="..."`	Names the style sheet. Unnamed style sheets are always applied. Named style sheets are applied by default or provided as options, depending on the REL attribute used.

To link a style sheet to an HTML document, follow these steps:

1. Start with a complete HTML `<HEAD>` section, such as the following code:

   ```
   <!DOCTYPE HTML PUBLIC "-//W3C//DTD HTML 4.0
   Transitional//EN">
   <HTML>
   <HEAD>
   <TITLE>ASR Outfitters</TITLE>
   </HEAD>
   <BODY>
   </BODY>
   </HTML>
   ```

2. Add the `<LINK>` tag.

   ```
   <!DOCTYPE HTML PUBLIC "-//W3C//DTD HTML 4.0
   Transitional//EN">
   <HTML>
   <HEAD>
   <TITLE>ASR Outfitters</TITLE>
   <LINK>
   </HEAD>
   <BODY>
   </BODY>
   </HTML>
   ```

3. Specify the `REL` and `TYPE` values of `StyleSheet` and `text/css` to link to a standard style sheet.

   ```
   <LINK REL="StyleSheet" TYPE="text/css">
   ```

4. Specify the address of the style sheet with the HREF= attribute. Specify either a relative URL, as in the sample code, or an absolute URL.

```
<LINK REL="StyleSheet" HREF="blue.css" TYPE="text/css">
```

There you go! To link your HTML document to more than one style sheet, simply include multiple <LINK> tags, complete with each of the style sheets to which they link. For example, you might link an HTML document to a generic style sheet that contains basic style definitions and then also link it to a more specific style sheet that contains definitions suitable to a particular style of document—instructions, marketing, and so on. If you link to multiple style sheets, all take effect. If you define the same element in multiple sheets, however, the later links override the previous links.

The HTML specification indicates that you can also link your HTML documents to optional style sheets using the REV="Alternate Style Sheet" attribute so that visitors can choose which styles to use. Theoretically, you can provide optional style sheets that let visitors choose a low-bandwidth style for viewing over a modem connection or a high-bandwidth style with lots of cool images for viewing over a high-speed connection. Or, you can present choices for high-resolution and high color-depth monitors and provide alternatives for standard monitors at lower color-depth. At the time of writing, however, neither Internet Explorer nor Netscape Navigator supports optional style sheets.

Applying Style Sheets to Parts of Documents

So far, you've seen how to apply style sheets to entire HTML documents. You can also apply styles included in a style sheet to specific parts of HTML documents, as shown in Figure 16.5. This is called applying *style classes*, which you define in your style sheet. For example, suppose you specify in a style sheet that the first line of all paragraphs is indented. You might find, however, that paragraphs after a bulleted list should not be indented because they continue the information from the paragraph above the list. To address this issue, you can manually format the paragraph, which might be appropriate for a one-time occurrence. A better solution, however, is to set up a new class of paragraph tag within your style definition called, say, continue. You can use this new paragraph class whenever the first line of a paragraph should not be indented. Table 16.4 describes the tags and attributes you use to apply classes.

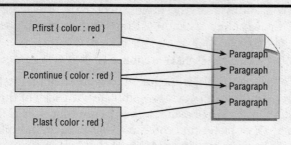

FIGURE 16.5: Applying style classes, you can specify how parts of HTML documents appear.

TABLE 16.4: Tags and Attributes for Applying Classes

TAG/ATTRIBUTE	DESCRIPTION
<SPAN>	Holds style attributes and applies them to the HTML code between the opening and closing tags. Surround letters and words with these tags.
<DIV>	Holds style attributes and applies them to the HTML code between the opening and closing tags. Surround paragraphs or other block-level elements with these.
CLASS="..."	References a style class to apply to a specified part of an HTML document.
ID="uniquen"	Specifies a unique name associated with a specific style definition. You can use this only once within a style sheet.

You can apply a class to an existing HTML tag, or you can use the <DIV> and <SPAN> tags to specify that the class apply to other elements—such as specific letters or words—not individually specified by an HTML tag.

Applying Classes to an HTML Tag   You apply a class to an existing HTML tag—such as <P>, <H1>, <UL>, and so on—to specify formatting for a group of items. To apply classes within an HTML document, follow these steps:

1. Start with an existing paragraph within an HTML document.
   ```
   <P>Many people buy ASR products despite the higher
   cost.</P>
   ```

2. Add the CLASS= attribute to the opening <P> tag, like this:

```
<P CLASS="">Many people buy ASR products despite the
higher cost.</P>
```

3. Add the name of the paragraph class. (You'll see how to define and name classes when you develop the style sheet later in this chapter.)

```
<P CLASS="continue">Many people buy ASR products despite
the higher cost.</P>
```

That's it!

If you have a specific formatting need—a one-time need—you can define a style ID and then apply the ID= attribute in place of the CLASS= attribute in the preceding example. You would end up with something like this:

```
<P ID="538fv1">Many people buy ASR products despite the
higher cost.</P>
```

We don't generally recommend this one-time formatting use, but it can be appropriate in some cases, including in particular Microsoft's Dynamic HTML implementation.

Applying Classes to Other Document Parts You can also apply classes to specific parts of an HTML document that do not have existing tags. For example, suppose you want to make the first few lines in the document body a different color. Because no specific tag exists to designate the first few lines (in CSS1), you must specify the paragraph or text to which the style applies.

To apply classes to specific parts of an HTML document, use the <DIV> and <SPAN> tags, described earlier in Table 16.4. These tags provide a place to apply class formatting when there's no existing HTML tag.

You use the <DIV> tag to apply classes to block-level sections of a document. Here are the steps:

1. Start with an existing HTML document and text.

```
<P>Many people buy ASR products despite the higher
cost.</P>
```

2. Add the <DIV> tags around the section.

```
<DIV>
<P>Many people buy ASR products despite the higher
cost.</P>
</DIV>
```

3. Add the appropriate CLASS= attribute.

```
<DIV CLASS="notice">
<P>Many people buy ASR products despite the higher
cost.</P>
</DIV>
```

Use the <SPAN> tag to apply classes to characters or words. For example, to apply the firstuse class (that you define elsewhere) to a word, follow these steps:

1. Start with an existing HTML document and text.

```
<P>Many people buy ASR products despite the higher
cost.</P>
```

2. Add the <SPAN> opening and closing tags.

```
<P>Many people buy <SPAN>ASR products</SPAN> despite the
higher cost.</P>
```

3. Add the appropriate CLASS= attribute.

```
<P>Many people buy <SPAN CLASS="firstuse">ASR
products</SPAN> despite the higher cost.</P>
```

TIP

You might use classes in conjunction with HTML 4 tables (covered in Chapter 11). Table tags accept CLASS= attributes to apply formatting to the table sections you specify rather than to individual cells, rows, and columns or to the table as a whole.

Applying Inline Style Definitions

Applying inline style definitions throughout an HTML document is similar to adding formatting extensions. For example, just as you can apply an alignment attribute to a paragraph, you can apply a style definition within the <P> tag, as Figure 16.6 shows. Of course, with style sheets you have far more formatting possibilities than with simple HTML formatting commands.

Although you wouldn't use this method to apply styles throughout an HTML document—it's time-consuming—you might use it to make exceptions to an existing style sheet. For example, your style sheet might specify that paragraphs appear in blue text. You can apply an inline style to specify that one specific paragraph appears in red. Table 16.5 lists the tags and attributes you use to apply inline styles.

TABLE 16.5: Tags and Attributes for Inline Style Sheets

Tag/Attribute	Description
Any HTML tag	All HTML tags within and including <BODY> can support style definitions.
STYLE="..."	Used for inline style definitions, which you apply as an attribute to HTML tags. Provide the style definition within quotes, and provide quoted elements within the STYLE="..." attribute within single quotes.

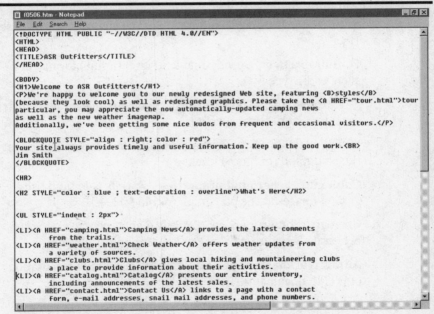

```
f0506.htm - Notepad                                                    _ 8 X
File  Edit  Search  Help
<!DOCTYPE HTML PUBLIC "-//W3C//DTD HTML 4.0//EN">
<HTML>
<HEAD>
<TITLE>ASR Outfitters</TITLE>
</HEAD>

<BODY>
<H1>Welcome to ASR Outfitters!</H1>
<P>We're happy to welcome you to our newly redesigned Web site, featuring <B>styles</B>
(because they look cool) as well as redesigned graphics. Please take the <A HREF="tour.html">tour
particular, you may appreciate the now automatically-updated camping news
as well as the new weather imagemap.
Additionally, we've been getting some nice kudos from frequent and occasional visitors.</P>

<BLOCKQUOTE STYLE="align : right; color : red">
Your site always provides timely and useful information. Keep up the good work.<BR>
Jim Smith
</BLOCKQUOTE>

<HR>

<H2 STYLE="color : blue ; text-decoration : overline">What's Here</H2>

<UL STYLE="indent : 2px">

<LI><A HREF="camping.html">Camping News</A> provides the latest comments
        from the trails.
<LI><A HREF="weather.html">Check Weather</A> offers weather updates from
        a variety of sources.
<LI><A HREF="clubs.html">Clubs</A> gives local hiking and mountaineering clubs
        a place to provide information about their activities.
<LI><A HREF="catalog.html">Catalog</A> presents our entire inventory,
        including announcements of the latest sales.
<LI><A HREF="contact.html">Contact Us</A> links to a page with a contact
        form, e-mail addresses, snail mail addresses, and phone numbers.
```

FIGURE 16.6: You apply inline style definitions within HTML code.

To add a style definition to an existing HTML tag, follow these steps:

1. Start with an existing HTML tag.

   ```
   <P>Many people buy ASR products despite the higher
   cost.</P>
   ```

2. Add the STYLE= attribute.

   ```
   <P STYLE="">Many people buy ASR products despite the
   higher cost.</P>
   ```

3. Add the style definition(s), separated by semicolons. Substitute single quotes for double quotes within the attribute; otherwise, you'll bring the attribute to a premature end.

```
<P STYLE="color : blue; font-family: 'Times New Roman',
Arial">Many people buy ASR products despite the higher
cost.</P>
```

Developing a Style Sheet

In the previous sections, you learned how to associate a style sheet with an HTML document. Your goal now is to develop the style sheet—that is, to specify the style definitions you want to include. A *style definition* specifies formatting characteristics.

You can choose from any combination of the eight categories of style properties.

Font properties   Specify character-level (inline) formatting such as the type face.

Text properties   Specify display characteristics for text, such as alignment or letter spacing.

Box properties   Specify characteristics for sections of text, at the paragraph (or block) level.

Color and background properties   Specify color and background images at the paragraph (or block) level.

Classification properties   Specify display characteristics of lists and elements (such as P or H1) as inline or block level.

Aural style sheet properties   Control the aural presentation of HTML documents (CSS2 only).

Printed style sheet properties   Add features specifically to control printed output of HTML documents (CSS2 only).

Positioning properties   Add features to precisely control the placement of elements on the display (CSS2 only).

When developing a style sheet, simplicity is key. You can easily get carried away with formatting options, but keep things simple. And, as you might guess, using even some of these options can quickly get complex.

Before we dive into developing a style sheet, let's take a look at some style sheet code:

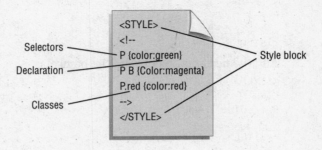

Here's what each part does:

- The style block includes style and comment tags, plus style definitions (or rules).

- Selectors are HTML elements. In this example, the P—as in a paragraph tag—is a selector.

- Declarations are the properties of the HTML elements, such as color, background, alignment, and font. In this example, color: green is the declaration. The style block is enclosed within brackets, { }.

- Classes specify an additional style definition associated with specific occurrences of the HTML element. For example, paragraphs tagged with <P CLASS=red> would use this style class.

- Each style definition can define the formatting associated with a specific HTML tag, with a specific CLASS, or with a specific ID. The formatting associated with HTML tags appears in the document without any special action on your part. Style definitions for CLASSes or IDs also require that you add the CLASS= or ID= attribute to the appropriate HTML document section before the formatting can appear in the HTML document.

To add these elements, follow these steps:

1. Be sure the style block is in place, like this.
   ```
   <STYLE>
   <!--
   -->
   </STYLE>
   ```

2. Add a selector and brackets, as shown here:

```
<STYLE>
<!--
P { }
-->
</STYLE>
```

3. Add the declaration between the brackets.

```
<STYLE>
<!--
P { color : aqua }
-->
</STYLE>
```

 STYLE SHEET TIPS

As you're building a style sheet, the process will be easier if you follow these guidelines:

▶ To include multiple selectors, place them on separate lines, like this:

```
<STYLE>
<!--
P {color: red}
H1 {color: blue}
BLOCKQUOTE {color: green}
-->
</STYLE>
```

▶ To provide multiple declarations for a single selector, group the declarations within the brackets, separated by a semicolon. For example, to define P as red with a yellow background, use the following code:

```
<STYLE>
<!--
P {color: red ; background: yellow}
-->
</STYLE>
```

▶ You might find the style definitions easier to read if you space them out somewhat, as in this example, and put only one declaration on a single line:

```
<STYLE>
```

CONTINUED ➡

```
<!--
P {color: red ;
background: yellow}
-->
</STYLE>
```

▶ Start at the highest level—the most general level—within your document, which is probably the body. Format the <BODY> as you want most of the document to appear, and then use specific style rules to override the <BODY> settings.

In addition, become familiar with ways to specify measurements and values, which are discussed in the next two sections.

Specifying Measurements

When specifying locations of elements, you might also want to specify their size. For example, when specifying that the first line of paragraphs indent, you can also specify the size of the indention. In general, provide measurements in the units shown in Table 16.6. You can also express most measurements as a percentage of the browser window.

Your measurement might look like this:

```
P { text-indent: 2px }
```

or like this:

```
P { text-indent: 1em }
```

TABLE 16.6: Units of Measure in Style Sheets

Unit	What It Is	Description
em	Em space	The width of a capital *M* in the typeface being used.
ex	X-height	The height of a lowercase letter *x* in the typeface being used.
in	Inch	
cm	Centimeter	
mm	Millimeter	
px	Pixel	The individual screen dots are one pixel.

CONTINUED ➡

TABLE 16.6 continued: Units of Measure in Style Sheets

Unit	What It Is	Description
pt	Point	A typographical measurement that equals 1/72 inch.
pc	Pica	A typographical measurement that equals 1/6 inch.

Specifying Colors in Style Rules

Using style sheets, you can specify colors in the standard HTML ways (as a #rrggbb value and as a color name), as well as in two other ways that use a slightly different approach to specify proportions of red, green, and blue. The following four lines show how to specify red in each method.

```
P { color : #FF0000 }
P { color : red }
P { color : rgb(255,0,0) }
P { color : rgb(100%,0%,0%) }
```

TIP

Although each of these is equally easy to use, we recommend using the #rrggbb option because it's likely to be more familiar, as it matches HTML color statements.

In the following sections, we'll show you how to develop an embedded style sheet. After you complete an embedded style sheet, you can move it to a separate document and import it or link it.

If you're following along with the example, have ready an HTML document with the complete structure tags.

Listing 16.1

```
<!DOCTYPE HTML PUBLIC "-//W3C//DTD HTML 4.0
Transitional//EN">
<HTML>
<HEAD>
<TITLE>ASR Outfitters</TITLE>
</HEAD>

<BODY>
<H1>Welcome to ASR Outfitters!</H1>
```

```
<P>We're happy to welcome you to our newly redesigned Web
site, featuring <B>styles</B>
(because they look cool) as well as redesigned graphics.
Please take the <A HREF="tour.html">tour of our site</A> if
you haven't been here in a while. In particular, you may
appreciate the now automatically-updated camping news as well
as the new weather imagemap.
Additionally, we've been getting some nice kudos from
frequent and occasional visitors.</P>
<BLOCKQUOTE>
Your site always provides timely and useful information. Keep
up the good work.<BR>
Jim Smith
</BLOCKQUOTE>
<HR>
<H2>What's Here</H2>
<UL>
<LI><A HREF="camping.html">Camping News</A> provides the
latest comments from the trails.
<LI><A HREF="weather.html">Check Weather</A> offers weather
updates from a variety of sources.
<LI><A HREF="clubs.html">Clubs</A> gives local hiking and
mountaineering clubs a place to provide information about
their activities.
<LI><A HREF="catalog.html">Catalog</A> presents our entire
inventory, including announcements of the latest sales.
<LI><A HREF="contact.html">Contact Us</A> links to a page
with a contact form, e-mail addresses, snail mail addresses,
and phone numbers. If it isn't here, you can't find us.
</UL>

<H2>What We Do</H2>
<P>In addition to providing the latest camping and outdoor
activities news, we do also provide mountaineering and
hiking equipment nationwide via mail order as well as
through our stores in the Rocky Mountains.
Please take a few minutes to look through our
<A HREF="catalog.html">online offerings</A>.</P>
<H2>Other Issues</H2>
<UL>
<LI>As you may know, our URL was misprinted in the latest
<I>Hiking News</I>. Please tell your hiking friends that
the correct URL is <TT>http://www.asroutfitters.com/</TT>.
<LI>To collect a $1000 reward, turn in the name of the person
who set the fire in the Bear Lake area last weekend.
<OL>
```

```
<LI>Call 888-555-1212.
<LI>Leave the name on the recording.
<LI>Provide contact information so we can send you the
reward.
</OL>
</UL>
<H2>What Would You Like To See?</H2>
<P>If you have suggestions or comments about the site or
other information we could provide, we'd love to know about
it. Drop us an e-mail at <A HREF="mailto:asroutfitters
@raycomm.com">asroutfitters@raycomm.com</A>.
Of course, you could also contact us more traditionally at
the following address: </P>
<ADDRESS>ASR Outfitters
<BR>
4700 N. Center <BR>
South Logan, UT 87654<BR>
801-555-3422</ADDRESS>
</BODY>
</HTML>
```

Without any styles or formatting other than the standard HTML/
browser defaults, this document looks something like that in Figure 16.7.

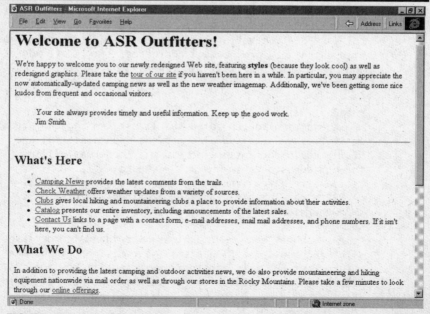

FIGURE 16.7: An HTML document without any special formatting or style sheets

To add a style block to the document, follow these steps:

1. Add a pair of opening and closing <STYLE> tags within the document head, as shown in the following code.

```
<!DOCTYPE HTML PUBLIC "-//W3C//DTD HTML 4.0 Transitional
//EN">
<HTML>
<HEAD>
<TITLE>ASR Outfitters</TITLE>
<STYLE>

</STYLE>
</HEAD>
```

2. Add an opening and closing comment (<!-- -->) tag within the <STYLE> tags, as shown here:

```
<STYLE>
<!--

-->
</STYLE>
```

After the <STYLE> and comment tags are in place, define the style sheet. Think of defining styles as specifying rules for what each element should look like. For example, specify that you want all text blue, all bullets indented, all headings centered, and so on.

Next, you specify style properties, such as fonts, text, boxes, colors, backgrounds, and classifications. The following sections do not build on one another; instead, they show you how to set each of the properties separately, based on the sample ASR Outfitters page. Through these examples, you'll see *some* of the many style sheet effects you can achieve.

Setting Font Properties

If the fonts you specify are not available on your visitors' computers, the browser will display text in a font that is available. To ensure that one of your preferred fonts is used, choose multiple font families. Table 16.7 shows some of the basic font properties and values.

TABLE 16.7: Font Properties

PROPERTY	VALUE
font-family	Times New Roman, Arial, serif, sans-serif, monospace
font-style	Normal, italic, oblique
font-variant	Normal, small-caps
font-weight	Normal, bold, bolder, lighter, 100, 200, 300, 400, 500, 600, 700, 800, 900
font-size	xx-small, x-small, small, medium, large, x-large, xx-large, or size measurement
Font	Any or all of the above properties

The following example sets a basic font for the whole document—everything between the opening and closing <BODY> tags. It sets the basic font for a document to Comic Sans MS, with Technical and Times New Roman as other choices and with a generic serif font as the last choice.

1. Within the style block, add a BODY selector.

```
<STYLE>
<!--
BODY
-->
</STYLE>
```

2. Add brackets.

```
<STYLE>
<!--
BODY {}
-->
</STYLE>
```

3. Add the property. To set only the typeface, use font-family.

```
<STYLE>
<!--
BODY { font-family }
-->
</STYLE>
```

4. Add a colon to separate the property from the value.

```
<STYLE>
<!--
BODY { font-family : }
```

```
-->
</STYLE>
```

5. Add the value `"Comic Sans MS"` (the first choice typeface).

```
<STYLE>
<!--
BODY { font-family : "Comic Sans MS" }
-->
</STYLE>
```

6. Add additional values, as you choose, separated by commas. If the font family name contains a space, put the name in quotes. Otherwise, quotes are optional. Conclude your list of fonts with either a serif or sans serif font that's bound to match something on the visitor's computer.

```
<STYLE>
<!--
BODY { font-family : "Comic Sans MS", Technical, "Times
New Roman", serif }
-->
</STYLE>
```

Here is the resulting page, complete with the new font for the document body.

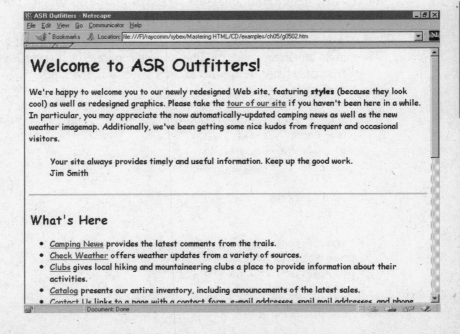

SETTING LINK CHARACTERISTICS

You use three special style classes (and font style rules) to control the colors of links in your document:

- ► A:link
- ► A:active
- ► A:visited

Use these within your style sheet definition to specify the rules that apply to links, active links, and visited links. For example, to set unvisited links to blue, active links to red, and visited links to magenta, your style block would look like this:

```
<STYLE>
<!--
A:link   { color :   blue }
A:active { color :   red }
A:visited { color :   magenta }
-->
</STYLE>
```

You can also define additional text styles within the document. For example, to set all headings to Arial italic, follow these steps:

1. Add a comma-separated list of all headings to the existing style block, as selectors. The comma-separated list specifies that the style rule applies to each selector individually.

```
<STYLE>
<!--
BODY { font-family : "Comic Sans MS", Technical, "Times
New Roman", serif }
H1, H2, H3, H4, H5, H6
-->
</STYLE>
```

2. Add brackets.

```
<STYLE>
<!--
BODY { font-family : "Comic Sans MS", Technical, "Times
New Roman", serif }
H1, H2, H3, H4, H5, H6 { }
-->
</STYLE>
```

3. Add the font-family property, with Arial as the first choice, Helvetica as the second choice, and sans serif as the third choice.

```
<STYLE>
<!--
BODY { font-family : "Comic Sans MS", Technical, "Times
New Roman", serif }
H1, H2, H3, H4, H5, H6 { font-family : Arial, Helvetica,
"sans-serif" }
-->
</STYLE>
```

4. After the font-family values, add a semicolon and a new line so that you can easily enter (and read) the font-style rule.

```
<STYLE>
<!--
BODY { font-family : "Comic Sans MS", Technical, "Times
New Roman", serif }
H1, H2, H3, H4, H5, H6 { font-family : Arial, Helvetica,
"sans-serif" ;
}
-->
</STYLE>
```

5. Add the font-style property, a colon, and the italic value.

```
<STYLE>
<!--
BODY { font-family : "Comic Sans MS", Technical, "Times
New Roman", serif }
H1, H2, H3, H4, H5, H6 { font-family : Arial, Helvetica,
"sans-serif" ;
font-style : italic }
-->
</STYLE>
```

6. Continue adding font properties, separated by a semicolon, if you want to define other aspects, such as font size or weight. The following lines of code show the headings set to a larger size and weight than usual. You'll see the results in Figure 16.8.

```
<STYLE>
<!--
BODY { font-family : "Comic Sans MS", Technical, "Times
New Roman", serif }
H1, H2, H3, H4, H5, H6 {
font-family : Arial, Helvetica, "sans-serif" ;
```

Part III

```
font-style : italic ;
font-size : x-large ;
font-weight : bolder ;
}
-->
</STYLE>
```

COMBINING MULTIPLE CHARACTERISTICS

With font properties, you can combine multiple characteristics into a single line—kind of like using shorthand. For example, you could reduce the sample heading definition to:

```
H1, H2, H3, H4, H5, H6 { font: Arial, Helvetica,
"sans-serif" italic x-large bolder }
```

Using this shorter definition has a few disadvantages. First, the reduced code is more difficult to interpret—particular for those just learning style sheets. Also, browser support is even sketchier for the shorter version than for the longer version, so visitors may not be able to view the effects.

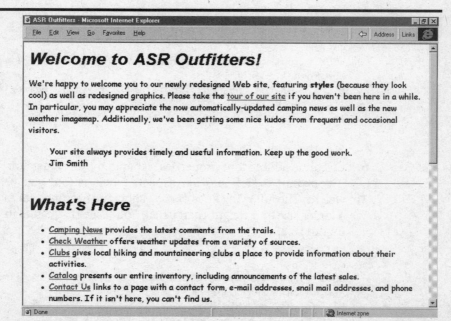

FIGURE 16.8: The results of setting the font family, style, size, and weight for headings

Setting Text Properties

Text properties specify the characteristics of text blocks (sections of text, not individual characters). Table 16.8 shows some of the most common text properties.

TABLE 16.8: Text Properties

PROPERTY	VALUE
word-spacing	Measurement
letter-spacing	Measurement
text-decoration	none, underline, overline, line-through, blink
vertical-align	baseline, super, sub, top, text-top, middle-bottom, text-bottom
text-transform	none, capitalize, uppercase, lowercase
text-align	left, right, center, justify
text-indent	Measurement or %

You apply these properties to selectors in the same way you apply font-level properties. To indent paragraphs and set up a special, nonindented paragraph class, follow these steps:

1. Within the style block, add a P selector.

   ```
   <STYLE>
   <!--
   P
   -->
   </STYLE>
   ```

2. Add brackets.

   ```
   <STYLE>
   <!--
   P {}
   -->
   </STYLE>
   ```

3. Add the text-indent property, with a value of 5% to indent all regular paragraphs by 5 percent of the total window width.

   ```
   <STYLE>
   <!--
   ```

```
P { text-indent : 5% }
-->
</STYLE>
```

4. Add the `P.noindent` selector on a new line within the style
    block. Using a standard selection, in conjunction with a
    descriptive term (that you make up), you create a new style
    class within the style sheet.

```
<STYLE>
<!--
P { text-indent : 5% }
P.noindent
-->
</STYLE>
```

5. Add brackets and the `text-indent` property, with a value of
    0% to specify no indent.

```
<STYLE>
<!--
P { text-indent : 5% }
P.noindent { text-indent : 0% }
-->
</STYLE>
```

6. To specify which text should be formatted without an indent,
    add a new `<P>` tag with a `CLASS="noindent"` attribute, as
    shown here.

```
<P>We're happy to welcome you to our newly redesigned
Web site, featuring <B>styles</B>
(because they look cool) as well as redesigned graphics.
Please take the <A HREF="tour.html">tour of our
site</A> if you haven't been here in a while. In
particular, you may appreciate the now automatically-
updated camping news as well as the new weather
imagemap. </P>
<P CLASS="noindent">Additionally, we've been getting
some nice kudos from frequent and occasional
 visitors.</P>
```

Figure 16.9 shows the results. All text tagged with `<P>` in the HTML
document is indented by 5 percent of the window width, and special formatting, set up with the `CLASS=` attribute, does not indent.

SPECIFYING GENERIC STYLE CLASSES

You can also specify a class without a selector, as in the following style block:

```
<STYLE>
<!--
.red { color : red }
-->
</STYLE>
```

You can use a generic class, such as red in this example, with any HTML tags in your document. If you specify an element with the class (P.red, for example), you can only use that class with <P> tags.

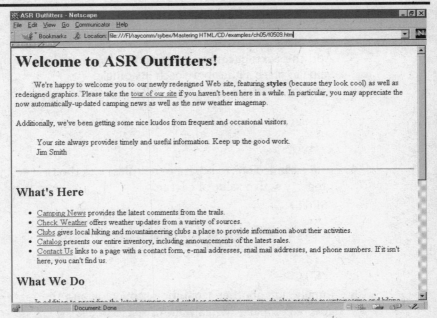

FIGURE 16.9: Setting text properties lets you customize your documents—the second paragraph is not indented, while the first one is, because of a style class.

You can also use text properties to apply special formatting to headings. To format all headings with a line below them, centered, and with extra spacing between the letters, follow these steps:

1. Add the list of heading selectors you want to format to your basic style sheet. To apply these formats to headings 1 through 3; for example, list H1, H2, H3.

    ```
    <STYLE>
    <!--
    H1, H2, H3
    -->
    </STYLE>
    ```

2. Add brackets following the selector.

    ```
    <STYLE>
    <!--
    H1, H2, H3 {  }
    -->
    </STYLE>
    ```

3. Add the text-decoration property with underline as the value to place a line above each heading.

    ```
    <STYLE>
    <!--
    H1, H2, H3 { text-decoration : underline }
    -->
    </STYLE>
    ```

4. Add a semicolon (to separate the rules) and the text-align property with a value of center.

    ```
    <STYLE>
    <!--
    H1, H2, H3 { text-decoration : underline ;
    text-align : center}
    -->
    </STYLE>
    ```

5. Finally, add another separation semicolon and the letter-spacing property with a value of 5px (5 pixels).

    ```
    <STYLE>
    <!--
    H1, H2, H3 { text-decoration : underline ;
    text-align : center ;
    letter-spacing : 5px }
    -->
    </STYLE>
    ```

The sample page looks like this:

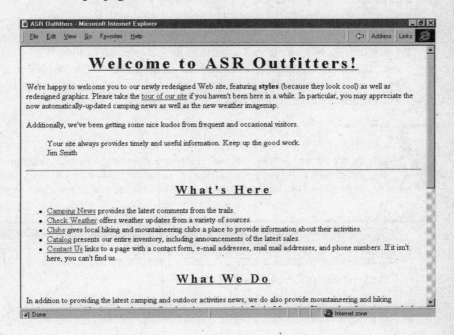

SPECIFYING STYLE IDS

You can specify an ID for a one-time use—for example, if you're developing a Dynamic HTML document. Use a # at the beginning of the ID selector, as in the following style block:

```
<STYLE>
<!--
#firstusered { color : red }
-->
</STYLE>
```

You can use an ID, such as firstusered in this example, with any single ID= attribute in your document. If you specify an element with the ID (<P ID=firstusered>, for example), you can only use that ID once in the document.

Setting Box Properties

You use box properties to create all sorts of box designs—a feature that's not available in standard HTML. You can box text, such as cautions or contact information, to call attention to it, as shown in Figure 16.10. You can adjust the margins to control how close text is to the border, and you can also remove the border to create floating text. Table 16.9 lists some commonly used box properties.

TIP

At the time of writing, Internet Explorer and Netscape Navigator support box properties differently—in particular, the relationship between the surrounding text and the box and the size of the box around text is quite inconsistent.

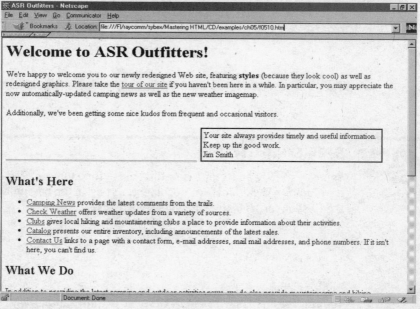

FIGURE 16.10: Floating boxes are handy for calling attention to information or making the page design more interesting.

TABLE 16.9: Box Properties

PROPERTY	VALUE
margin-top	Measurement, % of parent
margin-right	Measurement, % of parent
margin-bottom	Measurement, % of parent
margin-left	Measurement, % of parent
Margin	Measurement, % of parent
border-width	Measurement, thick, medium, thin
border-color	#rrggbb
border-style	none, dotted, dashed, solid, double, groove, ridge, inset, outset
Border	Any or all of the above attributes
Width	Measurement or %
Height	Measurement or %
Float	right, left, none
Clear	right, left, none, both

To create a box, apply these box-level characteristics to existing text in an HTML document, including, for example, paragraphs, block quotes, or headings. The following steps show you how to create a box using an existing block quote. This box will float close to the right margin with a 2-pixel border and will occupy only 50 percent of the window width.

1. Within the style block, add a BLOCKQUOTE selector.

```
<STYLE>
<!--
BLOCKQUOTE
-->
</STYLE>
```

2. Add brackets.

```
<STYLE>
<!--
BLOCKQUOTE {}
-->
</STYLE>
```

3. Add a WIDTH property, with a value of 50%.

```
<STYLE>
<!--
BLOCKQUOTE { width : 50% }
-->
</STYLE>
```

4. Add a semicolon as a separator and the FLOAT property with a value of right.

```
<STYLE>
<!--
BLOCKQUOTE { width : 50% ;
float : right }
-->
</STYLE>
```

5. Add another semicolon as a separator and the BORDER property. In this example, we provided the individual border properties together, rather than as individual entities.

```
<STYLE>
<!--
BLOCKQUOTE { width : 50% ;
float : right ;
border : 2px solid black }
-->
</STYLE>
```

Figure 16.11 shows the results.

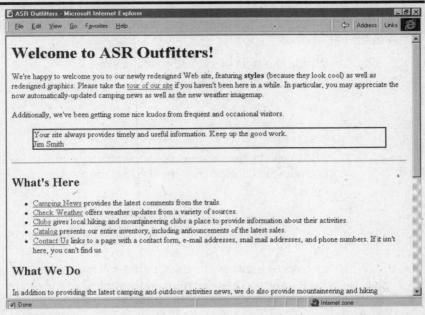

FIGURE 16.11: Using boxes is an excellent way to call attention to information.

Setting Color and Background Properties

To establish color and background properties for the sample document or for any block-level elements, use the properties and values shown in Table 16.10.

TABLE 16.10: Color and Background

PROPERTY	VALUE
Color	#rrggbb
background-color	#rrggbb, transparent
background-image	url(http://sampleurl.com)
background-repeat	repeat, repeat-x, repeat-y, no-repeat
Background	Any or all of the above properties

To include a background color, add the properties to the <BODY> element, as shown in the following steps, which add #FFFFCC (light yellow) to the background:

1. Within the style block, add a BODY selector.

    ```
    <STYLE>
    <!--
    BODY
    -->
    </STYLE>
    ```

2. Add brackets, the background-color attribute, and the #FFF-FCC value, which specifies the light yellow color.

    ```
    <STYLE>
    <!--
    BODY {background-color : #FFFFCC}
    -->
    </STYLE>
    ```

When viewed in a browser, the background will appear lightly colored, just as it would if the BGCOLOR= attribute were applied to the <BODY> tag. Each element within the document inherits the background color from the body.

You can also add a background image to the <BODY> tag or other block elements. Remember, block elements are any elements with a line break before and after, such as <BODY>, <P>, or <H1>.

As shown in the following steps, you can tile the background image either vertically or horizontally:

1. To add a background image to the document body, add the background-image property, separated from the previous property with a semicolon.

    ```
    <STYLE>
    <!--
    BODY {background-color : #FFFFCC ;
    background-image : }
    -->
    </STYLE>
    ```

2. Add the value for the background image as url(pattern .gif). Use any absolute or relative URL in the parentheses.

    ```
    <STYLE>
    <!--
    BODY {background-color : #FFFFCC ;
    ```

```
background-image : url(pattern.gif) }
-->
</STYLE>
```

3. Add `background-repeat: repeat-x` to specify that the background image repeat horizontally (in the direction of the x-axis). To repeat only vertically, use `repeat-y`; use `no-repeat` if you don't want a repeat.

```
<STYLE>
<!--
BODY {background-color : #FFFFCC ;
background-image : url(pattern.gif) ;
background-repeat : repeat-x ; }
-->
</STYLE>
```

Figure 16.12 shows this effect in Netscape Navigator.

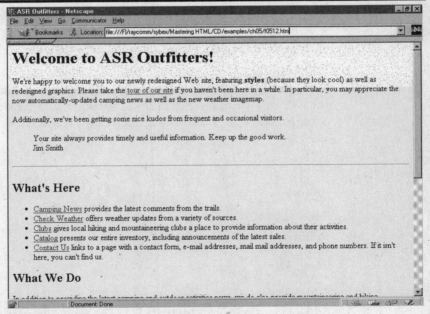

FIGURE 16.12: Style sheets let you easily add a background image.

Setting Classification Properties

You use classification properties to change specific elements from inline (such as I or B) to block elements with line breaks before and after (such as P and H1), as well as to control the display of lists. Table 16.11 lists some classification properties and their values.

TABLE 16.11: Classification Properties

PROPERTY	VALUE
Display	inline, block, list-item
line-height	Measurement or %
list-style-type	disc, circle, square, decimal, lower-roman, upper-roman, lower-alpha, upper-alpha, none
list-style-image	url(http://someurl.com/image.gif)

To specify that an unordered list use square bullets, follow these steps:

1. Within the style block, add a UL selector followed immediately by an LI selector on the same line. By combining these, the style rule will apply only to an <LI> within a <UL>. Setting a rule for only <LI> affects all numbered and bulleted lists.

```
<STYLE>
<!--
UL LI
-->
</STYLE>
```

2. Add brackets.

```
<STYLE>
<!--
UL LI {}
-->
</STYLE>
```

3. Add a list-style-type property with the value of square.

```
<STYLE>
<!--
UL LI { list-style-type : square }
-->
</STYLE>
```

You can also set a specific image for use as a bullet by using `list-style-image : url(figure.gif)`, as shown here:

```
<STYLE>
<!--
UL LI { list-style-image : url(figure.gif) }
-->
</STYLE>
```

By changing the display property, you can change a list from displaying as a vertical list, as is customary, to an inline list in which each item appears within a line of text. Use the following style rule:

```
<STYLE>
<!--
UL LI { display : inline }
-->
</STYLE>
```

Setting Aural Style Sheet Properties

One of the more recent additions to style sheet capabilities is *aural properties*, which allow you to set properties for documents that will be read aloud (as opposed to read on screen). Visually impaired visitors could use these, or you might use these as a supplement to a visual presentation or in situations in which reading is not possible—for example, in the car. Aural style sheet properties let you specify that documents be read aloud, specify sound characteristics, and specify other auditory options.

Table 16.12 lists some aural style sheet properties and their values.

TABLE 16.12: Aural Style Sheet Properties

PROPERTY	VALUES
Volume	Value, %, silent, x-soft, soft, medium, loud, x-loud
Pause	Value, %
speech-rate	Value, extra slow, slow, medium, fast, extra fast, faster, slower
pitch-range	Value

NOTE

Aural style sheets are part of the CSS2 specification and are only available in CSS2-compliant browsers.

To specify that the document be read aloud with loud volume and fast speech (for efficiency), follow these steps:

1. In a new style block, provide a BODY selector to make your settings apply to the entire document.

   ```
   <STYLE>
   <!--
   BODY
   -->
   </STYLE>
   ```

2. Add brackets.

   ```
   <STYLE>
   <!--
   BODY {}
   -->
   </STYLE>
   ```

3. Add a volume property with the value of loud.

   ```
   <STYLE>
   <!--
   BODY { volume : loud ; }
   -->
   </STYLE>
   ```

4. Add a speech-rate property with the value of fast.

   ```
   <STYLE>
   <!--
   BODY { volume : loud ; speech-rate : fast ;}
   -->
   </STYLE>
   ```

Setting Printed Media Properties

Printed media properties can help you accommodate visitors who print out your documents, rather than read them online. These CSS2 properties let you set values for the page box, which you might think of as the area of your printout. For example, in hardcopy, your page box might be the 8.5 × 11 piece of paper; the page box includes the content, margins, and edges. Table 16.13 lists some of the more common printed media properties and their values.

TABLE 16.13: Printed Media Style Sheet Properties

PROPERTY	VALUES
size	Value, automatic, portrait, landscape
marks	crop marks, cross marks
margin	Length, %, automatic
page-break-before	automatic, always, avoid, left, right
page-break-after	automatic, always, avoid, left, right
page-break-inside	automatic, always, avoid, left, right
page-break-before	automatic, always, avoid, left, right
orphans	Value
widows	Value

NOTE

Like aural style sheets, printed media properties are part of the CSS2 specification and are only available in CSS2-compliant browsers.

To specify that the printed document have a page break before all H1 elements, follow these steps:

1. In a style block, provide an H1 selector to apply your settings to all first-level headings in the entire document.

   ```
   <STYLE>
   <!--
   H1
   -->
   </STYLE>
   ```

2. Add brackets.

   ```
   <STYLE>
   <!--
   H1 {}
   -->
   </STYLE>
   ```

3. Add a page-break-before property with the value of always.

   ```
   <STYLE>
   <!--
   H1 { page-break-before : always ; }
   ```

```
-->
</STYLE>
```

Setting Positioning Properties

Using positioning, you can add properties to style rules to control element positioning. For example, you can identify specific locations for elements, as well as specify locations that are relative to other elements. Positioning properties are part of the CSS2 specification, so only CSS2-compliant browsers support them. Table 16.14 lists some positioning properties and their values.

TABLE 16.14: Positioning Properties

PROPERTY	VALUES
Position	static, absolute, relative, fixed
top, bottom, left, and right	Length, %, auto
Float	left, right, non-floating
Overflow	visible, scrolling, hidden, automatic

NOTE

Like aural style sheets, positioning properties are part of the CSS2 specification and are only available in CSS2-compliant browsers.

To specify that the .warning classes in the document float to the left with text wrapping around to the right, while the P.logo class just sits at the bottom of the window, follow these steps:

1. In a new style block, provide a .warning selector.

   ```
   <STYLE>
   <!--
   .warning
   -->
   </STYLE>
   ```

2. Add brackets.

   ```
   <STYLE>
   <!--
   .warning {}
   -->
   ```

```
</STYLE>
```

3. Add a float property with the value of left.

```
<STYLE>
<!--
.warning { float :  left }
-->
</STYLE>
```

4. Add a P.logo selector and brackets.

```
<STYLE>
<!--
.warning { float : left }
P.logo {}
-->
</STYLE>
```

5. Add a position property and fixed value.

```
<STYLE>
<!--
.warning { float : left }
P.logo { position : fixed }
-->
</STYLE>
```

6. Add bottom and right properties and length of 0 for each value.

```
<STYLE>
<!--
.warning { float : left }
P.logo { position : fixed ; bottom : 0px ; right : 0px }
-->
</STYLE>
```

WHAT'S NEXT

In this chapter, you learned how style sheets and HTML documents relate and how to develop style sheets for your own needs. As you can see, style sheets are certainly more comprehensive than any formatting option previously available in HTML.

In the next chapter, Deborah Ray and Eric Ray continue to teach you advanced Web design techniques. While you want visitors to see all that your site has to offer, you also want them to interact with your site, joining a newsletter list, e-mailing comments or ideas, or purchasing a product. You'll learn how to use forms to receive and process such input from your visitors.

Chapter 17

DEVELOPING HTML FORMS

When you submit credit card information to purchase something online, search the Web with AltaVista or HotBot, participate in a Web-based chat room, or even select a line from a drop-down menu, you're using a form. Within the scope of plain HTML—as opposed to extensions such as JavaScript, Java applets, and other embedded programs—forms are the only method of two-way communication between Web pages and Web sites.

Adapted from *Mastering HTML 4*, 2nd Edition, by Deborah S. Ray and Eric J. Ray

ISBN 0-7821-2523-9   912 pages $34.99

Perhaps because of the name, HTML developers tend to assume that forms are just for collecting pages of data. Actually, you can use forms to get any kind of information from visitors without giving them the feeling of "filling out a form"—a form could be (and often is) as simple as a blank field to fill out and a Submit button.

In this chapter, we'll look at how to develop forms using standard tags and attributes, which virtually all browsers support. We'll develop a form for ASR Outfitters piece by piece.

TIP

Check out the HTML Master's Reference for a comprehensive list of form tags and attributes.

You can create forms using any HTML development tools—alone or in combination. For example, if you plan to develop a lot of forms, you might consider using a WYSIWYG editor to create the basic form. These editors don't produce consistently good results, but they help ensure that you don't leave out any tags or necessary attributes. You can then manually modify the formatting as necessary. If you'll only be doing one or two forms, however, creating them manually or with the help of a code-based editor is more than adequate and is probably easier than learning how to use a WYSIWYG editor effectively.

DETERMINING FORM CONTENT

The first step in developing a form is determining which information to include and how to present it—that is, how to break it down into manageable pieces. You then need to ensure that visitors can easily provide the information you want from them, which means that your form needs to be both functional and visually appealing.

Information Issues

When deciding which information to include and how to break it down, consider your purposes for creating the form. You might begin by answering these questions:

- ▶ What information do I want? Customer contact information? Only e-mail addresses so that I can contact visitors later? Opinions about the site?

- ► Why will visitors access the form? To order something online? To request information? To submit comments or questions about products or services?

- ► What information can visitors readily provide? Contact information? Description of their product use? Previous purchases?

- ► How much time will visitors be willing to spend filling out the form? Would they be willing to describe something in a paragraph or two, or would they just want to select from a list?

After determining what information you want and what information your visitors can provide, break the information into the smallest chunks possible. For example, if you want visitors to provide contact information, divide contact information into name, street address, and city/state/zip. Go a step further, however, and collect the city, state, and zip code as separate items so that you can later sort data according to, say, customers in a particular city, state, or zip code. If you don't collect these items separately, you won't be able to sort on them individually.

TIP

Although it's possible to go back and change forms after you implement them, careful planning will save a lot of trouble and work later. For example, if you complete and implement a form and then discover that you forgot to request key information, the initial responses to the form will be less useful or skew the resulting data. Fixing the form takes nearly as much time as doing it carefully at first.

ASR Outfitters includes a form on its Web site to collect targeted addresses for future product and sale announcements. Although ASR could just as easily (but not as cheaply) use regular mailings by purchasing mailing lists, a Web site form avoids the cost of traditional mailings, collects information from specifically interested visitors, and keeps the Internet-based company focused on the Net.

Because filling out a Web page form takes some time, ASR created a form, as shown in Figure 17.1, that includes only the essentials. In this case, a little demographic information is needed.

Thank you for your interest in getting e-mailed information from ASR Outfitters. We assure you that we do not resell or distribute these addresses in any form. We use this information exclusively to provide you with better service.

Information Request

	First Name
	Last Name
	E-mail Address
	Address

City [ ] State [ ] Zip or Postal Code

| | Country |

Please choose the most appropriate statement.
- ○ I regularly purchase items online.
- ○ I have on occasion purchased items online.
- ◉ I have not purchased anything online, but I would consider it.
- ○ I prefer to shop in real stores.

I'm interested in (choose all that apply):
- ☐ Hiking
- ☐ Mountain Biking
- ☐ Camping
- ☐ Rock Climbing
- ☐ Off-Road 4WD
- ☐ Cross-country Skiing

I learned about this site from:
[Print Ads ▼]

Comments:
```
Please type any additional comments here
```

[Submit] [Start Over]

ASR Outfitters
info@asroutfitters.com
4700 N. Center
South Logan, UT 87654
801-555-3422

FIGURE 17.1: ASR Outfitters' form collects only the basic demographic and marketing information.

First name This is necessary to help personalize responses.

Last name This is also necessary to help personalize responses.

E-mail address Collecting this information is the main purpose of the form.

Street address, city, state, zip, and country All are necessary for future snail mailings and for later demographic analysis. Collecting the address, even with no immediate intent to use it, is probably a wise move, because it would be difficult to ask customers for more information later.

Referral The marketing department wants to know how the audience found the Web site.

Online purchasing habits ASR wants to learn about the possible acceptance rate for taking orders over the Net.

Areas of interest ASR wants to find out about the customer's interests to determine areas in which to expand its online offerings.

Other comments It's always important to give visitors an opportunity to provide additional information.

Usability Issues

Usability, as it applies to forms, refers to how easily your visitors can answer your questions. Most online forms require some action of visitors and usually offer no concrete benefit or reward for their efforts. Therefore, if forms are not easy to use, you won't get many (or any) responses. Here are some usability guidelines to consider when you are creating forms.

Group Similar Categories

When you group similar categories, as you can see from Figure 17.1, the form appears less daunting, and visitors are more likely to fill it out and submit it. ASR can group the information it's soliciting from visitors into three main categories:

- ▶ Contact information
- ▶ Purchasing habits and areas of interest
- ▶ Referrals and other information

Make the Form Easy

If you've ever completed a long form, you know how tedious it can be.
Think tax form for an example of how *not* to do it. Although the specifics
depend greatly on the information you'll be collecting, some principles
remain constant:

▸ Whenever possible, provide a list from which visitors can choose
one or more items. Lists are easy to use, and they result in easy-
to-process information.

▸ If you can't provide a list, ask visitors to fill in only a small amount
of text. Again, this takes minimal time, and it provides you with
data that is fairly easy to process.

▸ If you absolutely must, ask visitors to fill in large areas of text.
Keep in mind, though, that this takes a lot of time—both for the
visitor and for you. Additionally, many visitors are likely to ignore
a request that requires them to enter a great deal of information.

NOTE

For more information about how to create lists and areas to fill in, see the section "Creating Forms," later in this chapter.

Provide Incentives

Provide visitors with incentives to fill out the form and submit it. Offer
them something, even if its value is marginal. Studies show that a penny
or a stamp included in mailed surveys often significantly improves the
response rate. Consider offering a chance in a drawing for a free product,
an e-mailed list of tips and tricks, or a discount on services.

ASR Outfitters might have offered anything from a free tote bag to an
e-mailed collection of hiking tips or a discount on the next purchase, but
chose to settle for a small coupon book available on the next visit to the
store.

Design Issues

Perhaps because of the need to address all the technical issues, Web
authors often neglect design issues. A well-designed form, however, helps
and encourages visitors to give you the information you want.

What constitutes good form design? Something visually appealing, graphically helpful, and consistent with the remainder of the site. A form at an intranet site that has a white background and minimal graphics and that is managed by conservative supervisors would likely have a simple, vertical design and be none the worse for it. A visually interesting or highly graphical Web site, however, calls for a form in keeping with the overall theme.

Although the visual interest of the form should not overwhelm the rest of the page, you'll want to make judicious use of color, alignment, small images, and font characteristics. Here are some guidelines:

▶ Use headings to announce each new group of information. This helps visitors move easily through the form.

▶ Be sure to visually separate groups. This makes the forms easier to use because sections become shorter and easier to wade through. You can use horizontal rules or the <FIELDSET> tag in HTML 4 to do this.

▶ Use text emphases to draw the audience to important information. Use emphases sparingly; emphasize only a few words so that they stand out on the page.

▶ Specify how visitors are to move through the form. Don't make your visitors scroll horizontally to access information. Consider making a narrow, longer form rather than a wider, shorter form to accommodate those who have lower monitor resolution. If your survey is in multiple columns, make different categories visually obvious.

▶ Use arrows to help visitors move through the page in a specified order.

▶ Be sure that it's clear which check boxes and fields go with the associated descriptive information. For example, if you have a long row of check boxes and labels, it's fairly confusing to figure out whether the check box goes with the text on the right or the text on the left. Use line breaks and spacing to clearly differentiate.

▶ Specify which fields are optional (and required). Some browsers and processing programs can reject forms that are incorrectly or not completely filled out.

- ▶ Use a background image. Forms with some texture tend to be less form-ish and more friendly. Be sure, though, that the image doesn't outweigh the content and that the text adequately contrasts with the image.

- ▶ Make all the text-entry fields the same width and put them on the left if you have a vertical column of name and address information—that way all the text will align vertically and look much better. If the text labels go on the left, the fields will not (cannot) align vertically and will therefore look more random and less professional.

CREATING FORMS

Forms have two basic parts:

- ▶ The part you can see (that a visitor fills out)

- ▶ The part you can't see (that specifies how the server should process the information)

In this section, we'll show you how to create the part that you can see. We'll show you how to create the other part later in the section "Processing Forms."

Understanding Widgets

Forms consist of several types of *widgets* (they're also called controls), which are fields you can use to collect data:

- ▶ Submit and Reset buttons send the form information to the server for processing and return the form to its original settings.

- ▶ Text fields are areas for brief text input. Use these for several-word responses, such as names, search terms, or addresses.

- ▶ Select lists are lists from which visitors can choose one or more items. Use them to present a long but finite list of choices. For example, choose your state from this list, or choose one of these 17 options.

- ▶ Check boxes allow visitors to select none, one, or several items from a list. Use them to elicit multiple answers. For example, ASR Outfitters uses check boxes to get information about the activities of its customers.

- ▶ Radio buttons give visitors an opportunity to choose only one item—for example, gender, a preference, or anything else that can be only one way.

- ▶ Text areas are areas for lengthy text input, as in open-ended comments or free-form responses.

Figure 17.2 shows a sample form that includes these widgets.

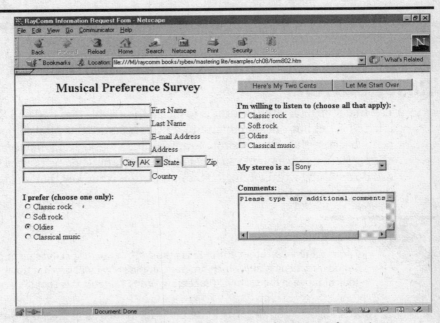

FIGURE 17.2: Forms give visitors different ways of entering information.

WHICH WIDGETS ARE BEST?

When deciding which widget to use, consider the information you want to collect. For example, start by seeing whether you can collect pieces of information using check boxes and radio buttons. These are generally the easiest for your visitors to use because they specify the options and require only the click of a mouse. Then, look for places you can use select lists, which are also easy to use. Finally, include text areas only if visitors need to respond in their own words.

CONTINUED ➡

In general, radio buttons, check boxes, and select lists are all better choices for accepting input than text areas. If visitors are selecting choices from a list, you need not be concerned with misspellings, inconsistent answers, or free-form answers that don't fit the categories. If you can provide choices and let visitors choose from among them, do so.

Creating a Form and Adding Submit and Reset Buttons

The first step in creating a form is to insert the <FORM> tags and add Submit and Reset buttons. Submit and Reset buttons are essential components because they allow visitors to submit information and, if necessary, clear selections. Although you must add other form fields before the form will do anything worthwhile, the Submit button is the key that makes the form go somewhere.

NOTE

Forms require two other attributes in the <FORM> tag to specify what happens to the form results and which program on the server will process them. We'll look at those in the section "Processing Forms," later in this chapter.

Table 17.1 lists and describes the basic form tags as well as the Submit and Reset buttons.

TABLE 17.1: Basic Form Tags

TAG/ATTRIBUTE	USE
<FORM>	Marks a form within an HTML document.
<INPUT TYPE="SUBMIT" VALUE="...">	Provides a Submit button for a form. The VALUE= attribute produces text on the button.
<INPUT TYPE="IMAGE" NAME="POINT" SRC="..." BORDER=0>	Provides a graphical Submit button. The SRC= attribute indicates the image source file, and the BORDER= attribute turns off the image border.
<INPUT TYPE="RESET" VALUE="...">	Provides a Reset button for a form. The VALUE= attribute produces text on the button.

In the following example, we'll create a form for the ASR Outfitters site as we show you how to start a form and then add Submit and Reset buttons. The following code produces the page shown in Figure 17.3.

```
<!DOCTYPE HTML PUBLIC "-//W3C//DTD HTML 4.0
Transitional//EN">
<HTML>
<HEAD>
<TITLE>ASR Outfitters Information Request Form</TITLE>
</HEAD>
<BODY BACKGROUND="" BGCOLOR="#ffffff" TEXT="#000000"
LINK="#0000ff" VLINK="#800080" ALINK="#ff0000">
<TABLE>
<TR>
<TD VALIGN=TOP>
<CENTER><IMG SRC="asrlogo.gif" ALT="ASR Outfitters Logo"
WIDTH="604" HEIGHT="192" BORDER="0" ALIGN=""><BR>
<FONT SIZE="7" FACE="Gill Sans">
<H2>Information Request</H2>
</FONT>
</CENTER>
<TD>
<FONT SIZE="3" FACE="Gill Sans">
Thank you for your interest in getting e-mailed information
from ASR Outfitters. We assure you that we do not resell or
distribute these addresses in any form. We use this
information exclusively to provide you with better service.
<P></FONT>
</TABLE>
<HR WIDTH=80% SIZE=8 NOSHADE>
<HR WIDTH=80% SIZE=8 NOSHADE>
<IMG SRC="asrlogosm.gif" ALIGN="LEFT" WIDTH="200" HEIGHT="84"
BORDER="0" ALT="ASR Small Logo">
<DIV ALIGN=RIGHT>
<ADDRESS ALIGN=RIGHT>
<FONT FACE="Gill Sans">
<BR>ASR Outfitters<BR>
<A HREF="mailto:info@asroutfitters.com">info@asroutfitters
.com</A>
<BR>
4700 N. Center<BR>
South Logan, UT 87654<BR>
801-555-3422<BR>
</FONT>
</ADDRESS>
</DIV>
</BODY>
</HTML>
```

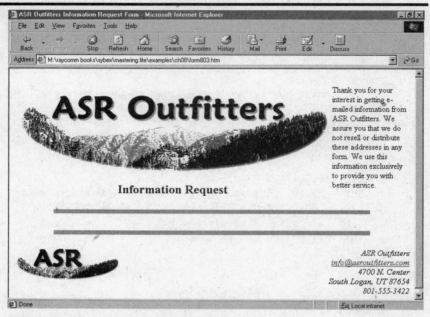

FIGURE 17.3: The ASR Outfitters form page, sans form

To add a form to the page, follow these steps:

1. Add the <FORM> tags where you want the form to be.

   ```
   <HR WIDTH=80% SIZE=8 NOSHADE>
   <FORM>
   </FORM>
   ```

TIP

You can avoid problems with your forms by properly nesting your form within other objects in the form. Be careful to place the form outside paragraphs, lists, and other structural elements. For example, you do not want to open a table within the form and close it after the end of the form. Also, be sure to test your forms carefully.

2. Create a Submit button by adding the <INPUT> tag, the TYPE= attribute, and the VALUE= attribute. Although the Submit button traditionally goes at the bottom of the form, immediately

above the </FORM> tag, it can go anywhere in the form. You can set the text on the face of the Submit button to anything you want—simply substitute your text for the text in the VALUE= attribute:

```
<HR WIDTH=80% SIZE=8 NOSHADE>
<FORM>
<INPUT TYPE="SUBMIT" VALUE="Submit">
</FORM>
```

3. Create a Reset button by adding the <INPUT> tag, the TYPE= attribute, and the VALUE= attribute. Again, although the Reset button traditionally goes at the bottom of the form with the Submit button, immediately above the closing </FORM> tag, it can go anywhere in the form. The Reset button can have any text on its face, based on the VALUE= attribute. The following example has *Start Over* on the face.

```
<HR WIDTH=80% SIZE=8 NOSHADE>
<FORM>
<INPUT TYPE="SUBMIT" VALUE="Submit">
<INPUT TYPE="RESET" VALUE="Start Over">
</FORM>
```

Figure 17.4 shows what the buttons look like in a completed form.

NOTE
You cannot control button size directly—the length of the text determines the size of the button.

If the appearance of your form is extremely important to you, consider using a graphical Submit button. Be sure, however, that your visitors will be using browsers that can handle these buttons.

Using images for Submit buttons can cause unexpected or unwanted results in older browsers. For example, they crash old versions of Netscape Navigator. Consider using browser detection scripts to improve your success with image-based Submit buttons. (See Chapter 10 for information about including images.)

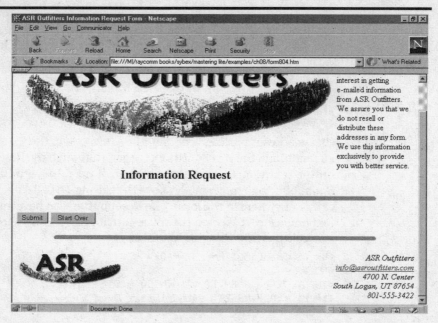

FIGURE 17.4: The Submit and Reset (Start Over) buttons are added to the form.

If you want to use an image for your Submit button, substitute the following code for the Submit button (substituting your own image for submitbutton.gif):

```
<INPUT TYPE="IMAGE" NAME="POINT" SRC="submitbutton.gif"
BORDER=0>
```

The TYPE="IMAGE" attribute specifies that an image will be used to click on and submit the form. The NAME="POINT" attribute specifies that the x,y coordinates where the mouse is located will be returned to the server when the image is clicked. Finally, the SRC= and BORDER= attributes work just as they do with regular images—they specify the URL of the image and turn off the border.

Figure 17.5 shows the complete ASR Outfitters form with a graphical Submit button.

HTML makes no provision for a Reset button with an image; so if you choose to use an image for your Submit button, dispense with a Reset button. If you don't, you'll have to deal with the potentially poor combination of an image and a standard Reset button.

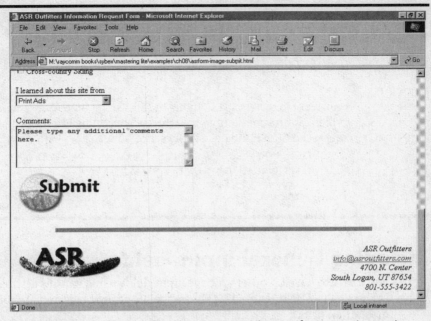

FIGURE 17.5: Graphical Submit buttons can make your form more interesting.

HTML 4 OPPORTUNITIES

If your visitors will be using HTML 4–compliant browsers, you can use the paired <BUTTON> tag, which creates a button that you can include instead of or in conjunction with Submit and Reset buttons. Buttons created with the <BUTTON> tag have no specific action associated with them, as do the Submit and Reset buttons. If you're so inclined, you can link the button to a JavaScript script. Doing so gives you all sorts of functional and flashy possibilities (see Chapter 20 for information on JavaScript).

To provide a Submit button, use code similar to the following:

```
<BUTTON TYPE="SUBMIT" VALUE="SUBMIT" NAME="SUBMIT">
Click to Submit Form
</BUTTON>
```

CONTINUED ➡

Part iii

To provide a graphical Reset button, use code similar to the following:

```
<BUTTON TYPE="RESET" VALUE="RESET" NAME="RESET">
<IMG SRC="gifs/resetbuttonnew.gif" ALT="Reset
button">
</BUTTON>
```

If you want to use a <BUTTON> tag to call a script that, for example, verifies a form's contents, you might use something like this, which creates a button that runs a verify script:

```
<BUTTON TYPE="BUTTON" VALUE="VERIFY" NAME="VERIFY"
onClick="verify(this.form)">
Click to Verify Form
</BUTTON>
```

Including General Input Fields

You can also develop other types of input fields using various attributes in the <INPUT> field. Table 17.2 shows the input field tags and attributes most often used.

TABLE 17.2: Input Field Tags and Attributes

Tag/Attribute	Use
<INPUT>	Sets an area in a form for visitor input.
TYPE="..."	Sets the type of input field. Possible values are TEXT, PASSWORD, CHECKBOX, RADIO, FILE, HIDDEN, IMAGE, BUTTON, SUBMIT, and RESET.
NAME="..."	Processes form results.
VALUE="..."	Provides content associated with NAME="...". Use this attribute with radio buttons and check boxes because they do not accept other input. You can also use this attribute with text fields to provide initial input.
SIZE="n"	Sets the visible size for a field. Use this attribute with text input fields.
MAXLENGTH="n"	Sets the longest set of characters that can be submitted. Use this attribute with text fields.
SELECTED	Indicates the default selection to be presented when the form is initially loaded or reset.
ACCEPT="..."	Specifies the acceptable MIME types for file uploads. Wildcards are acceptable, as in image/*.

Text Fields

A text field is a blank area within a form and is the place for visitor-supplied information. As you can see below, text fields are commonly used for a name, an e-mail address, and so on:

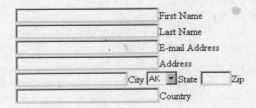

To add a text field to an existing form, follow these steps:

1. Add an `<INPUT>` tag where you want the field.

   ```
   <FORM>
   <INPUT>
   </FORM>
   ```

2. Specify the type of input field. In this case, use `TYPE="TEXT"`.

   ```
   <FORM>
   <INPUT TYPE="TEXT">
   </FORM>
   ```

3. Add the `NAME=` attribute to label the content. For example, one of the first fields in the ASR Outfitters form is for the first name of a visitor, so the field name is `"firstname"`.

   ```
   <INPUT TYPE="TEXT" NAME="firstname">
   ```

TIP

The values for `NAME=` should be unique within the form. Multiple forms on the same site (or even on the same page) can share values, but if different fields share a name value, the results will be unpredictable.

4. Specify the size of the field in the form by including the `SIZE=` attribute. Although this is optional, you can ensure your visitor has ample space and can make similar text fields the same size. For example, 30 is a generous size for a name, but still not overwhelmingly large, even on a low-resolution monitor.

   ```
   <INPUT TYPE="TEXT" NAME="firstname" SIZE="30">
   ```

5. Add the MAXLENGTH= attribute if you want to limit the number of characters your visitors can provide (for example, if the field passes into an existing database with length restrictions). Keep in mind that any MAXLENGTH= setting should not be less than the SIZE= attribute; otherwise, your visitors will be confused when they can't continue typing to the end of the field.

```
<INPUT TYPE="TEXT" NAME="firstname" SIZE="30"
MAXLENGTH="30">
```

6. Add text outside the <INPUT> field to indicate the information your visitor should provide. Remember that the name of the field is not visible in the browser; up to this point, you've created a blank area within the form, but you have not labeled that area in any way.

```
<INPUT TYPE="TEXT" NAME="firstname" SIZE="30"
MAXLENGTH="30"> First Name<BR>
```

Figure 17.6 shows the resulting text field in the context of the form. Use the same process to add other text fields.

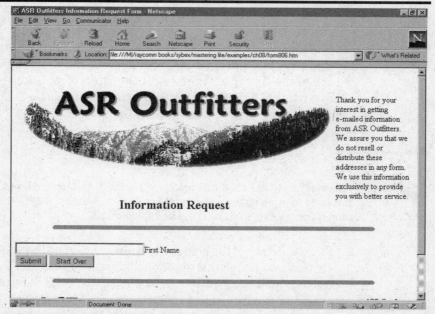

FIGURE 17.6: Visitors can enter information in text fields.

GUIDELINES FOR INCLUDING MULTIPLE TEXT FIELDS

As a rule, forms are much more attractive if the fields are aligned. If they are nearly, but not exactly, aligned, the form looks sloppy, just as a misaligned paper form looks sloppy.

Here are some guidelines to follow when you include multiple text fields in your form:

▶ Place the fields at the left margin of your page, followed by the descriptive text. If you place the descriptive text (such as "First Name" or "Last Name") to the left of the fields, the fields will not line up vertically. Alternatively, consider putting your form fields and descriptive text in a table so that the rows and columns can ensure even alignment. Set the text fields to the same size, when appropriate. Of course, you wouldn't set the field for entering the official state abbreviation to 30 characters, but there's no reason that first name, last name, and company name couldn't all be the same length.

▶ As you add descriptive labels, remember to also add line breaks (
 or <P>) in appropriate places. None of the form tags force a line break, so your form tags will all run together on a single line. In many cases, this is fine, but it can also look a little off.

▶ Optionally, add a VALUE= attribute to the text input tag to "seed" the field with a value or to provide an example of the content you want. For example, you could add VALUE="First Name Here" to the input field used for the first name to let your visitors know what to type.

If you are taking a survey, seeding a field is of questionable value. If your visitors can't figure out what to put in a field, you probably have a design problem. If you include some text, your visitors are likely not to complete the field (and submit your sample) or to accidentally leave part of your sample text in the field, thereby corrupting your data.

The best—possibly only—time to seed a field is if you do not have space on the form for descriptive labels.

Part III

Radio Buttons

A radio button is a type of input field that allows visitors to choose one option from a list. Radio buttons are so named because you can choose only one of them, just as you can select only one button (one station) at a time on your car radio. When viewed in a browser, radio buttons are usually small circles, as shown here:

I prefer (choose one only):
○ Classic rock
○ Soft rock
◉ Oldies
○ Classical music

In the ASR Outfitters questionnaire, we wanted to find out if visitors were inclined to make purchases online; the choices range from refusing to purchase to regularly purchasing online. Each choice is mutually exclusive—choosing one excludes the remainder. Radio buttons were our obvious choice.

To add radio buttons to a form, follow these steps:

1. Add any introductory text to lead into the buttons, at the point where the buttons should appear. Also put in the descriptive text and formatting commands as appropriate. The text of the ASR Outfitters example looks like the following:

    ```
    <P>
    Please choose the most appropriate statement.
    <BR>I regularly purchase items online.
    <BR>I have on occasion purchased items online.
    <BR>I have not purchased anything online, but I would
    consider it.
    <BR>I prefer to shop in real stores.
    ```

2. Add the <INPUT> tag where the first radio button will go.

    ```
    <BR><INPUT>I regularly purchase items online.
    ```

3. Add the TYPE="RADIO" attribute.

    ```
    <BR><INPUT TYPE="RADIO">I regularly purchase items
    online.
    ```

4. Add the NAME= attribute. The name applies to the collection of buttons, not just to this item, so be sure the NAME= attribute is generic enough to apply to all items in the set.

    ```
    <BR><INPUT TYPE="RADIO" NAME="buying">I regularly
    purchase items online.
    ```

5. Add the VALUE= attribute. In text input areas, the value is
    what the visitor types; however, you must supply the value
    for radio buttons (and check boxes). Choose highly descrip-
    tive, preferably single-word values (such as "regular" rather
    than "yes" or "of course").

    ```
    <BR><INPUT TYPE="RADIO" NAME="buying" VALUE="regular">
    I regularly purchase items online.
    ```

6. Add the attribute CHECKED to one of the items to indicate the
    default selection. Remember, only one radio button can be
    selected, so only one button can carry the CHECKED attribute.

    ```
    <BR><INPUT TYPE="RADIO" NAME="buying" VALUE="regular"
    CHECKED>I regularly purchase items online.
    ```

TIP

In general, make the most likely choice the default option, both to make a visitor's job easier and to minimize the impact of their not checking and verifying
the entry for that question. Although adding the CHECKED attribute is optional,
it ensures that the list records a response.

7. Add the remaining radio buttons.

Use the same NAME= attribute for all radio buttons in a set. Browsers
use the NAME attribute on radio buttons to specify which buttons are
related and therefore which ones are set and unset as a group. Different
sets of radio buttons within a page use different NAME attributes.

The completed set of radio buttons for the ASR Outfitters form looks
like the following:

```
<P>
Please choose the most appropriate statement.
<BR><INPUT TYPE="RADIO" NAME="buying" VALUE="regular">
I regularly purchase items online.
<BR><INPUT TYPE="RADIO" NAME="buying" VALUE="sometimes">
I have on occasion purchased items online.
<BR><INPUT TYPE="RADIO" NAME="buying" VALUE="might" CHECKED>
I have not purchased anything online, but I would consider
it.
<BR><INPUT TYPE="RADIO" NAME="buying" VALUE="willnot">
I prefer to shop in real stores.
<BR>
```

When viewed in a browser, the radio buttons look like those in Figure 17.7.

Part iii

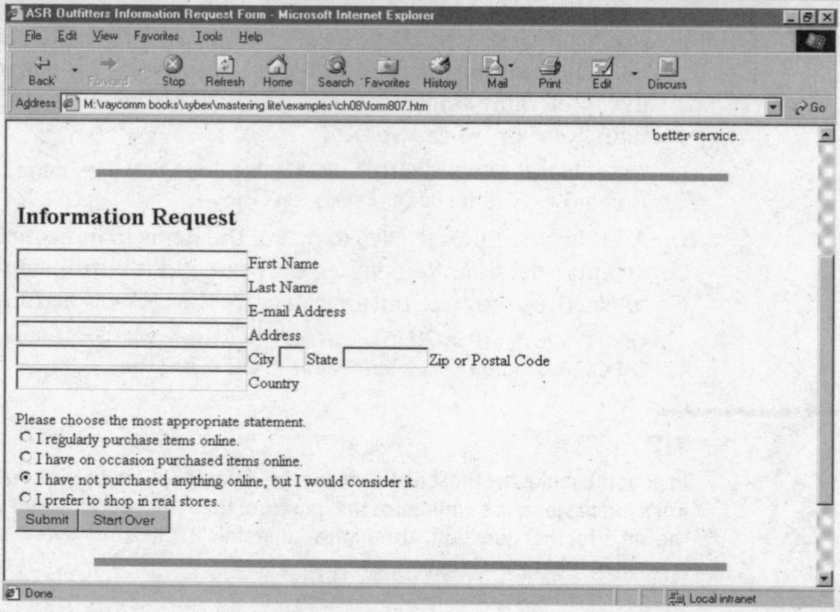

FIGURE 17.7: A visitor can select a radio button to choose an item from a list.

HTML 4 OPPORTUNITIES

HTML 4 lets you easily group related items using the <FIELDSET> tag. For example, in the ASR Outfitters form, several fields collect personal information, and you could group them within a <FIELD-SET> tag, like this:

```
<FIELDSET>
…various input fields for personal information go
here.
</FIELDSET>
```

Additionally, by adding <LEGEND> tags (aligned to the TOP, BOTTOM, LEFT, or RIGHT), you can clearly label content:

```
<FIELDSET>
<LEGEND ALIGN="TOP">Personal Information</LEGEND>
…various input fields for personal information go
here.
</FIELDSET>
```

Check Boxes

Visitors can also use check boxes to select an item from a list. Each check box works independently from the others; visitors can select or deselect any combination of check boxes. Using check boxes is appropriate for open questions or questions that have more than one "right" answer.

In most browsers, check boxes appear as little squares that contain a check mark when selected:

> **I'm willing to listen to (choose all that apply):**
> ☐ Classic rock
> ☐ Soft rock
> ☐ Oldies
> ☐ Classical music

The ASR Outfitters form is designed to find out about activities that interest customers. Any combination of answers from none to all might be possible, so this is a good place to use check boxes.

To add check boxes to your form, follow these steps:

1. Enter the lead-in text and textual cues for each item, as in the following code sample.

   ```
   <P>I'm interested in (choose all that apply):
   <BR>Hiking
   <BR>Mountain Biking
   <BR>Camping
   <BR>Rock Climbing
   <BR>Off-Road 4WD
   <BR>Cross-country Skiing
   ```

TIP

The <BR> tags could just as easily go at the end of the lines, but after entering the form tags, placing the <BR> tags at the beginning of the lines will make the code easier to read.

2. Add an <INPUT> tag between the <BR> and the first choice from the list.

   ```
   <BR><INPUT>Hiking
   ```

3. Add the TYPE="CHECKBOX" attribute to set the input field as a check box.

   ```
   <BR><INPUT TYPE="CHECKBOX">Hiking
   ```

4. Add the NAME= attribute to label the item. For check boxes, unlike radio buttons, each item has a separate label. Although the check boxes visually appear as a set, logically the items are completely separate.

```
<BR><INPUT TYPE="CHECKBOX" NAME="hiking">Hiking
```

5. Add the VALUE= attribute for the item. In the ASR Outfitters form, the value could be yes or no—indicating that hiking is or is not an activity of interest. However, when the form is returned through e-mail, it's useful to have a more descriptive value. If the value here is hiking, the word *hiking* returns for a check mark, and nothing returns for no check mark. The e-mail recipient can decipher this easier than a yes or a no.

```
<BR><INPUT TYPE="CHECKBOX" NAME="hiking" VALUE=
"hiking">Hiking
```

6. Add a CHECKED attribute to specify default selections. Although you can, with check boxes, include a CHECKED attribute for multiple items, be careful not to overdo. Each CHECKED attribute that you include is an additional possible false positive response to a question.

```
<BR><INPUT TYPE="CHECKBOX" NAME="hiking" VALUE="hiking"
CHECKED>Hiking
```

7. Repeat this process for each of the remaining check boxes, remembering to use different NAME= attributes for each one (unlike radio buttons).

In the ASR Outfitters form, the final code looks like this:

```
<P>I'm interested in (choose all that apply):
<BR><INPUT TYPE="CHECKBOX" NAME="hiking"
VALUE="hiking">Hiking
<BR><INPUT TYPE="CHECKBOX" NAME="mbiking"
VALUE="mbiking">Mountain Biking
<BR><INPUT TYPE="CHECKBOX" NAME="camping"
VALUE="camping">Camping
<BR><INPUT TYPE="CHECKBOX" NAME="rock" VALUE="rock">
Rock Climbing
<BR><INPUT TYPE="CHECKBOX" NAME="4wd" VALUE="4wd">
Off-Road 4WD
<BR><INPUT TYPE="CHECKBOX" NAME="ccskiing"
VALUE="ccskiing">Cross-country Skiing
<BR>
```

When viewed in a browser, the check boxes look like those in Figure 17.8.

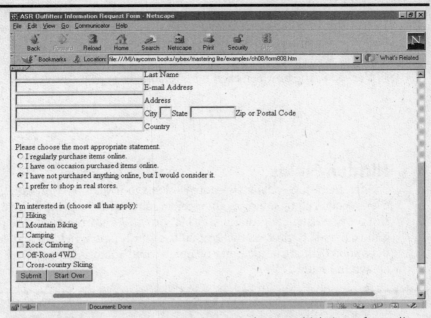

FIGURE 17.8: Visitors can use check boxes to choose multiple items from a list.

Password Fields

Password fields are similar to text fields, except the contents of the field are not visible on the screen. Password fields are appropriate whenever the content of the field might be confidential—as in passwords, but also in some cases for Social Security numbers or the mother's maiden name. For example, if a site is accessed from a public place and requires confidential information, a visitor will appreciate your using a password field. Of course, because your visitors cannot see the text they type, the error rate and problems with the data rise dramatically.

To establish a password field, follow these steps:

1. Add the <INPUT> field.

   <INPUT>Password

2. Set the TYPE="PASSWORD" attribute.

   <INPUT **TYPE="PASSWORD"**>Password

3. Add the NAME= attribute.

   <INPUT TYPE="PASSWORD" **NAME="newpass"**>Password

4. Specify the visible size and, if appropriate, the maximum size for the input text by using the MAXLENGTH= attribute.

```
<INPUT TYPE="PASSWORD" NAME="newpass" SIZE="10"
MAXLENGTH="10">Password
```

Viewed in the browser, each typed character appears as an asterisk (*):

 Password

Hidden Fields

Hidden fields are—obviously—not visible to your visitors. They are, however, recognized by the program receiving the input from the form and can provide useful additional information. ASR Outfitters uses the program cgiemail to process the form; it accepts a hidden field to reference a page shown after the customer completes and submits the form, as shown in Figure 17.9.

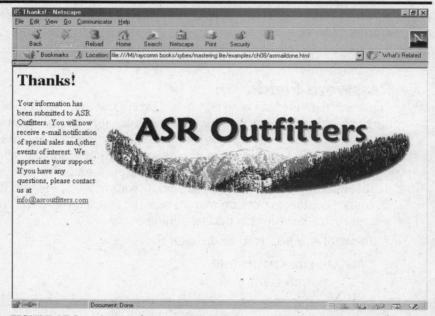

FIGURE 17.9: A hidden field can tell the server to send a reference page to the visitor.

NOTE

The cgiemail program, which is software for a Unix Web server to return form results with e-mail, is discussed at length in the final section of this chapter, "One Solution: Processing Using cgiemail."

If you need hidden fields, the program that requires them usually includes specific documentation for the exact values. The cgiemail program that ASR Outfitters uses requires a hidden field such as the following:

```
<INPUT TYPE="HIDDEN" NAME="success" VALUE="http://www
.xmission.com/~ejray/asr/asrmaildone.html">
```

The TYPE="HIDDEN" attribute keeps it from being shown, and the NAME= and VALUE= attributes provide the information that cgiemail expects.

Hidden fields can go anywhere in your form, but it's usually best to place them at the top, immediately after the opening <FORM> tag, so that they aren't misplaced or accidentally deleted when you edit the form.

File Fields

HTML also supports a special input field, a file field, to allow visitors to upload files. For example, if you want visitors to submit information—say, a picture, a scanned document, a spreadsheet, or a word-processed document—they can use this field to simply upload the file without the hassle of using FTP or e-mailing the file.

This feature must be implemented both in the Web browser and in the Web server, because of the additional processing involved in uploading and manipulating uploaded files. After verifying that the server on which you'll process your form supports file uploads, you can implement this feature by following these steps:

1. Add the appropriate lead-in text to your HTML document.
   ```
   Please post this photo I took in your gallery!
   ```

2. Add an <INPUT> field.
   ```
   Please post this photo I took in your gallery!
   <INPUT>
   ```

3. Add the TYPE="FILE" attribute.
   ```
   Please post this photo I took in your gallery!
   <INPUT TYPE="FILE">
   ```

4. Add an appropriate NAME= attribute to label the field.
   ```
   Please post this photo I took in your gallery!
   <INPUT TYPE="FILE" NAME="filenew">
   ```

5. Optionally, specify the field's visible and maximum length
    with the SIZE= and MAXLENGTH= attributes.

    ```
    Please post this photo I took in your gallery!
    <INPUT TYPE="FILE" NAME="filenew" SIZE="30"
    MAXLENGTH="200">
    ```

6. Optionally, specify which file types can be uploaded by using
    the ACCEPT= attribute. For example, add ACCEPT="image/*" to
    accept any image file.

    ```
    Please post this photo I took in your gallery!
    <INPUT TYPE="FILE" NAME="filenew" SIZE="20"
    ACCEPT="image/*">
    ```

The values for the ACCEPT= attribute are MIME types. If you accept
only a specific type, such as image/gif, you can specify that. If you'll take
any image file, but no other files, you could use image/* as ASR Outfitters
does. Finally, if you will accept only a few types, you can provide a list of
possible types, separated by commas:

```
<INPUT TYPE="FILE" NAME="filenew" SIZE="20"
ACCEPT="image/gif, image/jpeg">
```

This code results in a text area plus a button that allows visitors to
browse to a file, when rendered in most browsers, as shown in Figure 17.10.

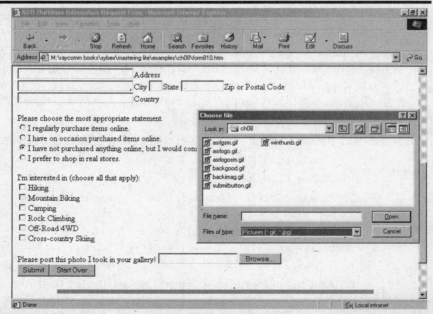

FIGURE 17.10: You can use file fields to upload files.

Including Text Areas

Text areas are places within a form for extensive text input. One of the primary uses for text areas is to solicit comments or free-form feedback from visitors, as shown here:

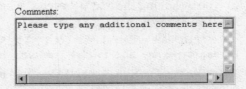

Table 17.3 lists and describes the most commonly used tags and attributes for text areas within HTML forms.

TABLE 17.3: Text Area Tags and Attributes

TAG/ATTRIBUTE	USE
<TEXTAREA>	Sets an area in a form for lengthy visitor input. Initial content for the text area goes between the opening and closing tags.
NAME="..."	Establishes a label for an input field. The NAME= attribute is used for form processing.
ROWS="n"	Sets the number of rows for the visible field.
COLS="n"	Sets the number of columns for the visible field.

TIP

Don't confuse text fields with text areas. *Text fields* are appropriate for shorter input; *text areas* are appropriate for longer input.

To include a text area in a form, follow these steps:

1. Enter any lead-in text to set up the text area.

<P>Comments:

2. Add an opening and closing <TEXTAREA> tag.

<P>Comments:
   <TEXTAREA></TEXTAREA>

3. Add a NAME= attribute to label the field.
   <TEXTAREA **NAME="comments"**></TEXTAREA>

4. Add ROWS= and COLS= attributes to set the dimensions of the text area. The ROWS= attribute sets the height of the text area in rows, and COLS= sets the width of the text area in characters.

```
<TEXTAREA NAME="comments" ROWS="5" COLS="40"></TEXTAREA>
```

5. Enter some sample information to let your visitors know what to type by adding the text between the opening and closing <TEXTAREA> tags.

```
<TEXTAREA NAME="comments" COLS="40" ROWS="5">
Please type any additional comments here.</TEXTAREA>
```

This <TEXTAREA> code produces a text area field in the HTML document like the one shown in Figure 17.11.

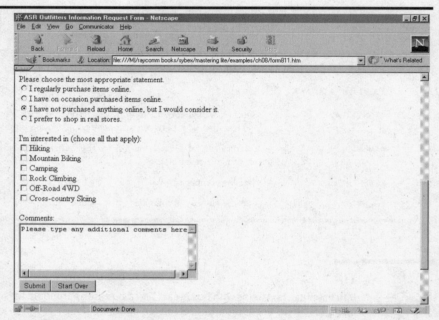

FIGURE 17.11: A visitor can type comments in a text area.

Including Select Fields

Select fields are some of the most flexible fields used in developing forms because you can let visitors select single and multiple responses. For example, suppose you need visitors to tell you the state in which they live. You could list the states as a series of radio buttons, but that would take up tons of page space. Or, you could provide a text field, but visitors could make a typing mistake or spelling error.

Your best bet is to use a select field, which lets you list all 50 states in a minimal amount of space. Visitors simply select a state from the list without introducing spelling errors or typos.

Select fields, as shown here, can either provide a long (visible) list of items or a highly compact listing, similar to the Fonts drop-down list in a word-processing program.

Table 17.4 lists and describes the most commonly used tags and attributes for creating select fields.

TABLE 17.4: Select Field Tags and Attributes

TAG/ATTRIBUTE	USE
`<SELECT>`	Sets an area in a form for a select field that can look like a drop-down list or a larger select field.
`NAME="..."`	Establishes a label for an input field. The NAME= attribute is used for form processing.
`SIZE="n"`	Sets the visible size for the select field. The default (1) creates a drop-down list. You can change the default (to 2 or higher) if you want more options to be visible.
`MULTIPLE`	Sets the select field to accept more than one selection. Use this attribute along with the SIZE= attribute to set a number as large as the maximum number of likely selections.
`<OPTION>`	Marks the items included in the select field. You'll have an `<OPTION>` tag for each item you include. The closing tag is optional.
`VALUE="..."`	Provides the content associated with the NAME= attribute.
`SELECTED`	Lets you specify a default selection, which will appear when the form is loaded or reset.

Use a select field any time you need to list many items or ensure that visitors don't make spelling or typing errors. To include a select field in a form, follow these steps:

1. Enter the lead-in text for the select field.

   `<BR>I learned about this site from:<BR>`

2. Add opening and closing `<SELECT>` tags.

   `<BR>I learned about this site from:<BR>`

```
<SELECT>
</SELECT>
```

3. Enter a NAME= attribute to label the select field.

```
<SELECT NAME="referral">
</SELECT>
```

4. Add the choices that your visitors should see. Because the select field takes care of line breaks and other formatting, do not include any line break tags.

```
<BR>I learned about this site from:<BR>
<SELECT NAME="referral">
 Print Ads
 In-Store Visit
 Friend's Recommendation
 Sources on the Internet
 Other
</SELECT>
```

5. Add an <OPTION> tag for each possible selection. The closing </OPTION> tag is optional.

```
<SELECT NAME="referral">
 <OPTION>Print Ads
 <OPTION>In-Store Visit
 <OPTION>Friend's Recommendation
 <OPTION>Sources on the Internet
 <OPTION>Other
</SELECT>
```

6. Provide a VALUE= attribute for each option tag. These values are what you will see when the form is submitted, so make them as logical and descriptive as possible.

```
<BR>I learned about this site from:<BR>
<SELECT NAME="referral">
 <OPTION VALUE="print">Print Ads
 <OPTION VALUE="visit">In-Store Visit
 <OPTION VALUE="rec">Friend's Recommendation
 <OPTION VALUE="internet">Sources on the Internet
 <OPTION VALUE="other">Other
</SELECT>
```

7. Optionally, let visitors select multiple items from the list by including the MULTIPLE attribute in the opening <SELECT> tag.

```
<BR>I learned about this site from:<BR>
<SELECT NAME="referral" MULTIPLE>
 <OPTION VALUE="print">Print Ads
 <OPTION VALUE="visit">In-Store Visit
 <OPTION VALUE="rec">Friend's Recommendation
```

```
<OPTION VALUE="internet">Sources on the Internet
<OPTION VALUE="other">Other
</SELECT>
```

TIP

If you choose to include MULTIPLE, your visitor can select one or all options; you cannot restrict the choices to only, say, two of four items.

8. Optionally, add the SELECTED attribute to the <OPTION> tag to specify a default selection. You can offer more than one default setting if you used the MULTIPLE attribute.

```
<BR>I learned about this site from:<BR>
<SELECT NAME="referral" MULTIPLE>
 <OPTION VALUE="print" SELECTED>Print Ads
 <OPTION VALUE="visit">In-Store Visit
 <OPTION VALUE="rec">Friend's Recommendation
 <OPTION VALUE="internet">Sources on the Internet
 <OPTION VALUE="other">Other
</SELECT>
```

With this, the basic select field is complete. Browsers display this select field as a drop-down list, as in Figure 17.12.

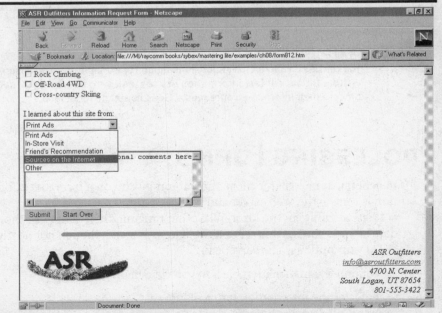

FIGURE 17.12: Select fields let you provide many choices in a compact format.

DESIGNING LONG SELECT FIELDS

When developing particularly long select fields—ones that include many items—be sure to make the area as easy to use as possible. Here are some guidelines:

► Be sure that the select field appears within one screen; don't make visitors scroll to see the entire select field.

► Add a SIZE= attribute to the opening <SELECT> tag to expand the drop-down list to a list box, like this:

```
<SELECT NAME="referral" MULTIPLE SIZE="5">
```

The list box can have a vertical scrollbar, if necessary, to provide access to all items, as shown below. (Select boxes are horizontally fixed, meaning that they cannot scroll horizontally.)

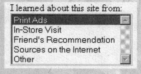

NOTE

You can use JavaScript to validate form input. For example, you can ensure that visitors fill out contact information or the credit card numbers you need to process their information or requests. See Chapter 20 for details.

PROCESSING FORMS

In general, after a visitor clicks the Submit button on a form, the information is sent to the Web server and to the program indicated by the ACTION= attribute in the form. What that program then does with the data is up to you. In this section, we'll look at some, though not nearly all, of your options. The server can:

► Send the information back to you via e-mail.

► Enter the information into a database.

► Post the information to a newsgroup or a Web page.

▶ Use the input to search a database.

When you're working out what to do with the data you collect or if you're just checking out what others have done to get some inspiration, your first stop should always be your Web server administrator. In particular, ask which programs are installed to process form input. Depending on what's available, you might be able to take advantage of those capabilities.

Regardless of how you want the information processed, you include specific attributes in the opening <FORM> tag, as explained in Table 17.5.

TABLE 17.5: Attributes for the <FORM> Tag

ATTRIBUTE	USE
ACTION="..."	Indicates the program on the HTTP server that will process the output from the form.
METHOD="..."	Tells the browser how to send the data to the server, with either the POST method or the GET method.

The ACTION= and METHOD= attributes depend on the server-side program that processes the form.

In general, the documentation that came with your form-processing script or with your Web server will tell you what to use for POST and GET. For example, ASR Outfitter's ISP (www.xmission.com) publishes information on its Web site about how to set up a form to mail the results (using a CGI script called cgiemail, discussed later in this chapter). In this case, the proper opening <FORM> tag is:

```
<FORM METHOD="POST" ACTION="http://www.xmission
.com/cgi-bin/cgiemail/~user/user-mail.txt">
```

Of course, the attributes you use depend on the program processing the information. By changing the attributes, you can also specify a different program. Because this single line of code within an HTML form determines how the information is processed, you can change what happens to the data without significantly changing the form itself.

Why would you want to change what happens to the data? You'd do so primarily because you discover better ways to manipulate the data. For example, if you're looking for feedback about your company's new product, you want the quickest way to get started collecting the data, which is probably having it e-mailed to you. Later on, after the crisis is over, you might investigate ways to have the data written directly into an automated

Part iii

database—which isn't as speedy to set up as e-mail, but can save you some work.

Some Web servers have built-in scripts or commands to process form results; others, particularly Unix servers, require additional programs.

In the following sections, we discuss your form-processing options—sending with e-mail, writing to a database, posting to a Web page, and other possibilities. Because your ISP's particular setup can vary significantly, we've provided general information that you can apply to your specific situation—probably with the help of your server administrator. The final section in this chapter, though, gives you a specific example of setting up an e-mail return—an option you're likely to encounter.

ABOUT USING FORM DATA

Getting a good response rate is the single biggest challenge to survey takers. Using an HTML form to collect information puts you in a similar role, with the added complication that your visitors must find your Web site to complete it. Once you get the data, however, you need to use it wisely. Here are some guidelines:

▶ Carefully consider the source, and don't read more into the data than you should. It's quite tempting to assume that the available information is representative of what you might collect from an entire population (customers, users, and so on).

▶ Take the time to analyze your data carefully, determining what it does and doesn't tell you.

For example, after ASR Outfitters implements its form and receives a few hundred responses, it will have a general idea of how many customers would be willing to make purchases online, how many are located in specific areas, how many have certain interests, and even how many use online services. Much of this information will not have been previously available to ASR, and it will be tempting to assume that the data is representative of all ASR customers.

The results of ASR's online survey reflect only the preferences and opinions of that small set of customers who use the Internet, *and* visited the site, *and* took the time to fill out the survey. Even if 95 percent of the people who complete the survey express interest in more rock-climbing gear, that might not reflect the interests of the overall ASR customer base.

NOTE

To learn your form-processing options, check with your server administrator or visit your ISP's Web site.

Processing Forms via E-Mail

Having the server return form results to you via e-mail isn't always ideal (although it can be), but it is often useful, it is nearly always expedient, and it is cheap. Using e-mail to accept form responses simply sends the information the visitor submits to you (or someone you designate) in an e-mail message. At that point, you have the information and can enter it (manually) in a database, send a response (manually), or do anything else you want with the data.

If you're collecting open comments from a relatively small number of people, using a program to e-mail the results is a reasonable, long-term solution. That is, it's a reasonable solution if you—or whoever gets the e-mail—can easily address the volume of form responses. E-mail is also a good solution if you do not know what level of response to expect. If the volume turns out to be manageable, continue. If the volume is high, consider other solutions, such as databases.

Database Processing

Writing the information that respondents submit into a database is a good solution to a potentially enormous data management problem. If you are collecting information about current or potential customers or clients, for example, you will probably want to quickly call up these lists and send letters, send e-mail, or provide demographic information about your customers to potential Web site advertisers. To do that, you'll want to use a database.

Although the specifics of putting form data into a database depend on the server and the software, we can make some generalizations. If you work in a fairly large company that has its own Web server on site, you'll encounter fewer problems with tasks such as putting form results directly into a database or sending automatic responses via e-mail. If you represent a small company and rely on an Internet Service Provider for Web hosting, you may have more of a challenge.

If your Web server uses the same platform on which you work—that is, if you're a Windows person and your Web server is a Windows NT Web server—feeding the form results directly into a database is manageable.

Part III

However, if your Web server is, for example, on a Unix platform but you work on a Macintosh as a rule, you may face some additional challenges in getting the information from a form into a readily usable database.

Posting to a Web Page

Depending on the information you're collecting, you might want to post the responses to a Web page or to a discussion group. For example, if ASR Outfitters sets up a form to collect information about hiking conditions, the natural output might be a Web page.

A program called Ceilidh (pronounced *kay-lee*) offers a good environment for online discussion or teaching applications, as shown in Figure 17.13.

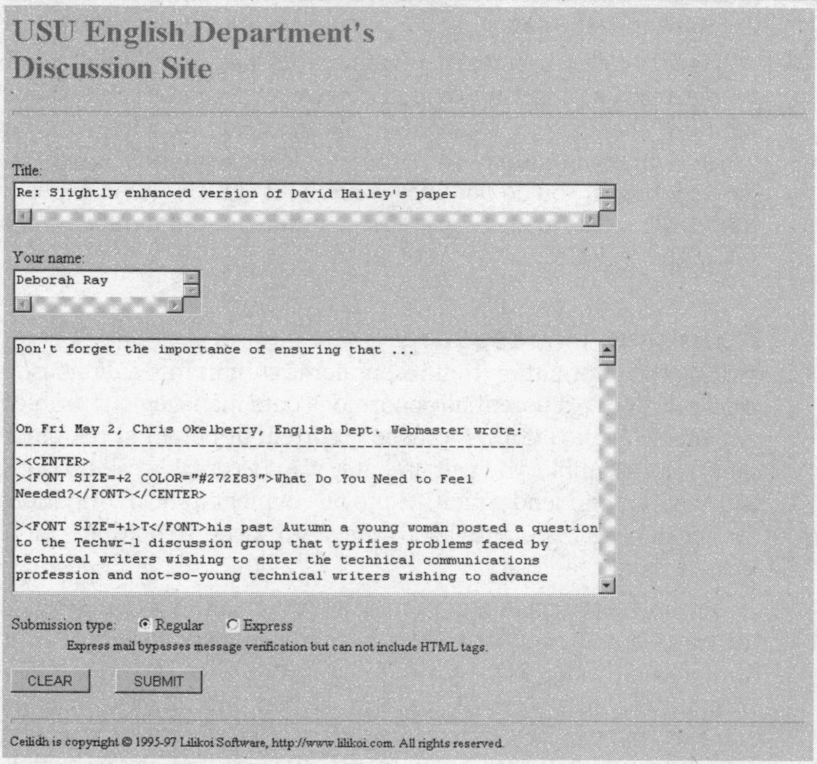

USU English Department's Discussion Site

Title:
Re: Slightly enhanced version of David Hailey's paper

Your name:
Deborah Ray

Don't forget the importance of ensuring that ...

On Fri May 2, Chris Okelberry, English Dept. Webmaster wrote:

><CENTER>
><FONT SIZE=+2 COLOR="#272E83">What Do You Need to Feel Needed?</FONT></CENTER>

><FONT SIZE=+1>T</FONT>his past Autumn a young woman posted a question to the Techwr-1 discussion group that typifies problems faced by technical writers wishing to enter the technical communications profession and not-so-young technical writers wishing to advance

Submission type: ⦿ Regular ○ Express
   Express mail bypasses message verification but can not include HTML tags.

    CLEAR   SUBMIT

Ceilidh is copyright © 1995-97 Lilikoi Software, http://www.lilikoi.com. All rights reserved.

FIGURE 17.13: Ceilidh offers outstanding online discussion and teaching applications.

Other Options

If you find that the options available on your system do not meet your needs, check out Matt's Script Archive (at www.worldwidemart.com/scripts/) or Selena Sol's Public Domain CGI Scripts (at www.extropia.com).

These scripts offer a starting point, for either you or your server administrator, to handle form processing effectively. In particular, the form-processing script from Selena's archive offers everything from database logging to giving audiences the opportunity to verify the accuracy of the data they enter.

Keep in mind, if you choose to install and set up these scripts yourself, that the installation and debugging of a server-side script is considerably more complex and time-consuming than installing a new Windows program. Not that it isn't possible for the novice to do it, and do it successfully, but set aside some time.

If you do choose to download and use scripts from the Net, be sure that you get them from a reliable source and that you or your server administrator scan the scripts for possible security holes. Form-processing programs must take some special steps to ensure that a malicious visitor does not use the form to crash the server or worse. Without taking precautions, forms can pass commands directly to the server, which will then execute them, with potentially disastrous results.

One Solution: Processing Using cgiemail

Because you will likely choose—at least initially—to have form results e-mailed to you, we will walk you through a form-to-e-mail program. The cgiemail program is produced and distributed for free by MIT, but it is only available for Unix servers. Check out:

```
web.mit.edu/wwwdev/cgiemail/index.html
```

for the latest news about cgiemail. This program is a good example because many ISPs offer access to it and because it is also commonly found on corporate Internet and intranet servers.

TIP

Comparable programs exist for both Macintosh and Windows 95/98/NT. You can find MailPost for the Macintosh at www.mcenter.com/mailpost/, and you can find wcgimail for Windows 95/98/NT at www.spacey.net/rickoz/wcgimail.stm.

Here is the general process for using cgiemail:

1. Start with a complete form—the one developed earlier in this chapter or a different one. Without a functional form, you cannot get the results sent to you via e-mail.

2. Add the ACTION= and METHOD= attributes with values you get from your server administrator. (See the "Processing Forms" section, earlier in this chapter, for more information about the ACTION= and METHOD= attributes.)

3. Develop a template for the e-mail message to you. This template includes the names of each of your fields and basic e-mail addressing information.

4. Develop a response page that the visitor sees after completing the form.

Now, let's look at how ASR Outfitters can use cgiemail to implement its form.

1. The Form

You don't need to do anything special to forms to use them with cgiemail. You have the option of requiring some fields to be completed, but that is not essential. For example, because the purpose of the ASR Outfitters form is to collect e-mail addresses, ASR would do well to make the e-mail address required.

The solution? Rename the name field from emailaddr to required-emailaddr. The cgiemail program will then check the form and reject it if that field is not complete. The actual code for that line of the form would look like this:

```
<BR><INPUT TYPE="TEXT" NAME="required-emailaddr" SIZE="30">
E-mail Address
```

Optionally, add required- to each field name that must be completed.

2. The ACTION= and METHOD= Attributes

The server administrator provided ASR Outfitters with the ACTION= and METHOD= attributes shown in the following code:

```
<FORM METHOD="POST" ACTION="http://www.xmission.com/
cgi-bin/cgiemail/~ejray/asr/ejray-asr-mail.txt">
```

The file referenced in the ACTION= line is the template for an e-mail message. In this case, the http://www.xmission.com/cgi-bin/cgiemail

part of the ACTION= line points to the program itself, and the following part
(/~ejray/asr/ejray-asr-mail.txt) is the server-relative path to the file.
(Remember, with a server-relative path, you can add the name of the
server to the front of the path and open the document in a Web browser.)

3. The Template

The plain text template includes the bare essentials for an e-mail message, fields in square brackets for the form field values, and any line
breaks or spacing needed to make it easier to read.

In general, you can be flexible in setting up the template, but you must
set up the e-mail headers exactly as shown here. Don't use leading
spaces, but do capitalize and use colons as shown. The parts after the
colons are fields for the From e-mail address, your e-mail address (in both
the To: line and in the Errors-To: line), and any subject field you choose.

```
From: [emailaddr]
To: ASR Webmaster <webmaster@asroutfitters.com>
Subject: Web Form Submission
Errors-To: ASR Webmaster <webmaster@asroutfitters.com>
```

Format the rest of the template as you choose—within the constraints
of plain text files. If you want to include information from the form, put
in a field name (the content of a NAME= attribute). The resulting e-mail will
contain the value of that field (either what a visitor enters or the VALUE=
attribute you specify in the case of check boxes and radio buttons).

Be liberal with line breaks, and enter descriptive values as you set up
the template. E-mail generated by forms may make sense when you're up
to your ears in developing the form, but later on it's likely to be so cryptic
that you can't understand it.

Following is the complete content of the ejray-asr-mail.txt file.

```
From: [emailaddr]
To: ASR Webmaster <webmaster@asroutfitters.com>
Subject: Web Form Submission
Errors-To: ASR Webmaster <webmaster@asroutfitters.com>

Results from Information Request Web Form:

[firstname] [lastname]
[emailaddr]
[address]
[city], [state] [zip]
[country]
```

Part III

```
Online Purchasing:
[buying]

Interested In:
[hiking]
[mbiking]
[camping]
[rock]
[4wd]
[ccskiing]

Referral:
[referral]

Comments:
[comments]
```

The cgiemail program completes this template with the values from the form, resulting in an e-mail message like the following:

```
Return-path: <www@krunk1.xmission.com>
Envelope-to: asroutfitters@raycomm.com
Delivery-date: Sat, 24 May 1997 10:03:55 -0600
Date: Sat, 24 May 1997 10:03:51 -0600 (MDT)
X-Template: /home/users/e/ejray/public_html/asr/
ejray-asr-mail.txt
From: mjones@raycomm.com
To: ASR Webmaster <asroutfitters@raycomm.com>
Subject: Web Form Submission
Errors-To: ASR Webmaster <asroutfitters@raycomm.com>

Results from Information Request Web Form:

Molly Jones
mjones@raycomm.com
402 E 4th
South Logan, UT 84341
USA

Online Purchasing:
might

Interested In:
hiking

camping
rock
```

```
Referral:
rec

Comments:
I'd also like information about
outdoor gear.
Thanks!
```

4. Success Page

The only remaining step is to set up a success page, a document that is returned to the visitor indicating that the form has been received. Although a success page is optional, we recommend that you use one. In the form code, a "success" field is actually a hidden <INPUT> field that looks like this:

```
<INPUT TYPE="HIDDEN" NAME="success" VALUE="http://www
.xmission.com/~ejray/asr/asrmaildone.html">
```

A success page can contain any content you choose. If you want, you can point the success page back to your home page or to any other page on your site. On the other hand, many HTML developers use the success page as a place to thank the visitor for taking the time to fill out the form and to offer an opportunity to ask questions or make comments.

WARNING

A nonstandard way of returning forms is to use a mailto: URL in the ACTION= line. This hack only works with Netscape Navigator, and not with all versions at that. A much better solution, unless you can closely control the browsers your visitors use, is a server-based e-mail program.

WHAT'S NEXT

In this chapter, you learned how to determine what information to include in forms and to develop them using a variety of widgets. Additionally, you learned about the different ways to process forms and to get the data back. Now we'll move on to another method for adding sophistication to your pages—Dynamic HTML (DHTML). In the next chapter, Joseph Schmuller will introduce you to the advanced effects and functionality that are possible with DHTML.

Part iii

Chapter 18

EXPLORING AND NAVIGATING DYNAMIC HTML

With the explosion of interest in the World Wide Web, Hypertext Markup Language (HTML) has assumed a prominent place in the computer world. HTML has evolved to meet the increasing demand for eye-catching—and mind-catching—Web sites. Until recently, however, the evolutionary process mostly involved new and improved tags and attributes. The end-products, static Web pages that often required repeated time-consuming round-trips between client and server machines, clearly showed that a new direction was in order.

Adapted from *Dynamic HTML: Master the Essentials*, by Joseph Schmuller

ISBN 0-7821-2277-9   608 pages $29.99

Dynamic HTML (DHTML) is that new direction. It combines HTML with cascading style sheets (CSS) and scripting languages. What role does each member of this combination play?

▶ As you're undoubtedly aware, HTML specifies a Web page's elements, like a table, a heading, a paragraph, or a bulleted list.

▶ CSS enables you to decide how a Web browser renders those elements: you can use a CSS to determine (i.e., to *style*) an element's size, color, position, and a number of other features.

▶ Scripting languages enable you to manipulate the Web page's elements, so that the styles you assigned to them can change in response to an end user's input.

That last point is extremely important. Before DHTML, you often had to jump through complicated hoops to give end users the ability to change a Web page's features after it downloaded. One of those hoops, as I mentioned before, involved repeated communication with the server machine. This takes a lot of time, and it detracts from the Web-surfing experience. How many times have you clicked your browser's Stop button because everything was just taking too long? DHTML makes Web page events seemingly instantaneous: they occur within the browser after the page has downloaded. With DHTML, Web pages become very much like other software applications.

Microsoft and Netscape, the companies behind the two most popular Web browsers, each have a version of DHTML. Both are called "DHTML," and each vendor's version is compatible only with its own browser. Microsoft and Netscape have proposed separate versions of DHTML to the World Wide Web Consortium. Each, of course, hopes the Consortium adopts its proposal and stamps it the official version, but it's probably the case that a sort of hybrid will emerge.

SETTING UP

We'll jump into DHTML in the next section, but first we need to set up a template to use in the exercises later in this chapter. If you have a favorite text editor, feel free to use it throughout the exercises. If not, Windows 95/98/NT/2000 provides one for you: Notepad.

You can set up Notepad to act as a convenient HTML editor:

1. Find Notepad in your system, open it, and select File ➤ New.

2. Next, select File ➤ Save As. Save the file as `Template`.

3. In this file, type these lines:

```
<HTML>
<HEAD>
<TITLE>New Page</TITLE>
</HEAD>
<BODY>

</BODY>
</HTML>
```

4. Select File ➤ Save.

Whenever you have to create an HTML file, you can open `Template` and then save it under a new name with the extension `.htm`.

Your `Template` file should look like this:

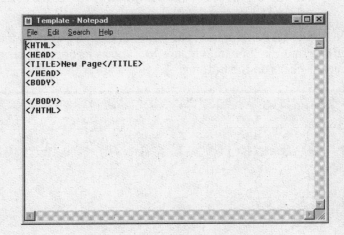

You now have a starting point for creating any HTML document.

Using DHTML in Internet Explorer

Now, as promised, you're going to dive right into DHTML. You'll work with HTML, CSS, and scripting. You'll start with a page in Internet Explorer and you'll endow it with a number of *dynamic effects*—effects that depend on user actions. Here are the dynamic effects you'll build into your first page:

► Moving your mouse through a heading on the top of the page will cause a hidden text display to appear and will change the color of the heading.

► Moving your mouse through the heading will also change the color and the content of a small box on the page.

► Clicking on the heading will cause a box in the center of the page to split into four boxes that move outward toward the corners of the page, revealing a short message in the center of the page.

► The centered message will appear to be layered above the text display.

► Moving the mouse out of the heading will return the page to its original appearance.

Figure 18.1 shows what the page will look like when you first open it in Internet Explorer, and Figure 18.2 shows its appearance after a few mouse-clicks on the heading.

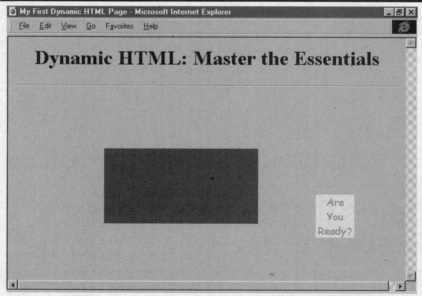

FIGURE 18.1: Your first DHTML Web page, opened in Internet Explorer

FIGURE 18.2: The Web page after several mouse-clicks on the heading

The Heading and the Horizontal Line

Let's get started. Open your Template file, select File ➢ Save As, and save the file as First Dynamic IE.htm. Change the title of the page by typing **My First Dynamic Web Page** between <TITLE> and </TITLE> in place of New Page. Inside the <BODY> tag, type **Style = "background-color : 'Silver'"** to give your page that macho silver-gray color you see in many applications. This expression is called a *style sheet*. Because it's inside a tag, it's an *inline* style sheet. As you can see, in this context, Style is an attribute and its value is a string. The string contains a style property, a colon, and the value of the property. A style sheet can hold more than one property-value pair, and when it does, a semicolon separates adjacent pairs. (You'll see an example of this in the next section, "The Hidden Message.") For much more about style sheets, see Chapter 16.

NOTE

If you've worked with HTML 3.x, you've probably used the bgcolor attribute to specify a Web page's background color. In HTML 4.0, this attribute is *deprecated*, meaning that (1) newer features of the language provide Web developers with greater capabilities, and (2) it may become obsolete in future versions of HTML.

Next, center an H1 heading by typing:

```
<H1 Style = "text-align:center">Dynamic HTML: Master the
Essentials</H1>
```

after the <BODY> tag. To follow the heading with a horizontal line, type **<HR>**.

At this point, we're going to add an extremely important attribute to the <H1> tag. This attribute, ID, will give us a way of referring to the header when we have to work with it in a scripting language. Inside the <H1> tag, type **ID = h1Header**.

Your document should look like this:

```
<HTML>
<HEAD>
<TITLE>My First Dynamic HTML Page</TITLE>
</HEAD>
<BODY Style = "background-color:'silver'">
<H1 ID = h1Header Style = "text-align:center">Dynamic HTML:
Master the Essentials</H1>
<HR>
</BODY>
</HTML>
```

The page in Internet Explorer looks like Figure 18.1, but without anything below the line under the heading.

WHAT'S IN A NAME?

When I assign an ID to an HTML element, I'll begin the ID with a lowercase prefix. That prefix will be the element tag (like h1, div, or p). The rest of the ID will be a descriptive term that tells you something about the element. It will begin with an uppercase letter, and all the rest will be lowercase (h1Header, for example).

This is similar to a naming convention that software developers use in other contexts. The prefix usually is an abbreviation, but every HTML element has a short name, so I'll use that name as the prefix.

If you're familiar with object-oriented programming, you've already seen this kind of notation. Is this naming convention subtly trying to tell you that DHTML turns HTML elements into objects? Exactly!

The Hidden Message

To create the remaining elements of the page, we'll divide the page into segments called DIVs. Each segment starts with <DIV> and ends with </DIV>. After we've created our segments, we'll script them to exhibit the desired effects.

Let's create a segment to hold the hidden message that you see in a large, bold, white font in Figure 18.2. Just after the <HR> tag, type:

```
<DIV ID = divMessage>
</DIV>
```

Next, type the message between these two DIV tags. Put the message in a paragraph (that is, enclose it with a <P> and a </P>) and make it a bulleted list. Here's the HTML to type between the DIV tags:

```
<P> Topics in this book include
<UL>
<LI> Scripting
<LI> Cascading Style Sheets
<LI> Animation
<LI> ... And Many More!
</UL>
</P>
```

We've typed the message, but so far its appearance in Internet Explorer would be pretty nondescript. We haven't colored the text white, enlarged it, or made it bold. We also haven't positioned the message on the page.

To take care of the message's size, appearance, and position, we'll add information to the <DIV> tag. We add the information as a group of styling specifications in an inline style sheet. Within the <DIV> tag, type:

```
Style = "Position:Absolute;Left:5%;Top:10%;
Visibility:Hidden;z-index:-1;font-style:normal;
font-weight:bold;font-family:Normal;font-size:50;
color:'White'"
```

The first property-value pair, Position:Absolute, tells the browser to position the DIV with respect to the top edge and left edge of the browser window.

NOTE

Another possible value for Position is Relative. In contrast to Absolute, Relative situates an element in relation to other elements on the page.

Part iii

The next two property-value pairs show one way that style sheets let you specify position—via percentages of distance from the left edge and the top edge of the browser window. The first of the two pairs positions the DIV's left side 5 percent of the distance from the left edge to the right, and the second positions its top edge 10 percent of the distance from the top of the browser to the bottom. The fourth pair, Visibility:Hidden, keeps the message invisible when the page opens.

The next pair positions the DIV in the "third dimension." If you look closely at Figure 18.2, you'll see that the large, white-lettered message appears to be underneath the message in the center of the screen and underneath the page's heading. The z-index styling property determines this kind of layering: the lower the z-index, the deeper the apparent layer of its element.

NOTE

The word *layer* is important in Netscape's version of DHTML. For this reason, I'll try to avoid this word during our discussion of Internet Explorer.

The remaining property-value pairs determine the message font's size, weight, appearance, and color. The font-size attribute's value, 50, specifies a font whose size is 50 pixels.

NOTE

In HTML 3.x, developers used the <FONT> tag to specify a font's aspects. In HTML 4.0, the <FONT> tag is *deprecated*. As I said in a previous note, this means that (1) newer features of the language provide Web developers with greater capabilities, and (2) this element may become obsolete in future versions of HTML. Font-size is a good example of "greater capabilities." Through its Size attribute, the <FONT> tag supports only seven possible font sizes. The newer font-size style property, on the other hand, can give you pixel-level precision when you specify the size of a font.

The Message at the Center of the Page

Now we'll create the message at the center of the page. Create a <DIV> tag called divLearn, and then position it by pixels, rather than percentages. We'll position it 180 pixels from the left edge of the page and 200 pixels from the top edge:

```
<DIV ID = divLearn Style ="Position:Absolute;Left:180;
Top:200;">
```

It will be helpful to confine the message to a specific width—say, 210 pixels—so that we can make its text cover three lines. To overlay the message on top of the large white-font text display, we'll give it a z-index of 0. (Remember that the text display's z-index is −1.) Adding these specifications to the style sheet gives us:

```
<DIV ID = divLearn Style ="Position:Absolute;Left:180;
Top:200;Width:210;z-index:0;">
```

The message will reside in a paragraph:

```
<P>
Learn how to create striking effects on your Web pages.
</P>
```

and we'll add some styling information to the <P> tag. In this tag, we can specify an appearance, size, and weight for the font. The entire <P> tag should look like this:

```
<P ID = pLearn Style = "font-family:cursive;font-size:15pt;
font-weight:bold">
```

Here's the HTML for the DIV:

```
<DIV ID = divLearn Style
="Position:Absolute;Left:180;Top:200;Width:210;z-index:0;">
<P ID = pLearn Style = "font-family:cursive;font-size:15pt;
font-weight:bold">
Learn how to create striking effects on your Web pages.
</P>
</DIV>
```

The Moving Boxes

To create the effect of a box that splits into four boxes, we position four boxes in the center of the page and give them all the same background color. Each box will be a separate DIV. I used blue as the background color, but you can pick any color you like. I also specified a color property and a text-align property, because we'll use them in an exercise.

Here is one way to write the DIVs for the boxes:

```
<DIV ID = divBox1 Style="background-color:blue;color:blue;
text-align:center;Position:Absolute;Left:150;Top:180;
Width:120;Height:60;z-index:1 ">
</DIV>

<DIV ID = divBox2 Style="background-color:blue;color:blue;
text-align:center;Position:Absolute;Left:270;TOP:180;Width:
120;Height:60;z-index:1">
```

```
</DIV>

<DIV ID = divBox3 Style="background-color:blue;color:blue;
text-align:center;Position:Absolute;Left:150;Top:240;Width:
120;Height:60;z-index:1">
</DIV>

<DIV ID = divBox4 Style="background-color:blue;color:blue;
text-align:center;Position:Absolute;Left:270;Top:240;Width:
120;Height:60;z-index:1">
</DIV>
```

If you write the DIVs this way, you'll create the boxes in Figures 18.1 and 18.2, but the CSS syntax presents another possibility. Instead of writing the colors, text alignment, width, and height four times, we can put the style specifications for these properties at the beginning of the document, between <HEAD> and </HEAD>; give those specifications a name; and then use that name within each box's <DIV> tag.

Here's how to do it. After the <HEAD> tag in your document, type:

```
<STYLE Type = "text/css">
</STYLE>
```

We'll put the style information between these two tags. To give a name ("bluebox") to the style specifications and specify the background color, color, text alignment, width, and height for the boxes, type:

```
.bluebox {background-color:blue;
        color:blue;
        text-align:center;
        width:120;
        height:60}
```

after your newly created <STYLE> tag. When you preface the name of a style with a dot, you create a style *class*. Note the consistent syntax for the style sheet. We still use a colon to separate a property from its value and a semicolon to separate adjacent property-value pairs.

TIP

In the Microsoft version of DHTML, you can omit Type = "text/css", as CSS is the only type of style sheet that Microsoft supports. In the Netscape version, you can't omit this expression, because Netscape supports another type of style sheet in addition to CSS.

With the style specified as a class in the head of your document, you insert the name of the class in each box's DIV. Here's the HTML for the movable boxes:

```
<DIV ID = divBox1 Class = "bluebox" Style="Position:Absolute;
Left:150;Top:180;z-index:1">
</DIV>

<DIV ID = divBox2 Class = "bluebox" Style="Position:Absolute;
Left:270;Top:180;z-index:1">
</DIV>

<DIV ID = divBox3 Class = "bluebox" Style="Position:Absolute;
Left:150;Top:240;z-index:1">
</DIV>

<DIV ID = divBox4 Class = "bluebox" STYLE="Position:Absolute;
Left:270;Top:240;z-index:1">
</DIV>
```

Save your work and open the page in Internet Explorer; you'll see a display that looks like Figure 18.1, but without the little box in the lower right corner.

Here's the exercise that uses the `color` and `text-align` properties you just set. It will show you how style sheets can combine to determine an HTML element's appearance. Follow these steps:

1. For the first movable box, between <DIV> and </DIV>, insert a paragraph that identifies the box:

   `<P>Box<BR>1</P>`

2. Do the same for the fourth movable box:

   `<P>Box<BR>4</P>`

3. In the first movable box's inline style sheet, add:

   `color:white`

4. In the fourth movable box's inline style sheet, add:

   `background-color:white`

In your document, the HTML for the movable boxes should now look like this:

```
<DIV ID = divBox1 Class = "bluebox" Style="Position:Absolute;
Left:150;Top:180;z-index:1;color:white">
<P>Box<BR>1</P>
</DIV>
```

```
<DIV ID = divBox2 Class = "bluebox" Style="Position:Absolute;
Left:270;Top:180;z-index:1">
</DIV>

<DIV ID = divBox3 Class = "bluebox" Style="Position:Absolute;
Left:150;Top:240;z-index:1">
</DIV>

<DIV ID = divBox4 Class = "bluebox" STYLE="Position:Absolute;
Left:270;Top:240;z-index:1; background-color:white">
<P>Box<BR>4</P>
</DIV>
```

Figure 18.3 shows the appearance of your page in Internet Explorer with these changes in place.

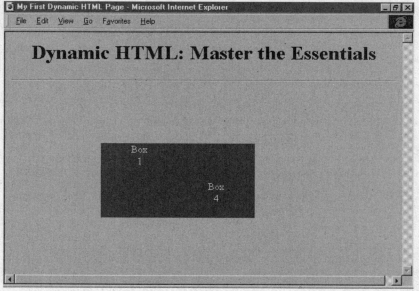

FIGURE 18.3: Your page in Internet Explorer, with modified styling specifications for two of the movable boxes

The effects of these changes show you that you can combine styles from the specification at the beginning of the document (between the <STYLE> and </STYLE> tags) and style from inline specifications. This combination is referred to as *cascading*—the *C* in CSS.

Remove those changes from divBox1 and divBox4, and we'll move on to the next element.

The Changeable Box

We finish off the page design by creating the box in the lower right corner. The box changes color and content when you pass the mouse through the heading at the top of the page. You can see this by comparing Figure 18.1 to Figure 18.2. By now, you've probably guessed that we'll implement the effect by writing two DIVs, assigning them different z-indices, and making one visible and one invisible. We'll write a script that switches the visibility of the DIVs when the mouse passes into the heading and returns to the original values when the mouse passes out of the heading.

Here's the HTML that sets up the two DIVs:

```
<DIV ID = divReady Style = "Position:Absolute;
Top:70%;Left:80%;Width:10%;z-index:1;Visibility:Visible">
<P Align = Center Style = "font-family:cursive;
Background-Color:'Beige';Color:Chocolate">
Are<BR>You<BR>Ready?</P>
</DIV>

<DIV ID = divStarted Style =
"Position:Absolute;Top:70%;Left:80%;Width:10%;z-index:0;
Visibility:Hidden">
<P Align = Center Style = "font-family:cursive;
Background-Color:'BlanchedAlmond';Color:Blue">
Let's<BR>Get<BR>Started</P>
</DIV>
```

A Word about Color

We've used numerous color names in the HTML for our first page. What other color names can you use in your code? The appendix presents some of the colors that Internet Explorer and Navigator can render and their hexadecimal codes. It's important to test a color in both browsers. As our work with Netscape later in this chapter will show, the browsers react differently to different color names.

Scripting the Dynamic Effects

We've set up a number of segments in our Web page, and if you open it in Internet Explorer at this point, you'll see a display that looks like Figure 18.1. However, a user can't interact with this page in its present form to make it look like Figure 18.2. To enable interactivity, we have to add scripts.

Scripts make a Web page come alive. If we think of the elements on a page as actors on a stage, then a script tells them how to behave and interact with one another.

You write a script in a *scripting language*, a computer language designed to work inside a specific environment, such as an HTML document. Two scripting languages are prominent. One, VBScript, is a subset of Microsoft's popular Visual Basic. The other, JavaScript, has some of the syntax of Java, but is very different from Java. Both VBScript and JavaScript work with software structures called *objects*.

NOTE
You'll learn more about JavaScript and working with objects in Chapter 20.

Unlike programming languages that can create applications that run by themselves, a scripting language requires a piece of software called an *interpreter* to run its programs. Internet Explorer has built-in interpreters for VBScript and JavaScript, and Navigator has a built-in interpreter for JavaScript. In this first Internet Explorer–based exercise, we'll work with VBScript.

In an HTML document, one way to write scripts is to put them inside this set of tags:

```
<SCRIPT Language = "VBScript">
<!--
-->
</SCRIPT>
```

You place this code in your document somewhere between <HEAD> and </HEAD>.

You put the body of your script between <!-- and -->. These two structures represent the beginning and end of a comment. Since a browser ignores comments, it won't process your script if it doesn't have the interpreter specified by the Language attribute in the <SCRIPT> tag.

Our script will set up the behaviors for the Web page elements for these situations:

- ▶ The mouse passes into the heading.
- ▶ Mouse-clicks occur with the cursor in the heading.
- ▶ The mouse passes out of the heading.

The Mouse Passes into the Heading

As I said earlier, when the mouse passes into the heading, we want the color of the heading to change, the large-font message to become visible, and the box in the lower right corner to change its colors and its content.

Passing the cursor into the heading is an *onMouseOver* event. (Think of an *event* as a signal to the Web page from the outside world.) Remember that we've given the heading an ID so we can refer to it in our script. We'll write a *subroutine* for the heading's onMouseOver event.

We start the subroutine with this line:

```
Sub h1Header_onMouseOver
```

Sub lets the browser know that a subroutine definition follows, h1Header is the ID we gave the heading, and onMouseOver is the specific event that causes the subroutine to respond.

One of the behaviors that we want to happen as a result of this event is the change in the heading's color. We represent the heading's color as:

```
h1Header.Style.Color
```

You can read this expression as "h1Header's Style's Color." In this context, a dot is like an apostrophe followed by *s*.

NOTE

A more detailed explanation is that h1Header is an object, Style is a property of the object, and Color is a property of Style.

To change the heading's color from the default black to something a bit livelier, like goldenrod, type:

```
h1Header.Style.Color = "Goldenrod"
```

Next, we'll make the message with the large font visible. The ID for that message is divMessage, so the code to make it visible is:

```
divMessage.Style.Visibility = "Visible"
```

Part iii

Similarly, we switch the `Visibility` property for the two boxes in the lower right corner of the page:

```
divReady.Style.Visibility = "Hidden"
divStarted.Style.Visibility = "Visible"
```

We must end every subroutine with:

```
End Sub
```

The entire subroutine for the heading's `onMouseOver` event is:

```
Sub h1Header_onMouseOver
   h1Header.Style.Color = "Goldenrod"
   divMessage.Style.Visibility = "Visible"
   divReady.Style.Visibility = "Hidden"
   divStarted.Style.Visibility = "Visible"
End Sub
```

The script in this subroutine illustrates a fundamental principle of DHTML—it changes CSS information in response to a user event.

Mouse-Clicks Occur with the Cursor in the Heading

When the mouse passes into the heading and the user clicks the mouse, the message in the middle of the page becomes visible, and the box in the middle of the page splits into four boxes that move toward the corners of the page with each click. The effect is something like animation, as the boxes appear to move across the page.

You already know how to make an element visible:

```
pLearn.Style.Visibility = "Visible"
```

Now for the tricky part—moving the boxes. Let's say we want the first box, `divBox1`, to move 20 pixels to the left and 20 pixels toward the top each time we click the mouse. This composite movement will take `divBox1` toward the upper left corner. The box to its immediate right, `divBox2`, should go 20 pixels to the right and 20 toward the top (i.e., toward the upper right corner). `divBox3` should move 20 to the left and 20 toward the bottom, and `divBox4` should move 20 to the right and 20 toward the bottom. (You can use other numbers of pixels if you like.) In the coordinate system of browsers, the upper left corner is at (0,0) so that movement toward the right is positive, movement toward the left is negative, movement toward the bottom is positive, and movement toward the top is negative.

With all these considerations in mind, we can set up the desired movement with:

```
Call MoveElementBy(divBox1,-20,-20)
Call MoveElementBy(divBox2,20,-20)
Call MoveElementBy(divBox3,-20,20)
Call MoveElementBy(divBox4,20,20)
```

Each line calls the subroutine MoveElementBy, which takes three *arguments* (items a subroutine needs in order to do its job)—the ID of the element to move, the number of pixels to move it in the horizontal direction, and the number of pixels to move it in the vertical direction.

This is all very straightforward, except for one problem: VBScript has no built-in subroutine called MoveElementBy. Where will this subroutine come from? We have to build it ourselves. The first line of the subroutine's definition should look like this:

```
Subroutine MoveElementBy(ElementID, LeftMovementAmount,
TopMovementAmount)
```

Setting this up is a little more challenging than it looks, because MoveElementBy has to move an element a specified number of pixels. The positional information of an element, however, is not in numerical form—it's in a string. For example, if divBox1 is 200 pixels from the left edge of the window, the value of divBox1.Style.Left isn't the number 200, it's the string "200px". We somehow have to turn "200px" into the number 200.

NOTE
There's a way around this, but I want to take the opportunity to show you some of the aspects of VBScript.

Fortunately, VBScript provides some help. We'll use two built-in *functions* to turn the string "200px" into the string "200", and another built-in function to convert the string "200" into the integer 200. (In VBScript, a function is like a subroutine except that it returns a value.)

The function InStr searches a string for the presence of a target string. If InStr finds the target, it returns the position in which the target begins. For example:

```
InStr("200px", "px")
```

returns 4. Our strategy, then, will be to set a variable equal to:

```
InStr(ElementID.Style.Left,"px")
```

Part iii

and another variable equal to:

```
InStr(ElementID.Style.Top,"px")
```

where `ElementID` is the ID of the element we're moving:

```
intPxPositionLeft = InStr(ElementID.Style.Left,"px")
intPxPositionTop = InStr(ElementID.Style.Top,"px")
```

The `int` prefix indicates that the variables hold integer information. We then use these variables in another built-in function, called `Left`. This function starts from the leftmost character in a string and returns a specified number of characters. The expression:

```
Left("200px",3)
```

returns the string `"200"`. We'll take the value that `Left` returns and use it as the argument for the VBScript function `CInt`, which converts a string into an integer. The expression:

```
CInt(Left(ElementID.Style.Left, intPxPositionLeft-1))
```

turns an element's `Left` edge location into an integer, and:

```
CInt(Left(ElementID.Style.Top, intPxPositionTop-1))
```

turns the element's `Top` edge location into an integer.

Here's the VBScript for moving the boxes in response to a mouse-click:

```
Sub h1Header_onClick
  pLearn.Style.Visibility = "Visible"
  Call MoveElementBy(divBox1,-20,-20)
  Call MoveElementBy(divBox2,20,-20)
  Call MoveElementBy(divBox3,-20,20)
  Call MoveElementBy(divBox4,20,20)
End Sub
Sub
MoveElementBy(ElementID,LeftMovementAmount,TopMovementAmount)
  dim intPxPositionLeft
  dim intPxPositionTop
  intPxPositionLeft = InStr(ElementID.Style.Left,"px")
  intPxPositionTop = InStr(ElementID.Style.Top,"px")
  ElementID.Style.Left = _
   CInt(Left(ElementID.Style.Left,intPxPositionLeft-1)) + _
    LeftMovementAmount
  ElementID.Style.Top = _
   CInt(Left(ElementID.Style.Top,intPxPositionTop-1)) +
    TopMovementAmount
End Sub
```

NOTE
The underscore is VBScript's line-continuation character.

In the second subroutine, the dim statement defines the variables we use to store the returned values of the InStr function. VBScript allows you to create variables on the fly, but it's a good idea to define them explicitly, as we've done here.

The Mouse Passes Out of the Heading

After the scripting you've just created, the script for moving the mouse out of the heading is pretty tame:

```
Sub h1Header_onMouseOut
    h1Header.Style.Color = "Black"
    divBox1.Style.Top = 200
    divBox1.Style.Left = 150
    divBox2.Style.Top = 200
    divBox2.Style.Left = 270
    divBox3.Style.Top = 235
    divBox3.Style.Left = 150
    divBox4.Style.Top = 235
    divBox4.Style.Left = 270
    divMessage.Style.Visibility = "Hidden"
    divReady.Style.Visibility = "Visible"
    divStarted.Style.Visibility = "Hidden"
    pLearn.Style.Visibility = "Hidden"
End Sub
```

This Sub just returns all the elements to their original settings.

An Important Tip

If you save your work and open the page in Internet Explorer, it will look like Figure 18.1 and your scripts will enable you to perform mouse actions that activate the dynamic effects. You'll encounter one problem, however. Moving the mouse into and out of the heading will result in flicker; because it's text, the heading sets off an irregularly shaped area—sometimes the cursor is in that area, sometimes it's not, and it's not always obvious which is which. The irregularity of the heading area's shape causes another problem—mouse-clicks on the heading might not work as you'd like them to.

You can easily solve these problems by wrapping the heading in a DIV and positioning the DIV at the top of the page. Here's what the HTML for the heading should look like:

```
<DIV Style = "Position:Absolute;Left:10;Top:0;Width:100%">
<H1 ID = h1Header Style = "text-align:center">Dynamic HTML:
Master the Essentials</H1>
<HR>
</DIV>
```

Including the <HR> tag in the DIV preserves the positional relationship between the heading and the horizontal line.

The Whole File

Here's the entire First Dynamic IE.htm file:

Listing 18.1   First Dynamic IE.htm

```
<HTML>
<HEAD>
<STYLE Type = "text/css">
.bluebox {background-color:blue;
    color:blue;
    text-align:center;
    width:120;
    height:60}
</STYLE>

<SCRIPT LANGUAGE = "VBSCRIPT">

Sub h1Header_onMouseOver
    h1Header.Style.Color = "Goldenrod"
    divMessage.Style.Visibility = "Visible"
    divReady.Style.Visibility = "Hidden"
    divStarted.Style.Visibility = "Visible"
End Sub

Sub h1Header_onMouseOut
    h1Header.Style.Color = "Black"
    divBox1.Style.Top = 180
    divBox1.Style.Left = 150
    divBox2.Style.Top = 180
    divBox2.Style.Left = 270
    divBox3.Style.Top = 240
    divBox3.Style.Left = 150
    divBox4.Style.Top = 240
    divBox4.Style.Left = 270
```

```
    divMessage.Style.Visibility = "Hidden"
    divReady.Style.Visibility = "Visible"
    divStarted.Style.Visibility = "Hidden"
End Sub

Sub h1Header_onClick
    pLearn.Style.Visibility = "Visible"
    Call MoveElementBy(divBox1,-20,-20)
    Call MoveElementBy(divBox2,20,-20)
    Call MoveElementBy(divBox3,-20,20)
    Call MoveElementBy(divBox4,20,20)
End Sub

Sub
MoveElementBy(ElementID,LeftMovementAmount,TopMovementAmount)
    pPositionTop = InStr(ElementID.Style.Top,"px")
    pPositionLeft = InStr(ElementID.Style.Left,"px")
    ElementID.Style.Top = _
      CInt(Left(ElementID.Style.Top,pPositionTop-1)) + _
      TopMovementAmount
    ElementID.Style.Left = _
      CInt(Left(ElementID.Style.Left,pPositionLeft-1)) + _
      LeftMovementAmount
End Sub

</SCRIPT>
<TITLE>My First Dynamic HTML Page</TITLE>
</HEAD>
<BODY Style = "background-color:'Silver'">
<DIV Style = "Position:Absolute;Left:10;Top:0;Width:100%">
<H1 ID = h1Header Style = "text-align:center">Dynamic HTML:
Master the Essentials</H1>
<HR>
</DIV>
<DIV ID = divMessage Style =
"Position:Absolute;Left:5%;Top:10%;Visibility:Hidden;z-
index:-1;font-style:normal;font-weight:bold;font-
family:Normal;font-size:50;color:'White'">
<P> Topics in this book include
<UL>
<LI> Scripting
<LI> Cascading Style Sheets
<LI> Animation
<LI> ... And Many More!
</UL>
</P>
</DIV>
```

```
<DIV ID = divLearn
Style="Position:Absolute;Left:180;Top:200;Width:210;z-
index:0;">
<P ID = pLearn Style = "font-family:cursive;font-
size:15pt;font-weight:bold">
Learn how to create striking effects on your Web pages.
</P>
</DIV>

<DIV ID = divBox1 Class = "bluebox"
Style="Position:Absolute;Left:150;Top:180;z-index:1">
</DIV>

<DIV ID = divBox2 Class = "bluebox"
Style="Position:Absolute;Left:270;Top:180;z-index:1">
</DIV>

<DIV ID = divBox3 Class = "bluebox"
Style="Position:Absolute;Left:150;Top:240;z-index:1">
</DIV>

<DIV ID = divBox4 Class = "bluebox"
STYLE="Position:Absolute;Left:270;Top:240;z-index:1">
</DIV>

<DIV ID = divReady Style =
"Position:Absolute;Top:70%;Left:80%;Width:10%;z-index:1;
Visibility:Visible">
<P Style = "text-align:center;font-family:cursive;Background-
Color:'Beige';Color:Chocolate">
Are<BR>You<BR>Ready?</P>
</DIV>

<DIV ID = divStarted Style =
"Position:Absolute;Top:70%;Left:80%;Width:10%;z-index:0;
Visibility:Hidden">
<P Style = "text-align:center;font-family:cursive;Background-
Color:'BlanchedAlmond';Color:Blue">
Let's<BR>Get<BR>Started</P>
</DIV>

</BODY>
</HTML>
```

Open this file in Internet Explorer to see all the effects that turn Figure 18.1 into Figure 18.2.

USING DHTML IN NAVIGATOR

To round out your introduction to Dynamic HTML, let's put a similar page together for Netscape Navigator. We'll have to make a few changes, but most of the effects will remain:

- ▶ Moving the mouse into the heading will change the color of the heading and make a large-font message appear.

- ▶ Mouse-clicks will make boxes in the middle of the page move out toward the corners. In this version, the mouse-click will occur on an on-screen button, rather than on the heading.

- ▶ A mouse-click on another button will return all the elements to their original settings.

I've eliminated the small changeable box from this page, but you can put it in as an exercise. Figure 18.4 shows what this page looks like in Netscape with the dynamic effects visible.

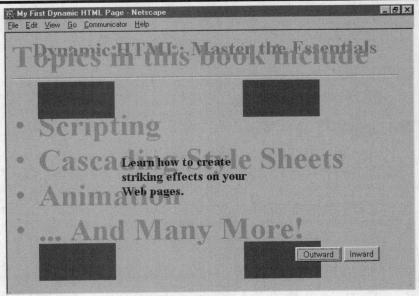

FIGURE 18.4: Your DHTML page in Navigator, with dynamic effects visible

To start things off, open your Template, save it as First Dynamic Nav.htm, and change the title to **My First Dynamic Web Page**. Next, change the background color to silver. In the Internet Explorer version, you did this by putting the style sheet:

```
Style = "background-color:'silver'"
```

into the <BODY> tag. If you do that in the Navigator version, you'll run into trouble. As you'll see again and again, Navigator is quirky when it comes to rendering colors specified in style sheets. (Future versions of Navigator will no doubt solve this problem.) To work around this, insert the deprecated attribute Bgcolor into the <BODY> tag:

```
Bgcolor = "Silver"
```

The Heading and the Horizontal Line

We start out as before, by creating the heading and the horizontal line beneath it. The HTML is the same as before, so your file should look like this:

```
<HTML>
<HEAD>
</HEAD>
<TITLE>My First Dynamic HTML Page</TITLE>
<BODY Bgcolor = "Silver">
<Center>
<H1>Dynamic HTML: Master the Essentials</H1></Center>
<HR>
</BODY>
</HTML>
```

The <LAYER> Tag

In our Internet Explorer version, we used <DIV> tags to divide our page into segments. We then used VBScript to apply dynamic effects to those divisions.

To segment a Web page, Navigator provides the <LAYER> tag. You begin a segment with <LAYER> and end it with </LAYER>. Although both <LAYER> and <DIV> segment a page and support the z-index, they differ in important ways.

Netscape designed the <LAYER> tag to behave like a piece of transparent paper laid on top of a Web page. Between <LAYER> and </LAYER>, you insert HTML elements. You provide the <LAYER> tag with an ID (via either ID or Name) and with attributes and values that specify its appearance and position. You use JavaScript to change those values in response to user events. Dynamic effects result from these scripted changes.

NOTE

As I write this, <LAYER> is a cornerstone of Netscape's Dynamic HTML. This may change, however, because the World Wide Web Consortium has rejected the <LAYER> tag.

One of the important differences between <DIV> and <LAYER> is that the <LAYER> tag doesn't work with inline style sheets. You can use inline style sheets to set styles for HTML elements that reside inside a layer, but you can't assign IDs to these elements and then script them. You can only script behaviors for the <LAYER> tag, and programmatically change only the attributes that the <LAYER> tag supports. This limits the type of scripting you can do, compared with the Microsoft version. To create similar effects from one browser to the other, you often have to exercise some ingenuity, as you'll see later in this chapter.

Default positioning presents another important difference. If you don't include values for TOP and LEFT, a <DIV> tag defaults to a position based on where it appears in the flow of the HTML document. A <LAYER> tag, on the other hand, defaults to a position 7 pixels from the left edge of the browser window and 7 pixels from the top. With multiple layers this can get messy, as they will all default to the same position.

Back to the Heading and the Horizontal Line

Now that you know about Netscape's <LAYER> tag, let's put the heading and the horizontal line into a layer. Remember, we start with <LAYER> and end with </LAYER>, and we have to provide positional information:

```
<LAYER Name = layerHeader Left = 10 Top = 10 z-index = 0
<Center>
<H1>Dynamic HTML: Master the Essentials</H1></Center>
<HR>
</LAYER>
```

Notice the Name attribute, and note also that we've provided a z-index value. This value, 0, puts the layer at the same level as the document. Higher numbers make the layer appear on top of the document; negative numbers make the layer appear below the document.

We added the z-index because we can't reference the heading and change its color with a script. Instead, we have to exercise the ingenuity I mentioned in the last section. To make the heading appear to change color, we'll create another heading, which resides in a layer just below this one; give the new heading a different color; make the layer invisible; and script a visibility swap. Here's the other heading and its enclosing layer:

```
<LAYER Name = layerUnderHeader Left = 10 Top = 10 z-index =
-1Visibility = "hide">
<Center>
<H1 Style = "color:'khaki'">Dynamic HTML: Master the
Essentials</H1></Center>
<HR>
</LAYER>
```

The z-index, -1, and the Visibility value, "hide", hint at the script that will appear to change the color of the page's heading.

NAVIGATOR, COLORS, AND CSS

I didn't use goldenrod for the new heading color this time, because Navigator renders it as darkish green when you specify this color in a CSS. Of course, Navigator renders khaki as darkish green in this context, too. As I pointed out before, Navigator—at least my release—is iffy when you specify colors in a CSS. If you use the code values instead of the names, you'll get the same result.

You can prove to yourself that Navigator understands the colors listed in the appendix, however. Within any of the <LAYER> tags that we create in this exercise, set the Bgcolor attribute equal to any of the color names in the appendix. You'll find them rendered very nicely as background colors when you open the file in Navigator. In fact, we'll use one of those colors when we set up our movable boxes. (Remember that we used Bgcolor as a substitute for Style = "background-color: 'Silver'" when we set the background color for the body of the page.)

The Hidden Message

As in the Internet Explorer version, we'll implement the large-font hidden message by putting it inside a paragraph, and we'll provide the styling specifications in an inline style sheet:

```
<P Style = "color:'green'; font-size:50px; font-weight:bold">
Topics in this book include
<UL Style = "color:'green'; font-size:50px; font-weight:bold">
```

```
<LI> Scripting
<LI> Cascading Style Sheets
<LI> Animation
<LI> ... And Many More!
</UL>
</P>
```

.You'll immediately see three differences between the Internet Explorer version and this one:

▸ In the Internet Explorer version, we didn't put a style sheet in the `<UL>` tag. In Internet Explorer, the `<UL>` tag inherited the `<P>` tag's style. In Navigator, it doesn't, although the `<LI>` elements do inherit the `<UL>`'s style.

▸ In Internet Explorer, we didn't put px after the font-size value. With no unit after the value, Internet Explorer defaults to px; Navigator does not. If you omit the unit name after the value, Navigator defaults to normal-sized font.

▸ Although Figure 18.4 isn't in color, you probably noticed that the color of the large-font message isn't white. As you can see from the style sheets, we've set it to green. Why? In the context of a style sheet, Navigator doesn't render white as a text color—it defaults to black. (This is consistent with the situation I described in the sidebar "Navigator, Colors, and CSS.") Later releases of Navigator 4.*x* will probably clear this up. If you like, you can use the `<FONT>` tag to set the text color to white, but I'd prefer that you became accustomed to working with style sheets rather than with deprecated elements.

Now let's put this message in a layer and give the layer a name, a position, a visibility, and a z-index. Precede the `<P>` tag with:

```
<LAYER ID = layerMessage Left=10 Top=10 Visibility = "hide"
z-index = -2 >
```

and follow the `</P>` tag with:

```
</LAYER>
```

The Message at the Center of the Page

The paragraph that holds the centered message is the same as the one in the Internet Explorer version, except that it has no ID. The `<LAYER>` tag that precedes it holds the position, width, and z-index specifications:

```
<LAYER NAME = layerLearn LEFT = 180 TOP = 200 Width = 210
z-index = 0>
```

```
<P Style="font-family:Cursive;font-weight:bold;
font-size:15pt">
Learn how to create striking effects on your Web pages.
</P>
</LAYER>
```

The Movable Boxes

The easiest way to implement the movable boxes is to create each one as a separate layer and position them appropriately. To make them appear as blue boxes, we set the (somewhat infamous) Bgcolor attribute to blue:

```
<LAYER NAME = layerBox1 Bgcolor = "blue" LEFT = 150 TOP = 180
Width = 120 Height = 60 z-index = 1>
</LAYER>

<LAYER NAME = layerBox2 Bgcolor = "blue" LEFT = 270 TOP = 180
Width = 120 Height = 60 z-index = 1>
</LAYER>

<LAYER NAME = layerBox3 Bgcolor = "blue" LEFT = 150 TOP = 240
Width = 120 Height = 60 z-index = 1>
</LAYER>

<LAYER NAME = layerBox4 Bgcolor = "blue" LEFT = 270 TOP = 240
Width = 120 Height = 60 z-index = 1>
</LAYER>
```

The Clickable Buttons

This version of our Web page has two buttons in the lower right corner. One is labeled Outward, and the other is labeled Inward. Clicking on the Outward button will move the boxes toward the corners, and clicking on the Inward button will return them to their original positions.

I put these buttons on the page because they support the onClick event. The <LAYER> tag does not support this event, so clicking on the heading would have no effect. Since I wanted a mouse-click to move the boxes, I added these buttons.

The buttons are examples of *form controls*, so named because they reside between <FORM> and </FORM> tags. You specify a button inside an <INPUT> tag by assigning the value button to the Type attribute. You label the button by assigning a string to the Value attribute:

```
<FORM>
<INPUT Type = button Value = "Outward">
```

```
<INPUT Type = button Value = "Inward">
</FORM>
```

We wrap the form in a layer so that we can position it within the page. Precede the <FORM> tag with:

```
<LAYER Left = 450 Top = 350>
```

and follow the </FORM> tag with </LAYER>.

Scripting the Dynamic Effects

Once again, we'll write scripts to make our Web page come alive. This time we'll write our scripts in JavaScript, the only scripting language Navigator supports.

In our Internet Explorer version, we put VBScript between <SCRIPT> and </SCRIPT> tags. In this version, we'll write our JavaScript inline (i.e., inside HTML tags). It's not necessary to do it this way—I'm just illustrating another way to add script. Both ways, tagged and inline, work in both browsers.

The Mouse Passes into and out of the Heading

We begin our inline scripting with the events associated with the heading. The heading, you'll remember, resides in a LAYER called layerHeader. Since we're concerned with the mouse moving into and out of the heading, we'll write script for the onMouseOver and onMouseOut events inside the <LAYER> tag for layerHeader.

When the mouse moves into the heading, we want to make the large-font message appear and have the heading's color change. We're making the heading seem to change colors by making layerHeader invisible and layerUnderHeader visible. This means that we'll want these settings:

```
layerMessage.visibility = "show"
layerHeader.visibility = "hide"
layerUnderHeader.visibility = "show"
```

To put these settings into inline JavaScript code, you write them inside a quoted string and separate them with semicolons. (Make sure you change the double quotes around the attribute values to single quotes.) Then you set this string as the value of onMouseOver and put the whole thing inside the <LAYER> tag:

```
<LAYER Name = layerHeader Left = 10 Top = 10 z-index = 0
onMouseOver = "layerMessage.visibility = 'show';
        layerHeader.visibility = 'hide';
        layerUnderHeader.visibility = 'show'"
```

Part iii

Don't add the closing angle bracket yet, because you still have to add the code for onMouseOut, which returns the settings to their starting values:

```
onMouseOut = "layerMessage.visibility = 'hide';
        layerUnderHeader.visibility = 'hide'
        layerHeader.visibility = 'show'" >
```

Note the closing angle bracket, indicating that we've finished scripting the behaviors for this layer.

WARNING

JavaScript is case-sensitive, so don't even think about beginning visibility with an uppercase V.

Mouse-Clicks Occur on the Response Buttons

We finish by scripting behaviors for the onClick event in the tags that define the on-screen response buttons. When we click the button labeled Outward, we want the boxes to move outward, and when we click the button labeled Inward, we want the boxes to move back into their starting positions.

Fortunately, JavaScript layers have built-in *methods* that will handle these effects for us. (Think of a method as a procedure that the layer knows how to follow.) The first method, offset, is something like the MoveElementBy subroutine we wrote. It takes two arguments—the distance to move the layer in the horizontal direction and the distance to move it in the vertical direction. Here's the code to write inside the first response button's <INPUT> tag:

```
<INPUT Type = button Value = "Outward"
  onClick = "layerBox1.offset(-20,-20);
        layerBox2.offset(20,-20);
        layerBox3.offset(-20,20);
        layerBox4.offset(20,20);">
```

The second built-in method is called moveTo. As its name suggests, moveTo moves a layer to a location specified by the method's two arguments:

```
<INPUT Type = button Value = "Inward"
  onClick = "layerBox1.moveTo(150,180);
        layerBox2.moveTo(270,180);
        layerBox3.moveTo(150,240);
        layerBox4.moveTo(270,240);">
```

The Whole File

Here's the entire First Dynamic Nav.htm listing:

Listing 18.2   First Dynamic Nav.htm

```
<HTML>
<HEAD>
</HEAD>
<TITLE>My First Dynamic HTML Page</TITLE>
<BODY Bgcolor = "Silver">
<LAYER Name = layerHeader Left = 10 Top = 10 z-index = 0
onMouseOver = "layerMessage.visibility = 'show';
               layerHeader.visibility = 'hide';
               layerUnderHeader.visibility = 'show'"

onMouseOut = "layerMessage.visibility = 'hide';
              layerUnderHeader.visibility = 'hide'
              layerHeader.visibility = 'show'" >
<Center>
<H1>Dynamic HTML: Master the Essentials</H1></Center>
<HR>
</LAYER>

<LAYER Name = layerUnderHeader Left = 10 Top = 10 z-index =
-1 Visibility = "hide">
<Center>
<H1 Style = "color:'khaki'">Dynamic HTML: Master the
Essentials</H1></Center>
<HR>
</LAYER>
<Layer ID = layerMessage Left=10 Top=10
Visibility = "hide" z-index = -2 >

<P Style = "color:'green'; font-size:50px;
font-weight:bold">Topics in this book include
<UL Style = "color:'green'; font-size:50px;
font-weight:bold">
<LI> Scripting
<LI> Cascading Style Sheets
<LI> Animation
<LI> ... And Many More!
</UL>
</P>
</LAYER>

<LAYER NAME = layerLearn LEFT = 180 TOP = 200 Width = 210
z-index = 0>
```

```
<P Style="font-family:Cursive;font-weight:bold;
font-size:15pt">
Learn how to create striking effects on your Web pages.
</P>
</LAYER>

<LAYER NAME = layerBox1 Bgcolor = "blue" LEFT = 150 TOP = 180
Width = 120 Height = 60 z-index = 1>
</LAYER>

<LAYER NAME = layerBox2 Bgcolor = "blue" LEFT = 270 TOP = 180
Width = 120 Height = 60 z-index = 1>
</LAYER>

<LAYER NAME = layerBox3 Bgcolor = "blue" LEFT = 150 TOP = 240
Width = 120 Height = 60 z-index = 1>
</LAYER>

<LAYER NAME = layerBox4 Bgcolor = "blue" LEFT = 270 TOP = 240
Width = 120 Height = 60 z-index = 1>
</LAYER>

<LAYER Left = 450 Top = 350>
<FORM>
<INPUT Type = button Value = "Outward"
   onClick = "layerBox1.offset(-20,-20);
          layerBox2.offset(20,-20);
          layerBox3.offset(-20,20);
          layerBox4.offset(20,20);">

<INPUT Type = button Value = "Inward"
   onClick = "layerBox1.moveTo(150,180);
          layerBox2.moveTo(270,180);
          layerBox3.moveTo(150,240);
          layerBox4.moveTo(270,240);">

</FORM>
</LAYER>
</BODY>
</HTML>
```

Open this file in Navigator to see the scripted effects. Mousing over the heading will make the heading's color appear to change and will display the hidden message. Moving the mouse out of the header will return the heading color to its starting value. Clicking the Outward button will make the box in the middle split apart, and the resulting four boxes will move toward the four corners of the Web page. Clicking the Inward button will immediately move all the boxes back to the center.

WHAT'S NEXT?

You now have an idea of what you can achieve with DHTML and its combination of HTML, cascading style sheets, and scripting. You also have a feel for the similarities and differences between the dueling DHTMLs from Microsoft and Netscape. In Part IV, you'll move beyond HTML to learn about some of the programming languages that will help you develop advanced content. Leading the way in Chapter 19 is Erik Strom, who will introduce you to Perl and the Common Gateway Interface (CGI).

Part iii

PART iV

BEYOND HTML

Chapter 19

INTRODUCING PERL AND CGI

The Internet has become—perhaps arguably—the most important communication medium in the world. There is virtually no argument, however, about the World Wide Web. It is the Internet's most important channel of communication. If you want to deal with the Net, pretty soon you'll have to deal with the Web.

Adapted from *Perl CGI Programming: No experience required,* by Erik Strom

ISBN 0-7821-2157-8   448 pages $29.99

You'll learn about one of the most important aspects of the Web in this chapter. The *Common Gateway Interface* (CGI) and applications written in the Perl programming language give you the tools to create dynamic, informative Web pages, with which you can fashion a Web site that your visitors will find truly useful and worth revisiting.

A good Web site is not just a collection of pretty pictures. It has to *do* something. With Perl and CGI, you can make it do just that.

WHY PERL?

A Web page is a text document that is formatted with a set of commands—a programming language, if you will—called the *Hypertext Markup Language*, or HTML. The name is descriptive: HTML is a "markup" language; that is, it controls the way a document looks. HTML instructions tell a Web browser, such as Netscape's Navigator or Microsoft's Internet Explorer, how it should go about displaying the page on screen. But HTML by itself has practically no facilities for making a Web page do things. You have to rely on other means for that.

The Perl programming language is hands-down the most popular method of making a Web page "do" something, mainly because Perl is freely available and will run on every computer platform that can host a Web server. Coupled with the Common Gateway Interface (CGI), Perl is used on the vast majority of Web sites to create Web pages that have to do more than sit there and look pretty.

There are a couple of other tools you can use to create a dynamic Web page:

- Java
- Proprietary languages

The following sections will look at each of them.

Java

Java, which was originally invented by Sun Microsystems to control toasters, is a popular and highly touted method for making interactive Web pages these days. As a programming language, Java is a very rich resource, one that will allow you to do almost anything you desire with your page. However, different Web browsers support Java to varying degrees, so by including an *applet* written in that language in your page, you run the risk of excluding some visitors.

TIP

An *applet* in Java is a program that is run by the Web browser, if the browser is capable of running it (many Web browsers aren't).

To work properly, Java depends on the browser software that your visitors use. If the browser supports Java, your applets work. If not, and you are a kind Webmaster, your visitors will get a message telling them essentially to buy another browser. If you are unkind, they will get either a blank screen or some wonderfully obscure HTTP error message that, if nothing else, will ensure that they never return to your Web page again.

Proprietary Languages

Along the same lines as Java are the proprietary packages, notably Visual Basic Script (VBScript) from Microsoft and Netscape's JavaScript.

TIP

Proprietary software packages usually target a specific hardware and/or software platform. They won't work with everything.

VBScript is, of course, based on Visual Basic, Microsoft's heavily Windows-laden version of the BASIC programming language. JavaScript is an *interpreted* flavor of Java, which means that the Web browser interprets and executes each line in the script. While the intent of both—essentially extending HTML to make the Web page itself more dynamic—probably is laudable, neither will run on any but the newer browsers from both companies, because the older browsers were written before these tools existed.

They're slick, yes. By taking advantage of a specific platform, the proprietary tools can run faster and do more than a generic package that is intended to run on *all* platforms. But they don't allow you to accommodate every visitor to your site because not all visitors will have the hardware or software that the proprietary tools target (see Figure 19.1). Not all visitors will be using Intel-based PCs, nor will all visitors be running a version of Navigator or Internet Explorer, or Windows 95/98 or NT/2000.

Some visitors may not even be able to display graphics. But *all* of them need to be considered when you set up a site.

NOTE

The proprietary methods extend HTML by creating programs that run on a visitor's computer, rather than at your site on your Web server. As a result, they depend totally on the computer and software the visitor is using.

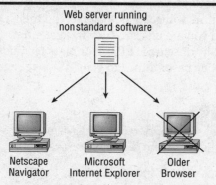

FIGURE 19.1: Proprietary languages can exclude some visitors from your Web site.

CGI

Long before Java, there was the Common Gateway Interface, or CGI for short. CGI is the most common method for passing information from an HTML document to a program that can process the information. CGI doesn't care what browser you're using; even nongraphical Lynx-type software will work.

Unlike Java and its more proprietary cousins, CGI is not a programming language, nor does it load itself onto the visitor's machine to run. CGI is, as its name spells out, an interface, a set of rules. It resides on the Web-server computer, providing a way for the page to communicate in a rough fashion with the server. CGI allows you to write programs to deal with the page in *any* language—including Perl.

Perl's Ancient History

There is only one reason that Perl programs—or *scripts*, which is a lexical convention that will be explained shortly—are so universal in World Wide Web programming. The simple fact of the matter is, until the last few years, virtually every Web server in existence was running on a Unix system, and Perl is among the most useful of Unix tools.

The first *Hypertext Transfer Protocol* (HTTP) servers were written for Unix, too, and freely distributed among system administrators who wanted to try out the Web. CGI was developed as a standard of communication on these systems. In a sense, Perl, HTTP, and CGI *all* became standards for doing Web work (see Figure 19.2).

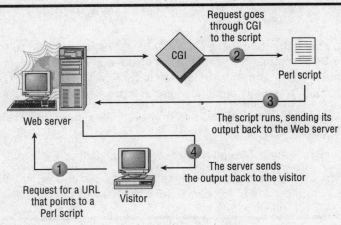

FIGURE 19.2: The HTTP-CGI-Perl connection

The beauty of standards is that they usually transcend the platforms on which they originated. The number of non-Unix Web servers and Web sites on the Internet increases every day. Yet the HTTP-CGI-Perl connection remains the same because it was lifted intact into the newer platforms.

Unix is, in a very large sense, an operating system written by and, most importantly, *for* programmers. It really was never intended for humans to use easily, which is why so many people have gone to such extraordinary lengths to make Unix more friendly, with X Windows and various other graphical interfaces. These interfaces require tremendous amounts of processing power, so in many cases system designers have simply given up and relegated bare-bones Unix to the background, running it on the system server and hanging Macintoshes or other workstations running Windows on the network for users.

The beauty of Unix, for those who have taken the time to learn it, is in the rich set of software tools that it provides. Unadorned Unix is like a box of wonderful Swiss Army knives; with any one of them, you can carve any masterpiece your imagination can conjure.

Perl is one of the most useful of those Swiss Army knives.

THE UNIX TOOLBOX

Consider some of the more obscure tools you can pull out of Unix:

grep   Allows you to search through files, directories, or entire disks for words or phrases.

sh, csh, ksh   Some of the Unix "shells," which are akin to the MS-DOS command line but are considerably more powerful. Shell scripts are like DOS batch files with turbochargers attached. You really don't need another programming language.

ed, sed, vi   The Unix editors that everyone hates...and everyone uses.

whereis   Finds files anywhere; actually a shell script.

man   Calls up the manual pages for programs and other utilities, often serving to further confuse the hapless user.

We Owe It All to Larry Wall: A History of Perl

Larry Wall is a linguist-turned-programmer who, as of this writing, is an associate at O'Reilly & Associates, a technical publishing company. Legend has it that he began working on Perl nearly 10 years ago while attempting a sticky project for Unisys.

NOTE

The Perl language grew out of the classic Unix philosophy: if the system doesn't allow you to do your job easily, then you simply write another tool to solve the problem.

Perl actually is an acronym whose most accepted expanded version is *Practical Extraction and Report Language*, though Unix wags have come up with many more earthy descriptions, such as "Pathologically Eclectic Rubbish Lister." It was derived in large part from sed and awk, jackhammers of the Unix toolbox for those who understand them, utterly unintelligible command programs for those who don't. After all, what can one say about a program whose most famous error message is awk: bailing out near Line 1?

The strengths of sed and awk, and their offspring Perl, lie mainly in their built-in capabilities for processing text through pattern-matching, searching for and replacing phrases—or "strings"—in entire groups of files, and using Unix's obscure yet extremely powerful regular expressions.

REGULAR EXPRESSIONS: BANE AND BOON

Regular expressions are among the most useful—and most difficult to master—tools in the Unix array.

You can think of them as supercharged search-and/or-replace operations. While most any text editor will let you find phrases and replace them with other phrases throughout a file, regular expressions add a great deal of power to the operation. For example, you can use regular expressions to look for strings at the beginning or end of a line, or in a word, or for a specific number of occurrences.

But it's not easy. A Perl regular expression that swaps the first two words in a line of text looks like this:

```
s/^([^ ]*) *([^ ]*)/$2 $1/;
```

Doesn't make much sense, does it? But that could be a very useful operation, couldn't it? Let's just say that you will find many uses for them.

The bedrock of Unix is the C programming language—most of it is written in C. But C, in its position at the foundation of the operating system, adheres to the minimalist philosophy of Unix, which means that you often have to write scads of C code to accomplish relatively simple tasks. A trivial search-and-replace operation on a text file, written in C, requires the programmer at least to scan the file character by character and could easily grow from a simple subroutine into an entire application (see Figure 19.3).

But the same operation can be accomplished in a few lines of Perl code (see Figure 19.4).

TIP

Perl is a challenge to learn, but it is infinitely more efficient for the programmer (read: "fewer lines of code") and easier to use than C.

```
WebPage - [C:\usr\erik\PERL-CGI\ADDGUEST.CPP]                          _ □ ×
File  Edit  Search  Window  Help                                        _ 8 ×

    ZeroMemory (&GuestEntry, sizeof (GUEST_ENTRY));    // Hose out the structure.

    char*   INFO_ARRAY [] =
    {
        GuestEntry.FirstName,
        GuestEntry.LastName,
        GuestEntry.City,
        GuestEntry.State,
        GuestEntry.Country,
        GuestEntry.EMail,
        GuestEntry.Comments,
        NULL
    };

    char*   o;                      // Couple of pointers for string manipulation.
    char*   p = buf;
    int     n = 0;                  // Counter.

    while ((o = strchr (p, '&')) != NULL)
        {
        *o = NULL;                  // End the substring here.
        strcpy (INFO_ARRAY [n++], p);   // Copy the data into the correct spot.
        p = ++o;                    // Get the next one.
        }
```

FIGURE 19.3: An example of code written in C++

Unix programmers snapped up Perl as a tool of choice almost immediately for tasks ranging from "quick and dirty" to horribly complex. Because you have the ability to call most of the standard Unix system services from a Perl script, including the internetworking functions, you probably could write an entire operating system in it. It would be very slow, but it would run a computer.

To this day, almost every serious Unix systems programmer works with Perl almost daily. It's just too useful for programmers to ignore.

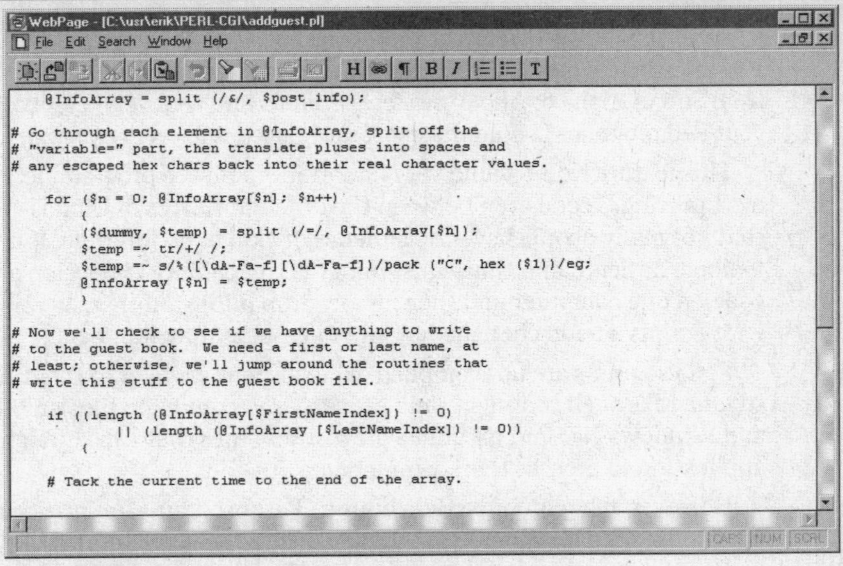
WebPage - [C:\usr\erik\PERL-CGI\addguest.pl]
File Edit Search Window Help
@InfoArray = split (/&/, $post_info);
# Go through each element in @InfoArray, split off the
# "variable=" part, then translate pluses into spaces and
# any escaped hex chars back into their real character values.
for ($n = 0; @InfoArray[$n]; $n++)
{
($dummy, $temp) = split (/=/, @InfoArray[$n]);
$temp =~ tr/+/ /;
$temp =~ s/%([\dA-Fa-f][\dA-Fa-f])/pack ("C", hex ($1))/eg;
@InfoArray [$n] = $temp;
}
# Now we'll check to see if we have anything to write
# to the guest book. We need a first or last name, at
# least; otherwise, we'll jump around the routines that
# write this stuff to the guest book file.
if ((length (@InfoArray[$FirstNameIndex]) != 0)
|| (length (@InfoArray [$LastNameIndex]) != 0))
{
# Tack the current time to the end of the array.
CAPS NUM SCRL

FIGURE 19.4: An example of code written in Perl

Perl and the World Wide Web

Perl has become popular for Web work because in most of its incarnations it is an *interpreted* language, like the first versions of BASIC, rather than a *compiled* language, such as C or C++. However, this isn't strictly true, because Perl compilers are available from many sources, just as there are many C interpreters to be had. The essential difference between a compiled application and an interpreted one is that a compiled program has been translated into the machine language of the computer on which it will run by another program called a *compiler*. The translated, or compiled, file will run all by itself. An *interpreted* program, on the other hand, is actually translated and run on-the-fly by a program called an *interpreter*.

Because they consist of machine-language instructions, compiled programs generally run faster. But for the same reason, they are not portable from one computer platform to another. Code compiled for a Sun box or a Macintosh won't run on an Intel-based PC because the different processors that power these machines all speak radically different tongues. Your program would have to be recompiled for the target machine before it would work. It may even have to be rewritten.

There are no such restrictions on interpreted Perl code. All you need is some version of the Perl interpreter—called *perl*—on the target computer. Perl interpreters have been written for every popular computer platform, from Sun to Alpha to Apple to Intel and more, and with very few exceptions your Perl programs should transport unchanged into every environment.

This feature won't sound very important to novice programmers. However, porting C code even between the different flavors of Unix is an art that not many people have the patience or skill to do full time. It is tedious, difficult, and time-consuming. The capability to develop and test code on one computer and then simply drop it into another, as you can with Perl, is a boon cherished by all professional programmers.

Perl programs are not compiled, which is why we refer to them as *scripts*. Like shell scripts in Unix or batch and command files on MS-DOS and Windows NT, Perl programs are just text files that run through an application to process their commands.

However, make no mistake about it: Perl programs are just that—programs, with all the power and versatility the word implies. If you've never written a line of code in your life, Perl will forever spoil you against the more traditional programming languages. If you are a programmer but this is your introduction to Perl, you will find yourself using it more and more as your familiarity with it increases, because it makes things so *easy*.

For the nuts and bolts of Web site processing, administration, and maintenance, tedious system chores that should *always* be hidden from users, and the creation of truly dynamic Web pages, Perl can't be beat.

BUILDING A PERL SCRIPT

Now that you have a little background, you're going to write your first Perl program. It's a simple example that gives you the basic idea of how a Perl script is written and run. All of our subsequent examples will build on this one.

"Hello World" probably seems kind of dumb, but those of us who have been programming for a while have a soft spot for this snippet of code. It's the first programming example given in the monumental *C Programming Language,* by Brian Kernighan and Dennis Ritchie, which was published in 1976. Many programmers cut their teeth on this work; forgive us, please, if we remember it fondly.

USING EXISTING PERL SCRIPTS

Perl scripts are simply text files that you can create using your favorite text editor. Perl is the language of choice for Web developers these days because of its ease of use on Unix machines. Its popularity also has other benefits: for one thing, a huge body of existing code out there in the ether. Most of it is free, which means you can simply drop it into your Web server and run it, regardless of the operating system that powers your computer. Most of that code was written, tested, and debugged by Unix programmers who had their own Web sites to maintain. You can find lots of stuff in Usenet—go to comp.lang.perl. Or try one of the Web search engines such as Yahoo!.

So it makes sense for you to be running Perl on your Web site, if only from the standpoint of the effort you want to put into writing software. If you have a task to perform and someone else has already written the code to perform it—and has no compunction at all about you using it—then why shouldn't you avoid reinventing wheels?

First Things First: Perls before Code

You can't do anything without the Perl language interpreter. Make sure you have a copy of it before you go further or you'll get snotty error messages from whatever operating system you're using.

TIP

You can get Perl for Win32—Windows NT and Windows 95/98—by pointing your Web browser to http://www.ActiveState.com/. Unix sources for Perl are numerous and ever-changing; the best way to find them is in the Internet newsgroups at comp.sources.unix. MacPERL for the Macintosh is available at http://www.iis.ee.ethz.ch/~neeri/macintosh/perl.html.

I'll make very few assumptions about the computer you are using or the operating system that it runs. However, most of the really good Perls that can be obtained are intended to run on Windows NT/2000 and Windows 95/98 or Unix, and most of our examples will emphasize those two platforms.

Installing the Perl interpreter can be as simple as running a setup program or as complicated as extracting the source code and compiling it yourself.

Fortunately, Perl is included in many Unix distributions these days. If that's the case on your system, obviously you don't have to do anything. The Perl executable for NT/2000 and Windows 95/98 can be downloaded for free from Microsoft's Web site and several others. It performs flawlessly.

COMPILING YOUR OWN PERL INTERPRETER...

Compiling the Perl source code yourself is the method preferred by Unix system administrators, who usually have a rather macho attitude about such things. Because the most freely available C code for Perl was written primarily for Unix systems, it compiles easily most of the time.

Likewise, compiling the code for Windows NT/2000 and Windows 95/98 is possible, but only for the most daring of systems gurus; the process certainly is beyond the scope of this book. Both of the latest versions of the most popular C/C++ development packages available for Windows—Visual C++ from Microsoft and Borland C++ for Windows from Borland International—contain quirks that prevent a straightforward compilation of the Perl source code. Unless you want to change the functionality of Perl (which is an exercise of dubious logical value in itself) and devote hours to debugging someone else's code, you're much better off simply using whatever executable files you can find for the operating system you're using.

Loading the Interpreter

Regardless of your operating system, once you have the Perl interpreter, you're ready to go. On Unix, things will be a little easier if you put the Perl interpreter in a subdirectory that is included in your PATH environment string, which is a system variable that maps out where the operating system should look when you type the name of a program at the command line. In other words, if you have loaded PATH by typing **PATH=/usr/bin;/usr/me;/pub/local/etc** at the command line and you then enter **perl**, the operating system will look in each of those directories for Perl before it gives up and complains to you that the command couldn't be found. The same is true in Windows NT/2000 and Windows 95/98.

TIP

The setup program for the Win32 Perl at www.activeware.com will ask you if you want Perl to be added to your PATH. If you answer affirmatively, the change will take place the next time you restart your computer.

As we discussed earlier, Perl scripts are simple text files that you can create using your favorite text editor. To put together your first Perl program, start that text editor now and enter the following lines:

```
#!/usr/bin/perl

print "Hello World!", "\n";

#      End hello.pl
```

NOTE

The first line in the program begins with Perl's "comment" character (#), which will be ignored by the interpreter. However, it must contain the path to your Perl interpreter. If your system's Perl interpreter is not in /usr/bin, change the path to the correct subdirectory.

That's fairly easy, isn't it? We'll explain what's going on in the next section; for now, save the file as hello.pl ("hello.pl" in quotes if you're using Notepad on Windows 95/98 or NT/2000), and close your text editor.

Running the "Hello" Example

The hello.pl is about as tiny as programs get, both in the writing and in the execution. It is intended to be run from the *command line*, which means the shell in Unix, the console command processor in Windows NT/2000, or cmd.exe or command.com in Windows 95/98.

TIP

To avoid the confusion of having to refer to both operating system methods when the term *command line* is used, we'll henceforth refer to the Unix shell and the NT/2000/95/98 console as the command line. Also, because Perl adheres to the Unix convention of specifying path names with the forward slash (/) rather than Microsoft's backslash (\), we will adhere to it, too, in the text of our examples. Remember the difference when you're typing commands in the NT console.

Open a command-line window (a shell in Unix, a command console or MS-DOS window in Windows 95/98 and NT/2000). Because Perl is an interpreted language, you won't be running your first Perl program directly. You have to run `perl` with your Perl program as an argument to it. If, when you installed the Perl software on your system, you put it somewhere in your PATH, then you can simply type:

```
perl hello.pl
```

Otherwise you'll have to type in the full path to `perl` followed by the name of your program. For example, if you installed Perl in /myprogs/ perl, and that subdirectory is not in your PATH environment variable, you would have to type:

```
/myprogs/perl hello.pl
```

In any event, when you run the program, the result should look something like Figure 19.5.

Notice that the program prints "Hello World!" with a line-ender to the screen.

Congratulations! You are now a Perl programmer.

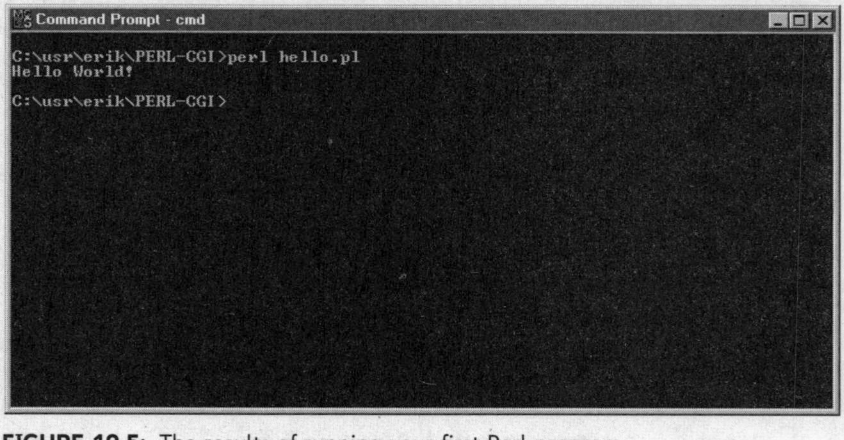

FIGURE 19.5: The results of running your first Perl program

How Perl Programs Run

In a technical sense, the Perl interpreter is a language compiler that doesn't write its translated output to a file on the disk. Its "output file" is the screen, which is called *standard output,* or *stdout,* in systems parlance.

If a program name is given on the command line, the interpreter first checks the validity of each line, dumping out error messages for incorrect code and stopping if it finds any. If your program passes muster, the interpreter executes each of its lines of code.

One of the convenient aspects of doing it this way is that you find out immediately if your program does something wrong—and programs inevitably do! Most developers work on "windowed" systems, and they run the text editor with their Perl program code in one window and keep the command-line screen in another (see Figure 19.6). It is then quite easy to pop from window to window, writing and fixing code in the text editor and testing the code from the command line. With Perl, you get all your errors at once, and that speeds up the coding process. With a compiled language such as C or C++, you have to write the code, compile it, fix any errors that have cropped up in the compilation, compile it again, link it to the external libraries it needs, then—*whew!*—run it and see what errors occur there. Then you get to start all over again. It's little wonder that Perl has become so popular!

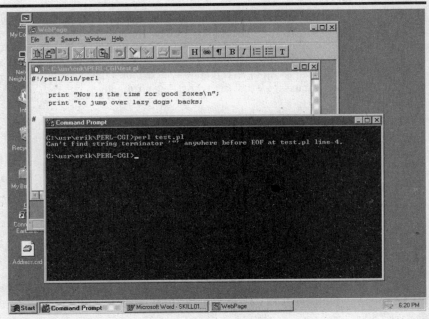

FIGURE 19.6: The two-window debugging process

Dissecting the "Hello" Example

We have briefly covered the first line in the program. We'll now take apart this line, `#!/usr/bin/perl`, piece by piece:

 # (pound sign)   This is Perl's "comment" character, which means that anything following it up to the end of the line is ignored by the interpreter. This is where you can document your program so that others (or *you* after you haven't touched the program in a few months!) can understand what is being accomplished in the code.

! (exclamation point)   This *first* comment line is a special case. Unix aficionados will read to the exclamation point (!) and recognize it as an instruction to the shell—a command for the command line. Strictly speaking, this tells the shell to run the Perl interpreter with the program code as its input.

NOTE

The first line is required, and it should always contain the full path to your Perl interpreter, which may or may not be in /usr/bin. I used /usr/bin as an example because it is a common place to put it. Oddly, though there is no direct way under Windows 95/98 or NT/2000 to run a command with the ! character, the Win32 Perl interpreter requires you to follow this convention. You will get an error message if the path is specified incorrectly.

The Heart of the Program: print

We have used only one real Perl function in this short program—`print`. This function is a real workhorse, especially in Web programming, where you will use Perl to construct HTML pages. You very likely will use `print` in every program you write.

How does `print` work? We'll go into a detailed description later, because `print` can do a lot. For now, let's look at what it does in `hello.pl`:

```
print "Hello World!", "\n";
```

The unadorned `print`, as we have used it in the example program, takes a list of *strings*—that is, text enclosed by quotation marks—as its *arguments,* or *parameters.*

TIP

The terms *argument* and *parameter* will be used interchangeably in reference to the data you will use with Perl functions.

In this case, we are telling `print` that we want it to "print" the phrases "Hello World!" and "\n" to the screen. Notice that the two phrases, which are the `print` function's arguments, are separated by a comma. It is also important that the line ends with a semicolon. *All* code lines in Perl must end with the semicolon; the interpreter will complain bitterly if you forget to do this, and it's usually the first thing you will do wrong. Be forewarned!

WARNING

All code lines in Perl must end in a semicolon. Why? The interpreter can't decide for itself where a code statement ends, because it may extend for more than one line. The semicolon tells the interpreter, "This statement ends here."

The Strange \n

"Hello World!" is easy enough to figure out, but what is this \n? C-language programmers and others who are, by necessity, familiar with Unix conventions know this as the *newline* character. If you've never seen this before, remember carefully the backslash (\) that precedes the n. This is called an *escape* character because it gives a special meaning to the character that follows it. The \n specifically refers to the linefeed character, with a value of 10 in the ASCII character set.

The linefeed is the standard line-ender in Unix; the MS-DOS convention, which has been retained by Windows 95/98 and NT/2000, is to end each line with a carriage return *and* a linefeed, which in a Perl `print` command would be set up as \r\n. However, the Perl interpreter knows what operating system it's running on and makes certain allowances for these differences. For now, whether you compose your code on Unix or Windows NT, you can use the simple \n as a line-ender.

Table 19.1 lists some other Perl "escaped" characters.

NOTE

Table 19.1 doesn't list all of the Perl special "escaped" characters. These are just the most common.

Part IV

TABLE 19.1: Some of the Perl Special Characters

CHARACTER STRING	DOES THIS
\n	Newline or linefeed
\r	Carriage return
\t	Tab
\f	Formfeed
\b	Backspace
\033	ASCII 27 (Escape) in octal
\x1B	Same in hexadecimal
\cD	Control-D
\\	Backslash
\"	Double quote
\'	Single quote
\u	Uppercase next character
\U	Uppercase following characters
\l, \L	Same as above, but lowercase
\E	End \U or \L

The escaped double quote (\") can be somewhat confusing. It is used when you want to actually use the double-quote character in a string, rather than use it to *delimit* the string. For example, the Perl code:

```
print "Hello World!", "\n";
print "\"", "Hello World!","\"", "\n";
```

would result in the following output to the screen:

```
Hello World!
"Hello World!"
```

Perl also allows a construct to keep you from loading up your strings with backslashes. You may use q/STRING/ and qq/STRING/ too, where STRING is the phrase enclosed between the slashes.

Goodbye to "Hello"

We have done just about all we can with this first version of "Hello World!" You should now be familiar with Perl comment lines, with emphasis on the important first line, which actually is an instruction. Additionally, you've gained a passing acquaintance with the workhorse print function and some of the things that you can do with it.

The results of running the new version of the script are illustrated in Figure 19.7.

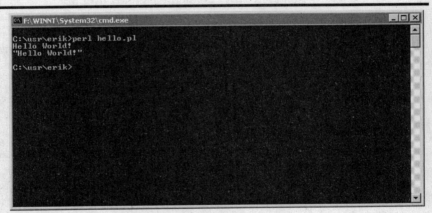

FIGURE 19.7: The new results of running hello.pl

There's one more line in the program, however, and we shouldn't move on without explaining it:

```
#           End hello.pl
```

This is a comment line, as you have learned, but why? Obviously, it's the end of the program because there's no more program after it.

Yes, it *is* quite obvious in a tiny snippet of code such as we've typed into hello.pl. However, other programs will be much more complicated and much larger, and it won't be as clear where one subroutine starts or another ends.

It is simply good programming practice to document your code well, not just for others but for your own benefit. And good documentation starts with clearly marking the beginning and end of important sections of code.

Variables, Scalars, and Lists in Perl

The code we've written so far is simple. Let's make it a bit more complicated—and therefore useful—by introducing three new concepts:

Variable   Data stored in specific memory location

Scalar   A single variable that defines either numeric or string (character) data

List   A number of scalars stored sequentially in one variable

Perl Variables: What's in a Name

The capability to store data in locations that have specific names lies at the heart of any useful programming language. Moving data to a specific spot in memory and being able to recall them by name (or location) at a later time is known as working with *variables*. Perl is no different in this respect.

If you have done any programming at all, you will be familiar with the concept of variables. However, the conventions used in Perl can be a little weird for the uninitiated, so if you're thinking of skipping this section, please don't!

Storing data in a variable is as straightforward as picking a name and setting it equal to a value. Complex programming languages, such as C, have lots of complex rules for what types of data can be stored where; in C, for example, integers have to go into `int` variables and strings of characters are stored as `char` arrays. Variables have to be declared and given types before they can be used.

Perl, despite all that it owes to C, plays very fast and loose with those rules. In Perl, you declare a variable merely by using it, which helps to make the Perl development process somewhat quicker and easier than programming in C.

WARNING

The rules of good, structured programming apply to Perl as they do to any other language: make your Perl code readable by using lots of comments. Just because a language allows a fast and loose form of variable declaration is no excuse for writing "spaghetti code."

Introducing Scalars

The most fundamental data in Perl are called *scalars*. The word can be intimidating to beginners because its meaning is not immediately apparent. A scalar is nothing more than a single piece of data. Scalars differ from another fundamental Perl data type, the *list* (defined in the "Perl Lists" section below).

Perl regards numeric *and* string data as scalar values, and in most cases it's pretty good at telling the difference between the two and acting properly.

NOTE

In most programming languages, "strings" are simply strings of characters. "Now is the time for all good folks to come to the aid of their party" is a string. Notice that it is enclosed in quotes. This is important in Perl.

The important thing to remember about scalar variables is that they always begin with a dollar sign ($). You can call them anything you want—just never forget the dollar sign.

WARNING

Perl is a case-sensitive language, which means that it distinguishes between uppercase and lowercase letters in names. Thus, it will regard $VariableName and $variablename as two different scalar variables.

We can create a second version of hello.pl to illustrate the concept of storing data in scalar variables. Type the following lines into your text editor and save the file as hello2.pl:

```perl
#!/usr/bin/perl

# hello2, a slightly more sophisticated "Hello World"

$Hello = "Hello, World";   # String variable
$TimeAround = 2;           # Numeric variable

print $Hello, " for the ", $TimeAround, "nd time!", "\n";

#    End hello2.pl
```

Now run the program as we ran the one we created earlier. You'll see this on your screen (see Figure 19.8):

```
Hello, World for the 2nd time!
```

Part iv

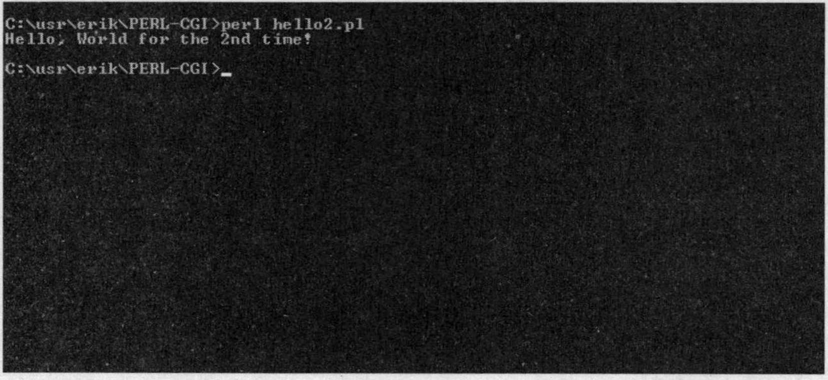

```
C:\usr\erik\PERL-CGI>perl hello2.pl
Hello, World for the 2nd time!
C:\usr\erik\PERL-CGI>_
```

FIGURE 19.8: Using variables in your Perl script

You were able to set the two variables, $Hello and $TimeAround, to two entirely unrelated types, yet the print function knew precisely what to do with them and assembled the resulting output string flawlessly. The print function is even smarter than we've made it appear here; the line could have been written to include the variables in one long string argument, such as the following:

```
print "$Hello for the ${TimeAround}nd time!";
```

The important thing to note here is that TimeAround was enclosed in curly braces to set it off from the nd. But you can see that print has no trouble culling the variables from the other parts of the string and behaving properly.

This "shorthand" capability is one of Perl's great strengths, as you will see when you begin working with more complicated programs. However, brevity in code is not necessarily an ideal to strive for, unless it directly leads to more efficient code. Writing a program that is clear and understandable is much more important.

Perl Lists

You have learned so far that scalar variables handle and store individual pieces of data. But what if you have a collection of related data? It would be convenient to store *all* of them in a variable, wouldn't it?

Perl lists are intended to do just that. Lists are similar to arrays in many other programming languages, where the variable name defines a starting point, index 0, and the members are stored consecutively. You just increase the index and add it to the starting point to arrive at the array member you want.

NOTE

A Perl *list* is the equivalent of an *array* in Visual Basic, C++, and many other languages. The terms will be used interchangeably.

The C language requires that all members of the array are of the same *type*, which really only means that they are all the same size. Perl doesn't care about type at all. Any old thing can go into a list—strings, numbers, characters, anything—and they all happily coexist.

What's in a List?

List notation in Perl is as specific as scalar notation. List names begin with the @ character; after that, you can call them anything you want.

Setting a list equal to something, or loading it with data, is a bit more complex, but we can make it understandable with a few examples.

An array of numbers would be set up like this:

```
@Numbers = (1, 2, 3, 4, 5, 6);
```

We now have an array of six consecutive numbers called @Numbers. In Perl, as in many other languages, arrays start at position 0, so if we were to set a scalar variable to the value of the first member of @Numbers:

```
$OneNumber = $Numbers[0];
```

$OneNumber would be equal to 1.

Notice that the notation changed a little in the last line: we referred to the first element of @Numbers with a dollar sign in front of it. But isn't that how we note a *scalar* value?

Yes, it is. And the notation is correct because just one member of a list *is* a scalar, so you must use the dollar sign in front of it. The *subscript,* which is the part of $Numbers[0] enclosed in brackets, is where you tell Perl which member of the array you want.

STREAMLINED PERL...

Here's a handy Perl shortcut. Because the members of the array are consecutive numbers, you could have initialized it like this:

```
@Numbers = (1..6);
```

It's the same as specifying each of the numbers from 1 to 6, as far as Perl is concerned.

Lists of Strings

When you load strings into an array, they need to be distinguished somehow. The Perl convention departs slightly from what we have learned so far, which is to enclose strings of characters in double quotes. This can be done with lists, but it is considered more correct to delimit lists of strings with single quotes (' ').

Table 19.2 illustrates some of the things you can do with strings.

TABLE 19.2: Perl List Examples

INITIALIZATION	COMMENT
@list = (4..8);	same as @list = (4,5,6,7,8)
@list1 = ('red', 'green', 'blue');	array of colors
@list2 = (1, 'yellow', @list1);	same as @list2 = (1, 'yellow', 'red', 'green', 'blue');
@list3 = ();	null (empty) list
@list4 = (0,1, @list3, 3);	same as @list4 = (0,1,3);

Perl lists have numerous other features, which you'll see when you approach more complex programming topics. For now, you should know what a list is, how to initialize it, and how to access one of its members.

NOTE

Presumably, we're all fully qualified computer nerds here, so we are allowed to use "access" as a verb. Be advised, however, that the practice in common usage drives English-language purists to scowling fidgets.

PERL AND THE COMMON GATEWAY INTERFACE

You've learned a little about the Perl programming language. But how does it fit into the World Wide Web? The Common Gateway Interface (CGI) is the key. CGI has been used for many years as a facility for passing information from a Web page to a program that can process the information.

CGI, despite what many programmers put on their resumes, is not a programming language. It is, as the name states explicitly, an *interface*. It allows you to write a program that will take all of its input from an HTML document—a page on the World Wide Web—and *do something* with that input. You can regard CGI as a kind of pipeline between your Web page and a Perl program (see Figure 19.9): whatever is entered on the page is available to your program through CGI.

HTML is quite good at describing how a Web page should look in a browser, but the language all by itself has virtually no facilities for processing information or making even rudimentary decisions.

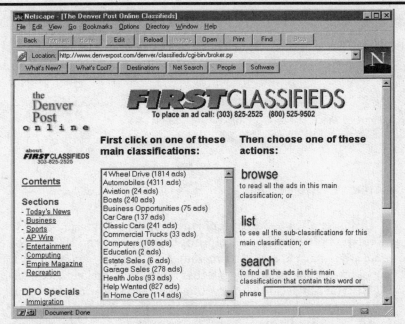

FIGURE 19.9: A search phrase or a list selection entered in this form will be processed by a Perl program through CGI.

WARNING

Some browsers include extensions to HTML that support all kinds of fancy interpretation. In the real world, however, you cannot depend on your Web site visitors possessing the latest and greatest browsers with all of their nonstandard HTML extensions.

Part iv

When you run a Perl program from the command line, it takes its input, generally, from you, at your keyboard, and it sends its output, generally, back to you, on the screen. CGI reroutes those standard conventions. The Perl program's input comes from the Web page. Most importantly, CGI sends your program's output back to the Web server. If the output happens to be formatted correctly in HTML, the server will put it out as an HTML document to whatever browser is connected to it. In other words, a print statement from within your Perl program will be printing to the Web server, not to the screen (see Figure 19.10).

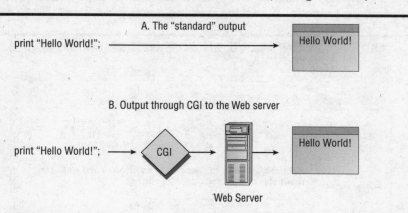

FIGURE 19.10: The difference between "standard" and CGI output

This is a difficult concept for many neophytes to grasp, but it is the foundation of using CGI as a pipeline between Perl and HTML. You can *draw a Web page* from a Perl program. And, because Perl is a fully functional programming language, rather than a markup language such as HTML, you can decide within your program *what to draw* based on what has been entered in the page and sent to you.

Of course, this facility isn't limited to Perl. You can interface with CGI using *any* program written in *any* language (provided, of course, that it will run on your computer!). Indeed, there may be occasions when you need the brute force of C/C++ or some other high-level compiled language to tackle some process that would bring your Web server to its knees if the program were written in Perl. For example, a program that does a lot of heavy number crunching would be much more efficient in C or C++ than in Perl. Those occasions will be rare, however. Most of what you need to do can be accomplished more easily from a Perl script than from a compiled program. Additionally, your Perl program won't have to be rewritten and recompiled if you move to another operating system or computer platform.

What Is CGI, Anyway?

Does *Common Gateway Interface* mean much, if anything, to you? Probably not. Without CGI, however, there would be no reason to talk about Perl and Web pages because there would be no way to link the two.

CGI as a *concept* has been applied to many systems other than links between Web servers and application programs. For example, it would provide a clean and near-universal interface for database servers and their clients without the barriers introduced by proprietary systems. Software manufacturers sometimes seem to worry about making sure that you only do business with them, but a "common gateway" from one system to another provides a standard of sorts to which the manufacturers must adhere; if they can't deal with it, no one will buy their applications.

For now, anyone who actually knows what you're talking about when you bandy about terms such as *CGI* will assume that you're talking exclusively about World Wide Web applications. In that context, without the Web, there would be no CGI. And without the Internet, there would be no Web.

CGI: The Force behind the Web

Whereas HTML gives the World Wide Web its *look*, CGI makes it *functional*. It is what its name implies: a "common gateway" between the Web server and applications that can be useful to the server, but that doesn't run as a part of it. CGI is the only way the server can communicate with these other applications, such as a database.

NOTE

Keep in mind that no support exists for CGI outside of HTTP servers. In other words, CGI only works with HTTP servers. Its uses outside that realm have been interesting, but strictly marginal.

A Common Gateway

In technical terms, a *gateway* is an interface or an application that allows two systems to pass information between them.

For example, Microsoft's old Mail program and its newer Exchange are limited to sending mail only to other Microsoft Mail users. A separate product provides a Simple Mail Transfer Protocol (SMTP) gateway so that mail can be sent to and received from the Internet.

Likewise with your Web server. It doesn't know Perl from Adam, but through the mechanism of CGI it can handle requests from *clients*, or visitors to your site, and pass the results back.

Because the server is only following a set of rules for passing information, it does not know or care what you use in the background to process what it sends you. The functions are totally independent of one another. Thus, you can write CGI programs in *any* programming language. The only requirement is that the information you send back has to be formatted in a way that the server recognizes.

TIP

You can find a great deal of information on the formal CGI specification at http://hoohoo.ncsa.uiuc.edu/cgi/interface.html.

The CGI Environment

MS-DOS, Unix, and, to a limited extent, Windows users should be at least a little familiar with the concept of *environment variables.* For example, on both MS-DOS and Unix, an environment variable called PATH stores the list of directories through which the operating system will search when you type a program name on the command line.

To the operating system, whether it's Windows or Unix, the *environment* is a block of memory where variable names can be stored as string values, such as PATH=c:/bin;c:/usr/bin;c:/usr/local/bin. Taking this example further, whenever the user refers to %PATH% (on NT and 95/98) or $PATH (on Unix), the operating system substitutes c:/bin;c:/usr/bin;c:/usr/local/bin.

Programs can get into this block of memory, too. What makes this facility especially useful is that the environment is in *global* memory, which means that anything there is accessible by other programs running at the same time.

The Web server fills in a standard list of environment variables when it runs; it fills in others when requests are made of it. Because the Web server runs all the time, anything it places in the environment can be read by another program, such as your Perl script, if the other program knows the names of the variables to read.

In the simplest sense, this is how CGI gets information between the server and your program (see Figure 19.11). The details are a little more complicated, however.

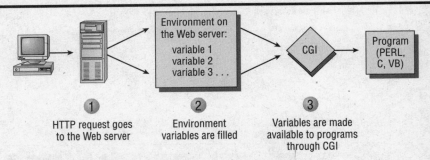

1	2	3
HTTP request goes to the Web server	Environment variables are filled	Variables are made available to programs through CGI

FIGURE 19.11: The Web server, CGI, and the environment

CGI PROGRAMMING LANGUAGES

This chapter deals with Perl as the preferred programming vehicle for CGI applications. However, the HTTP-CGI gateway has no requirements or preferences when it comes to the language in which a CGI application is written. Let's examine briefly the advantages and disadvantages of some of the most widely used languages.

C, C++

C and, more recently, C++ are the most popular languages for application and systems development. Figure 19.12 shows a snippet of code in C++.

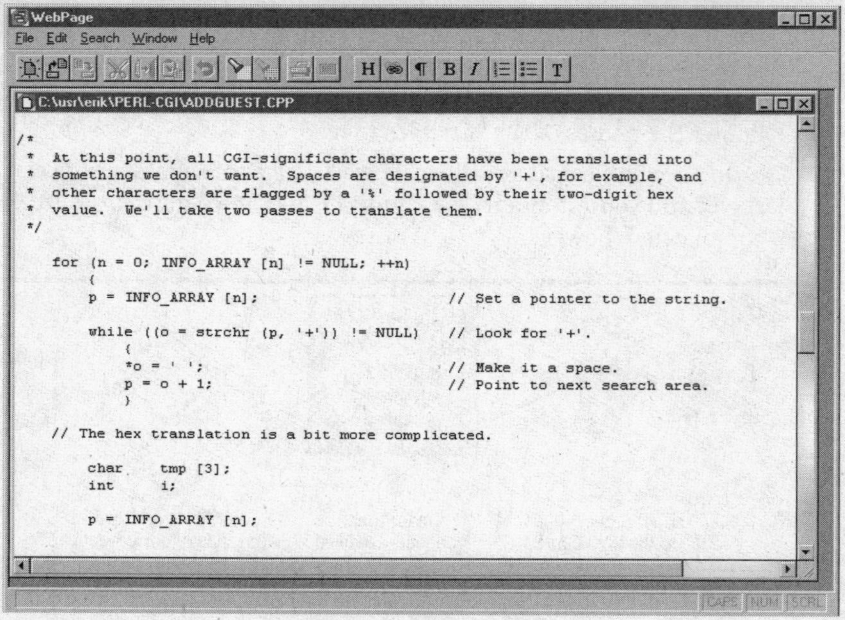

```
WebPage                                                            _ □ ×
File  Edit  Search  Window  Help

  [toolbar]  H  ∞ ¶ B I ≔ ≔ T

 C:\usr\erik\PERL-CGI\ADDGUEST.CPP                                 _ □ ×

/*
 *  At this point, all CGI-significant characters have been translated into
 *  something we don't want.  Spaces are designated by '+', for example, and
 *  other characters are flagged by a '%' followed by their two-digit hex
 *  value.  We'll take two passes to translate them.
 */

    for (n = 0; INFO_ARRAY [n] != NULL; ++n)
       {
       p = INFO_ARRAY [n];                    // Set a pointer to the string.

       while ((o = strchr (p, '+')) != NULL)  // Look for '+'.
          {
          *o = ' ';                           // Make it a space.
          p = o + 1;                          // Point to next search area.
          }

    // The hex translation is a bit more complicated.

       char   tmp [3];
       int    i;

       p = INFO_ARRAY [n];
```

FIGURE 19.12: A C++ code snippet, which is very similar to C

Advantages

These are some of advantages of C and C++:

▶ When it comes to sheer, raw power, it is very difficult to beat these two compiled languages for either CGI or normal applications. For extremely large and complicated CGI projects, C or C++ probably is a better choice than Perl, especially on a busy Web site where processing speed will be a concern.

▶ Both languages are common on both Unix and Windows NT systems, so generally there are few problems porting code between the platforms.

▶ The popularity of C/C++ means that there is a large body of existing code that you can tap into.

Disadvantages

Some of the disadvantages of these two languages are:

▶ As you learned earlier, there are so many nifty shortcuts built into Perl that you generally can accomplish a lot more in a lot less code than you can in C or C++. Perl's string-manipulation functions, especially, are so much stronger that it's almost ridiculous to try to do the same thing in C/C++.

▶ Here's something else to keep in mind: it would not be an exaggeration to say that upward of 90 percent of all CGI programs involve heavy string manipulation.

Visual Basic

Visual Basic (VB) is Microsoft's workhorse language for simple Windows application development. Figure 19.13 shows some VB code in a Word macro.

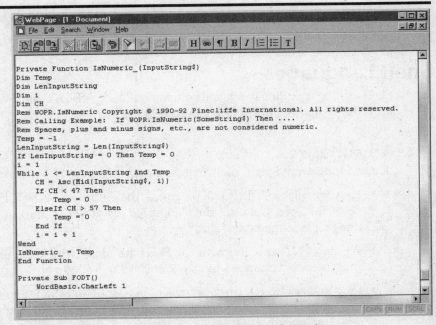

FIGURE 19.13: A Visual Basic example in a Microsoft Word macro

Part iv

Advantages

Some of the advantages of VB in a CGI context are:

▶ VB is Microsoft's version of the BASIC language, which has been around for decades and is familiar to just about anyone who's ever done any programming.

▶ It is easy to learn, easy to use, fast, and popular.

▶ In a totally Microsoft environment, it can work quickly and efficiently for CGI applications.

Disadvantages

Some of VB's disadvantages are:

▶ VB was developed primarily for doing Windows applications, so at least half of its power is wasted on CGI programs, which most often run in the background and depend on sending properly formatted HTML to a Web browser for display.

▶ VB would be extremely difficult, if not impossible, to port over to a Unix system.

Shell Languages

Shell scripts, including batch and command files on MS-DOS and Windows 95/98 and NT, are easy to use and easy to write.

Advantages

Some of the advantages of shell languages are:

▶ For very quick and dirty CGI programs, these utilities can be very powerful tools. The Unix shell languages are powerful programming tools in their own right.

▶ Windows NT complies with the Posix standard, which means that the most common Unix tools, such as sh, will run on it, too.

▶ Programs written in these languages are small and tight, don't involve the overhead of the Perl interpreter, and easily port from one system to another.

Disadvantages

Some of the disadvantages of shell languages are:

▶ Shell programs don't allow any of the flexibility and powerful control structures that "real" programming languages do.

▶ You constantly need to call other utilities such as grep or sed (or even Perl!).

WARNING

Anything of more than a minimum level of complexity should be avoided in the shell languages. They are slow, difficult to maintain, and generally not worth the trouble.

Proprietary CGI Methods

Some of the proprietary CGI methods, such as ActiveX from Microsoft and JavaScript from Netscape, are worth mentioning. These are very powerful tools, make no mistake about it, and we'll look at them in further detail in later chapters. Because they take full and specific advantage of the hardware/software platforms on which they run, the proprietary packages are naturally much faster and much more efficient than more "traditional" CGI software.

After all, there's just no comparison between a program that runs according to a strictly imposed set of rules, basically on top of the operating system, and a program that is able to utilize even the most bare-metal of operating system functions.

However, it is not in the spirit of CGI to adhere to a particular hardware or software platform. Like the spirit of the Internet, it is to let as many people as possible, with as many varied machines as possible, become part of the community.

No restrictions—that's the way it's supposed to be.

WHAT'S NEXT?

Now you know enough about Perl to create and run a simple program, and you have an understanding of the CGI environment and how Perl and CGI work together on the Web. In the next chapter, Jamie Jaworski will show you how JavaScript works and how to embed JavaScript statements into your HTML documents.

Part iv

Chapter 20

INTRODUCING JAVASCRIPT AND JSCRIPT

This chapter introduces you to the JavaScript language. I'll show you how JavaScript works with both the Netscape and Microsoft browsers and Web servers, and how to embed JavaScript statements in HTML documents. I'll then cover JavaScript's use of *types* and *variables* and show you how to use *arrays*. By the time you have finished this chapter, you'll be able to write simple scripts and include them in your Web pages.

Adapted from *Mastering JavaScript Premium Edition*, by James Jaworski
ISBN 0-7821-2819-X   1,056 pages $49.99

JavaScript and Browsers, JavaScript and Servers

JavaScript is a script-based programming language that supports the development of both client and server components of Web-based applications. On the client side, it can be used to write programs that are executed by a Web browser within the context of a Web page. On the server side, it can be used to write Web server programs that can process information submitted by a Web browser and then update the browser's display accordingly. Figure 20.1 provides an overview of how JavaScript supports both client and server Web programming.

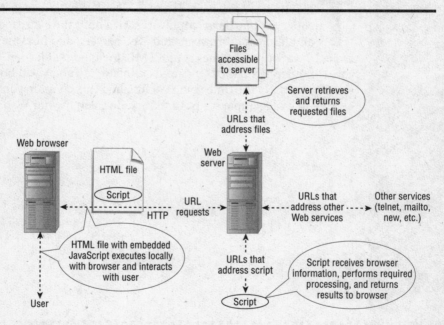

FIGURE 20.1: JavaScript supports both client and server Web applications.

NOTE

Microsoft's version of JavaScript is named JScript. I use "JavaScript" to refer to both JavaScript and JScript unless I'm referring to one but not the other. In these cases, I'll refer to "Netscape's JavaScript" and "Microsoft's JScript."

On the left side of the figure, a Web browser displays a Web page. This a result of the browser acting on the instructions contained in an HTML file. The browser reads the HTML file and displays elements of the file as they are encountered. In this case, the HTML file (which the browser has retrieved from a Web server, seen on the right) contains embedded JavaScript code. The process of reading the HTML file and identifying the elements contained in the file is referred to as *parsing*. When a script is encountered during parsing, the browser executes the script before continuing with further parsing.

The script can perform actions, such as generating HTML code that affects the display of the browser window. It can perform actions that affect the operation of plug-ins, Java applets, or ActiveX components. The script can also define JavaScript language elements that are used by other scripts. Figure 20.2 summarizes the parsing of HTML files that contain JavaScript scripts.

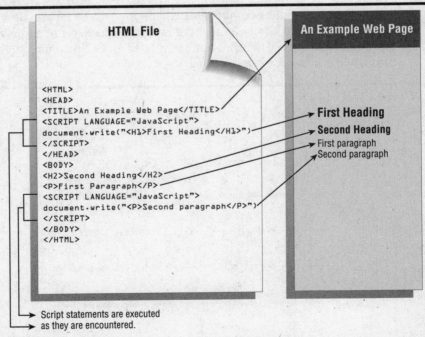

FIGURE 20.2: HTML files are parsed and displayed one element at a time.

Some scripts may define functions for handling *events* that are generated by user actions. For example, you might write a script to define a function for handling the event "submitting a form" or "clicking a link."

The event handlers can then perform actions such as validating the form's data, generating a custom URL for the link, or loading a new Web page.

JavaScript's event-handling capabilities provide greater control over the user interface than HTML alone. For example, when a user submits an HTML form, a browser that isn't implementing JavaScript handles the "submit form" event by sending the form data to a CGI program for further processing. The CGI program processes the form data and returns the results to the Web browser, which displays the results to the user. By comparison, when a user submits an HTML form using a browser that *does* implement JavaScript, a JavaScript event-handling function may be called to process the form data. This processing may vary from validating the data (that is, checking to see that the data entered by the user is appropriate for the fields contained in the form) to performing all of the required form processing, eliminating the need for a CGI program. In other words, JavaScript's event-handling capabilities allow the *browser* to perform some, if not all, of the form processing. Figure 20.3 compares JavaScript's event-handling capabilities to those provided by HTML. Besides providing greater control over the user interface, these event-handling capabilities help to reduce network traffic, the need for CGI programs, and the load on the Web server.

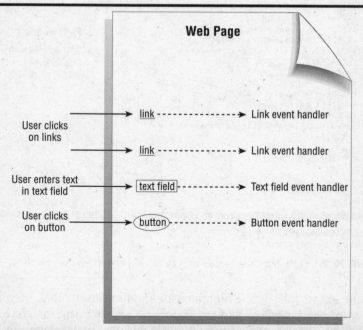

FIGURE 20.3: Event-handling functions enable scripts to respond to user actions.

While JavaScript's browser programming capabilities can eliminate the need for *some* server-side programs, others are still required to support more advanced Web applications, such as those that access database information, support electronic commerce, or perform specialized processing. Server-side JavaScript scripts are used to replace traditional CGI programs. Instead of a Web server calling a CGI program to process form data, perform searches, or implement customized Web applications, a JavaScript-enabled Web server can invoke a precompiled JavaScript script to perform this processing. The Web server automatically creates JavaScript objects that tell the script how it was invoked and the type of browser requesting its services; it also automatically communicates any data supplied by the browser. The script processes the data provided by the browser and returns information to the browser, via the server. The browser then uses this information to update the user's display. Figure 20.4 illustrates how server-side scripts are used.

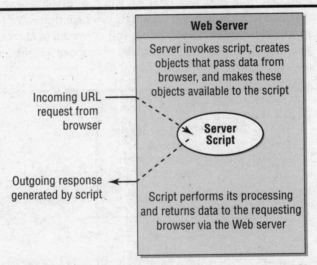

FIGURE 20.4: Server-side scripts are used to replace CGI programs.

There are several advantages to using server-side JavaScript scripts on Netscape and Microsoft Web servers:

▶ Because these Web servers have been specially designed for executing JavaScript scripts, they are able to minimize the processing overhead that is usually associated with invoking the script, passing data, and returning the results of script processing.

► You can use JavaScript to replace CGI scripts written in other languages. This eliminates the problems that are usually associated with managing multiple CGI programs, which may have been written in an OS shell language, Perl, tcl, C, and other languages. It also provides tighter control over the security of these server-side applications.

► The database extensions integrated within these servers provide a powerful capability for accessing information contained in compatible external databases. These database extensions may be used by server-side scripts.

The database connectivity supported by these servers enables even beginning programmers to create server-side JavaScript programs to update databases with information provided by browsers (usually through forms) and to provide Web users with Web pages that are dynamically generated from database queries. You can imagine how exciting this is for researchers gathering and reporting information over the Web and for entrepreneurs who have catalogs full of products and services to sell over the Web. Figure 20.5 illustrates the use of JavaScript to provide database connectivity to Web applications.

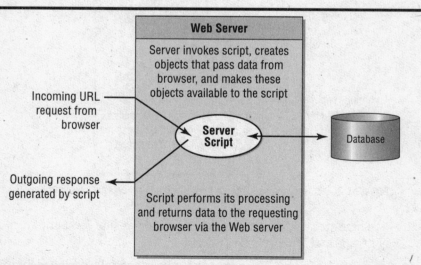

FIGURE 20.5: Netscape and Microsoft Web servers provide database connectivity to server-side scripts.

NOTE

In this section, I've provided an overview of the different ways in which JavaScript can be used for browser and server-side Web applications. JavaScript's syntax is the same for both client (browser) and server programming; however, the examples I will be using in this chapter mainly reflect how JavaScript relates to browser programming.

EMBEDDING JAVASCRIPT IN HTML

JavaScript statements can be included in HTML documents by enclosing the statements between an opening `<script>` tag and a closing `</script>` tag. Within the opening tag, the `language` attribute is set to `"JavaScript"` to identify the script as being JavaScript as opposed to some other scripting language, such as Visual Basic Script (VBScript). The script tag is typically used as follows:

```
<script language="JavaScript">
 JavaScript statements
</script>
```

The script tag may be placed in either the *head* or the *body* of an HTML document. In many cases, it is better to place the script tag in the head of a document to ensure that all JavaScript definitions have been made before the body of the document is displayed. You'll learn more about this in the subsection, "Use of the Document Head," later in this section.

The traditional first exercise with any programming language is to write a program to display the text *Hello World!* This teaches the programmer to display output, a necessary feature of most programs. A JavaScript script that displays this text is shown in Listing 20.1.

Listing 20.1:   Hello World!

```
<html>
<head>
<title>Hello World!</title>
</head>
<body>
<script language="JavaScript">
document.write("Hello World!")
</script>
</body>
</html>
```

The body of our example document (the lines between the <body> and the </body> tags) contains a single element: a script, identified by the <script> and </script> tags. The opening script tag has the attribute language="JavaScript" to identify the script as JavaScript. The script has a single statement, document.write("Hello World!"), that writes the text *Hello World!* to the body of the current document object. Figure 20.6 shows how the HTML document is displayed by a JavaScript-enabled browser—Netscape Navigator. The text written by the script becomes part of the HTML document displayed by the browser.

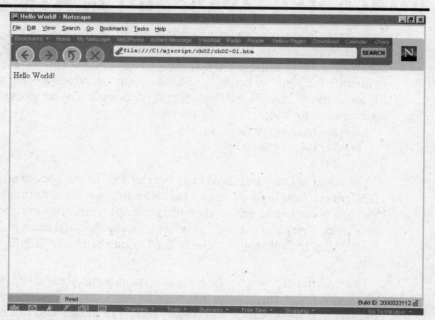

FIGURE 20.6: The very simple result of Listing 20.1, Hello World!, displayed by Netscape Navigator

Other Language Attributes

All JavaScript-capable browsers will process JavaScript code if the language attribute is set to "JavaScript". However, the language attribute can also be set to the following other values in order to limit the browsers that are able to process JavaScript code:

JavaScript1.1   Used to limit execution of a script to browsers that support JavaScript 1.1. These browsers are Navigator 3

and later, Internet Explorer 4 and later, HotJava 2.0 and later, and Opera 3.5 and later.

JavaScript1.2   Used to limit execution of a script to browsers that support JavaScript 1.2. These browsers are Navigator 4 and later, Internet Explorer 4 and later, and HotJava 3.0 and later.

JavaScript1.3   Used to limit execution of a script to browsers that support JavaScript 1.3. These browsers are limited to Navigator 4.06 and later, Internet Explorer 5.0 and later, and HotJava 3.0 and later.

JavaScript1.5   Used to limit execution of a script to browsers that support JavaScript 1.5. These browsers are limited to Navigator 6.0 and later and Internet Explorer 5.5 and later.

JScript   Used to limit execution of a script to browsers that support JScript. These browsers are limited to Internet Explorer 3 and later.

Table 20.1 identifies which of the above attributes are supported by popular browsers. If a browser does not support an attribute, it will simply ignore the <SCRIPT> tags.

TABLE 20.1: Browser Support of the LANGUAGE Attribute

BROWSER	JAVASCRIPT	1.1	1.2	1.3	1.5	JSCRIPT
Navigator 2	X					
Navigator 3	X	X				
Navigator 4	X	X	X			
Navigator 4.06	X	X	X	X		
Navigator 6.0	X	X	X	X	X	
Internet Explorer 3	X					X
Internet Explorer 4	X	X	X			X
Internet Explorer 5	X	X	X	X		X
Internet Explorer 5.5	X	X	X	X	X	X
Opera 3.62	X	X	X	X	X	X
HotJava 3.0	X	X	X	X		

You may wonder whatever happened to JavaScript 1.4? JavaScript 1.4 corresponds to ECMAScript Revision 2. The only browser that recognizes and supports the `JavaScript1.4` attribute value is HotJava 3.0. The Opera browser recognizes the `JavaScript1.4` attribute value but does not support the language features.

NOTE

The Opera browser reports that it supports all language attribute values, but it only supports up to JavaScript version 1.1 as of Opera 3.62.

TIP

To ensure that more browsers are able to execute your scripts, set the language attribute to "JavaScript". Your JavaScript code can then perform checks to detect which type and version of browser is currently executing a script.

NOTE

In addition to the language attribute, Internet Explorer 4 and later support the use of conditional compilation directives. These directives are used to limit script execution to selected portions of scripts.

Telling Non-JavaScript Browsers to Ignore Your Code

Not all browsers support JavaScript. Older browsers, such as Netscape Navigator 1, Internet Explorer 2, and the character-based Lynx browser, do not recognize the script tag and, as a consequence, display as text all the JavaScript statements that are enclosed between <script> and </script>. Figures 20.7 and 20.8 show how the preceding JavaScript script is displayed by Internet Explorer 2 and by DosLynx.

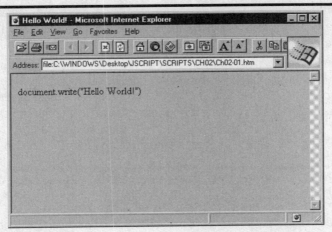

FIGURE 20.7: Internet Explorer 2 displays the Hello World! script of Listing 20.1 instead of executing it.

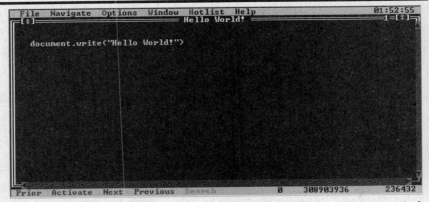

FIGURE 20.8: DosLynx displays the Hello World! script of Listing 20.1 instead of executing it.

Fortunately, HTML provides a method to conceal JavaScript statements from such JavaScript-challenged browsers. The trick is to use HTML *comment* tags to *surround* the JavaScript statements. Because HTML comments are displayed only within the code used to create a Web page, they do not show up as part of the browser's display. The use of HTML comment tags is as follows:

```
<!-- Begin hiding JavaScript
JavaScript statements
// End hiding JavaScript -->
```

The `<!--` tag begins the HTML comment and the `-->` tag ends the comment. The `//` string identifies a JavaScript comment, as you'll learn later in this chapter in the section, "JavaScript Comments."

The comment tags cause the JavaScript statements to be treated as comments by JavaScript-challenged browsers. JavaScript-enabled browsers, on the other hand, know to ignore the comment tags and process the enclosed statements as JavaScript. Listing 20.2 shows how HTML comments are used to hide JavaScript statements. Figure 20.9 shows how Internet Explorer 2 displays the HTML document shown in Listing 20.2.

Listing 20.2: **Using HTML Comments to Hide JavaScript Code**

```html
<html>
<head>
<title>Using HTML comments to hide JavaScript code</title>
</head>
<body>
<script language="JavaScript">
<!-- Begin hiding JavaScript
document.write("Hello World!")
// End hiding JavaScript -->
</script>
</body>
</html>
```

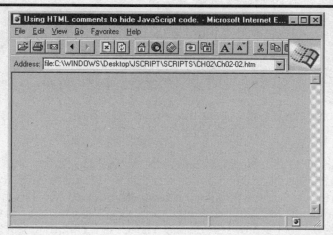

FIGURE 20.9: Result of using HTML comments (Listing 20.2) with Internet Explorer 2. Compare to Figures 20.7 and 20.8.

The Noscript Tag

Versions 2 and later of Netscape Navigator and versions 3 and later of Microsoft Internet Explorer support JavaScript. These browsers account for nearly 90 percent of browser use on the Web and their percentage of use is increasing. This means that most browser requests come from JavaScript-capable browsers. However, there are still popular browsers, such as Lynx, that do not support JavaScript. In addition, both Navigator and Internet Explorer provide users with the option of *disabling* JavaScript. The <noscript> tag was created for those browsers that can't or won't process JavaScript. It is used to display markup that is an alternative to executing a script. The HTML instructions contained inside the tag are displayed by JavaScript-challenged browsers (as well as by JavaScript-capable browsers that have JavaScript disabled). The script shown in Listing 20.3 illustrates the use of the noscript tag. Figure 20.10 shows the Web page of Listing 20.3 as displayed by a JavaScript-capable browser. Compare that display to Figure 20.11, which shows how it is displayed by Internet Explorer 2, a non-JavaScript browser.

Listing 20.3:   Using the <noscript> Tag

```
<html>
<head>
<title>Using the noscript tag.</title>
</head>
<body>
<script language="JavaScript">
<!-- Begin hiding JavaScript
document.write("Hello World!")
// End hiding Javascript -->
</script>
<NOSCRIPT>
[JavaScript]
</NOSCRIPT>
</body>
</html>
```

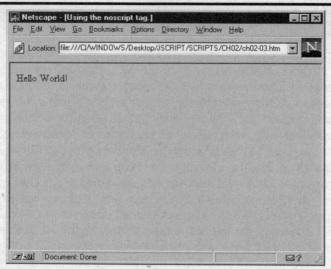

FIGURE 20.10: Using the noscript tag with Navigator, a JavaScript-capable browser (Listing 20.3)

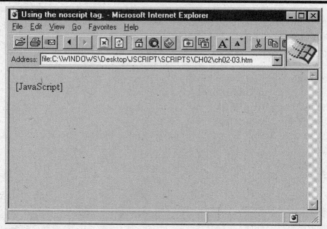

FIGURE 20.11: Using the noscript tag with Internet Explorer 2, a non-JavaScript browser (Listing 20.3)

The Script Tag's SRC Attribute

The script tag itself provides another way to include JavaScript code in an HTML document, via the tag's SRC attribute, which may be used to specify a *file* containing JavaScript statements. Here's an example of the use of the SRC attribute:

```
<script language="JavaScript" SRC="src.js">
</script>
```

In the above example, the file src.js is a file containing JavaScript statements. (The file could have been named anything, but it should end with the .js extension; I just chose src.js to help you remember the SRC attribute.) Note that the closing </script> tag is still required.

If the file src.js contains the following code:

```
<!-- Begin hiding JavaScript document.write("This text was
generated by code in the src.js file.")
// End hiding JavaScript -->
```

then the HTML document shown in Listing 20.4 would produce the browser display shown in Figure 20.12.

Listing 20.4:   Inserting Source JavaScript Files

```
<html>
<head>
<title>Using the SRC attribute of the script tag.</title>
</head>
<body>
<script language="JavaScript" SRC="src.js">
</script>
</body>
</html>
```

NOTE

The SRC attribute may have a URL as its attribute value. Web servers that provide the source file, however, must report the file's MIME type as application/x-javascript; otherwise, browsers will not load the source file.

Part IV

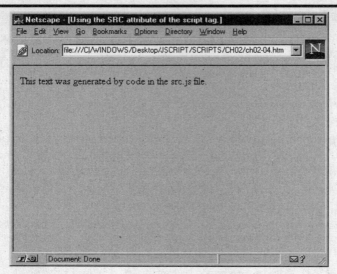

FIGURE 20.12: Using the SRC attribute of the script tag to include JavaScript code (Listing 20.4)

JavaScript Entities

JavaScript entities allow the value of an HTML attribute to be provided by a JavaScript *expression*. This allows attribute values to be dynamically calculated during the loading of a Web page.

A JavaScript entity begins with &{ and ends with };. The following example shows how the HREF attribute of a link may be specified by the JavaScript linkTo variable:

```
<A HREF="&{linkTo};">Click here.</A>
```

The value of linkTo, which must be calculated earlier in the script, must be a valid URL.

NOTE

You'll learn about variables in the section, "Variables—Value Storehouses," later in this chapter.

Listing 20.5 shows how the above tag can be used to create a link to the Web page of the book from which this chapter came.

Listing 20.5:   Using JavaScript Entities

```
<html>
<head>
<title>Using the JavaScript entities.</title>
<script language="JavaScript"><!--
linkTo="http://www.courseone.com/javascript"
// -->
</script>
</head>
<body>
<A HREF="&{linkTo};">Click here.</A>
</body>
</html>
```

WARNING

Microsoft Internet Explorer does not support JavaScript entities. Use of entities with Internet Explorer may lead to scripting errors.

JavaScript Comments

The JavaScript language provides comments of its own. These comments are used to insert notes and processing descriptions into scripts. The comments are ignored (as intended) when the statements of a script are parsed by JavaScript-enabled browsers.

JavaScript comments use the syntax of C++ and Java. The // string identifies a comment that continues to the end of a line. An example of a single line comment follows:

```
// This JavaScript comment continues to the end of the line.
```

The /* and */ strings are used to identify comments that may span multiple lines. The comment begins with /* and continues up to */. An example of a multiple line comment follows:

```
/* This is
an example
of a multiple
line comment */
```

The script shown in Listing 20.6 illustrates the use of JavaScript comments. The script contains four statements that, if they weren't ignored, would write various capitalizations of the text *Hello World!* to the current document. However, since the first three of these statements are contained in comments, and since browsers ignore comments, these statements have no effect on the Web page generated by the script. Figure 20.13 shows how the JavaScript comments in Listing 20.6 are handled by a JavaScript-capable browser.

Listing 20.6:   Using JavaScript Comments

```
<html>
<head>
<title>Using JavaScript comments</title>
</head>
<body>
<script language="JavaScript">
<!-- Begin hiding JavaScript
// document.write("hello world!")
/* document.write("Hello world!")
document.write("Hello World!") */
document.write("HELLO WORLD!")
// End hiding Javascript -->
</script>
</body>
</html>
```

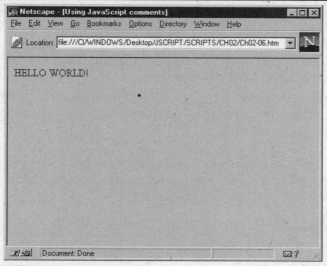

FIGURE 20.13: How JavaScript comments are handled by a JavaScript-capable browser (Listing 20.6)

NOTE

Throughout the rest of this chapter, all browser references will be to JavaScript-capable browsers, unless otherwise specified.

Use of the Document Head

The head of an HTML document provides a great place to include JavaScript definitions. Since the head of a document is processed before its body, placing definitions in the head will cause them to be defined before they are used. This is important because any attempt to use a variable before it is defined results in an error. Listing 20.7 shows how JavaScript definitions can be placed in the head of an HTML document. The script contained in the document head defines a variable named *greeting* and sets its value to the string *Hi Web surfers!* (You'll learn all about variables in the section, "Variables–Value Storehouses," later in this chapter.) The script contained in the document's body then writes the value of the `greeting` variable to the current document. Figure 20.14 shows how this document is displayed.

Listing 20.7:   Using the Head for Definitions

```
<HTML>
<HEAD>
<TITLE>Using the HEAD for definitions</TITLE>
<SCRIPT language="JavaScript">
<!--
greeting = "Hi Web surfers!"
// -->
</SCRIPT>
</HEAD>
<BODY>
<SCRIPT language="JavaScript">
<!--
document.write(greeting)
// -->
</SCRIPT>
</BODY>
</HTML>
```

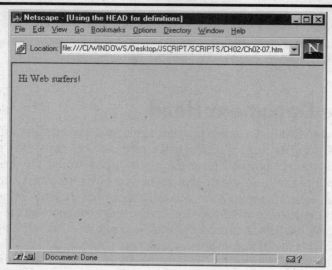

FIGURE 20.14: How the greeting variable is displayed (Listing 20.7)

It is important to make sure that all definitions occur before they are used; otherwise an error will be displayed when your HTML document is loaded by a browser. Listing 20.8 contains an HTML document that will generate a "use before definition" error. In this listing, the head contains a JavaScript statement that writes the value of the greeting variable to the current document; however, the greeting variable is not defined until the body of the document. Figure 20.15 shows how this error is displayed by a browser.

Listing 20.8:   Example of Use before Definition

```
<HTML>
<HEAD>
<TITLE>Use before definition</TITLE>
<SCRIPT language="JavaScript">
<!--
document.write(greeting)
// -->
</SCRIPT>
</HEAD>
<BODY>
<SCRIPT language="JavaScript">
<!--
greeting = "Hi Web surfers!"
```

```
// -->
</SCRIPT>
</BODY>
</HTML>
```

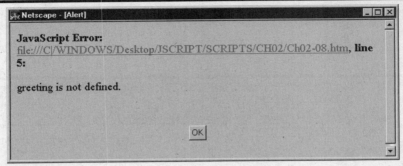

FIGURE 20.15: JavaScript generates an error when a variable is used before it is defined (Listing 20.8).

GENERATING HTML

The examples presented so far have shown how you can use JavaScript to write simple text to the document object. By including HTML tags in your JavaScript script, you can also use JavaScript to generate HTML elements that will be displayed in the current document. The example shown in Listing 20.9 illustrates this concept. Figure 20.16 shows how the Web page generated by this script is displayed.

Listing 20.9:   Using JavaScript to Create HTML Tags

```
<HTML>
<HEAD>
<TITLE>Using JavaScript to create HTML tags</TITLE>
<SCRIPT LANGUAGE="JavaScript">
<!--
greeting = "<H1>Hi Web surfers!</H1>"
welcome = "<P>Welcome to <CITE>HTML Complete</CITE>.</P>"
nextline = "<P>Chapter 20: Learning JavaScript and
JScript.</P>"
// -->
</SCRIPT>
</HEAD>
<BODY>
```

Part iv

```
<SCRIPT LANGUAGE="JavaScript">
<!--
document.write(greeting)
document.write(welcome)
document.write(nextline)
// -->
</SCRIPT>
</BODY>
</HTML>
```

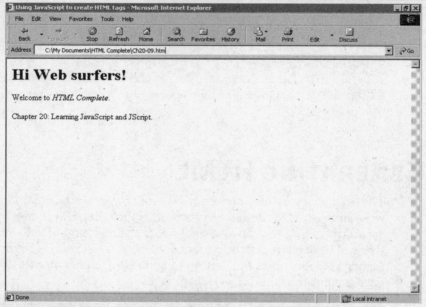

FIGURE 20.16: Generating HTML from JavaScript (Listing 20.9)

In the script contained in the head of the HTML document, the variables greeting, welcome, and nextline are assigned text strings containing embedded HTML tags. These text strings are displayed by the script contained in the body of the HTML document:

▶ The greeting variable contains the heading *Hi Web surfers!*, which is surrounded by the HTML heading tags <H1> and </H1>.

▶ The welcome variable is assigned the string *Welcome to HTML Complete*.

- ▶ The citation tags , <CITE> and </CITE>, cause the welcome variable's string to be cited as a literary reference (which means it shows up in italic).

- ▶ The paragraph tags, <P> and </P>, which surround the welcome text, are used to mark it as a separate paragraph.

▶ The nextline variable is assigned the string *Chapter 20: Learning JavaScript and JScript*.

The resulting HTML document generated by the script is equivalent to the following:

```
<HTML>
<HEAD>
<TITLE>Using JavaScript to create HTML tags</TITLE>
</HEAD>
<BODY>
<H1>Hi Web surfers!</H1>
<P>Welcome to <CITE>HTML Complete</CITE>.</P>
<P>Chapter 20: Learning JavaScript and JScript.</P>
</BODY>
</HTML>
```

So far, I've been making use of variables, such as greeting and welcome, without having explicitly defined what they are. In the next section, I formally introduce variables.

VARIABLES—VALUE STOREHOUSES

JavaScript, like other programming languages, uses variables to store values so they can be used in other parts of a program. Variables are names that are associated with these stored values. For example, the variable imageName may be used to refer to the name of an image file to be displayed and the variable totalAmount may be used to display the total amount of a user's purchase.

Variable names can begin with an uppercase letter (A through Z), lowercase letter (a through z), underscore character (_), or dollar sign character ($). The remaining characters can consist of letters, the underscore character, the dollar sign character, or digits (0 through 9). Examples of variable names are as follows:

```
orderNumber2
_123
SUM
```

Part iv

Image7
Previous_Document

Variable names are case-sensitive. This means that a variable named sum refers to a different value than one named Sum, sUm, or SUM.

WARNING

Since variable names are case-sensitive, it is important to make sure that you use the same capitalization each time you use a variable.

WARNING

The dollar sign ($) character is reserved for machine-generated code and should not be used in your scripts. In particular, it should not be used for scripts that will be run by earlier browsers that are not fully ECMAScript-compatible.

Types and Variables

Unlike Java and some other programming languages, JavaScript does not require you to specify the *type* of data contained in a variable. (It doesn't even allow it.) In fact, the same variable may be used to contain a variety of different values, such as the text string *Hello World!*, the integer *13*, the floating-point value *3.14*, or the logical value *true*. The JavaScript interpreter keeps track of and converts the type of data contained in a variable.

JavaScript's automatic handling of different types of values is a double-edged sword. On one side, it frees you from having to explicitly specify the type of data contained in a variable and from having to convert from one data type to another. On the other side, since JavaScript automatically converts values of one type to another, it is important to keep track of what types of values should be contained in a variable and how they are converted in expressions involving variables of other types. The next section, "Types and Literal Values," identifies the types of values that JavaScript supports. The later section, "Conversion between Types," discusses important issues related to type conversion.

Types and Literal Values

JavaScript supports five primitive types of values and supports complex types, such as arrays and objects. *Primitive types* are types that can be assigned a single literal value, such as a number, string, or Boolean value. Here are the primitive types that JavaScript supports:

Number   Consists of integer and floating-point numbers and the special NaN (not a number) value. Numbers use a 64-bit IEEE 754 format.

Boolean   Consists of the logical values true and false.

String   Consists of string values that are enclosed in single or double quotes.

The null type   Consists of a single value, null, which identifies a null, empty, or nonexistent reference.

The undefined type   Consists of a single value, undefined, which is used to indicate that a variable has not been assigned a value.

WARNING

The undefined value was introduced with the ECMAScript specification and is not supported by browsers that are not fully ECMAScript-compatible. This includes Navigator 4.05 and earlier and Internet Explorer 3 and earlier.

NOTE

You'll learn about the Object type later in this chapter under the section, "The Object Type and Arrays."

In JavaScript, you do not declare the type of a variable as you do in other languages, such as Java and C++. Instead, the type of a variable is implicitly defined based on the literal values that you assign to it. For example, if you assign the integer *123* to the variable total, then total will support number operations. If you assign the string value *The sum of all accounts* to total, then total will support string operations. Similarly, if you assign the logical value *true* to total, then it will support Boolean operations.

It is also possible for a variable to be assigned a value of one type and then later in the script's execution be assigned a value of another type. For example, the variable total could be assigned *123*, then *The sum of all accounts*, and then *true*. The type of the variable would change with the type of value assigned to it. The different types of literal values that can be assigned to a variable are covered in the following subsections.

Number Types—Integers and Floating-Point Numbers

When working with numbers, JavaScript supports both integer and floating-point values. It transparently converts from one type to another as values of one type are combined with values of other types in numerical expressions. For example, integer values are converted to floating-point values when they are used in floating-point expressions.

Integer Literals

Integers can be represented in JavaScript in decimal, hexadecimal, or octal form:

- A *decimal* (base 10) integer is what nonprogrammers are used to seeing—the digits 0 through 9, with each new column representing a higher power of 10.

- A *hexadecimal* (base 16) integer in JavaScript must always begin with the characters 0x or 0x in the two leftmost columns. Hexadecimal uses the digits 0 through 9 to represent the values 0 through 9 and the letters A through F to represent the values normal people know as 10 through 15.

- An *octal* (base 8) integer in JavaScript must always begin with the character 0 in the leftmost column. Octal uses only the digits 0 through 7.

Examples of decimal, hexadecimal, and octal integers are provided in Table 20.2.

TABLE 20.2: Examples of Decimal, Hexadecimal, and Octal Integers for the Same Values

DECIMAL NUMBER	HEXADECIMAL EQUIVALENT	OCTAL EQUIVALENT
19	0x13	023
255	0xff	0377
513	0x201	01001
1024	0x400	02000
12345	0x3039	030071

The program shown in Listing 20.10 illustrates the use of JavaScript hexadecimal and octal integers. Figure 20.17 shows how the Web page generated by this program is displayed. Note that the hexadecimal and octal integers are converted to decimal before they are displayed.

Listing 20.10: Using JavaScript Integers

```
<HTML>
<HEAD>
<TITLE>Using JavaScript integers</TITLE>
</HEAD>
<BODY>
<SCRIPT LANGUAGE="JavaScript">
<!--
document.write("0xab00 + 0xcd = ")
document.write(0xab00 + 0xcd)
document.write("<BR>")
document.write("0xff - 0123 = ")
document.write(0xff - 0123)
document.write("<BR>")
document.write("-0x12 = ")
document.write(-0x12)
// -->
</SCRIPT>
</BODY>
</HTML>
```

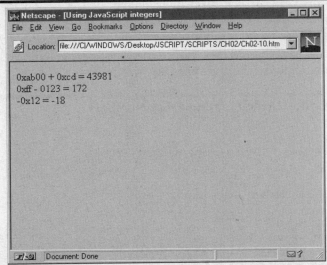

FIGURE 20.17: Using hexadecimal and octal integers (Listing 20.10)

Floating-Point Literals

Floating-point literals are used to represent numbers that require the use of a decimal point, or very large or small numbers that must be written using exponential notation.

A floating-point number must consist of either a number containing a decimal point or an integer followed by an exponent. The following are valid floating-point numbers:

-4.321

55.

12e2

1e-2

7e1

-4e-4

.5

As you can see in the examples above, floating-point literals may contain an initial integer, followed by an optional decimal point and fraction, followed by an optional exponent (*e* or *E*) and its integer exponent value. For example, 4e6 equals 4×10 to the sixth power, which equals 4,000,000. Also, the initial integer and integer exponent value may be signed as positive or negative (+ or −). Up to 20 significant digits may be used to represent floating-point values.

The script shown in Listing 20.11 and Figure 20.18 illustrates how JavaScript displays these values. Notice that JavaScript simplifies the display of these numbers whenever possible.

Listing 20.11:   Using Floating-Point Numbers

```
<HTML>
<HEAD>
<TITLE>Using floating-point numbers</TITLE>
</HEAD>
<BODY>
<SCRIPT LANGUAGE="JavaScript">
<!--
document.write(-4.321)
document.write("<BR>")
document.write(55.)
document.write("<BR>")
```

```
document.write(12e2)
document.write("<BR>")
document.write(1e-2)
document.write("<BR>")
document.write(7e1)
document.write("<BR>")
document.write(-4e-4)
document.write("<BR>")
document.write(.5)
// -->
</SCRIPT>
</BODY>
</HTML>
```

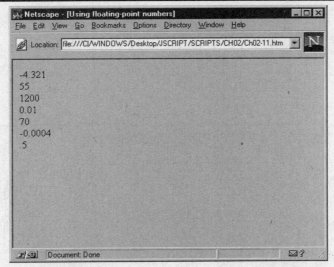

FIGURE 20.18: How JavaScript displays floating-point numbers (Listing 20.11)

Boolean Values

JavaScript, like Java, supports a pure Boolean type that consists of the two values true and false. Several logical operators may be used in Boolean expressions. JavaScript automatically converts the Boolean values true and false into 1 and 0 when they are used in numerical expressions. The script shown in Listing 20.12 illustrates this automatic conversion. Figure 20.19 shows the results of this conversion as displayed by Navigator.

NOTE

A *Boolean value* is a value that is either true or false. The word *Boolean* is taken from the name of the mathematician George Boole, who developed much of the fundamental theory of mathematical logic.

Listing 20.12: Conversion of Logical Values to Numeric Values

```
<HTML>
<HEAD>
<TITLE>Conversion of logical values to numeric values</TITLE>
</HEAD>
<BODY>
<SCRIPT LANGUAGE="JavaScript">
<!--
document.write("true*5 + false*7 = ")
document.write(true*5 +false*7)
// -->
</SCRIPT>
</BODY>
</HTML>
```

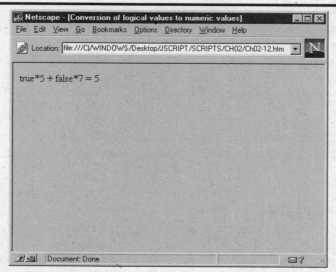

FIGURE 20.19: How logical values are converted to other types (Listing 20.12)

String Values

JavaScript provides built-in support for strings of characters. A string is a sequence of zero or more characters that are enclosed by double (") or single quotes ('). If a string begins with a double quote, then it must end with a double quote. Likewise, if a string begins with a single quote, then it must end in a single quote.

To insert a single or double quote character in a string, you must precede it by the backslash (\) escape character. The following are examples of the use of the escape character to insert quotes into strings:

```
"He asked, \"Who owns this book?\""
'It\'s Bill\'s book.'
```

The script shown in Listing 20.13 illustrates the use of quotes within strings. Figure 20.20 shows how the strings are displayed. Note that single quotes do not need to be coded with escape characters when they are used within double-quoted strings. Similarly, double quotes do not need to be coded when they are used within single-quoted strings.

Listing 20.13:   Using Quotes within Strings

```html
<HTML>
<HEAD>
<TITLE>Using quotes within strings</TITLE>
</HEAD>
<BODY>
<SCRIPT LANGUAGE="JavaScript">
<!--
document.write("He said, \"That's mine!\"<BR>")
document.write('She said, "No it\'s not."<BR>')
document.write('That\'s all folks!')
// -->
</SCRIPT>
</BODY>
</HTML>
```

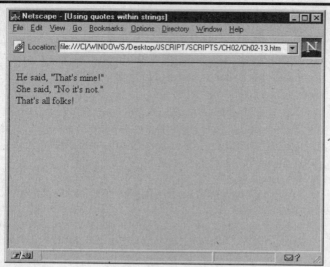

FIGURE 20.20: How quotes are inserted into strings (Listing 20.13)

JavaScript defines special formatting characters for use in strings. These characters are identified in Table 20.3.

TABLE 20.3: Special Formatting Characters

CHARACTER	MEANING
\'	single quote
\"	double quote
\\	backslash
\n	new line
\r	carriage return
\f	form feed
\t	horizontal tab
\b	backspace
\v	vertical tab

The script shown in Listing 20.14 shows how these formatting characters are used. Figure 20.21 displays the Web page generated by this script. The Web page uses the HTML *preformatted text* tags to prevent the formatting characters from being treated as HTML whitespace characters. Notice that the backspace character is incorrectly displayed, the form feed character is ignored, and that the carriage return character is displayed in the same manner as the new line character. Even though these characters are not fully supported in the display of Web pages, they may still be used to insert formatting codes within data and files that JavaScript produces.

NOTE

Any Unicode character may be encoded using a special escape sequence consisting of \uxxxx, where each x is a hexadecimal digit, and the four digits provide the Unicode value for the character. For example, \u0041 is the escape sequence for the letter *A*.

Listing 20.14:   Using Special Formatting Characters

```
<HTML>
<HEAD>
<TITLE>Using special formatting characters</TITLE>
</HEAD>
<BODY>
<PRE>
<SCRIPT LANGUAGE="JavaScript">
<!--
document.write("This shows how the \bbackspace character
works.\n")
document.write("This shows how the \ttab character works.\n")
document.write("This shows how the \rcarriage return
character works.\n")
document.write("This shows how the \fform feed character
works.\n")
document.write("This shows how the \nnew line character
works.\n")
// -->
</SCRIPT>
</PRE>
</BODY>
</HTML>
```

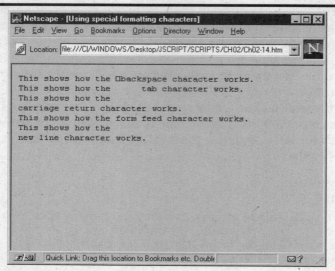

FIGURE 20.21: This is how formatting characters are handled (Listing 20.14). Note that your Web browser does not process all characters.

The null Value

The null value is common to all JavaScript types. It is used to set a variable to an initial value that is different from other valid values. Use of the null value prevents the sort of errors that result from using uninitialized variables. The null value is automatically converted to default values of other types when used in an expression, as you'll see in the following section, "Conversion between Types."

The undefined Value

The undefined value indicates that a variable has been created but not assigned a value. Like the null value, the undefined value is common to all JavaScript types and is automatically converted to default values of these types. The undefined value is converted to NaN for numeric types, false for Boolean, and "undefined" for strings.

Conversion between Types

JavaScript automatically converts values from one type to another when they are used in an expression. This means that you can combine different types in an expression and JavaScript will try to perform the type conversions that are necessary for the expression to make sense. For example, the expression `"test"` + 5 will convert the numeric 5 to a string `"5"` and append it to the string `"test"`, producing `"test5"`. JavaScript's automatic type conversion also allows you to assign a value of one type to a variable and then later assign a value of a different type to the same variable.

How does JavaScript convert from one type to another? The process of determining when a conversion should occur and what type of conversion should be made is fairly complex. JavaScript converts values when it evaluates an expression or assigns a value to a variable. When JavaScript assigns a value to a variable, it changes the type associated with the variable to the type of the value that is assigns.

When JavaScript evaluates an expression, it parses the expression into its component unary and binary expressions based upon the order of precedence of the operators it contains. It then evaluates the component unary and binary expressions of the parse tree. Figure 20.22 illustrates this process. Each expression is evaluated according to the operators involved. If an operator takes a value of a type that is different than the type of an operand, then the operand is converted to a type that is valid for the operator.

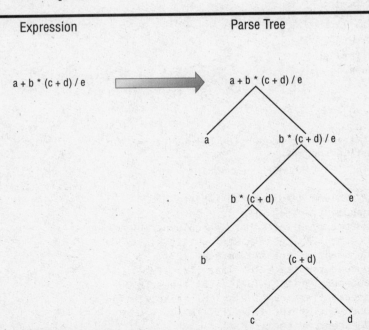

FIGURE 20.22: Expressions are evaluated based on the types of operators involved.

Some operators, such as the + operator, may be used for more than one type. For example, "a"+"b" results in the string "ab" when the + operator is used with string values, but it assumes its typical arithmetic meaning when used with numeric operands. What happens when JavaScript attempts to evaluate "a"+3? JavaScript converts the integer 3 into the string "3" and yields "a3" for the expression. In general, JavaScript will favor string operators over all others, followed by floating-point, integer, and logical operators.

The script shown in Listing 20.15 illustrates JavaScript conversion between types when the + operator is used. Figure 20.23 shows how the Web page resulting from this script is displayed.

Listing 20.15: Automatic Conversion between Types

```
<HTML>
<HEAD>
<TITLE>Implicit conversion between types</TITLE>
<SCRIPT LANGUAGE="JavaScript">
<!--
s1="test"
s2="12.34"
i=123
r=.123
lt=true
lf=false
n=null
// -->
</SCRIPT>
</HEAD>
<BODY>
<H1>Implicit conversion between types</H1>
<TABLE BORDER=2>
<SCRIPT LANGUAGE="JavaScript">
<!--
// Column headings for table
document.write("<TR>")
document.write("<TH>row + column</TH>")
document.write("<TH>string \"12.34\"</TH>")
document.write("<TH>integer 123</TH>")
document.write("<TH>float .123</TH>")
document.write("<TH>logical true</TH>")
document.write("<TH>logical false</TH>")
document.write("<TH>null</TH>")
document.write("</TR>")
```

```
// First operand is a string
document.write("<TR>")
document.write("<TH>string \"test\"</TH>")
document.write("<TD>")
document.write(s1+s2)
document.write("</TD><TD>")
document.write(s1+i)
document.write("</TD><TD>")
document.write(s1+r)
document.write("</TD><TD>")
document.write(s1+lt)
document.write("</TD><TD>")
document.write(s1+lf)
document.write("</TD><TD>")
document.write(s1+n)
document.write("</TD>")
document.write("</TR>")
// First operand is an integer
document.write("<TR>")
document.write("<TH>integer 123</TH>")
document.write("<TD>")
document.write(i+s2)
document.write("</TD><TD>")
document.write(i+i)
document.write("</TD><TD>")
document.write(i+r)
document.write("</TD><TD>")
document.write(i+lt)
document.write("</TD><TD>")
document.write(i+lf)
document.write("</TD><TD>")
document.write(i+n)
document.write("</TD>")
document.write("</TR>")
// First operand is a float
document.write("<TR>")
document.write("<TH>float .123</TH>")
document.write("<TD>")
document.write(r+s2)
document.write("</TD><TD>")
document.write(r+i)
document.write("</TD><TD>")
document.write(r+r)
document.write("</TD><TD>")
document.write(r+lt)
document.write("</TD><TD>")
```

```
document.write(r+lf)
document.write("</TD><TD>")
document.write(r+n)
document.write("</TD>")
document.write("</TR>")
// First operand is a logical true
document.write("<TR>")
document.write("<TH>logical true</TH>")
document.write("<TD>")
document.write(lt+s2)
document.write("</TD><TD>")
document.write(lt+i)
document.write("</TD><TD>")
document.write(lt+r)
document.write("</TD><TD>")
document.write(lt+lt)
document.write("</TD><TD>")
document.write(lt+lf)
document.write("</TD><TD>")
document.write(lt+n)
document.write("</TD>")
document.write("</TR>")
// First operand is a logical false
document.write("<TR>")
document.write("<TH>logical false</TH>")
document.write("<TD>")
document.write(lf+s2)
document.write("</TD><TD>")
document.write(lf+i)
document.write("</TD><TD>")
document.write(lf+r)
document.write("</TD><TD>")
document.write(lf+lt)
document.write("</TD><TD>")
document.write(lf+lf)
document.write("</TD><TD>")
document.write(lf+n)
document.write("</TD>")
document.write("</TR>")
// First operand is null
document.write("<TR>")
document.write("<TH>null</TH>")
document.write("<TD>")
document.write(n+s2)
document.write("</TD><TD>")
document.write(n+i)
```

```
document.write("</TD><TD>")
document.write(n+r)
document.write("</TD><TD>")
document.write(n+lt)
document.write("</TD><TD>")
document.write(n+lf)
document.write("</TD><TD>")
document.write(n+n)
document.write("</TD>")
document.write("</TR>")
// -->
</SCRIPT>
</TABLE>
</BODY>
</HTML>
```

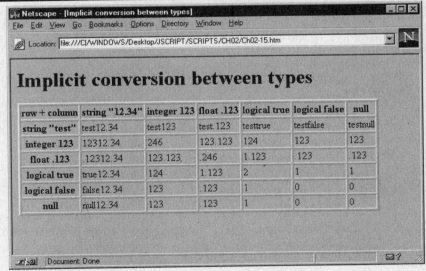

FIGURE 20.23: Conversion table for the + operator (Listing 20.15)

Note that in all cases where string operands are used with a nonstring operator, JavaScript converts the other operator into a string:

▶ Numeric values are converted to their appropriate string value.

▶ Boolean values are converted to 1 and 0 to support numerical operations.

► The null value is converted to "null" for string operations, false for logical operations, and 0 for numerical operations.

Let's take a look at Listing 20.15. The script in the document head defines the variables to be used in the table's operations. The s1 and s2 variables are assigned string values. The i and r variables are assigned integer and floating-point values. The lt and lf variables are assigned logical values. The n variable is assigned the null value.

The script in the document body is fairly long. However, most of the script is used to generate the HTML tags for the cells of the conversion table. The script is surrounded by the tags <TABLE BORDER=2> and </TABLE>. The script then generates the cells of the table one row at a time. The <TR> and </TR> tags mark a row of the table. The <TH> and </TH> tags mark header cells. The <TD> and </TD> tags identify normal nonheader table cells.

First, the column header row is displayed. Then each row of the table shown in Figure 20.23 is generated by combining the operand at the row heading with the operand at the table heading using the + operator.

NOTE

Internet Explorer displays Figure 20.23 slightly differently. If a decimal number has a magnitude less than 1, then Internet Explorer prepends a 0 when displaying the number or converting it to a string value. For example, .123 is displayed as 0.123.

Conversion Functions

Functions are collections of JavaScript code that perform a particular task and often return a value. A function may take zero or more parameters. These parameters are used to specify the data to be processed by the function.

JavaScript provides three functions that are used to perform explicit type conversion. These are eval(), parseInt(), and parseFloat().

NOTE

Functions are referenced by their name with the empty parameter list () appended. This makes it easier to differentiate between functions and variables in the discussion of scripts.

The eval() function can be used to convert a string expression to a numeric value. For example, the statement total = eval("432.1*10") results in the value 4321 being assigned to the total variable. The eval() function takes the string value "432.1*10" as a parameter and returns the numeric value 4321 as the result of the function call. If the string value passed as a parameter to the eval() function does not represent a numeric value, then use of eval() results in an error being generated.

The parseInt() function is used to convert a string value into an integer. Unlike eval(), parseInt() returns the first integer contained in the string or 0 if the string does not begin with an integer. For example, parseInt ("123xyz") returns 123 and parseInt("xyz") returns 0. The parseInt() function also parses hexadecimal and decimal integers.

The parseFloat() function is similar to the parseInt() function. It returns the first floating-point number contained in a string or 0 if the string does not begin with a valid floating-point number. For example, parseFloat("2.1e4xyz") returns 21000 and parseFloat("xyz") returns 0.

The script shown in Listing 20.16 illustrates the use of JavaScript's explicit conversion functions. Figure 20.24 shows how the Web page that this script generates is displayed.

Listing 20.16:   Explicit Conversion Functions

```
<HTML>
<HEAD>
<TITLE>Using Explicit Conversion Functions</TITLE>
</HEAD>
<BODY>
<H1 ALIGN="CENTER">Using Explicit Conversion Functions</H1>
<SCRIPT LANGUAGE="JavaScript"><!--
document.write('eval("12.34*10") = ')
document.write(eval("12.34*10"))
document.write("<BR>")
document.write('parseInt("0x10") = ')
document.write(parseInt("0x10"))
document.write("<BR>")
document.write('parseFloat("5.4321e6") = ')
document.write(parseFloat("5.4321e6"))
// --></SCRIPT>
</BODY>
</HTML>
```

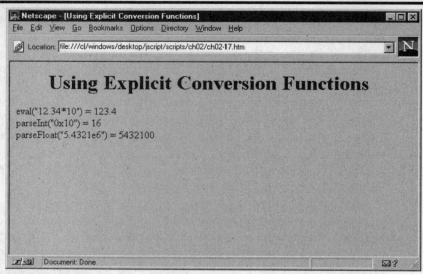

FIGURE 20.24: Using the JavaScript conversion functions (Listing 20.16)

The Object Type and Arrays

In addition to the primitive types discussed in the previous sections, JavaScript supports the Object type. This type is referred to as a complex data type because it is built from the primitive types. Next, I'll cover a special JavaScript object—the array.

NOTE

Arrays are a special type of JavaScript object.

Arrays—Accessing Indexed Values

Arrays are objects that are capable of storing a sequence of values. These values are stored in indexed locations within the array. For example, suppose you have a company with five employees and you want to display the names of your employees on a Web page. You could keep track of their names in an array variable named `employee`. You would construct the array using the statement:

```
employee = new Array(5)
```

and store the names of your employees in the array using the following statements:

```
employee[0] = "Bill"
employee[1] = "Bob"
employee[2] = "Ted"
employee[3] = "Alice"
employee[4] = "Sue"
```

You could then access the names of the individual employees by referring to the individual elements of the array. For example, you could display the names of your employees using statements such as the following:

```
document.write(employee[0])
document.write(employee[1])
document.write(employee[2])
document.write(employee[3])
document.write(employee[4])
```

The script shown in Listing 20.17 illustrates the use of arrays. Figure 20.25 shows how the Web page this script generates is displayed.

Listing 20.17:   Using JavaScript Arrays

```
<HTML>
<HEAD>
<TITLE>Using Arrays</TITLE>
</HEAD>
<BODY>
<H1 ALIGN="CENTER">Using Arrays</H1>
<SCRIPT LANGUAGE="JavaScript"><!--
employee = new Array(5)
employee[0] = "Bill"
employee[1] = "Bob"
employee[2] = "Ted"
employee[3] = "Alice"
employee[4] = "Sue"
document.write(employee[0]+"<BR>")
document.write(employee[1]+"<BR>")
document.write(employee[2]+"<BR>")
document.write(employee[3]+"<BR>")
document.write(employee[4])
// --></SCRIPT>
</BODY>
</HTML>
```

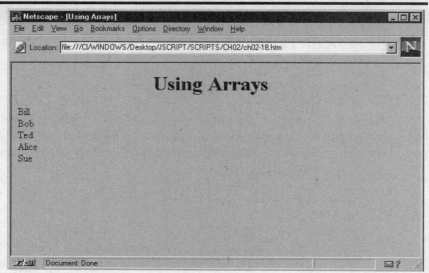

FIGURE 20.25: Arrays allow multiple values to be stored with a single variable (Listing 20.17).

The *length* of an array is the number of elements that it contains. In the example script of Listing 20.17, the length of the employee array is 5. The individual elements of an array are referenced using the name of the array followed by the index of the array element enclosed in brackets. Because the first index is 0, the last index is one less than the length of the array. For example, suppose that you have an array named day of length 7 that contains the names of the days of the week. The individual elements of this array would be accessed as day[0], day[1], ..., day[6].

Constructing Arrays

An array object must be constructed before it is used. An array may be constructed using either of the following two statement forms:

- ▶ arrayName = new Array(arrayLength)

- ▶ arrayName = new Array()

NOTE
A third form of array construction is discussed in the following subsection, "Constructing Dense Arrays."

In the first form, the length of the array is explicitly specified. An example of this form is:

```
days = new Array(7)
```

In the above example, days corresponds to the array name and 7 corresponds to the array length.

In the second array construction form, the length of the array is not specified and results in the creation of an array of length 0. An example of using this type of array construction follows:

```
order = new Array()
```

This constructs an array of length 0 that is used to keep track of customer orders. JavaScript automatically extends the length of an array when new array elements are initialized. For example, the following statements create an order array of length 0 and then subsequently extend the length of the array to 100 and then 1000.

```
order = new Array()
order[99] = "Widget #457"
order[999] = "Delux Widget Set #10"
```

When JavaScript encounters the reference to order[99], in the above example, it extends the length of the array to 100 and initializes order[99] to "Widget #457". When JavaScript encounters the reference to order[999] in the third statement, it extends the length of order to 1000 and initializes order[999] to "Delux Widget Set #10".

Even if an array is initially created with a fixed initial length, it still may be extended by referencing elements that are outside the current size of the array. This is accomplished in the same manner as with zero-length arrays. Listing 20.18 shows how fixed-length arrays are expanded as new array elements are referenced. Figure 20.26 shows the how the Web page that this script generates is displayed.

Listing 20.18:   Extending the Length of an Array

```
<HTML>
<HEAD>
<TITLE>Extending Arrays</TITLE>
</HEAD>
<BODY>
<H1 ALIGN="CENTER">Extending Arrays</H1>
<SCRIPT LANGUAGE="JavaScript"><!--
order = new Array()
document.write("order.length = "+order.length+"<BR>")
order[99] = "Widget #457"
```

Part iv

```
document.write("order.length = "+order.length+"<BR>")
order[999] = "Delux Widget Set #10"
document.write("order.length = "+order.length+"<BR>")
// --></SCRIPT>
</BODY>
</HTML>
```

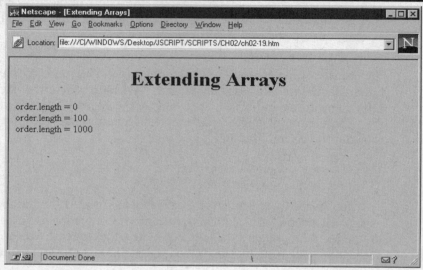

FIGURE 20.26: An array's length dynamically expands as new elements are referenced (Listing 20.18).

Constructing Dense Arrays　A *dense array* is an array that is initially constructed with each element being assigned a specified value. Dense arrays are used in the same manner as other arrays. They are just constructed and initialized in a more efficient manner. Dense arrays are specified by *listing* the values of the array elements, in place of the array length. Dense array declarations take the following form:

```
arrayName = new Array(value₀, value₁, ... , valueₙ)
```

In the above statement, because we start counting at zero, the length of the array is n+1.

When creating short length arrays, the dense array declaration is very efficient. For example, an array containing the three-letter abbreviations for the days of the week may be constructed using the following statement:

```
day = new Array('Sun','Mon','Tue','Wed','Thu','Fri','Sat')
```

The Elements of an Array   JavaScript does not place any restrictions on the values of the elements of an array. These values could be of different types, or could refer to other arrays or objects. For example, you could create an array as follows:

```
junk = new Array("s1",'s2',4,3.5,true,false,null,new
Array(5,6,7))
```

The `junk` array has length 8 and its elements are as follows:

```
junk[0]="s1"
junk[1]='s2'
junk[2]=4
junk[3]=3.5
junk[4]=true
junk[5]=false
junk[6]=null
junk[7]=a new dense array consisting of the values 5, 6, & 7
```

The last element of the array, `junk[7]`, contains an array as its value. The three elements of `junk[7]` can be accessed using *a second set of subscripts*, as follows:

```
junk[7][0]=5
junk[7][1]=6
junk[7][2]=7
```

The script shown in Listing 20.19 illustrates the use of arrays within arrays. Figure 20.27 shows the Web page that results from execution of this script.

Listing 20.19:   An Array within an Array

```
<HTML>
<HEAD>
<TITLE>Arrays within Arrays</TITLE>
</HEAD>
<BODY>
<H1 ALIGN="CENTER">Arrays within Arrays</H1>
<SCRIPT LANGUAGE="JavaScript"><!--
junk = new Array("s1",'s2',4,3.5,true,false,null,new
Array(5,6,7))
document.write("junk[0] = "+junk[0]+"<BR>")
document.write("junk[1] = "+junk[1]+"<BR>")
document.write("junk[2] = "+junk[2]+"<BR>")
document.write("junk[3] = "+junk[3]+"<BR>")
document.write("junk[4] = "+junk[4]+"<BR>")
document.write("junk[5] = "+junk[5]+"<BR>")
document.write("junk[6] = "+junk[6]+"<BR>")
```

```
document.write("junk[7][0] = "+junk[7][0]+"<BR>")
document.write("junk[7][1] = "+junk[7][1]+"<BR>")
document.write("junk[7][2] = "+junk[7][2])
// --></SCRIPT>
</BODY>
</HTML>
```

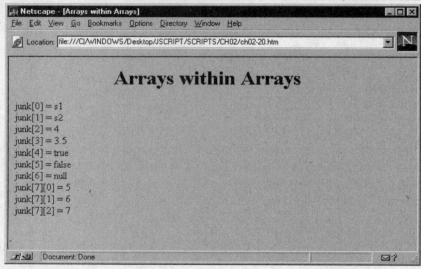

FIGURE 20.27: An array may contain another array as the value of one of its elements (Listing 20.19).

Objects and the Length Property

JavaScript arrays are implemented as objects. *Objects* are named collections of data that have properties and may be accessed via methods. A *property* returns a value that identifies some aspect of the state of an object. *Methods* are used to read or modify the data contained in an object.

The length of an array is a property of an array. You can access the property of any object in JavaScript by appending a period (.) plus the name of the property to the name of the object, as shown here:

objectName.propertyName

For example, the length of an array is determined as follows:

arrayName.length

Now, consider the following array:

```
a = new Array(2,4,6,8,10)
```

The value returned by a.length is 5.

In addition to the length property, arrays also support several methods.

SUMMARY

This chapter introduced you to the JavaScript language. You learned how JavaScript works and how JavaScript statements are embedded in HTML documents. You learned about JavaScript's use of types and variables, and how JavaScript automatically converts values of one type to another.

WHAT'S NEXT

In the next chapter, Kurt Cagle introduces you to the Extensible Markup Language (XML), the emerging Web technology that will change the way we design and deploy Web documents.

Chapter 21

XML Introduction and History

Mastering the *Extensible Markup Language*, or *XML*, will likely end up changing the way you think about programming, communications, and even the notion of meaning and context. Even though the language itself is simple—indeed, that's one of its strengths—XML is likely to completely rearrange the computer landscape. In this chapter, you'll learn why XML will likely be the data language of tomorrow and why it's so important that you learn how to work with it now.

Adapted from *XML Developer's Handbook*,
by Kurt Cagle
ISBN 0-7821-2704-5   704 pages $49.99

THE NEED FOR CONTEXT

What is meaning? This is one of those questions that first-year philosophy students inevitably trip up on. Until recently, meaning hasn't impacted computer programming significantly, but the answer to this question will ultimately prove to be the cornerstone of computing for the next several decades. The reason for this is simple: we have too much data and too little meaning.

We live in an age when data is everywhere. From the moment you crawl out of bed, you are blasted with data—the alarm clock kicking on and broadcasting news happening in Washington, D.C., and weather forecasts for the next five days. We open our papers and scan dozens of stories written less than 24 hours beforehand, get the RBIs of our favorite baseball players, and examine near-microscopic print to find out how many fractions of a dollar our mutual funds have risen or fallen since the last time we checked.

At work, we increasingly spend our lives juggling data, trying to make sense of a dip in sales figures in the western region, attempting to understand why the compiler is generating error -43225, and making sure that the hours billed are properly categorized. The *knowledge worker,* an appellation that covers everyone from a data entry clerk to the CEO of a large company, has replaced the blue-collar laborer as the typical wage earner. The computer revolution has rebuilt our entire society around knowledge, information, *meaning.*

Ironically, while too little data can lead to a false understanding of an issue, if you have too much data you usually have to expend a significant amount of energy and/or time to extract information from that data. For the vast period of human history, perhaps up to 1950 or so, data was expensive and relatively scarce, and the idea that one could have too much data was almost laughable.

This situation has completely reversed itself in the past 50 years as the means of creating, processing, and displaying data has leapt forward at an exponential pace. The famous prediction called *Moore's Law,* first observed by IBM chairman Gordon Moore, has proven reliable witness to this: roughly every 18 months, processing power (and, consequently, the ability to both acquire and display data) has doubled. Perhaps somewhat frightening, even this pace has sped up in the last decade.

Connectivity has played a big part in the dramatic advances of recent years. Networks have been a part of computing since the 1960s, but it was only when people started connecting personal computers, with their high concentration of processing power, with other such computers that structures like the Internet became possible. Unfortunately, one of the characteristics of most networks is that, as they grow, the interactions between different parts of the network can often cause feedback and other unexpected phenomena, making it more difficult to build tightly integrated systems.

Data + Context = Information

Moreover, *data is not information*. Data is the raw material, the input that forms information, but, in general, data exists in a separate context than the information it generates. For example, consider a small weather station that keeps track of such pieces of data as humidity, temperature, wind speed, and barometric pressure for a particular location, an airport. It transmits this data to a central system at regular intervals, adding the newly captured data (such as a location and a timestamp) to this basic record.

The air traffic controller at the airport will transmit this information to aircraft to help them anticipate dangerous weather conditions. A news station weather person will collect this data as well as similar data from other locations in the region to display on a regional weather map. A meteorologist will take this data, plus others from a much wider region, to prepare a short-range forecast of how the weather will change in a given area in the next few days. A climatologist will pull the data as a sample to combine with other data in order to perform a long-term modeling of weather patterns spanning years or decades.

Each of these individuals use the same data, either alone or in conjunction with other data, but they manipulate this data within different contexts. Even if all systems technically could communicate transparently, they would still require some way of shifting the data context easily. To date, most of this shifting is performed through the use of expensive, programmer-intensive solutions. (If the number of want ads for Web developers is any indication, this demand for programmers is far outstripping the supply.)

This weather example provides a good rule of thumb: data without any underlying framework, without context, is essentially just white noise. Information can only be retrieved from data if that data is placed into some form of context. You can think of context in this light as a function; working with the raw data, it filters out unnecessary data and returns what's relevant. To the air traffic controller, the present wind speed is a highly important value, so the amount of processing, the context, is fairly minimal. On the other hand, to the climatologist, the wind speed at 2:00 P.M. on March 3, 2000, at the Olympia airport is largely irrelevant, except as it provides one point in a large and complex data sample.

The Birth of the Internet

As networks increase in size and number, the amount of data that these networks produce grows as well, and has long since surpassed the point where it can be effectively managed by human beings. Sometime around the summer of 1997, the amount of data being held in electronic form surpassed the total number of words in all the written works ever produced. By the time this book is published, it is estimated that that number will have grown to four times the total number of words in all of human literature, with it effectively doubling every 18 months thereafter.

The Internet is obviously the world's largest network, so it's not surprising that many of the problems dealing with information overload first surfaced there. The most apparent (though by no means the only) part of the Internet is the World Wide Web, the system of interconnected HTML pages, server pages, and similar resources that has ended up consuming so many otherwise-productive office hours. While historians can point to any number of possible events that culminated in today's Internet, the World Wide Web was essentially the invention of one man, Tim Berners-Lee, at the time (1990) a programmer working for the CERN High-Energy Research Lab in Geneva, Switzerland and currently one of the principle members of the World Wide Web Consortium.

NOTE

The World Wide Web Consortium, also known as the W3C, is the final arbiter for most of the information standards currently in use on the Internet. The latest XML and HTML standards can be found at the W3C Web site: http://www.w3.org.

Berners-Lee's objective when he created the basic protocols of the Web—the Hypertext Transfer Protocol (HTTP) and the Hypertext Markup Language (HTML)—was hardly world domination. Instead, several scientists at CERN needed to store and transmit documents in a way that would allow easy reference by other scientists within the organization and would let scientists reference each other's pages via hypertext; Berners-Lee set out to address this need.

While hypertext systems had been around for several years before that time, they were principally proprietary in nature. The primary difference in Berners-Lee's design was that he distributed the document viewer (the first browser) as a low-bandwidth application and made both the protocols and the software freely available. Needless to say, word about the applications (and the applications themselves) spread quickly, especially once the combination of HTML and HTTP made its way to educational institutions.

The Historical Relationship between HTML and XML

The history of HTML is well known, but one facet that relates to XML is worth stressing: *HTML was originally designed to be used as a way to transmit and display physics abstracts.* Most of the abstracts at CERN made use of the Standard Generalized Markup Language, or SGML, a description language used primarily to store theses, reports, product help information, and other related documentation.

SGML can trace its roots back to the 1960s, when its precursor, the Generalized Markup Language (GML), was developed by Charles Goldfarb, Edward Mosher, and Raymond Lorie at IBM in order to help organize the vast amount of documentation that the company was beginning to produce. By 1978, the American National Standards Institute (ANSI) took the basics of GML and fashioned a nationwide standard called GCA 101-1983. Six years later, after GCA had proven so demonstratively successful at document management, the International Organization for Standardization (ISO) began work on a global version, which became *Information Processing—Text and Office Systems—Standard Generalized Markup Language (SGML)*, ISO 8879:1986, in 1986.

Berners-Lee created HTML as an instance of SGML; he used the rules laid down by SGML to set up the tags that the abstracts would be written in. The heading structure and similar elements that formed the earliest versions of HTML worked well in a number of circumstances, but the appearance of tags such as CITE at least hint that the structure Berners-Lee set up was never intended to go beyond creating abstracts.

Go beyond it the language did, however. By the early 1990s, HTML pages output by HTTP servers took research facilities and universities by storm. The language began to get stretched this way and that as young programmers began playing around with HTTP servers and HTML viewers (also known as browsers). One of the most successful HTTP browsers by far was Mosaic, created by Marc Andreesen and others at the newly opened National Center for Supercomputing Applications (NCSA) at the University of Illinois at Champaign.

NOTE

A personal note: I was a student at the University of Illinois when the NCSA opened, although I missed working with Andreesen (and, no doubt, becoming a multi-billionaire) by about six months.

Mosaic put a graphical face on the Web. In the original HTML spec, an image reference was a hypertext link to a graphics document, which was then opened up in a separate viewer application. With the advent of Mosaic, you could embed graphic images directly into a document, in essence turning what had been a very dry tool for navigating physics documents into a medium for mass communication. Mosaic became *the* killer application for the World Wide Web, and Silicon Graphics founder James Clark joined forces with Andreesen to launch Netscape, Inc.

Did the Browser Wars Kill HTML?

Back to context for a moment. As previously indicated, HTML's initial purpose was to describe scientific abstracts. It had a very definite structure to it, with the principle headers (such as <h1>, <h2>, and <h3>) echoing primary and subordinate header information, the paragraph tag (<p>) containing paragraphs of information, the citation tags indicating document citations, and so forth. If you set up such a document, then you could reasonably expect that a program could load the document, parse it, and produce a very credible abstract based upon the tag types. In other words, the earliest HTML had a fairly well-defined context.

The allure of incorporating graphics into presentations, coupled with the extremely rapid growth of the Netscape browser market, introduced a problem. The vast majority of people are not SGML experts (thankfully). Those who started playing with Web pages designed by the seats of their pants, initially with little to no documentation about why the language had the structure it had. Graphical elements began creeping into documents not simply as informational elements (the reason they were there originally) but more and more often as navigation buttons, image maps, and related components. Netscape then lowered the bar on entry, making the HTML parser extremely tolerant of sloppy code—an open paragraph mark became implicit, image tags and rules didn't need to be closed, emphasis (<EM>) and strong (<S>) tags became bold (<B>) and italic (<I>) respectively.

In other words, HTML began to shift from being a context-based markup language to being a typographic markup language. This is not totally surprising. Typographic languages emphasize visual presentation, and the reason that people were creating Web pages was to make visual displays, not to reference scholastic abstracts. A Web builder for an ad agency wanting to make a strong display for a client, for example, didn't need abstraction; she needed a way to translate the precise layout control that she was used to with programs like QuarkXPress and Aldus (now Adobe) PageMaker.

The browser wars of the mid-1990s contributed to this problem. Stung by critics for being late to embrace the Internet, Bill Gates chose December 7, 1995, to sound a battle cry against the dominant Internet browser company, Netscape, and he stated his determination to make Microsoft an Internet-centric company. (Whether they've managed to pull it off is still subject to some debate.) In the ensuing four years, Microsoft and Netscape battled for both mind-share of the browser market and greater control of the HTTP server market. In the end, Netscape folded. In 1999, America Online and Sun Microsystems jointly acquired the company, changing the name on the letterhead (and in the "About Box") to iPlanet, and effectively finishing off the spoils.

However, one of the major casualties in the war was context. Proposals for new tags were submitted to the W3C almost every other day, with such notorious ideas as the blink tag (Netscape) and the marquee tag (Microsoft) both superlative examples of truly useless (and semantically bankrupt) elements that were included to attract users.

Yet if the blink tag was egregious, other tags rendered what little context that had been in the original document language largely moot. The TABLE, for example, is a semantically empty container for tabular data. The ability to span multiple columns or rows with a single cell meant that even basic table header information could no longer be relied upon to determine the meaning of a column programmatically. Furthermore, differences between tables in the Netscape-vs.-Microsoft model meant that it was almost impossible to impart some type of context into a table even if you wanted to.

The FRAME is another example of an HTML element with dubious consequences for context. With frames, trying to understand the meaning of a given Web page became practically impossible. It also made navigation in Web pages much more complex, and differing degrees of support for the HTML version 3 standard made programming uniformly against frames a nightmare for the Web developer.

However, perhaps the low point for making contextually rich HTML documents came with the font tag. The font tag lets you specify a span's size, font name, and color. If you wanted to, you could create a font tag that made paragraph text appear identical to h1 text (or vice versa). While the original intention was fairly noble (separating the presentation layer from the context layer), most people and many applications used the font tag as a lazy way of formatting a Web page without putting any thought into the structure of the program.

Of course, all of these elements were exacerbated by the dueling standards that both Microsoft and Netscape engaged in. Both companies attempted to create features that would give them an advantage in the burgeoning browser market, and these enhancements to HTML meant that designing for the two primary browsers typically involved writing two sets of code (or more as newer versions broke older standards). The best solutions for writing dual code ultimately came down to relying on such proprietary solutions as Macromedia's Shockwave, applications that made sure that the Web experience was the same on both systems but were also essentially invisible to search engines and indexers.

The Presentation Layer Breaks Loose

By 1996, it was becoming obvious to most Web developers that HTML was badly broken. Incompatibilities between browsers, tags that stressed presentation over content, and the rise in third-party "solutions" had all weakened the standard to such an extent that the technique of simply adding more tags no longer seemed quite so viable.

About this time, the W3C convened a working group to study the viability of implementing a style sheet language into the Web standard. Style sheets have been a part of the publishing landscape for some time. In essence, with a style sheet you can map a set of attributes to a named style and then apply the style to a selection of text (or some other element on the page).

A couple of different approaches were considered. One of the first involved adapting SGML's Document Style Semantics and Specification

Language (DSSSL), a transformation language that essentially processes tags and creates a formalized output from them. DSSSL is a very rich and robust language, capable of actually manipulating the order and other essential characteristics of a document, but it has the disadvantage of also being a fairly complex language, sufficiently so as to make DSSSL difficult to write for novice Web builders.

Over time, the consensus of the W3C members shifted to Cascading Style Sheets (CSS). In CSS, each style was represented by a rule, which consisted of zero or more attributes grouped together into a single unit. The rule could be applied to a single HTML element, or it could be applied as a class to specific tags. While not as robust as DSSSL, CSS was considerably simpler to use, and it more readily fit the document object model that Microsoft was beginning to push.

In December, 1996, the CSS1 model was approved, marking the beginning of Dynamic HTML, HTML code that could be changed on the fly by altering CSS attributes. A second draft of CSS (CSS2) was ratified in May, 1998, covering media specifications and internationalization. The third draft of CSS (CSS3) is currently under consideration and will likely examine behavioral extensions, Scalable Vector Graphics (SVG) integration, and incorporation of input item characteristics into the CSS2 model.

TIP

To find out more about the current developments in CSS, check the Web site at http://www.w3.org/Style/css.

THE EMERGENCE OF XML

Perhaps one of the most important things to come out of the search for a better style sheet language was the awareness on the part of many experts in the Web community that it was perhaps time to reexamine the reason for HTML in the first place. As mentioned previously, HTML is basically a language for dealing with abstracts, although by 1995 it had evolved into an editorial language. This worked fairly well for editorial content—stories, articles, dissertations—but seemed to be increasingly inadequate for businesses wanting to sell their wares online, for companies that saw the Internet as a way to get crucial information out to agents in the field, or for heavily multimedia-driven sites.

Part iv

The tag- and attribute-based notation used in HTML had become a standard convention by 1995, and companies increasingly began to come up with their own proprietary extensions to HTML, although these were principally for server-side code creation. Allaire's ColdFusion was one of the first to build a consistent set of proprietary tags for use in building Web pages, and Microsoft used a tag and percent notation to implement the foundation language for their MSN system, which in time became Active Server Pages.

However, such systems pretty much worked exclusively on the server since the client browser had no understanding of how to interpret the tags. The SGML proponents raised the suggestion of using SGML itself on the Web, but this particular approach had a number of problems. While SGML is not itself a proprietary system, it is an incredibly complex one; the specification for the language runs several hundreds of pages, and is most notable for the bewildering varieties of rules and exceptions that the metalanguage has.

While this complexity is necessary for the sophisticated corporate applications that use it, the demands of a Web-based solution mean that the version of SGML would have to be:

- ▶ Lightweight

- ▶ Easy to use

- ▶ Unambiguous (with as few exceptions as possible)

- ▶ Extensible (easily modified)

Of these requirements, SGML only satisfied the extensibility criterion. However, given that HTML was an SGML instance, it seemed reasonable to create a new markup language that embodied the best features of SGML but demonstrated the simplicity that had been one of the most defining characteristics of HTML. In 1997, the W3C convened a working group of Web and SGML experts to try to resolve this dilemma, and on February 10, 1998, the proposal for the Extensible Markup Language (XML) version 1 was accepted as a recommendation.

TIP

The XML version 1 specification, also known as REC-xml-19980210, can be found at http://www.w3.org/TR/REC-xml.

A Quick Lexicon

A typical XML structure looks much like an oddly named HTML file, although, for a number of reasons, most XML documents in use today actually are fairly highly structured. A simple example might be a purchase order that could look something like Listing 21.1.

Listing 21.1:   A Purchase Order for ACME Rockets, as an XML Document

```
<?xml version="1.0"?>
<purchaseOrder type="1125" processed="false">
    <header>
        <orderFrom>Wiley E. Coyote</orderFrom>
        <orderTo>ACME Rocket Company</orderTo>
        <address>
            <street>1105 N. Sonoma Way</street>
            <city>Death Valley</city>
            <state>Arizona</state>
            </country>
        </address>
    </header>
    <body>
        <!-- The last rockets exploded prematurely. Please do
        watch your quality control. - WEC -->
        <lineItem>
            <name>Mark X Rocket</name>
            <description><![CDATA[Big, powerful red rockets,
suitable for chasing highly mobile desert birds.]]>
        </description>
            <number>24</number>
            <filter>if &gt; 15</filter>
            <unit>Individual</unit>
            <price>3.25</price>
            <priceUnit>USD</priceUnit>
            <discount>22.15</discount>
            <priceUnit>USD</priceUnit>
        </lineItem>
    </body>
</purchaseOrder>
```

While simple, this particular example shows most of the major elements of a stand-alone XML document—stand-alone in that there are no Document Type Definitions (DTDs) or schema information. In the preceding example, seven basic types of objects make up the document: processing instructions tags, elements tags, attributes, text, CDATA sections, entities, and comments, which have the characteristics detailed in the following sections:

Processing Instructions (PIs)

A *processing instruction* is bracketed by opening and closing question tags, as shown in the following example:

```
<? This is a processing instruction ?>
```

Processing instructions provide information outside of the normal scope of the XML structure for use by either the parser or third-party utilities. For example, you could use processing instructions to specify which display set to use when outputting the XML data. Formal XML structures should always start out with the `<?xml version="1.0"?>` PI to indicate that this is an XML document, although most parsers will not generate errors if this first line is not included.

Elements

An *element* consists of an open angle bracket immediately followed by a single word tag and zero or more name/value pairs (called attributes) terminated by a closing angle bracket, as shown in the following example:

```
<purchaseOrder type="1125" processed="false">
```

The closing tag is similar to the format of an HTML tag, with the terminating tag starting with a `</` string (instead of `<`), as in the following line:

```
</purchaseOrder>
```

In HTML, certain elements don't need to be explicitly terminated, such as the `<BR>` tag. In XML, on the other hand, if an element doesn't contain any text or other elements, you still need to terminate it. However, you can use an abbreviated form for such elements, in which the forward slash is moved to the end of the tag. In that case, you don't need an explicit closing tag, as demonstrated in the following line:

```
<country/>
```

Attributes

An *attribute* is a name/value pair that's associated with a given element. For example, in the `purchaseOrder` tag, both `type` and `processed` are the names of attributes, as shown in the following example:

```
<purchaseOrder type="1125" processed="false">
```

What should constitute an attribute versus an element has spawned more than a few heated debates upon list servers and newsgroups and is a subject that will be revisited in depth later in this chapter. As a general rule of thumb, elements give you added flexibility for processing, though at the possible cost of speed, while attributes are easily accessible but are not as flexible. An attribute cannot contain a line break or XML symbols, such as < or &, and many parsers place an upper limit (typically around 256 characters) on the length of such an attribute.

Comments

A *comment* in an XML structure is a note added for clarification or coding purposes and is designated with an exclamation note and two dashes, as shown in the following example:

```
<!-- This is a single line note -->
```

Comments can include white space (such as character spaces, line breaks, tabs, and related elements) but can't include embedded comments. In other words:

```
<!-- This is a <!-- single --> line note -->
```

will generate an error since the close bracket after `single` is recognized only as the termination of the outermost comment.

WARNING

Avoid the temptation to place code information inside comments. Many parsers will actually strip comment information out of the XML document for the sake of efficiency. Use PIs instead.

Text

Text in XML can be any Unicode character (that is, any 16-bit character encoding that follows the ISO Unicode standard), with a few important exceptions. While you can have XML tags embedded within text, XML treats these tags as subordinate elements (however, see the following "CDATA Sections" section). Thus, while the following highlighted characters are considered to be text:

```
<name>Mark X Rocket</name>
```

only the words `Mark` and `Rocket` are considered to be text elements:

```
<name>Mark <X/>Rocket</name>
```

While different parsers handle text differently, the standard behavior (and the one that the Microsoft parser displays) is to define the text for an element to be the set of text for all of its children elements. So the text for the element name in the next example is made up of the text for firstName followed by the text for lastName (for example, *Joe Smith*):

```
<name>
    <firstName>Joe</firstName>
    <lastName>Smith</lastName>
    </name>
```

The element text's default behavior is to strip excess white space (such as tabs, line breaks, and leading and trailing spaces) from the text when that text is retrieved. There are ways of using schemas to modify this default behavior, preserving some or all of the white space information.

CDATA Sections

There are times when you want to include markup text in an XML document but you don't want the text to be parsed as part of the document. For example, you may have descriptive text that's marked up in HTML; you don't necessarily want this text to be interpreted as part of the XML document, especially if the HTML uses tags without terminators (such as the aforementioned <BR> tag. This is the domain of *CDATA sections*, as shown in the following example:

```
<description><![CDATA[The <B>Mark X Rocket</B>
can be used for targeting highly mobile
<I>desert birds</I>]]></description>
```

A CDATA (for character *data*) section is delimited by the somewhat unwieldy brackets, as in <![CDATA[and]]>. As with a comment, the only thing you can't put into a CDATA section is another CDATA section, since the closing brackets of]]> are the only way that the parser can tell where the CDATA section ends. CDATA sections retain information about line breaks and other white space, so they're actually quite useful for keeping things like JavaScript code in one piece.

Entities

Entities come from SGML and let you use convenient short names for longer blocks of text, even text that conceivably can contain additional XML markup (or even contain entire documents). XML currently supports only a handful of inbuilt entities, including < (*less than*) for the < character, > (*greater than*) for >, and & (*ampersand*) to represent the & character. In the preceding XML structure, the filter element's text contains an entity, as shown in the following line:

```
<filter>if &gt; 15</filter>
```

When the text is later retrieved, the output will end up looking like the following line:

```
if > 15
```

You can define additional entities through Document Type Definitions, and the current draft of the XML Schema specification calls for an equivalent structure called an XML variable.

This is not the entire zoo of XML critters, but it's a fairly representative cross section. With these building blocks, you should be able to build nearly any XML structure that you need.

THE ROLES OF XML

You may wonder why I dwell so little on the DTD, the dictionary that defines an XML structure. This actually reflects a deliberate bias on my part to focus on how to work with XML as objects or as data, rather than to stick with the more traditional approach of seeing XML as documents.

There are a number of different viewpoints as to what constitutes the best way of working with XML, each of which has an appropriate place. Perhaps the best advice I can give in this regard is to say that you should use the approach to XML that best fits your own particular needs:

▶ A document-centric approach works well for editorial content but poorly for sending information.

▶ A data-centric viewpoint can prove limiting with standard markup text but can vastly simplify programming for displaying tables or other information.

The strength of XML ultimately is its ability to conform to the need at the moment (although, as with many strengths, this can be its weakness as well).

Throughout this section, I examine the different faces of XML and then try to show why none of them should be considered the "preferred" way of structuring your XML formats or writing your code. However, most XML documents tend to fall into one of the following patterns:

▶ Document format

Part iv

- ▶ Document management format

- ▶ Data store or transmitter

- ▶ Filter mechanism

- ▶ Object description

- ▶ Multimedia format

As a caveat, you need to remember that XML is still a new technology and, as with most new technologies, that the deep thinking about the fundamental characteristics of XML—its meta-characteristics, if you will—has a ways to go yet.

XML As a Document Format

SGML is a document metalanguage, capable of creating sophisticated vocabularies for all types of documents. It is also immensely complicated, in great part because documents seem to have this singular resistance to being categorized. Human thought processes are wildly nonlinear, so it's perhaps not terribly surprising that the documents we create have a linear structure simply by dint of history. (The book is essentially a linear device, even though, with some effort, it can be made nonlinear.) When we have to categorize them by concept or idea, the nice, neat, logical structures we impose on them frequently have a tendency to leak around the edges.

For this reason, while XML was originally designed for use as a more sophisticated document representation language to supplant HTML on the Web, this particular aspect of XML (the creation and application of vocabularies) has been slow to take off, for a number of reasons:

- ▶ To date, only Internet Explorer 5 supports the use of XML within the browser, but it does so inconsistently with the standards.

- ▶ To create a full document description language, you need to be able to break a document, in abstract, into multiple logical units; this is often a more difficult undertaking when working with documents than when dealing with well-defined data.

- ▶ There is typically more than one mapping of a document that's appropriate for the situation, and resolving what makes up the best such mapping can typically be a time-consuming and a frequently politically perilous occupation.

> ▶ Documents are more likely to have a requirement for a consistent display, and because of the sheer scope of such documents, this can mean creating highly complex display mechanisms.

When XML itself was in development, most of the working group responsible for creating XML came from a background in SGML, a technology that is highly geared toward document creation and management. So it is neither surprising that much of the early focus on XML concentrated on XML's document aspect (especially as a replacement for HTML) nor surprising, at least in retrospect, that this usage of XML has yet to really take off.

For the record, document-based XML is usually referred to as being *loosely structured*; elements typically can be placed in nearly any order, text can mix freely with elements within container elements, and elements can usually have fairly complex sets of attributes with many of the attribute values defaulted. In SGML, the relationship between the elements is defined in a separate document called a Document Type Definition, which XML also supports. However, in the future, DTDs will almost certainly be deprecated in favor of XML Schemas. (See the "XML As a Data Format" section later in this chapter for details.)

Perhaps the best example to demonstrate a document-centric approach is XHTML, which is an XML-compliant version of HTML. With XHTML, you have the mixed benefits of being able to parse the structure as an XML document (scanning for heads and subheads, for example) while still being able to read it in a Web browser.

TAKING XHTML TO THE LIMIT

In all likelihood, XHTML will become the default document markup language of the Web within a few years. While this may not necessarily completely solve the context problem, it makes it much easier for a WebBot to decipher and understand a Web page, and it also means that you could ultimately retrieve a Web page at a much higher level of resolution using the XML query language, XPath.

Once you have XML Web servers in place, I anticipate that you can do such things as embed a table from one document into the body of another through the use of a reference tag and an XML query string, like in the following example:

```
<h1>Sales figures</h1>
<p>Current sales are up, as can be shown by the
```

CONTINUED ➡

```
sales figures for the last three quarters:</p>
<table href="http://www.acmeRocket.com/sales/
salesFigures.xmp/table[(@id= 'salesFigures1']/
tr[td(2).value() $gt$ 19991001]" />
```

Note that in addition to pulling out an explicit structure from a document, you could conceivably query this document to retrieve specific information (in this case, all rows of the salesFigures1 table where td(2) is greater than October 1, 1999).

Currently, this syntax and behavior are still hypothetical, although there are a number of servers coming to market as I write this, which should provide exactly this sort of behavior.

XML As a Document Management Format

I want to make a distinction here between document formats and document management formats. Document management formats are very closely allied to the other current rage in computing circles these days, directories.

While the conventional example of a directory is something like a phone book, I personally have had more than my share of problems with this description. In computer circles, a directory is essentially a hierarchical structure that can be queried to retrieve information about a computer system, the file structure on a network drive, user information, and so forth.

If the mention of the word *hierarchical* is ringing some bells here, then you're beginning to get a feel for working with XML. In theory, you could represent a directory system through the use of an XML document. The Lightweight Directory Access Protocol (LDAP) architecture that is currently deployed in numerous servers is built around the older X.500 protocol as a way of using a directory-like notation to retrieve information about a system. Servers that convert LDAP results into XML (or that accept XML XPath syntax for retrieving LDAP information) are likely to become commonplace by the time this book is published, as the two formats are not that dissimilar.

Similarly, XML can be used to create one or more *topic maps* into a document space. A topic map can be thought of as a hierarchical table of contents for a whole Web site. The advantage of a topic map is that it can arrange documents by their content rather than their location in a directory. For example, a simple topic map for XML might look like the following:

```
<topicMap>
    <topic>
        <title>XML Basics</title>
        <author>Kurt Cagle</author>
        <href>xmlDocs/xmlPrimary.xml</href>
        <keywords>
            <keyword>XML</keyword>
            <keyword>XSL</keyword>
            <keyword>W3C</keyword>
        </keywords>
        <topic>
            <title>A Look at XML</title>
            <author>Denise Santaro</author>
        <href>xmlDocs/XMLIntro.xml</href>
            <keyword>XML</keyword>
            <keyword>W3C</keyword>
        </topic>
    </topic>
     <topic>
        <title>XSL Basics</title>
        <author>Phileus Potts</author>
        <href>xmlDocs/xslPrimary.xml</href>
        <keywords>
            <keyword>XSL</keyword>
            <keyword>W3C</keyword>
        </keywords>
    </topic>
</topicMap>
```

While the structure here is regular (making it more of a data-centric XML document), its primary purpose is to create a relational map to documents (or, conceivably, to subdocuments, depending on the documents and the server) in what amounts to a concept space. In its simplest form, such a space would probably be expressed as a tree-view of some sort, but, more importantly, it is a way of abstracting relationships without tying them into an explicit file directory structure. It also reduces redundancy of documents since you don't need such a document in more than one place to show a relationship.

Topic maps and XML-enabled directories will change the way that we look at document management, and will ultimately even change the way we think about documents themselves. Since more than one topic map can be assigned to a document space, topic maps essentially enable the capability of shifting your perspective about the information you have available to you. As we move increasingly into a data-rich environment (even, perhaps, into one where data is considered pollution), XML's role in document management will become critical.

XML As a Data Format

A funny thing happened on the road to XML adoption as the next HTML: several people simultaneously discovered that a table is a data structure. For example, consider a simple table of line items from a purchase order (Table 21.1).

TABLE 21.1: Purchase Order Line Items

PRODUCT NAME	PRODUCT CODE	COST PER UNIT	NUMBER OF UNITS
Acme Big Bang	BigBang	$35.59	6
Acme Little Popper	LittlePop	$10.24	12
Acme Giant Slingshot	GslingShot	$25.99	2
Acme Suction Cups	SuctCups	$10.59	24
Acme Illusionary Paint	IllPaint	$129.95	1

Anyone who has ever had to put together a Web site knows that the HTML for that site can get a little cryptic, since the language concentrates on the display of data rather than providing any real meaning to the structure, as in the following example:

```
<table>
  <tr>
    <th>Product Name</th>
    <th>Product Code</th>
    <th>Cost Per Unit</th>
    <th>Number of Units</th>
  </tr>
  <tr>
    <td>Acme Big Bang</td>
    <td>BigBang</td>
    <td>35.59</td>
    <td>6</td>
  </tr>
```

```
<tr>
    <td>Acme Little Popper</td>
    <td>LittlePop</td>
    <td>10.24</td>
    <td>12</td>
</tr>
    <!-- more of the same -->
</table>
```

The HTML tells you very little—the structure is a table, the table has headers and rows, there are four elements in each row. With a little work, you could probably get code to associate each header name with its given column, but this is meaning that you impose upon the table; by all rights, the columns could, in fact, have no association with the column headers in this organization.

Suppose, however, that you could create your own HTML to deal with this problem, substituting purchaseOrder for table, lineItem for tr, and then labeling each td element with the name of the property it contains. Note the following example:

```
<purchaseOrder>
    <lineItem>
        <productName>Acme Big Bang</productName>
        <productCode>BigBang</productCode>
        <costPerUnit>35.59</costPerUnit>
        <numberOfUnits>6</numberOfUnits>
    </lineItem>
    <lineItem>
        <productName>Acme Little Popper</productName>
        <productCode>LittlePop</productCode>
        <costPerUnit>10.24</costPerUnit>
        <numberOfUnits>12</numberOfUnits>
    </lineItem>
    <!-- Additional line items -->
</purchaseOrder>
```

Comparing the HTML with the POML (for Purchase Order Markup Language, an imaginary HTML language), the difference that such a name change makes is dramatic. Just at a glance, you can tell that a purchase order is comprised of line items, which, in turn, include names, codes, unit costs, and number of units. You can intuit the purpose of the table, and a largely anonymous table suddenly becomes a very clear object model.

The Purchase Order Markup Language is, of course, actually an instance of XML, and therein lies the irony. SGML has always had the data structuring capability, but given the complexity of both the tools and the language itself, using SGML as a data description language was simply not cost-effective. However, by cutting out a significant part of the overhead that SGML represents, the whole notion that a document is simply one form of a data structure quickly emerges.

This realization didn't bypass programmers. Most programming languages have basic data structures that are built into the language—linked lists, vectors, collections—but these are, for the most part, linear structures. One structure in particular, the associative array, does let you associate a label with a given entity in a list, and if that entity itself is an associative array, then you can build a structure similar to what XML offers. (And, in some languages, XML parsers are built in precisely this manner.)

The problem with such tree structures, however, comes from the fact that there is no consistent methodology for creating such trees; in essence, to build a logical tree, you need to write your own techniques for populating the tree, for navigating it, for querying elements within it, and so on. This problem is only made worse because such tree structures occur all the time in programming. Perhaps this is because programmers tend to organize things in hierarchical chunks, or maybe it is an intrinsic characteristic of information (one consequence of the Data + Context = Information aphorism previously related).

Describing the Data

With XML, programmers ended up with two things for free: a mechanism for creating and navigating a hierarchical data tree (the XML parser) and a way of representing hierarchy in a consistent and easily controllable fashion. Thus, even as the SGML contingent of the XML community figure out ways of adding more document-centric features, Web and application developers start incorporating XML into their applications to handle the smaller, more immediate hierarchies that they face every day.

One of the characteristics of most databases is that they retain more than just the actual data of the elements in their tables; they also contain information about the data type of the element, constraints upon an element's possible value, whether a given field can be blank, and so forth. In short, a good database should also contain *metadata* about its information.

SGML has some serious shortcomings with respect to metadata. Because the language intrinsically treats its documents at all times as collections of text characters, the need to specify whether a given element has the characteristics of a date, or a real number, or an integer doesn't exist. SGML can specify that an element or attribute have data that comes from a specific set of tokens, but, even then, the capability is considerably less useful from a data standpoint because the tokens have significant limitations on how they can be formed (no spaces, no punctuation, no line breaks; just alphanumeric characters).

A *data schema language* would let developers set characteristics in their XML document that make them more database-like. For example, while the preceding version of the POML language lets you work with each entity as text, a schema expands the capabilities of POML extensively, as presented in the following example:

```
<element name="lineItem">
    <element name="productName" type="string"/>
    <element name="productCode" type="string" />
    <element name="costPerUnit" type="currency">
        <minInclusive>0.00</minInclusive></minInclusive>
    </element>
    <element name="numberOfUnits" type="integer">
        <minInclusive>1</minInclusive>
    </element>
</element>
```

This description indicates that an element with the tag name of `lineItem` contains the four elements `productName`, `productCode`, `costPerUnit`, and `numberOfUnits`, as you would expect from the initial markup. However, while the product name and product code elements are strings, the `costPerUnit` is presented as a currency (which is a unit that was defined elsewhere) and `numberOfUnits` is always an integer. Furthermore, you can never have a negative unit cost (`<minInlusive>0.00 </minInclusive>`), nor can you have less than one unit of the indicated item on the purchase order.

The preceding fragment shows a small piece of the XML Schema language that is being proposed by the W3C to define XML documents. While XML Schema offers a number of benefits over the older SGML DTDs, one of the most significant is that it is itself written in XML and can thus be manipulated with the same tools as the XML it describes. Additionally, XML Schema lays the foundation for treating XML as an object-oriented data language, complete with such features as inheritance and polymorphism.

XML As a Transformation Language

In the preceding section, I introduced the notion of converting a table into an XML representation. While this makes the meaning of the table somewhat more tractable, it does raise the obvious question: "Well, yes, but how does the HTML browser know to display it as a table now?"

It doesn't. HTML has no contingencies for recognizing such tags as productCode, nor should it; the plethora of unnecessary tags was what made HTML unstable in the first place. However, in order to make XML viewable outside of anything beyond a text editor, you need some mechanism to convert the XML into a different format, such as HTML.

The Extensible Style Language fits the bill. The name can be a little deceptive, especially if you come from the Web world and are used to HTML 4 Cascading Style Sheets. When the W3C was still looking at XML as principally being a document format, CSS made perfect sense: you could create a style sheet and associate one style rule with an XML element in a similar manner to the way that you worked with HTML tags.

The problem with CSS arises when you start treating XML as data. To format the invoice list in a table, you'd have to be able to map the XML nodes back to their HTML equivalents. However, CSS doesn't have an option to format an element as a table or a row. You could get away with it by using overlapping DIV elements, but you would have to manipulate this through Internet Explorer's object model, which loses your portability.

Furthermore, with CSS, there's no way to reorder the data, nor to filter it. Since a significant proportion of data operations are built around those two operations, this meant that you would need to programmatically manipulate the XML using some other language (such as the XML Document Object Model, covered in the next section) for even the simplest of operations.

SGML's DSSSL language, considered once for CSS and rejected, was brought back under consideration as a possible tool to allow more complex transformations. While the capabilities that it offered were attractive—the ability to reorder or filter out entities, limited search capabilities, a programmatic syntax—DSSSL suffered the same basic limitation that DTDs suffered: it wasn't written in XML.

Keeping in mind the characteristics of DSSSL, however, the XML Style Group of the W3C decided to use some of the programmatic abilities of DSSSL to create a new language, called the Extensible Style Language, or XSL. This language is written in XML and is meant to be applied either as a style sheet (a lá CSS) or through a programmatic call from the Document Object Model.

XSL's primary purpose is simple, albeit very powerful: it transforms one XML document into another document. That other document could be in HTML format. It could be an XML document. It could be an XSL document, or a SQL Script, or a text file, or a Rich Text Format (RTF) file. While there are a few classes of documents that would be hard to write XSL filters for, in theory XSL should still be able to produce them. That's the goal, anyway.

However, wrapping your brain around XSL can take a little bit of work. XSL is built around the notion of templates. Each template provides a pattern to match, and when an XML element matches the pattern, the template is run, generating text that is added to a growing string of text. The XSL parser travels down the original XML document an element at a time, opening up child elements before going to the next sibling element. Put another way, XSL works recursively so that an XSL document can be remarkably compact compared to the more linear forms of procedural languages. Of course, XSL can also get considerably more cryptic for precisely the same reason.

A simple XSL script can convert the purchaseOrder into a table for output, as demonstrated by the following example:

NOTE

This and any subsequent style sheets will probably have to be transformed to the http://www.w3.org/1999/XSL/Transform namespace instead.

```
<xsl:stylesheet xmlns:xsl="
http://www.w3.org/1999/XSL/Transform">
    <xsl:template match="/">
        <xsl:apply-templates select="purchaseOrder"/>
    </xsl:template>

    <xsl:template match="purchaseOrder">
        <table>
        <tr>
        <xsl:for-each select="lineItem/*">
            <th><xsl:nodeName></th>
        </xsl:for-each>
        <xsl:apply-templates select="lineItem"/>
        </table>
    </xsl:template>
```

Part IV

```
        <xsl:template match="lineItem">
          <tr>
          <xsl:apply-templates select="*"/>
          </tr>
        </xsl:template>

        <xsl:template match="*">
          <td><xsl:value-of/></td>
        </xsl:template>
      </xsl:stylesheet>
```

The gist of the preceding code can be seen by realizing that there are four templates:

▶ The first matching the top most element in the XML structure

▶ The second matching the purchase order

▶ The third designed to trap line items

▶ The fourth writing out each of the line item properties

The `apply-templates` statement essentially instructs the XSL parser to run any applicable templates against the children or other descendents of the current element.

XSL can be considerably more complex than this and, honestly, is one of the most difficult aspects of XML to comprehend. However, once you have mastered XSL, you will find that it opens up entirely new vistas for XML applications.

Consider the following sequence: A query against a database generates an XML object, but that object may not be in quite the form that you need. So you transform that object with an XSL transform and send the resultant data across the wire to another process, which reads the relevant data (possibly using another XSL script) and transforms that XML into HTML output for possible display.

One of the most exciting aspects of XSL transforms is that (at least with the Microsoft implementation) you can apply logic code to the nodes within an XSL script. This means that you can perform such things as computations on specific elements or the validation of an XML structure strictly through XSL means. Coupled with a suitable server, this has the potential to transform XML itself from a simple data language into a processing (or even event-driven) programming language.

XML As a Programming Language

When I originally proposed writing this section, we scrutinized it closely. After all, the notion that XML is not a programming language has become a truism in the short time that XML has been around. I just don't feel it's true.

XML works surprisingly well within the context of object-oriented languages as a data structure. In a way, I would argue that up until now there has been a serious disconnect between the need to express objects as discrete entities and the fundamentally linear way that most procedural languages, such as Visual Basic, Java, or C++, handle such objects.

Within XML, you can create objects implicitly by organization, or you can use some of the more recent additions to XML Schema, such as Archetypes, to explicitly define objects, data types, collections, and all of the other OOP (object-oriented programming) entities that have appeared in recent years. As mentioned in the previous section, with the aid of XSL, the XML language is essentially geared toward transforming data from one form to another. Oddly enough, if you count mapping an object to a graphical interface or to a device driver, this is precisely the same thing that happens with more traditional programs.

The one principle difference between XML and procedural languages is that XML isn't really event-driven. However, even in this context, it's worth thinking about what happens when people program in more traditional languages, such as VB. For a given data class or component, the programmer sets up a map, as in the following example, that associates the event with a routine:

```
Sub Form_OnLoad()
    'Initialize the form
    me.title="My Title"
    me.width=400
    me.height=300
End Form_OnLoad()

Sub Form_OnResize()
    'Resize the form's components
    me.textbox.width=me.width-10
    me.textbox.height=me.height-5
End Form_OnLoad()
```

It's not that much of a stretch to see an XML-based language that's built around the same notion, as demonstrated by the following example:

```
<xll:component name="Form1" type="VBA.Form">
```

```
<xll:event name="onload">
    <!-- Initialize the form -->
    <xll:object ref="me">
            <width>400</width>
            <height>300</height>
            <title>My Title</title>
</xll:event>
<xll:event name="onresize">
    <!-- Resize the form's components -->
    <xll:object ref="me.textbox">
            <width>me.width-10</width>
            <height>me.height-5</height/>
</xll:event>
</xll:component>
```

While you would still need some mechanism that actually takes into account the association between an event map and the actual event that calls it, the structure here effectively means that you could write a script as a series of object definitions and references that are essentially built around an XML structure. You technically make the jump between XML as an object definition and XML as a programming language.

Note that while, at the moment, the xll namespace described above is a fiction, a number of different programming initiatives are taking place to create a conceptually similar language in the near future. The benefits of using such an encoding are significant, as outlined in the following list:

▶ Languages become considerably easier to document because the tags for various actions are more explicitly spelled out than they are in normal parsed form.

▶ Different machines can parse the same document with different tools and still be able to reconstruct the primary actions of the code.

▶ Such code can be encoded with the objects upon which they act, reinforcing the notion of encapsulation, while the ability to refer to (and import or export) schemas means that an object's functionality can be changed simply by switching the namespace of the entity.

▶ Reflection, or the ability to read an object's property set at run time, becomes trivial because all you would need to do to get the property list of an object is query the XML structure.

> ► Internationalization and localization also become fairly easy since both text content and property specifications for different cultures can be contained within separate documents.

Couple the preceding benefits with the ability to refer to code from any location, and the very nature of what we mean by programming begins to shift from a number of procedures run on disparate machines to a pool of intelligent objects.

XML As a Multimedia Format

Multimedia seems a strange place to find XML. After all, what could be farther from a simple text representation of data than video, graphics, and sound? Ironically, XML promises to play a large part in the future of media, especially as it moves in force onto the Web.

One of the characteristics that seems to repeatedly define XML is *management*. Topic maps are crucial to document management, middleware applications are equally key for data management. If you look upon multimedia not as graphics and video and sound but as the time or spatial management of resources, then the association between XML and multimedia should become clear.

Programs like Macromedia Director are effective because they provide a convenient mechanism for indicating when specific events occur—when graphics change position, when sounds are played, when videos are started or stopped. The Synchronized Multimedia Integration Language (SMIL) performs this same function using an XML format. This format isn't specifically Web-based, by the way; it is simply a way of providing one or more timelines that a SMIL-compatible viewer can use to animate elements.

Microsoft raised the valid issue that the SMIL format isn't terribly well optimized for use within a browser and chose to release an extension written in XML called HTML+TIME. This format provides a mechanism for animating Web elements and is built into the Internet Explorer 5 browser.

However, looking at multimedia from the standpoint of pictures appearing within a browser, XML again will play a role. One of the major problems that the Web faces is the download time of images. Most graphics on the Web are bitmaps; every pixel in an image is represented internally as one or more bytes. While, for photographic images, such resolution is necessary, many of the graphics that do exist on the Web are relatively flat images—logos, lines, arcs, and so forth. This problem becomes even more critical when animated GIFs come into play, as even simple graphics can drag a Web page down to the point where there are 200 frames of the animation.

Macromedia's Flash (under the original name Future Splash) was one of the first products to use vector graphics on the Web, in which the shapes that make up the images are given as equations rather than pixel values. This approach, coupled with a superb graphics editor, has made Flash viewer (one of a couple of flavors of Macromedia Shockwave) one of the most popular third-party extensions on the Web today.

Because vector graphics have proven so popular (and because they are vital if the Web is to ever have the capability to reproduce well as a print medium), Macromedia and Microsoft teamed up to produce a non-proprietary vector graphic solution called Vector Markup Language (VML). Adobe, Netscape, and Sun simultaneously proposed a different vector graphic format based upon the popular postscript form that Adobe uses, under the name Precision Graphics Markup Language (PGML).

The W3C took both formats under consideration in a working committee and split the difference, coming up with a hybrid format called Scalable Vector Graphics (SVG). SVG encodes each of the graphical elements as an XML element and provides sophisticated capabilities, such as clipping paths, text kerning, bitmap integration, and the ability to animate these elements using script or SMIL.

Ironically, the initial releases of Internet Explorer 5 contain the older VML implementation, although Microsoft will be releasing an SVG plug-in in its 5.1 release, and it should become a standard feature in any subsequent browser.

NOTE

The most recent SVG specification can be found at http://www.w3.org/TR/1999/WD-SVG-19991203/.

How Can I Use XML?

Given the evolving nature of XML, it's natural to wonder where, exactly, XML can be used. Sure, it's interesting technology, but the level of hype about XML tends to obscure what it's really for.

XML actually does have a wide variety of uses, and as more companies develop for it, the scope of the language will widen at a rate comparable to the spread of Java. To best get an idea about where you can start leveraging XML technology, however, it's worth recapping both its strengths and its weaknesses.

The following are XML's pluses:

- ► Works especially well as a data transfer format.

- ► Is intrinsically flexible. You can quickly add or delete elements on-the-fly and can create XML subtrees automatically.

- ► Echoes the hierarchical structure that people are familiar with from using file directories.

- ► Is a transformational language; you can filter it, change it into other formats (such as HTML), and order it by multiple criteria crossing several layers.

- ► Is a standard, which means that even two disparate machines running different operating systems half a world apart can still communicate with it.

- ► Supports (with XML Schema) data typing and lends itself readily to object-oriented programming.

The following are XML's minuses:

- ► Isn't a large-scale database. It's not suited for searching or retrieving tens of thousands of records (at once).

- ► Is much more complex than HTML since it is a metalanguage rather than a language.

- ► Isn't a procedural language.

- ► Is still evolving, and, like any evolving technology, carries a certain intrinsic risk in using it.

These attributes point to applications where XML really shines: customizing Web sites, component development, document/directory management, state management, database intermediation, and multimedia management. It also works reasonably well in support roles with initialization and localization files and performs credibly as a way to communicate between applications.

Part iv

Customizing Web Sites

XML was originally designed to customize Web sites, and while there have been a few bumps on the road to making this viable, the ability to change your Web sites depending upon any number of conditions is one of the real power-applications for XML.

Consider the fundamental problems that most Web pages face at the start of the 21st century:

▶ The browser market is split between Internet Explorer and iPlanet (née Netscape) Navigator, although Navigator's share is shrinking quickly. Additionally, several million people use America Online or WebTV to browse the Net, and these implement only a subset of the full features of either browser.

▶ Several different versions of each of the browsers are currently in use, and the browsers are frequently not completely backward-compatible.

▶ The support for scripting languages is inconsistent, and advanced script features frequently generate errors in older browsers (assuming that scripting is available at all).

▶ Increasingly, people are using PDAs, cellular phones, and other hand-held devices to interact with the Web. These devices often don't have the processing power to handle complex scripting and frequently support fairly basic HTML only.

The Internet is facing profound balkanization, and adding another browser (or another browser version) only exacerbates rather than helps the problem. One consequence of this is that while the latest browsers have features such as the ability to display formatted XML on the client side, Web site developers are rightly leery of coding XML to the client in this fashion because the vast majority of all browsers out there do not support XML.

Therefore, developers have been moving to server-side scripting solutions for a while. Technologies such as Active Server Pages (ASP), Java Server Pages (JSP), and ColdFusion let developers write script pages that process information or data on the server and then format the results in an HTML format that can be sent to the client. Any of these can determine what type of client they are writing to and then adjust their output accordingly.

There are problems with this approach. Concentrating on Active Server Pages, the traditional architecture of a server page lets developers intermingle formatting code (HTML) with data manipulation code (server side VBScript or JavaScript), often resulting in a difficult-to-follow and computational mess, especially when client-side scripting exists as well (as demonstrated by the following example):

```
<%@Language="VBScript"%>
<html><head>
<%dim title
title=request.queryString("title")
%>
<title><%=title%></title>
</head>
<%dim bgImage
bgImage=request.queryString("bgimage")
%>
<body background="<%=bgImage%>">
<h1><%=title%></h1>
<%
dim bc
set browserObj=createObject("XMLUtils.Browser")
if bc.browserName="Internet Explorer" then
%>
<script language="JavaScript">
    window.status='<%=request.queryString("windowStatus")%>';
</script>
<% end if %>
<p>This is perfectly legible, right?</p>
..
</body></html>
```

While it is possible to follow what's going on in this example, the combination of bracketed tags within tags, multiple intermixed script languages, and the lack of any programmatic flow makes such an ASP difficult to use and completely impossible to migrate to different systems. The irony here is that the preceding code is typical of how ASP pages are written on the Web, although the language itself is capable of producing far cleaner results.

Without getting into details about what's inside the XML or XSL files, the same script could effectively be reproduced using ASP in conjunction with XML, as demonstrated in the following example:

```
<%@Language="VBScript"%>
<%
Sub Main()
```

```
' Dimension and create the objects to be used
' in the script
dim pageName
dim xmlDoc
dim xslDoc
dim bc
dim paramObj

set xmlDoc=createObject("Microsoft.XMLDOM")
set xslDoc=createObject("Microsoft.XMLDOM")
set browserObj=createObject("XMLUtils.Browser")
set paramObj=createObject("XSLUtils.Parameters")

pageName=request("pageName")
' set the right source for the transformation
' document, based upon the browser
select case browserObject.browserName
    case "Internet Explorer"
        xslDoc.load pageName+"_IE.xsl"
    case "Netscape Navigator"
        xslDoc.load pageName+"_NS.xsl"
end select

' set the parameters that come from the HTML query
' string into the XSL filter
paramObj.QueryString=Request.QueryString
' load the xml source document
xmlDoc.load pageName+".xml"
' then transform the output
response.write xmlDoc.transformNode(xslDoc)
End Sub

Main
%>
```

This sample includes two objects: XMLUtils.Browser, which gets
browser capabilities information, and XSLUtils.Parameters, which sets
parametric information within XSL documents. Notice here that the
actual names of the files to be retrieved are passed as query string parameters. As a consequence, you can use the same ASP script for any page
that has both an Internet Explorer and a Netscape XSL filter.

While the code is perhaps a little denser in the preceding example, it's
only because there isn't much actual output text in the first ASP page.
XML can significantly reduce the overhead of ASP files and speed up
their execution because the bulk of the actual processing takes place

within optimized DLLs rather than in slower, interpreted code. Moreover, it becomes easier to separate the data preparation layers from the presentation layer; the preceding script could be rewritten to take an XML object as a parameter, and you could then substitute the XML retrieved from a database query or passed as an object from a post command rather than load an explicit XML file from the server.

XML has become an integral part of Microsoft's future development efforts, from data access to document storage and retrieval to messaging systems and distributed computing. This is very much in keeping with their efforts to make data access a seamless part of the operating environment, with that data increasingly expressed as XML.

Creating Components and Scripts

If you are fortunate enough to be able to limit your browser to Internet Explorer 5 (IE5), you can also take advantage of several features that this browser supports. IE5 was essentially the first Internet browser to support XML features implicitly, although Internet Explorer 4 did have a crude XML parser that was available as an ActiveX control.

Behaviors easily rank as the most useful of these features. A behavior can be thought of as a way of extending HTML tags through scripting. Indeed, Microsoft's implementation of such features as Vector Markup Language (VML) is accomplished through precisely this mechanism. Moreover, you can create behaviors, such as animated clocks, that you can then insert into your code through a simple HTML declaration, like the following:

```
<DIV style="behavior:url(clock.htc);"
timezone="-8" format="hh:mm:ss.dd AM"/>
```

Or you can declare an XML namespace and create a style sheet reference, as in the following example:

```
<html xmlns:a="http://www.xmldevhandbook.com/clockspace">
<style>
   a\:clock {behavior:url(clock.htc);}
</style>
<body>
This is a clock:
<a:clock timezone="-8" format="hh:mm:ss.dd AM"/>
</body>
</html>
```

Behaviors are especially useful in creating components for use within your Web page without the complications of building ActiveX controls. On a recent project, for example, I built a component for converting a SQL server call into a formatted table. The component talked to an ASP page on the server for processing the SQL query and returning it as an XML document, and then it called a parameterized XSL file to output the data as a table. Behaviors maintained state and event information so that the table could respond to mouse-over and click events.

However, it is possible to build similar components without resorting to IE; as long as you have access to the object model, you can use the same principles for any Web browser that supports a scripting language and can capture events. These components are built on the server with the client-side scripting code included as part of the page, and XML is a remarkably powerful way to both organize and customize these server-side components.

An example of where this could be useful is a help system in which a roll-over on an item identified beforehand brings up a floating help balloon that contains more extensive information about an element's function.

As languages such as Visual Basic and Java start to become more XML-centric, many of the standard components will have options for using XML as the data source. For example, the TreeView control in Visual Basic version 6 seems almost ideally suited for use by XML, but you have to have a fairly good knowledge of XML to actually take advantage of this. Over time, even standard controls will provide options for both importing or exporting data and for saving or loading in visual state information.

One of the lesser-known but more useful additions that Internet Explorer 5 brought with it was the Windows Scripting Host, which lets you apply scripting behavior to the operating system itself. As an indication of Microsoft's future programming goals, the Scripting Host is written around an XML shell and gives you a way of using XML to set various applications' configurations.

Managing Documents and Data Spaces

The task of managing documents has moved from being a fairly simple operation of maintaining a decent naming convention on your 20MB hard drive to keeping track of tens of thousands of documents produced by thousands of people over a network that could extend all across the world. Without the ability to keep track of documents, a company's primary asset—its information—slowly melts away in a sea of undocumented electrons. This is already happening on the Internet, where significant portions of the Web are simply inaccessible unless you happen to know exactly where something is located. However, information entropy is likely to become a significant factor in the corporate workspace before too long, even restricting the domain to corporate intranets.

In the near term, XML's use in managing documents is likely to be oriented toward simple indexing schemes that work by mirroring file structures in XML. However, as XML concept editors and document filters become more prevalent, it's likely that many documents will be archived in an XML format (even if they're not originally written in such a format).

Directory structures, as mentioned before, currently are most frequently represented using the LDAP protocol. However, the hierarchical structure of LDAP could be fairly easily modified into an XML format (and vice versa), which means that the same system for representing document information could also work with computer state information (user names, resource locations, business data, and so forth).

In a similar fashion, as databases become more integrated with XML standards, applications that can translate between SQL and the XPath language will become more common. SQL is not a language that lends itself to use on the Internet; its structure is verbose, the level of information that you need in order to perform a basic query can run several lines or pages, and the data that is contained within fields is often of a sensitive or protected nature that you don't necessarily want exposed. Typically, ASP acts as a buffer between the data and the outside world, but because each ASP essentially has to be generated from scratch, this can make for expensive Web interfaces.

Increasingly, XML is replacing complex ASP in this middle tier. The XML information can be easily changed from one format to another, it can provide both simple and complex validation of data, and it can determine through the use of an XSL transform whether a given record is valid before attempting an expensive write to the database. Moreover, with the ability to integrate with messaging, an XML solution can take the data that is created from a SQL query and export it to the client as a single unit, without necessarily forcing the entire client to refresh itself.

E-commerce

The ability to handle transactions easily without a lot of ASP pre-processing makes XML an ideal mechanism for handling the emerging frontier of e-commerce. Indeed, much of the drive to handle data types has come from the nascent e-commerce sector.

Electronic transactions in commerce are not new. Approximately 20 years ago, the increasingly connected business sector in the United States realized that commerce data could be sent between large companies through the new 1200bps modems. The problem, of course, came in the language used; no two companies had precisely the same set of information for accounting purposes. A secondary problem was that the slow bit speed in the modems effectively meant that any language that was used had a need to be as compact and efficient as possible.

A coalition of companies started focusing on the problem in the late 1970s, trying to find a standard that would have both the flexibility to accommodate multiple accounting systems and the efficiency to work with the slow modems of the time. The result of this effort—first in the United States and then in the United Nations—was a format called Electronic Data Interchange (EDI).

EDI has been a very effective standard, but it has some profound limitations. For example, in order to accommodate the ways that different companies performed business transactions, it exposed a large number of properties—so large a number, in fact, that one company would often choose one property while another would choose a different one for the same piece of information. The solution to this was the rise of the Value Added Networks (VANs), which, for a significant fee, kept the mappings of different companies and wrote translation routines for converting one to another.

A quarter century later, the Internet is pervasive and allows connections that are thousands of times faster than those early modems. Moreover, the number of companies that need to perform transactions has exploded, and many of them are small companies that find the EDI VAN fees prohibitively expensive.

The pressure from small companies to perform business-to-business transactions has coupled with the rise of XML to provide an incentive to change the EDI architecture to a common format. Initially, the larger EDI companies and the VANs pushed for an EDI/XML format in which the XML Schema essentially matched the field definitions of the older EDI architecture. However, as the capabilities of XML became more evident, this early EDI/XML approach was abandoned in favor of a new schema.

Microsoft, which has been one of the leading companies to push for the adoption of XML Schema, also has set up an XML standard called BizTalk, which is meant to be an XML-Schema-compliant framework for performing transactions in which companies register prospective XML architectures. Trade organizations, most notably the Organization for the Advancement of Structured Information Standards (OASIS), have also proposed XML standards for various e-commerce transactions (such as invoicing, purchasing, and account queries). In all likelihood, there will be a plethora of different standards for several years to come, although XSL minimizes the possible fracturing effects of these competing schemas.

However, e-commerce extends beyond business-to-business transactions. Business-to-consumer e-commerce has seen the more visible development over the last five years as the World Wide Web has become the World Wide Shopping Mall. XML will probably be slower to move into this realm since most business-to-consumer transactions take place through Internet browsers, so the XML transactions that are likely to occur will more likely happen on the server side. However, even given that XML has a role to play in presenting the information and maintaining intermediate state information before a purchase is finalized, we'll see more of XML on the browser side in the context of e-commerce.

Integrating Applications

As with most contemporary technologies, XML exposes an object model (usually called a Document Object Model, or DOM, in the case of XML) that allows programmers to write applications using specific methods of XML. These methods let developers walk an XML tree, retrieve individual elements or attributes, determine schema information, transform subtrees, and perform validation, among a number of other options.

While much has been made of XSL's transformational capabilities, the ability to use the XML DOM means that you, as a programmer, can integrate XML into your own applications, whether they are completely generated from scratch or they use the object model of other applications, such as Microsoft Office.

Microsoft Office 2000 does not have much built-in XML support (save for a few XML constructs called data islands that are used to retain information in HTML pages created by Office), but you can use XML to persist data that may exist in an Excel spreadsheet and then transform it through the use of DOM (or by the clever application of XSL) to create a table in Word or a chart in PowerPoint.

One advantage to this approach over traditional OLE (which also lets you transfer data among applications) is that OLE requires that both applications be run simultaneously. (For resource-intensive applications, like Word or Excel, running several such applications could easily leave you short of memory.) An XML stream uses the relatively lightweight MSXML component instead and doesn't even require that the data come from Excel. (For example, you may want it to come from a persisted XML file on the Web instead, or perhaps from a SQL Server database.)

This integration becomes even more important when the source of the data is located on a machine different than the consumer of the data. With XML, it is possible to use Excel as a remote server, generating data to a PowerPoint presentation, or perhaps to a Visio document, or maybe even—heavens forefend—to a Java applet running in a Netscape browser. It is this ability to facilitate remote transactions in an inexpensive, platform-independent manner that points to one of the principal uses of XML in the future.

A related venue to this is the area of messaging. Web connections aren't always possible, especially if you are in a travel-intensive occupation, such as sales. Messaging lets a salesperson write relevant information through a Web browser or other client application into a message cache if the machine isn't connected to the Internet or a private network. When they return to the office (or their cellular modem comes back within range of a transmitter, as is increasingly the case), a messaging manager sends the information that was cached on to the client. While sophisticated caching systems are needed for standard client applications, if you're simply going through a Web interface you can leverage XML's persistence capabilities and structuring to store information until the transaction can be completed.

The barrier here between data and programming language blurs, as I indicated earlier in this chapter, and that point serves to highlight yet another axiom that XML introduces: there really is, in the end, no difference between program and data, between actor and action; they are one and the same.

IN SUMMARY

XML looks like such a trivial thing, but it will probably have more impact on the evolution of computing than any technology since the advent of HTML. XML is fundamentally a language to manage resources, whether those resources are documents, data, graphics, programs, or concepts. It has evolved out of the realization that we are becoming adrift in a sea of too much data and too little information.

Ironically, as XML has taken shape through countless hours of wrangling in conferences and newsgroups and e-mail, people have realized that the nature of information transcends the notion of a document. E-commerce systems talk money while researchers seek out context, yet the tool for both is becoming the same. Our views about programming, objects, and applications are shifting, subtly at first, but with more and more alacrity over time.

Oh, by the way, to revisit the question that started this chapter:

What is Meaning?

Simple. Anything you want it to be. Have fun....

WHAT'S NEXT

In the next chapter, A. Russell Jones takes you on a tour of Active Server Pages (ASP) technology. Developed by Microsoft, ASP lets you build multiuser applications, so that your Web server can handle the throngs of visitors who will flock to your site.

Part iv

Chapter 22

BEHIND THE SCENES—HOW ACTIVE SERVER PAGES WORK

Active Server Pages (ASP) technology is actually a very simple idea. Wouldn't Web sites be powerful tools if you could mix HTML and code? And they are, as you will see. ASP lets you use the power of a Web server to process user requests and provide dynamic, individualized content based on logic, file, and database data, and also process the user's individualized data. In other words, ASP lets multiple users simultaneously run a program on your Web server. Essentially, you have the power of a mainframe computer, coupled with the graphics-processing ability of a local workstation, all wrapped up in a cross-platform viewer—the browser—and packaged in a world-standard communications mechanism—the Web. This book shows you how to tap into that power to deliver flexible, individualized applications.

Adapted from *Mastering Active Server Pages 3*,
by A. Russell Jones
ISBN 0-7821-2619-7   864 pages $49.99

In essence, a Web application consists of a series of short conversations between a Web server and a browser. Remember in *Gone with the Wind* when Scarlett O'Hara was surrounded by a group of young men at the Twelve Oaks barbecue, all trying to engage Scarlett in conversation. The eager young men initiated the conversation and Scarlett responded to them. The user/server relationship operates in much the same way. Each user (browser) initiates requests from the server, and the server, much like Scarlett, responds quickly to each request. Each user, while engaging your Web page, feels as though they have your full attention. Your goal in a Web application is to be Scarlett. You want to capture everyone's attention and respond to each individual while showing preference to none.

ASP lets you treat users as unique entities, even though all of them are running the same program on the same machine—your Web server. Obviously, running a complex program for multiple users on one computer takes a lot of resources. Fortunately, Microsoft makes sure those resources are at your disposal. ASP provides:

- A way to save individualized data for each user

- Access to the file system

- Access to databases

- A means to launch and control any Component Object Model (COM) component

In short, ASP allows you to build multiuser applications, which means you can leverage ASP to provide application scalability. If you plan your ASP applications carefully, they can scale from a single-server application that can handle 30-100 simultaneous users and a few thousand hits per day to multi-server (Web farm) applications handling thousands of simultaneous users and millions of requests per day.

ASP isn't a single technology. Using ASP effectively requires that you learn a collection of tools, languages, techniques, and technologies. These didn't spring into being suddenly; each is a topic in its own right, with an evolutionary history that began before ASP. Before we jump into ASP technology, a little history lesson.

INTRODUCTION TO ASP

The best way to introduce ASP is to give a little background on the technologies that existed before ASP, why new capabilities were needed, and how ASP meets those needs.

Beyond HTML

Hypertext Markup Language (HTML) is a tagged text file format used to format Web content for display—usually in a browser. HTML is a very simple language with only a few commands. That's part of the reason HTML instantly became popular. Until HTML, the only way for a non-programmer to display text and graphics easily was to use a What-You-See-Is-What-You-Get (WYSIWYG) word processor. Unfortunately, everybody had to have the same operating system, the same word processor, and sometimes even the same version of the word processor to view your documents. HTML changed all that, and changed the world as well. Today, even though HTML is considerably more complex than it was originally, a few hours of instruction still suffices to train people well enough so they can create fairly complicated pages.

HTML's simplicity was one important factor in its rapid adoption; another equally important factor is its ability to navigate easily between files. By pointing and clicking with a mouse, a user can move between files without knowing where those files are located. Such navigation is called *hypertext*, a concept invented by Ted Nelson over 30 years before HTML brought hypertext navigation to the world.

Despite, or perhaps because of its simplicity, HTML rapidly became the display language of choice for the World Wide Web (WWW). Paeans were written describing how the Web would become the new panacea for delivering timely information to millions of eager readers all over the world. But that scenario wasn't quite right. Sure, people formatted millions of pages of text and graphics and placed them on the Web, but those eager readers immediately started complaining that the information wasn't specific enough for them. They wanted personalized pages that acted like their favorite Windows programs, sites that remembered their personal preferences, communications, interactivity—in short, they wanted applications, not just information.

Enter CGI

HTML needed some help. As a simple layout language, HTML is without peer, but as an application engine, it leaves a great deal to be desired. Help quickly appeared in the form of Common Gateway Interface (CGI) applications. A CGI application runs entirely on the server. When a browser contacts the server and makes a file request, the CGI application returns HTML just as if it were an HTML file. The difference is that the CGI program can process information sent by the browser and return HTML that differs in response to varying conditions. CGI programs can send one type of information to one user, and another type of information to another user, or send different files based on the type and version of browser the user is running.

Although you can write CGI programs in almost any language, most early CGI programmers used Perl, a language with powerful text-processing capabilities. Because Perl is a scripting language, many CGI programs are called CGI scripts. A scripting language is a relatively small, usually interpreted (not compiled) language. Web site designers immediately began using pre-written CGI scripts to perform simple calculations, such as counting the number of users who visited their pages. Other CGI programs backed the Web search engines, indexing content and storing the indexes in powerful databases.

These CGI programs used HTML forms to accept search requests from users, search the databases, and provide customized responses. CGI programs were the forerunners of the new, active Web. Simple, stored pages sufficed for information display, but people now used Web applications to find those pages. Web site programmers began to use CGI programs to provide dynamic content rather than static HTML.

Unfortunately, CGI programs had several shortcomings. The Web is a world of small transactions. Each transaction consists of a single request or a series of short requests by the browser. When you request a page, the Web server supplies the page, and then forgets about you. For busy sites, such requests may happen at the rate of 100 requests per second or more. The first generation of CGI programs consisted of executables that had to be loaded into memory for each request. The CGI program would then process the request and terminate. All of this loading and unloading used up time and resources on the server. It obviously takes considerably more memory and central processing unit (CPU) time to load a program and execute it than it does to simply return the contents of an HTML file. Web server designers began to look for a more efficient method to deliver dynamic content.

ISAPI and NSAPI

For post-CGI programming, the leading vendors of Web server software decided to provide hooks into the Web server itself. The concept they standardized on is called Internet Server Application Programming Interface (ISAPI), or on Netscape servers, Netscape Server Application Programming Interface (NSAPI). Using these hooks, programmers working in C and other general-purpose programming languages could write applications to process requests and return dynamic content like CGI programs. Unlike CGI programs, these new ISAPI programs remained loaded in memory in the server's address space. Thus ISAPI programs could perform the same tasks as CGI programs, but without the overhead of loading and terminating the program for each request.

Microsoft introduced two different kinds of ISAPI programs: filters, which intercept Web requests before the server sees them, and applications, which process Web requests. Officially, ASP is an ISAPI application. Don't confuse the term application with the applications you build with ASP. In this chapter, I'll refer to the ASP application as the ASP engine. The ISAPI ASP application is a single Dynamic Link Library (DLL) (`asp.dll`) that parses files and executes the code they contain.

BENEFITS OF ASP

There are many benefits to ASP, and they will be discussed throughout this chapter. However, the following are a couple of general reasons why ASP is the choice for so many.

ASP Is Language-Independent

The ASP engine does not depend on a single language. In fact, the ASP engine doesn't actually execute the code you write. Instead, ASP is a language-independent scripting host. The ASP engine works with any scripting language that is compatible with the Microsoft Scripting Host requirements. It can even work with code written in multiple scripting languages on the same page.

The ASP engine differentiates scripting code from HTML, and then asks the appropriate scripting engine(s) to execute it. VBScript is the default ASP scripting language, but you'll also see a significant amount of JavaScript and some PerlScript.

ASP Is for Non-Programmers

One of the holy grails of computing is to find a language that ordinary people (read "non-programmers") can use to perform programmer-type tasks. It's based on the idea that programmers will create reusable, general-purpose entities (the blocks), and anybody with a few hours to spare can then hook them together to create complex programs. Don't worry. Simplicity in programming is a moving target.

In the earliest days of computing, programmers used machine language, flipping switches to manipulate bits and bytes. Assembly language changed all that—assembler was the glue that let non-programmers manipulate the bits and bytes easily. As assembler grew increasingly complex, languages like FORTRAN and C became the glue that connected assembly-language modules. Back in the pre-Windows, Disk Operating System (DOS) days, a simple scripting language used in batch files was supposed to be the glue. You could hook simple batch files together to automate other programs and perform complex tasks. However, the original batch language grew until only programmers could use it. Just a few years ago, Visual Basic was the glue language; now Visual Basic is the language that creates the building blocks. Today the glue language is ASP— and it's true that ASP, as it exists today, is better suited for glue-like tasks than it is for mainstream processing, but that may change.

Nevertheless, you should understand that ASP is not a low-level programming language. It's not a database language either, although you can access databases from it. If you're thinking about using ASP as a front-end for your data warehouse/data-scrubbing functions, think again. ASP is not a component-building language. If you're planning to learn ASP to create the next great word processor or spreadsheet, plan harder. ASP is not a mathematical modeling language, it's not a graphics manipulation language, and it's not a Graphical User Interface (GUI) builder.

ASP's strength lies in providing simple decision-making capability to what would otherwise be static HTML pages, and in coordinating and monitoring back-end components to return quick HTML responses to disparate clients. In other words, ASP is the glue.

But it's not yet simple glue. Although you may not need to be a programmer to build simple ASP pages, you need to become a programmer to build ASP applications. Becoming a programmer is more a state of mind, of talent, and of practice, than a matter of education. In other words, given talent and time to practice, you can learn to be a programmer.

As with all arts, there's a healthy dose of technical craftsmanship involved with ASP applications programming. Your aim should be to make the underlying code generation so automatic that you can focus on the larger problems. If you want to be successful with ASP, write lots of small programs, work on them until they're elegant, and then combine them into larger, more complex programs as you become comfortable with the basics. Along the way, you'll find that ASP is not, in itself, a complete programming solution. You'll find other areas, equally as interesting as ASP, that will help you build useful and aesthetic Web applications.

OTHER METHODS FOR DELIVERING DYNAMIC CONTENT

ASP is not the only method for delivering dynamic content—it's just one of the newest. Other methods preceded ASP (and yet other methods will follow). In the mid-90s the hot Web technology was CGI programs, which let Web servers do something besides serve up static HTML pages.

What Is a CGI Program?

CGI programs are small executables that the server executes in response to a request from a browser. The CGI program processes the request in code and returns HTML to the browser. The difference between a CGI program and a static Web page is that the HTML returned to the browser can be different based on who's making the request, where they are, what time it is—almost anything you can think of. Fortunately, Microsoft recognized that CGI programs aren't the most efficient way to process requests for active content. The reason they're inefficient is that the server must load the CGI program for each request.

The underlying explanation has its roots deep in Hypertext Transfer Protocol (HTTP). An HTTP request is a short transaction between a client and a server. Neither the server nor the client remembers each other once the transaction is complete.

Imagine two people wandering through a party. Every time they pass each other they introduce themselves, have a short conversation, then drift apart, but never remember meeting each other. Alternately, consider the movie *Groundhog Day*, in which one day continuously repeats itself. The people in the film do the same things and say the same things each day. The only one who realizes that they're living the same day repeatedly is the leading character, played by Bill Murray. Web requests are like that, except there's no Bill Murray character to notice.

Because both the server and client treat each HTTP transaction as a brand-new entity, they must go through an elaborate series of handshakes for each request. Worse, because the server forgets the client after each transaction, it also destroys any CGI program that it invoked to process the request. The server must then reload the CGI program for the next request. Loading executable programs often takes longer than executing the program. For a Web site, loading programs is a non-productive activity; the point is to use the server as efficiently as possible.

What Is ISAPI?

To help eliminate the overhead associated with CGI applications, Microsoft introduced the Internet Server Application Programming Interface (ISAPI). It takes just as long to load an ISAPI application as a CGI program, but the server doesn't destroy ISAPI applications at the end of each request. Instead, they stay loaded, either as long as the server is running or for a pre-determined length of time. There are two types of ISAPI programs: ISAPI applications and ISAPI filters.

ISAPI Applications

ISAPI applications run *after* the Web server has seen the request. ISAPI applications let you add functionality to a Web server while still taking advantage of all the other features the server offers. The ASP engine is an ISAPI application. Internet Information Server (IIS) passes requests for ASP files to the ASP engine, which processes the request to provide dynamic content.

ISAPI Filters

ISAPI filters run *before* the Web server has seen the request. ISAPI filters let you monitor or intercept requests for special processing. For example, a program to categorize requests and allot server bandwidth based on the requesting user's IP address would be a good candidate for an ISAPI filter. The program would intercept the requests and filter them before they reached the Web server. Alternatively, a filter could function like a firewall, to block requests from non-trusted sources.

What Are the Advantages of ASP over HTML?

HTML is a simple and flexible formatting and layout language, but it has no programming constructs. If you need to display static text and images, HTML is perfect. If you need to display content that changes often, or if you need to display content tailored for individuals, HTML is sadly lacking. The problem is that HTML lacks any decision-making capability.

For example, suppose you want to display the nationwide voting results based on voter interviews. You set up the infrastructure to place the results in a database. Your HTML front-end displays a map of the United States. When a client selects one or more of the states, you want to display a table showing a breakdown, by county, of the anticipated voting results for that state.

If you were creating the site weeks after the election when all the results had been tallied, HTML would serve perfectly. But to display the live data implies that the results may change hour-to-hour or minute-by-minute. Even a small army of HTML coders would have a hard time keeping up with the election results. To display live data, you need a programming language, and HTML is not a programming language.

ASP scripting provides the functionality you would need to read the database, obtain the up-to-the-minute results for that state, group them by county, and create a custom HTML response based on the fresh data.

Content that changes with each request is called *dynamic content*. Sites that provide only static content can quickly become boring. Dynamic sites dominate the Web today. Sites that provide dynamic content, especially those in which the user interacts with the content rather than simply pointing and clicking to change pages, are called Web applications.

WHAT IS ASP'S COMPETITION?

The Web is the new paradigm for delivering applications because it is globally accessible; allows for centralized administration; provides immediate, single-point upgrades; and delivers an application to multiple clients on several operating systems using the same code base. Everybody's working in this new paradigm. Therefore, ASP has plenty of competition. Of course, it depends how you define competition. The various vendors are busily differentiating their products by positioning them as something more than Web development environments.

Also, ASP is a difficult product to categorize; it isn't a development environment per se (you can develop ASP pages with any text editor); and it isn't a language (you can develop ASP pages using any of several scripting languages). Similarly, you can use ASP to build simple Web sites or complex applications.

ASP's major competitors in the application arena are Application Server vendors, Sun's JavaServer Pages, Java itself, C++ ISAPI applications, and Visual Basic. Microsoft's preferred tool for building ASP sites is Visual InterDev. Its major competitors in the site-building arena are FrontPage, HomeSite, Dreamweaver, and a host of shareware and freeware site builders/HTML editors.

Application Server Vendors

ASP's high-end competitors started out as Web application development environments. Some of them have since metamorphosed into Application Server vendors. This simply means they're bundling their application development environments as enterprise-level software—usually with hardware and service contracts. Cold Fusion, Bluestone, and NetDynamics are three competitors in this category. All three provide HTML tag extensions and custom commands that let you easily access databases, format pages, and deliver customized content. All are powerful (and relatively expensive) solutions.

The main advantage of Application Servers is that they make it less difficult to build complex pages that scale easily. Their main disadvantages are that they require custom server installations, they often charge by the number of clients, and may obscure the low-level details—some even hide the code—which makes it difficult to make changes to differentiate your site from others built with the same packages.

JavaServer Pages

Sun recently introduced JavaServer Pages (JSP), which I believe will, in the long run, become ASP's principal competition. JSPs run on several different Web servers already, including Apache (Unix), Netscape, and IIS servers. ASP can also run on Unix via ChiliSoft's Chili!ASP product, but at the loss of some functionality.

Java

Sun originally touted Java as the universal client-side language for the Web, but it soon became apparent that its performance wasn't going to be sufficient for that purpose. Recently though, Java has found a new home on the server. Java is similar to C++, but has some features, such as automatic memory management, that make it a better rapid development environment. In addition, Java development environments have improved considerably in the past few years—several are now equally as full-featured as Microsoft's Visual Studio suite.

Java itself is an excellent language that, like Microsoft's Visual Basic, can be either interpreted or compiled. When compiled into native code, Java is nearly as fast as compiled C code.

A large number of C and C++ developers found it easy to move to Java because of the similarity in the syntax of the two languages. The development of Enterprise Java Beans (similar to Microsoft's COM technology) coupled with Java's ability to run on several different operating systems may make Java the language of choice for developing business connectivity Web applications.

VB IIS Applications

Microsoft itself competes with ASP technology on both the low and high end of the scale. On the high end, Visual Basic 6 added a class module called WebClasses. WebClasses build on ASP technology, but let you compile your code into ActiveX DLLs.

Theoretically, compiled code should make applications run faster. In practice, the speed of your application depends on many variables, most of which are unrelated to whether your code is compiled or interpreted. The main advantage of compiled applications is that when you sell code, the clients can't see the code; they can use the application, but can't modify it. The main disadvantage is that you must register the compiled ActiveX DLLs on the server, which means you can't modify the code as easily after deploying the application.

Others (e.g., C++)

You can write Web applications with almost any language, but many development shops select C++ because it has the best low-level access to Windows, it's extremely fast, and C++ code is even somewhat portable to other operating systems. Although C++ isn't strictly an ASP competitor, I've included it here because it's an excellent choice for commercial application development. If you're planning to use ASP to develop commercial applications, you should be aware that your competition might be using faster technology.

How ASP Compares with its Competition

ASP has several major advantages over most other Web application development languages or environments, especially for intranet development.

ASP code resides in text files.   Text files are easy to modify, even after deployment. It's a tremendous advantage to be able to fix a problem remotely using a text editor. Web applications that depend on compiled code or registered ActiveX objects are much more difficult to maintain and upgrade. Beyond that, I can assure you that you'll be able to edit the code you write today with a text editor tomorrow—there are no Integrated Development Environment (IDE) version dependencies with text files. That's not the case with most other code development environments because they constantly improve, and frequently change. They're usually (but not always) backwardly compatible with their own earlier versions, but they're rarely editable with another environment's editors. With ASP files, anyone can edit the code with a text editor.

ASP code times out.   IIS stops executing ASP pages after 90 seconds by default. You can (and normally should) adjust this to a shorter value. Therefore, if you accidentally write an endless loop, or allow someone to request a million records, you won't tie up the server beyond the timeout interval. Many Internet Service Providers (ISPs) who won't usually host compiled applications will host ASP applications—partly because the scripts time out.

ASP code is server-safe.   ASP code runs in a limited space—for example, you can't natively read or write binary files with ASP. It's very difficult, if not impossible, to completely crash an IIS server with native ASP script. That's another reason many

ISPs will host ASP applications when they refuse to host Web applications developed with other technologies.

ASP code doesn't require registration.   The IIS install program installs the ASP runtime DLLs, scripting DLLs, Microsoft ActiveX Data Objects (ADO) DLLs, and the Microsoft Scripting Runtime DLL—and that's the only code you need to run ASP applications. Most other development tools require additional server-side installs and registry operations. Some require you to install special server applications. This may not seem like much trouble on a development server, but it causes problems in production, especially when you just want to correct a misspelling or make a minor change.

ASP applications are usually small.   Because all the DLLs are already installed on the server, you need only deliver the code files, images, and support files to make an ASP application run—and those files are usually small and highly compressible. Note that this becomes less and less true as you add compiled ActiveX components to your application.

You can upgrade ASP applications without stopping IIS. Although it may not sound like it, this is a major advantage. It's no advantage at all when your application is the only one running on the server, but when there are dozens of applications running on the same server (typical of larger businesses), no one wants to stop or shut down the server to make changes in your application. You must usually schedule such changes, often well in advance. The problem is that no one can predict what the effect of stopping the server will have on all the applications running on that server. Put yourself in a user's position. You wouldn't want to have your application suddenly stop responding and possibly lose data just so someone else could upgrade an application.

How to Use ASP

Now that you know more about ASP's capabilities, how should you approach using it to build your applications? The way to use ASP depends on the size of your application, the number of clients you expect to have, the capacity of your server(s), whether your application is for an intranet or the Internet, and the time and resources you have available for development. The most scalable sites use ASP's scripting capabilities as a front-end to Microsoft Transaction Server (MTS) components that do all the database access and most of the business logic processing. But you don't have to use ASP that way. At the cost of some speed and a lot of scalability, ASP is perfectly capable of handling quite a few users without help from external COM objects or MTS.

I recommend that you use ASP alone for learning. As your scripting and database capabilities grow, you can begin to build and use COM objects. When your scalability requirements outgrow ASP's intrinsic capabilities, you can begin to use MTS.

Simple Text Processing

Use ASP script for simple text processing. This is ASP's strong point, as it usually involves a series of simple decisions about how to format responses. Avoid using ASP script for complex string manipulations, especially in loops, because it's too slow.

Complex Decision Making

Use ASP for complex decision-making. Computers are extremely fast at making simple decisions, and ASP scripts, although they're not the fastest languages around, are more than adequate for making such decisions. When you combine decision-making with text processing, you have the building blocks to create personalized, interactive applications.

Intermediary between Browser and COM Components

As your decision-making and data processing requirements grow, you can purchase or build COM components. As you increase your use of server-based COM components, ASP becomes the intermediary between the browser and these back-end components. As I said earlier—ASP is glue.

HOW *NOT* TO USE ASP

Just as ASP has its strong points, it also has its weak points, which are:

- ► ASP is an interpreted, not a compiled language, therefore it's inherently slower than other, compiled solutions.

- ► ASP doesn't have strong variable typing—all variables are Variants. Variants are convenient, but are also larger and slower than typed variables.

- ► ASP must insert `include` files each time they're used.

- ► ASP treats all `object` variables as late-bound objects. It must request information about the object for each property or method access, which slows down the response.

In contrast, compiled languages usually have strong variable typing, which means the programmer must specify the type and range of content each variable will have. That means more work for the programmer, but less work for the program, because it eliminates decisions. Similarly, `include` files in compiled programs are included only once, at compile time, and object references can be early-bound, which means the compiler checks property and method names and parameters at compile time, not at runtime.

As Business Logic

ASP isn't at its best when implementing business rules for two reasons. First, such rules often involve many object property or database accesses. Languages like VB or C++ use *early binding* to access `object` variables. That means that the compiler knows the set of properties, methods, arguments, and return values exposed by an object at compile time. In contrast, ASP must ask the object for a list of its properties and methods at runtime—and it must do this for each property or method access. That type of object access is called *late binding*. Late binding, as you can imagine, is several times slower than early binding. Late binding isn't usually a problem unless you need to access an object many times, such as in a loop, or in implementing complex business rules.

Second, and probably more important, the ideal program model places business rules into objects to create a clean separation between the rule implementation and the interface. Placing business rule code in ASP pages along with formatting and interface code violates that separation, not least because the code may be repeated in many places. If you need to change a rule that has been isolated in a single object, you can replace that object with minimal effect on the rest of the application code. If the business rule code is intermixed with interface and formatting code, it can be much more difficult to change. Note that separating business rules also allows you to test those rules separately from the program, and to reuse the same rule code in other applications.

As Database Access Logic

ASP isn't meant to be a data-access component. Just like business rules, and for the same reasons, ASP works better when you use it to format the results returned by data-access objects than when you use ASP script to communicate directly with the database. As long as you're making read-only queries, there's little difference between using data-access objects and ADO code in ASP pages. But when your applications need to update a database in complex ways, you're much better off isolating the data-access code in an external object.

As a Primary Means of Complex Data Processing

ASP can perform complex decisions, but you shouldn't ask or expect it to perform well for data-intensive operations. Remember, ASP doesn't have typed variables, can't perform early binding, and is an interpreted language. For data-intensive operations you want as much speed as possible. Often, you'll want to offload processing from your Web server to another server, and that's possible only if you place the code into external COM objects.

WHAT YOU CAN DO WITH ASP

ASP lets you perform several operations that are difficult or impossible with straight HTML. I'll list most of them in this book, but you should understand that just because you *can* do something with ASP doesn't mean you *should* perform that operation with ASP. The goal of all Web sites and applications is to respond to the client as quickly as possible, making the site an interactive experience rather than an exercise in patience.

Make If...Then Decisions

Most programming is about making simple decisions. For example, when a user selects an item from a drop-down list, your application will do one thing or another depending on which item is selected. That implies that your application can make a decision. In pseudocode:

```
If user clicked TX then
     'Save user's selection in a variable
     Session("LastUserSelection") = "TX"
     Show list of state parks in Texas
ElseIf user clicked TN then
     ' Save user's selection in a variable
     Session("LastUserSelection") = "TN"
     Show list of state parks in Tennessee
End If
```

The code shows that you're going to make a decision based on which state abbreviation a user selected from a list of states. You want to save the user's selection for future use, and then display a new list of state parks for the selected state.

Similarly, when the user returns to the list after looking at the state park list, you'll probably want to leave the list in the same state it was in when the user left it—with either TX or TN selected. The following pseudocode loop checks the value of the Session("LastUserSelection") variable saved in the previous code listing:

```
For Each State In StateList
     If Session("LastUserSelection") = State then
         ' Display the item as selected
     Else
         ' Display the item unselected
     End If
Next
```

Most programming consists of a series of such decisions. Note that the first decision—that of displaying a list of state parks based on a selection—is semi-possible with HTML. For example, you could present a list of state abbreviations formatted as hypertext links, each of which redirected the user to the appropriate state park page; but the second decision—that of reselecting the user's last choice—is not possible with HTML because there's no way to remember which link the user chose last.

Process Information from Clients

HTML has the capability to create interactive forms—no doubt you've seen many of them. A form is a place for the user to enter or select data. HTML also has the capability to send or *submit* that data to the server for processing. However, HTML does not have the ability to process the submitted data. To process data you must have a programming language, and HTML is a layout language.

ASP provides several native objects that let you access data sent by clients. You can store data, make decisions, alter the data, send it back to the client—basically, you can do whatever you want. The ASP objects make it easy to process client data.

Access Databases and Files

ASP by itself has no database connectivity or file-reading abilities; however, you can use the ADO objects installed with ASP to access databases and the Microsoft Scripting Runtime FileSystemObject and TextStream objects (also installed with ASP) to read and write text files. HTML has no access to external data other than through hyperlinks. You can link two documents together with an <a> anchor tag containing a Uniform Resource Locator (URL) to display data, but you can't read or write files.

Format Responses

With ASP you can respond differently to different clients. That means you can take the results of a database query or data from a file, format it on the fly, and return the results to a client. For example, you can hide or show data based on a client's permission level. In a student report card application, for example, you would want to let teachers and school administrators view and change data for their own students—but you wouldn't want to let students change the data! Similarly, you would want students to see only their own report cards, not those of other students.

With ASP you can use the same data set for all users, but format the responses based on identity. You can also easily change the look and feel of the response, change colors and controls, adjust to multiple screen resolutions, and more by running condition-specific code on the server. HTML is static—a page is a page is a page. You can't show only part of a page, you can't show different pages based on identity, and you can't change page results for a single user without changing them for all users.

Launch and Communicate with COM Objects

With ASP you aren't limited to the capabilities of scripting languages or to the properties and methods of the intrinsic ASP objects. ASP can launch Component Object Model (COM) objects. A COM object may contain almost any kind of functionality, but all COM objects have one thing in common—they can communicate with one another. ASP ships with several COM objects, including `Scripting.Dictionary`, `Scripting.FileSystem`, `MSWC.BrowserType`, and `TextStream`. You can purchase, download, or create your own COM objects with Visual Basic, C++, or any of several other languages. You can even create COM objects with a text editor with VBScript or Jscript, using a technology known originally as Remote Scripting, and now included as part of the Windows Scripting Host. Initially, you could use these text file-based COM objects to run code on the server from a browser, thus the term *remote scripting*.

Regardless of the language used to create your COM objects, you can launch and control them from an ASP page. COM objects you can use with ASP pages have several names. You'll see them advertised and described as MTS components, ActiveX controls, ActiveX Documents, and Active Template Library (ATL) objects. But they're all exactly the same thing—COM objects. Some COM objects run on the server and some run (on Internet Explorer) on the client. You can easily extend the functionality of your applications through COM components in exactly the same way other developers extend their Windows applications. There are many commercial, free, and shareware COM components available on the Web, at Microsoft's site, and from third-party vendors.

Control Transactions

You can use ASP to create mission-critical transactional applications. A *transaction* is any set of tasks that must either all complete successfully or all fail completely. The classic example is a financial transaction. When you pay by check or credit card, the bank must remove the money from your account and credit the merchant's account. If either part fails, you want both parts to fail. Forcing failure is a difficult process, because it means you have to undo the parts of the transaction that have already completed.

Fortunately, there's software available to help you monitor and control transactions. IIS 4 ships with a transaction monitor called Microsoft

Transaction Server (MTS), which manages the process for you. In Windows 2000 (which includes IIS 5) MTS is part of a group of services called COM+, but from a programmer's point of view, both versions manage transactions the same way. All you need to do is group the operations into a transaction. If the transaction fails, MTS can automatically roll back the parts of the transaction that have already been completed.

Applications that use transactions typically must monitor the transaction to determine its status, and not all transactions complete instantaneously. Some transactions take minutes or days to complete. In addition, transactions may not all occur on machines or in code under your control. In the financial transaction, for example, the merchant's account may not be (and probably isn't) with the same bank as your account. Transactions that occur on more than one system are called *distributed transactions*. MTS manages transactions on disk, using a program called the Microsoft Distributed Transaction Coordinator (MS DTC). MTS prepares each part of the transaction. When all the parts have signaled their readiness, MTS issues a commit command. As each part of the transaction completes, it notifies MTS, which logs a completion message. MTS notifies the transaction owner (in this case, your ASP page) about the state of the transaction and the outcome.

In Windows 2000, MTS has become part of COM+, and COM objects running in MTS are now called COM+ applications. That's confusing terminology, but it's part of Microsoft's strategy to eliminate monolithic applications. Instead of creating large applications, you should begin to think about and design your applications as a set of reusable, small, and lightweight components.

How Web Requests Work

Whenever a user enters a URL into a browser's address field, clicks a link, or submits a form, the browser packages up information about itself, the URL, and (in some cases) the user, and sends that information to the server as a Web request. The ASP engine consists of a collection of objects that contain information about the request, the scripting technology used to make decisions about how to handle the request (the code), and the Web server itself. Before you can understand much about what the ASP engine can do, you need to know what happens before the user's request reaches the code in your ASP page.

A Web request requires two components: a Web server and a client. The client is usually a browser, but could be another type of program, such as a spider (a program that walks Web links gathering information) or an agent (a program tasked with finding specific information, often using search engines). The server and the browser are usually on two separate computers, but that's not a requirement. You can use a browser to request pages from a Web server running on the same computer. The point is that whether the Web server and the browser are on the same computer, or whether they're on opposite sides of the world, the request works almost exactly the same way.

Both the server and the client must use a defined protocol to communicate with each other. A protocol is simply an agreed-upon method for initiating a communications session, passing information back and forth, and terminating the session. There are several protocols used for Web communications; the most common are Hypertext Transfer Protocol (HTTP) and File Transfer Protocol (FTP). Regardless of the protocol used, Web requests are carried over an underlying network protocol called Transmission Control Protocol/Internet Protocol (TCP/IP), which is a global communications standard that determines the rules two computers follow when they exchange information.

The server computer runs an endless loop to check for communication initialization. The client sends an initialization to begin a session. The initialization is a defined series of bytes. The byte content isn't important; the only important thing is that both computers recognize the byte series as an initialization. When the server receives the initialization request, it acknowledges the transmission by returning another series of bytes to the client. The conversation between the two computers continues in this back-and-forth manner. If computers spoke in words, you can imagine the conversation being conducted as follows:

Client Hello?

Server Hello. I speak English.

Client I speak English too.

Server What do you want?

Client I want the file /mySite/myFiles/file1.htm.

Server That file has moved to /mySite/oldFiles/file1.htm.

Client Sorry. Goodbye

Server   Goodbye.

Client   Hello?

Server   Hello. I speak English.

Client   I speak English too.

Server   What do you want?

Client   I want the file /mySite/oldFiles/file1.htm.

Server   Here's some information about that file.

Client   .Thanks, please send the data.

Server   Starting data transmission.

Client   I got packet 1. Send packet 2.

Server   Sending packet 2.

Etc.

Server   All packets sent.

Client   All packets received in good condition. Goodbye.

Server   Goodbye.

TCP/IP is only one of many computer communication protocols, but due to the popularity of the Internet, it has become ubiquitous. You won't need to know much more than that about TCP/IP to use it—the underlying protocol is almost entirely transparent. You do, however, need to know how one machine finds another machine to initiate a communications session.

How a Client Requests Content

When you type a request into the browser address bar or click a hyperlink, the browser packages the request and sends it to a *naming server*. The naming server maintains a database of names, each of which is associated with an IP address. Computers don't understand words very well, so the naming server translates the requested address into a number. The text name you see in the link or the address bar is actually a human-friendly version of an IP address. The IP address is a set of four numbers between 0 and 255, separated by periods. For example: 204.225.113.34.

Each IP address uniquely identifies a single computer. If the first naming server doesn't have the requested address in its database, it forwards the request to a naming server further up the hierarchy. Eventually, if no naming server can translate the requested name to an IP address, the request reaches one of the powerful naming servers that maintain master lists of all publicly registered IP addresses. If no naming server can translate the address, the failed response travels back through the naming server hierarchy until it reaches your browser. At that point, you'll see an error message.

If the naming server can find the request, it caches the request so it won't have to contact higher-level naming servers for the next request to the same server. The naming server returns the IP address to the browser, which uses the IP address to contact the Web server associated with the address. Many Web pages contain references to other files that the Web server must provide for the page to be complete; however, the browser can request only one file at a time. For example, images referenced in a Web page require a separate request for each image.

Thus, the process of displaying a Web page is usually a series of short conversations between the browser and the server. Typically, the browser receives the main page, searches it for other required file references, and then begins to display the main page while requesting the referenced files. That's why you often see image placeholders when a page is loading. The main page contains the references to other URLs that contain the images, but not the images themselves.

What the Server Does with the Request

From the Web server's point of view, each conversation is a brand new contact. By default, a Web server services requests on a first-come, first-served basis. Web servers don't remember any specific browser from one request to another. (Actually, the latest version of the HTTP protocol, HTTP 1.1, does have the ability to maintain a connection over multiple requests, which speeds up your Web access considerably.)

Parts of a URL

The line that you type into the browser address field is a Uniform Resource Locator (URL). The server breaks the requested URL into its component parts. Forward slashes, colons, periods, question marks, and ampersands, called delimiters, make it easy to separate the parts. Each part has a specific function. Here's a sample URL request (the URL doesn't really exist):

```
http://www.someSite.com/VisualBasic/default.htm?Page=1&Para=2
```

Table 22.1 shows the name and function of each part.

TABLE 22.1: URL Parts and Description

URL Item	Function	Description
http	Protocol	Tells the server which protocol it should use to respond to the request.
www.someSite.com	Domain name	This part of the URL translates to the IP address. The domain name consists of several parts separated by periods: the host name—www; the enterprise domain name—someSite; and the top-level Internet domain name—com. There are several other top-level Internet domain names, including org (organization), gov (government), and net (network).
VisualBasic	Virtual directory	The server translates this name into a physical path on a hard drive.
default.htm	Filename	The server will return the contents of the file. If the file were an executable file (such as an ASP file) rather than an HTML file, the server would execute the program contained in the file and return the results rather than return the file contents.
? (question mark)	Separator	The question mark separates the file request from additional parameters sent with the request. The example URL contains two parameters, Page=1 and Para=2.
Page	Parameter name	Programs you write, such as ASP pages, can read the parameters and use them to supply information.
= (equals sign)		The equals sign separates a parameter name from the parameter value.
1	Parameter value	The parameter named Page has a value of 1. Note that all parameter values are sent as string data. Your programs are free to interpret the values as numbers, but you will have to cast or change them to numeric form.
& (ampersand)	Separator	The ampersand separates parameter=value pairs.
Para=2		Second parameter and value.

Server Translates the Path

You don't make Web requests with real or physical paths; instead, you request pages using a virtual path. After parsing the URL, the server translates the virtual path to a physical path name. For example, the virtual directory in the URL http://myServer/myPath/myFile.asp is myPath. The myPath virtual directory maps to a local directory like c:\inetpub\wwwroot\VB\myFile.asp, or to a network Universal Naming Convention (UNC) name like \\someServer\somePath\VB\myFile.asp.

Server Checks for the Resource

The server checks for the requested file. If it doesn't exist, the server returns an error message—usually HTTP 404 - File Not Found. You've probably seen this error message while browsing the Web; if not, you're luckier than I am.

Server Checks Permissions

After locating the resource, the server checks to see if the requesting account has sufficient permission to access the resource. For example, if the requesting account is the anonymous account, and the user has requested a file for which that account has no read permission, the server returns an error message—usually HTTP 403 - Access Denied. The actual error text depends on the exact error generated. There are several sub-levels for 403 error messages. You can find a complete list of error messages in the IIS Default Web Site Property dialog box. The contents of most error messages are customizable. By default, the server reads error message text from the HTML files in your $windows$\help\common\ directory, where $windows$ is the name of your NT directory, usually named WINNT.

How the Server Responds

Graphics files, Word documents, HTML files, ASP files, executable files, CGI scripts—how does the server know how to process the requested file? Actually, servers differentiate file types in several different ways.

Internet Information Server (IIS) differentiates file types based on file extensions (such as .asp, .htm, .exe, and so forth) just like Windows Explorer. When you double-click on a file or icon in Windows Explorer, it looks up the file extension in the *Registry*, a special database that holds system and application information. The Registry contains one entry for each registered file extension. Each extension has an associated file type entry. Each file type entry, in turn, has an associated executable file or file handler. The server strips the file extension from the filename, looks up the associated program, and then launches that program to return the file. IIS follows the same series of steps to determine how to respond to requests.

Most Web servers also use file extensions to determine how to process a file request, but they don't use Registry associations. Instead, they use an independent list of file extension-to-program associations. The entries in these lists are called MIME types, which stands for Multipurpose Internet Mail Extensions, because e-mail programs need to know the type of content included with messages. Each MIME type, just like the Registry associations, is associated with a specific action or program. The Web server searches the list for an entry that matches the file extension of the requested file.

Most servers handle unmatched file extensions by offering to download the file to your computer. Some servers also provide a default action if you request a URL that doesn't contain a filename. In this case, most servers try to return one of a list of default filenames—usually a file called default.htm or index.htm. You may be able to configure the default filename(s) for your server, either globally for all virtual directories on that server, or for each individual virtual directory on that server.

The server can begin streaming the response back to the client as it generates the response, or it can buffer the entire response and send it all at once when the response is complete. There are two parts to the response: the response header and the response body. The response header contains information about the type of response. Among other things, the response header can contain a response code, the MIME type of the response, the date and time after which the response is no longer valid, a redirection URL, and any cookie values the server wants to store on the client. *Cookies* are text strings that the browser saves in memory or on the client computer's hard drive. The cookie may last for the duration of the browser session, until a specified expiration date, or permanently. The browser sends cookies associated with a site back to the server for each subsequent request for that site.

What the Client Does with the Response

The client, usually a browser, needs to know the type of content with which the server has responded. The client reads the MIME type header to determine the content type. For most requests, the MIME type header is either text/html or an image type such as image/gif, but it might also be a word-processing file, a video or audio file, an animation, or any other type of file. Browsers, like servers, use registry values and MIME type lists to determine how to display the file. For standard HTML and image files, browsers use a built-in display engine. For other file types, browsers call upon the services of helper applications or plug-ins that can display the information. The browser assigns all or part of its window area as a canvas onto which the helper program, or plug-in, paints its content.

When the response body consists of HTML, the browser parses the file to separate markup from content. It then uses the markup to determine how to lay out the content on screen. Modern HTML files may contain several different types of content in addition to markup, text, and images; browsers handle each one differently. Among the additional content types are:

Cascading Style Sheets (CSS)   CSS style sheets contain information about how to format the content. Modern browsers use CSS styles to assign fonts, colors, borders, visibility, positioning, and other formatting information to elements on the page.

Script   All modern browsers can execute JavaScript, although they don't always execute it the same way. The term JavaScript applies specifically to script written in Netscape's JavaScript scripting language, but two close variants, Microsoft's Jscript and the ECMA-262 specification (ECMAScript), have essentially the same syntax and support an almost identical command set. In addition to JScript, Internet Explorer supports VBScript, which is a subset of Visual Basic for Applications (which, in turn, is a subset of Microsoft's Visual Basic language).

NOTE
The complete ECMA-262 specification can be found at http://www.ecma.ch/ecma1/stand/ecma-262.htm.

ActiveX components or Java applets   These small programs execute on the client rather than the server. ActiveX components only run in Internet Explorer on Windows platforms, (roughly 60 percent of the total market when this book was written), whereas Java applets run on almost all browsers and almost all platforms.

XML   Extensible Markup Language (XML) is similar to HTML—both consist of tags and content. That's not surprising, because both are derived from Standard Generalized Markup Language (SGML). HTML tags describe how to display the content, and to a limited degree, the function of the content. XML tags describe what the content is. In other words, HTML is primarily a formatting and display language, whereas XML is a content-description language. The two languages complement each other well. XML was first used in Internet Explorer 4 as channels. With Internet Explorer 5, Microsoft has extended the browser's understanding of and facility with XML so that today you can use it to provide data islands in HTML files. You can also deliver a combination of XML and Extensible Stylesheet Language (XSL) (a rules language written in XML that's similar in purpose to CSS) to generate the HTML code on the client. The XML/XSL combination lets you offload processing from the server, thus improving your site's scalability.

How ASP Requests Differ from HTM Requests

Until a request for an ASP file reaches the server, it is identical to an HTM request. The naming server finds the host server in the same way, and the browser makes exactly the same request as it does for an HTM file. At that point, however, the server routes the request to the ASP engine rather than the default IIS response engine. The ASP engine reads the requested file, either from disk or from the IIS file cache, and then parses the file.

The ASP engine then takes three actions, in this order:

1. The ASP engine inserts any include files. Include files are separate files that IIS can place into a requested file. After the insertion, IIS processes the file exactly as if the inserted file were part of the originally requested file. The insertion of include files occurs before the ASP engine processes any code.

2. The ASP engine begins to interpret the code. It interprets code in sequence, except for code sections marked as Functions or Subs. Refer to the "Methods, Functions, Routines,

and Subroutines" sidebar for an explanation of the terminology used in this book.

3. The ASP engine returns the response. You can control whether the engine begins to return the response immediately (unbuffered response) or whether it stores the response string until the response is complete (buffered response) via IIS settings.

Bear in mind that the browser knows nothing about what technology is running on the server. To the browser, all responses are simply a string of characters or numbers. The MIME type of the response determines how the browser treats the response.

METHODS, FUNCTIONS, ROUTINES, AND SUBROUTINES

In VBScript you can write inline code, which is code that executes in the physical order in which the code appears in the file. You can also write code methods, which are blocks of code you can call by name. A method usually (but not always) consists of reusable code—the kind of thing you might want to do over and over again. In VBScript there are two kinds of methods: *subs*, also called subroutines, which perform a unit of work but do not return a result, and *functions*, which are exactly the same as subroutines except they do return a result. Subs and functions are often interchangeable. It's a matter of much debate and programming style whether you need to return a result.

For example, a good candidate for a subroutine is the process of appending text to a file. To append text to a file, you need to open the file, append the text, and close the file. It's easy to write that as inline code, but you will probably need to write almost exactly the same routine over and over again as you build applications. Therefore, you can move the code to a subroutine instead. You might call the routine appendTofile. You pass the subroutine the name of the file and the text to append, and the subroutine opens the file and appends the text. For example:

```
Sub appendToFile(aFilename, someText)
    ' open the file aFilename
    ' append the text
    ' close the file
End Sub
```

CONTINUED ➞

By wrapping the inline code in a subroutine you've made it reusable, because the same code will now work with any file and any text. You can make it a subroutine rather than a function because you don't need to return any result.

In contrast, a good candidate for a function is the process of adding an arbitrary set of numbers together. You might call the function addNumbers. You pass the addNumbers function a Variant array of numbers. The function adds the numbers and returns the result. For example:

```
Function addNumbers(vNumberArray)
    Dim i
    Dim result
    For i = 0 to ubound(vNumberArray)
    For i = 0 result = result + vNumberArray(i)
    Next
    addNumbers = result
End Function
```

Both functions and subroutines are known generically as methods. You may also see the word *routines*, which means exactly the same thing. Methods typically refer to code packaged in objects, whereas routines typically refer to code packaged in code modules, but you'll find them used more or less interchangeably in the industry.

What Is the asp.dll?

The ASP Dynamic Link Library (DLL) is the code behind the ASP engine. There are at least three versions of the asp.dll; version 3 ships with Windows 2000. Although I have no doubt that internally the DLL has changed significantly since version 1, unlike most Microsoft technology, the public interface has remained almost exactly the same. That's because ASP is not a language—it's a scripting host. Therefore, it doesn't need to change unless the basic requirements of a scripting host change.

What Is Script?

I've mentioned script several times, but what is script? Unfortunately, I don't have a very clear answer for you because the answer depends on whom you ask. To Microsoft, script is any ActiveX programming language that exposes an interface compatible with the Windows Scripting Host. The two most common scripting languages for Microsoft applications are VBScript and JScript or JavaScript, although there are other compatible scripting languages—PerlScript for example. To Netscape, script means JavaScript. To Sun Microsystems, script means JavaScript that runs on the server as JavaServer Pages (JSPs), a recent ASP knock-off.

To almost everyone, script means a small, relatively limited interpreted language. You need to know what interpreted code is to understand the previous sentence. Computers don't understand code as you write it. Instead, other programs translate the code you write into machine instructions. There are two ways to make the translation. You can translate the code at runtime, which means the computer reads a line or block of code from your code file, makes the translation, and then executes the code. That process is called interpreting the code, and it's done by a program called an interpreter.

Alternatively, you can translate the code and store the resulting machine code in a file. When you execute the file, the computer reads the machine instructions directly. That kind of translation is not performed at runtime; a program called a compiler translates the code before the computer begins to execute it. The compiler and the interpreter do much the same thing, but the compiler is more efficient because it isn't under any time constraints. It compiles the code offline. The interpreter is less efficient, because it has to translate the code to machine instructions and run it almost instantaneously.

Script languages are small only in comparison with full-featured languages. VBScript is a subset of the Visual Basic language. In contrast, JavaScript is not a subset of Java, although the two languages share much of the same syntax. Netscape invented JavaScript because they needed a safe way to run code inside a browser. JScript and JavaScript are not quite identical, but they will evolve to become identical over time, due to the ECMA standards. Almost all browsers can execute JavaScript. Internet Explorer is the only browser that can execute VBScript.

You are perfectly free to use any ActiveX-compatible scripting languages—and you may want to consider doing so if you're familiar with Java, C, or Perl, or if your applications will demand much client-side scripting. Yes, that's right; script code can run either on the server or the client. This is probably the most confusing point for beginning ASP programmers. Just remember this, if it's ASP code, it will run on the server before the response has been completed. If it's client-side code, it will run on the client only after the browser has begun to receive the response.

NOTE

JScript and JavaScript are not the same thing. Although they have an almost identical feature set, they are completely independent, created and marketed by Microsoft and Netscape, respectively.

If the majority of your target audience uses Netscape browsers, if you're creating applications for the public that will run on the Internet, or if you think your application's user base is broader than Windows, you should use JavaScript for all your client-side script.

How Does the Server Separate Script from Content?

When the ASP engine parses the file, it separates server-side script from content in two ways. As the programmer, you must separate your script from content with a delimiter, which is an arbitrary character or sequence of characters that separates values. Delimited text files often have only a single delimiter—the comma or tab character. ASP script has two delimiters, one to mark the beginning of a code block and another to mark the end of the code block. The ASP code start delimiter is a left angle-bracket and a percent sign, and the end delimiter is the percent sign followed by a right angle-bracket; for example: <% your code here %>.

You may also separate code from script using a more traditional, HTML-like syntax. Using this method, the code begins with a <script> tag and ends with a </script> tag. To use this syntax with ASP script, write the script as follows:

```
<script language="JScript" RunAt="Server">
' your code here
</script>
```

Note the text RunAt="Server" in the <script> tag. If you don't include that text (called an attribute), the server will ignore the script, but the browser will try to execute the script on the client side. In other words, <script> tags by default delimit client-side script. To force the ASP engine to process scripts as server-side code, you must add the RunAt="Server" attribute.

My advice is not to use the <script RunAt="Server"> syntax—it's too easy to confuse the syntax and cause unnecessary errors. Use the bracket-percent delimiters instead. In some editors, like HomeSite, FrontPage, and Visual InterDev, the editor will change the text color for script between the bracket-percent delimiters, which can help you differentiate script from HTML.

How/When Does the Server Process Script?

When the server invokes the ASP scripting engine, it first parses the file and inserts any `include` files. It then collects the script portion by finding all the script delimiters. The ASP engine treats all non-script content as strings that it writes verbatim back to the client. Next, the scripting engine creates variables and external components invoked by the script. Finally, it begins interpreting the script, executing each command and sending results to the client (or buffering the results, depending on server settings).

At the completion of script processing, the scripting engine destroys variables and external components created for the script. If the results were buffered, the server returns the contents of the buffer to the client.

How Does the Browser Act with ASP Sites?

This is important because it is one of the most common misconceptions of beginning ASP programmers: the browser has no concept of ASP sites, HTML sites, or any other kind of site. The browser is completely, utterly, and totally ignorant of the way a server processes its requests. To a browser, there's no difference between an ASP page and an HTM file. Browsers don't request specific kinds of content; they just request that the conversation with the server follows one of the standard communications protocols.

What's Next

In the final chapter of this book, Ann Navarro introduces you to XHTML.

Chapter 23

INTRODUCTION TO XHTML

Since 1997, when the World Wide Web Consortium (W3C) first introduced HTML 4.0 to the general public, there's been much speculation about where HTML would go beyond version 4. Many people were in favor of HTML 5.0, with even more new elements and presentational features than were found in HTML 4.0. Others wanted to drop development of HTML altogether in favor of making XML the new language of the Web.

Written for *HTML Complete,* 2nd Editon
by Ann Navarro

The W3C decided to hold a two-day workshop in May of 1998, where nearly 100 experts from around the world gathered to discuss what should be done with HTML. Should it go on? Should we all move to XML? Or was there another solution?

By the end of the event, the consensus was clear. The Web needed a transition between the HTML of the time (version 4) and XML. This "bridge" would help the Web authoring community move into the world of XML, which provides both the freedom to create your own elements and the requirements of clean code. This new language eventually came to be known as XHTML, the *Extensible Hypertext Markup Language*.

WHAT IS XHTML?

You know that XHTML is "extensible" HTML, but what that means to the average Web author isn't readily apparent. If you recall your HTML history, you'll remember that HTML is based on SGML. XHTML, on the other hand, is an application of XML, the *Extensible Markup Language*. While XML is also based upon SGML, the result is something entirely different.

Where HTML defines elements and attributes that are to be rendered in a specified manner, XML provides a framework for defining other languages. Instead of being constrained to paragraphs, lists, and tables, you can define elements just for names, addresses, telephone numbers, part numbers, or structures representing just about anything you can think of.

Yet with all the structural freedom found in XML, programmers and authors still need to provide information best suited to basic document structures. That's where XHTML comes in. XHTML provides the tried and true features of HTML in syntax compatible with the XML framework. As mentioned, XHTML is often described as a "bridge" between HTML and XML.

The first step across this bridge is codified in the XHTML 1.0 Recommendation published by the W3C in early 2000. The object was to simply transform HTML 4.0 into XML syntax, removing or modifying only what was necessary to do so. The "extensible" portion of XHTML occurs when new XML elements and attributes are introduced to the language.

This mix of HTML and XML comes using a technique known as the *Modularization of XHTML*. Using the framework provided by XML, the custom elements and attributes needed are defined in a document type definition (DTD) or Schema, and then combined with standard XHTML modules to create a unique language that is a part of the XHTML family of document types.

One of the most obvious implementations for XHTML is in e-commerce. Data about items for sale is usually stored in a database by the shop owner. Product names, prices, and other data used to manage inventory are stored in the various database fields. If that information is extracted and placed into an HTML page, the context is lost when it must be formatted using paragraphs, line breaks, and other generalized structures.

Using XML, the data can be kept in structures related to the database fields, such as this:

```
<product category="computer">
<manufacturer>IBM</manufacturer>
<type>laptop</type>
<model>Thinkpad 1421i</model>
<price currency="dollar">1299</price>
</product>
```

Web site developers don't want to re-create basic functions such as headings and paragraphs, so they create a customized e-commerce module.

The final step required is to write a style sheet, typically either in CSS (Cascading Style Sheets) or XSL (the Extensible Stylesheet Language). Without a style sheet, today's browser won't know how to present the data within the page.

Armed with the new document type and the style sheet, the author can then create a document that retains the necessary level of detail in the product information yet can be displayed in today's browsers!

Two terms that you'll see repeatedly are *well-formed* and *valid*. A document is considered well-formed if all its elements are complete (that is, all required components are present, such as opening and closing tags, and attribute values are fully quoted). A well-formed document can also be considered valid if it conforms directly to the requirements of the DTD against which it was written.

Validity has been a desirable state for as long as HTML has been around. The concept of well-formedness, however, comes to us with XML. Some of HTML's appeal (or problems, depending on who you ask!) is that the implementation of the language in Web browsers has been very forgiving. The programmers have "taught" the browser how to interpret what the author might have intended when writing their documents, instead of insisting that elements and attributes be written exactly as specified in the DTDs.

How Is XHTML Different from HTML?

Aside from the obvious differences related to extensibility discussed in the previous sections, you'll need to be aware of some other important differences.

As you begin to explore XHTML, you'll quickly realize that it's much more similar to HTML than it is different. The changes aren't really changes at all, but a more "law and order" approach to document development. What may be optional in HTML, such as closing </p> tags, are now required in XHTML. The W3C has published 13 specific guidelines for authors who wish to quickly understand the differences between the two languages. We'll highlight five of them here. The remainder can be found in Appendix C of the XHTML 1.0 Recommendation, at http://www.w3.org/TR/xhtml1/#guidelines.

Element Minimization

Many elements in HTML have been defined with optional closing tags. You'll frequently see this with paragraph tags and list items, or any element Web authors have found isn't affected by the "short hand" of omitting the closing tag. The act of omission is known as *element minimization*. A minimized paragraph could look like this:

```
<p>This is a very short paragraph.
```

In HTML, this is a perfectly valid paragraph structure. In XHTML, though, minimization is not allowed, and the closing </p> tag must be present:

```
<p>This is a very short paragraph.</p>
```

This seems simple, but requires a little bit of thought when working with elements contained within other elements. Consider a set of nested lists. Many XHTML novices will first try to construct them as follows:

```
<ol>
<li>Item One</li>
<li>Item Two</li>
<ul>
<li>Item Two-A</li>
<li>Item Two-B</li>
</ul>
<li>Item Three</li>
</ol>
```

When viewed in a current browser, this construction looks "correct." However, the content model for an ordered list allows only one or more list item elements. The list item element, on the other hand, is allowed to contain other elements such as additional list elements.

To properly create a nested list set, the second list must be contained within the list item after which it appears; it's actually a part of that element. The list item is then closed *after* the nested list is fully completed.

```
<ol>
<li>Item One</li>
<li>Item Two
<ul>
<li>Item Two-A</li>
<li>Item Two-B</li>
</ul>
</li>
<li>Item Three</li>
</ol>
```

Empty Elements

Empty elements are those that don't have any content between opening and closing tags. For instance, the unordered list element has content: one or more list items:

```
<ul>
<li>This list item is content in the UL element.</li>
</ul>
```

The image element, on the other hand, doesn't have a closing tag—just a single tag with attributes, and therefore no content:

```
<img src="picture.gif" height="100" width="100" alt="my
picture">
```

NOTE

Don't confuse the information stored in attributes within the element as *content*. Element content is the data contained within the bounds of the opening and closing tags. Other empty elements commonly used in HTML are the <br> and <hr> elements.

When we discussed element minimization, you learned that closing tags must always be used. This creates a bit of a problem for empty elements.

The solution, however, is quite simple. Each empty element now has a corresponding closing tag. The image element can then be written as:

```
<img src="picture.gif" height="100" width="100" alt="my
picture"></img>
```

Further shorthand has been developed, allowing authors to write both the opening and closing tags at the same time. This is done by inserting a slash before the terminal > character, for example:

```
<hr/>
```

To achieve backward compatibility with today's popular Web browsers, an additional space should be inserted before the slash:

```
<hr />
```

A proper XML parser will collapse the white space, which results in the same <hr/>.

TIP

The "space-slash" shorthand is the most compatible method of writing empty elements. Many existing Web browsers will be confused by the closing tags added to empty elements, but will happily ignore the slash, provided it's separated from the rest of the element by that space.

An important distinction should be made here between an element that happens to have no content and a truly *empty* element. For instance, a table may have several empty cells, but the content model for the <td> element is not EMPTY. In these cases, the element must be written as <td></td> and not <td />.

Boolean Attributes

A Boolean attribute is one that is activated simply by its presence, rather than by the traditional attribute="value" pair format of most attributes. For example, in HTML a horizontal rule can be rendered without shading by writing <hr noshade>. In XHTML, Boolean attributes are not permitted. Instead, the author must expand the attribute—that is, transform it into the expected attribute="value" pair form. For the noshade attribute, this would be noshade="noshade", resulting in:

```
<hr noshade="noshade">
```

Ampersands in Attribute Values

One of the peskiest validation issues many authors face is the URLs used to link to dynamically generated Web pages. Quite often, they make use of the ampersand character. The problem is that ampersands are the result of processing a character entity, and they can't be written directly in the document. That is, instead of writing simply &, you need to write &.

Many authors are concerned that they can't "change" the URL for these sites. The key is that validity is checked prior to the document being fully rendered. The link isn't seen until the document is displayed in the browser, at which time the rendering is finished. This means that the character entities have all been processed, and so what starts in the document as & will appear on the page as &. Thus the link hasn't been "changed," yet it will still be valid.

Case Sensitivity

More than any other decision made by the HTML Working Group, the issue of case sensitivity in elements and attributes generated more debate and complaints by at least several orders of magnitude. Despite the seemingly arbitrary decision that was made, careful examination of the possibilities did take place.

The problem began as this: XML was designed as being case-sensitive, whereas HTML, with a very few exceptions, is case-insensitive. With XHTML being an application of XML, it must follow the same rules and had to become case-sensitive. Based on the way XHTML documents served with XML-based MIME types interact with the XML Document Object Model (the details of which are beyond the scope of this book), the choice was made to go with lowercase.

TIP

For those of you who find uppercase HTML tags preferable based on the ease of picking them out in a sea of characters on a page, consider using one of the many text editors that offer color-coding of characters enclosed in brackets. Many authors find the color offset even easier to manage than the simple change in case.

Implementing XHTML

Once you begin to think about the myriad of possibilities available when writing custom modules to use in XHTML family document types, you'll quickly realize many of the advantages. Beyond the obvious extensibility, several key points make all versions XHTML, including the basic XHTML 1.0, very attractive to Web developers.

Well-formed and valid documents are predictable documents.   Many of the display problems encountered on Web pages are the result of incomplete or erroneous HTML. Forget the closing <table> tag, and you'll likely see a giant blank page rather than your well-laid out design when using one popular browser. By conforming to the XML-based requirements of well-formedness and validity, you greatly increase the chances of your documents displaying as you intended.

XHTML documents are XML-conformant.   We've said this before, but it's worth repeating here. XHTML is an application of XML, and therefore any valid XHTML document is automatically a well-formed and valid XML document. This allows documents to be viewed and edited by any standard XML tool, not just a Web browser.

XHTML documents may be viewed in today's browsers as well as future XHTML-based browsers.   This point is pretty self-explanatory. Using the guidelines discussed in this chapter, and the additional information provided by the W3C, authors can ensure that their documents can be viewed in both today's HTML-based browsers, such as Netscape Navigator, Internet Explorer, and Opera (to name just a few), and in tomorrow's XHTML-based applications.

XHTML can access either the HTML or XML Document Object Model.   Because XHTML is backward-compatible with HTML and an application of XML, it is possible for applets and scripts to interact with either Document Object Models during processing, giving increased flexibility.

XHTML offers tighter integration with uniquely structured data.   Through modularization, data that needs to retain structure and semantics associated with a database can be readily added to common Web documents without losing their original context. This ability allows for quicker and cleaner exchanges of data for e-commerce and other data-exchange scenarios.

There are so many possibilities available to Web authors with XHTML that it's a difficult prospect to discuss any *dis*advantages of using the language. But in fairness, there are a few things to watch out for during this transition to an XML-based Web.

One of the advantages of XHTML can also present difficulties to Web authors not used to dealing with such constraints. Most of today's Web-authoring tools, both WYSIWYG and HTML authoring environments, don't include such basic necessities as a document type declaration (required by XHTML), and often provide inconsistent use of quotes around attribute values and case in elements and attributes.

Additionally, the very nature of a WYSIWYG tool has proven difficult to translate into valid documents. The programmers responsible for the development of these applications instead tend to rely upon the rendering conventions of one or two popular browsers for a determination of "correct" behavior rather than validating against the HTML Recommendations.

If an author using one of these tools wants to create XHTML documents, some hand-editing will be required. Depending on the tool in use, this can be a very simple operation or a labor-intensive endeavor that could literally take longer than authoring the document by hand.

The other issue that may challenge some Web authors is the need to create style sheets to manage the display of custom modules. Many developers have experimented with CSS, especially now that support has been increasing with the newest browsers, but quite a few more have little to no experience with style languages. This can create a longer learning curve, resulting in increased development time.

Who Should Use XHTML?

Developers who may be interested in XHTML will generally fall into three camps:

- ▶ Web site authors who need to incorporate XML data into a Web page

- ▶ Application programmers who need to deliver device-, platform-, and language-independent structured data to a Web environment

▶ Web developers creating new sites or updating existing sites who wish to be prepared for quick integration of new data in uncertain formats

In addition, those just learning HTML for the first time might consider adopting XHTML techniques as they learn. Doing so while first experimenting with HTML will make the transition to an XML-based world practically transparent. As you've seen in this chapter, the HTML you've learned previously in this book needs very little change to be XHTML-compliant.

LEARNING MORE ABOUT XHTML

As the XHTML Recommendations continue to evolve, many new tutorials, references, and demo implementations will certainly be published. Books available today cover the XHTML 1.0 Recommendation and the initial public information on the Modularization of XHTML and new XHTML applications. Additional works, such as Sybex's *Mastering XHTML* and *Effective Web Design*, delve further into the process of integrating XHTML into your Web development skill set.

Online resources include:

▶ The W3C Hypertext Markup pages: `http://www.w3.org/MarkUp/`

▶ Web Developer's Virtual Library – Introduction to XHTML: `http://www.wdvl.com/Authoring/Languages/XML/XHTML/`

▶ XML.com Guide to XHTML: `http://www.xml.com/pub/Guide/XHTML`

WHAT'S NEXT

In this chapter you've learned about the next step in Web authoring: the Extensible Hypertext Markup Language. As an application of XML, XHTML 1.0 begins as a simple transformation of HTML 4.0 into XML syntax. Moving further into XHTML development, we have the Modularization of XHTML, which blends the familiar structure of HTML's document construction with custom elements and attributes.

Over the course of this book, our authors have given you a solid background in HTML and its implementation in site design. In addition, they've introduced you to other languages that you can use to augment

HTML and enhance your pages even more. The next step is up to you. You should now feel free to experiment with what you've learned while building sites of your own—just be sure to keep this book handy. In addition to the chapters you've just completed, the appendix—a comprehensive guide to HTML tags and their attributes, HTML special characters, and HTML color codes—will prove invaluable as you venture further into site design.

APPENDIX

HTML MASTER'S REFERENCE

Adapted from *Mastering HTML 4.0*,
by Deborah S. Ray and Eric J. Ray
ISBN 0-7821-2102-0   1,040 pages $49.99

HTML Tags and Attributes

This section is a comprehensive reference guide to all HTML tags, including standard tags and those introduced by Netscape Navigator and Microsoft Internet Explorer. For each tag, we've provided sample code and indicated the following:

▶ The version of HTML with which the tag is associated

▶ Whether browsers widely support the tag

▶ Whether to pair the tag with a closing tag

For each tag's attributes, we've provided sample code and indicated the following:

▶ The version of HTML with which the attribute is associated

▶ Whether browsers widely support the attribute

If tags and attributes appear in the HTML 4 standard, in the HTML 3.2 standard, or in the HTML 2 standard, the version number appears next to Standard. We indicate tags or attributes that are specific to a browser, such as Internet Explorer. In general, a variety of browsers recognize technology-specific tags, such as those for frames, and other browsers rarely recognize browser-specific tags. HTML 2 was the first official HTML standard. The number of tags that this standard defined is small compared with what is in use today. HTML 2 did not support tables, client-side imagemaps, or frames. You can safely use all HTML 2 tags and attributes.

HTML 3.2 remains backward-compatible with HTML 2, but provides many new tags. Included in HTML 3.2 is support for tables, client-side imagemaps, embedded applets, and many new attributes that help control alignment of objects within documents. You can assume that most browsers support or soon will support all HTML 3.2 tags and attributes.

HTML 4 remains backward-compatible with other versions of HTML and expands the capabilities to better address multiple languages and browser technologies such as speech or Braille. Additionally, most formatting tags and attributes are deprecated (strongly discouraged) in HTML 4 in favor of style sheets.

Specifying that a tag or an attribute is Common means that approximately 75 to 80 percent of browsers in common use accommodate the tag. All recent versions of both Internet Explorer and Netscape Navigator recognize Common tags and attributes.

We indicate variables as follows:

Variable	What You Substitute
n	A number (such as a size)
URL	Some form of address (as in a hyperlink)
#RRGGBB	A color value or a color name
...	Some other value, such as a title or a name

!

<!-- -->

Inserts comments into a document. Browsers do not display comments, although comments are visible in the document source.

Standard: HTML 2
Common: Yes
Paired: Yes
Sample:

```
<!-- Here is the picture of Fido -->
<IMG SRC="fidopic.jpg">
```

<!DOCTYPE>

Appears at the beginning of the document and indicates the HTML version of the document.

The HTML 2 standard is:

```
<!DOCTYPE HTML PUBLIC
"-//IETF//DTD HTML 2 //EN">
```

The HTML 3.2 standard is:

```
<!DOCTYPE HTML PUBLIC
"-//W3C//DTD/ HTML 3.2 Final//EN">
```

The HTML 4 standard is:

```
<!DOCTYPE HTML PUBLIC
"-//W3C//DTD/ HTML 4 Final//EN">
```

Standard: HTML 2
Common: Yes
Paired: No
Sample:

```
<!DOCTYPE HTML PUBLIC
"-//W3C//DTD/ HTML 4 Final//EN">
```

A

<A>

Also called the *anchor* tag, identifies a link or a location within a document. You commonly use this tag to create a hyperlink, using the HREF= attribute. You can also use the <A> tag to identify sections within a document, using the NAME= attribute.

Standard: HTML 2

Common: Yes
Paired: Yes
Sample:

```
<A HREF="http://www.raycomm
.com/">Visit RayComm</a>
```

Attribute Information

ACCESSKEY="..."

Assigns a key sequence to the element.

Standard: HTML 4
Common: No
Sample:

```
<A HREF="help.html"
ACCESSKEY="H">HELP</a>
```

CHARSET="..."

Specifies character encoding of the data designated by the link. Use the name of a character set defined in RFC2045. The default value for this attribute, appropriate for all Western languages, is "ISO-8859-1".

Standard: HTML 4
Common: No
Sample:

```
<A HREF="help.html" CHARSET="ISO-
8859-1">HELP</a>
```

CLASS="..."

Indicates the style class to apply to the <A> element.

Standard: HTML 4
Common: No
Sample:

```
<A HREF="next.html"
CLASS="casual">Next</A>
```

COORDS="*x1, y1, x2, y2*"

Identifies the coordinates that define a clickable area. Measure coordinates, in pixels, from the top-left corner of the image.

Standard: HTML 4
Common: No
Sample:

```
<A SHAPE="RECT" COORDS="20,8,46,30"
HREF="food.html">
```

HREF="*URL*"

Specifies the relative or absolute location of a file to which you want to provide a hyperlink.

Standard:	HTML 2
Common:	Yes
Sample:	

```
<A HREF="details.html">More Info</a>
```

ID="..."

Assigns a unique ID selector to an instance of the <A> tag. When you then assign a style to that ID selector, it affects only that one instance of the <A> tag.

Standard:	HTML 4
Common:	No
Sample:	

```
<A HREF="next.html" ID="123">Next</A>
```

NAME="..."

Marks a location within the current document with a name. The browser can then quickly move to specific information within a document. You can link to existing named locations in a document by using a fragment URL, consisting of a pound sign (#) and the name (from within that document), or by using a more complete URL, including a pound sign and a name (from other documents or sites).

Standard:	HTML 2
Common:	Yes
Sample:	

```
<A HREF="#ingredients">
Ingredients</A><BR><A
NAME="ingredients"><H1>
Ingredients</H1>
```

REL="..."

Specifies relationship hyperlinks.

Standard:	HTML 3.2
Common:	No
Sample:	

```
<A REV="made"
HREF="mailto:bob@company.com">
```

REV="..."

Specifies reverse relationship hyperlinks.

Standard:	HTML 3.2
Common:	No
Sample:	

```
<A REV="Previous" HREF="http://
www.raycomm.com/firstdoc.htm">
```

SHAPE="{RECT, CIRCLE, POLY, DEFAULT}"

Specifies the type of shape used to represent the clickable area. SHAPE=RECT indicates that the shape is rectangular. SHAPE=CIRCLE specifies that the shape is a circle. SHAPE=POLY indicates that the shape is a polygon represented by three or more points.

Standard:	HTML 4
Common:	No
Sample:	

```
<A SHAPE="RECT" COORDS="20,8,46,30"
HREF="food.html">
```

STYLE="..."

Specifies style sheet commands that apply to the contents within the <A> tags.

Standard:	HTML 4
Common:	No
Sample:	

```
<A STYLE="background: red"
HREF="page2.html">Page 2</A>
```

TABINDEX="n"

Indicates where the element appears in the tabbing order of the document.

Standard:	HTML 4
Common:	No
Sample:	

```
<A HREF="food.html"
TABINDEX="4">Food</A>
```

TARGET="..."

Indicates the name of a specific frame into which you load the linked document. You establish frame names within the <FRAME> tag. The value of this attribute can be any single word.

Standard:	HTML 4
Common:	Yes
Sample:	

```
<A HREF="/frames/frame2.html"
TARGET="pages">Go to Page 2</a>
```

TITLE="..."

Specifies text assigned to the tag that you can use for context-sensitive help within the document. Browsers may use this to show tool tips over the hyperlink.

Standard:	HTML 4

Common: Yes
Sample:

```
<A HREF="page2.html" TITLE="Go to the
next page">
```

Other Attributes

This tag also accepts the TYPE, LANG, DIR, HREFLANG, onFocus, onBlur, onClick, onDblClick, onMouseDown, onMouseUp, onMouseOver, onMouseMove, onMouseOut, onKeyPress, onKeyDown, and onKeyUp attributes. See the Element-Independent Attributes section of this reference for definitions and examples.

<ABBR>

Specifies an abbreviated structure for this element.

Standard: HTML 4
Common: Yes
Paired: Yes
Sample:

```
<ABBR TITLE="Hypertext Markup
Language">HTML</ABBR>
```

Attribute Information

CLASS="..."

Indicates the style class to apply to the <ABBR> element.

Standard: HTML 4
Common: No
Sample:

```
<ABBR CLASS="casual" TITLE="Hypertext
Markup Language"> HTML</ABBR>
```

ID="..."

Assigns a unique ID selector to <ABBR>.

Standard: HTML 4
Common: No
Sample:

```
<ABBR ID="123" TITLE="Hypertext
Markup Language">HTML</ABBR>
```

STYLE="..."

Specifies style sheet commands.

Standard: HTML 4
Common: Yes

Sample:

```
<ABBR STYLE="background: red"
TITLE="Hypertext Markup
Language">HTML</ABBR>
```

TITLE="..."

Specifies text assigned to the tag.

Standard: HTML 4
Common: Yes
Sample:

```
<ABBR TITLE="Hypertext Markup
Language">HTML</ABBR>
```

Other Attributes

This tag also accepts the LANG, DIR, onClick, onDblClick, onMouseDOwn, onMouseUp, onMouseOver, onMouseMove, onMouseOut, onKeyPress, onKeyDown, and onKeyUp attributes.

<ACRONYM>

Indicates an acronym in a document.

Standard: HTML 4
Common: No
Paired: Yes
Sample:

```
<P><ACRONYM>HTTP</ACRONYM> stands for
HyperText Transfer Protocol</P>
```

Attribute Information

CLASS="..."

Indicates which style class applies to the <ACRONYM> element.

Standard: HTML 4
Common: No
Sample:

```
<P><ACRONYM CLASS="casual">HTTP
</ACRONYM> stands for HyperText
Transfer Protocol</P>
```

ID="..."

Assigns a unique ID selector to an instance of the <ACRONYM> tag. When you then assign a style to that ID selector, it affects only that one instance of the <ACRONYM> tag.

Standard: HTML 4
Common: No

Sample:

```
<P><ACRONYM ID="123">HTTP
</ACRONYM> stands for HyperText
Transfer Protocol</P>
```

STYLE="..."

Specifies style sheet commands that apply to the definition.

> **Standard:** HTML 4
> **Common:** No
> **Sample:**

```
<P><ACRONYM STYLE="background: blue;
color: white">ESP</ACRONYM> stands
for extra-sensory
perception.</P>
```

TITLE="..."

Specifies text assigned to the tag. For the <ACRONYM> tag, use this to provide the expansion of the term. You might also use this attribute for context-sensitive help within the document. Browsers may use this to show tool tips over the text.

> **Standard:** HTML 4
> **Common:** No
> **Sample:**

```
<P><ACRONYM TITLE="Hypertext Transfer
Protocol">HTTP</ACRONYM> stands for
Hypertext Transfer Protocol</P>
```

Other Attributes

This tag also accepts the LANG, DIR, onClick, onDblClick, onMouseDown, onMouseUp, onMouseOver, onMouseMove, onMouseOut, onKeyPress, onKeyDown, and onKeyUp attributes. See the Element-Independent Attributes section of this reference for definitions and examples.

<ADDRESS>

In a document, distinguishes an address from normal document text.

> **Standard:** HTML 2
> **Common:** Yes
> **Paired:** Yes
> **Sample:**

```
I live at:
<ADDRESS>123 Nowhere Ave<BR>City,
State 12345</ADDRESS>
```

Attribute Information

ALIGN={LEFT, RIGHT, CENTER}

Indicates how the address text is aligned within the document. ALIGN=LEFT positions the address text flush with the left side of the document. ALIGN=RIGHT positions the address text flush with the right side of the document. ALIGN=CENTER centers the address text between the left and right edges of the document.

> **Standard:** HTML 3.2; deprecated in favor of style sheets
> **Common:** Yes
> **Sample:**

```
<ADDRESS ALIGN="CENTER">123 Anywhere
St.</ADDRESS>
```

CLASS="..."

Indicates the style class to apply to the <ADDRESS> element.

> **Standard:** HTML 4
> **Common:** No
> **Sample:**

```
<ADDRESS CLASS="casual">123 First
Ave.</ADDRESS>
```

ID="..."

Assigns a unique ID selector to an instance of the <ADDRESS> tag. When you then assign a style to that ID selector, it affects only that one instance of the <ADDRESS> tag.

> **Standard:** HTML 4
> **Common:** No
> **Sample:**

```
<ADDRESS ID="123">1600
Pennsylvania</ADDRESS>
```

STYLE="..."

Specifies style sheet commands that apply to the contents within the <ADDRESS> tags.

> **Standard:** HTML 4
> **Common:** Yes
> **Sample:**

```
<ADDRESS STYLE="background: red">
```

TITLE="..."

Specifies text assigned to the tag. You might use this attribute for context-sensitive help within the document. Browsers may use this to show tool tips over the address text.

Standard: HTML 4
Common: No
Sample:

`<ADDRESS TITLE="Address">`

Other Attributes

This tag also accepts the LANG, DIR, onClick, onDblClick, onMouseDown, onMouseUp, onMouseOver, onMouseMove, onMouseOut, onKeyPress, onKeyDown, and onKeyUp attributes. See the Element-Independent Attributes section of this reference for definitions and examples.

`<APPLET>`

Embeds a Java applet object into an HTML document. Typically, items that appear inside the `<APPLET>` tags allow browsers that do not support Java applets to view alternative text. Browsers that do support Java ignore all information between the `<APPLET>` tags.

Standard: HTML 3.2; deprecated in HTML 4 in favor of `<OBJECT>`
Common: Yes
Paired: Yes
Sample:

`<APPLET CODE="game.class">It appears your browser does not support Java. You're missing out on a whole world of neat things!</APPLET>`

Attribute Information

ALIGN={LEFT, MIDDLE, RIGHT, TOP, BOTTOM, }

Specifies the horizontal alignment of the Java applet displayed. For example, a value of MIDDLE tells the browser to place the applet evenly spaced between the left and right edges of the browser window.

Standard: HTML 3.2; deprecated in HTML 4 in favor of style sheets
Common: No

Sample:

`<APPLET ALIGN=MIDDLE CODE=""http://www.raycomm.com/ checkers.class">You lose. Would you like to play again? Hit the RELOAD button.<BR></APPLET>`

ALT="..."

Displays a textual description of a Java applet, if necessary.

Standard: HTML 3.2
Common: No
Sample:

`<APPLET CODE=""http://www .raycomm.com/checkers.class">ALT="A game of checkers">We could have had a relaxing game of checkers if your browser supported Java applets. I'll gladly play with you if you enable Java applets or upgrade to a browser that supports Java.</APPLET>`

CODE="*URL*"

Specifies the relative or absolute location of the Java bytecode file on the server.

Standard: HTML 3.2
Common: No
Sample:

`<APPLET CODE="http://www .raycomm.com/checkers.class"> Dang! Your browser does not support Java applets. You may want to consider installing a newer Web browser. </APPLET>`

CODEBASE="*URL*"

Specifies the directory where you can find all necessary Java class files on the WWW server. If you set this attribute, you need not use explicit URLs in other references to the class files. For example, you would not need an explicit reference in the CODE= attribute.

Standard: HTML 3.2
Common: No
Sample:

`<APPLET CODEBASE="http://www .raycomm.com/checkers.class" CODE="checkers.html">`
If your browser supported inline Java applets, you'd be looking at a very

attractive checkerboard right now.
</APPLET>

HEIGHT="*n*"
Specifies the height (measured in pixels) of
the Java applet object within the document.

> **Standard:** HTML 3.2
> **Common:** No
> **Sample:**

```
<APPLET HEIGHT="200"
CODE="checkers.class">
Since your browser does not support
inline Java applets, we won't be
playing checkers today.
</APPLET>
```

HSPACE="*n*"
Specifies an amount of blank space (mea-
sured in pixels) to the left and right of the
Java applet within the document.

> **Standard:** HTML 3.2
> **Common:** No
> **Sample:**

```
<APPLET HSPACE="10"
CODE="/checkers.class">
Sorry. Due to the fact your browser
does not support embedded Java
applets, you'll have to play checkers
the old way today.
</APPLET>
```

NAME="..."
Assigns the applet instance a name so that
other applets can identify it within the document.

> **Standard:** Internet Explorer
> **Common:** No
> **Sample:**

```
<APPLET SRC="/checkers.class"
NAME="Checkers">
</APPLET>
```

PARAM *NAME*="..."
Passes program parameters to the Java
applet.

> **Standard:** HTML 3.2
> **Common:** No
> **Sample:**

```
<APPLET CODE="/checkers.class" PARAM
COLOR="red">
Since your browser does not support
```

inline Java applets, I win this game
of checkers by forfeit.
</APPLET>

TITLE="..."
Specifies text assigned to the tag. You might
use this attribute for context-sensitive help
within the document. Browsers may use this
to show tool tips over the embedded applet.

> **Standard:** HTML 4
> **Common:** No
> **Sample:**

```
<APPLET SRC="/java/thing.class"
TITLE="Thing">
```

VSPACE="*n*"
Specifies the amount of vertical space (measured in pixels) above and below the Java
applet.

> **Standard:** HTML 3.2
> **Common:** No
> **Sample:**

```
<APPLET VSPACE="10"
CODE="/checkers.class">
If you had a Java-capable browser,
you could be playing checkers!
</APPLET>
```

WIDTH="*n*"
Specifies the width (measured in pixels) of a
Java applet within a document.

> **Standard:** HTML 3.2
> **Common:** No
> **Sample:**

```
<APPLET WIDTH="350"
CODE="/checkers.class">
Checkers can be a lot of fun, but
it's more fun if your browser
supports Java. Sorry.
</APPLET>
```

Other Attributes
This tag also accepts the LANG, DIR, ARCHIVE,
OBJECT, ID, CLASS, and STYLE attributes. See
the Element-Independent Attributes section
and other tag listings in this reference for definitions and examples.

<AREA>

Defines an area within a client-side imagemap
definition (see the <MAP> tag). It indicates an

area where visitors can choose to link to another document.

Standard:	HTML 3.2
Common:	Yes
Paired:	No
Sample:	

```
<AREA SHAPE=RECT COORDS="20,8,46,30"
HREF="food.html">
```

Attribute Information

ALT="..."
Provides a textual description for visitors who have text-only browsers.

Standard:	HTML 4
Common:	Yes
Sample:	

```
<AREA ALT="This blue rectangle links
to blue.html" HREF="blue.html">
```

CLASS="..."
Indicates the style class you want to apply to the <AREA> element.

Standard:	HTML 4
Common:	No
Sample:	

```
<AREA CLASS="casual" SHAPE="RECT"
COORDS="20,8,46,30" HREF="food.html">
```

COORDS="x1, y1, x2, y2"
Identifies the coordinates within an imagemap that define the imagemap area. Measure coordinates, in pixels, from the top-left corner of the image.

Standard:	HTML 3.2
Common:	Yes
Sample:	

```
<AREA SHAPE="RECT"
COORDS="20,8,46,30" HREF="food.html">
```

HREF="URL"
Identifies the location of the document you want to load when the indicated imagemap area is selected.

Standard:	HTML 3.2
Common:	Yes
Sample:	

```
<AREA SHAPE="RECT"
COORDS="20,8,46,30" HREF="food.html">
```

ID="..."
Assigns a unique ID selector to an instance of the <AREA> tag. When you then assign a style to that ID selector, it affects this instance of the <AREA> tag.

Standard:	HTML 4
Common:	No
Sample:	

```
<AREA ID="123">
```

NOHREF
Defines an imagemap area that does not link to another document.

Standard:	HTML 3.2
Common:	Yes
Sample:	

```
<AREA SHAPE="RECT"
COORDS="20,8,46,30" NOHREF>
```

NOTAB
Excludes the imagemap area from the tab order.

Standard:	Internet Explorer
Common:	Yes
Sample:	

```
<AREA SHAPE="RECT"
COORDS="20,8,46,30" HREF="food.html"
NOTAB>
```

SHAPE="{RECT, CIRCLE, POLY}"
Specifies the type of shape used to represent the imagemap area. SHAPE=RECT indicates that the shape of the imagemap area is rectangular. SHAPE=CIRCLE specifies that the shape of the imagemap area is a circle. SHAPE=POLY indicates that the shape of the imagemap area is a polygon represented by three or more points.

Standard:	HTML 3.2
Common:	Yes
Sample:	

```
<AREA SHAPE="RECT"
COORDS="20,8,46,30" HREF="food.html">
```

STYLE="..."
Specifies style sheet commands that apply to the imagemap area.

Standard:	HTML 4
Common:	No

Sample:

```
<AREA SHAPE="RECT"
COORDS="20,8,46,30" HREF="food.html"
STYLE="background: red">
```

TABINDEX="n"

Indicates where the imagemap area appears in the tabbing order of the document.

Standard: HTML 4
Common: Yes
Sample:

```
<AREA SHAPE="RECT"
COORDS="20,8,46,30" HREF="food.html"
TABINDEX=4>
```

TARGET="..."

Identifies which named frame the linked document selected should load. For example, when visitors select an area within an imagemap, the linked document may load in the same frame or in a different frame, specified by TARGET="...".

Standard: HTML 4
Common: Yes
Sample:

```
<AREA SHAPE="RECT"
COORDS="20,8,46,30" HREF="food.html"
TARGET="leftframe">
```

TITLE="..."

Specifies text assigned to the tag. You might use this attribute for context-sensitive help within the document. Browsers may use this to show tool tips over the imagemap area.

Standard: HTML 4
Common: No
Sample:

```
<AREA SHAPE="RECT"
COORDS="20,8,46,30" HREF="food.html"
NAME="Food!">
```

Other Attributes

This tag also accepts the LANG, DIR, ACCESSKEY, onFocus, onBlur, onClick, onDblClick, onMouseDown, onMouseUp, onMouseOver, onMouseMove, onMouseOut, onKeyPress, onKeyDown, and onKeyUp attributes. See the Element-Independent Attributes section and other tag listings in this reference for definitions and examples.

B

<B>

Indicates text that should appear in boldface.

Standard: HTML 2
Common: Yes
Paired: Yes
Sample:

```
The afternoon was <B>so</B> hot!
```

Attribute Information

CLASS="..."

Indicates which style class applies to the <B> element.

Standard: HTML 4
Common: No
Sample:

```
<B CLASS="casual">Boom!</B>
```

ID="..."

Assigns a unique ID selector to an instance of the <B> tag. When you assign a style to that ID selector, it affects only that one instance of the <B> tag.

Standard: HTML 4
Common: No
Sample:

```
I work for <B ID="123">Widgets
Inc.</B>
```

STYLE="..."

Specifies style sheet commands that apply to the contents within the <B> tags.

Standard: HTML 4
Common: No
Sample:

```
<B STYLE="background: red">
```

TITLE="..."

Specifies text assigned to the tag. You might use this attribute for context-sensitive help within the document. Browsers may use this to show tool tips over the boldface.

Standard: HTML 4
Common: No

Sample:
```
<B TITLE="Species">Dog Species</B>
```

Other Attributes
This tag also accepts the LANG, DIR, onClick, onDblClick, onMouseDown, onMouseUp, onMouseOver, onMouseMove, onMouseOut, onKeyPress, onKeyDown, and onKeyUp attributes. See the Element-Independent Attributes section of this reference for definitions and examples.

<BASE>

Identifies the location where all relative URLs in your document originate.

Standard:	HTML 2
Common:	Yes
Paired:	No

Sample:
```
<BASE HREF="http://www.raycomm
.com/info/">
```

Attribute Information

HREF="*URL*"
Indicates the relative or absolute location of the base document.

Standard:	HTML 2
Common:	Yes

Sample:
```
<BASE HREF="http://www.raycomm
.com/">
```

TARGET="..."
Identifies in which named frame you load a document (see the HREF= attribute).

Standard:	HTML 4
Common:	Yes

Sample:
```
<BASE HREF="http://www.raycomm
.com/frames/" TARGET="main">
```

<BASEFONT>

Provides a font setting for normal text within a document. Font settings (see the <FONT> tag) within the document are relative to settings specified with this tag. Use this tag in the document header (between the <HEAD> tags).

Standard:	HTML 3.2; deprecated in HTML 4 in favor of style sheets
Common:	Yes
Paired:	No

Sample:
```
<BASEFONT SIZE="5">
```

Attribute Information

COLOR="*#RRGGBB*" or "..."
Sets the font color of normal text within a document. Color names may substitute for the explicit RGB hexadecimal values.

Standard:	HTML 3.2; deprecated in HTML 4 in favor of style sheets
Common:	Yes

Sample:
```
<BASEFONT SIZE="2" COLOR="#FF00CC">
```

FACE="...,..."
Specifies the font face of normal text within a document. You can set this attribute to a comma-separated list of font names. The browser selects the first name matching a font available.

Standard:	HTML 3.2; deprecated in HTML 4 in favor of style sheets
Common:	Yes

Sample:
```
<BASEFONT FACE="Avant Guard,
Helvetica, Arial">
```

SIZE="*n*"
Specifies the font size of normal text within a document. Valid values are integer numbers in the range 1 to 7 with 3 being the default setting.

Standard:	HTML 3.2; deprecated in HTML 4 in favor of style sheets
Common:	Yes

Sample:
```
<BASEFONT SIZE="5">
```

Other Attributes
This tag also accepts the ID, CLASS, LANG, DIR, TITLE, and STYLE attributes. See the

Element-Independent Attributes section and other tag listings in this reference for definitions and examples.

<BDO>

Indicates text that should appear with the direction (left to right or right to left) specified, overriding other language-specific settings.

Standard:	HTML 4
Common:	No
Paired:	Yes
Sample:	

```
<P LANG="IW" DIR="RTL">This Hebrew
text contains a number,
<BDO="LTR">29381</BDO>, that must
appear left to right.</P>
```

Attribute Information

This tag accepts the ID, LANG, CLASS, and DIR attributes. See the Element-Independent Attributes section of this reference for definitions and examples.

<BGSOUND>

Embeds a background sound file within documents. Use in the document head of documents intended for visitors who use Internet Explorer.

Standard:	Internet Explorer
Common:	Yes
Paired:	No
Sample:	

```
<BGSOUND SRC="scream.wav">
```

Attribute Information

LOOP="{n, INFINITE}"

Specifies the number of times a background sound file repeats. The value INFINITE is the default.

Standard:	Internet Explorer
Common:	No
Sample:	

```
<BGSOUND SRC="bugle.wav" LOOP="2">
```

SRC="*URL*"

Indicates the explicit or relative location of the sound file.

Standard:	Internet Explorer
Common:	No
Sample:	

```
<BGSOUND SRC="wah.wav">
```

<BIG>

Indicates that text display in a larger font.

Standard:	HTML 3.2
Common:	Yes
Paired:	Yes
Sample:	

```
<BIG>Lunch</BIG>
<p>Lunch will be served at 2 p.m.
```

Attribute Information

CLASS="..."

Indicates which style class applies to the <BIG> element.

Standard:	HTML 4
Common:	No
Sample:	

```
<BIG CLASS="casual">
Instructions</BIG>
```

ID="..."

Assigns a unique ID selector to an instance of the <BIG> tag. When you then assign a style to that ID selector, it affects only that one instance of the <BIG> tag.

Standard:	HTML 4
Common:	No
Sample:	

```
<BIG ID="123">REMINDER:</BIG>
Eat 5 servings of fruits and
vegetables every day!
```

STYLE="..."

Specifies style sheet commands that apply to the contents within the <BIG> tags.

Standard:	HTML 4
Common:	No
Sample:	

```
<BIG STYLE="background: red">
```

TITLE="..."

Specifies text assigned to the tag. You might use this attribute for context-sensitive help within the document. Browsers may use this to show tool tips over the text inside the <BIG> tags.

Standard: HTML 4
Common: No
Sample:

```
<BIG TITLE="Bigger">
```

Other Attributes

This tag also accepts the LANG, DIR, onClick, onDblClick, onMouseDown, onMouseUp, onMouseOver, onMouseMove, onMouseOut, onKeyPress, onKeyDown, and onKeyUp attributes. See the Element-Independent Attributes section of this reference for definitions and examples.

<BLINK>

A Netscape-specific tag that makes text blink on and off.

Standard: Netscape Navigator; style sheets offer the same functionality in a more widely recognized syntax.
Common: No
Paired: Yes
Sample:

```
<P><BLINK>NEW INFO</BLINK>:
We moved!
```

Attribute Information

CLASS="..."

Indicates which style class applies to the <BLINK> element.

Standard: HTML 4
Common: No
Sample:

```
<BLINK CLASS="casual">NEW
INFORMATION</BLINK>
```

ID="..."

Assigns a unique ID selector to an instance of the <BLINK> tag. When you then assign a style to that ID selector, it affects only that one instance of the <BLINK> tag.

Standard: HTML 4
Common: No
Sample:

```
<BLINK ID="123">12 Hour Sale!</BLINK>
```

STYLE="..."

Specifies style sheet commands that apply to the contents within the <BLINK> tags.

Standard: HTML 4
Common: No
Sample:

```
<BLINK STYLE="background: red">
```

<BLOCKQUOTE>

Provides left and right indention of affected text and is useful for quoting a direct source within a document. Use for indention is deprecated. Use <BLOCKQUOTE> to signify only a block quotation.

Standard: HTML 2
Common: Yes
Paired: Yes
Sample:

```
Dr. Henry's remarks are
below:<BLOCKQUOTE>I really like the
procedure.</BLOCKQUOTE>
```

Attribute Information

CITE="..."

Specifies a reference URL for the quotation.

Standard: HTML 4
Common: No
Sample:

```
<BLOCKQUOTE CITE="http://www
.clement.moore.com/xmas.html">
Twas the night...</BLOCKQUOTE>
```

CLASS="..."

Indicates which style class applies to the <BLOCKQUOTE> element.

Standard: HTML 4
Common: No
Sample:

```
<BLOCKQUOTE CLASS="casual">

Twas the night before
Christmas...</BLOCKQUOTE>
```

ID="..."

Assigns a unique ID selector to an instance of the <BLOCKQUOTE> tag. When you then assign a style to that ID selector, it affects only that one instance of the <BLOCKQUOTE> tag.

Standard: HTML 4
Common: No
Sample:

On July 12, John wrote a profound
sentence in his diary:

<BLOCKQUOTE ID="123">I woke up this
morning at nine and it was
raining.</BLOCKQUOTE>

STYLE="..."

Specifies style sheet commands that apply to the contents within the <BLOCKQUOTE> tags.

Standard: HTML 4
Common: No
Sample:

<BLOCKQUOTE STYLE="background: red">

TITLE="..."

Specifies text assigned to the tag. You might use this attribute for context-sensitive help within the document. Browsers may use this to show tool tips over the quoted text.

Standard: HTML 4
Common: No
Sample:

<BLOCKQUOTE TITLE="Quotation">

Other Attributes

This tag also accepts the LANG, DIR, onClick, onDblClick, onMouseDown, onMouseUp, onMouseOver, onMouseMove, onMouseOut, onKeyPress, onKeyDown, and onKeyUp attributes. See the Element-Independent Attributes section of this reference for definitions and examples.

<BODY>

Acts as a container for the body of the document. It appears after the <HEAD> tag and is followed by the </HTML> tag. In HTML 3.2, the <BODY> tag also sets various color settings and background characteristics of the document; however, in HTML 4, those formatting attributes are deprecated in favor of style sheets.

Standard: HTML 2
Common: Yes
Paired: Yes
Sample:

<BODY>
<H1>HELLO!</H1>
</BODY>

Attribute Information

ALINK="#*RRGGBB*" or "..."

Indicates the color of hyperlink text while the text is selected. Color names can substitute for the RGB hexadecimal values.

Standard: HTML 3.2; deprecated in HTML 4 in favor of style sheets
Common: Yes
Sample:

<BODY BGCOLOR="#000ABC"
TEXT="#000000" LINK="#FFFFFF"
VLINK="#999999" ALINK="#FF0000">

BACKGROUND="*URL*"

Specifies the relative or absolute location of an image file that tiles across the document's background.

Standard: HTML 3.2; deprecated in HTML 4 in favor of style sheets
Common: Yes
Sample:

<BODY BACKGROUND=
"images/slimey.gif">

BGCOLOR="#*RRGGBB*" or "..."

Indicates the color of a document's background. Color names can substitute for the RGB hexadecimal values.

Standard: HTML 3.2; deprecated in HTML 4 in favor of style sheets
Common: Yes
Sample:

<BODY BGCOLOR="#000ABC"
TEXT="#000000" LINK="#FFFFFF"
VLINK="#999999" ALINK="#FF0000">

BGPROPERTIES="FIXED"

Specifies the behavior of the background image (see the BACKGROUND attribute.)

BGPROPERTIES=FIXED indicates that the background image remains in place as you scroll the document, creating a watermark effect.

Standard: Internet Explorer
Common: No
Sample:

```
<BODY BACKGROUND="waves.jpg"
BGPROPERTIES="FIXED">
```

CLASS="..."

Indicates which style class applies to the <BODY> element.

Standard: HTML 4
Common: No
Sample:

```
<BODY CLASS="casual">
```

ID="*n*"

Assigns a unique ID selector to the <BODY> tag.

Standard: HTML 4
Common: No
Sample:

```
<BODY ID="123">
```

LEFTMARGIN="*n*"

Specifies the width (in pixels) of a margin of white space along the left edge of the entire document.

Standard: Internet Explorer
Common: No
Sample:

```
<BODY LEFTMARGIN="30">
```

LINK="*#RRGGBB*" or "..."

Indicates the color of hyperlink text within the document, which corresponds to documents not already visited by the browser. Color names can substitute for the RGB hexadecimal values.

Standard: HTML 3.2; deprecated in HTML 4 in favor of style sheets
Common: Yes
Sample:

```
<BODY BGCOLOR="#000ABC"
TEXT="#000000" LINK="#FFFFFF"
VLINK="#999999" ALINK="#FF0000">
```

SCROLL="{YES, NO}"

Indicates whether scrolling is possible within the document body.

Standard: Internet Explorer 4
Common: No
Sample:

```
<BODY BGCOLOR="silver" SCROLL="NO">
```

STYLE="..."

Specifies style sheet commands that apply to the document body.

Standard: HTML 4
Common: No
Sample:

```
<BODY STYLE="background: red">
```

TEXT="*#RRGGBB*" or "..."

Indicates the color of normal text within the document. Color names can substitute for the RGB hexadecimal values.

Standard: HTML 3.2; deprecated in HTML 4 in favor of style sheets
Common: Yes
Sample:

```
<BODY BGCOLOR="#000ABC"
TEXT="#000000" LINK="#FFFFFF"
VLINK="#999999" ALINK="#FF0000">
```

TITLE="..."

Specifies text assigned to the tag. You might use this attribute for context-sensitive help within the document. Browsers may use this to show tool tips.

Standard: HTML 4
Common: No
Sample:

```
<BODY TITLE="Document body">
```

TOPMARGIN="*n*"

Specifies the size (in pixels) of a margin of white space along the top edge of the entire document.

Standard: Internet Explorer
Common: No
Sample:

```
<BODY TOPMARGIN="10">
```

VLINK="#*RRGGBB*" or "..."

Indicates the color of hyperlink text within the document, which corresponds to documents already visited by the browser. Color names can substitute for the RGB hexadecimal values.

Standard:	HTML 3.2; deprecated in HTML 4 in favor of style sheets
Common:	Yes
Sample:	

```
<BODY BGCOLOR="#000ABC"
TEXT="#000000" LINK="#FFFFFF"
VLINK="#999999" ALINK="#FF0000">
```

Other Attributes

This tag also accepts the LANG, DIR, onload, onunload, onClick, onDblClick, onMouseDown, onMouseUp, onMouseOver, onMouseMove, onMouseOut, onKeyPress, onKeyDown, and onKeyUp attributes. See the Element-Independent Attributes section of this reference for definitions and examples.

Breaks a line of continuous text and prevents text alignment around images.

Standard:	HTML 2
Common:	Yes
Paired:	No
Sample:	

```
I live at:<P>123 Nowhere Ave<BR>New
York, NY 12345
```

Attribute Information

CLASS="..."

Indicates which style class applies to the element.

Standard:	HTML 4
Common:	No
Sample:	

```
<BR CLASS="casual">
```

CLEAR="{ALL, LEFT, RIGHT, NONE}"

Discontinues alignment of text to inline graphic images. The sample demonstrates how you can force the text to appear after the image and not alongside it.

Standard:	HTML 3.2

Common:	Yes
Sample:	

```
<IMG SRC="portrait.jpg"
ALIGN="RIGHT"><BR CLEAR="ALL">
<P>The above photo was taken when I
was in Florida.
```

ID="..."

Assigns a unique ID selector to an instance of the <BR> tag. When you then assign a style to that ID selector, it affects only that one instance of the <BR> tag.

Standard:	HTML 4
Common:	No
Sample:	

```
<BR ID="123">
```

STYLE="..."

Specifies style sheet commands that apply to the <BR> tag.

Standard:	HTML 4
Common:	No
Sample:	

```
<BR STYLE="background: red">
```

TITLE="..."

Specifies text assigned to the tag. You might use this attribute for context-sensitive help within the document. Browsers may use this to show tool tips.

Standard:	HTML 4
Common:	No
Sample:	

```
<BR CLEAR="ALL" TITLE="Stop
image wrap">
```

<BUTTON>

Sets up a button to submit or reset a form as well as to activate a script. Use the <IMG> tag between the opening and closing <BUTTON> tags to specify a graphical button.

Standard:	HTML 4
Common:	No
Paired:	Yes
Sample:	

```
<BUTTON TYPE="BUTTON" VALUE="Run
Program" onclick(doit)>Click
it</BUTTON>
```

Attribute Information

ACCESSKEY="..."
Associates a key sequence with the button.

Standard: HTML 4
Common: Yes
Sample:
```
<BUTTON ACCESSKEY="B">Click
Me!</BUTTON>
```

CLASS="..."
Indicates which style class applies to the <BUTTON> element.

Standard: HTML 4
Common: No
Sample:
```
<BUTTON CLASS="casual"
TYPE="SUBMIT" VALUE="Submit">
```

DISABLED
Denies access to the input method.

Standard: HTML 4
Common: No
Sample:
```
<BUTTON TYPE="SUBMIT" NAME="Pass"
DISABLED>
```

ID="n"
Assigns a unique ID selector to an instance of the <INPUT> tag. When you then assign a style to that ID selector, it affects only that one instance of the <INPUT> tag.

Standard: HTML 4
Common: No
Sample:
```
<BUTTON ID="123" TYPE="SUBMIT"
VALUE="Submit">
```

NAME="..."
Gives a name to the value you pass to the form processor.

Standard: HTML 4
Common: Yes
Sample:
```
<BUTTON TYPE="BUTTON" NAME=
RUNPROG" VALUE="Click to Run">
```

STYLE="..."
Specifies style sheet commands that apply to the element.

Standard: HTML 4

Common: No
Sample:
```
<BUTTON STYLE="background: red".
TYPE="BUTTON" NAME="RUNPROG"
VALUE="Click to Run">
```

TABINDEX="n"
Specifies where the input method appears in the tab order. For example, TABINDEX=3 places the cursor at the button element after the visitor presses the Tab key three times.

Standard: HTML 4
Common: No
Sample:
```
<BUTTON TYPE="BUTTON" NAME=
"RUNPROG" VALUE="Click to Run"
TABINDEX="3">
```

TITLE="..."
Specifies text assigned to the tag. You might use this attribute for context-sensitive help within the document. Browsers may use this to show tool tips over the input method.

Standard: HTML 4
Common: No
Sample:
```
<BUTTON TYPE="SUBMIT" NAME="cc"
VALUE="visa" TITLE="Visa">
```

TYPE="..."
Indicates the kind of button to create. SUBMIT produces a button that, when selected, submits all the name-value pairs to the form processor. RESET sets all the input methods to their empty or default settings. BUTTON creates a button with no specific behavior that can interact with scripts.

Standard: HTML 4
Common: Yes
Sample:
```
<BUTTON TYPE="BUTTON" VALUE="Send
Data..." onclick(verify())>
</FORM>
```

VALUE="..."
Sets the default value for the button face.

Standard: HTML 4
Common: No
Sample:
```
<BUTTON TYPE="BUTTON" NAME="id"
VALUE="Press Me">
```

Other Attributes

This tag also accepts the LANG, DIR, onfocus, onblur, onClick, onDblClick, onMouseDown, onMouseUp, onMouseOver, onMouseMove, onMouseOut, onKeyPress, onKeyDown, and onKeyUp attributes. See the Element-Independent Attributes section of this reference for definitions and examples.

C

<CAPTION>

Used inside <TABLE> tags to specify a description for a table.

Standard:	HTML 3.2
Common:	Yes
Paired:	Yes
Sample:	

```
<TABLE>
  <CAPTION VALIGN="TOP"
  ALIGN="CENTER">  Test Grades
  For COOKING 101  </CAPTION>
  <TR>

  <TH>Student</TH><TH>Grade</TH>
  </TR>
  <TR>
    <TD>B. Smith</TD><TD>88</TD>
  </TR>
  <TR>
    <TD>J. Doe</TD><TD>45</TD>
  </TR>
</TABLE>
```

Attribute Information

ALIGN="{TOP, BOTTOM, LEFT, RIGHT}"

Indicates whether the caption appears at the top, bottom, left, or right of the table.

Standard:	HTML 3.2; LEFT and RIGHT added in HTML 4
Common:	Yes
Sample:	

```
<CAPTION ALIGN="TOP">Seattle Staff
DIRectory</CAPTION>
```

CLASS="..."

Indicates which style class applies to the <CAPTION> element.

Standard:	HTML 4
Common:	No
Sample:	

```
<CAPTION CLASS="casual">Hydrogen vs
Oxygen</CAPTION>
```

ID="..."

Assigns a unique ID selector to an instance of the <CAPTION> tag. When you then assign a style to that ID selector, it affects only that one instance of the <CAPTION> tag.

Standard:	HTML 4
Common:	No
Sample:	

```
<TABLE>
  <CAPTION ID="123">Great
  Painters</CAPTION>
```

STYLE="..."

Specifies style sheet commands that apply to the contents of the <CAPTION> tags.

Standard:	HTML 4
Common:	No
Sample:	

```
<CAPTION STYLE="background: red">
```

TITLE="..."

Specifies text assigned to the tag. You might use this attribute for context-sensitive help within the document. Browsers may use this to show tool tips over the caption.

Standard:	HTML 4
Common:	Yes
Sample:	

```
<CAPTION TITLE="Table caption">
```

Other Attributes

This tag also accepts the LANG, DIR, onClick, onDblClick, onMouseDown, onMouseUp, onMouseOver, onMouseMove, onMouseOut, onKeyPress, onKeyDown, and onKeyUp attributes. See the Element-Independent Attributes section of this reference for definitions and examples.

<CENTER>

Positions text an equal distance between the left and right edges of the document. This tag, now officially replaced by the <DIV ALIGN="CENTER"> attribute, was included in HTML 3.2 only because of its widespread use.

Standard:	HTML 3.2; deprecated in HTML 4
Common:	Yes
Paired:	Yes
Sample:	

```
<CENTER><BLINK><H1>ONE-DAY
SALE!</H1></BLINK></CENTER>
```

<CITE>

Provides an in-text citation of a proper title such as the title of a book. Most browsers display the text inside the <CITE> tags in italics.

Standard:	HTML 2
Common:	Yes
Paired:	Yes
Sample:	

```
I just finished reading <CITE>Being
Digital</CITE> by Nicholas
Negroponte.
```

Attribute Information

CLASS="..."
Indicates which style class applies to the <CITE> element.

Standard:	HTML 4
Common:	No
Sample:	

```
This came from <CITE CLASS=
"casual">Thoreau's Walden Pond</CITE>
```

ID="..."
Assigns a unique ID selector to an instance of the <CITE> tag. When you then assign a style to that ID selector, it affects only that one instance of the <CITE> tag.

Standard:	HTML 4
Common:	No
Sample:	

```
I read about this in
<CITE ID="123">
World Weekly News</CITE>
```

STYLE="..."
Specifies style sheet commands that apply to the contents within the <CITE> tags.

Standard:	HTML 4
Common:	No
Sample:	

```
<CITE STYLE="background: red">
```

TITLE="..."
Specifies text assigned to the tag. You might use this attribute for context-sensitive help within the document. Browsers may use this to show tool tips over the cited text.

Standard:	HTML 4
Common:	No
Sample:	

```
<CITE TITLE="Citation">FDA Vegetable
Pamphlet</CITE>
```

Other Attributes
This tag also accepts the LANG, DIR, onClick, onDblClick, onMouseDown, onMouseUp, onMouseOver, onMouseMove, onMouseOut, onKeyPress, onKeyDown, and onKeyUp attributes. See the Element-Independent Attributes section of this reference for definitions and examples.

<CODE>

Embeds excerpts of program source code into your document text. This is useful if you want to show program source code inline within a paragraph of normal text. For showing formatted segments of source code longer than one line, use the <PRE> tag.

Standard:	HTML 2
Common:	Yes
Paired:	Yes
Sample:	

```
To display the value of the cost
variable use the
<CODE>printf("%0.2f\n", cost);
</CODE> function call.
```

Attribute Information

CLASS="..."
Indicates which style class applies to the <CODE> element.

Standard: HTML 4
Common: No
Sample:

```
<CODE CLASS="casual">x++;</CODE>
```

ID="..."

Assigns a unique ID selector to an instance of the <CODE> tag. When you then assign a style to that ID selector, it affects only that one instance of the <CODE> tag.

Standard: HTML 4
Common: No
Sample:

```
<CODE ID="123">while(x)
x-;</CODE>
```

STYLE="..."

Specifies style sheet commands that apply to the contents within the <CODE> tags.

Standard: HTML 4
Common: No
Sample:

```
<BODY STYLE="background: red">
```

TITLE="..."

Specifies text assigned to the tag. You might use this attribute for context-sensitive help within the document. Browsers may use this to show tool tips over the code text.

Standard: HTML 4
Common: No
Sample:

```
<CODE TITLE="C Code">exit(1);</CODE>
```

Other Attributes

This tag also accepts the LANG, DIR, onClick, onDblClick, onMouseDown, onMouseUp, onMouseOver, onMouseMove, onMouseOut, onKeyPress, onKeyDown, and onKeyUp attributes. See the Element-Independent Attributes section of this reference for definitions and examples.

<COL>

Specifies attributes for a table column.

Standard: HTML 4
Common: No
Paired: No

Sample:

```
<TABLE>
<COLGROUP>
  <COL ALIGN="RIGHT">
  <COL ALIGN="CENTER">
<TR>
  <TD>This cell is aligned
  right</TD>
  <TD>This cell is centered</TD>
</TR>
</TABLE>
```

Attribute Information

ALIGN="{LEFT, RIGHT, CENTER, JUSTIFY, CHAR}"

Specifies how text within the table columns will line up with the edges of the table cells, or if ALIGN=CHAR, on a specific character (the decimal point).

Standard: HTML 4
Common: No
Sample:

```
<COL ALIGN="CENTER">
```

CHAR="..."

Specifies the character on which cell contents will align, if ALIGN="CHAR". If you omit CHAR=, the default value is the decimal point in the specified language.

Standard: HTML 4
Common: No
Sample:

```
<COL ALIGN="CHAR" CHAR=",">
```

CHAROFF="n"

Specifies the number of characters from the left at which the alignment character appears.

Standard: HTML 4
Common: No
Sample:

```
<COL ALIGN="CHAR" CHAR=","
CHAROFF="7">
```

ID="..."

Assigns a unique ID selector to an instance of the <COL> tag. When you assign a style to that ID selector, it affects only that one instance of the <COL> tag.

Standard: HTML 4
Common: No

Sample:
```
<COL ID="123">
```

SPAN="*n*"
Indicates the number of columns in the group.

Standard: HTML 4
Common: No
Sample:
```
<COLGROUP>
    <COL ALIGN="RIGHT" SPAN="2">
```

STYLE="..."
Specifies style sheet commands that apply to the contents of the <COL> tags.

Standard: HTML 4
Common: No
Sample:
```
<COL STYLE="background: black">
```

TITLE="..."
Specifies text assigned to the tag. You might use this attribute for context-sensitive help within the document. Browsers may use this to show tool tips over the table column.

Standard: HTML 4
Common: No
Sample:
```
<COL TITLE="Table column">
```

WIDTH="*n*"
Specifies the horizontal dimension of a column (in pixels or as a percentage). Special values of "0*" force the column to the minimum required width, and "2*" requires that the column receive proportionately twice as much space as it otherwise would.

Standard: HTML 4
Common: No
Sample:
```
<COL WIDTH="100">
```

VALIGN="{TOP, BOTTOM, BASELINE, MIDDLE}"
Vertically positions the contents of the table column. VALIGN="TOP" positions the contents flush with the top of the column. VALIGN="BUTTON" positions the contents flush with the bottom. VALIGN="CENTER"

positions the contents at the center of the column. VALIGN="BASELINE" aligns the contents with the baseline of the current text font.

Standard: HTML 4
Common: No
Sample:
```
<COL VALIGN="TOP">
```

Other Attributes
This tag also accepts the LANG, DIR, onClick, onDblClick, onMouseDown, onMouseUp, onMouseOver, onMouseMove, onMouseOut, onKeyPress, onKeyDown, and onKeyUp attributes. See the Element-Independent Attributes section of this reference for definitions and examples.

<COLGROUP>
Specifies characteristics for a group of table columns.

Standard: HTML 4
Common: No
Paired: Yes
Sample:
```
<TABLE>
<COLGROUP VALIGN="TOP">
    <COL ALIGN="RIGHT">
    <COL ALIGN="CENTER">
<TR>
    <TD>This cell is aligned top
    and right</TD>
    <TD>This cell is aligned top
    and centered</TD>
</TR>
</TABLE>
```

Attribute Information

ALIGN="{LEFT, RIGHT, CENTER, JUSTIFY, CHAR}"
Specifies how text within the table columns lines up with the edges of the table cells, or if ALIGN=CHAR, on a specific character (the decimal point).

Standard: HTML 4
Common: No
Sample:
```
<COLGROUP ALIGN="CENTER">
```

CHAR="..."

Specifies the character on which cell contents align, if ALIGN="CHAR". If you omit CHAR=, the default value is the decimal point in the specified language.

Standard: HTML 4
Common: No
Sample:

```
<COLGROUP ALIGN="CHAR" CHAR=",">
```

CHAROFF="n"

Specifies the number of characters from the left at which the alignment character appears.

Standard: HTML 4
Common: No
Sample:

```
<COLGROUP ALIGN="CHAR" CHAR=","
CHAROFF="7">
```

ID="..."

Assigns a unique ID selector to an instance of the tag. When you then assign a style to that ID selector, it affects only that one instance of the tag.

Standard: HTML 4
Common: No
Sample:

```
<COLGROUP ID="123">
```

SPAN="n"

Indicates how many consecutive columns exist in the column group and to which columns the specified attributes apply.

Standard: HTML 4
Common: No
Sample:

```
<COLGROUP>
    <COL ALIGN="RIGHT" SPAN="2">
```

STYLE="..."

Specifies style sheet commands that apply to the contents of the <COLGROUP> tags.

Standard: HTML 4
Common: No
Sample:

```
<COLGROUP STYLE="color: red">
```

TITLE="..."

Specifies text assigned to the tag. You might use this attribute for context-sensitive help within the document. Browsers may use this to show tool tips over the column group.

Standard: HTML 4
Common: No
Sample:

```
<COLGROUP TITLE="Column Group">
```

WIDTH="n"

Specifies the horizontal dimension of columns within the column group (in pixels or as a percentage). Special values of "0*" force the column to minimum required width, and "2*" requires that the column receive proportionately twice as much space as it otherwise would.

Standard: HTML 4
Common: No
Sample:

```
<COLGROUP WIDTH=100>
    <COL ALIGN="RIGHT">
```

VALIGN="{TOP, BOTTOM, BASELINE, MIDDLE}"

Vertically positions the contents of the table column. VALIGN="TOP" positions the contents flush with the top of the column. VALIGN="BOTTOM" positions the contents flush with the bottom. VALIGN="CENTER" positions the contents at the vertical center of the column. VALIGN="BASELINE" aligns the contents with the baseline of the current text font.

Standard: HTML 4
Common: No
Sample:

```
<COLGROUP VALIGN="TOP">
```

Other Attributes

This tag also accepts the CLASS, LANG, DIR, onClick, onDblClick, onMouseDown, onMouseUp, onMouseOver, onMouseMove, onMouseOut, onKeyPress, onKeyDown, and onKeyUp attributes. See the Element-Independent Attributes section of this reference for definitions and examples.

<COMMENT>

Indicates an author comment. Because these tags are Netscape-specific, we encourage you to use the `<!--...-->` tags instead.

Standard: Netscape Navigator
Common: Yes
Paired: Yes
Sample:

```
<COMMENT>This document was created
September 19, 1997.
</COMMENT>
```

D

<DD>

Contains a definition in a definition list. Use this tag inside `<DL>` tags. This tag can contain block-level elements.

Standard: HTML 2
Common: Yes
Paired: Yes, optional
Sample:

```
<DL><DT>Butter
<DD>Butter is a dairy product.
</DL>
```

Attribute Information

CLASS="..."
Indicates which style class applies to the `<DD>` element.

Standard: HTML 4
Common: No
Sample:

```
<DL>
  <DT>HTML
  <DD CLASS="casual">Hypertext
  Markup LANGuage
</DD>
```

ID="..."
Assigns a unique ID selector to an instance of the `<DD>` tag. When you then assign a style to that ID selector, it affects only that one instance of the `<DD>` tag.

Standard: HTML 4
Common: No

Sample:

```
<DL>
  <DT>RS-232C
  <DD ID="123">A standard for
  serial communication between
  computers.
</DL>
```

STYLE="..."
Specifies style sheet commands that apply to the definition.

Standard: HTML 4
Common: No
Sample:

```
<DD STYLE="background: blue; color:
white">
```

TITLE="..."
Specifies text assigned to the tag. You might use this attribute for context-sensitive help within the document. Browsers may use this to show tool tips over the definition.

Standard: HTML 4
Common: No
Sample:

```
<DD TITLE="Definition">
```

Other Attributes
This tag also accepts the LANG, DIR, onClick, onDblClick, onMouseDown, onMouseUp, onMouseOver, onMouseMove, onMouseOut, onKeyPress, onKeyDown, and onKeyUp attributes. See the Element-Independent Attributes section of this reference for definitions and examples.

<DEL>

Indicates text marked for deletion in the document. May be either block-level or inline, as necessary.

Standard: HTML 4
Common: No
Paired: Yes
Sample:

```
<P>HTTP stands for HyperText
Transfer <DEL>Transport</DEL>
Protocol.</P>
```

Attribute Information

CITE="*URL*"

Indicates address of reference (definitive source, for example) for deletion.

Standard: HTML 4
Common: No
Sample:

```
<DEL CITE="http://www.w3.org/">
HTML 3.0 was used for 10 years.</DEL>
```

CLASS="..."

Indicates which style class applies to the <DEL> element.

Standard: HTML 4
Common: No
Sample:

```
<DEL CLASS="casual">POP stands for
Post Office Protocol.</DEL>
```

DATETIME="..."

Indicates the date and time in precisely this format: YYYY-MM-DDThh:mm:ssTZD. For example, 2000-07-14T08:30:00-07:00 indicates July 14, 2000, at 8:30 AM, in U.S. Mountain Time (7 hours from Greenwich time). This time could also be presented as 2000-07-14T08:30:00Z.

Standard: HTML 4
Common: No
Sample:

```
<DEL DATETIME="2000-07-
14T08:30:00Z">POP stands for Post
Office Protocol.</DEL>
```

ID="..."

Assigns a unique ID selector to an instance of the tag. When you then assign a style to that ID selector, it affects only that one instance of the <DEL> tag.

Standard: HTML 4
Common: No
Sample:

```
<DEL ID="123">WWW stands for World
Wide Web.</DEL>
```

STYLE="..."

Specifies style sheet commands that apply to the deleted text.

Standard: HTML 4
Common: No
Sample:

```
<DEL STYLE="background: blue; color:
white">ESP stands for extra-sensory
perception.</DEL>
```

TITLE="..."

Specifies text assigned to the tag. You might use this attribute for context-sensitive help within the document. Browsers may use this to show tool tips over the text.

Standard: HTML 4
Common: No
Sample:

```
<DEL TITLE="Definition">More deleted
text.</DEL>
```

Other Attributes

This tag also accepts the LANG, DIR, onClick, onDblClick, onMouseDown, onMouseUp, onMouseOver, onMouseMove, onMouseOut, onKeyPress, onKeyDown, and onKeyUp attributes. See the Element-Independent Attributes section of this reference for definitions and examples.

<DFN>

Indicates the definition of a term in the document.

Standard: HTML 3.2
Common: No
Paired: Yes
Sample:

```
<DFN>HTTP stands for HyperText
Transfer Protocol.</DFN>
```

Attribute Information

CLASS="..."

Indicates which style class applies to the <DFN> element.

Standard: HTML 4
Common: No
Sample:

```
<DFN CLASS="casual">POP stands for
Post Office Protocol.</DFN>
```

ID="..."

Assigns a unique ID selector to an instance of the <DFN> tag. When you then assign a style to that ID selector, it affects only that one instance of the <DFN> tag.

Standard:	HTML 4
Common:	No

Sample:

```
<DFN ID="123">WWW stands for World
Wide Web.</DFN>
```

STYLE="..."

Specifies style sheet commands that apply to the definition.

Standard:	HTML 4
Common:	No

Sample:

```
<DFN STYLE="background: blue; color:
white">ESP stands for extra-sensory
perception.</DFN>
```

TITLE="..."

Specifies text assigned to the tag. You might use this attribute for context-sensitive help within the document. Browsers may use this to show tool tips over the definition text.

Standard:	HTML 4
Common:	No

Sample:

```
<DFN TITLE="Definition">
```

Other Attributes

This tag also accepts the LANG, DIR, onClick, onDblClick, onMouseDown, onMouseUp, onMouseOver, onMouseMove, onMouseOut, onKeyPress, onKeyDown, and onKeyUp attributes. See the Element-Independent Attributes section of this reference for definitions and examples.

<DIR>

Contains a directory list. Use the <LI> tag to indicate list items within the list. Use <UL>, rather than this deprecated tag.

Standard:	HTML 2; deprecated in HTML 4. Use <UL> instead.
Common:	Yes
Paired:	Yes

Sample:

```
Choose a music genre:<DIR>
```

```
<LI><A HREF="rock/">Rock</A>
<LI><A HREF="country/
">Country</A>
<LI><A HREF="na/">New Age</A>
</DIR>
```

Attribute Information

CLASS="..."

Indicates which style class applies to the <DIR> element.

Standard:	HTML 4
Common:	No

Sample:

```
<DIR CLASS="casual">
  <LI>Apples
  <LI>Kiwis
  <LI>Mangos
  <LI>Oranges
</DIR>
```

COMPACT

Causes the list to appear in a compact format. This attribute probably will not affect the appearance of the list as most browsers do not present lists in more than one format.

Standard:	HTML 2; deprecated in HTML 4
Common:	No

Sample:

```
<DIR COMPACT>...
</DIR>
```

ID="..."

Assigns a unique ID selector to an instance of the <DIR> tag. When you then assign a style to that ID selector, it affects only that one instance of the <DIR> tag.

Standard:	HTML 4
Common:	No

Sample:

```
<DIR ID="123">
  <LI>Thingie 1
  <LI>Thingie 2
</DIR>
```

STYLE="..."

Specifies style sheet commands that apply to the <DIR> element.

Standard:	HTML 4
Common:	No

Sample:
```
<DIR STYLE="background: blue; color:
white">
  <LI>Thingie 1
  <LI>Thingie 2
</DIR>
```

TITLE="..."

Specifies text assigned to the tag. You might use this attribute for context-sensitive help within the document. Browsers may use this to show tool tips over the directory list.

Standard: HTML 4
Common: No
Sample:

```
<DIR TITLE="DIRectory List">
```

Other Attributes

This tag also accepts the LANG, DIR, onClick, onDblClick, onMouseDown, onMouseUp, onMouseOver, onMouseMove, onMouseOut, onKeyPress, onKeyDown, and onKeyUp attributes. See the Element-Independent Attributes section of this reference for definitions and examples.

<DIV>

Indicates logical divisions within a document. You can use these to apply alignment, line-wrapping, and particularly style sheet attributes to a section of your document. <DIV ALIGN=CENTER> is the official replacement for the <CENTER> tag.

Standard: HTML 3.2
Common: No
Paired: Yes
Sample:

```
<DIV ALIGN="CENTER"
STYLE="background: blue">
<FONT SIZE=+2>All About Formic
Acid</FONT>
</DIV>
```

Attribute Information

ALIGN="{LEFT, CENTER, RIGHT, JUSTIFY}"

Specifies whether the contents of the section align with the left or right margins (LEFT, RIGHT), are evenly spaced between them (CENTER), or if the text stretches between the left and right margins (JUSTIFY).

Standard: HTML 3.2; deprecated in HTML 4 in favor of style sheets
Common: No
Sample:

```
<DIV ALIGN="RIGHT">
Look over here!</DIV>
<DIV ALIGN="LEFT">
Now, look over here!</DIV>
```

CLASS="..."

Indicates which style class applies to the <DIV> element.

Standard: HTML 4
Common: No
Sample:

```
<DIV CLASS="casual">
```

DATAFLD="..."

Selects a column from a previously identified source of tabulated data (see the DATASRC= attribute).

Standard: Internet Explorer 4
Common: No
Sample:

```
<DIV DATASRC="#data_table">
<DIV DATAFLD="name"></DIV>
</DIV>
```

DATAFORMATAS="{TEXT, HTML, NONE}"

Indicates how tabulated data formats within the <DIV> element.

Standard: Internet Explorer 4
Common: No
Sample:

```
<DIV DATAFORMATAS="HTML"
DATASRC="#data_table">
```

DATASRC="..."

Specifies the source of data for data binding.

Standard: Internet Explorer 4
Common: No
Sample:

```
<DIV DATASRC="#data_table">
```

ID="..."

Assigns a unique ID selector to an instance of the <DIV> tag. When you then assign a style to that ID selector, it affects only that one instance of the <DIV> tag.

Standard:	HTML 4
Common:	No
Sample:	

```
<DIV ID="123">
```

NOWRAP

Disables line-wrapping for the section.

Standard:	Netscape Navigator
Common:	No
Sample:	

```
<HR>
<DIV ALIGN="LEFT" NOWRAP>
The contents of this section will not
automatically wrap as you size the
window.
</DIV><HR>
```

STYLE="..."

Specifies style sheet commands that apply to the contents within the <DIV> tags.

Standard:	HTML 4
Common:	No
Sample:	

```
<DIV STYLE="background: red">
```

TITLE="..."

Specifies text assigned to the tag. You might use this attribute for context-sensitive help within the document. Browsers may use this to show tool tips over the contents of the <DIV> tags.

Standard:	HTML 4
Common:	No
Sample:	

```
<DIV TITLE="Title" CLASS="casual">
```

Other Attributes

This tag also accepts the LANG, DIR, onClick, onDblClick, onMouseDown, onMouseUp, onMouseOver, onMouseMove, onMouseOut, onKeyPress, onKeyDown, and onKeyUp attributes. See the Element-Independent Attributes section of this reference for definitions and examples.

<DL>

Contains the <DT> and <DD> tags that form the term and definition portions of a definition list.

Standard:	HTML 2
Common:	Yes
Paired:	Yes
Sample:	

```
<DL><DT>Hygiene
<DD>Always wash your hands before
preparing meat.</DL>
```

Attribute Information

CLASS="..."

Indicates which style class applies to the <DL> element.

Standard:	HTML 4
Common:	No
Sample:	

```
<DL CLASS="casual">
  <DT>RAM
  <DD>Random Access Memory
</DL>
```

COMPACT

Causes the definition list to appear in a compact format. This attribute probably will not affect the appearance of the list as most browsers do not present lists in more than one format.

Standard:	HTML 2; deprecated in HTML 4
Common:	No
Sample:	

```
<DL COMPACT>...
</DL>
```

ID="..."

Assigns a unique ID selector to an instance of the <DD> tag. When you then assign a style to that ID selector, it affects only that one instance of the <DD> tag.

Standard:	HTML 4
Common:	No
Sample:	

```
<DL ID="123">
  <DT>Food
  <DD>We will be eating 3
```

```
meals/day.
</DL>
```

STYLE="..."

Specifies style sheet commands that apply to contents within the <DL> tags.

Standard:	HTML 4
Common:	No

Sample:

```
<DL STYLE="background: red">
```

TITLE="..."

Specifies text assigned to the tag. You might use this attribute for context-sensitive help within the document. Browsers may use this to show tool tips over the definition list.

Standard:	HTML 4
Common:	No

Sample:

```
<DL TITLE="Definition List">
```

Other Attributes

This tag also accepts the LANG, DIR, onClick, onDblClick, onMouseDown, onMouseUp, onMouseOver, onMouseMove, onMouseOut, onKeyPress, onKeyDown, and onKeyUp attributes. See the Element-Independent Attributes section of this reference for definitions and examples.

<DT>

Contains the terms inside a definition list. Place the <DT> tags inside <DL> tags.

Standard:	HTML 2
Common:	Yes
Paired:	Yes, optional

Sample:

```
<DL><DT>Hygiene
<DD>Always wash your hands before
preparing meat.</DL>
```

Attribute Information

CLASS="..."

Indicates which style class applies to the <DT> element.

Standard:	HTML 4
Common:	No

Sample:

```
<DL>
  <DT CLASS="casual">CUL8R
  <DD>See You Later.
</DL>
```

ID="..."

Assigns a unique ID selector to an instance of the <DT> tag. When you then assign a style to that ID selector, it affects only that one instance of the <DT> tag.

Standard:	HTML 4
Common:	No

Sample:

```
<DL>
  <DT ID="123">Caffeine
  <DD>Avoid caffeine during the
stress management course.
</DL>
```

STYLE="..."

Specifies style sheet commands that apply to the contents within the <DT> tags.

Standard:	HTML 4
Common:	No

Sample:

```
<DT STYLE="background: red">
```

TITLE="..."

Specifies text assigned to the tag. You might use this attribute for context-sensitive help within the document. Browsers may use this to show tool tips over the definition term.

Standard:	HTML 4
Common:	No

Sample:

```
<DT TITLE="Term">Programmer</DT>
<DD>A method for converting coffee
into applications.
```

Other Attributes

This tag also accepts the LANG, DIR, onClick, onDblClick, onMouseDown, onMouseUp, onMouseOver, onMouseMove, onMouseOut, onKeyPress, onKeyDown, and onKeyUp attributes. See the Element-Independent Attributes section of this reference for definitions and examples.

E

<EM>

Makes the text stand out. Browsers usually do this with italic or boldface.

Standard:	HTML 2
Common:	Yes
Paired:	Yes

Sample:

```
It is <EM>very</EM> important to read
the instructions before beginning.
```

Attribute Information

CLASS="..."

Indicates which style class applies to the <EM> element.

Standard:	HTML 4
Common:	No

Sample:

```
Did you say my house was on<EM
CLASS="casual">FIRE?!</EM>
```

ID="..."

Assigns a unique ID selector to an instance of the <EM> tag. When you then assign a style to that ID selector, it affects only that one instance of the <EM> tag.

Standard:	HTML 4
Common:	No

Sample:

```
I have complained <EM
ID="123">ten</EM>times about the
leaking faucet.
```

STYLE="..."

Specifies style sheet commands that apply to the contents within the <EM> tags.

Standard:	HTML 4
Common:	No

Sample:

```
<EM STYLE="background: red">
```

TITLE="..."

Specifies text assigned to the tag. You might use this attribute for context-sensitive help within the document. Browsers may use this to show tool tips over the emphasized text.

Standard:	HTML 4
Common:	No

Sample:

```
<EM TITLE="Emphasis">
```

Other Attributes

This tag also accepts the LANG, DIR, onClick, onDblClick, onMouseDown, onMouseUp, onMouseOver, onMouseMove, onMouseOut, onKeyPress, onKeyDown, and onKeyUp attributes. See the Element-Independent Attributes section of this reference for definitions and examples.

<EMBED>

Places an embedded object into a document. Examples of embedded objects include MIDI files and digital video files. Because the <EMBED> tag is not standard, we suggest you use the <OBJECT> tag instead. If the browser does not have built-in support for an object, visitors will need a plug-in to use the object within the document.

Standard:	Netscape Navigator, supported by Internet Explorer
Common:	No
Paired:	No

Sample:

```
<EMBED SRC="fur_elise.midi">
```

Attribute Information

ACCESSKEY="..."

Specifies a key sequence that binds to the embedded object.

Standard:	Internet Explorer 4
Common:	No

Sample:

```
<EMBED SRC="st.ocx" ACCESSKEY="E">
```

ALIGN="{LEFT, RIGHT, CENTER, ABSBOTTOM, ABSMIDDLE, BASELINE, BOTTOM, TEXTTOP, TOP}"

Indicates how an embedded object is positioned relative to the document borders and surrounding contents. ALIGN="LEFT", ALIGN="RIGHT", or ALIGN="CENTER" makes the embedded object float between the edges of the frame either to the left, right, or evenly between. The behavior is similar to that of the ALIGN= attribute of the <IMG> tag. ALIGN="TEXTTOP" or ALIGN="TOP" lines up the top of the embedded object with the top of the current text font. ALIGN=" ABSMIDDLE" lines up the middle of the embedded object with the middle of the current text font. ALIGN="ABSBOTTOM" lines up the bottom of the embedded object with the bottom of the current text font. ALIGN="BASELINE" or ALIGN=" BOTTOM" lines up the bottom of the embedded object with the baseline of the current text font.

Standard:	Internet Explorer 4
Common:	No
Sample:	

```
<EMBED SRC="song.mid" ALIGN="CENTER">
```

HEIGHT="*n*"

Specifies the vertical dimension of the embedded object. (See the UNITS= attribute for how to measure dimensions.)

Standard:	Netscape Navigator
Common:	No
Sample:	

```
<EMBED SRC="rocket.avi" WIDTH="50"
HEIGHT="40">
```

HIDDEN

Indicates that the embedded object should not be visible.

Standard:	Internet Explorer 4
Common:	No
Sample:	

```
<EMBED SRC="song.mid" HIDDEN>
```

NAME="..."

Gives the object a name by which other objects can refer to it.

Standard:	Netscape Navigator
Common:	No
Sample:	

```
<EMBED SRC="running.avi"
NAME="movie1">
```

OPTIONAL PARAM="..."

Indicates additional parameters. For example, AVI movies accept the AUTOSTART attribute.

Standard:	Netscape Navigator

Common:	No
Sample:	

```
<EMBED SRC="explode.avi"
AUTOSTART="true">
```

PALETTE="#*RRGGBB*|#*RRGGBB*"

Indicates the foreground and background colors for the embedded object. You can specify colors with hexadecimal RGB values or with color names.

Standard:	Netscape Navigator
Common:	No
Sample:	

```
<EMBED SRC="flying.avi"
PALETTE="Red|Black">
```

SRC="*URL*"

Indicates the relative or absolute location of the file containing the object you want to embed.

Standard:	Netscape Navigator
Common:	No
Sample:	

```
<EMBED SRC="beethoven_9.midi">
```

TITLE="..."

Specifies text assigned to the tag. You might use this attribute for context-sensitive help within the document. Browsers may use this to show tool tips over the embedded object.

Standard:	Internet Explorer 4
Common:	No
Sample:	

```
<EMBED SRC="explode.avi"
TITLE="movie">
```

UNITS="{PIXELS, EN}"

Modifies the behavior of the HEIGHT= and WIDTH= attributes. UNITS=PIXELS measures attributes in pixels. UNITS=EN measures dimensions in EN spaces.

Standard:	Netscape Navigator
Common:	No
Sample:	

```
<EMBED SRC="rocket.avi" WIDTH="50"
HEIGHT="40">
```

WIDTH="*n*"

Indicates the horizontal dimension of the embedded object. (See the UNITS= attribute for how to measure dimensions.)

Standard: Netscape Navigator
Common: No
Sample:

```
<EMBED SRC="cartoon.avi" WIDTH="50">
```

Other Attributes

This tag also accepts the LANG, DIR, onClick, onDblClick, onMouseDown, onMouseUp, onMouseOver, onMouseMove, onMouseOut, onKeyPress, onKeyDown, and onKeyUp attributes. See the Element-Independent Attributes section of this reference for definitions and examples.

F

<FIELDSET>

Groups related form elements.

Standard: HTML 4
Common: No
Paired: Yes
Sample:

```
<FORM ...>
<FIELDSET>
...logically related field
elements...
</FIELDSET>
</FORM>
```

Attribute Information

CLASS="..."

Indicates which style class applies to the <FIELDSET> element.

Standard: HTML 4
Common: No
Sample:

```
<FIELDSET CLASS="casual">Group
Rates</FIELDSET>
```

ID="..."

Assigns a unique ID selector to an instance of the <FIELDSET> tag. When you then assign a style to that ID selector, it affects only that one instance of the <FIELDSET> tag.

Standard: HTML 4
Common: No

Sample:

```
<FIELDSET ID="123">now! </FIELDSET>
```

STYLE="..."

Specifies style sheet commands that apply to the contents within the <FIELDSET> tags.

Standard: HTML 4
Common: No
Sample:

```
<FIELDSET STYLE="background: red">
```

TITLE="..."

Specifies text assigned to the tag. You might use this attribute for context-sensitive help within the document. Browsers may use this to show tool tips over the font text.

Standard: HTML 4
Common: No
Sample:

```
<FIELDSET TITLE="Personal data
fields">
```

Other Attributes

This tag also accepts the LANG, DIR, onClick, onDblClick, onMouseDown, onMouseUp, onMouseOver, onMouseMove, onMouseOut, onKeyPress, onKeyDown, and onKeyUp attributes. See the Element-Independent Attributes section of this reference for definitions and examples.

<FONT>

Alters or sets font characteristics of the font the browser uses to display text.

Standard: HTML 3.2; deprecated in HTML 4 in favor of style sheets
Common: Yes
Paired: Yes
Sample:

```
The cat was really <FONT
SIZE="+3">BIG!</FONT>
```

Attribute Information

COLOR="#*RRGGBB*" or "..."

Indicates the color the browser uses to display text. Color names can substitute for the RGB hexadecimal values.

> **Standard:** HTML 3.2; deprecated in HTML 4 in favor of style sheets
> **Common:** Yes
> **Sample:**

```
<FONT COLOR=#FF0000><H2>Win A
Trip!</H2></FONT> <FONT
COLOR="lightblue"><p>That's right! A
trip to Hawaii can be yours if you
scratch off the right number!</FONT>
```

FACE="...,..."

Specifies a comma-separated list of font names the browser uses to render text. If the browser does not have access to the first named font, it tries the second, then the third, and so forth.

> **Standard:** Netscape Navigator and Internet Explorer, not introduced in standard HTML in favor of style sheets
> **Common:** Yes
> **Sample:**

```
<FONT SIZE=+1 FACE="Avant Guard,
Helvetica, Lucida Sans, Arial">
```

SIZE=*n*

Specifies the size of the text affected by the FONT tag. You can specify the size relative to the base font size (see the <BASEFONT> tag) which is normally 3. You can also specify the size as a digit in the range 1 through 7.

> **Standard:** HTML 3.2; deprecated in HTML 4 in favor of style sheets
> **Common:** Yes
> **Sample:**

```
<BASEFONT SIZE=4>
```

```
<FONT SIZE=+2>This is a font of size
6.</FONT> <FONT SIZE=1>This is a font
of size 1.</FONT>
```

Other Attributes

This tag also accepts the LANG, DIR, ID, CLASS, TITLE, and STYLE attributes. See the Element-Independent Attributes section and other tag listings in this reference for definitions and examples.

<FORM>

Sets up a container for a form tag. Within the <FORM> tags, you can place form input tags such as <FIELDSET>, <INPUT>, <SELECT>, and <TEXTAREA>.

> **Standard:** HTML 2
> **Common:** Yes
> **Paired:** Yes
> **Sample:**

```
<FORM METHOD=POST
ACTION="/cgi-bin/search.pl">
```

```
Search : <INPUT TYPE=TEXT NAME="name"
SIZE=20><BR>
```

```
<INPUT TYPE=SUBMIT VALUE="Start
Search"> </FORM>
```

Attribute Information

ACCEPT-CHARSET="..."

Specifies the character encodings for input data that the server processing the form must accept. The value is a list of character sets as defined in RFC2045, separated by commas.

> **Standard:** HTML 4
> **Common:** No
> **Sample:**

```
<FORM METHOD=POST
ACCEPT-CHARSET="ISO-8859-1"
ACTION="/stat-collector.cgi">
```

ACCEPT="..."

Specifies a list of MIME types, separated by commas, that the server processing the form will handle correctly.

> **Standard:** HTML 4
> **Common:** No
> **Sample:**

```
<FORM METHOD=POST ACCEPT="image/ gif,
image/jpeg "ACTION="/
image-collector.cgi">
```

ACTION="*URL*"

Specifies the explicit or relative location of the form processing CGI application.

> **Standard:** HTML 2

Common: Yes
Sample:

```
<FORM METHOD=POST
ACTION="/stat-collector.cgi">
```

CLASS="..."

Indicates which style class applies to the <FORM>.

Standard: HTML 4
Common: No
Sample:

```
<FORM METHOD=POST CLASS="casual"
ACTION="/stat-collector.cgi">
```

ENCTYPE="..."

Specifies the MIME type used to submit (post) the form to the server. The default value is "application/x-www-form-urlencoded". Use the value "multipart/form-data" when the returned document includes files.

Standard: HTML 4
Common: No
Sample:

```
<FORM METHOD=POST ENCTYPE=
"application/x-www-
form-urlencoded"ACTION=
"/stat-collector.cgi">
```

ID="..."

Assigns a unique ID selector to an instance of the <FORM> tag. When you then assign a style to that ID selector, it affects only that one instance of the <FORM> tag.

Standard: HTML 4
Common: No
Sample:

```
<FORM ACTION="/cgi-bin/ttt.pl"
METHOD=GET ID="123">
```

METHOD={POST,GET}

Changes how form data is transmitted to the form processor. When you use METHOD=GET, the form data is given to the form processor in the form of an environment variable (*QUERY_STRING*). When you use METHOD=POST, the form data is given to the form processor as the standard input to the program.

Standard: HTML 2
Common: Yes

Sample:

```
<FORM METHOD=POST
ACTION="/cgi-bin/www-search">

Enter search keywords:
<INPUT TYPE=TEXT NAME="query"
SIZE=20>

<INPUT TYPE=SUBMIT VALUE="Search">

</FORM>
```

NAME="..."

Assigns the form a name accessible by bookmark, script, and applet resources.

Standard: Internet Explorer
Common: No
Sample:

```
<FORM METHOD=POST
ACTION="/cgi-bin/ff.pl"NAME="ff">
```

STYLE="..."

Specifies style sheet commands that apply to the contents within the <FORM> tags.

Standard: HTML 4
Common: No
Sample:

```
<FORM STYLE="background: red">
```

TARGET="..."

Identifies in which previously named frame the output from the form processor should appear.

Standard: HTML 4
Common: Yes
Sample:

```
<FORM TARGET="output" METHOD=GET
ACTION="/cgi-bin/thingie.sh">
```

TITLE="..."

Specifies text assigned to the tag. You might use this attribute for context-sensitive help within the document. Browsers may use this to show tool tips over the fill-out form.

Standard: HTML 4
Common: No
Sample:

```
<FORM METHOD=POST ACTION="/cgi-
bin/ff.pl"TITLE="Fill-out form">
```

Other Attributes

This tag also accepts the LANG, DIR, onsubmit, onreset, onClick, onDblClick, onMouseDown, onMouseUp, onMouseOver, onMouseMove, onMouseOut, onKeyPress, onKeyDown, and onKeyUp attributes. See the Element-Independent Attributes section of this reference for definitions and examples.

<FRAME>

Defines a frame within a frameset (see the <FRAMESET> tag). The <FRAME> tag specifies the source file and visual characteristics of a frame.

Standard: HTML 4
Common: Yes
Paired: No
Sample:

```
<FRAMESET ROWS="*,70">
  <FRAME SRC="frames/body.html"
NAME="body">
  <FRAME SRC="frames/buttons
.html" NAME="buttons" SCROLLING
=NO NORESIZE>
</FRAMESET>
```

Attribute Information

BORDER="n"

Specifies the thickness of the border (in pixels) around a frame. Use BORDER=0 to specify a frame with no border.

Standard: Netscape Navigator
Common: Yes
Sample:

```
<FRAME SRC="hits.html"
BORDER="2">
```

BORDERCOLOR="#RRGGBB" or "..."

Specifies the color of the border around the frame. Use the color's hexadecimal RGB values or the color name.

Standard: Internet Explorer, Netscape Navigator
Common: Yes
Sample:

```
<FRAME SRC="hits.html"
BORDERCOLOR="red">
```

FRAMEBORDER={1,0}

Indicates whether the frame's border is visible. A value of 1 indicates that the border is visible, and a value of 0 indicates that it is not visible.

Standard: HTML 4
Common: No
Sample:

```
<FRAME SRC="weather.html"
FRAMEBORDER=0>
```

MARGINHEIGHT="n"

Specifies the vertical dimension (in number of pixels) of the top and bottom margins in a frame.

Standard: HTML 4
Common: No
Sample:

```
<FRAME SRC="cats.html"
MARGINHEIGHT=10>
```

MARGINWIDTH="n"

Specifies the horizontal dimension (in pixels) of the left and right margins in a frame.

Standard: HTML 4
Common: No
Sample:

```
<FRAME SRC="dogs.html"
MARGINWIDTH=10>
```

NAME="..."

Gives the frame you are defining a name. You can use this name later to load new documents into the frame (see the TARGET= attribute) and within scripts to control attributes of the frame. Reserved names with special meaning include _blank, _parent, _self, and _top.

Standard: HTML 4
Common: Yes
Sample:

```
<FRAME SRC="/cgi-bin/weather.cgi"
NAME="weather">
```

NORESIZE

Makes a frame's dimensions unchangeable. Otherwise, if a frame's borders are visible, visitors can resize the frame by selecting a border and moving it with the mouse.

Standard: HTML 4

Common: Yes
Sample:

```
<FRAME SRC="bottom.html"
NAME="bottom" NORESIZE SCROLLING=NO>
```

SCROLLING={YES, NO, AUTO}

Indicates whether a scrollbar is present within a frame when text dimensions exceed the dimensions of the frame. Set SCROLLING=NO when using a frame to display only an image.

Standard: HTML 4
Common: Yes
Sample:

```
<FRAME NAME="titleimg"
SRC="title.html" SCROLLING=NO>
```

SRC="*URL*"

Specifies the relative or absolute location of a document that you want to load within the defined frame.

Standard: HTML 4
Common: Yes
Sample:

```
<FRAME NAME="main" SRC="intro.html">
```

Other Attributes

This tag also accepts the LONGDESC, ID, CLASS, TITLE, and STYLE attributes. See the Element-Independent Attributes section and other tag listings in this reference for definitions and examples.

\<FRAMESET>

Contains frame definitions and specifies frame spacing, dimensions, and attributes. Place \<FRAME> tags inside \<FRAMESET> tags.

Standard: HTML 4
Common: Yes
Paired: Yes
Sample:

```
<FRAMESET COLS="*,70">

  <FRAME SRC="frames/body.html"
  NAME="body">

  <FRAME SRC="frames/side.html"
  NAME="side">

</FRAMESET>
```

Attribute Information

BORDER="n"

Specifies the thickness of borders (in pixels) around frames defined within the frameset. You can also control border thickness with the \<FRAME> tag.

Standard: Netscape Navigator
Common: No
Sample:

```
<FRAMESET COLS="*,150" BORDER=5>

  <FRAME SRC="left.html"
  NAME="main">

  <FRAME SRC="side.html"
  NAME="side">

</FRAMESET>
```

BORDERCOLOR="#*RRGGBB*" or "..."

Sets the color of the frame borders. Color names can substitute for the hexadecimal RGB color values.

Standard: Netscape Navigator, Internet Explorer
Common: Yes
Sample:

```
<FRAMESET BORDERCOLOR="Red"
ROWS="100,*">

  <FRAME SRC="top.html"
  NAME="title">
  <FRAME SRC="story.html"
  NAME="Story">
</FRAMESET>
```

COLS="..."

Specifies the number and dimensions of the vertical frames within the current frameset.

Set COLS= to a comma-separated list of numbers or percentages to indicate the width of each frame. Use the asterisk (*) to represent a variable width. A frame of variable width fills the space left over after the browser formats space for the other frames (\<FRAMESET COLS="100, 400,10% *">).

Setting COLS= with percentage values controls the ratio of frame horizontal space relative to the amount of space available within the browser (\<FRAMESET COLS="10%,*">).

You cannot use COLS= and ROWS= in the same tag.

Standard:	HTML 4
Common:	Yes

Sample:

```
<FRAMESET COLS="*,100,*">
  <FRAME SRC="left.html"
  NAME="left">
  <FRAME SRC="middle.html"
  NAME="middle">
  <FRAMESET ROWS=2>
<FRAME SRC="top.html"
NAME="top">
    <FRAME SRC="bottom.html"
    NAME="bottom">
  </FRAMESET>
</FRAMESET>
```

FRAMESPACING="n"

Specifies the space (in pixels) between frames within the browser window.

Standard:	Internet Explorer
Common:	No

Sample:

```
<FRAMESET ROWS="*,100"
FRAMESPACING=10>
  <FRAME SRC="top.html"
  NAME="top">
  <FRAME SRC="middle.html"
  NAME="middle">
</FRAMESET>
```

ROWS="..."

Specifies the number and dimensions of the horizontal frames within the current frameset.

Set ROWS= to a comma-separated list of numbers or percentages to indicate the height of each frame. Use the asterisk (*) to represent a variable height. A frame of variable height fills the space remaining after the browser formats space for the other frames (<FRAMESET ROWS="100,400,*">).

Setting ROWS= to a comma-separated list of percentages allows you to control the ratio of frame vertical space relative to the space available within the browser (<FRAMESET ROWS="10%,*">).

You cannot use ROWS= and COLS= in the same tag.

Standard:	HTML 4
Common:	Yes

Sample:

```
<FRAMESET ROWS="*,100,*">
  <FRAME SRC="top.html"
  NAME="top">

  <FRAME SRC="middle.html"
  NAME="middle">

  <FRAMESET COLS=2>

    <FRAME SRC="bottom1.html"
    NAME="left">

    <FRAME SRC="bottom2.html"
    NAME="right">

  </FRAMESET>

</FRAMESET>
```

Other Attributes

This tag also accepts the ID, CLASS, TITLE, STYLE, onLoad and onUnload attributes. See the Element-Independent Attributes section of this reference for definitions and examples.

H

<Hn>

Specifies headings in a document. Headings are numbered 1–6, with <H1> representing the heading for the main heading in the document and <H3> representing a heading for a nested subtopic. Generally, text inside heading tags appears in boldface and may be larger than normal document text.

Standard:	HTML 2
Common:	Yes
Paired:	Yes

Sample:

```
<H1>Caring For Your Canary</H1>
This document explains how you should
take care of a canary. With proper
care, you and your new bird will have
a lasting, happy relationship.
<H2>Feeding</H2>
```

Attribute Information

ALIGN={LEFT, CENTER, RIGHT, JUSTIFY}

Positions the heading in the left, right, or center of a document.

Standard: HTML 3.2; deprecated
in HTML 4 in favor of style
sheets

Common: Yes

Sample:

```
<H3 ALIGN=RIGHT>History Of The
Platypus</H3>
```

CLASS="..."

Indicates which style class applies to the `<Hn>`
element.

Standard: HTML 4

Common: No

Sample:

```
<H1 CLASS="casual" ALIGN=LEFT>River
Tours</H1>
```

ID="..."

Assigns a unique ID selector to an instance of
the `<Hn>` tag. When you then assign a style to
that ID selector, it affects only that one
instance of the `<Hn>` tag.

Standard: HTML 4

Common: No

Sample:

```
<H2 ID="123">Paper Products</H2>
```

STYLE="..."

Specifies style sheet commands that apply to
the heading.

Standard: HTML 4

Common: No

Sample:

```
<H1 STYLE="background: red">
```

TITLE="..."

Specifies text assigned to the tag. You might
use this attribute for context-sensitive help
within the document. Browsers may use this
to show tool tips over the heading.

Standard: HTML 4

Common: No

Sample:

```
<H1 TITLE="Headline">
```

Other Attributes

This tag also accepts the LANG, DIR, onClick,
onDblClick, onMouseDown, onMouseUp,
onMouseOver, onMouseMove, onMouseOut,
onKeyPress, onKeyDown, and onKeyUp attributes. See the Element-Independent Attributes
section of this reference for definitions and
examples.

<HEAD>

Contains document head information. You
can place any of the following tags within the
document head: `<LINK>`, `<META>`, `<TITLE>`,
`<SCRIPT>`, `<BASE>`, and `<STYLE>`.

Standard: HTML 2

Common: Yes

Paired: Yes

Sample:

```
<HTML>
<HEAD>
<TITLE>Making a Peanut-Butter and
Jelly Sandwich</TITLE>
<LINK REL=Parent
HREF="sandwiches.html">
</HEAD>
```

Attribute Information

PROFILE="*URL*"

Specifies the address of data profiles. You
might use this attribute to specify the location of, for example, `<META>` tag information.

Standard: HTML 4

Common: No

Sample:

```
<HEAD PROFILE="http://www
.raycomm.com/general.html">
</HEAD<
```

Other Attributes

This tag also accepts the LANG and DIR attributes. See the Element-Independent Attributes
section of this reference for definitions and
examples.

<HR>

Draws horizontal lines (rules) in your document. This is useful for visually separating
document sections.

Standard: HTML 2

Common: Yes

Paired: No

Sample:

```
<H2>Birthday Colors</H2>
<HR ALIGN=LEFT WIDTH="60%">
<P>Birthdays are usually joyous
celebrations so we recommend bright
colors.
```

Attribute Information

ALIGN={LEFT, CENTER, RIGHT}

Positions the line flush left, flush right, or in the center of the document. These settings are irrelevant unless you use the WIDTH= attribute to make the line shorter than the width of the document.

Standard:	HTML 3.2; deprecated in HTML 4 in favor of style sheets
Common:	Yes

Sample:

```
<H2 ALIGN=LEFT>Shopping List</H2>
<HR WIDTH="40%" ALIGN=LEFT>
<UL TYPE=SQUARE>
<LI>Eggs
<LI>Butter
<LI>Bread
<LI>Milk
</UL>
```

CLASS="..."

Indicates which style class applies to the <HR> element.

Standard:	HTML 4
Common:	No

Sample:

```
<HR CLASS="casual" WIDTH="50%">
```

COLOR="#RRGGBB" or "..."

Specifies the color of the line. The color name can substitute for the hexadecimal RGB values.

Standard:	Internet Explorer; style sheets provide equivalent functionality.
Common:	No

Sample:

```
<HR COLOR=#09334C>
```

ID="n"

Assigns a unique ID selector to an instance of the <HR> tag. When you then assign a style to that ID selector, it affects only that one instance of the <HR> tag.

Standard:	HTML 4
Common:	No

Sample:

```
<HR ID="123">
```

NOSHADE

Specifies that the browser not shade the line.

Standard:	HTML 3.2
Common:	Yes

Sample:

```
<HR NOSHADE ALIGN=CENTER WIDTH="50%">
<IMG SRC="Bobby.jpg" ALIGN=CENTER
BORDER=0 ALT="Bobby">
<BR CLEAR=ALL>
<HR NOSHADE ALIGN=CENTER WIDTH="50%">
```

SIZE="n"

Specifies the thickness of the line (in pixels).

Standard:	HTML 3.2; deprecated in HTML 4 in favor of style sheets
Common:	Yes

Sample:

```
<HR SIZE=10>
```

STYLE="..."

Specifies style sheet commands that apply to the horizontal rule.

Standard:	HTML 4
Common:	No

Sample:

```
<HR WIDTH="50%" STYLE="color: red">
```

TITLE="..."

Specifies text assigned to the tag. You might use this attribute for context-sensitive help within the document. Browsers may use this to show tool tips over the horizontal rule.

Standard:	HTML 4
Common:	No

Sample:

```
<HR TITLE="A line">
```

WIDTH="n"

Specifies the length of the line. You can specify the value with an absolute number of pixels or as a percentage to indicate how much of the total width available is used.

Standard: HTML 3.2; deprecated in HTML 4 in favor of style sheets

Common: Yes

Sample:

```
<H2 ALIGN=CENTER>The End!</H2>
<HR WIDTH="85%">
<P ALIGN=CENTER>
<A HREF="/index.html">Home</A> |
<A HREF="Story3.html">Next
Story</A> |
<A HREF="Story1.html">Prev Story</A>
```

Other Attributes

This tag also accepts the onClick, onDblClick, onMouseDown, onMouseUp, onMouseOver, onMouseMove, onMouseOut, onKeyPress, onKeyDown, and onKeyUp attributes. See the Element-Independent Attributes section of this reference for definitions and examples.

\<HTML\>

Contains the entire document. Place these tags at the top and bottom of your HTML file.

Standard: HTML 2

Common: Yes

Paired: Yes

Sample:

```
<HTML>
<HEAD><TITLE>Test Page</TITLE></HEAD>
<BODY>
   <H1>Is this working?</H1>
</BODY>
</HTML>
```

Attribute Information

This tag accepts the LANG and DIR attributes. See the Element-Independent Attributes section of this reference for definitions and examples.

\<I\>

Italicizes text.

Standard: HTML 2

Common: Yes

Paired: Yes

Sample:

```
After this, Tom told me to
read<I>Mastering HTML</I>. I had no
choice but to do so.
```

Attribute Information

CLASS="..."

Indicates which style class applies to the \<I\> element.

Standard: HTML 4

Common: No

Sample:

```
This mouse is
<I CLASS="casual">enhanced</I>.
```

ID="..."

Assigns a unique ID selector to an instance of the \<I\> tag. When you then assign a style to that ID selector, it affects only that one instance of the \<I\> tag.

Standard: HTML 4

Common: No

Sample:

```
He called it a <I ID="123">
Doo-Dad</I>!
```

STYLE="..."

Specifies style sheet commands that apply to italicized text.

Standard: HTML 4

Common: No

Sample:

```
<I STYLE="color: green">
```

TITLE="..."

Specifies text assigned to the tag. You might use this attribute for context-sensitive help within the document. Browsers may use this to show tool tips over the italicized text.

Standard: HTML 4

Common: No

Sample:

```
<I TITLE="Italicized">
```

Other Attributes

This tag also accepts the LANG, DIR, onClick, onDblClick, onMouseDown, onMouseUp, onMouseOver, onMouseMove, onMouseOut, onKeyPress, onKeyDown, and onKeyUp attributes. See the Element-Independent Attributes section of this reference for definitions and examples.

<IFRAME>

Creates floating frames within a document. Floating frames differ from normal frames because they are independently manipulable elements within another HTML document.

Standard:	HTML 4
Common:	No
Paired:	Yes
Sample:	

```
<IFRAME NAME="new_win"
SRC="http://www.raycomm.com">
</IFRAME>
```

Attribute Information

ALIGN={LEFT, CENTER, RIGHT, JUSTIFY}

Specifies how the floating frame lines up with respect to the left and right sides of the browser window.

Standard:	HTML 4; deprecated usage. Use style sheets instead.
Common:	No
Sample:	

```
<IFRAME ALIGN=LEFT
SRC="goats.html"NAME="g1">
```

BORDER="n"

Indicates the thickness of a border around a floating frame (in pixels).

Standard:	Internet Explorer 4
Common:	No
Sample:	

```
<IFRAME SRC="joe.html"
NAME="Joe"BORDER=5>
```

BORDERCOLOR="#RRGGBB" or "..."

Specifies (in hexadecimal RGB values or the color name) the color of the border around a floating frame.

Standard:	Internet Explorer 4
Common:	No
Sample:	

```
<IFRAME SRC="joe.html"
NAME="Joe"BORDERCOLOR=#5A3F2E>
```

FRAMEBORDER={0,1}

Indicates whether the floating frame has visible borders. A value of 0 indicates no border, and a value of 1 indicates a visible border.

Standard:	HTML 4
Common:	No
Sample:	

```
<IFRAME SRC="main.html"
NAME="main"FRAMEBORDER=0>
```

FRAMESPACING="n"

Indicates the space (in pixels) between adjacent floating frames.

Standard:	Internet Explorer 4
Common:	No
Sample:	

```
<IFRAME SRC="joe.html" NAME="Joe"
FRAMESPACING=10>
```

HEIGHT="n"

Specifies the vertical dimension (in pixels) of the floating frame.

Standard:	HTML 4
Common:	No
Sample:	

```
<IFRAME SRC="joe.html"
NAME="Joe"WIDTH=500 HEIGHT=200>
```

HSPACE="n"

Indicates the size (in pixels) of left and right margins within the floating frame.

Standard:	Internet Explorer 4
Common:	No
Sample:	

```
<IFRAME SRC="joe.html"
NAME="Joe"HSPACE=10 VSPACE=10>
```

ID="..."

Assigns a unique ID selector to an instance of the <IFRAME> tag. When you then assign a style to that ID selector, it affects only that one instance of the <IFRAME> tag.

Standard:	HTML 4
Common:	No

```
<IFRAME SRC="Joe.html" NAME="Joe"
ID="123">
```

MARGINHEIGHT="*n*"

Specifies the size of the top and bottom margins (in pixels) within the floating frame.

Standard: HTML 4
Common: No
Sample:

```
<IFRAME SRC="top.html"
NAME="topbar" MARGINHEIGHT=50>
```

MARGINWIDTH="*n*"

Specifies the size of the left and right margins (in pixels) within the floating frame.

Standard: HTML 4
Common: No
Sample:

```
<IFRAME SRC="body.html"
NAME="body"MARGINWIDTH=50>
```

NAME="..."

Assigns the frame a unique name. You can use this name within other frames to load new documents in the frame and to manipulate the attributes of the frame.

Standard: HTML 4
Common: No
Sample:

```
<IFRAME SRC="joe.html" NAME="Joe"
WIDTH=500 HEIGHT=200>
```

NORESIZE

Specifies that the floating frame cannot resize. Because the HTML 4 specification forbids resizable inline frames, this attribute is only relevant to Internet Explorer.

Standard: Internet Explorer
Common: No
Sample:

```
<IFRAME SRC="joe.html"
NAME="Joe"NORESIZE>
```

SCROLLING={YES, NO, AUTO}

Indicates whether the floating frame has scrollbars.

Standard: HTML 4
Common: No

Sample:

```
<IFRAME SRC="top.html" SCROLLING=NO>
```

SRC="*URL*"

Specifies the relative or absolute location of the document file to load in the floating frame.

Standard: HTML 4
Common: No
Sample:

```
<IFRAME NAME="pics" SRC="pics/">
```

STYLE="..."

Specifies style sheet commands that apply to the floating frame.

Standard: HTML 4
Common: No
Sample:

```
<IFRAME SRC="dots.html" NAME="dots"
STYLE="background: red">
```

WIDTH="*n*"

Specifies the horizontal dimension (in pixels) of the floating frame.

Standard: HTML 4
Common: No
Sample:

```
<IFRAME SRC="joe.html" NAME="Joe"
WIDTH=500 HEIGHT=200>
```

VSPACE="*n*"

Indicates the size (in pixels) of top and bottom margins within the floating frame.

Standard: Internet Explorer 4
Common: No
Sample:

```
<IFRAME SRC="joe.html" NAME="Joe"
HSPACE=10 VSPACE=10>
```

Other Attributes

This tag also accepts the LONGDESC, CLASS, TITLE, LANG, DIR, onClick, onDblClick, onMouseDown, onMouseUp, onMouseOver, onMouseMove, onMouseOut, onKeyPress, onKeyDown, and onKeyUp attributes. See the Element-Independent Attributes section of this reference for definitions and examples.

<IMG>

Places an inline image in a document. You can use the attributes ISMAP= and USEMAP= with the <IMG> tag to implement imagemaps.

Standard:	HTML 2
Common:	Yes
Paired:	No
Sample:	

```
<IMG SRC="images/left_arrow.gif"
ALT="<-">
```

Attribute Information

ALIGN={LEFT, RIGHT, TOP, MIDDLE, BOTTOM}

Specifies the appearance of text that is near an inline graphic image. For example, if you use RIGHT, the image appears flush to the right edge of the document, and the text appears to its left. Using LEFT produces the opposite effect.

HTML 2 mentions only attribute values of TOP, MIDDLE, and BOTTOM. TOP aligns the top of the first line of text after the <IMG> tag to the top of the image. BOTTOM (the default) aligns the bottom of the image to the baseline of the text. MIDDLE aligns the baseline of the first line of text with the middle of the image.

HTML 3.2 added LEFT and RIGHT to the list of attribute values.

You can use the <BR> tag to control specific points where text stops wrapping around an image and continues below the instance of the image.

Standard:	HTML 2; deprecated in HTML 4 in favor of style sheets
Common:	Yes
Sample:	

```
<IMG SRC="red_icon.gif" ALIGN=LEFT>
It's about time for volunteers to
pitch in.<BR CLEAR=ALL>
```

ALT="..."

Provides a textual description of images, which is useful for visitors who have text-only browsers. Some browsers may also display the ALT= text as a floating message when the visitor places the mouse pointer over the image.

Standard:	HTML 2
Common:	Yes
Sample:	

```
<IMG SRC="smiley.gif" ALT=":-)">
```

BORDER="n"

Specifies the width (in pixels) of a border around an image. The default value is usually 0 (no border). The border color is the color of normal text within your document.

Standard:	HTML 3.2
Common:	Yes
Sample:	

```
<IMG SRC="portrait.jpg" BORDER=2>
```

CLASS="..."

Indicates which style class applies to the <IMG> element.

Standard:	HTML 4
Common:	No
Sample:	

```
<IMG CLASS="casual" SRC="dots.gif">
```

CONTROLS

If the image is a video file, indicates the playback controls that appear below the image.

Standard:	Internet Explorer 2
Common:	No
Sample:	

```
<IMG DYNSRC="foo.avi" CONTROLS>
```

DATAFLD="..."

Indicates a column in previously identified tabular data.

Standard:	Internet Explorer 4
Common:	No
Sample:	

```
<IMG SRC="thing.gif" DATAFLD="color">
```

DATASRC="..."

Specifies the location of tabular data to be bound.

Standard:	Internet Explorer 4
Common:	No
Sample:	

```
<IMG SRC="thing.gif"
DATASRC="#data_table">
```

DYNSRC="*URL*"

Specifies the relative or absolute location of a dynamic image (VRML, video file, and so on).

Standard: Internet Explorer 2
Common: No
Sample:

```
<IMG DYNSRC="foo.avi">
```

HEIGHT="*n*"

Specifies the vertical dimension of the image (in pixels). If you don't use this attribute, the image appears in the default height. Use this attribute, along with the WIDTH= attribute, to fit an image within a space. You can fit a large image into a smaller space, and you can spread a smaller image. Some Web designers use the WIDTH= and HEIGHT= attributes to spread a single pixel image over a large space to produce the effect of a larger solid-color image.

Standard: HTML 3.2
Common: Yes
Sample:

```
<IMG SRC="images/smiley.jpg" WIDTH=50
HEIGHT=50>
```

HSPACE="*n*"

Establishes a margin of white space (in pixels) to the left and right of a graphic image. (See the VSPACE= attribute for how to control the top and bottom margins around an image.)

Standard: HTML 3.2
Common: Yes
Sample:

```
<IMG SRC="pics/pinetree.jpg"
HSPACE=20 VSPACE=15>
```

ID="*n*"

Assigns a unique ID selector to an instance of the <IMG> tag. When you then assign a style to that ID selector, it affects only that one instance of the <IMG> tag.

Standard: HTML 4
Common: No
Sample:

```
<IMG SRC="grapes.jpg" ID="123">
```

ISMAP

Indicates that the graphic image functions as a clickable imagemap. The ISMAP= attribute instructs the browser to send the pixel coordinates to the server imagemap CGI application when a visitor selects the image with the mouse pointer. When HTML 2 established the ISMAP= attribute, imagemaps were implemented in a server-side fashion only. Now, client-side imagemaps are more popular (see the USEMAP= attribute).

Standard: HTML 2
Common: Yes
Sample:

```
<A HREF="/cgi-bin/
imagemap/mymap">
<IMG ISMAP SRC="images/main.gif"></A>
```

LOWSRC="*URL*"

Indicates the absolute or relative location of a lower resolution version of an image.

Standard: Netscape Navigator
Common: No
Sample:

```
<IMG SRC="bigpic.jpg"
LOWSRC="lilpic.jpg">
```

LOOP={*n*, INFINITE}

Indicates the number of times a video file plays back.

Standard: Internet Explorer 2
Common: No
Sample:

```
<IMG DYNSRC="bar.avi"
LOOP=INFINITE>
```

NAME="..."

Specifies a name by which bookmarks, scripts, and applets can reference the image.

Standard: Internet Explorer 4
Common: No
Sample:

```
<IMG SRC="tweakie.jpg" NAME="img_1">
```

SRC="*URL*"

Specifies the relative or absolute location of a file that contains the graphic image you want to embed in a document.

Standard: HTML 2
Common: Yes

Sample:

```
<IMG SRC="images/left_arrow.gif"
ALT="<-">
```

START={FILEOPEN, MOUSEOVER}

Specifies the event that triggers the playback of a dynamic image. START=FILEOPEN starts playback when the browser has completely downloaded the file. START=MOUSEOVER starts playback when a visitor places the mouse pointer over the image.

Standard: Internet Explorer 2
Common: No
Sample:

```
<IMG DYNSRC="ship.vrm"
START=MOUSOVER>
```

STYLE="..."

Specifies style sheet commands that apply to the inline image.

Standard: HTML 4
Common: No
Sample:

```
<IMG SRC="dots.gif"
STYLE="background: red">
```

TITLE="..."

Specifies text assigned to the tag. You might use this attribute for context-sensitive help within the document. Browsers may use this to show tool tips over the image.

Standard: HTML 4
Common: No
Sample:

```
<IMG SRC="pics/jill.jpg"
TITLE="Image">
```

USEMAP="URL"

Specifies the location of the client-side imagemap data (see the <MAP> tag). Because the <MAP> tag gives the map data an anchor name, be sure to include the name with the URL of the document that contains the map data.

Standard: HTML 3.2
Common: Yes
Sample:

```
<IMG ISMAP SRC="map1.gif"
USEMAP="maps.html#map1">
```

VRML="..."

Specifies the absolute or relative location of a VRML world to embed in a document.

Standard: Internet Explorer 4
Common: No
Sample:

```
<IMG VRML="vr/myroom.vrml">
```

VSPACE="n"

Establishes a margin of white space (in pixels) above and below a graphic image. (See the HSPACE= attribute for how to control the left and right margins of an image.)

Standard: HTML 3.2
Common: Yes
Sample:

```
<IMG SRC="pics/pinetree.jpg"
HSPACE=20 VSPACE=15>
```

WIDTH="n"

Specifies the horizontal dimension of the image (in pixels). If you don't use this attribute, the image appears in the default width. Use this attribute, along with the HEIGHT= attribute, to fit an image within a space. You can fit a large image into a smaller space, and you can spread a smaller image. Some Web designers use WIDTH= and HEIGHT= to spread a single pixel image over a large space to produce the effect of a larger solid-color image.

Standard: HTML 3.2
Common: Yes
Sample:

```
<IMG SRC="images/smiley.jpg" WIDTH=50
HEIGHT=50>
```

Other Attributes

This tag also accepts the LONGDESC, LANG, DIR, onClick, onDblClick, onMouseDown, onMouseUp, onMouseOver, onMouseMove, onMouseOut, onKeyPress, onKeyDown, and onKeyUp attributes. See the Element-Independent Attributes section of this reference for definitions and examples.

<INPUT>

Identifies several input methods for forms. This tag must appear between the opening and closing <FORM> tags.

Standard:	HTML 2
Common:	Yes
Paired:	No
Sample:	

```
<FORM ACTION="/cgi-bin/order/"
METHOD=POST>=
<INPUT NAME="qty" TYPE="TEXT" SIZE=5>
<INPUT TYPE="submit" VALUE="Order">
</FORM>
```

Attribute Information

ACCEPT="..."

Specifies a list of acceptable MIME types for submitted files.

Standard:	HTML 4
Common:	No
Sample:	

```
<INPUT TYPE=FILE ACCEPT="image/gif">
Please submit a GIF image.
```

ALIGN={LEFT, CENTER, RIGHT, JUSTIFY}

Lines up a graphical submit button (TYPE=IMAGE). The behavior of this tag is identical to that of the ALIGN= attribute of the <IMG> tag.

Standard:	HTML 3.2; deprecated in HTML 4 in favor of style sheets
Common:	Yes
Sample:	

```
<INPUT TYPE=IMAGE SRC="picture.gif"
ALIGN=RIGHT>
```

CHECKED

Use with TYPE=RADIO or TYPE=CHECKBOX to set the default state of those input methods to True.

Standard:	HTML 2
Common:	Yes
Sample:	

```
<INPUT TYPE=CHECKBOX CHECKED
NAME="foo" VALUE="1"><BR>

2 <INPUT TYPE=CHECKBOX NAME="foo"
VALUE="2"><BR>
```

CLASS="..."

Indicates which style class applies to the <INPUT> element.

Standard:	HTML 4
Common:	No
Sample:	

```
<INPUT CLASS="casual" TYPE=TEXT
NAME="age">
```

DATAFLD="..."

Selects a column from previously identified tabular data.

Standard:	Internet Explorer 4
Common:	No
Sample:	

```
<DIV DATASRC="#data_table">

<INPUT TYPE=TEXT NAME="color"
DATAFLD="colorvals">
```

DATASRC="..."

Specifies the location of tabular data to be bound.

Standard:	Internet Explorer 4
Common:	No
Sample:	

```
<INPUT TYPE=TEXT
DATASRC="#data_table"
DATAFLD="dataval1">
```

DISABLED="..."

Disables an instance of the input method so that data cannot be accepted or submitted.

Standard:	HTML 4
Common:	No
Sample:	

```
<INPUT TYPE=PASSWORD NAME="Pass"
DISABLED>
```

ID="*n*"

Assigns a unique ID selector to an instance of the <INPUT> tag. When you then assign a style to that ID selector, it affects only that one instance of the <INPUT> tag.

Standard:	HTML 4
Common:	No
Sample:	

```
Age:
<INPUT TYPE=TEXT NAME="age" ID="123">
```

MAXLENGTH="*n*"

Indicates the number of characters you can enter into a text input field and is only useful to input methods of type TEXT or PASSWORD. Contrary to the SIZE= attribute, MAXLENGTH= does not affect the size of the input field shown on the screen.

Standard:	HTML 2
Common:	Yes

Sample:

```
Phone: <INPUT TYPE=TEXT NAME="phone"
MAXLENGTH=11>
```

NAME="..."

Gives a name to the value you pass to the form processor. For example, if you collect a person's last name with an input method of type TEXT, you assign the NAME= attribute something like "lastname." This establishes a *name-value pair* for the form processor.

Standard:	HTML 2
Common:	Yes

Sample:

```
Enter your phone number: <INPUT
TYPE="text" NAME="phone" SIZE=10>
```

NOTAB

Removes the input element from the tab order.

Standard:	Internet Explorer
Common:	No

Sample:

```
Hair color:
<INPUT TYPE=TEXT NAME="hcolor" NOTAB>
```

READONLY

Indicates that changes to the input method data cannot occur.

Standard:	HTML 4
Common:	No

Sample:

```
<INPUT TYPE=TEXT NAME="desc"
VALUE="1/4 inch fLANGe assy"
READONLY>
```

SIZE="n"

Specifies the width of the input method (in characters). This applies only to input methods of type TEXT or PASSWORD. HTML 4 specifies size measurements in pixels for all other input methods, but pixel size specification is little supported.

Standard:	HTML 2

Common:	Yes

Sample:

```
Your Age: <INPUT TYPE="text"
NAME="Age" SIZE=5><BR>
```

SRC="*URL*"

Implements a graphic image for a submit button. For this to work, indicate TYPE=IMAGE.

Standard:	HTML 3.2
Common:	Yes

Sample:

```
<INPUT TYPE=IMAGE SRC="/images/push-
button.gif">
```

STYLE="..."

Specifies style sheet commands that apply to the input element.

Standard:	HTML 4
Common:	No

Sample:

```
<INPUT TYPE=RADIO NAME="food"
VALUE="1" STYLE="background: red">
```

TABINDEX="*n*"

Specifies where the input method appears in the tab order. For example, TABINDEX=3 places the cursor at the input element after the visitor presses the Tab key three times.

Standard:	Internet Explorer
Common:	No

Sample:

```
Credit card number:
<INPUT TYPE=TEXT
NAME="ccard"TABINDEX=5>
```

TITLE="..."

Specifies text assigned to the tag. You might use this attribute for context-sensitive help within the document. Browsers may use this to show tool tips over the input method.

Standard:	HTML 4
Common:	No

Sample:

```
<INPUT TYPE=RADIO NAME="cc"
VALUE="visa" TITLE="Visa">
```

TYPE="..."

Indicates the kind of input method to use. Valid values are TEXT, PASSWORD, RADIO,

CHECKBOX, SUBMIT, RESET, IMAGE, FILE, HIDDEN, and BUTTON.

TEXT produces a simple one-line text input field that is useful for obtaining simple data such as a person's name, a person's age, a dollar amount, and so on. To collect multiple lines of text, use the <TEXTAREA> tag.

PASSWORD gives the visitor a simple one-line text input field similar to the TEXT type. When visitors enter data into the field, however, they do not see what they type.

TYPE=RADIO produces a small radio button that can be turned on and off. Use radio buttons when you want a visitor to select only one of several items. For multiple-value selections, see the CHECKBOX type or the <SELECT> tag.

SUBMIT produces a button that, when selected, submits all the name-value pairs to the form processor.

RESET sets all the input methods to their empty or default settings.

TYPE=IMAGE replaces the submit button with an image. The behavior of this value is identical to that of the submit button, except that the x,y coordinates of the mouse position over the image when selected are also sent to the form processor.

BUTTON creates a button with no specific behavior that can interact with scripts.

> **Standard:** HTML 2
> **Common:** Yes
> **Sample:**

```
<FORM METHOD=POST ACTION="/cgi-
bin/thingie">
Name: <INPUT TYPE=TEXT
NAME="name"><BR>
Password: <INPUT TYPE=PASSWORD
NAME="pass"><BR>
Ice Cream:  Vanilla<INPUT TYPE=RADIO
VALUE="1" CHECKED NAME="ice_cream">
Chocolate<INPUT TYPE=RADIO VALUE="2"
NAME="ice_cream"><br>
<INPUT TYPE=SUBMIT VALUE="Send
Data..."> 
</FORM>
```

USEMAP="*URL*"
Indicates the relative or absolute location of a client-side imagemap to use with the form.

> **Standard:** HTML 4
> **Common:** No
> **Sample:**

```
<INPUT SRC="mapimage.gif"
USEMAP="maps.html#map1">
```

VALUE="..."
Sets the default input value method. Required when <INPUT> is set to TYPE=RADIO or CHECKBOX.

> **Standard:** HTML 2
> **Common:** Yes
> **Sample:**

```
<INPUT TYPE=HIDDEN NAME="id"
VALUE="123">
```

Other Attributes
This tag also accepts the ALT, ISMAP, ACCESSKEY, LANG, DIR, onFocus, onBlur, onSelect, onChange, onClick, onDblClick, onMouseDown, onMouseUp, onMouseOver, onMouseMove, onMouseOut, onKeyPress, onKeyDown, and onKeyUp attributes. See the Element-Independent Attributes section of this reference for definitions and examples.

<INS>

Indicates text to be inserted in the document. May be either block-level or inline, as necessary.

> **Standard:** HTML 4
> **Common:** No
> **Paired:** Yes
> **Sample:**

```
<P>HTTP stands for Hypertext
<INS>Transfer</INS>Protocol</P>
```

Attribute Information

CITE="*URL*"
Indicates address of reference (definitive source, for example) for insertion.

> **Standard:** HTML 4
> **Common:** No
> **Sample:**

```
<INS CITE="http://www.w3.org/">
HTML 2 was used for 2 years.
</INS>
```

CLASS="..."

Indicates which style class applies to the <INS> element.

Standard: HTML 4
Common: No
Sample:

```
<INS CLASS="joeadd">POP stands for
Post Office Protocol.</INS>
```

DATETIME="..."

Indicates the date and time in precisely this format: YYYY-MM-DDThh:mm:ssTZD. For example, 2000-07-14T08:30:00-07:00 indicates July 14, 2000, at 8:30 AM, in U.S. Mountain Time (7 hours from Greenwich time). This time could also be presented as 2000-07-14T08:30:00Z.

Standard: HTML 4
Common: No
Sample:

```
<INS DATETIME="2000-07-
14T08:30:00Z">POP stands for Post
Office Protocol.</INS>
```

ID="..."

Assigns a unique ID selector to an instance of the <INS> tag. When you then assign a style to that ID selector, it affects only that one instance of the <INS> tag.

Standard: HTML 4
Common: No
Sample:

```
<INS ID="123">WWW stands for World
Wide Web</INS>
```

STYLE="..."

Specifies style sheet commands that apply to the inserted text.

Standard: HTML 4
Common: No
Sample:

```
<INS STYLE="background: blue; color:
white">ESP stands for extra-sensory
perception.</INS>
```

TITLE="..."

Specifies text assigned to the tag. You might use this attribute for context-sensitive help within the document. Browsers may use this to show tool tips over the inserted text.

Standard: HTML 4
Common: No
Sample:

```
<INS TITLE="Definition">More deleted
text.</INS>
```

Other Attributes

This tag also accepts the LANG, DIR, onClick, onDblClick, onMouseDown, onMouseUp, onMouseOver, onMouseMove, onMouseOut, onKeyPress, onKeyDown, and onKeyUp attributes. See the Element-Independent Attributes section of this reference for definitions and examples.

<ISINDEX>

Inserts an input field into the document so that visitors can enter search queries. The queries then go to a CGI application indicated by the ACTION= attribute.

Standard: HTML 2; deprecated in HTML 4 in favor of <FORM>
Common: Yes
Paired: No
Sample:

```
<ISINDEX PROMPT="Keyword Search"
ACTION="/cgi-bin/search.cgi">
```

Attribute Information

ACTION="*URL*"

Specifies the URL of the application that processes the search query. If you don't include ACTION=, the query goes to a URL formed from the document base (see the <BASE> tag).

Standard: HTML 2
Common: Yes
Sample:

```
<ISINDEX ACTION="/cgi-bin/index-
search">
```

PROMPT="..."

Changes the input prompt for keyword index searches. If you don't specify PROMPT=, the browser displays a default prompt.

Standard: HTML 3.2
Common: Yes

Sample:

```
<ISINDEX PROMPT="Search for
something.">
```

Other Attributes

This tag also accepts the ID, CLASS, LANG, DIR, TITLE, and STYLE attributes. See the Element-Independent Attributes section and other tag listings in this reference for definitions and examples.

K

`<KBD>`

Specifies keyboard input within a document.

Standard:	HTML 2
Common:	Yes
Paired:	Yes
Sample:	

```
Press <KBD>CTRL+S</KBD> to save your
document.
```

Attribute Information

CLASS="..."

Indicates which style class applies to the `<KBD>` element.

Standard:	HTML 4
Common:	No
Sample:	

```
Now press the <KBD
CLASS="casual">F4</KBD> key!
```

ID="..."

Assigns a unique ID selector to an instance of the `<KBD>` tag. When you then assign a style to that ID selector, it affects only that one instance of the `<KBD>` tag.

Standard:	HTML 4
Common:	No
Sample:	

```
Press <KBD ID="123">F1</KBD> for
help.
```

STYLE="..."

Specifies style sheet commands that apply to the text within the `<KBD>` tags.

Standard:	HTML 4

Common: No

Sample:

```
<KBD STYLE="background:
red">F10</KBD>
```

TITLE="..."

Specifies text assigned to the tag. You might use this attribute for context-sensitive help within the document. Browsers may use this to show tool tips over the keyboard text.

Standard:	HTML 4
Common:	No
Sample:	

```
Now press the <KBD TITLE=
"Keyboard stuff">F4</KBD> key.
```

Other Attributes

This tag also accepts the LANG, DIR, onClick, onDblClick, onMouseDown, onMouseUp, onMouseOver, onMouseMove, onMouseOut, onKeyPress, onKeyDown, and onKeyUp attributes. See the Element-Independent Attributes section of this reference for definitions and examples.

L

`<LABEL>`

Provides identifying text for a form widget.

Standard:	HTML 4
Common:	No
Paired:	Yes
Sample:	

```
<LABEL FOR="idname">First
Name</LABEL>
<INPUT TYPE="TEXT" ID="idname">
```

Attribute Information

ACCESSKEY="..."

Assigns a keystroke to the element.

Standard:	HTML 4
Common:	No
Sample:	

```
<LABEL FOR="idname" ACCESSKEY=H>
```

CLASS="..."

Indicates which style class applies to the
<LABEL> element.

> **Standard:** HTML 4
> **Common:** No
> **Sample:**

```
<LABEL FOR="idname"
CLASS="short">First Name</LABEL>
<INPUT TYPE="TEXT" ID="idname">
```

FOR="..."

Specifies the ID of the widget associated with
the label.

> **Standard:** HTML 4
> **Common:** No
> **Sample:**

```
<LABEL FOR="idname">First
Name</LABEL>
<INPUT TYPE="TEXT" ID="idname">
```

ID="*n*"

Assigns a unique ID selector to an instance of
the <INPUT> tag. When you then assign a
style to that ID selector, it affects only that
one instance of the <INPUT> tag.

> **Standard:** HTML 4
> **Common:** No
> **Sample:**

```
<LABEL FOR="idname" ID="234">First
Name</LABEL>
<INPUT TYPE="TEXT" ID="idname">
```

STYLE="..."

Specifies style sheet commands that apply to
the input element.

> **Standard:** HTML 4
> **Common:** No
> **Sample:**

```
<LABEL FOR="idname"
STYLE="background : red">
First Name</LABEL>
<INPUT TYPE="TEXT" ID="idname">
```

TITLE="..."

Specifies text assigned to the tag. You might
use this attribute for context-sensitive help
within the document. Browsers may use this
to show tool tips over the input method.

> **Standard:** HTML 4
> **Common:** No

> **Sample:**

```
<INPUT TYPE=RADIO NAME="cc"
VALUE="visa" TITLE="Visa">
```

Other Attributes

This tag also accepts the LANG, DIR, onfocus,
onblur, onselect, onchange, onClick,
onDblClick, onMouseDown, onMouseUp,
onMouseOver, onMouseMove, onMouseOut,
onKeyPress, onKeyDown, and onKeyUp attributes. See the Element-Independent Attributes
section of this reference for definitions and
examples.

<LAYER>

Defines a layer within a document, which you
can than manipulate with JavaScript. Specify
the layer's contents by placing HTML
between the <LAYER> tags or by using the
SRC= attribute.

> **Standard:** Netscape Navigator 4
> **Common:** No
> **Paired:** Yes
> **Sample:**

```
<LAYER SRC="top.html" HEIGHT=100
WIDTH=100 Z-INDEX=4 NAME="top"
VISIBILITY=SHOW>
</LAYER>
```

Attribute Information

ABOVE="..."

Specifies the name of a layer above which the
current layer should appear.

> **Standard:** Netscape Navigator 4
> **Common:** No
> **Sample:**

```
<LAYER SRC="grass.gif" Z-INDEX=1
NAME="Grass" VISIBILITY=SHOW>
<LAYER SRC="dog.gif"
ABOVE="Grass"NAME="Dog">
```

BACKGROUND="*URL*"

Specifies the relative or absolute location of
an image file that the browser tiles as the
background of the layer.

> **Standard:** Netscape Navigator 4
> **Common:** No

Sample:
```
<LAYER Z-INDEX=5 NAME="info"
BACKGROUND="goo.gif">
<H1>Hi there</H1></LAYER>
```

BELOW="..."

Specifies the name of a layer below which the current layer should appear.

Standard: Netscape Navigator 4
Common: No
Sample:
```
<LAYER BELOW="road.jpg" NAME="Road"
UNDER="Car">
</LAYER>
```

BGCOLOR="#*RRGGBB*" or "..."

Specifies the background color of the layer. Use either the hexadecimal RGB values or the color name.

Standard: Netscape Navigator 4
Common: No
Sample:
```
<LAYER BGCOLOR=#FF0011><DIV
ALIGN=CENTER>
   <H1><BLINK>EAT AT
   JOES!</BLINK></H1>
</DIV>
</LAYER>
```

CLIP="*x1, y1, x2, y2*"

Indicates the dimensions of a clipping rectangle that specifies which areas of the layer are visible. Areas outside this rectangle become transparent.

You can give the x and y coordinates in pixels or as percentages to indicate relative portions of the layer. You can omit *x1* and *y1* if you want to clip from the top-left corner of the layer.

Standard: Netscape Navigator 4
Common: No
Sample:
```
<LAYER SRC="hawk.jpg" CLIP="20%,20%">
</LAYER>
```

HEIGHT="*n*"

Specifies the vertical dimension of the layer (in pixels or as a percentage of the browser window height).

Standard: Netscape Navigator 4
Common: No

Sample:
```
<LAYER SRC="frame.gif"
ABOVE="bg"NAME="frame"
WIDTH=200 HEIGHT=200>
```

LEFT="*n*"

Specifies the layer's horizontal position (in pixels) relative to the left edge of the parent layer. Use the TOP= attribute for vertical positioning.

Standard: Netscape Navigator 4
Common: No
Sample:
```
<LAYER LEFT=100 TOP=150>This layer is
at {100,150}</LAYER>
```

NAME="..."

Gives the layer a name by which other layer definitions and JavaScript code can reference it.

Standard: Netscape Navigator 4
Common: No
Sample:
```
<LAYER SRC="car.gif"
NAME="CarPic"ABOVE="Road">
</LAYER>
```

SRC="*URL*"

Specifies the relative or absolute location of the file containing the contents of the layer.

Standard: Netscape Navigator 4
Common: No
Sample:
```
<LAYER SRC="ocean.jpg"></LAYER>
```

TOP="*n*"

Specifies the layer's vertical position (in pixels) relative to the top edge of the parent layer. Use the LEFT= attribute for horizontal positioning.

Standard: Netscape Navigator 4
Common: No
Sample:
```
<LAYER LEFT=100 TOP=150>This layer is
at {100,150}</LAYER>
```

VISIBILITY={SHOW, HIDE, INHERIT}

Indicates whether the layer is initially visible. VISIBILITY=SHOW indicates the layer is initially visible. VISIBILITY=HIDE indicates the layer is not initially visible.

VISIBILITY=INHERIT indicates the layer has the same initial visibility attribute as its parent layer.

Standard: Netscape Navigator 4
Common: No
Sample:

```
<LAYER SRC="grass.gif" Z-INDEX=1
NAME="Grass" VISIBILITY=SHOW>
```

WIDTH="*n*"

Specifies the horizontal dimension of the layer (in pixels or as a percentage of the browser window width).

Standard: Netscape Navigator 4
Common: No
Sample:

```
<LAYER SRC="frame.gif"
ABOVE="bg"NAME="frame"
WIDTH=200 HEIGHT=200>
```

Z-INDEX="*n*"

Specifies where the layer appears in the stack of layers. Higher values indicate a position closer to the top of the stack.

Standard: Netscape Navigator 4
Common: No
Sample:

```
<LAYER Z-INDEX=0 NAME="Bottom">
You may never see this text if other
layers are above it.
</LAYER>
```

<LEGEND>

Specifies a description for a fieldset. Use inside <FIELDSET> tags.

Standard: HTML 4
Common: No
Paired: Yes
Sample:

```
<FORM><FIELDSET>
 <LEGEND VALIGN=TOP
 ALIGN=CENTER>
 Test Grades For COOKING 101
 </LEGEND>...
</FORM>
```

Attribute Information

ALIGN={TOP, BOTTOM, LEFT, RIGHT}

Indicates whether the legend appears at the top, bottom, left, or right of the fieldset.

Standard: HTML 4
Common: No
Sample:

```
<LEGEND ALIGN=TOP>
Seattle Staff DIRectory
</LEGEND>
```

CLASS="..."

Indicates which style class applies to the <LEGEND> element.

Standard: HTML 4
Common: No
Sample:

```
<LEGEND CLASS="casual">Hydrogen vs.
Oxygen</LEGEND>
```

ID="..."

Assigns a unique ID selector to an instance of the <LEGEND> tag. When you then assign a style to that ID selector, it affects only that one instance of the <LEGEND> tag.

Standard: HTML 4
Common: No
Sample:

```
<LEGEND ID="123">Great
Painters</LEGEND>
```

STYLE="..."

Specifies style sheet commands that apply to the contents of the
<LEGEND> tags.

Standard: HTML 4
Common: No
Sample:

```
<LEGEND STYLE="background: red">
```

TITLE="..."

Specifies text assigned to the tag. You might use this attribute for context-sensitive help within the document. Browsers may use this to show tool tips over the legend.

Standard: HTML 4
Common: Yes
Sample:

```
<LEGEND TITLE="of Sleepy Hollow">
```

Other Attributes

This tag also accepts the LANG, DIR, onClick, onDblClick, onMouseDown, onMouseUp, onMouseOver, onMouseMove, onMouseOut, onKeyPress, onKeyDown, and onKeyUp attributes. See the Element-Independent Attributes section of this reference for definitions and examples.

\<LI\>

Places items into ordered (see the \<OL\> tag), menu (see the \<MENU\> tag), directory (see the \<DIR\> tag), and unordered (see the \<UL\> tag) lists.

Standard:	HTML 2
Common:	Yes
Paired:	Yes, optional
Sample:	

```
My favorite foods are:<UL>
  <LI>Pepperoni Pizza
  <LI>Lasagna
  <LI>Taco Salad
  <LI>Bananas
</UL>
```

Attribute Information

CLASS="..."

Indicates which style class applies to the \<LI\> element.

Standard:	HTML 4
Common:	No
Sample:	

```
<LI CLASS="casual">Dogs
```

ID="*n*"

Assigns a unique ID selector to an instance of the \<LI\> tag. When you then assign a style to that ID selector, it affects only that one instance of the \<LI\> tag.

Standard:	HTML 4
Common:	No
Sample:	

```
<LI ID="123">Bees</LI>
```

STYLE="..."

Specifies style sheet commands that apply to the list item.

Standard:	HTML 4
Common:	No

Sample:

```
<LI STYLE="background: red">
```

TITLE="..."

Specifies text assigned to the tag. You might use this attribute for context-sensitive help within the document. Browsers may use this to show tool tips over the list item.

Standard:	HTML 4
Common:	No
Sample:	

```
<LI TITLE="List Item">Thingie
```

TYPE="..."

Specifies the bullets for each unordered list item (see the \<UL\> tag) or the numbering for each ordered list item (see the \<OL\> tag). If you omit the TYPE= attribute, the browser chooses a default type. Valid TYPE values for unordered lists are DISC, SQUARE, and CIRCLE. Valid TYPE values for ordered lists are 1 for Arabic numbers, a for lowercase letters, A for uppercase letters, i for lowercase Roman numerals, and I for uppercase Roman numerals.

Standard:	HTML 3.2
Common:	Yes
Sample:	

```
<UL>
 <LI TYPE=SQUARE>Food
 <OL>
   <LI TYPE=1>Spaghetti
   <LI TYPE=1>Tossed Salad
 </OL>
</UL>
```

VALUE="..."

Sets a number in an ordered list. Use this attribute to continue a list after interrupting it with something else in your document. You can also set a number in an ordered list with the START= attribute of the \<OL\> tag.

Because unordered lists do not increment, the VALUE= attribute is meaningless when used with them.

Standard:	HTML 3.2
Common:	Yes
Sample:	

```
<OL TYPE=1>
  <LI VALUE=5>Watch
  <LI>Compass
</OL>
```

Other Attributes

This tag also accepts the LANG, DIR, onClick, onDblClick, onMouseDown, onMouseUp, onMouseOver, onMouseMove, onMouseOut, onKeyPress, onKeyDown, and onKeyUp attributes. See the Element-Independent Attributes section of this reference for definitions and examples.

<LINK>

Establishes relationships between the current document and other documents. Use this tag within the <HEAD> section. For example, if you access the current document by choosing a hyperlink from the site's home page, you can establish a relationship between the current document and the site's home page (see the REL= attribute). At this time, however, most browsers don't use most of these relationships. You can place several <LINK> tags within the <HEAD> section of your document to define multiple relationships. With newer implementations of HTML, you can also use the <LINK> tag to establish information about cascading style sheets. Some other relationships that the <LINK> tag defines include the following:

CONTENTS: A table of contents.

INDEX: An index.

GLOSSARY: A glossary of terms.

COPYRIGHT: A copyright notice.

NEXT: The next document in a series (use with REL=).

PREVIOUS: The previous document in a series (use with REV=).

START: The first document in a series.

HELP: A document offering help or more information.

BOOKMARK: A bookmark links to a important entry point within a longer document.

STYLESHEET: An external style sheet.

ALTERNATE: Different versions of the same document. When used with LANG, ALTERNATE implies a translated document; when used with MEDIA, it implies a version for a different medium.

Standard: HTML 2
Common: Yes

Paired: No
Sample:

```
<HEAD>
<TITLE>Prices</TITLE>
<LINK REL=Top HREF="http://www
.raycomm.com/">
<LINK REL=Search HREF="http://www
.raycomm.com/search.html">
</HEAD>
```

Attribute Information

HREF="*URL*"

Indicates the relative or absolute location of the resource you are establishing a relationship to/from.

Standard: HTML 2
Common: Yes
Sample:

```
<LINK REL=Prev HREF="page1.html">
```

MEDIA="..."

Specifies the destination medium for style information. It may be a single type or a comma-separated list. Media types include the following:

SCREEN: For online viewing (default setting)

PRINT: For traditional printed material and for documents on-screen viewed in print preview mode

PROJECTION: For projectors

BRAILLE: For Braille tactile feedback devices

SPEECH: For a speech synthesizer

ALL: Applies to all devices

Standard: HTML 4
Common: No
Sample:

```
<LINK MEDIA=SCREEN REL="STYLESHEET"
HREF="/global.css">
```

NAME="..."

Specifies a name by which bookmarks, scripts, and applets can reference the relationship.

Standard: Internet Explorer 4
Common: No

Sample:
```
<LINK REL="Search"
HREF="/search.html"NAME="Search">
```

REL="..."

Defines the relationship you are establishing between the current document and another resource. The HTML 3.2 specification includes several standard values for the REL= attribute. REL=Top defines the site home page or the top of the site hierarchy. REL=Contents usually defines the location of a resource that lists the contents of the site. REL=Index provides a link to an index of the site. REL=Glossary indicates the location of a glossary resource. REL=Copyright indicates the location of a copyright statement. REL=Next and REL=Previous establish relationships between documents or resources in a series. REL=Help indicates the location of a help resource. REL=Search specifies the location of a search resource. REL=style sheet specifies information about style sheets.

> **Standard:** HTML 2
> **Common:** Yes
> **Sample:**

```
<LINK REL=Help HREF="/Help/
index.html">
<LINK REL=style sheet
HREF="sitehead.css">
</HEAD>
```

REV="..."

Establishes reverse relationships between the current document and other resources. One common use is REV="made", after which you can set the HREF= attribute to a mailto: URL to contact the author of the document.

> **Standard:** HTML 2
> **Common:** Yes
> **Sample:**

```
<LINK REV=made HREF="mailto:
jdoe@somewhere.com">
```

TARGET="..."

Specifies the name of a frame in which the referenced link appears.

> **Standard:** Internet Explorer 4
> **Common:** No

Sample:
```
<LINK TARGET="_blank" REL="Home"
HREF="http://www.mememe.com/">
```

TITLE="..."

Specifies text assigned to the tag that can be used for context-sensitive help within the document. Browsers may use this to show tool tips.

> **Standard:** HTML 4
> **Common:** Yes
> **Sample:**

```
<LINK REL=Top HREF="/index.html"
TITLE="Home Page">
```

TYPE="..."

Specifies the MIME type of a style sheet to import with the <LINK> tag.

> **Standard:** HTML 4
> **Common:** No
> **Sample:**

```
<LINK REL=STYLESHEET TYPE="text/
css"HREF="/style/main.css">
```

Other Attributes

This tag also accepts the CHARSET, HREFLANG, ID, CLASS, STYLE, LANG, DIR, onFocus, onBlur, onChange, onSelect, onClick, onDblClick, onMouseDown, onMouseUp, onMouseOver, onMouseMove, onMouseOut, onKeyPress, onKeyDown, and onKeyUp attributes. See the Element-Independent Attributes section of this reference for definitions and examples.

<LISTING>

Specifies preformatted text to include within a document. Unlike the <PRE> tags, the browser does not interpret HTML tags within the <LISTING> tags. HTML 3.2 declared this tag obsolete, so use <PRE> instead.

> **Standard:** Obsolete
> **Common:** Yes
> **Paired:** Yes

Sample:

The output from these reports is shown below.

```
<LISTING>
Company      Q1     Q2      Q3     Q4
---------    ----   -----   ----   ----
Widget Inc.  4.5m   4.6m    6.2m   4.5m
Acme Widget  5.9m   10.2m   7.3m   6.6m
West Widget  2.2m   1.3m    3.1m   6.1m
</LISTING>
```

M

<MAP>

Specifies a container for client-side imagemap data. Inside the <MAP> container, you place instances of the <AREA> tag.

Standard:	HTML 3.2
Common:	Yes
Paired:	Yes
Sample:	

```
<MAP NAME="mainmap"> <AREA NOHREF
ALT="Home" SHAPE=RECT
COORDS="0,0,100,100">
  <AREA HREF="yellow.html"
  ALT="Yellow" SHAPE=RECT
  COORDS="100,0,200,100">

  <AREA HREF="blue.html"
  ALT="Blue" SHAPE=RECT
  COORDS="0,100,100,200">
  <AREA HREF="red.html" ALT="Red"
  SHAPE=RECT
  COORDS="100,100,200,200">
</MAP>
```

Attribute Information

CLASS="..."

Indicates which style class applies to the element.

Standard:	HTML 4
Common:	No
Sample:	

```
<MAP CLASS="casual" NAME="simba">
```

ID="..."

Indicates an identifier to associate with the map. You can also use this to apply styles to the object.

Standard:	HTML 4
Common:	No
Sample:	

```
<MAP ID="123" NAME="simba">
```

NAME="..."

Establishes a name for the map information you can later reference by the USEMAP= attribute of the <IMG> tag.

Standard:	HTML 3.2
Common:	Yes
Sample:	

```
<MAP NAME="housemap">
...
<IMG SRC="house.gif"
USEMAP="#housemap" BORDER=0 ALT="Map
of House">
```

STYLE="..."

Specifies style sheet commands that apply to the contents within the <MAP> tags.

Standard:	HTML 4
Common:	No
Sample:	

```
<MAP STYLE="background: black">
```

TITLE="..."

Specifies text assigned to the tag. You might use this attribute for context-sensitive help within the document. Browsers may use this to show tool tips.

Standard:	HTML 4
Common:	No
Sample:	

```
<MAP TITLE="imagemap spec">
```

Other Attributes

This tag also accepts the LANG, DIR, onClick, onDblClick, onMouseDown, onMouseUp, onMouseOver, onMouseMove, onMouseOut, onKeyPress, onKeyDown, and onKeyUp attributes. See the Element-Independent Attributes section of this reference for definitions and examples.

<MARQUEE>

Displays a scrolling text message within a document. Only Internet Explorer recognizes this tag.

Standard:	Internet Explorer
Common:	No

Paired: Yes
Sample:

```
<MARQUEE DIRECTION=LEFT
BEHAVIOR=SCROLL SCROLLDELAY=250
SCROLLAMOUNT=10>Big sale today on
fuzzy wuzzy widgets!</MARQUEE>
```

Attribute Information

ALIGN={LEFT, CENTER, RIGHT, TOP, BOTTOM}

Specifies the alignment of text outside the marquee.

Standard: Internet Explorer
Common: No
Sample:

```
<MARQUEE WIDTH=200 HEIGHT=50
ALIGN=LEFT DIRECTION=LEFT>
How To Groom Your Dog</MARQUEE>
```

BEHAVIOR={SLIDE, SCROLL, ALTERNATE}

Indicates the type of scrolling. BEHAVIOR=
SCROLL scrolls text from one side of the
marquee, across, and off the opposite side.
BEHAVIOR= SLIDE scrolls text from one side
of the marquee, across, and stops when the
text reaches the opposite side. BEHAVIOR=
ALTERNATE bounces the marquee text from
one side to the other.

Standard: Internet Explorer
Common: No
Sample:

```
<MARQUEE DIRECTION=LEFT
BEHAVIOR=ALTERNATE>GO BEARS! WIN WIN
WIN!</MARQUEE>
```

BGCOLOR="#RRGGBB" or "..."

Specifies the background color of the marquee. Use a hexadecimal RGB color value or a
color name.

Standard: Internet Explorer
Common: No
Sample:

```
<MARQUEE BGCOLOR="red"
DIRECTION=LEFT>Order opera
tickets here!</MARQUEE>
```

DATAFLD="..."

Selects a column from a block of
tabular data.

Standard: Internet Explorer 4
Common: No
Sample:

```
<MARQUEE DATASRC="#data_table"
DATAFLD="nitems">
```

DATAFORMATAS={TEXT, HTML, NONE}

Specifies how items selected from
tabular data format within the document.

Standard: Internet Explorer 4
Common: No
Sample:

```
<MARQUEE DATASRC="#data_table"
DATAFLD="nitems" DATAFORMATAS=HTML>
```

DATASRC="..."

Specifies the location of tabular data to be
bound within the document.

Standard: Internet Explorer 4
Common: No
Sample:

```
<MARQUEE DATASRC="#data_table"
DATAFLD="nitems">
```

DIRECTION={LEFT, RIGHT}

Indicates the direction in which the marquee
text scrolls.

Standard: Internet Explorer
Common: No
Sample:

```
<MARQUEE DIRECTION=LEFT>Order opera
tickets here!</MARQUEE>
```

HEIGHT="n"

Specifies the vertical dimension of the marquee (in pixels).

Standard: Internet Explorer
Common: No
Sample:

```
<MARQUEE WIDTH=300 HEIGHT=50>
GO BEARS!</MARQUEE>
```

HSPACE="n"

Specifies the size of the margins (in pixels) to
the left and right of the marquee.

Standard: Internet Explorer
Common: No
Sample:

```
<MARQUEE DIRECTION=LEFT
HSPACE=25>Check out our detailed
product descriptions!</MARQUEE>
```

ID="..."

Assigns a unique ID selector to an instance of the <MARQUEE> tag. When you then assign a style to that ID selector, it affects only that one instance of the <MARQUEE> tag.

Standard: Internet Explorer 4
Common: No
Sample:

```
<MARQUEE ID="3d4">
```

LOOP={n, INFINITE}

Controls the appearance of the marquee text.

Standard: Internet Explorer
Common: No
Sample:

```
<MARQUEE LOOP=5>December 12 is our
big, all-day sale!</MARQUEE>
```

SCROLLAMOUNT="n"

Indicates how far (in pixels) the marquee text shifts between redraws. Decrease this value for a smoother (but slower) scroll; increase it for a faster (but bumpier) scroll.

Standard: Internet Explorer
Common: No
Sample:

```
<MARQUEE SCROLLAMOUNT=10
SCROLLDELAY=40>Plant a tree for Arbor
Day!
</MARQUEE>
```

SCROLLDELAY="n"

Indicates how often (in milliseconds) the marquee text redraws. Increase this value to slow the scrolling action; decrease it to speed the scrolling action.

Standard: Internet Explorer
Common: No
Sample:

```
<MARQUEE DIRECTION=RIGHT
SCROLLDELAY=30>Eat at
Joe's!</MARQUEE>
```

STYLE="..."

Specifies style sheet commands that apply to the text within the <MARQUEE> tags.

Standard: Internet Explorer 4
Common: No
Sample:

```
<MARQUEE STYLE="background: red">
```

TITLE="..."

Specifies text assigned to the tag. You might use this attribute for context-sensitive help within the document. Browsers may use this to show tool tips over the marquee.

Standard: Internet Explorer 4
Common: No
Sample:

```
<MARQUEE TITLE="Scrolling Marquee">
```

VSPACE="n"

Specifies the size of the margins (in pixels) at the top and bottom of the marquee.

Standard: Internet Explorer
Common: No
Sample:

```
<MARQUEE DIRECTION=LEFT
VSPACE=25>Check out our detailed
product descriptions!</MARQUEE>
```

WIDTH="n"

Specifies the horizontal dimension (in pixels) of the marquee.

Standard: Internet Explorer
Common: No
Sample:

```
<MARQUEE WIDTH=300>

Go Bears!</MARQUEE>
```

<MENU>

Defines a menu list. Use the <LI> tag to indicate list items. Use <UL> instead of this deprecated element.

Standard: HTML 2; deprecated in HTML 4
Common: No
Paired: Yes
Sample:

```
Now you can:<MENU>
  <LI>Eat the sandwich
```

```
<LI>Place the sandwich in the
fridge
<LI>Feed the sandwich to the
dog
</MENU>
```

Attribute Information

CLASS="..."

Indicates which style class applies to the
<MENU> element.

Standard:	HTML 4
Common:	No
Sample:	

```
<MENU CLASS="casual">
  <LI>Information
  <LI>Members
  <LI>Guests
</MENU>
```

COMPACT

Specifies that the menu list appear in a space-
saving form.

Standard:	HTML 2; deprecated in HTML 4
Common:	Yes
Sample:	

```
<H2>Drinks Available</H2>
<MENU COMPACT>
  <LI>Cola</LI>
  <LI>Fruit Drink</LI>
  <LI>Orange Juice</LI>
  <LI>Water</LI>
</MENU>
```

ID="..."

Assigns a unique ID selector to an instance of
the <MENU> tag. When you then assign a style
to that ID selector, it affects only that one
instance of the <MENU> tag.

Standard:	HTML 4
Common:	No
Sample:	

```
You'll need the following:
<MENU ID="123">
  <LI>Extra socks
  <LI>Snack crackers
  <LI>Towel
</MENU>
```

STYLE="..."

Specifies style sheet commands that apply to
the menu list.

Standard:	HTML 4
Common:	Yes
Sample:	

```
<MENU STYLE="background: black;
color: white">
```

TITLE="..."

Specifies text assigned to the tag. You might
use this attribute for context-sensitive help
within the document. Browsers may use this
to show tool tips over the menu list.

Standard:	HTML 4
Common:	No
Sample:	

```
<MENU TITLE="Menu List">
```

Other Attributes

This tag also accepts the LANG, DIR, onClick,
onDblClick, onMouseDown, onMouseUp,
onMouseOver, onMouseMove, onMouseOut,
onKeyPress, onKeyDown, and onKeyUp attributes. See the Element-Independent Attributes
section of this reference for definitions and
examples.

<META>

Specifies information about the document to
browsers, applications, and search engines.
Place the <META> tag within the document
head. For example, you can use the <META>
tag to instruct the browser to load a new document after 10 seconds (client-pull), or you
can specify keywords for search engines to
associate with your document.

Standard:	HTML 2
Common:	Yes
Paired:	No
Sample:	

```
<HEAD>
<TITLE>Igneous Rocks In North
America</TITLE>
<META HTTP-EQUIV="Keywords"
CONTENT="Geology, Igneous, Volcanos">
</HEAD>
```

Attribute Information

CONTENT="..."

Assigns values to the HTTP header field.
When using the REFRESH HTTP header,

assign a number along with a URL to the CONTENT= attribute; the browser then loads the specified URL after the specified number of seconds.

Standard: HTML 2
Common: Yes
Sample:

```
<META HTTP-EQUIV="Refresh"
CONTENT="2; URL=nextpage.html">
```

HTTP-EQUIV="..."

Indicates the HTTP header value you want to define, such as Refresh, Expires, or Content-LANGUAGE. Other header values are listed in RFC2068.

Standard: HTML 2
Common: Yes
Sample:

```
<META HTTP-EQUIV="Expires"
CONTENT="Tue, 04 Aug 2000 22:39:22
GMT">
```

NAME="..."

Specifies the name of the association you are defining, such as Keywords or Description.

Standard: HTML 2
Common: Yes
Sample:

```
<META NAME="Keywords"
CONTENT="travel,automobile">
<META NAME="Description"
CONTENT="The Nash Metro moves fast
and goes beep beep.">
```

Other Attributes

This tag also accepts the SCHEME, LANG, and DIR attributes. See the Element-Independent Attributes section of this reference for definitions and examples.

<MULTICOL>

Formats text into newspaper-style columns.

Standard: Netscape Navigator 4
Common: No
Paired: Yes
Sample:

```
<MULTICOL COLS=2 GUTTER=10>
...
</MULTICOL>
```

Attribute Information

COLS="n"

Indicates the number of columns.

Standard: Netscape Navigator 4
Common: No
Sample:

```
<MULTICOL COLS=4>
```

GUTTER="n"

Indicates the width of the space (in pixels) between multiple columns.

Standard: Netscape Navigator 4
Common: No
Sample:

```
<MULTICOL COLS=3 GUTTER=15>
```

WIDTH="n"

Indicates the horizontal dimension (in pixels or as a percentage of the total width available) of each column.

Standard: Netscape Navigator 4
Common: No
Sample:

```
<MULTICOL COLS=2 WIDTH="30%">
```

N

<NOBR>

Disables line-wrapping for a section of text. To force a word break within a <NOBR> clause, use the <WBR> tag.

Standard: Netscape Navigator
Common: Yes
Paired: Yes
Sample:

```
<NOBR>This entire line of text will
remain on one single line in the
browser window until the closing tag
appears. That doesn't happen until
right now.</NOBR>
```

Attribute Information

CLASS="..."

Indicates which style class applies to the element.

Standard: Netscape Navigator

Common: No

Sample:

```
<NOBR CLASS="casual">
```

ID="..."

Assigns a unique ID selector to an instance of the <NOBR> tag. When you then assign a style to that ID selector, it affects only that one instance of the <NOBR> tag.

Standard: Netscape Navigator

Common: No

Sample:

```
You'll need the following:
<NOBR ID="123">
```

STYLE="..."

Specifies style sheet commands that apply to the nonbreaking text.

Standard: Netscape Navigator

Common: Yes

Sample:

```
<NOBR STYLE="background: black">
```

<NOFRAMES>

Provides HTML content for browsers that do not support frames or are configured not to present frames. You can include a <BODY> tag within the <NOFRAMES> section to provide additional formatting and style sheet features.

Standard: HTML 4

Common: Yes

Paired: Yes

Sample:

```
<FRAMESET COLS="*,70">
  <FRAME SRC="frames/body.html"
  NAME="body">
  <FRAME SRC="frames/side.html"
  NAME="side">
</FRAMESET>
<NOFRAMES>
  <p>Your browser doesn't support
  frames. Please follow the links
  below for the rest of the story.
  <p><a href="Prices.html">
  Prices</a> | <a href="About.
  html">About Us</a> | <a href
  ="Contact.html">Contact Us</a>
</NOFRAMES>
```

Attribute Information

TITLE="..."

Specifies text assigned to the tag. You might use this attribute for context-sensitive help within the document. Browsers may use this to show tool tips.

Standard: HTML 4

Common: No

Sample:

```
<NOFRAMES TITLE="HTML for nonframed
browsers">
```

Other Attributes

This tag also accepts ID, CLASS, STYLE, LANG, DIR, onClick, onDblClick, onMouseDown, onMouseUp, onMouseOver, onMouseMove, onMouseOut, onKeyPress, onKeyDown, and onKeyUp attributes. See the Element-Independent Attributes section and other tag listings in this reference for definitions and examples.

<NOSCRIPT>

Provides HTML content for browsers that do not support scripts. Use the <NOSCRIPT> tags inside a script definition.

Standard: HTML 4

Common: No

Paired: Yes

Sample:

```
<NOSCRIPT>
Because you can see this, you can
tell that your browser will not run
(or is set not to run) scripts.
</NOSCRIPT>
```

Other Attributes

This tag also accepts ID, CLASS, STYLE, TITLE, LANG, DIR, onClick, onDblClick, onMouseDown, onMouseUp, onMouseOver, onMouseMove, onMouseOut, onKeyPress, onKeyDown, and onKeyUp attributes. See the Element-Independent Attributes section and other tag listings in this reference for definitions and examples.

O

<OBJECT>

Embeds a software object into a document. The object can be an ActiveX object, a Quick-Time movie, or any other objects or data that a browser supports.

Use the <PARAM> tag to supply parameters to the embedded object. You can place messages and other tags between the <OBJECT> tags for browsers that do not support embedded objects.

Standard:	HTML 4
Common:	No
Paired:	Yes
Sample:	

```
<OBJECT CLASSID="/thingie.py">
<PARAM NAME="thing" VALUE=1>
Sorry. Your browser does not
support embedded objects. If it
supported these objects you
would not see this message.
</OBJECT>
```

Attribute Information

ALIGN={LEFT, CENTER, RIGHT, TEXTTOP, MIDDLE, TEXTMIDDLE, BASELINE, TEXTBOTTOM, BASELINE}

Indicates how the embedded object lines up relative to the edges of the browser windows and/or other elements within the browser window. Using ALIGN=LEFT, ALIGN=RIGHT, or ALIGN=CENTER will cause the embedded object to *float* between the edges of the window either to the left, right, or evenly between. The behavior is similar to that of the ALIGN= attribute of the <IMG> tag. ALIGN=TEXTTOP aligns the top of the embedded object with the top of the surrounding text. ALIGN=TEXTMIDDLE aligns the middle of the embedded object with the middle of the surrounding text. ALIGN=TEXTBOTTOM aligns the bottom of the embedded object with the bottom of the surrounding text. ALIGN=BASELINE aligns the bottom of the embedded object with the baseline of the surrounding text. ALIGN=MIDDLE aligns the middle of the embedded object with the baseline of the surrounding text.

Standard:	HTML 4; deprecated in favor of style sheets
Common:	No
Sample:	

```
<OBJECT DATA="shocknew.dcr"
TYPE="application/DIRector" WIDTH=288
HEIGHT=200 ALIGN=RIGHT>
```

BORDER="*n*"

Indicates the width (in pixels) of a border around the embedded object. BORDER=0 indicates no border.

Standard:	HTML 4
Common:	No
Sample:	

```
<OBJECT DATA="shocknew.dcr"
TYPE="application/DIRector" WIDTH=288
HEIGHT=200 BORDER=10>
```

CODEBASE="..."

Specifies the absolute or relative location of the base directory in which the browser will look for data and other implementation files.

Standard:	HTML 4
Common:	No
Sample:	

```
<OBJECT CODEBASE="/~fgm/code/">
</OBJECT>
```

CODETYPE="..."

Specifies the MIME type for the embedded object's code.

Standard:	HTML 4
Common:	No
Sample:	

```
<OBJECT CODETYPE="application/
x-msword">
</OBJECT>
```

CLASS="..."

Indicates which style class applies to the element.

Standard:	HTML 4
Common:	No
Sample:	

```
<OBJECT CLASS="casual"
CODETYPE="application/x-msword">
</OBJECT>
```

CLASSID="..."
Specifies the URL of an object resource.

Standard: HTML 4
Common: No
Sample:

```
<OBJECT CLASSID="http://www
.raycomm.com/bogus.class">
```

DATA="*URL*"
Specifies the absolute or relative location of the embedded object's data.

Standard: HTML 4
Common: No
Sample:

```
<OBJECT DATA="/~fgm/goo.AVI">
</OBJECT>
```

DATAFLD="..."
Selects a column from a block of tabular data.

Standard: Internet Explorer 4
Common: No
Sample:

```
<OBJECT DATA="dataview.ocx"
DATASRC="#data_table"
DATAFLD="datafld1">
```

DATASRC="..."
Specifies the location of tabular data to be bound within the document.

Standard: Internet Explorer 4
Common: No
Sample:

```
<OBJECT DATA="dataview.ocx"
DATASRC="#data_table">
```

DECLARE
Defines the embedded object without actually loading it into the document.

Standard: HTML 4
Common: No
Sample:

```
<OBJECT CLASSID="clsid:99B42120-6EC7-
11CF-A6C7-00AA00A47DD3" DECLARE>
</OBJECT>
```

HEIGHT="*n*"
Specifies the vertical dimension (in pixels) of the embedded object.

Standard: HTML 4

Common: No
Sample:

```
<OBJECT DATA="shocknew.dcr"
TYPE="application/DIRector" WIDTH=288
HEIGHT=200 VSPACE=10 HSPACE=10>
```

HSPACE="*n*"
Specifies the size of the margins (in pixels) to the left and right of the embedded object.

Standard: HTML 4
Common: No
Sample:

```
<OBJECT DATA="shocknew.dcr"
TYPE="application/DIRector" WIDTH=288
HEIGHT=200 VSPACE=10 HSPACE=10>
```

ID="..."
Indicates an identifier to associate with the embedded object. You can also use this to apply styles to the object.

Standard: HTML 4
Common: No
Sample:

```
<OBJECT DATA="shocknew.dcr"
TYPE="application/DIRector" WIDTH=288
HEIGHT=200 VSPACE=10 HSPACE=10
ID="swave2">
```

NAME="..."
Specifies the name of the embedded object.

Standard: HTML 4
Common: No
Sample:

```
<OBJECT CLASSID="clsid:99B42120-6EC7-
11CF-A6C7-00AA00A47DD3" NAME="Very
Cool Thingie">
</OBJECT>
```

STANDBY="..."
Specifies a message that the browser displays while the object is loading.

Standard: HTML 4
Common: No
Sample:

```
<OBJECT STANDBY="Please wait. Movie
loading." WIDTH=100 HEIGHT=250>
<PARAM NAME=SRC VALUE="TheEarth.AVI">
<PARAM NAME=AUTOSTART VALUE=TRUE>
<PARAM NAME=PLAYBACK VALUE=FALSE>
</OBJECT>
```

TABINDEX="*n*"
Indicates the place of the embedded object in the tabbing order.

> **Standard:** HTML 4
> **Common:** No
> **Sample:**

```
<OBJECT CLASSID="clsid:99B42120-6EC7-
11CF-A6C7-00AA00A47DD3" TABINDEX=3>
</OBJECT>
```

TITLE="..."
Specifies text assigned to the tag. You might use this attribute for context-sensitive help within the document. Browsers may use this to show tool tips over the embedded object.

> **Standard:** HTML 4
> **Common:** No
> **Sample:**

```
<OBJECT TITLE="Earth Movie" WIDTH=100
HEIGHT=250>
 <PARAM NAME=SRC
 VALUE="TheEarth.AVI">/
 <PARAM NAME=AUTOSTART
 VALUE=TRUE>
 <PARAM NAME=PLAYBACK
 VALUE=FALSE>
</OBJECT>
```

TYPE="..."
Indicates the MIME type of the embedded object.

> **Standard:** HTML 4
> **Common:** No
> **Sample:**

```
<OBJECT DATA="shocknew.dcr"
TYPE="application/x-DIRector"
WIDTH=288 HEIGHT=200
VSPACE=10 HSPACE=10>
```

USEMAP="*URL*"
Indicates the relative or absolute location of a client-side imagemap to use with the embedded object.

> **Standard:** HTML 4
> **Common:** No
> **Sample:**

```
<OBJECT USEMAP="maps.html#map1">
```

VSPACE="*n*"
Specifies the size of the margin (in pixels) at the top and bottom of the embedded object.

> **Standard:** HTML 4
> **Common:** No
> **Sample:**

```
<OBJECT DATA="shocknew.dcr"
TYPE="application/DIRector" WIDTH=288
HEIGHT=200 VSPACE=10 HSPACE=10>

</OBJECT>
```

WIDTH="*n*"
Indicates the horizontal dimension (in pixels) of the embedded object.

> **Standard:** HTML 4
> **Common:** No
> **Sample:**

```
<OBJECT DATA="shocknew.dcr"
TYPE="application/DIRector" WIDTH=288
HEIGHT=200 VSPACE=10 HSPACE=10>
```

Other Attributes
This tag also accepts the ARCHIVE, STYLE, LANG, DIR, onClick, onDblClick, onMouseDown, onMouseUp, onMouseOver, onMouseMove, onMouseOut, onKeyPress, onKeyDown, and onKeyUp attributes. See the Element-Independent Attributes section of this reference for definitions and examples.

<OL>

Contains a numbered (ordered) list.

> **Standard:** HTML 2
> **Common:** Yes
> **Paired:** Yes
> **Sample:**

```
<OL TYPE=i>
 <LI>Introduction
 <LI>Part One
 <OL TYPE=A>
  <LI>Chapter 1
  <LI>Chapter 2
 </OL>
</OL>
```

Attribute Information

CLASS="..."
Indicates which style class applies to the <OL> element.

> **Standard:** HTML 4
> **Common:** No

Sample:

```
<OL CLASS="casual">
  <LI>Check engine oil
  <LI>Check tire pressures
  <LI>Fill with gasoline
<OL>
```

COMPACT

Indicates that the ordered list appears in a compact format. This attribute may not affect the appearance of the list as most browsers do not present lists in more than one format.

Standard:	HTML 2, deprecated in HTML 4
Common:	No

Sample:

```
<OL COMPACT>
```

ID="*n*"

Assigns a unique ID selector to an instance of the <OL> tag. When you then assign a style to that ID selector, it affects only that one instance of the <OL> tag.

Standard:	HTML 4
Common:	No

Sample:

```
Recommended bicycle accessories:
<OL ID="123">
  <LI>Water bottle
  <LI>Helmet
  <LI>Tire pump
</OL>
```

START="..."

Specifies the value at which the ordered list should start.

Standard:	HTML 2
Common:	Yes

Sample:

```
<OL TYPE=A START=F>
```

STYLE="..."

Specifies style sheet commands that apply to the ordered list.

Standard:	HTML 4
Common:	Yes

Sample:

```
<OL STYLE="background: black; color:
white">
```

TITLE="..."

Specifies text assigned to the tag. You might use this attribute for context-sensitive help within the document. Browsers may use this to show tool tips over the ordered list.

Standard:	HTML 4
Common:	No

Sample:

```
<OL TITLE="Ordered list">
```

TYPE="..."

Specifies the numbering style of the ordered list. Possible values are 1 for Arabic numbers, i for lowercase Roman numerals, I for uppercase Roman numerals, a for lowercase letters, and A for uppercase letters.

Standard:	HTML 2
Common:	Yes

Sample:

```
<OL TYPE=a>
  <LI>Breakfast
  <LI>Mrs. Johnson will speak
  <LI>Demonstration
  <LI>Lunch
</OL>
```

Other Attributes

This tag also accepts the LANG, DIR, onClick, onDblClick, onMouseDown, onMouseUp, onMouseOver, onMouseMove, onMouseOut, onKeyPress, onKeyDown, and onKeyUp attributes. See the Element-Independent Attributes section of this reference for definitions and examples.

<OPTGROUP>

Logically groups items together.

Standard:	HTML 4
Common:	No
Paired:	Yes

Sample:

```
<OPTGROUP
LABEL="TypesOfHomes"></OPTGROUP>
```

Attribute Information

CLASS="..."

Indicates which style class applies.

Standard:	HTML 4
Common:	No

Sample:

```
<OPTGROUP CLASS="casual">
```

ID="..."

Assigns a unique ID selector to an instance of <OPTGROUP>.

Standard:	HTML 4
Common:	No

Sample:

```
<OPTGROUP ID="123">
```

LABEL="..."

Labels the option group with a name.

Standard:	HTML 4
Common:	Yes

Sample:

```
<OPTGROUP LABEL="TypesOfHomes">
  <OPTION>Ranch</OPTION>
  <OPTION>Mansion</OPTION>
</OPTGROUP>
```

Other Attributes

This tag also accepts the LANG, DIR, STYLE, TITLE, onClick, onDblClick, onMouseDown, onMouseUp, onMouseMove, onMouseOver, onMouseOut, onKeyPress, onKeyDown, and onKeyUp attributes. See the Element-Independent Attributes section and other tag listings in this reference for definitions and examples.

<OPTION>

Indicates items in a fill-out form selection list (see the <SELECT> tag).

Standard:	HTML 2
Common:	Yes
Paired:	No

Sample:

```
Select an artist from the
1970s:<SELECT NAME="artists">
 <OPTION>Boston
 <OPTION SELECTED>Pink Floyd
 <OPTION>Reo Speedwagon
</SELECT>
```

Attribute Information

CLASS="..."

Indicate which style class applies to the element.

Standard:	HTML 4
Common:	No

Sample:

```
<OPTION NAME="color" CLASS="casual">
```

DISABLED="..."

Denies access to the input method.

Standard:	HTML 4
Common:	No

Sample:

```
<OPTION VALUE="Bogus"
DISABLED>Nothing here
```

ID="*n*"

Assigns a unique ID selector to an instance of the <OPTION> tag. When you then assign a style to that ID selector, it affects only that one instance of the <OPTION> tag.

Standard:	HTML 4
Common:	No

Sample:

```
<OPTION ID="123">Mastercard
```

SELECTED

Marks a selection list item as preselected.

Standard:	HTML 2
Common:	Yes

Sample:

```
<OPTION SELECTED VALUE=1>Ice
Cream</OPTION>
```

TITLE="..."

Specifies text assigned to the tag. You might use this attribute for context-sensitive help within the document. Browsers may use this to show tool tips over the selection list option.

Standard:	HTML 4
Common:	No

Sample:

```
<OPTION TITLE="Option">Thingie
```

VALUE="..."

Indicates which data is sent to the form processor if you choose the selection list item. If the VALUE= attribute is not present within the <OPTION> tag, the text between the <OPTION> tags is sent instead.

Standard:	HTML 2
Common:	Yes

Sample:

```
<OPTION VALUE=2>Sandwiches
</OPTION>
```

Other Attributes

This tag also accepts the LABEL, LANG, DIR, onClick, onDblClick, onMouseDown, onMouseUp, onMouseOver, onMouseMove, onMouseOut, onKeyPress, onKeyDown, and onKeyUp attributes. See the Element-Independent Attributes section of this reference for definitions and examples.

P

<P>

Indicates a paragraph in a document.

Standard:	HTML 2
Common:	Yes
Paired:	Yes, optional

Sample:

```
<P >As soon as she left, the phone
began ringing. "Hello," I said after
lifting the receiver.</P>
<P>"Is she gone yet?" said the voice
on the other end.</P>
```

Attribute Information

ALIGN={LEFT, CENTER, RIGHT, JUSTIFY}

Aligns paragraph text flush left, flush right, or in the center of the document.

Standard:	HTML 3.2; deprecated in HTML 4 in favor of style sheets
Common:	Yes

Sample:

```
<P ALIGN=CENTER>There will be fun and
games for everyone!
```

CLASS="..."

Indicates which style class applies to the <P> element.

Standard:	HTML 4
Common:	No

Sample:

```
<P CLASS="casual">Tom turned at the
next street and stopped.
```

ID="n"

Assigns a unique ID selector to an instance of the <P> tag. When you then assign a style to that ID selector, it affects only that one instance of the <P> tag.

Standard:	HTML 4
Common:	No

Sample:

```
<P ID="123">This paragraph is yellow
on black!
```

STYLE="..."

Specifies style sheet commands that apply to the contents of the paragraph.

Standard:	HTML 4
Common:	No

Sample:

```
<P STYLE="background: red; color:
white">
```

TITLE="..."

Specifies text assigned to the tag. You might use this attribute for context-sensitive help within the document. Browsers may use this to show tool tips over the paragraph.

Standard:	HTML 4
Common:	No

Sample:

```
<P TITLE="Paragraph">
```

WIDTH="n"

Specifies the horizontal dimension of the paragraph (in pixels).

Standard:	Internet Explorer 4
Common:	No

Sample:

```
<P WIDTH=250>
```

Other Attributes

This tag also accepts the LANG, DIR, onClick, onDblClick, onMouseDown, onMouseUp, onMouseOver, onMouseMove, onMouseOut, onKeyPress, onKeyDown, and onKeyUp attributes. See the Element-Independent Attributes section of this reference for definitions and examples.

<PARAM>

Specifies parameters passed to an embedded object. Use the <PARAM> tag within the <OBJECT> or <APPLET> tags.

> **Standard:** HTML 4
> **Common:** No
> **Paired:** No
> **Sample:**

```
<OBJECT CLASSID="/thingie.py">
<PARAM NAME="thing" VALUE=1>
Sorry. Your browser does not
support embedded objects.
</OBJECT>
```

Attribute Information

DATAFLD="..."

Selects a column from a block of tabular data.

> **Standard:** Internet Explorer 4
> **Common:** No
> **Sample:**

```
<PARAM DATA="dataview.ocx"
DATASRC="#data_table"
DATAFLD="datafld1">
```

DATASRC="..."

Specifies the location of tabular data to be bound within the document.

> **Standard:** Internet Explorer 4
> **Common:** No
> **Sample:**

```
<PARAM DATA="dataview.ocx"
DATASRC="#data_table">
```

NAME="..."

Indicates the name of the parameter passed to the embedded object.

> **Standard:** HTML 4
> **Common:** No
> **Sample:**

```
<PARAM NAME="startyear" VALUE="1920">
```

TYPE="..."

Specifies the MIME type of the data found at the specified URL. Use this attribute with the VALUETYPE=REF attribute.

> **Standard:** HTML 4
> **Common:** No

> **Sample:**

```
<PARAM NAME="data"
VALUE="/data/sim1.zip"
VALUETYPE=REF
TYPE="application/
x-zip-compressed">
```

VALUE="..."

Specifies the value associated with the parameter passed to the embedded object.

> **Standard:** HTML 4
> **Common:** No
> **Sample:**

```
<PARAM NAME="startyear" VALUE="1920">
```

VALUETYPE={REF, OBJECT, DATA}

Indicates the kind of value passed to the embedded object. VALUETYPE=REF indicates a URL passed to the embedded object. VALUETYPE=OBJECT indicates that the VALUE attribute specifies the location of object data. VALUETYPE=DATA indicates that the VALUE= attribute is set to a plain text string. Use this for passing alphanumeric data to the embedded object.

> **Standard:** Internet Explorer 3,
>   HTML 4
> **Common:** No
> **Sample:**

```
<PARAM NAME="length" VALUE="9"
VALUETYPE=DATA>
```

Other Attributes

This tag also accepts the ID attribute.

<PLAINTEXT>

Specifies that text appears as preformatted. This tag is obsolete; the <PRE> tag has replaced it.

> **Standard:** Obsolete
> **Common:** No
> **Paired:** Yes
> **Sample:**

```
<PLAINTEXT>Now go to the store and
buy:
Wrapping paper
Tape
Markers
</PLAINTEXT>
```

<PRE>

Contains preformatted plain text. This is useful for including computer program output or source code within your document.

Standard:	HTML 2
Common:	Yes
Paired:	Yes
Sample:	

```
Here's the source code:
<PRE>
#include <stdio.h>
void main()
{
  printf("Hello World!\n");
}
</PRE>
```

Attribute Information

CLASS="..."
Indicates which style class applies to the <PRE> element.

Standard:	HTML 4
Common:	No
Sample:	

```
<PRE CLASS="casual">BBQ INFO</PRE>
```

ID="..."
Assigns a unique ID selector to an instance of the <PRE> tag. When you then assign a style to that ID selector, it affects only that one instance of the <PRE> tag.

Standard:	HTML 4
Common:	No
Sample:	

```
An example of an emotion:
<PRE ID="123">
  :-)
</PRE>
```

STYLE="..."
Specifies style sheet commands that apply to the contents within the <PRE> tags.

Standard:	HTML 4
Common:	Yes
Sample:	

```
<PRE STYLE="background : red">
```

TITLE="..."
Specifies text assigned to the tag. You might use this attribute for context-sensitive help within the document. Browsers may use this to show tool tips over the preformatted text.

Standard:	HTML 4
Common:	No
Sample:	

```
<PRE TITLE="preformatted text">
```

WIDTH="n"
Specifies the horizontal dimension of the preformatted text (in pixels).

Standard:	HTML 4
Common:	No
Sample:	

```
<PRE WIDTH=80>
```

Other Attributes
This tag also accepts the LANG, DIR, onClick, onDblClick, onMouseDown, onMouseUp, onMouseOver, onMouseMove, onMouseOut, onKeyPress, onKeyDown, and onKeyUp attributes. See the Element-Independent Attributes section of this reference for definitions and examples.

Q

<Q>

Quotes a direct source within a paragraph. Use <Q> to signify only a longer or block quotation.

Standard:	HTML 4
Common:	No
Paired:	Yes
Sample:	

```
Dr. Henry remarked <Q>I really like
the procedure.</Q>
```

Attribute Information

CITE="..."
Specifies a reference URL for a quotation.

Standard:	HTML 4
Common:	No

Sample:

```
<Q CITE="http://www.clement.moore
.com/xmas.html">
Twas the night…
</Q>
```

CLASS="…"

Indicates which style class applies to the <Q> element.

Standard: HTML 4
Common: No
Sample:

```
<Q CLASS="casual">
Twas the night before Christmas…</Q>
```

ID="…"

Assigns a unique ID selector to an instance of the <Q> tag. When you then assign a style to that ID selector, it affects only that one instance of the <Q> tag.

Standard: HTML 4
Common: No
Sample:

```
On July 12, John wrote a profound
sentence in his diary:
<Q ID="123">I woke up this morning at
nine and it was raining.</Q>
```

STYLE="…"

Specifies style sheet commands that apply to the contents within the <Q> tags.

Standard: HTML 4
Common: No
Sample:

```
<Q STYLE="background: red">
```

TITLE="…"

Specifies text assigned to the tag. You might use this attribute for context-sensitive help within the document. Browsers may use this to show tool tips over the quoted text.

Standard: HTML 4
Common: No
Sample:

```
<Q TITLE="Quotation">
```

Other Attributes

This tag also accepts the LANG, DIR, onClick, onDblClick, onMouseDown, onMouseUp, onMouseOver, onMouseMove, onMouseOut, onKeyPress, onKeyDown, and onKeyUp attributes. See the Element-Independent Attributes section of this reference for definitions and examples.

S

<SAMP>

Indicates a sequence of literal characters.

Standard: HTML 2
Common: Yes
Paired: Yes
Sample:

```
An example of a palindrome is the
word <SAMP>TOOT</SAMP>.
```

Attribute Information

CLASS="…"

Indicates which style class applies to the <SAMP> element.

Standard: HTML 4
Common: No
Sample:

```
The PC screen read:
<SAMP CLASS="casual">Command Not
Found</SAMP>
```

ID="…"

Assigns a unique ID selector to an instance of the <SAMP> tag. When you then assign a style to that ID selector, it affects only that one instance of the <SAMP> tag.

Standard: HTML 4
Common: No
Sample:

```
Just for fun, think of how many words
end with the letters
<SAMP ID="123">ing</SAMP>.
```

STYLE="…"

Specifies style sheet commands that apply to the contents within the <SAMP> tags.

Standard: HTML 4
Common: Yes
Sample:

```
<SAMP STYLE="background: red">
```

TITLE="..."

Specifies text assigned to the tag. You might use this attribute for context-sensitive help within the document. Browsers may use this to show tool tips.

Standard: HTML 4
Common: No
Sample:

```
<SAMP TITLE="Sample">
```

Other Attributes

This tag also accepts the LANG, DIR, onClick, onDblClick, onMouseDown, onMouseUp, onMouseOver, onMouseMove, onMouseOut, onKeyPress, onKeyDown, and onKeyUp attributes. See the Element-Independent Attributes section of this reference for definitions and examples.

<SCRIPT>

Contains browser script code. Examples include JavaScript and VBScript. It is a good idea to place the actual script code within the comment tags so that browsers that don't support the <SCRIPT> tag code can ignore it.

Standard: HTML 3.2
Common: Yes
Paired: Yes
Sample:

```
<SCRIPT LANGUAGE="JavaScript">
<!- ... ->
</SCRIPT>
```

Attribute Information

LANGUAGE="..."

Indicates the type of script.

Standard: HTML 4,
            Internet Explorer
Common: Yes
Sample:

```
<SCRIPT LANGUAGE="JavaScript">
```

SRC="*URL*"

Specifies the relative or absolute location of a script to include in the document.

Standard: HTML 4,
            Internet Explorer
Common: Yes

Sample:

```
<SCRIPT type="text/javascript"
SRC="http://www.some.com/sc/
script.js">
</SCRIPT>
```

TYPE="..."

Indicates the MIME type of the script. This is an alternative to the LANGUAGE attribute for declaring the type of scripting.

Standard: HTML 3.2
Common: Yes
Sample:

```
<SCRIPT TYPE="text/javascript">
  document.write
  ("<EM>Great!</EM>")
</SCRIPT>
```

Other Attributes

This tag also accepts the CHARSET and DEFER attributes.

<SELECT>

Specifies a selection list within a form. Use the <OPTION> tags to specify items in the selection list.

Standard: HTML 2
Common: Yes
Paired: Yes
Sample:

```
What do you use our product for?<BR>
```

```
<SELECT MULTIPLE NAME="use">

  <OPTION VALUE=1>Pest control
  <OPTION VALUE=2>Automotive
  lubricant
  <OPTION VALUE=3>Preparing
  pastries
  <OPTION SELECTED VALUE=4>
  Personal hygiene
  <OPTION VALUE=5>Other

</SELECT>
```

Attribute Information

CLASS="..."

Indicates which style class applies to the element.

Standard: HTML 4
Common: No

Sample:

```
<SELECT NAME="color" CLASS="casual">
```

DATAFLD="..."

Indicates a column from previously identified tabular data.

Standard: Internet Explorer 4
Common: No
Sample:

```
<SELECT NAME="color"
DATASRC="#data_table" DATAFLD="clr">
```

DISABLED

Denies access to the selection list.

Standard: HTML 4
Common: No
Sample:

```
<SELECT NAME="color" DISABLED>
```

ID="..."

Assigns a unique ID selector to an instance of the <SELECT> tag. When you then assign a style to that ID selector, it affects only that one instance of the <SELECT> tag.

Standard: Internet Explorer 4
Common: No
Sample:

```
<SELECT ID="123" NAME="salary">
```

MULTIPLE

Indicates that a visitor can select more than one selection list item at the same time.

Standard: HTML 2
Common: Yes
Sample:

```
<SELECT MULTIPLE>
```

NAME="..."

Gives a name to the value you are passing to the form processor. This establishes a *name-value pair* with which the form processor application can work.

Standard: HTML 2
Common: Yes
Sample:

```
What is your shoe size?

<SELECT SIZE=4 NAME="size">
  <OPTION>
  <OPTION>
```

```
  <OPTION>
  <OPTION>
  <OPTION>
  <OPTION>
</SELECT>
```

READONLY

Indicates that your visitor cannot modify values within the selection list.

Standard: Internet Explorer 4
Common: No
Sample:

```
<SELECT NAME="color" READONLY>
```

SIZE="n"

Specifies the number of visible items in the selection list. If there are more items in the selection list than are visible, a scrollbar provides access to the other items.

Standard: HTML 2
Common: Yes
Sample:

```
<SELECT SIZE=3>
```

STYLE="..."

Specifies style sheet commands that apply to the contents within the <SELECT> tags.

Standard: HTML 4
Common: Yes
Sample:

```
<SELECT STYLE="background: red"
NAME="color">
```

TABINDEX="n"

Indicates where in the tabbing order the selection list is placed.

Standard: HTML 4
Common: No
Sample:

```
<SELECT NAME="salary" TABINDEX=3>
```

TITLE="..."

Specifies text assigned to the tag. You might use this attribute for context-sensitive help within the document. Browsers may use this to show tool tips over the selection list.

Standard: HTML 4
Common: No

Sample:

```
<SELECT TITLE="Select List"
NAME="Car">
```

Other Attributes

This tag also accepts the LANG, DIR, onFocus, onBlur, onChange, onSelect, onClick, onDblClick, onMouseDown, onMouseUp, onMouseOver, onMouseMove, onMouseOut, onKeyPress, onKeyDown, and onKeyUp attributes. See the Element-Independent Attributes section of this reference for definitions and examples.

<SMALL>

Specifies text that should appear in a small font.

Standard:	HTML 3.2
Common:	Yes
Paired:	Yes
Sample:	

```
<P>Our lawyers said we need to
include some small print:

<P><SMALL>By reading this document,
you are breaking the rules and will
be assessed a $2000 fine.</SMALL>
```

Attribute Information

CLASS="..."

Indicates which style class applies to the <SMALL> element.

Standard:	HTML 4
Common:	No
Sample:	

```
<SMALL CLASS="casual">Void where
prohibited</SMALL>
```

ID="..."

Assigns a unique ID selector to an instance of the <SMALL> tag. When you then assign a style to that ID selector, it affects only that one instance of the <SMALL> tag.

Standard:	HTML 4
Common:	No
Sample:	

```
Most insects are <SMALL
ID="123">small</SMALL>.
```

STYLE="..."

Specifies style sheet commands that apply to the contents within the <SMALL> tags.

Standard:	HTML 4
Common:	Yes
Sample:	

```
<SMALL STYLE="background: red">
```

TITLE="..."

Specifies text assigned to the tag. You might use this attribute for context-sensitive help within the document. Browsers may use this to show tool tips over the text inside the <SMALL> tags.

Standard:	HTML 4
Common:	No
Sample:	

```
<SMALL TITLE="Legalese">Actually
doing any of this will subject you to
risk of criminal prosecution.</SMALL>
```

Other Attributes

This tag also accepts the LANG, DIR, onClick, onDblClick, onMouseDown, onMouseUp, onMouseOver, onMouseMove, onMouseOut, onKeyPress, onKeyDown, and onKeyUp attributes. See the Element-Independent Attributes section of this reference for definitions and examples.

<SPACER>

A Netscape-specific tag that specifies a blank space within the document. We recommend using style sheets or other formatting techniques unless you're developing documents exclusively for visitors using Netscape Navigator.

Standard:	Netscape Navigator 4
Common:	No
Paired:	No
Sample:	

```
<SPACER TYPE=HORIZONTAL SIZE=150>
Doctors Prefer MediWidget 4 to 1
```

Attribute Information

SIZE="n"

Specifies the dimension of the spacer (in pixels).

Standard:	Netscape Navigator 3

Common: No

Sample:

```
<SPACER TYPE=HORIZONTAL SIZE=50>
<IMG SRC="rosebush.jpg">
```

TYPE={HORIZONTAL, VERTICAL}

Indicates whether the spacer measures from left to right or from top to bottom.

Standard: Netscape Navigator 3
Common: No
Sample:

```
<P>After you've done this, take a
moment to review your work.
<SPACER TYPE=VERTICAL SIZE=400>
<P>Now, isn't that better?
```

`<SPAN>`

Defines an inline section of a document affected by style sheet attributes. Use `<DIV>` to apply styles at the block-element level.

Standard: HTML 4
Common: No
Paired: Yes
Sample:

```
<SPAN STYLE="background:
red">...</SPAN>
```

Attribute Information

CLASS="..."

Indicates which style class applies to the `<SPAN>` element.

Standard: HTML 4
Common: No
Sample:

```
<SPAN CLASS="casual">
```

DATAFLD="..."

Selects a column from a previously identified source of tabular data (see the `DATASRC=` attribute).

Standard: Internet Explorer 4
Common: No
Sample:

```
<SPAN DATASRC="#data_table">
  <SPAN DATAFLD="name"></SPAN>
</SPAN>
```

DATAFORMATAS={TEXT, HTML, NONE}

Indicates the format of tabular data within the `<SPAN>` element.

Standard: Internet Explorer 4
Common: No
Sample:

```
<SPAN DATAFORMATAS=HTML
DATASRC="#data_table">
```

DATASRC="..."

Specifies the source of data for data binding.

Standard: Internet Explorer 4
Common: No
Sample:

```
<SPAN DATASRC="#data_table">
```

ID="..."

Assigns a unique ID selector to an instance of the `<SPAN>` tag. When you then assign a style to that ID selector, it affects only that one instance of the `<SPAN>` tag.

Standard: HTML 4
Common: No
Sample:

```
<SPAN ID="123">
```

STYLE="..."

Specifies style sheet commands that apply to the contents within the `<SPAN>` tags.

Standard: HTML 4
Common: No
Sample:

```
<SPAN STYLE="background: red">
```

TITLE="..."

Specifies text assigned to the tag. You might use this attribute for context-sensitive help within the document. Browsers may use this to show tool tips.

Standard: HTML 4
Common: No
Sample:

```
<SPAN TITLE="Section"
STYLE="background: red">
```

Other Attributes

This tag also accepts the LANG, DIR, onClick, onDblClick, onMouseDown, onMouseUp, onMouseOver, onMouseMove, onMouseOut, onKeyPress, onKeyDown, and onKeyUp attributes. See the Element-Independent Attributes section of this reference for definitions and examples.

<STRIKE>, <S>

Indicate a strikethrough text style.

Standard:	HTML 3.2; deprecated in HTML 4 in favor of style sheets
Common:	Yes
Paired:	Yes
Sample:	

My junior high biology teacher was
<STRIKE>sorta</STRIKE> really smart.

Attribute Information

CLASS="..."
Indicates which style class applies to the <STRIKE> element.

Standard:	HTML 4
Common:	No
Sample:	

<STRIKE CLASS="casual">Truman
</STRIKE> lost.

ID="..."
Assigns a unique ID selector to an instance of the <STRIKE> tag. When you then assign a style to that ID selector, it affects only that one instance of the <STRIKE> tag.

Standard:	HTML 4
Common:	No
Sample:	

Don <STRIKE ID="123">ain't
</STRIKE>isn't coming tonight.

STYLE="..."
Specifies style sheet commands that apply to the contents within the <STRIKE> tags.

Standard:	HTML 4
Common:	No
Sample:	

<STRIKE STYLE="background: red">

TITLE="..."
Specifies text assigned to the tag. You might use this attribute for context-sensitive help

within the document. Browsers may use this to show tool tips over the text.

Standard:	HTML 4
Common:	No
Sample:	

He was <STRIKE TITLE="omit">
Ambitious</STRIKE>
<B>Enthusiastic</B>.

Other Attributes
This tag also accepts the LANG, DIR, onClick, onDblClick, onMouseDown, onMouseUp, onMouseOver, onMouseMove, onMouseOut, onKeyPress, onKeyDown, and onKeyUp attributes. See the Element-Independent Attributes section of this reference for definitions and examples.

<STRONG>

Indicates strong emphasis. The browser will probably display the text in a boldface font.

Standard:	HTML 2
Common:	Yes
Paired:	Yes
Sample:	

If you see a poisonous spider in the room then <STRONG>Get out of there!</STRONG>

Attribute Information

CLASS="..."
Indicates which style class applies to the <STRONG> element.

Standard:	HTML 4
Common:	No
Sample:	

Did you say my dog is
<STRONG CLASS="casual">DEAD?!
</STRONG>

ID="..."
Assigns a unique ID selector to an instance of the <STRONG> tag. When you then assign a style to that ID selector, it affects only that one instance of the <STRONG> tag.

Standard:	HTML 4
Common:	No

Sample:

```
Sure, you can win at gambling. But
it's more likely you will <STRONG
ID="123">lose</STRONG>.
```

STYLE="..."

Specifies style sheet commands that apply to the contents within the <STRONG> tags.

Standard:	HTML 4
Common:	No

Sample:

```
<STRONG STYLE="background: red">
```

TITLE="..."

Specifies text assigned to the tag. You might use this attribute for context-sensitive help within the document. Browsers may use this to show tool tips over the emphasized text.

Standard:	HTML 4
Common:	No

Sample:

```
I mean it was <STRONG
TITLE="emphasis">HOT!</STRONG>
```

Other Attributes

This tag also accepts the LANG, DIR, onClick, onDblClick, onMouseDown, onMouseUp, onMouseOver, onMouseMove, onMouseOut, onKeyPress, onKeyDown, and onKeyUp attributes. See the Element-Independent Attributes section of this reference for definitions and examples.

<STYLE>

Contains style sheet definitions and appears in the document head (see the <HEAD> tag). Place style sheet data within the comment tags (<!--… -->) to accommodate browsers that do not support the <STYLE> tag.

Standard:	HTML 3.2
Common:	No
Paired:	Yes

Sample:

```
<HTML>
<HEAD>
<TITLE>Edible Socks: Good or
Bad?</TITLE>
<STYLE TYPE="text/css">
<!--
 @import url(http://www.raycomm
.com/mhtml/styles.css)
```

```
H1 { background: black; color:
yellow }
LI DD { background: silver; color:
black }
-->
</STYLE>
</HEAD>
```

Attribute Information

MEDIA="..."

Specifies the destination medium for style information. It may be a single type or a comma-separated list. Media types include the following:

SCREEN: For online viewing (default setting)

PRINT: For traditional printed material and for documents on screen viewed in print preview mode

PROJECTION: For projectors

BRAILLE: For Braille tactile feedback device

SPEECH: For a speech synthesizer

ALL: Applies to all devices

Standard:	HTML 4
Common:	No

Sample:

```
<HEAD>
<TITLE>Washington DC Taverns</TITLE>
<STYLE TYPE="text/css" MEDIA="ALL">
<!--
 @import http://www.somewebsite.com
 H1 { background: black; color:
 white}
 LI DD { background: silver; color:
 darkgreen }
-->
</STYLE>
</HEAD>
```

TITLE="..."

Specifies text assigned to the tag. You might use this attribute for context-sensitive help within the document. Browsers may use this to show tool tips.

Standard:	HTML 4
Common:	No

Sample:

```
<STYLE TITLE="Stylesheet 1"
TYPE="text/css">
<!-- H1 { background: black; color:
yellow }
  LI DD { background: silver; color:
black }
-->
</SCRIPT>
```

TYPE="..."

Specifies the MIME type of the style sheet specification standard used.

Standard:	HTML 4
Common:	No

Sample:

```
<HEAD>
<TITLE>Washington DC Taverns</TITLE>
<STYLE TYPE="text/css">
<!--
  @import http://www.somewebsite.com
  H1 { background: black; color:
  white}
  LI DD { background: silver; color:
  darkgreen }
-->
</STYLE>
</HEAD>
```

Other Attributes

This tag also accepts the LANG and DIR attributes. See the Element-Independent Attributes section of this reference for definitions and examples.

<SUB>

Indicates subscript text.

Standard:	HTML 3.2
Common:	Yes
Paired:	Yes

Sample:

```
<P>Chemists refer to water as
H<SUB>2</SUB>O.
```

Attribute Information

CLASS="..."

Indicates which style class applies to the <SUB> element.

Standard:	HTML 4
Common:	No

Sample:

```
<SUB CLASS="casual">2</SUB>
```

ID="..."

Assigns a unique ID selector to an instance of the <SUB> tag. When you then assign a style to that ID selector, it affects only that one instance of the <SUB> tag.

Standard:	HTML 4
Common:	No

Sample:

```
. . . At the dentist I ask for lots
of
NO<SUB ID="123">2</SUB>.
```

STYLE="..."

Specifies style sheet commands that apply to the contents within the <SUB> tags.

Standard:	HTML 4
Common:	No

Sample:

```
<SUB STYLE="background: red">
```

TITLE="..."

Specifies text assigned to the tag. You might use this attribute for context-sensitive help within the document. Browsers may use this to show tool tips over the subscripted text.

Standard:	HTML 4
Common:	No

Sample:

```
Before he died, he uttered,
"Groovy."<SUB
TITLE="Footnote">2</SUB>
```

Other Attributes

This tag also accepts the LANG, DIR, onClick, onDblClick, onMouseDown, onMouseUp, onMouseOver, onMouseMove, onMouseOut, onKeyPress, onKeyDown, and onKeyUp attributes. See the Element-Independent Attributes section of this reference for definitions and examples.

<SUP>

Indicates superscript text.

Standard:	HTML 3.2
Common:	Yes
Paired:	Yes

Sample:

```
<P>Einstein's most famous equation is
probably E=mc<SUP>2</SUP>.
```

Attribute Information

CLASS="..."

Indicates which style class applies to the
<SUP> element.

Standard:	HTML 4
Common:	No
Sample:	

```
<STYLE>
<!--
  SUP.casual {background: black;
    color: yellow}
-->
</STYLE>
...
z<SUP CLASS="casual">2</SUP> = x<SUP
CLASS="casual">2</SUP> +
y<SUP CLASS="casual">2</SUP>
```

ID="..."

Assigns a unique ID selector to an instance of
the <PRE> tag. When you then assign a style
to that ID selector, it affects only that one
instance of the <SUP> tag.

Standard:	HTML 4
Common:	No
Sample:	

```
<STYLE>
<!--
  #123 {background: black;
    color: yellow}
-->
</STYLE>
... Pythagorean theorem says
z<SUP ID="123">2</SUP>=4+16.
```

STYLE="..."

Specifies style sheet commands that apply to
the contents within the <SUP> tags.

Standard:	HTML 4
Common:	No
Sample:	

```
<SUP STYLE="background: red">
```

TITLE="..."

Specifies text assigned to the tag. You might
use this attribute for context-sensitive help

within the document. Browsers may use this
to show tool tips over the superscripted text.

Standard:	HTML 4
Common:	No
Sample:	

```
x<SUP TITLE="Exponent">2</SUP>
```

Other Attributes

This tag also accepts the LANG, DIR, onClick,
onDblClick, onMouseDown, onMouseUp,
onMouseOver, onMouseMove, onMouseOut,
onKeyPress, onKeyDown, and onKeyUp attributes. See the Element-Independent Attributes
section of this reference for definitions and
examples.

T

<TABLE>

Specifies a container for a table within your
document. Inside these tags you can place
<TR>, <TD>, <TH>, <CAPTION>, and other
<TABLE> tags.

Standard:	HTML 3.2
Common:	Yes
Paired:	Yes
Sample:	

```
<TABLE BORDER=0>  <TR>
    <TD><IMG SRC="Pine.jpg"
    BORDER=0 ALT="Pine"></TD>

    <TD VALIGN=MIDDLE><P>Pine
    trees naturally grow at
    higher elevations.

    They require less water and
    do not shed leaves in the
    fall.</TD>  </TR>
</TABLE>
```

Attribute Information

ALIGN={LEFT, CENTER, RIGHT}

Positions the table flush left, flush right, or in
the center of the window.

Standard:	HTML 3.2
Common:	Yes
Sample:	

```
<TABLE ALIGN=CENTER>
```

BACKGROUND="*URL*"
Specifies the relative or absolute location of a graphic image file loaded as a background image for the entire table.

Standard:	Internet Explorer 3, Netscape Navigator 4
Common:	No
Sample:	

`<TABLE BACKGROUND="paper.jpg">`

BGCOLOR="*#RRGGBB*" or "..."
Specifies the background color within all table cells in the table. You can substitute color names for the hexadecimal RGB values.

Standard:	Deprecated in HTML 4 in favor of style sheets
Common:	No
Sample:	

`<TABLE BGCOLOR="Peach">`

BORDER="*n*"
Specifies the thickness (in pixels) of borders around each table cell. Use a value of 0 to produce a table with no visible borders.

Standard:	HTML 3.2
Common:	Yes
Sample:	

`<TABLE BORDER=0>`

BORDERCOLOR="*#RRGGBB*" or "..."
Specifies the color of the borders of all the table cells in the table. You can substitute color names for the hexadecimal RGB values.

Standard:	Internet Explorer 3.0
Common:	No
Sample:	

`<TABLE BORDERCOLOR=#3F9A11>`

BORDERCOLORDARK="*#RRGGBB*" or "..."
Specifies the darker color used to draw 3-D borders around the table cells. You can substitute color names for the hexadecimal RGB values.

Standard:	Internet Explorer 4
Common:	No
Sample:	

`<TABLE BORDERCOLORDARK="silver">`

BORDERCOLORLIGHT="*#RRGGBB*" or "..."
Specifies the lighter color used to draw 3-D borders around the table cells. You can substitute color names for the hexadecimal RGB values.

Standard:	Internet Explorer 4
Common:	No
Sample:	

`<TABLE BORDERCOLORLIGHT="white">`

CELLPADDING="*n*"
Specifies the space (in pixels) between the edges of table cells and their contents.

Standard:	HTML 3.2
Common:	Yes
Sample:	

`<TABLE CELLPADDING=5>`

CELLSPACING="*n*"
Specifies the space (in pixels) between the borders of table cells and the borders of adjacent cells.

Standard:	HTML 3.2
Common:	Yes
Sample:	

`<TABLE BORDER=2 CELLSPACING=5>`

CLASS="..."
Indicates which style class applies to the <TABLE> element.

Standard:	HTML 4
Common:	No
Sample:	

`<TABLE CLASS="casual" BORDER=2>`

COLS="*n*"
Specifies the number of columns in the table.

Standard:	HTML 4
Common:	No
Sample:	

`<TABLE BORDER=2 COLS=5>`

FRAME={VOID, BORDER, ABOVE, BELOW, HSIDES, LHS, RHS, VSIDES, BOX}
Specifies the external border lines around the table. For the FRAME= attribute to work, set the BORDER= attribute with a non-zero value.

FRAME=VOID indicates no border lines. FRAME=BOX or FRAME=BORDER indicates border lines around the entire table. This is the default. FRAME=ABOVE specifies a border line along the top edge. FRAME=BELOW draws a border line along the bottom edge. FRAME=HSIDES draws border lines along the top and bottom edges. FRAME=LHS indicates a border line along the left side. FRAME=RHS draws a border line along the right edge. FRAME=VSIDES draws border lines along the left and right edges.

Standard:	HTML 4
Common:	No
Sample:	

```
<TABLE BORDER=2 RULES=ALL
FRAME=VSIDES>
```

ID="n"

Assigns a unique ID selector to an instance of the <TABLE> tag. When you then assign a style to that ID selector, it affects only that one instance of the <TABLE> tag.

Standard:	HTML 4
Common:	No
Sample:	

```
<TABLE ID="123">
```

RULES={NONE, ROWS, COLS, GROUPS, ALL}

Specifies where rule lines appear inside the table. For the RULES= attribute to work, set the BORDER= attribute. RULES=NONE indicates no rule lines. RULES=ROWS indicates rule lines between rows. RULES=COLS draws rule lines between columns. RULES=ALL draws all possible rule lines. RULES=GROUPS specifies rule lines between the groups defined by the <TFOOT>, <THEAD>, <TBODY>, and <COLGROUP> tags.

Standard:	HTML 4
Common:	No
Sample:	

```
<TABLE BORDER=2 RULES=BASIC>
```

STYLE="..."

Specifies style sheet commands that apply to the contents of cells in the table.

Standard:	HTML 4
Common:	No

Sample:

```
<TABLE STYLE="background: red">
```

TITLE="..."

Specifies text assigned to the tag. You might use this attribute for context-sensitive help within the document. Browsers may use this to show tool tips over the table.

Standard:	HTML 4
Common:	No
Sample:	

```
<TABLE TITLE="Table">
```

WIDTH="n"

Specifies the width of the table. You can set this value to an absolute number of pixels or to a percentage amount so that the table is proportionally as wide as the available space.

Standard:	HTML 3.2
Common:	Yes
Sample:	

```
<TABLE ALIGN=CENTER WIDTH="60%">
```

Other Attributes

This tag also accepts the SUMMARY, LANG, DIR, onClick, onDblClick, onMouseDown, onMouseUp, onMouseOver, onMouseMove, onMouseOut, onKeyPress, onKeyDown, and onKeyUp attributes. See the Element-Independent Attributes section of this reference for definitions and examples.

<TBODY>

Defines the table body within a table. This tag must *follow* the <TFOOT> tag.

Standard:	HTML 4
Common:	No
Paired:	Yes
Sample:	

```
<TABLE>
<THEAD>...
 </THEAD>
<TFOOT>...
 </TFOOT>
 <TBODY>...
 </TBODY>
```

Attribute Information

ALIGN="{LEFT, RIGHT, CENTER, JUSTIFY, CHAR}"

Specifies how text within the table footer will line up with the edges of the table cells, or if ALIGN=CHAR, on a specific character (the decimal point).

Standard: HTML 4
Common: Yes
Sample:

```
<TBODY ALIGN=CENTER>
Television</TBODY>
```

CHAR="..."

Specifies the character on which cell contents will align, if ALIGN="CHAR". If you omit CHAR=, the default value is the decimal point in the specified language.

Standard: HTML 4
Common: No
Sample:

```
<THEAD ALIGN="CHAR" CHAR=",">
```

CHAROFF="n"

Specifies the number of characters from the left at which the alignment character appears.

Standard: HTML 4
Common: No
Sample:

```
<THEAD ALIGN="CHAR" CHAR=","
CHAROFF="7">
```

CLASS="..."

Indicates which style class applies to the <TBODY> element.

Standard: HTML 4
Common: No
Sample:

```
<TBODY CLASS="casual">
```

ID="n"

Assigns a unique ID selector to an instance of the <TBODY> tag. When you then assign a style to that ID selector, it affects only that one instance of the <TBODY> tag.

Standard: HTML 4
Common: No
Sample:

```
<TBODY ID="123">
```

STYLE="..."

Specifies style sheet commands that apply to the contents between the <TBODY> tags.

Standard: HTML 4
Common: No
Sample:

```
<TBODY STYLE="background: red">
```

TITLE="..."

Specifies text assigned to the tag. You might use this attribute for context-sensitive help within the document. Browsers may use this to show tool tips over the table body.

Standard: HTML 4
Common: No
Sample:

```
<TBODY TITLE="Table Body">
```

VALIGN={TOP, BOTTOM, MIDDLE, BASELINE}

Specifies the vertical alignment of the contents of the table body.

Standard: Internet Explorer 4
Common: No
Sample:

```
<TBODY VALIGN=MIDDLE>
```

Other Attributes

This tag also accepts the LANG, DIR, onClick, onDblClick, onMouseDown, onMouseUp, onMouseOver, onMouseMove, onMouseOut, onKeyPress, onKeyDown, and onKeyUp attributes. See the Element-Independent Attributes section of this reference for definitions and examples.

<TD>

Contains a table cell. These tags go inside the <TR> tags.

Standard: HTML 3.2
Common: Yes
Paired: Yes
Sample:

```
<TR>
  <TD>Bob Jones</TD>
  <TD>555-1212</TD>
  <TD>Democrat</TD>
</TR>
```

Attribute Information

ALIGN={LEFT, RIGHT, CENTER, JUSTIFY, CHAR}

Specifies how text within the table header will line up with the edges of the table cells, or if ALIGN=CHAR, on a specific character (the decimal point).

Standard: HTML 4
Common: Yes
Sample:

```
<TR>
  <TD ALIGN=CENTER>Television</TD>
  <TD> <IMG SRC="tv.gif" ALT="TV"
  BORDER=0> </TD>
</TR>
```

ABBR="..."

Specifies an abbreviated cell name.

Standard: HTML 4
Common: No
Sample:

```
<TD ABBR="TV"><B>Television</B>
</TD>
```

AXES="..."

Lists axis values that pertain to the cell.

Standard: HTML 4
Common: No
Sample:

```
<TD AXES="TV,
Programs"><B>Television</B></TD>
```

BACKGROUND="URL"

Specifies the relative or absolute location of a graphic image file for the browser to load as a background graphic for the table cell.

Standard: Internet Explorer, Netscape Navigator
Common: No
Sample:

```
<TD BACKGROUND="waves.gif">
```

BGCOLOR="#RRGGBB" or "..."

Specifies the background color inside a table cell. You can substitute the hexadecimal RGB values for the appropriate color names.

Standard: Deprecated in HTML 4 in favor of style sheets
Common: No

Sample:

```
<TR><TD BGCOLOR="Pink">Course
Number</TD>
<TD BGCOLOR="Blue">Time
taught</TD></TR>
```

BORDERCOLOR="#RRGGBB" or "..."

Indicates the color of the border of the table cell. You can specify the color with hexadecimal RGB values or by the color name.

Standard: Internet Explorer 2
Common: No
Sample:

```
<TR><TD BORDERCOLOR="Blue">
```

BORDERCOLORDARK="#RRGGBB" or "..."

Indicates the darker color used to form 3-D borders around the table cell. You can specify the color with its hexadecimal RGB values or with its color name.

Standard: Internet Explorer 4
Common: No
Sample:

```
<TD BORDERCOLORLIGHT=#FFFFFF
BORDERCOLORDARK=#88AA2C>
```

BORDERCOLORLIGHT="#RRGGBB" or "..."

Indicates the lighter color used to form 3-D borders around the table cell. You can specify the color with its hexadecimal RGB values or with its color name.

Standard: Internet Explorer 4
Common: No
Sample:

```
<TD BORDERCOLORLIGHT=#FFFFFF
BORDERCOLORDARK=#88AA2C>
```

CHAR="..."

Specifies the character on which cell contents will align, if ALIGN="CHAR". If you omit CHAR=, the default value is the decimal point in the specified language.

Standard: HTML 4
Common: No
Sample:

```
<TD ALIGN="CHAR" CHAR=",">
```

CHAROFF="*n*"

Specifies the number of characters from the left at which the alignment character appears.

Standard: HTML 4

Common: No

Sample:

```
<TD ALIGN="CHAR" CHAR=","
CHAROFF="7">
```

CLASS="..."

Indicates which style class applies to the <TD> element.

Standard: HTML 4

Common: No

Sample:

```
<TD CLASS="casual">Jobs Produced</TD>
```

COLSPAN="*n*"

Specifies that a table cell occupy one column more than the default of one. This is useful when you have a category name that applies to more than one column of data.

Standard: HTML 3.2

Common: Yes

Sample:

```
<TR><TD COLSPAN=2>Students</TD>
</TR>
<TR><TD>Bob Smith</TDH><TD>John
Doe</TD></TR>
```

ID="*n*"

Assigns a unique ID selector to an instance of the <TD> tag. When you then assign a style to that ID selector, it affects only that one instance of the <TD> tag.

Standard: HTML 4

Common: No

Sample:

```
<TD ID="123">
```

NOWRAP

Disables the default word-wrapping within a table cell, thus maximizing the amount of the cell's horizontal space.

Standard: Deprecated in HTML 4 in favor of style sheets

Common: No

Sample:

```
<TD NOWRAP>The contents of this cell
will not wrap at all</TD>
```

ROWSPAN="*n*"

Specifies that a table cell occupy more rows than the default of 1. This is useful when several rows of information are related to one category.

Standard: HTML 3.2

Common: Yes

Sample:

```
<TR><TD VALIGN=MIDDLE ALIGN=RIGHT
ROWSPAN=3>Pie Entries</TD>
<TD>Banana Cream</TD>
<TD>Mrs. Robinson</TD></TR>
<TR><TD>Strawberry Cheesecake</TD>
<TD>Mrs. Barton</TD></TR>
<TR><TD>German Chocolate</TD>
<TD>Mrs. Larson</TD></TR>
```

STYLE="..."

Specifies style sheet commands that apply to the contents of the table cell.

Standard: HTML 4

Common: No

Sample:

```
<TD STYLE="background: red">
```

TITLE="..."

Specifies text assigned to the tag. You might use this attribute for context-sensitive help within the document. Browsers may use this to show tool tips over the table header.

Standard: HTML 4

Common: No

Sample:

```
<TD TITLE="Table Cell Heading">
```

VALIGN={TOP, MIDDLE, BOTTOM, BASELINE}

Aligns the contents of a cell with the top, bottom, baseline, or middle of the cell.

Standard: HTML 3.2

Common: Yes

Sample:

```
<TD VALIGN=TOP>
<IMG SRC="images/bud.gif"
BORDER=0></TD>
```

WIDTH="*n*"

Specifies the horizontal dimension of the cell in pixels or as a percentage of the table width.

Standard: HTML 3.2; not listed in HTML 4

Common: Yes
Sample:

```
<TD WIDTH=200 ALIGN=LEFT><H2>African
Species</H2></TD>
```

Other Attributes

This tag also accepts the HEADERS, SCOPE, LANG, DIR, onClick, onDblClick, onMouseDown, onMouseUp, onMouseOver, onMouseMove, onMouseOut, onKeyPress, onKeyDown, and onKeyUp attributes. See the Element-Independent Attributes section of this reference for definitions and examples.

<TEXTAREA>

Defines a multiple-line text input field within a form. Place the <TEXTAREA> tags inside the <FORM> tags. To specify a default value in a <TEXTAREA> field, place the text between the <TEXTAREA> tags.

Standard: HTML 2
Common: Yes
Paired: Yes
Sample:

```
Enter any comments here:

<TEXTAREA NAME="comments" COLS=40
ROWS=5>

No Comments.

</TEXTAREA>
```

Attribute Information

ACCESSKEY="..."

Assigns a keystroke sequence to the <TEXTAREA> element.

Standard: HTML 4
Common: No
Sample:

```
<TEXTAREA COLS=40 ROWS=10
NAME="Story" ACCESSKEY=S>
```

CLASS="..."

Indicates which style class applies to the <TEXTAREA> element.

Standard: HTML 4
Common: No
Sample:

```
<TEXTAREA CLASS="casual">
```

COLS="n"

Indicates the width (in character widths) of the text input field.

Standard: HTML 2
Common: Yes
Sample:

```
<TEXTAREA NAME="desc" COLS=50
ROWS=3></TEXTAREA>
```

DATAFLD="..."

Selects a column from a previously identified source of tabular data (see the DATASRC= attribute).

Standard: Internet Explorer 4
Common: No
Sample:

```
<TEXTAREA DATASRC="#data_table"
DATAFLD="name" NAME="st1">
```

DATASRC="..."

Specifies the source of data for data binding.

Standard: Internet Explorer 4
Common: No
Sample:

```
<TEXTAREA DATASRC="#data_table"
DATAFLD="name" NAME="st1">
```

DISABLED

Denies access to the text input field.

Standard: HTML 4
Common: No
Sample:

```
<TEXTAREA ROWS=10 COLS=10
NAME="Comments" DISABLED>
```

ID="n"

Assigns a unique ID selector to an instance of the <TEXTAREA> tag. When you then assign a style to that ID selector, it affects only that one instance of the <TEXTAREA> tag.

Standard: HTML 4
Common: No
Sample:

```
<TEXTAREA ID="123">
```

NAME="..."

Names the value you pass to the form processor. For example, if you collect personal feedback, assign the NAME= attribute something like "comments". This establishes a *name-value pair* with which the form processor can work.

> **Standard:** HTML 2
> **Common:** Yes
> **Sample:**

```
<TEXTAREA COLS=30 ROWS=10
NAME="recipe"></TEXTAREA>
```

READONLY
Specifies that the visitor cannot change the contents of the text input field.

> **Standard:** HTML 4
> **Common:** No
> **Sample:**

```
<TEXTAREA ROWS=10 COLS=10
NAME="Notes" READONLY>
```

ROWS="*n*"
Indicates the height (in lines of text) of the text input field.

> **Standard:** HTML 2
> **Common:** Yes
> **Sample:**

```
<TEXTAREA NAME="desc" COLS=50
ROWS=3></TEXTAREA>
```

STYLE="..."
Specifies style sheet commands that apply to the <TEXTAREA> tag.

> **Standard:** HTML 4
> **Common:** No
> **Sample:**

```
<TEXTAREA STYLE="background: red">
```

TABINDEX=*n*
Indicates where <TEXTAREA> appears in the tabbing order.

> **Standard:** HTML 4
> **Common:** No
> **Sample:**

```
<TEXTAREA ROWS=5 COLS=40 NAME="story"
TABINDEX=2>
```

TITLE="..."
Specifies text assigned to the tag. You might use this attribute for context-sensitive help within the document. Browsers may use this to show tool tips over the text entry input method.

> **Standard:** HTML 4
> **Common:** No
> **Sample:**

```
<TEXTAREA COLS=10 ROWS=2 NAME="tt"
TITLE="Text Entry Box">
```

Other Attributes
This tag also accepts the LANG, DIR, onFocus, onBlur, onChange, onSelect, onClick, onDblClick, onMouseDown, onMouseUp, onMouseOver, onMouseMove, onMouseOut, onKeyPress, onKeyDown, and onKeyUp attributes. See the Element-Independent Attributes section of this reference for definitions and examples.

<TFOOT>

Defines a table footer within a table. It must *precede* the <TBODY> tag.

> **Standard:** HTML 4
> **Common:** No
> **Paired:** Yes
> **Sample:**

```
<TFOOT>
<TR>
<TD>Totals</TD><TD>$100.25</TD>
</TR>
</TFOOT>
</TABLE>
```

Attribute Information

ALIGN={LEFT, RIGHT, CENTER, JUSTIFY, CHAR}
Specifies how text within the table footer will line up with the edges of the table cells, or if ALIGN=CHAR, on a specific character (the decimal point).

> **Standard:** HTML 4
> **Common:** Yes
> **Sample:**

```
<TR>
 <TFOOT ALIGN=LEFT>
  <TH><B>Television</B></TH>
  <TH> <IMG SRC="tv.gif"
  ALT="TV" BORDER=0>  </TH>
 </TFOOT>
</TR>
```

CHAR="..."

Specifies the character on which cell contents will align, if ALIGN="CHAR". If you omit CHAR=, the default value is the decimal point in the specified language.

> **Standard:**   HTML 4
> **Common:**   No
> **Sample:**

```
<TFOOT ALIGN="CHAR" CHAR=",">
```

CHAROFF="n"

Specifies the number of characters from the left at which the alignment character appears.

> **Standard:**   HTML 4
> **Common:**   No
> **Sample:**

```
<TFOOT ALIGN="CHAR" CHAR=","
CHAROFF="7">
```

CLASS="..."

Indicates which style class applies to the <TFOOT> element.

> **Standard:**   HTML 4
> **Common:**   No
> **Sample:**

```
<TFOOT CLASS="casual">
```

ID="n"

Assigns a unique ID selector to an instance of the <TFOOT> tag. When you then assign a style to that ID selector, it affects only that one instance of the <TFOOT> tag.

> **Standard:**   HTML 4
> **Common:**   No
> **Sample:**

```
<TFOOT ID="123">
```

STYLE="..."

Specifies style sheet commands that apply to the contents between the <TFOOT> tags.

> **Standard:**   HTML 4
> **Common:**   No
> **Sample:**

```
<TFOOT STYLE="background: red">
```

TITLE="..."

Specifies text assigned to the tag. You might use this attribute for context-sensitive help within the document. Browsers may use this to show tool tips over the table footer.

> **Standard:**   HTML 4
> **Common:**   No
> **Sample:**

```
<TFOOT TITLE="Table Footer">
```

VALIGN={TOP, BOTTOM, MIDDLE, BASELINE}

Aligns the contents of the table footer with the top, bottom, or middle of the footer container.

> **Standard:**   Internet Explorer 4
> **Common:**   No
> **Sample:**

```
<TFOOT ALIGN=CENTER VALIGN=TOP>
```

Other Attributes

This tag also accepts the LANG, DIR, onClick, onDblClick, onMouseDown, onMouseUp, onMouseOver, onMouseMove, onMouseOut, onKeyPress, onKeyDown, and onKeyUp attributes. See the Element-Independent Attributes section of this reference for definitions and examples.

<TH>

Contains table cell headings. The <TH> tags are identical to the <TD> tags except that text inside <TH> is usually emphasized with bold-face font and centered within the cell.

> **Standard:**   HTML 3.2
> **Common:**   Yes
> **Paired:**   Yes, optional
> **Sample:**

```
<TABLE>
<TH>Name</TH><TH>Phone No</TH>
<TD>John Doe</TD>
<TD>555-1212</TD>
<TD>Bob Smith</TD>
<TD>555-2121</TD>
</TABLE>
```

Attribute Information

ALIGN={LEFT, RIGHT, CENTER, JUSTIFY, CHAR}

Specifies how text within the table header will line up with the edges of the table cells, or if ALIGN=CHAR, on a specific character (the decimal point).

> **Standard:**   HTML 4

Common: Yes
Sample:

```
<TR>
  <TH ALIGN=CENTER>Television</TH>
  <TH> <IMG SRC="tv.gif"
  ALT="TV" BORDER=0> </TH>
</TR>
```

ABBR="..."

Specifies an abbreviated cell name.

Standard: HTML 4
Common: No
Sample:

```
<TH ABBR="TV">
<B>Television</B></TH>
```

AXES="..."

Lists axis values that pertain to the cell.

Standard: HTML 4
Common: No
Sample:

```
<TH AXES="TV, Programs">
<B>Television</B></TH>
```

BACKGROUND="*URL*"

Specifies the relative or absolute location of a graphic image file for the browser to load as a background graphic for the table cell.

Standard: Internet Explorer, Netscape
                 Navigator
Common: No
Sample:

```
<TH BACKGROUND="waves.gif">
```

BGCOLOR="*#RRGGBB*" or "..."

Specifies the background color inside a table cell. You can substitute the hexadecimal RGB values for the appropriate color names.

Standard: Deprecated in HTML 4 in
                 favor of style sheets
Common: No
Sample:

```
<TR><TH BGCOLOR="Pink">Course
Number</TH>
<TH BGCOLOR="Blue">Time
taught</TH></TR>
```

BORDERCOLOR="*#RRGGBB*" or "..."

Indicates the color of the border of the table cell. You can specify the color with hexadecimal RGB values or by the color name.

Standard: Internet Explorer 2
Common: No
Sample:

```
<TR><TH BORDERCOLOR="Blue">
```

BORDERCOLORDARK="*#RRGGBB*" or "..."

Indicates the darker color used to form 3-D borders around the table cell. You can specify the color with its hexadecimal RGB values or with its color name.

Standard: Internet Explorer 4
Common: No
Sample:

```
<TH BORDERCOLORLIGHT="#FFFFFF"
BORDERCOLORDARK="#88AA2C">
```

BORDERCOLORLIGHT="*#RRGGBB*" or "..."

Indicates the lighter color used to form 3-D borders around the table cell. You can specify the color with its hexadecimal RGB values or with its color name.

Standard: Internet Explorer 4
Common: No
Sample:

```
<TH BORDERCOLORLIGHT="#FFFFFF"
BORDERCOLORDARK="#88AA2C">
```

CHAR="..."

Specifies the character on which cell contents align, if ALIGN="CHAR". If you omit CHAR=, the default value is the decimal point in the specified language.

Standard: HTML 4
Common: No
Sample:

```
<TH ALIGN="CHAR" CHAR=",">
```

CHAROFF="*n*"

Specifies the number of characters from the left at which the alignment character appears.

Standard: HTML 4
Common: No
Sample:

```
<TH ALIGN="CHAR" CHAR=","
CHAROFF="7">
```

CLASS="..."

Indicates which style class applies to the <TH> element.

Standard: HTML 4
Common: No
Sample:

```
<TH CLASS="casual">Jobs Produced</TH>
```

COLSPAN="n"

Specifies that a table cell occupy more columns than the default of one. This is useful if a category name applies to more than one column of data.

Standard: HTML 3.2
Common: Yes
Sample:

```
<TR><TH COLSPAN=2>
Students</TH></TR>
<TR><TD>Bob Smith</TDH>
<TD>John Doe</TD></TR>
```

ID="n"

Assigns a unique ID selector to an instance of the <TH> tag. When you then assign a style to that ID selector, it affects only that one instance of the <TH> tag.

Standard: HTML 4
Common: No
Sample:

```
<TH ID="123">
```

NOWRAP

Disables default word-wrapping within a table cell, maximizing the the cell's horizontal space.

Standard: Deprecated in HTML 4 in favor of style sheets
Common: No
Sample:

```
<TH NOWRAP>The contents of this cell
will not wrap at all.</TH>
```

ROWSPAN="n"

Specifies that a table cell occupy more rows than the default of 1. This is useful if several rows of information relate to one category.

Standard: HTML 3.2
Common: Yes

Sample:

```
<TR><TH VALIGN=MIDDLE ALIGN=RIGHT
ROWSPAN=3>Pie Entries</TH>
<TD>Banana Cream</TD>
<TD>Mrs. Robinson</TD></TR>
<TR><TD>Strawberry Cheesecake</TD>
<TD>Mrs. Barton</TD></TR>
<TR><TD>German Chocolate</TD>
<TD>Mrs. Larson</TD></TR>
```

STYLE="..."

Specifies style sheet commands that apply to the contents of the table cell.

Standard: HTML 4
Common: No
Sample:

```
<TH STYLE="background: red">
```

TITLE="..."

Specifies text assigned to the tag. You might use this attribute for context-sensitive help within the document. Browsers may use this to show tool tips over the table header.

Standard: HTML 4
Common: No
Sample:

```
<TH TITLE="Table Cell Heading">
```

VALIGN={TOP, MIDDLE, BOTTOM, BASELINE}

Aligns the contents of a cell with the top, bottom, baseline, or middle of the cell.

Standard: HTML 3.2
Common: Yes
Sample:

```
<TH VALIGN=TOP>
<IMG SRC="images/bud.gif
BORDER=0></TH>
```

WIDTH=n

Specifies the horizontal dimension of the cell in pixels or as a percentage of the table width.

Standard: HTML 3.2; not listed in HTML 4
Common: Yes
Sample:

```
<TH WIDTH=200 ALIGN=LEFT>
<H2>African Species</H2></TH>
```

Other Attributes

This tag also accepts the HEADERS, SCOPE, LANG, DIR, onClick, onDblClick, onMouseDown, onMouseUp, onMouseOver, onMouseMove, onMouseOut, onKeyPress, onKeyDown, and onKeyUp attributes. See the Element-Independent Attributes section of this reference for definitions and examples.

<THEAD>

Defines a table header section. At least one table row must go within <THEAD>.

Standard:	HTML 4
Common:	No
Paired:	Yes
Sample:	

```
<TABLE RULES=ROWS>
 <THEAD>
 <TR><TD>Column 1
 <TD>Column 2
 </THEAD>
```

Attribute Information

ALIGN={LEFT, RIGHT, CENTER, JUSTIFY, CHAR}

Specifies how text within the table header will line up with the edges of the table cells, or if ALIGN=CHAR, on a specific character (the decimal point).

Standard:	HTML 4
Common:	Yes
Sample:	

```
<TR>
 <THEAD ALIGN=CENTER>
 <TH><B>Television</B></TH>
 <TH> <IMG SRC="tv.gif"
 ALT="TV" BORDER=0> </TH>
 </THEAD>
</TR>
```

CHAR="..."

Specifies the character on which cell contents align, if ALIGN="CHAR". If you omit CHAR=, the default value is the decimal point in the specified language.

Standard:	HTML 4
Common:	No
Sample:	

```
<THEAD ALIGN="CHAR" CHAR=",">
```

CHAROFF="n"

Specifies the number of characters from the left at which the alignment character appears.

Standard:	HTML 4
Common:	No
Sample:	

```
<THEAD ALIGN="CHAR" CHAR=","
CHAROFF="7">
```

CLASS="..."

Indicates which style class applies to the <THEAD> element.

Standard:	HTML 4
Common:	No
Sample:	

```
<THEAD CLASS="casual">
```

ID="n"

Assigns a unique ID selector to an instance of the <THEAD> tag. When you then assign a style to that ID selector, it affects only that one instance of the <THEAD> tag.

Standard:	HTML 4
Common:	No
Sample:	

```
<THEAD ID="123">
```

STYLE="..."

Specifies style sheet commands that apply to the contents between the <THEAD> tags.

Standard:	HTML 4
Common:	No
Sample:	

```
<THEAD STYLE="background: red">
```

TITLE="..."

Specifies text assigned to the tag. You might use this attribute for context-sensitive help within the document. Browsers may use this to show tool tips over the table head.

Standard:	HTML 4
Common:	No
Sample:	

```
<THEAD TITLE="Table Heading">
```

VALIGN={TOP, MIDDLE, BOTTOM, BASELINE}

Aligns the contents of the table header with respect to the top and bottom edges of the header container.

Standard: HTML 4
Common: No
Sample:

```
<THEAD ALIGN=LEFT VALIGN=TOP>
```

Other Attributes

This tag also accepts the LANG, DIR, onClick, onDblClick, onMouseDown, onMouseUp, onMouseOver, onMouseMove, onMouseOut, onKeyPress, onKeyDown, and onKeyUp attributes. See the Element-Independent Attributes section of this reference for definitions and examples.

<TITLE>

Gives the document an official title. The <TITLE> tags appear inside the document header inside the <HEAD> tags.

Standard: HTML 2
Common: Yes
Paired: Yes
Sample:

```
<HTML>
<HEAD>
<TITLE>How To Build A
Go-Cart</TITLE>
</HEAD>
```

Attribute Information

This tag also accepts the LANG and DIR attributes. See the Element-Independent Attributes section of this reference for definitions and examples.

<TR>

Contains a row of cells in a table. You must place the <TR> tags inside the <TABLE> container, which can contain <TH> and <TD> tags.

Standard: HTML 3.2
Common: Yes
Paired: Yes, optional
Sample:

```
<TABLE>
<TR><TH COLSPAN=3>Test
Scores</TH></TR>
<TR>
  <TD>Bob Smith</TD>
  <TD>78</TD>
  <TD>85</TD>
</TR>
<TR>
  <TD>John Doe</TD>
  <TD>87</TD>
  <TD>85</TD>
</TR>
</TABLE>
```

Attribute Information

ALIGN={LEFT, RIGHT, CENTER, JUSTIFY, CHAR}

Specifies how text within the table row will line up with the edges of the table cells, or if ALIGN=CHAR, on a specific character (the decimal point).

Standard: HTML 4
Common: Yes
Sample:

```
<TR ALIGN=CENTER >
  <TD><B>Television</B></TD>
  <TD> <IMG SRC="tv.gif"
  ALT="TV" BORDER=0> </TD>
</TR>
```

BGCOLOR="#*RRGGBB*" or "..."

Specifies the background color of table cells in the row. You can substitute the color names for the hexadecimal RGB values.

Standard: Deprecated in HTML 4 in favor of style sheets
Common: No
Sample:

```
<TR BGCOLOR="Yellow">

  <TD><IMG SRC="Bob.jpg"
  ALT="Bob" BORDER=0></TD>
  <TD ALIGN=LEFT VALIGN=MIDDLE>
  Bob Smith sitting at his desk
  on a July afternoon.</TD>
</TR>
```

BORDERCOLOR="#*RRGGBB*" or "..."

Specifies the color of cell borders within the row. Currently, only Internet Explorer accepts this attribute. You can substitute color names for the hexadecimal RGB values.

Standard: Internet Explorer 2
Common: No
Sample:

```
<TR BORDERCOLOR="#3F2A55">
  <TD ALIGN=RIGHT VALIGN=MIDDLE>
  Computers</TD>
  <TD><IMG SRC="Computers.jpg">
  </TD>
</TR>
```

BORDERCOLORDARK="#*RRGGBB*" or "*...*"

Indicates the darker color for the 3-D borders around the table row. You can specify the color with its hexadecimal RGB values or with its color name.

Standard: Internet Explorer 4
Common: No
Sample:

```
<TR BORDERCOLORLIGHT="silver"
BORDERCOLORDARK="black">
```

BORDERCOLORLIGHT="#*RRGGBB*" or "*...*"

Indicates the lighter color for 3-D borders around the table row. You can specify the color with its hexadecimal RGB values or with its color name.

Standard: Internet Explorer 4
Common: No
Sample:

```
<TR BORDERCOLORLIGHT="silver"
BORDERCOLORDARK="black">
```

CHAR="*...*"

Specifies the character on which cell contents align, if ALIGN="CHAR". If you omit CHAR=, the default value is the decimal point in the specified language.

Standard: HTML 4
Common: No
Sample:

```
<TR ALIGN="CHAR" CHAR=",">
```

CHAROFF="*n*"

Specifies the number of characters from the left at which the alignment character appears.

Standard: HTML 4
Common: No

Sample:

```
<TR ALIGN="CHAR" CHAR=","
CHAROFF="7">
```

CLASS="*...*"

Indicates which style class applies to the <TR> element.

Standard: HTML 4
Common: No
Sample:

```
<TR CLASS="casual">
  <TD>Uranium</TD>
  <TD>Plutonium</TD>
  <TD>Radon</TD>
</TR>
```

ID="*n*"

Assigns a unique ID selector to an instance of the <TR> tag. When you then assign a style to that ID selector, it affects only that one instance of the <TR> tag.

Standard: HTML 4
Common: No
Sample:

```
<TR ID="123">
```

NOWRAP

Indicates that text within table cells in the row not wrap. This may cause the table to expand beyond the horizontal dimensions of the current document.

Standard: Internet Explorer 3; deprecated in HTML 4 in favor of style sheets
Common: No
Sample:

```
<TR NOWRAP>
  <TD>In this table cell I'm
  going to type a lot of
  stuff.</TD>
  <TD>In this table cell I'm
  going to continue to type a
  lot of stuff.</TD>
</TR>
```

STYLE="*...*"

Specifies style sheet commands that apply to all cells in the table row.

Standard: HTML 4
Common: No

Sample:

```
<TR STYLE="background: red">
```

TITLE="..."

Specifies text assigned to the tag. You might use this attribute for context-sensitive help within the document. Browsers may use this to show tool tips.

Standard:	HTML 4
Common:	No

Sample:

```
<TR TITLE="Table Row">
```

VALIGN={TOP, MIDDLE, BOTTOM, BASELINE}

Specifies the vertical alignment of the contents of all cells within the row.

Standard:	HTML 3.2
Common:	Yes

Sample:

```
<TR VALIGN=TOP>
  <TD ALIGN=CENTER>John
Smith</TD>
  <TD ALIGN=CENTER>Bob Doe</TD>
</TR>
```

Other Attributes

This tag also accepts the LANG, DIR, onClick, onDblClick, onMouseDown, onMouseUp, onMouseOver, onMouseMove, onMouseOut, onKeyPress, onKeyDown, and onKeyUp attributes. See the Element-Independent Attributes section of this reference for definitions and examples.

<TT>

Displays text in a monospace font.

Standard:	HTML 2
Common:	Yes
Paired:	Yes

Sample:

```
After I typed in help, the words
<TT>help: not found</TT> appeared on
my screen.
```

Attribute Information

CLASS="..."

Indicates which style class applies to the <TT> element.

Standard:	HTML 4
Common:	No

Sample:

```
I sat down and began to type.
<P><TT CLASS="casual">It was a dark
and stormy night.</TT>
```

ID="n"

Assigns a unique ID selector to an instance of the <TT> tag. When you then assign a style to that ID selector, it affects only that one instance of the <TT> tag.

Standard:	HTML 4
Common:	No

Sample:

```
<TT ID="123">
```

STYLE="..."

Specifies style sheet commands that apply to the contents within the <TT> tags.

Standard:	HTML 4
Common:	No

Sample:

```
<TT STYLE="background: red">
```

TITLE="..."

Specifies text assigned to the tag. You might use this attribute for context-sensitive help within the document. Browsers may use this to show tool tips over the text within the <TT> tags.

Standard:	HTML 4
Common:	No

Sample:

```
Now, type <TT TITLE="User
Typing">MAIL</TT> and hit the
<KBD>ENTER</KBD> key.
```

Other Attributes

This tag also accepts the LANG, DIR, onClick, onDblClick, onMouseDown, onMouseUp, onMouseOver, onMouseMove, onMouseOut, onKeyPress, onKeyDown, and onKeyUp attributes. See the Element-Independent Attributes section of this reference for definitions and examples.

U

<U>

Underlines text in a document. Use this tag with moderation since underlined text can confuse visitors accustomed to seeing hyperlinks as underlined text.

Standard:	HTML 2; deprecated in HTML 4 in favor of style sheets
Common:	Yes
Paired:	Yes
Sample:	

```
After waterskiing, I was
<U>really</U> tired.
```

Attribute Information

CLASS="..."

Indicates which style class applies to the <U> element.

Standard:	HTML 4
Common:	No
Sample:	

```
Have you seen <U CLASS="casual">
True Lies</U> yet?
```

ID="n"

Assigns a unique ID selector to an instance of the <U> tag. When you then assign a style to that ID selector, it affects only that one instance of the <U> tag.

Standard:	HTML 4
Common:	No
Sample:	

```
<U ID="123">
```

STYLE="..."

Specifies style sheet commands that apply to the contents within the <U> tags.

Standard:	HTML 4
Common:	No
Sample:	

```
<U STYLE="background: red">
```

TITLE="..."

Specifies text assigned to the tag. You might use this attribute for context-sensitive help within the document. Browsers may use this to show tool tips over the underlined text.

Standard:	HTML 4
Common:	No
Sample:	

```
Read the book <U TITLE=
"BookTitle">Walden</U> and you'll be
enlightened.
```

Other Attributes

This tag also accepts the LANG, DIR, onClick, onDblClick, onMouseDown, onMouseUp, onMouseOver, onMouseMove, onMouseOut, onKeyPress, onKeyDown, and onKeyUp attributes. See the Element-Independent Attributes section of this reference for definitions and examples.

<UL>

Contains a bulleted (unordered) list. You can then use the <LI> (List Item) tag to add bulleted items to the list.

Standard:	HTML 2
Common:	Yes
Paired:	Yes
Sample:	

```
Before you can begin, you need:<UL>
    <LI>Circular saw
    <LI>Drill with Phillips bit
    <LI>Wood screws
</UL>
```

Attribute Information

CLASS="..."

Indicates which style class applies to the <UL> element.

Standard:	HTML 4
Common:	No
Sample:	

```
<UL CLASS="casual">
    <LI>Hexagon</LI>
    <LI>Pentagon</LI>
    <LI>Octagon</LI>
</UL>
```

COMPACT

Indicates that the unordered list appears in a compact format. This attribute may not affect the appearance of the list as most browsers do not present lists in more than one format.

Standard: HTML 2; deprecated in HTML 4
Common: No
Sample:

```
<UL COMPACT>
  <LI>Flour
  <LI>Sugar
  <LI>Wheat
  <LI>Raisins
</UL>
```

ID="*n*"

Assigns a unique ID selector to an instance of the <UL> tag. When you then assign a style to that ID selector, it affects only that one instance of the <UL> tag.

Standard: HTML 4
Common: No
Sample:

```
<UL ID="123">
```

STYLE="..."

Specifies style sheet commands that apply to the contents of the unordered list.

Standard: HTML 4
Common: No
Sample:

```
<UL STYLE="background: red">
```

TITLE="..."

Specifies text assigned to the tag. You might use this attribute for context-sensitive help within the document. Browsers may use this to show tool tips over the unordered list.

Standard: HTML 4
Common: No
Sample:

```
<UL TITLE="Food List">
  <LI>Spaghetti
  <LI>Pizza
  <LI>Fettuccini Alfredo
</UL>
```

TYPE={SQUARE, CIRCLE, DISC}

Specifies the bullet type for each unordered list item. If you omit the TYPE= attribute, the browser chooses a default type.

Standard: HTML 2
Common: Yes
Sample:

```
<UL TYPE=DISC>
  <LI>Spaghetti
  <UL TYPE=SQUARE>
    <LI>Noodles
    <LI>Sauce
    <LI>Cheese
  </UL>
</UL>
```

Other Attributes

This tag also accepts the LANG, DIR, onClick, onDblClick, onMouseDown, onMouseUp, onMouseOver, onMouseMove, onMouseOut, onKeyPress, onKeyDown, and onKeyUp attributes. See the Element-Independent Attributes section of this reference for definitions and examples.

V

<VAR>

Indicates a placeholder variable in document text. This is useful when describing commands for which the visitor must supply a parameter.

Standard: HTML 2
Common: Yes
Paired: Yes
Sample:

```
To copy a file in DOS type <SAMP>COPY
<VAR>file1</VAR>
<VAR>file2</VAR></SAMP> and press the
ENTER key.
```

Attribute Information

CLASS="..."

Indicates which style class applies to the <VAR> element.

Standard: HTML 4
Common: No

Sample:

```
I, <VAR CLASS="casual">your
name</VAR>, solemnly swear to tell
the truth.
```

ID="n"

Assigns a unique ID selector to an instance of the <VAR> tag. When you then assign a style to that ID selector, it affects only that one instance of the <VAR> tag.

Standard: HTML 4
Common: No
Sample:

```
<VAR ID="123">
```

STYLE="..."

Specifies style sheet commands that apply to the contents within the <VAR> tags.

Standard: HTML 4
Common: No
Sample:

```
<VAR STYLE="background: red">
```

TITLE="..."

Specifies text assigned to the tag. You might use this attribute for context-sensitive help within the document. Browsers may use this to show tool tips over the text within the <VAR> tags.

Standard: HTML 4
Common: No
Sample:

```
Use a H<VAR TITLE="Heading Level
Number">n</VAR> tag.
```

Other Attributes

This tag also accepts the LANG, DIR, onClick, onDblClick, onMouseDown, onMouseUp, onMouseOver, onMouseMove, onMouseOut, onKeyPress, onKeyDown, and onKeyUp attributes. See the Element-Independent Attributes section of this reference for definitions and examples.

W

<WBR>

Forces a word break. This is useful in combination with the <NOBR> tag to permit line breaks where they could otherwise not occur.

Standard: Netscape Navigator
Common: No
Paired: No
Sample:

```
<NOBR>
This line would go on forever, except
that I have this neat tag called WBR
that does <WBR>this!
</NOBR>
```

X

<XMP>

Includes preformatted text within a document. Unlike the <PRE> tag, the browser does not interpret HTML tags within the <XMP> tags. HTML 3.2 declared this tag obsolete; so use <PRE> instead.

Standard: Obsolete
Common: No
Paired: Yes
Sample:

```
The output from these reports is
shown below.
<XMP>
Company       Q1      Q2      Q3     Q4
----------   ---     ---     ---    ---
Widget Inc   4.5m    4.6m   6.2m   4.5m
Acme Widget  5.9m   10.2m   7.3m   6.6m
West Widget  2.2m    1.3m   3.1m   6.1m
</XMP>
```

Element-Independent Attributes and Event Handlers

Many HTML elements accept the attributes and event handlers described in this section. See the cross-references from individual elements for specific support information.

Attributes

DIR="{LTR, RTL}"

Specifies the direction (left to right or right to left) for the text used within the section. This attribute is used most often within documents to override site-wide language direction specifications.

Standard: HTML 4
Common: No
Sample:

```
<P>The following quote is in Hebrew,
therefore written right to left, not
left to right.
<Q LANG="IW" DIR="RTL">Hebrew text
goes here and is presented right to
left, not left to right. </Q></P>
```

LANG="..."

Specifies the language used within the section. This attribute is used most often within documents to override site-wide language specifications. Use standard codes for languages, such as DE for German, FR for French, IT for Italian, and IW for Hebrew. See ISO Specification 639 at www.sil.org/sgml/iso639a.html for more information about language codes.

Standard: HTML 4
Common: No
Sample:

```
<P>The following quote is in German.
<Q LANG="DE">Guten Tag!</Q></P>
```

Event Handlers

Each of the following event handlers helps link visitor actions to scripts.

onLoad="..."

Occurs when the browser finishes loading a window or all frames within a <FRAMESET>. This handler works with <BODY> and <FRAMESET> elements.

onUnload="..."

Occurs when the browser removes a document from a window or frame. This handler works with <BODY> and <FRAMESET> elements.

onClick="..."

Occurs when a visitor clicks the mouse over an element. This handler works with most elements.

onDblClick="..."

Occurs when a visitor double-clicks the mouse over an element. This handler works with most elements.

onMouseDown="..."

Occurs when a visitor presses the mouse button over an element. This handler works with most elements.

onMouseUp="..."

Occurs when a visitor releases the mouse button over an element. This handler works with most elements.

onMouseOver="..."

Occurs when a visitor moves the mouse over an element. This handler works with most elements.

onMouseMove="..."

Occurs when a visitor moves the mouse while still over an element. This handler works with most elements.

onMouseOut="..."

Occurs when a visitor moves the mouse away from an element. This handler works with most elements.

onFocus="..."

Occurs when a visitor moves the focus to an element either with the mouse or the Tab key. This handler works with <A>, <AREA>, <LABEL>, <INPUT>, <SELECT>, <TEXTAREA>, and <BUTTON>.

onBlur="..."

Occurs when a visitor moves focus from an element either with the mouse or the tab key.

This handler works with <A>, <AREA>, <LABEL>, <INPUT>, <SELECT>, <TEXTAREA>, and <BUTTON>.

onKeyPress="..."
Occurs when a visitor presses and releases a key over an element. This handler works with most elements.

onKeyDown="..."
Occurs when a visitor presses a key over an element. This handler works with most elements.

onKeyUp="..."
Occurs when a visitor releases a key over an element. This handler works with most elements.

onSubmit="..."
Occurs when a visitor submits a form. This handler works only with <FORM>.

onReset="..."
Occurs when a visitor resets a form. This handler works only with <FORM>.

onSelect="..."
Occurs when a visitor selects text in a text field. This handler works with the <INPUT> and <TEXTAREA> elements.

onChange="..."
Occurs when a visitor modifies a field and moves the input focus to a different control. This handler works with <INPUT>, <SELECT>, and <TEXTAREA>.

HTML Special Characters

Standard HTML Characters

The characters in Table A.1 were included in HTML 2 and HTML 3.2 and are also included in the current HTML 4 specification. Most browsers should display these characters, based on the mnemonic or numeric representation.

TABLE A.1: Standard HTML Characters

Symbol	Mnemonic Representation	Numeric Representation	Description
			Nonbreaking space
¡	&iexcl;	&#161;	Inverted exclamation mark
¢	&cent;	&#162;	Cent
£	&pound;	&#163;	Pound sterling
¤	&curren;	&#164;	General currency
¥	&yen;	&#165;	Yen
¦	&brvbar;	&#166;	Broken (vertical) bar
§	&sect;	&#167;	Section
¨	&uml;	&#168;	Umlaut (diaeresis)
©	&copy;	&#169;	Copyright sign
ª	&ordf;	&#170;	Ordinal indicator, feminine
«	&laquo;	&#171;	Angle quotation mark, left
¬	&not;	&#172;	Not
	&shy;	&#173;	Soft hyphen
®	&reg;	&#174;	Registered
¯	&macr;	&#175;	Macron
°	&deg;	&#176;	Degree
±	&plusmn;	&#177;	Plus-or-minus
2	&sup2;	&#178;	Superscript two
3	&sup3;	&#179;	Superscript three
´	&acute;	&#180;	Acute accent

TABLE A.1 continued: Standard HTML Characters

SYMBOL	MNEMONIC REPRESENTATION	NUMERIC REPRESENTATION	DESCRIPTION
µ	&micro;	&#181;	Micro
¶	&para;	&#182;	Pilcrow (paragraph)
·	&middot;	&#183;	Middle dot
¸	&cedil;	&#184;	Cedilla
¹	&sup1;	&#185;	Superscript one
º	&ordm;	&#186;	Ordinal indicator, masculine
»	&raquo;	&#187;	Angle quotation mark, right
¼	&frac14;	&#188;	Fraction one-quarter
½	&frac12;	&#189;	Fraction one-half
¾	&frac34;	&#190;	Fraction three-quarters
¿	&iquest;	&#191;	Inverted question mark
À	&Agrave;	&#192;	Uppercase A, grave accent
Á	&Aacute;	&#193;	Uppercase A, acute accent
Â	&Acirc;	&#194;	Uppercase A, circumflex
Ã	&Atilde;	&#195;	Uppercase A, tilde
Ä	&Auml;	&#196;	Uppercase A, diaeresis or umlaut mark
Å	&Aring;	&#197;	Uppercase A, angstrom
Æ	&AElig;	&#198;	Uppercase AE diphthong (ligature)
Ç	&Ccedil;	&#199;	Uppercase C, cedilla
È	&Egrave;	&#200;	Uppercase E, grave accent
É	&Eacute;	&#201;	Uppercase E, acute accent
Ê	&Ecirc;	&#202;	Uppercase E, circumflex
Ë	&Euml;	&#203;	Uppercase E, umlaut (diaeresis)
Ì	&Igrave;	&#204;	Uppercase I, grave accent
Í	&Iacute;	&#205;	Uppercase I, acute accent
Î	&Icirc;	&#206;	Uppercase I, circumflex
Ï	&Iuml;	&#207;	Uppercase I, umlaut (diaresis)

TABLE A.1 continued: Standard HTML Characters

Symbol	Mnemonic Representation	Numeric Representation	Description
Ð	&ETH;	&#208;	Uppercase Eth, Icelandic
Ñ	&Ntilde;	&#209;	Uppercase N, tilde
Ò	&Ograve;	&#210;	Uppercase O, grave accent
Ó	&Oacute;	&#211;	Uppercase O, acute accent
Ô	&Ocirc;	&#212;	Uppercase O, circumflex
Õ	&Otilde;	&#213;	Uppercase O, tilde
Ö	&Ouml;	&#214;	Uppercase O, umlaut (diaresis)
×	&times;	&#215;	Multiplication
Ø	&Oslash;	&#216;	Uppercase O, slash
Ù	&Ugrave;	&#217;	Uppercase U, grave accent
Ú	&Uacute;	&#218;	Uppercase U, acute accent
Û	&Ucirc;	&#219;	Uppercase U, circumflex
Ü	&Uuml;	&#220;	Uppercase U, umlaut (diaresis)
Ý	&Yacute;	&#221;	Uppercase Y, acute accent
þ	&THORN;	&#222;	Uppercase THORN, Icelandic
ß	&szlig;	&#223;	Small sharp s, German
à	&agrave;	&#224;	Lowercase a, grave accent
á	&aacute;	&#225;	Lowercase a, acute accent
â	&acirc;	&#226;	Lowercase a, circumflex
ã	&atilde;	&#227;	Lowercase a, tilde
ä	&auml;	&#228;	Lowercase a, umlaut (diaresis)
å	&aring;	&#229;	Lowercase a, angstrom
æ	&aelig;	&#230;	Lowercase ae diphthong (ligature)
ç	&ccedil;	&#231;	Lowercase c, cedilla
è	&egrave;	&#232;	Lowercase e, grave accent
é	&eacute;	&#233;	Lowercase e, acute accent
ê	&ecirc;	&#234;	Lowercase e, circumflex

TABLE A.1 continued: Standard HTML Characters

SYMBOL	MNEMONIC REPRESENTATION	NUMERIC REPRESENTATION	DESCRIPTION
ë	&euml;	&#235;	Lowercase e, umlaut (diaresis)
ì	&igrave;	&#236;	Lowercase i, grave accent
í	&iacute;	&#237;	Lowercase i, acute accent
î	&icirc;	&#238;	Lowercase i, circumflex
ï	&iuml;	&#239;	Lowercase i, umlaut (diaresis)
ð	&eth;	&#240;	Lowercase eth, Icelandic
ñ	&ntilde;	&#241;	Lowercase n, tilde
ò	&ograve;	&#242;	Lowercase o, grave accent
ó	&oacute;	&#243;	Lowercase o, acute accent
ô	&ocirc;	&#244;	Lowercase o, circumflex
õ	&otilde;	&#245;	Lowercase o, tilde
ö	&ouml;	&#246;	Lowercase o, umlaut (diaresis)
÷	&divide;	&#247;	Division
ø	&oslash;	&#248;	Lowercase o, slash
ù	&ugrave;	&#249;	Lowercase u, grave accent
ú	&uacute;	&#250;	Lowercase u, acute accent
û	&ucirc;	&#251;	Lowercase u, circumflex
ü	&uuml;	&#252;	Lowercase u, umlaut (diaresis)
ý	&yacute;	&#253;	Lowercase y, acute accent
þ	&thorn;	&#254;	Lowrcase thorn, Icelandic
ÿ	&yuml;	&#255;	Lowercase y, umlaut (diaresis)

HTML Color Codes

As we mentioned throughout the book, certain colors provide more uniform results than others. Table A.2 presents the named colors and "safe" colors together in a list. The numbered safe colors between named colors represent colors in the spectrum between those two points. For example, if you want to use a safe dark blue color, choose from the two "safe" colors—#000099 and #0000CC—that are between dark blue and medium blue in the table.

TABLE A.2: The Named Colors and the Safe Colors

NAME	CODE	NAME	CODE	NAME	CODE
Black	#000000	Darkgreen	#006699	Medium-springgreen	#00FA9A
	#000033		#0066CC		
	#000066		#0066FF	Lime	#00FF00
Navy	#000080	Green	#008000		#00FF00
Darkblue	#00008B	Teal	#008080		#00FF33
	#000099	Darkcyan	#008B8B		#00FF66
Darkblue	#0000CC		#009900	Springgreen	#00FF7F
Mediumblue	#0000CD		#009933		#00FF99
Blue	#0000FF		#009966	Springgreen	#00FFCC
	#0000FF		#009999	Aqua	#00FFFF
	#003300		#0099CC	Cyan	#00FFFF
	#003333		#0099FF		#00FFFF
Blue	#003366	Deepskyblue	#00BFFF	Midnightblue	#191970
	#003399		#00CC00	Dodgerblue	#1E90FF
	#0033CC		#00CC33	Lightseagreen	#20B2AA
	#0033FF		#00CC66	Forestgreen	#228B22
Darkgreen	#006400		#00CC99	Seagreen	#2E8B57
	#006600		#00CCCC	Darkslategray	#2F4F4F
	#006633		#00CCFF	Limegreen	#32CD32
	#006666	Darkturquoise	#00CED1		#330000

TABLE A.2 continued: The Named Colors and the Safe Colors

Name	Code	Name	Code	Name	Code
Limegreen	#330033	Limegreen	#33FF33	Cornflower-blue	#666600
	#330066		#33FF66		#666633
	#330099		#33FF99		#666666
	#3300CC		#33FFCC		#666699
	#3300FF		#33FFFF		#6666CC
	#333300	Medium-Seagreen	#3CB371		#669900
	#333333				#669933
	#333366	Turquoise seagreen	#40E0D0		#669966
	#333399	Royalblue	#4169E1		#669999
	#3333CC	Steelblue	#4682B4		#6699CC
	#3333FF	Darkslateblue	#483D8B		#6699FF
	#336600	Medium-turquoise	#48D1CC		#66CC00
	#336633				#66CC33
	#336666	Indigo	#4B0082		#66CC66
	#336699	Darkolivegreen	#556B2F		#66CC99
	#3366CC	Cadetblue	#5F9EA0		#66CCCC
	#3366FF	Cornflower-blue	#6495ED		#66CCFF
	#339900		#660000	Medium-aquamarine	#66CDAA
	#339933	Cornflower-blue	#660033		#66FF00
	#339966				#66FF33
	#339999		#660066		#6666FF
	#3399CC		#660099		#66FF66
	#3399FF		#6600CC		#66FF99
	#33CC00		#6600FF		#66FFCC
	#33CC33		#663300		#66FFFF
	#33CC66		#663333	Dimgray	#696969
	#33CC99		#663366	Slateblue	#6A5ACD
	#33CCCC		#663399	Olivedrab	#6B8E23
	#33CCFF		#6633CC	Slategray	#708090
	#33FF00		#6633FF		

TABLE A.2 continued: The Named Colors and the Safe Colors

Name	Code	Name	Code	Name	Code
Lightslategray	#778899	Darkorchid	#993300	Darkorchid	#99FFFF
Medium-slateblue	#7B68EE		#993333	Yellowgreen	#9ACD32
Lawngreen	#7CFC00		#993366	Sienna	#A0522D
Chartreuse	#7FFF00		#993399	Brown	#A52A2A
Aquamarine	#7FFFD4		#9933CC	Darkgray	#A9A9A9
Maroon	#800000		#9933FF	Lightblue	#ADD8E6
Purple	#800080		#996600	Greenyellow	#ADFF2F
Olive	#808000		#996633	Paleturquoise	#AFEEEE
Gray	#808080		#996666	Lightsteelblue	#B0C4DE
Skyblue	#87CEEB		#996699	Powderblue	#B0E0E6
Lightskyblue	#87CEFA		#9966CC	Firebrick	#B22222
Blueviolet	#8A2BE2		#9966FF	Dark-goldenrod	#B8860B
Darkred	#8B0000		#999900		
Darkmagenta	#8B008B		#999933	Medium-orchid	#BA55D3
Saddlebrown	#8B4513		#999966	Rosybrown	#BC8F8F
Darkseagreen	#8FBC8F		#999999	Darkkhaki	#BDB76B
Lightgreen	#90EE90		#9999CC	Silver	#C0C0C0
Medium purple	#9370DB		#9999FF	Medium-violetred	#C71585
Darkviolet	#9400D3		#99CC00		
Palegreen	#98FB98		#99CC33		#CC0000
	#990000		#99CC66		#CC0033
	#990033		#99CC99		#CC0066
	#990066		#99CCCC		#CC0099
	#990099		#99CCFF		#CC00CC
	#9900CC		#99FF00		#CC00FF
	#9900FF		#99FF33		#CC3300
Darkorchid	#9932CC		#99FF66		#CC3333
			#99FF99		#CC3366
			#99FFCC		#CC3399

TABLE A.2 continued: The Named Colors and the Safe Colors

NAME	CODE	NAME	CODE	NAME	CODE
Medium-violetred	#CC33CC	Chocolate	#D2691E	Linen	#FAF0E6
	#CC33FF	Tan	#D2B48C	Lightgolden-rodyellow	#FAFAD2
	#CC6600	Lightgrey	#D3D3D3		
	#CC6633	Thistle	#D8BFD8	Oldlace	#FDF5E6
	#CC6666	Orchid	#DA70D6	Red	#FF0000
	#CC6699	Goldenrod	#DAA520		#FF0000
	#CC66CC	Palevioletred	#DB7093		#FF0033
	#CC66FF	Crimson	#DC143C		#FF0066
	#CC9900	Gainsboro	#DCDCDC		#FF0099
	#CC9933	Plum	#DDA0DD		#FF00CC
	#CC9966	Burlywood	#DEB887	Fuchsia	#FF00FF
	#CC9999	Lightcyan	#E0FFFF	Magenta	#FF00FF
	#CC99CC	Lavender	#E6E6FA		#FF00FF
	#CC99FF	Darksalmon	#E9967A	Deeppink	#FF1493
	#CCCC00	Violet	#EE82EE		#FF3300
	#CCCC33	Palegoldenrod	#EEE8AA	Deeppink	#FF3333
	#CCCC66	Lightcoral	#F08080		#FF3366
	#CCCC99	Khaki	#F0E68C		#FF3399
	#CCCCCC	Aliceblue	#F0F8FF		#FF33CC
	#CCCCFF	Honeydew	#F0FFF0		#FF33FF
	#CCFF00	Azure	#F0FFFF	Orangered	#FF4500
	#CCFF33	Sandybrown	#F4A460	Tomato	#FF6347
	#CCFF66	Wheat	#F5DEB3		#FF6600
	#CCFF99	Beige	#F5F5DC		#FF6633
	#CCFFCC	Whitesmoke	#F5F5F5		#FF6666
	#CCFFFF	Mintcream	#F5FFFA		#FF6699
Indianred	#CD5C5C	Ghostwhite	#F8F8FF		#FF66CC
Peru	#CD853F	Salmon	#FA8072		#FF66FF
		Antiquewhite	#FAEBD7	Hotpink	#FF69B4
				Coral	#FF7F50

TABLE A.2 continued: The Named Colors and the Safe Colors

Name	Code	Name	Code	Name	Code
Darkorange	#FF8C00	Pink	#FFCC99	Seashell	#FFF5EE
	#FF9900		#FFCCCC	Cornsilk	#FFF8DC
	#FF9933		#FFCCFF	Lemonchiffon	#FFFACD
	#FF9966	Gold	#FFD700	Floralwhite	#FFFAF0
Darkorange	#FF9999	Peachpuff	#FFDAB9	Snow	#FFFAFA
	#FF99CC	Navajowhite	#FFDEAD	Yellow	#FFFF00
	#FF99FF	Moccasin	#FFE4B5		#FFFF33
Lightsalmon	#FFA07A	Bisque	#FFE4C4		#FFFF66
Orange	#FFA500	Mistyrose	#FFE4E1		#FFFF99
Lightpink	#FFB6C1	Blanched-almond	#FFEBCD		#FFFFCC
Pink	#FFC0CB			Lightyellow	#FFFFE0
	#FFCC00	Papayawhip	#FFEFD5	Ivory	#FFFFF0
	#FFCC33	Lavender blush	#FFF0F5	White	#FFFFFF
Pink	#FFCC66				

INDEX

C

E

J

M

O

X

About the Contributors

Some of the best—and best-selling—Sybex authors have contributed chapters from their current books to *HTML Complete,* 2nd Edition.

Kurt Cagle is a consultant specializing in XML and Microsoft technologies. He is a regular contributor to *Dr. Dobbs Journal,* *Visual Basic Programmer's Journal,* and *Web Builder* magazine. He is also the XML and DHTML Pro for the popular DevX programmers' Web site.

Pat Coleman writes about the Internet, Windows, and Windows applications and is the coauthor of *Mastering Intranets* and *Mastering Internet Explorer 4,* both from Sybex.

Vincent Flanders is the mastermind behind WebPagesThatSuck.com. He spent two years as a Webmaster for a large Internet Service Provider and has taught HTML and design courses.

Molly Holzschlag is the author of several best-selling Web design books, including two in the Laura Lemay series. A widely recognized Web design consultant and content provider, Molly also develops and teaches design courses for the New School University, the University of Phoenix, Pima Community College, and DigitalThink.

James Jaworski writes the SuperScripter column for www.builder.com, CNET's leading Web site for Webmasters. He is the author of *Mastering JavaScript*, *Mastering JavaScript and JScript*, *Do-It-Yourself Web Publishing with HotMetal,* and *The Java Developer's Guide.*

A. Russell Jones, Ph.D., a confessed former zookeeper and professional musician, now composes computer applications. He is a senior systems developer for VF Services Corporation in Greensboro, North Carolina. He is also the author of *Visual Basic Developer's Guide to ASP and IIS,* from Sybex.

Stephen Mack, a Web designer and consultant for several major companies, has written two books on the Internet and has dozens of magazine articles to his credit.

Deborah S. Ray and **Eric J. Ray** are owners of RayComm, Inc., a technical communications consulting firm that specializes in cutting-edge Internet and computing technologies. Together they have coauthored more than 10 computer books, including the first edition of *Mastering HTML 4* from Sybex. They also write a syndicated computer column, which is available in newspapers across North America.

Janan Platt Saylor has 13 years of experience as a controller and consultant teaching people how to use computers. She publishes multimedia poetry on the Web, often from her online poetry workshop, AlienFlower.

Joe Schmuller, an award-winning webmaster and consultant, has been the Editor-in-Chief at *PCAI Magazine* for several years. He is also the author of Sybex's *ActiveX: No experience required.*

Erik Strom is a programmer, systems consultant, and freelance writer in Hershey, PA. He has been programming for 18 years and has scores of computer articles to his credit.

Gene Weisskopf is a software applications developer whose articles are frequently published in computer magazines. He has written several books for Sybex, including *ABCs of FrontPage 97,* *ABCs of Excel 97,* and *FrontPage 98: No experience required.* He has also taught spreadsheet and introductory computer courses for many years.

Michael Willis, Vincent Flanders' bright and creative sidekick, has been a graphic designer for 18 years and has a successful Web/print design firm.

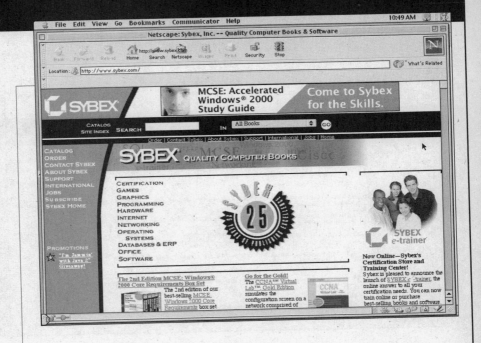

TELL US WHAT YOU THINK!

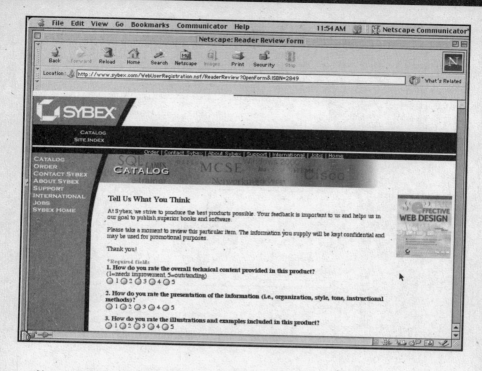

Your feedback is critical to our efforts to provide you with the best books and software on the market. Tell us what you think about the products you've purchased. It's simple:

1. Visit the Sybex website
2. Go to the product page
3. Click on **Submit a Review**
4. Fill out the questionnaire and comments
5. Click **Submit**

With your feedback, we can continue to publish the highest quality computer books and software products that today's busy IT professionals deserve.

www.sybex.com

SYBEX Inc. • 1151 Marina Village Parkway, Alameda, CA 94501 • 510-523-8233